DUE
D0712729

Wake Us When It's Over

Macmillan Publishing Company
866 Third Avenue, New York, N.Y. 10022
Collier Macmillan Canada, Inc.

Library of Congress Cataloging in Publication Data
Germond, Jack.
Wake us when it's over.
Includes index.
1. Presidents—United States—Election—1984.
2. United States—Politics and government—1981–
I. Witcover, Jules. II. Title.
E879.G47 1985 324.973'0927 85-7210
ISBN 0-02-630710-3

10 9 8 7 6 5 4 3 2 1

Printed in the United States of America

To Barbara, Mandi and Jessie

To Ed Campbell, who personifies what is good about politics

If I had any epitaph that I would rather have more than another, it would be to say that I had disturbed the sleep of my generation.

—ADLAI E. STEVENSON II

Contents

Acknowledgments

As American presidential campaigns go, the one in 1984 was no day at the beach. It seemed endless, and all of the competition was in one party. The level of bickering was high and of substantive dialogue low, in the general election especially. In many ways, the presidential campaign of 1984 embodied most of what is wrong today with the process of selecting the President of the United States.

Yet, for all that, the high stakes and the intensity of those seeking them always make a presidential campaign the stuff of high drama, and at close range the political competition of 1984 was no exception. In our effort to convey some sense of that drama, we have benefited first of all from personal observation of, and conversations with, the candidates and their principal strategists as we followed them in the many state primaries and caucuses of 1984 and in the general election campaign. Second, we have been greatly assisted by the extensive and candid recollections of more than a hundred active participants in the campaign in the weeks immediately after the election. Many are quoted here, but some, at their request, are not identified by name. However, all but a few of the interviews were tape-recorded. We wish to express our thanks to:

The two principal candidates, President Ronald Reagan and former Vice President Walter F. Mondale, for the generous amounts of time they gave us in reflective interviews in their offices after the election:

Their running mates, Vice President George Bush, for a long interview after the election, and former Representative Geraldine Ferraro, for helpful conversations during the campaign, although she declined to be interviewed after the election on grounds she was writing her own book;

All of the other major candidates—Senators Alan Cranston, John Glenn, Gary Hart and Fritz Hollings, former Senator George McGovern, former Governor Reubin Askew and the Reverend Jesse Jackson—for lengthy interviews during and after the election that were essential to this effort;

These members of the Reagan-Bush campaign: Lee Atwater, James Baker, Charles Black, Richard Darman, Michael Deaver, James Lake, Senator Paul Laxalt, Paul Manafort, Lyn Nofziger, Edward Rollins, Stuart Spencer, Roger Stone, Peter Teeley, Robert Teeter, William Timmons and Richard Wirthlin;

These members of the Mondale-Ferraro campaign: James Johnson, who was especially generous with his time; Robert Beckel, Michael Berman, Charles Campion, Tom Donilon, Michael Ford, Richard Goodstein, Frank Greer, Timothy Hagan, Peter Hart, David Ifshin, Paul Jensen, Elaine Kamarck, Martin Kaplan, Richard Leone, James Margolis, Richard Moe, James Quackenbush, John Reilly, Edward Rendell, John Sasso, Diane Thompson, Joseph Trippi and Anne Wexler;

From the Hart campaign: Kathy Bushkin, Patrick Caddell, Susan Casey, Senator Christopher Dodd, Keith Glaser, Kenneth Guido, Oliver Henkel, David Landau, Frank Mankiewicz, Jack Quinn, William Shore and Ray Strother;

From the Glenn campaign: Joseph Grandmaison, William Hamilton, Robert Keefe, Scott Miller, David Sawyer, Greg Schneiders and William White;

Also, Gerald Austin, former Senate Majority Leader Howard Baker, Ken Bode, Gerald Boyd, Ron Brown, Ed Campbell, Representative Richard Cheney, Milton Coleman, James Cunningham, Clark Clifford, David Garth, Judy Goldsmith, Senator Barry Goldwater, Karl Hess, Vernon Jordan, Fay Joyce, Lane Kirkland, Richard Koster, Bert Lance, David Lawsky, Representative Mickey Leland, Harry McPherson, Charles Manatt, John Perkins, Joe Reed, Timothy Russert, Charles Scalera, John Sears, Murray Seeger, Robert Strauss, Ed Theobald, Joseph White and Kathy Wilson;

Our particular thanks as well to Robert Fahs, librarian in the Washington bureau of *The Baltimore Sun*; Robert Stewart, our editor at Macmillan, and Sterling Lord, our agent. We also owe a debt to Chris Walters at Radio Shack in Washington, who helped us avert computer disasters on several occasions.

To these, and to all the many other participants in the campaign of 1984—campaign workers and our colleagues in the news media—who shared their experiences, their recollections and their time with us for the purposes of this book and in good fellowship, we are grateful.

JACK W. GERMOND
JULES WITCOVER

Washington, D.C.
March 1985

Introduction

The election of an American President, the civics textbooks tell us, is designed to be an elevating exercise, lofty in purpose and the ultimate expression of the public will in the world's greatest democratic nation. In its purest form, the seekers after the highest office in the land present themselves to the voters, opening themselves freely to the scrutiny of the electorate on all matters of past performance and future intention. The voters, for their part, absorb all the information offered by the candidates and seek out more, either by their own diligent research or, more often, through a searching free press—and, today, television. The whole process therefore becomes an open and comprehensive effort to arrive at a collective decision by the American people that is democratic, informed, just and wise.

That is what the civics textbooks tell us. In practice, however, the electing of the American President increasingly has become not an elevating exercise but a leveling one. In large part because the means of communication have mushroomed so rapidly and extensively since the advent of television, the elective process has been radically transformed. From a relatively simple and direct interplay between candidate and voter, the process has evolved into a complex and extremely costly maze through which both the candidate and the voter must pass before that one day every four years when the collective judgment of the electorate is made.

For various reasons, the growth in the complexity of the process has been accompanied by two critical developments. The first has been the emergence of a corps of well-trained and well-paid professionals in the art of practical politics to guide the candidates through the maze. And as these professionals have worked their will on the process, they have increasingly bent it out of shape to meet the particular short-run needs of their clients, leaving that process in a jumble of biases and contradictions that handicap many of the candidates and confuse even more voters. This situation leads to the second development: widespread voter disenchantment with, and distrust of, the process itself and the politicians who seek the presidency through it.

One rather superficial aspect of American politics remains the same: its language, and for obvious reasons. The political jargon is awash in the clichés of sports: winning or losing the game, campaign teams and their managers, public-opinion polls handicapping the horse race, candidates (often called "horses") jockeying for position and so on. The similarities between politics and sports are striking and obvious.

An election is, first of all, a contest among competitors striving for the same prize. If you work for one of them you are said to be, as in boxing, in his corner. In a debate, one candidate may score a knockout, or the event may be judged a draw. A single day on which several presidential primaries are held was originally called—what else?—Super Bowl Tuesday, now shortened to Super Tuesday. The language of the playing field or arena is too apropos to politics, and too integral, to be avoided in writing about a presidential campaign, and the reader will find this book no exception.

Yet the experience of witnessing seven such campaigns at close range in the last quarter century compels another less comfortable analogy: American presidential politics has become more like war than like sports; more like combat than like games-playing. And the favored formula for combat in the nuclear era—guerrilla warfare—has been copied and adapted in the world of political campaigning for the presidency.

Insurrections against the establishment—the incumbent President or the frontrunning candidate of the opposition party—begin with skirmishes in the countryside. They start in the form of straw polls or candidates' forums and then advance to the precinct caucuses of Iowa and the primary of little New Hampshire. The most successful combatants are usually those who, in the manner of the Vietcong in the Vietnam war, win acceptance of the populace at the grass-roots level. Literally, as in guerrilla warfare, their mostly young troops "live off the land"—depending on local support for food and lodging to survive.

Only later, as they build their political strength, are they able to move into the set-piece battles in the larger primary states where the establishment candidate has the strength of special-interest support such as labor (for the Democrats) or banking and business (for the Republicans). At this stage, the combat also becomes more dominated by the new weapons of political warfare, principally television.

The tremendous expenditure of time, money, talent and emotional commitment makes the seeking of the presidency comparable to a war of attrition. The candidates with superior resources attempt to wear out the opposition, who in turn are obliged to make desperate sacrifices, personal and political, to remain in the fight.

And in politics as in war, timing and the ability of one of the combatants to take advantage of unexpected turns of events can be critical. The right tactic, and in politics even the right phrase, at the right time can be decisive or can change the whole complexion of the fray.

If the similarity between presidential campaign politics and warfare were to end at this superficial level, the comparison would be nothing for the American public to be overly concerned about. But the similarity goes considerably further. As we hope this account will underscore, today's combat for the American presidency generates forces, mechanisms, ambitions and deceptions that threaten the integrity and effectiveness of the political process itself.

Rules and reforms written for a political playing field among law-abiding competitors become on the political battleground mere roadblocks to be circumvented—or even sabotaged if they stand in the way of a campaign juggernaut en route to a smashing victory.

At the same time, costly and elaborate propaganda machines are built and employed, sometimes to inform the populace but more often to deceive, confuse or simply lull it. And in the age of television, the combat on this front—the living rooms of America—can be persuasive beyond any jousting between the candidates themselves in the battlefield of primaries and caucuses in state after state and in the general election in the fall.

As the techniques of presidential campaigning have become more extensive and sophisticated, a small army of paid political professionals has emerged. Its leaders plot and pursue victory with all the cold calculation of generals in the field and, increasingly, with the same ruthlessness and single-minded determination to win at almost any cost. While many of these professionals are motivated by high political ideals or personal loyalty to party or candidate, they are mercenaries nonetheless—the Hessians of modern-day presidential politics.

These mercenaries are particularly conspicuous and influential in the field of television advertising. More than half of a candidate's campaign treasury—his war chest, as we now say—usually is spent in a battle of commercials in which accuracy, truth and the opponent's reputation are frequent casualties. So pronounced has the reliance on mercenaries in this area become that the incumbent seeking reelection in 1984 recruited professionals in television advertising who had no experience in politics but who were considered to be in the top ranks of commercial-product propagandizing.

The technology of politics, as in war, has become vastly more complex and dominant in shaping strategies and executing tactics. Campaign professionals determine where their candidates go, what they do, when and how to meet the demands and exploitative possibilities of television's eye. These professionals no longer place their priority focus on voters directly in the city squares and suburban plazas of the land. Through contrived "media events" that increasingly dominate candidates' schedules, their strategists zero in on those millions more voters whose eyes are glued to the small piece of the world outside their living rooms brought to them by television each night. The routine battle plan is simple: Get on the nightly news, and get on favorably.

On a more personal level, campaigning for the presidency under existing conditions and compulsions develops a wartime mentality among many who go into the political trenches. Men and women who in the normal pursuits of their lives would not think even of driving through a red light readily bring themselves, like men in battle, to commit violations of campaign law or ethics in the name of political survival—for their candidate or for their own vested interest in him. Spying on each others' campaigns becomes almost commonplace, and theft is not unheard of. And in the process, heretofore upstanding citizens are reduced to desperate opportunists doing whatever in their shaken judgment is required to stay in the fight. Sometimes that compulsion dictates illegal or unethical conduct regarding money; sometimes it leads to character assassination; sometimes to major distortions of the truth or to willful and destructive lying.

As in any war, many innocent people are hurt by the excesses of the combat. On the most basic level, voters are brainwashed, misled and deceived about what the candidates stand for, what they have done in the past and what they intend to do in the future. And on another level, the voters have their trust in public officials and their enthusiasm for the electoral process sapped by candidates' abuse of that process and by its confusing complexities and inordinate, wearying length.

Also hurt are many young people who embark on participation in the process and are either soured by it or themselves corrupted by the excesses practiced in their campaign's pursuit of survival or victory at all costs. And if they are not thus affected, many of them—even when campaign resources are gone—continue on their own from one state primary or caucus to another, like so many camp followers of old. Such is the enduring aphrodisiac of politics.

Finally, men and women who seek national office with the highest motives and sense of integrity bend under the pressure of political combat at close quarters. They emerge with at least their reputations and sometimes their very principles and standards of conduct badly tarnished or even demolished.

This picture of presidential politics—as guerrilla warfare escalating into broader, more technologically dominated combat with deplorable ramifications—may be entirely too harsh. Certainly many, many individuals from the precinct levels to the highest echelons of a presidential candidacy are able to traverse the political battlefield without inflicting or suffering casualty. But the mind-set of politics as war seems to us to be undeniably advancing, with unhappy consequences for the voters, for the candidates and for the country.

The presidential campaign of 1984 was, sadly, all too illustrative of this condition. Perhaps campaign strategists have always thought and talked the way one of those we interviewed described the mind-set in his campaign. "The mentality around there," he said, "was, 'Crush people. Crush campaigns. Crush candidates. Crush 'em.' " Such intensity may be commonplace in war and in sports, and we may be naive in suggesting that somehow it ought not reach quite that level in the business of electing the American President. But that such intensity exists and flourishes in national politics today cannot be refuted.

When a prominent political adviser submitted a lengthy paper on campaign strategy to his candidate in 1984, he prefaced it with two quotations. They were not from eminent political leaders of the past but from two of the great warlords of history, Sun-Tzu and Napoléon.

The quotation from Sun-Tzu's *The Art of War* said: "The military arts are like unto water; for water in its natural course runs away from high places and hastens downwards. So in war, then, to avoid what is strong is to strike what is weak. Water shapes its course according to the ground over which it flows; the soldier works out his victory in relation to the foe whom he is facing."

And Napoléon's advice was: "The whole art of war consists in a well-reasoned and extremely circumspect defensive, followed by rapid and audacious attack."

The application of these words of military wisdom to politics was obvious. In the long presidential campaign of 1984 that we have attempted to chronicle here—from the early straw polls to the primaries and caucuses, through the national conventions and the presidential nominees' debates to the election itself—there are many illustrations of the cunning, intensity, ruthlessness and deception more familiarly associated with warfare applied to the political process and those who participate in it. The result was yet another election boycotted or at least ignored by nearly half the eligible voters in the United States, and an election that offered precious little for the edification of those who did vote.

Already, as is the case after every recent presidential election, there are demands for electoral reforms, and commissions to study what those reforms should be. But before there can be hope for reforms, there must be a greater appreciation of why they are needed. This book, beyond being an account of what happened in the electing of the American President in 1984, attempts to indicate some of the reasons the process has become so unwieldy and subject to exploitation—and why the voters consequently have become so disillusioned, apathetic and even hostile to the process and to those who participate in it.

Political Calendar:
1984 Presidential Campaign

FEBRUARY 20	Iowa precinct caucuses
FEBRUARY 28	New Hampshire primary election
MARCH 4	Maine town caucuses
MARCH 6	Vermont primary
MARCH 13	Super Tuesday: Massachusetts, Rhode Island, Florida, Georgia and Alabama primaries; Oklahoma, Washington, Nevada and Hawaii Democratic caucuses
MARCH 17	Michigan caucuses
MARCH 20	Illinois primary
MARCH 27	Connecticut primary
APRIL 3	New York primary
APRIL 10	Pennsylvania primary
MAY 1	Tennessee primary
MAY 5	Texas caucuses
MAY 8	Ohio, Indiana, North Carolina and Maryland primaries
MAY 15	Nebraska and Oregon primaries

JUNE 5	California, New Jersey, West Virginia, South Dakota and New Mexico primaries
JULY 16–19	Democratic National Convention, San Francisco
AUGUST 20–23	Republican National Convention, Dallas
OCTOBER 7	First presidential debate, Louisville
OCTOBER 11	Vice-presidential debate, Philadelphia
OCTOBER 21	Second presidential debate, Kansas City
NOVEMBER 6	Election day

Wake Us When It's Over

1

One Hell of a One-liner

•

SUDDENLY, after months of following the campaign script to the letter, the President of the United States had stumbled. Leading by nearly twenty points in the public-opinion polls and apparently well on his way to reelection, he had performed just erratically enough in his first debate against his Democratic challenger, Walter F. Mondale, to raise in voters' minds—and in the news media hungry for an issue—the one question that might yet defeat him. Was Ronald Reagan, now seventy-three years old, slipping? Were his mental processes—already the subject of wide ridicule from his detractors—at last conspicuously deserting him, to the point that returning him to the White House for four more Republican years would be judged as simply too great a national risk?

This question was paramount as Reagan and Mondale, two weeks later, stood in opposite wings off the stage of the old theater at the Kansas City Convention Center, poised for their second and final debate of the 1984 presidential campaign. The date was October 21, and only sixteen days now remained before the voters would decide whether to keep Reagan on the job or replace him with the earnest but uninspiring Mondale. Until that first debate in Louisville two weeks earlier, there had not seemed to be much doubt about the outcome. But, inexplicably to all those closest to the President and to millions who admired him from a distance, that ninety-minute televised confrontation with Mondale revealed a different Ronald Reagan. The Great Communicator was strangely awkward, halting, even confused before the cameras that had been major instruments in his success, first as an actor, later as a politician.

Fritz Mondale, a thoroughly professional politician fully grounded in the issues, had always been underestimated by the Reagan camp. But his aggressive campaign rhetoric in advance of that first debate had led Reagan's political advisers to expect the challenger to come roaring out of his corner on the attack against the frontrunning President. Instead, Mondale—seventeen years Reagan's junior—was a model of decorum, treating Reagan with cool deference while scoring debating points heavily against the older man. Reagan's responses in that first debate, when examined later in print, did not seem exceptionally confused. But his delivery, captured so arrestingly by the medium that in the past had been so kind to him, indisputably conveyed a sense of uncertainty, a grappling for coherence, that triggered what the press at once labeled "the age issue."

In the days following the first debate, newspapers and television made Reagan's age and competence the centerpieces of their campaign coverage. The networks summoned not only physicians but also psychologists before their cameras to assess the effects of senility on its victims. The cartoonists, too, had a field day. One, Dwane Powell in the Raleigh *News and Observer*, drew a large Reagan head open at the left ear with springs, coils and gears flying out and an elephant representing the Republican Party rushing to the rescue with an oil can. For the first time in the 1984 campaign, there was some doubt about the heretofore one-sided Reagan-Mondale contest. Could the roof fall in on an incumbent President miles ahead in all the public-opinion polls? A suddenly intrigued nation tuned in an estimated one hundred million television sets to this second debate to find out.

The agreed-upon subject on this cool late October night in Kansas City was foreign policy. But the age issue was on the minds of all those who crowded into the classic old theater with its deeply slanted orchestra and overhanging balcony. In the two weeks since the first debate, as the question of Reagan's competence fueled a continuing stream of newspaper and television commentary, his campaign managers had sought to answer it by putting him on exhibition in the most favorable settings. The best of these had been an old-fashioned railroad whistlestop tour through western Ohio, arranged in advance of Reagan's poor first-debate performance but fortuitous nonetheless. The event made use of the same railroad car that had carried Democrat Harry Truman across the countryside in 1948. It was leased from a museum in Florida and moved north at considerable expense, but the cost was deemed an excellent investment. Reagan performed well on the whistlestop, and already the polls, which had narrowed after the first debate, were reflecting his earlier lead. Gallup, in fact, had him up slightly, from seventeen points ahead to twenty. Still, the President's political strategists well knew that a second poor debate could send his stock downward again.

Before the first debate, Reagan had gone through extensive rehearsals, armed with a detailed briefing book and assaulted by tough, aggressive debating points from the selected Mondale stand-in, David Stockman, Reagan's youthful and often arrogant budget director. Expecting Mondale to be equally tough, Stockman had hammered at his boss in a manner that Senator Paul Laxalt, the prime Reagan loyalist, later complained had "brutalized" the President. For this second debate, the word went out that the preparation had been more casual. If Reagan was to dispel the age issue, some like Laxalt said, he would do so only if his aides "let Reagan be Reagan"—relaxed and confident.

Part of doing so, his debate coaches decided, required them to employ a tactic most surprising in dealing with a professional actor of long experience. Their repeated criticisms of the President's answers in the rehearsals for the first debate had seemed to discourage him, so the second time around they intentionally applied an old-fashioned ego massage from time to time to keep his spirits up.

"We did a few things to build up his confidence," one of the coaches said. "We made him feel good about his practice sessions . . . by praising him when the answers were good and when the performance was good." Another said: "Having been an actor, he was very used to having people say, 'That's the perfect way to say it.' " And another recalled: "We'd throw a question at him, and when he'd answer it we'd say, 'Now you're getting there. That's a hell of an answer.' "

So the President of the United States, like any uncertain schoolboy, was given encouraging words when he came up with the right answers.

As for Mondale, he knew that this second debate was his big chance—probably his last chance—to make a race of it. Ever since Labor Day, he had been campaigning tirelessly, pleading with voters to direct their attention to the issues facing the country.

He had made an excellent start in the first debate on domestic policy, supposedly Reagan's stronger suit considering his success in slowing inflation and launching an economic recovery. Now, with foreign policy to be discussed in the second debate, and relations with the Soviet Union at Cold War levels and the American role in the Middle East in confusion, Mondale had a clear opportunity to score more telling points in another ninety minutes of serious dialogue.

As Reagan and Mondale strode onto the stage and the television camera lenses zoomed in for closeups, however, Mondale suffered an immediate setback. He looked extremely haggard, with conspicuously large bags under his eyes—the product, aides charged later, of lighting rearrangements insisted upon by the Reagan campaign. Whatever the reason, Mondale looked awful—a fact that was widely commented on in the audience and among reporters watching on television monitors. Still, how Mondale looked was not the critical matter now. It was how Reagan would handle himself.

With the two candidates standing at their lecterns awaiting the start of the debate, members of their families and campaign staffs gathered in separate viewing rooms backstage. At the same time, in a large basement hall before two huge television screens, several hundred members of the news media from across the country and abroad sat expectantly at long tables. Many of them were hunched over portable computers that made anachronisms of the old clacking portable typewriters of campaign lore. As the debate unfolded on the oversized television screens, some reporters typed frantically against early deadlines while most watched and listened in the manner of theater or movie critics, which in a sense many of them had become.

The debate, moderated by former NBC News commentator Edwin Newman, began on an appropriately serious note. Mondale was asked by the leadoff panelist, columnist Georgie Anne Geyer, about his emphasis on economic development, negotiations and a possible quarantine to cope with the unrest in Central America, where the United States was covertly supporting a war against the Sandinista regime in Nicaragua. Mondale responded by immediately charging that Reagan "had not pursued the diplomatic opportunities" available to him in the region, using the question to launch into an attack on Reagan as a leader. He deftly shifted the subject to Lebanon, charging that as a result of faulty presidential leadership "we have been humiliated and our opponents are stronger." From there, he jumped uninterrupted into a broader assault on Reagan, accusing the President of harboring a series of misconceptions about military matters—allegations he had been leveling in campaign speeches across the country.

"The bottom line of national strength," Mondale said, "is that the President must be in command. He must lead. And when a President doesn't know that submarine missiles are [not] recallable, says that 70 percent of our strategic forces are conventional, discovers three years into his administration that our arms control efforts have failed because he didn't know that most Soviet missiles were on land—these are things a President must know to command. A President is called the Commander-in-Chief. He is called that because he is supposed to be in charge of the facts and run our government and strengthen our nation."

Mondale's start was an aggressive and clever one, although he seemed at first a bit nervous, perhaps because he was aware of what was at stake. But he had moved at once to put Reagan on the defensive. Not only that, he had managed, by raising the questions about what the President knew and didn't know, to introduce at the debate's outset the matter of competence, which was after all at the root of the age issue.

In subsequent early answers, Mondale kept on the offensive, while President Reagan found himself, as a result of the panelists' questions and Mondale's attacks, on the defensive. Geyer's opening question to Reagan concerned the report then current about a Central Intelligence Agency manual prepared for anti-Sandinista guerrillas that, she said, "advocates not only assassinations of Sandinistas but the hiring of criminals to assassinate the guerrillas we are supporting, in order to create martyrs." Geyer asked the President: "Is this not, in effect, our own state-supported terrorism?"

Reagan rather lamely replied that he had ordered an investigation into the matter but that it appeared the whole affair had been a mixup. "The agency head" in Nicaragua—"the man in charge"—had excised some offensive pages in the manual, Reagan explained, but some unexcised copies nevertheless had slipped through. If anyone was at fault, he said, "we are certainly going to do something about that."

Reagan seemed to be acknowledging that the CIA was "in charge" of the anti-Sandinista war in Central America, and Geyer immediately jumped on him. "Mr. President," she asked, "are you implying, then, that the CIA in Nicaragua is directing the Contras [the anti-Sandinistas] there?" Reagan backed off. "I'm afraid I misspoke when I said a CIA head in Nicaragua. There is not someone there directing all of this activity. . . ."

Mondale, on rebuttal, pressed his sudden advantage. "What is a President charged with doing when he takes his oath of office?" he asked. "He raises his right hand and takes an oath of office to take care to faithfully execute the laws of the land. The President can't know everything, but a President has to know those things that are essential to his leadership and the enforcement of our laws." Mondale was going right at the competence issue again.

"This manual," he went on, "several thousands of which were produced, was distributed, ordering political assassinations, hiring of criminals and other forms of terrorism. Some of it was excised, but the part dealing with political terrorism was continued. How can this happen? How can something this serious occur in an administration and have a President of the United States, in a situation like this, say he didn't know? A President must know these things. I don't know which is worse—not knowing or knowing and not stopping it. . . ."

This first exchange was not going at all well for Reagan. In his own rebuttal to Mondale, he chose to ignore Mondale's allusions to ignorance or incompetence concerning the CIA manual and instead sought to defend himself against the allegations that he believed missiles were recallable. "I never, ever, conceived of such a thing," he protested. "I never said any such thing." What he had said, Reagan insisted, was that missile-bearing submarines and planes, once sent out on a mission, could be called back before they launched their missiles. "How anyone could think that any sane person would believe you could call back a nuclear missile, I think is as ridiculous as the whole concept has been," he said.

Mondale, however, continued to pound away at Reagan as a President not up to the job. Asked by panelist Marvin Kalb of NBC News about arms control, Mondale replied: "The President's failure to master, in my opinion, the essential elements of arms control has cost us dearly. . . . Three years into the administration, he said he just discovered that most Soviet missiles are on land,

and that's why his proposal didn't work." And ignoring Reagan's previous disclaimer, he added: "He said that these missiles on [submarines and planes] were less dangerous than ballistic [land-based] missiles because you could recall them if you decided there had been a miscalculation. A President must know those things."

Reagan sought to counter "these repetitions of the falsehoods that have already been stated here" by painting Mondale as soft on defense. He ridiculed a Mondale commercial showing him on the deck of the aircraft carrier *Nimitz*, observing that "if he had had his way when the *Nimitz* was being planned, he would have been deep in the water out there, because there wouldn't have been any *Nimitz* to stand on. He was against it." That one got a brief laugh from the audience, but Reagan wasn't playing for laughs at this point. He said of Mondale: "He was against the F-14 fighter; he was against the M-1 tank; he was against the B-1 bomber; he wanted to cut the salary of all of the military; he wanted to bring home half of the American forces in Europe. And he has a record of weakness with regard to our national defense that is second to none."

But Mondale didn't back off. Turning and looking directly at Reagan, he said: "Mr. President, I accept your commitment to peace, but I want you to accept my commitment to a strong national defense." The response drew the most sustained audience applause to that point. "Your definition of national strength," Mondale went on, "is to throw money at the Defense Department. . . . When you pay out five hundred dollars for a five-dollar hammer, you're not buying strength." The Mondale backers in the audience applauded again, drawing an admonition from Newman. They obviously thought their man was getting much the better of the exchanges.

Even when Mondale was asked by panelist Morton Kondracke of *The New Republic* magazine[1] whether he didn't leave the impression that he would never use force to protect American interests, the former Vice President turned his answer onto Reagan and the question of presidential competence. "In Lebanon," he said, "this President exercised American power all right, but the management of it was such that our Marines were killed; we had to leave in humiliation; the Soviet Union became stronger; ter-

1. Kondracke subsequently became Washington bureau chief for *Newsweek*.

rorists became emboldened. And it was because they did not think through how power should be exercised, did not have the American public with them on a plan that worked, that we ended up the way we did."

Reagan defended his actions in Lebanon in terms of propping up the embattled Lebanese regime. "And we were succeeding," he said. Then, always a man to strike a machismo chord when the opportunity presented, Reagan observed emphatically: "I will never send troops anywhere on a mission of that kind without telling them that if somebody shoots at them, they can darn well shoot back. . . . We withdrew because we were no longer able to carry out the mission for which we had been sent in. . . . I have no apologies for our going on a peace mission."

Well, the questioner wanted to know, what about his earlier view of "swift retaliation against terrorists." Didn't the failure to strike back after nearly 300 Americans had been killed by terrorist attacks in Lebanon "suggest that you're just bluffing?" Reagan replied that he would not retaliate indiscriminately, endangering innocent civilians, and that multi-national reaction was required.

Again Mondale leaped to the attack. "The Joint Chiefs of Staff urged the President not to put our troops in that [bombed] barracks because they were undefensible," he said. On three separate occasions adequate precautions had not been taken, he observed, and "the terrorists won each time. The President told the terrorists he was going to retaliate. He didn't. They called [his] bluff. And the bottom line is, the United States left in humiliation and our enemies are stronger."

Reagan was defensive. "First of all," he said, "Mr. Mondale should know that the President of the United States did not order the Marines into that barracks. That was a command decision made by the commanders on the spot and based with what they thought was best for the men there." Here was the Commander-in-Chief of the armed forces of the United States resorting to the old Army game—passing the buck to a subordinate! Surely Mondale would leap on this dodge the next chance he got.

Just then, however, another question rendered irrelevant all that went before and all that came after in this debate. As the two men had been engaging in serious and substantive exchange on the central foreign-policy issues of the day—just as Mondale had hoped—the former Vice President by any objective yardstick had been piling up points with his aggressive questions and answers. But many in the audience there in the Kansas City theater, in the millions of living rooms across the country, and especially in that basement press room were watching and listening to the President not so much for the substance of his replies as for how he looked and acted; how he handled himself. In other words, they were watching for anything that would give them a reading on the answer to the one question that mattered to them: Was Ronald Reagan getting too old to be President?

The final panelist was Henry Trewhitt, the veteran diplomatic correspondent of *The Baltimore Sun*, a mannerly man known for his professionalism and fair-mindedness. Trewhitt had prepared a question carefully to be certain that it qualified as legitimate for a debate confined to foreign-policy matters and yet could get to the heart of what the whole campaign really had come down to.

"Mr. President," he began, "I want to raise an issue that I think has been lurking out there for two or three weeks, and cast it specifically in national security terms. You already are the oldest President in history, and some of your staff say you were tired after your most recent encounter with Mr. Mondale. I recall, yet, that President Kennedy . . . had to go for days on end with very little sleep during the Cuban missile crisis. Is there any doubt in your mind that you would be able to function in such circumstances?"

This time Reagan was ready. He shifted position slightly and the trace of a smile crept across his face. "Not at all, Mr. Trewhitt," he said in the mock earnestness of the expert funny-story teller. "And I want you to know that also I will not make age an issue in this campaign. I am not going to exploit, for political purposes, my opponent's youth and inexperience."

All at once, for all practical purposes, the presidential election of 1984 was over. The audience in the theater broke into loud and prolonged laughter and applause. Even Mondale, caught in the camera's eye that peered over Reagan's shoulder at him, could not suppress a hapless grin that seemed to concede, "You got me!"

Down in the press room, reporters nodded knowingly to each other. But it was Trewhitt himself who best summed up the reaction and its instantaneous political effect. "Mr. President," he said, "I'd like to head for the fence and try to catch that one, but I'll go on to another question."

And Trewhitt did so, but he might have saved his breath for all that the subsequent questions and answers of the second debate mattered. The Reagan home run had not simply cleared the fence; it had gone right out of the ballpark. The age issue, which was born in the first debate, died just as quickly in the second, slain by one of the most resourceful weapons in Ronald Reagan's forensic arsenal—the good old one-liner.

In the Kansas City suburb of Overland Park, about twenty-five miles from the scene of the debate, the ever-efficient Reagan campaign was positioned to put a tape measure on the home run. Gathered in the conference room of a market research firm were forty voters selected from the Kansas City area phone book by random dialing—twenty Democrats, fifteen Republicans and five independents. The individuals were told only that they had been chosen to participate in a survey; they did not know it was being conducted under the direction of the Reagan campaign's chief pollster, Richard Wirthlin. Each of the forty was given a hand-held monitor bearing five buttons labeled A through E. If you felt very positive about something said in the debate as you watched it on a television screen in the room, you were to hold down A. If you felt very negative, you were to push E. If you felt somewhere in between, you were to push the appropriate button on the scale, with C representing a neutral reaction.

Sitting in the back of the room as silent observers were three representatives of Market Facts, a Chicago market research firm conducting the test for Wirthlin. When the President answered Trewhitt's question with his one-liner, the test viewers were so convulsed with laughter that some of them forgot to push any button. Still, the reaction registered high on the A or very positive scale, and interviewing by the market researchers after the debate established clearly that the Reagan quip was the high point—and the most memorable remark—of the ninety-minute confrontation.

Ronald Reagan, The Great Entertainer as well as The Great Communicator, had done it again. In his one debate with President Jimmy Carter in 1980, what most voters had remembered about his performance were two other one-liners: "There you go again" in alleging that Carter was misrepresenting his record on Medicare and, even more memorable, "Are you better off than you were four years ago?" But neither of those 1980 lines was the perfect squelch of an issue threatening Reagan that his putdown of the age issue was this time around.

The assumption in the press room that night was that Reagan's debate preparation team had come up with the one-liner and had orchestrated its use in one of the mock debates conducted in rehearsal for the real thing. Actually, most of Reagan's debate coaches insisted they had never thrown an age question at him. One did say a response had been prepared, but not the one Reagan used. The plan, he said, was that when and if the age issue came up, the President was to say, "Yes, age is an issue in this campaign. My opponent's ideas are too old." But that crack would have been a mere scratch single compared to Reagan's ad-lib homer.

White House Chief of Staff James Baker recalled later that sometime before the first debate, as he was riding in a White House limousine with the President, they started discussing the age issue, which had not surfaced in any serious way but was always in the background. Reagan told him: "Well, I might just say if I'm asked, 'If he doesn't question my age, I won't raise questions about his youth and inexperience.' " But nothing more was said about the subject after that, Baker said, and he was as surprised as anyone else when the one-liner leveled Mondale.

That the incumbent President could thus sweep away the only obstacle in his path to a landslide reelection with one clever remark—one that was not really responsive to the serious question about his stamina—said something about the quality of the presidential election campaign of 1984. Obviously there was much more to Ronald Reagan's smashing victory—forty-nine states and 525 electoral votes when America finally trooped to the polls sixteen days later—than his ability to obliterate the age issue with a quip. But the episode did clearly demonstrate how superficial much of the public's attitude was toward serious dialogue between Reagan and Mondale, when that remark could be judged the debate's highlight. Even one of the chief strategists within the White House observed to us after the election that it was "absurd" that Mondale's only chance for a comeback could be "undone by a single one-liner."

That circumstance was possible only because the presidential election of 1984 was never, in all its plodding months of campaigning by a host of Democratic challengers and an insulated, aloof Republican incumbent, a vehicle for a detailed, concentrated or intelligent examination of the vital issues facing the country.

On the Democratic side, the tortuous primary/caucus battle for the party's presidential nomination had degenerated into a very negative catfight. An unexpectedly strong challenge to Mondale from longshot Senator Gary Hart of Colorado did not trigger, as Hart had hoped, a substantive, constructive debate about the basic direction of an ailing party. Rather, it had produced only slashingly negative generalities from Mondale, such as his ludicrous "Where's the beef?" counterattack borrowed from a fast-food commercial. That deplorable but politically effective cheapening of the campaign dialogue in turn persuaded Hart to respond with negative attacks of his own, until the electorate was massively disenthralled. As a result, by the time Mondale was nominated he had so thoroughly diminished his own already shaky credibility in the eyes of voters that he could not force Reagan in the fall to engage in a serious exchange of views on the crucial issues of the day.

On the Republican side, the successful campaign formula of the aloof and insulated incumbency so calculatingly applied by Richard M. Nixon twelve years earlier against the hapless George McGovern provided the model for a Reagan reelection campaign that made Nixon's 1972 effort seem by comparison a kaleidoscope of candor. Reagan did not hide in the Rose Garden, to be sure. But beyond the two formal debates he never engaged in any elevating or even satisfactory communication with the voters that permitted a searching examination of his intent for the country's next four years. He did not hold a single press conference during the fall campaign; instead, he made a series of short sorties into the country in the manner of a political Music Man, playing Professor Harold Hill to both rural and urban River City crowds. He and his managers treated them to a disingenuously folksy road show long on emotional massage and flag-waving and short on specifics about the programmatic route ahead. In defense of this approach, one key White House strategist told us later: "We had our issues of patriotism, everything is hunky-dory, feel-good—which isn't bad."

In terms of what would facilitate the trouble-free election of an incumbent President, that Reagan aide's assessment could not be seriously disputed. But in terms of making the presidential election a democratic exercise of informed popular will, the Reagan campaign formula was an elaborate job of snake-oil salesmanship.

This is not to say that Ronald Reagan did not have legitimate positions to stake before the American people for their consideration; rather, that he was able to avoid doing so in any significant fashion.

To a considerable degree, the fault was in the unwillingness of the Reagan campaign to go beyond what, in its own coldly political calculations, was essential. But there were others to blame as well. Mondale, in his failure for a host of reasons to come through the nomination process as a credible candidate and to perform as one once nominated, was unable to bring a challenge of sufficient political strength to pressure Reagan out of his cocoon. The Democratic Party, in its failure to recognize the baggage of its past, the corrosive elements of its present and its bankruptcy of a vision for the future, did not provide Mondale with an adequate appeal on which to base a winning campaign.

The nominating process itself imposed on all the Democratic challengers a politically, financially, physically and emotionally debilitating marathon route to party endorsement. For all that had been written and said about the destructiveness of the process, "reforms" made in the four years since the 1980 election on balance only introduced new complications for the candidates. Meanwhile, nothing was done about some of the more obvious old problems—such as the bunching up of primaries and caucuses to the point that candidates were sentenced to physical exhaustion and voters to mental fatigue and, ultimately, political apathy.

The news media, and television particularly, came in for their share of responsibility for what was essentially a deplorable election. Collectively or individually, reporters and analysts too often yielded to the trivial, assigned excessive importance to the transparently self-serving and exaggerated the significance of way-station developments. The reporting on the contest for the Democratic nomination sometimes misinterpreted the strategic relevance of primary and caucus results in ways that seriously affected the outcome. And in covering the Republican side, too often newsprint space and television air time were given to Professor Harold Hill and his seventy-six trombones, without sufficient attention to the conditions in River City that the Music Man was glossing over.

Finally, too many voters once again revealed themselves in countless newspaper, radio and television interviews to be an intellectually lazy or at least apathetic lot—seemingly too engrossed in their personal problems and diversions to demand much from the candidates, especially from the incumbent who administered to them such heavy doses of soothing syrup. In a nation in which literally a torrent of specific information is available about political candidates and their views, too many citizens openly acknowledged that they cast their votes on superficial grounds—or, worse, didn't bother to vote at all. Although voter turnout inched up ever so slightly for the first time since 1960—seven-tenths of one percent over the 1980 turnout—nearly half the eligible voters in 1984 still stayed home on election day, in spite of intensive registration drives in both major parties.[2] Once again it was a case, for millions of Americans, of wake us when it's over.

Particularly distressing about this apathy is the fact that a most significant development in American political history was confirmed in the election of 1984. Conservatism, which had seemed a feeble, almost laughable political movement only twenty years earlier in the fervent but ineffectual presidential campaign of Senator Barry Goldwater of Arizona, had at last laid unmistakable claim to the support of a voting majority of the country. Four years earlier, when Ronald Reagan was first elected to the presidency, a large measure of his victory was attributed to an emphatic rejection of his Democratic opponent, Jimmy Carter, who after four years of incumbency was widely seen as weak and indecisive. Even now, there were many who credited Reagan's landslide reelection chiefly to his personal popularity rather than to the conservatism he espoused.

Along with Reagan's victory, however, the abysmal showing of Mondale as the Democratic standard-bearer obliged his party leaders to face something many of them had tried to put off through the 1970s and 1980s—years of such distractions or even aberrations as Vietnam, Watergate and the unloved Carter. They preferred not to face the evidence that their guiding light of half a century—the New Deal of Franklin D. Roosevelt and its successor mutations from Truman through Carter and Mondale—had been all but snuffed out by the voters as the preferred framework for governmental policy at the national level.

2. The nonpartisan Committee for the Study of the American Electorate reported in January 1985 that 92,707,218 Americans voted for President, or 53.3 percent of the eligible electorate, compared to 52.6 percent voting in 1980. Turnout among *registered* voters, however, declined 2.6 percent in 1984.

Thus, Reagan was elected and Mondale was routed at the apex of a conservative movement in the country that had developed almost inexorably in a period of great turmoil for the Republican Party—and at the nadir of an orthodox Democratic liberalism that had faded correspondingly.

Twenty years earlier, this same Ronald Reagan had been a new voice emerging from the wilderness of the right, at a time Fritz Mondale was about to enter the United States Senate as the disciple of and the appointed replacement for Minnesota's favorite son of the New Deal, Hubert H. Humphrey, just then elevated to the vice presidency. A brief look at that two-decade swing of the political pendulum is in order as a prelude to examining the presidential election of 1984 that was so triumphant for Reagan and conservatism and so dismal for Mondale and liberalism.

2

From Goldwater to Reagan

•

ALMOST TWENTY YEARS TO THE DAY before he buried Walter Mondale's faint 1984 hopes by vowing on nationwide television not to question his "youth and inexperience," Ronald Reagan had launched his own political career with an impassioned television plea for another lost cause—the conservative crusade of Barry Goldwater. In a paid fund-raising speech entitled "A Time for Choosing," motion-picture actor and television-drama host Reagan had told Americans across the country: "You and I have a rendezvous with destiny. We can preserve for our children this last best hope of man on earth, or we can sentence them to take the first step into a thousand years of darkness. If we fail, at least let our children and our children's children say of us we justified our brief moment here. We did all that could be done."

As drippingly melodramatic as that peroration was, the speech brought in $600,000 for the Goldwater campaign, an impressive amount by the standards of the politics of 1964. More significantly, it expressed the fervor of an emerging conservative movement in the United States that, while soon to be rejected overwhelmingly at the polls in the 1964 landslide of President Lyndon B. Johnson over Goldwater, ultimately would sweep this same Ronald Reagan into the White House. While the triumphant Johnson read his overwhelming victory as a mandate for expanding his Great Society program—the natural offspring, Texas-size, of Franklin D. Roosevelt's New Deal and Harry Truman's Fair Deal—the Goldwater conservatives hunkered down for the long haul. Like guerrillas driven into the hills, they fell back and regrouped, but did not give up the war.

Goldwater's chief speechwriter and political philosopher, a former news magazine editor named Karl Hess, subsequently wrote a book called *In a Cause That Will Triumph* in which he looked to the time conservatism would bury New Deal liberalism and make a prophet of Goldwater. "Senator Goldwater's vision of America is the one that lies just beyond the clouds of today's experimentation," Hess wrote. ". . . The elections of 1966 and even 1968 may see just the first rising of the tide. It may only be a ripple. But . . . it will be felt again. When it is, the dialogue truly will begin. And when that happens, many, many of the words will be familiar. Senator Goldwater will have said them."

Hess saw the 1964 election as a crucial fork in the road for the Republican Party. "In a certain realistic sense," he wrote, "it could be said that the Republican Party hasn't really existed in any meaningful sense for some thirty years. What it was supposed to stand for has certainly existed in the minds of a number of those who have called themselves Republicans. But there is no consistent representation of a political philosophy which is in any way comparable to that of the Democratic Party. We have had, therefore, in the ideological sense a one-party, not a two-party, system in this country ever since 1932." To rectify the situation, Hess wrote, "the 'out' party must turn to reform and ideology. . . . If the 'out' party cannot or will not grit its teeth and dig in for the long-haul fight that such a course requires, then it will become a non-party."

At least in that 1964 election, he wrote, "two men stood before the American people [who] represented two sets of values and ideas as clearly as though cast upon a stage." As a result, he said, millions of Americans "wonder as they see the Johnson poverty programs foundering on graft and confusion. They wonder when they hear their neighbor asking why he should work harder [when] the government will just take it anyway. They wonder when the union gets a raise for hard-working men and women only to have it wiped out by an equivalent boost in the cost of caring for people who will not work—not who can't, but who won't. They wonder when they watch a White House conference on national standards, so help us, of happiness, while they fidget and fret about the increasing drag of their own red-taped lives. . . . They wonder when they hear their children turn to a government text or a government counselor as authority higher than any parent. They must wonder. They must."

The words were written by Hess, but they easily could have been uttered then, or twenty years later, by Ronald Reagan. Those observations squared exactly with Reagan's philosophy as a convert from the Democratic Party in 1964, and ever thereafter.[3]

One of the many gaffes that plagued Goldwater in that 1964 campaign was his suggestion that Social Security be made voluntary. Critics jumped all over him, holding that any such move would fatally undermine the actuarial basis of the system. Yet Reagan in his televised speech in the closing days of the campaign had no hesitation in backing Goldwater on the issue. "Now, are we so lacking in business sense that we cannot put this program on a sound actuarial basis, so that those who depend on it won't come to the cupboard and find it bare?" he asked. "And at the same time can't we introduce voluntary features so that those who can make better provisions for themselves are allowed to do so?"

Reagan's views on Social Security were to plague him, too, over the next twenty years, until as a candidate for reelection to the presidency in 1984 he felt obliged to say he would never do anything to reduce or deny benefits to the elderly who qualified for them. But the system always seemed to symbolize for him, as it did for Goldwater, the dreaded "welfare state" to which America had been reduced by the New Deal and by "knee-jerk liberals."

In 1964, the use of such conservative code words by Goldwater elicited derisive laughter from the Democratic left and from the strong liberal-moderate eastern establishment of his own party as well. But by the time of Reagan's reelection to the presidency in 1984, few on the Democratic left were laughing anymore, and there was no longer any Republican left to speak of. Those code words had become part of the accepted political lexicon to convey what had been wrong with the country until the conservative tide

3. Hess concluded his book by pledging that "this is a cause in which I will spend my life." Within a few years, however, he underwent a startling transformation. The main difference Hess sees between the Goldwater of 1964 and the Reagan of 1985, he told us, is that Reagan is "all rhetoric" and is not bent on radical political or economic change, whereas Goldwater meant exactly what he said. Goldwater, in his own memoirs, *With No Apologies*, called Hess "a man who has been around the liberal-conservative bush so many times he would make Walter Lippmann look as though he had walked a perfectly straight line all of his life." Hess now calls himself a libertarian, and he lives in the small town of Kearneysville, West Virginia, near Harpers Ferry, where he makes furniture, which he trucks to Washington, D.C., and sells himself at the city's Eastern Market just off Capitol Hill where twenty years earlier he extolled the free-enterprise system as a Barry Goldwater apostle.

behind Reagan had manifested itself across the land, and in presidential electoral politics in particular.

The political transformation was barely perceptible for a considerable time. The immediate assumption after the inundation of Goldwater was that both the man and his ideology had been summarily buried by the voters. But Goldwater said in an interview after the 1984 reelection of Reagan that the fact there were "twenty-seven million people who thought I was right" encouraged the party's conservatives to persevere. He told us he knew from the start that he could not win the 1964 election, "so we set out to upset the Eastern seaboard, and we did. We moved the seat of the Republican Party to the West." By shifting the party's focus—and, very significantly, its financial base as well—away from the old moneyed and somewhat liberal interests in the East to the more conservative but relatively undeveloped Sun Belt, Goldwater said, the GOP was able to recapture and identify with the sense of a pioneer spirit that had inspired earlier Americans. By the time Reagan emerged as a national leader, Goldwater said, young people were looking to the western-oriented Republican Party as more sensitive to that old pioneer spirit.

The shift, however, was much more than geographical and financial. After years of Republican me-tooism in international affairs and on the liberal Democratic social agenda under such unsuccessful challengers to FDR as Wendell Willkie and Thomas E. Dewey, the ideological underpinnings of the Republican Party were now being questioned—as Hess had suggested they ought to be—by the conservatives. While having lost behind Goldwater in 1964, they were holding onto the party in many states, particularly in the West and South, and giving the GOP a much more orthodox conservative stripe than before.

That conservatism was succeeding in dominating the party and gaining real public support was not, however, widely perceived in the years right after the Goldwater defeat. For one thing, the country was still in the midst of its great internal revolution for social justice—the civil-rights movement. While Goldwater's emphasis on the issue of crime in the streets in the 1964 campaign had been seen as a thinly veiled way to inject racism into the contest and to play on white fears of black economic and social advances, many Republicans as well as Democrats were involved in that momentous revolution. Under the dominant leadership of Lyndon Johnson in the White House, those conservatives who dragged their heels or attempted to impede civil-rights progress were made to look petulantly futile.

At the same time, however, Johnson was being plagued by the increasingly unpopular and indecisive war in Vietnam. Four years after the Goldwater defeat, Johnson decided not to seek reelection and his Vice President and would-be successor, Hubert Humphrey, was narrowly defeated for the presidency by Richard Nixon in 1968. That result was generally attributed to public disfavor with Johnson's conduct of the war, rather than to any triumph of conservatism. Nixon after all was no conservative ideologue; he was a pragmatic politician who strove to occupy the center of the political spectrum while stroking leaders on the right and dutifully mouthing the conservative rhetoric in both domestic and foreign affairs. He talked tough on foreign policy and intimated that he had a secret plan to end the war in Vietnam that sensitivity, security and diplomacy required he not disclose in the 1968 campaign.

Once in office, Nixon continued and in some cases expanded the basic programs of the New Deal and the Great Society, while paying lip service to the growing unrest in the country toward greater government involvement in the lives of average Americans. In the view of Representative Richard Cheney of Wyoming, who was the White House Chief of Staff under President Gerald R. Ford before becoming chairman of the House Republican Policy Committee, "Nixon ballooned those [Democratic] programs like crazy. He was the big spender in recent decades. Johnson got a lot of that stuff on the books, but Nixon was the one who really funded the food stamp program along with housing and education."

It was also true, however, that with his Vice President, Spiro T. Agnew of Maryland, acting as point man, Nixon aggressively encouraged "the silent majority" of dissatisfied middle-class Americans to assert themselves—in his behalf. By Agnew especially, the encouragement was advanced with racial overtones that were deplored by liberals. But these innuendoes struck responsive chords among whites who were feeling increasingly threatened by the social and economic progress of blacks generated by the civil-rights revolution.

The continuing war in Vietnam and Nixon's politically fatal

Watergate affair, nevertheless, somewhat diverted attention from the conservative mood that was developing in the country. In 1976, though, Ronald Reagan provided the voice required to seize the national spotlight. He had engaged in a little-remembered, last-minute flirtation with the Republican presidential nomination in 1968 and had been emerging as an ever-stronger voice of conservatism after two terms as governor of California and as a top-drawer celebrity on the political fund-raising circuit. Now, in his challenge to Ford, the nation's first appointed President, Reagan publicly reinstituted the crusade that had suffered such ignominious defeat behind Goldwater twelve years before.

The same fervor that had fueled the 1964 Goldwater campaign drove the Reagan campaign in 1976. Only Ford's advantages of incumbency prevented Reagan from winning the Republican nomination, and quite possibly the presidency, in that year. With the defeat of Ford by Democrat Jimmy Carter, however, the way was cleared for Reagan and the conservative movement to make their successful drive for the White House in 1980. They achieved their goal not simply because of Reagan's personal appeal or the power of the conservative argument but because the twenty years since the Goldwater debacle had seen a steady erosion of the message and the political credibility of the New Deal and its successor variations and mutations.

The New Deal had been born in 1933 of economic desperation more than of any sociological tinkering. A prominent Democratic figure of the time, Washington lawyer and counselor to Presidents Clark Clifford, recalled in an interview after the 1984 election that "the New Deal came out of the agony of the Great Depression of the thirties. I remember so well. There really was no hope in the country in those early days. Franklin Roosevelt brought that hope when he came in in 1933. The whole social effort was directed toward getting people back to work, increasing the strength of labor unions so they could bargain on a more equal basis. Then came the great legislative enactments that corrected the gross abuses that had taken place, and the whole effort then was to try to lift the country up by its bootstraps. Franklin Roosevelt referred again and again to that one-third of our population who were ill-fed, ill-clothed and ill-housed, and much was done to lift them up."

Others who remembered that time, such as Goldwater, would

not concede that the New Deal pulled the country out of the Great Depression. "There were no liberal concepts that drew us out of that depression," he said. "It was World War Two."

But it was a time, he acknowledged, when conservatism was so distinctly out of favor that an old Democratic friend of the time named Ronald Reagan "used to call George Murphy [the actor, later a Republican senator] and me a couple of black fascist bastards" for their opposition to the strike of the Screen Actors' Guild, of which Reagan was president. World War II meant jobs, and that fact coupled with Democratic welfare programs generated political support for the New Deal. In a typical Goldwaterism, he put it this way: "The war more or less erased people's cares from their minds, because they all had jobs."

Clifford for his part conceded that preparations for World War II, and the intensive conduct of it, rejuvenated the nation's industrial machine and contributed greatly to solving the unemployment problem. But that development continued on well past the end of the war, he noted, into the 1950s and 1960s, "a period of fine prosperity for the country."

At the same time, however, Clifford recalled, "the tenor and the attitude of the country was changing because the people had advanced so generally and so steadily during these decades that the old concept of what was needed—to help the great mass of our citizens who were out of work and were doing badly—did not really exist in the same fashion that it did before. So many millions of our families had progressed to the point where they not only had a good job but they were owning their own home, they owned their own automobile and they were looking ahead to owning a second automobile and maybe a second home. The New Deal and the Fair Deal in my opinion were so basically successful in restoring prosperity to the country that they pretty well sounded their own death knell."

By the seventies, the situation had become much more complicated. "We still had the poor," Clifford said, "maybe not as many as we had before, but we had a much higher level of income and a much better living standard in the country." Accordingly, he said, people "became much more conscious of taxes. They began to get concerned too about the cost of government, and they got concerned about the question of whether the government was taking care of the people they need not take care of. So a whole new philosophy developed in the country, a more conservative philosophy, but conservative only in comparison to what had gone before."

Other observers of the New Deal phenomenon from a more conservative perspective agree in at least one basic regard—that it did attain its primary objectives. "Every aspiration the New Deal ever had for government programs, ways to have government help people, was satisfied," says Cheney. "There was nothing left on the agenda."

John Sears, the Washington lawyer who managed Reagan's presidential campaigns in 1976 and early 1980, concurs. "I don't know that the New Deal ever really declined," he says. "What the New Deal promised got done. There wasn't an obvious agenda left after that, so the liberals in the Democratic Party started getting into issues that were to some degree beyond the New Deal, and tried to cloak them in the garments of the New Deal.

"The purely social agenda of the Democratic Party was as much wrought by the fact that there weren't other things to do. Pro-abortion, pro other women's rights, anti-prayer in school—most of these things, whether people think they're right or wrong, are not pure political issues. They are things guys in bars talk about after they've run out of sports and sex, but they really have little to do with the guts of running the government or what general direction you should take in that. And out in the society, they are very divisive."

While it is true the Republicans, not the Democrats, were the ones who often injected such issues into the political debate as a result of Supreme Court rulings unfavorable to their viewpoint, the Democrats did permit themselves, Sears says, to be sidetracked into defending the unpopular view. The championing of civil rights came in time to fall into this unpopular category among many whites as they saw black progress less in terms of needed social progress and more as a threat to their own social or economic well-being.

Basic elements of the civil-rights revolution continued to draw substantial support from moderate as well as liberal whites. But as that revolution began to grapple with less conspicuous problems of discrimination and lack of opportunity in employment, housing and education that led to affirmative action programs and complex school busing formulas, white support often shied off. This trend was especially apparent against a backdrop of rising street crime and welfare costs, which became to many whites an easy handle for justifying their fears of growing black awareness and demands on the community at large. Liberals who failed to recognize these often middle-class white attitudes, or who ignored them, suffered an erosion of credibility in the eyes of those who held such attitudes.

At the same time the Republicans began to address themselves to questions touching on the high cost of government and its effectiveness—questions growing out of the heightened awareness of the new generation of taxpayers created by the very successes of the New Deal.

"The focus," Cheney says, "shifted away from the benefits that flowed to individuals and families from government action to the cost associated with it. Once government got to a certain size, once it began to consume a third of the gross national product, once you got runaway inflation and runaway federal spending and deficits, the economic consequences of operating a government that large, even in a strong economy like ours, became obvious to all and became the subject of political debate. In the fifties and sixties, when Barry Goldwater was arguing against Social Security, Medicare and so forth, it didn't mean he was wrong so much, but at the time the pain was only potential. It wasn't real."

When the economic pain at last did become real, the conservative movement that had been holding the fort in the Republican Party since the Goldwater takeover of 1964 was ready to take advantage of the situation.

"While the Democratic Party stalled out in terms of its economic agenda," Sears says, "the Republicans were able to pick out some things that did need to be changed. They got to be actually more of the activists on the normal domestic issues and the Democrats slowly came to be on the defensive on them. We are a very activist country, and the Democrats had been trusted since 1932 to define the activism and what should be done to bring it forward. But they were choosing now to use their activism on these social issues, and meanwhile the Republicans were being more activist on the more domestic economic issues."

There were, to be sure, remaining pure New Deal promises yet unfulfilled, particularly in the area of poverty. These were addressed massively during the Great Society of Lyndon Johnson and many of the prime remedies have endured—though with the continuing disparagement of conservative critics—food stamps, Medicaid, aid to dependent children, job training and the like.

"Most of the Great Society stuck," says Harry McPherson, yet another Washington lawyer who helped construct and publicize the program in the Johnson White House. "When most people say the Great Society failed, and that certainly is the conventional wisdom, it didn't. It is our life now. It is inconceivable to think of going back and having Grandma take care of her own medical bills. When we talk about the failure of the Great Society program, we're talking about the failure of the poverty program effort to end poverty. But in fact we have more families under the poverty line now than we had four or six years ago and we don't know what to do about it."

One obvious reason that Johnson's anti-poverty program was seen so widely as a failure, and that the expenditure of great sums of taxpayer money was increasingly resented, was that it over-promised at the outset and was oversold by its rhetoricians, Johnson foremost among them. The effort became "the war on poverty," and in this war as in most others, exaggeration of success became commonplace and self-defeating. Offshoots of simply feeding, clothing and housing the poor, such as efforts to assure their legal rights, became fights against City Hall that heightened political tensions and polarized the benefactors and the beneficiaries. What was intended as a means of eradicating inequities often served to highlight them and to fan passions over them.

"A few years later after the expending of a great deal of money," Sears says, "it seemed to people that it hadn't succeeded. And there were other things back at that time that began to make a lot of people think, 'We're glad to try to do this, but I guess you can't do it just by spending all this money. And, indeed, as I see some of this unfolding, I don't like it.' "

Such was the attitude about aid to education, especially with the growing student protests against the Vietnam war and the school busing controversy. "People began to think," Sears says, " 'What is my kid learning down there? And besides, he's got long hair.' And in this strange way, aid to education lost its credibility." With great regularity, local communities began to reject school bond issues for the first time in memory.

What's more, all this was happening in the context of the war in Vietnam, which Johnson insisted he could prosecute while still paying for all the Great Society domestic programs.

"People began to think for the first time since the beginning of the New Deal," Sears says, " 'What in the hell is happening with all this money we've been giving you? We don't seem to be getting much for it.' And for the first time since the Republicans were making the case, they began to be believed—that a lot of this wasn't worth the money. That was sort of a turning point."

There was also the matter of racial quotas in jobs and higher education supported by many in the Democratic Party, which did not always sit well with whites of modest income who felt their own interests were being jeopardized in the process.

"A lot of that was interpreted as latent racism," Sears says, "and on the part of some people it was. But on the part of a lot of other people it really wasn't. It wasn't that at the beginning they were dead set against some of these ideas. But as they got into them they began to scratch their heads and say, 'Well, I'm not sure. If I'm really going to go through this, I've got to see more benefit.' And it wasn't easy to show them."

On top of all this, frustrations deepened over the war in Southeast Asia, against a supposedly small but mysterious foe, that this great and powerful country did not seem able to win no matter how much manpower and money it poured in. And there was in charge now a President, Nixon, who turned out be so thoroughly devious and untrustworthy that he was forced to resign to avoid being impeached.

People concluded, Sears says, " 'I'd better take a better look at what we're doing here. There seem to be a lot of things wrong. I can't trust the President, and then this war, nobody's telling me straight on that.' They doubted everything more, and this inward process began to focus more attention on whether some of these things were worth the money."

The eventual political beneficiary, ironically, after the abbreviated caretaker administration of Gerald Ford, was a Democrat—Jimmy Carter. The one-term Georgia governor was able to come upon the revulsion to big-spending and corrupt government with clean hands.

"He simply said," Sears notes, " 'I'm different, I'm new, I've never been a part of this. I've never been to Washington.' He appeared to be an honest man, and by a slim margin people said, 'Let's give him a whirl at it.' "

Almost for the first time since 1932, when Roosevelt was elected and moved so aggressively and conclusively to bring activist government to Washington, it had become popular to run against Washington, even as a Democrat.

But just as the Republicans in the 1920s could not see that they were headed for political disaster, the Democrats in the late 1960s and 1970s did not seem able or willing to read the warning signals. When George Wallace flashed one with his surprisingly successful appeals to the expanded middle class, and particularly to white blue-collar workers in Northern industrial states in the 1968 and 1972 presidential primaries, the Democrats dismissed it as a mere ramification of racism, or a political aberration. They pressed on with what they saw as a natural extension of the New Deal agenda that had both inspired them and served them politically since FDR's first election.

"They got away from the New Deal themselves," Cheney says. "You could make the case that they forgot their roots. They got all caught up in things like affirmative action, gay rights. They moved beyond the point where government provided benefits for people, beyond the point where government was seeing to it that there was no discrimination against somebody because of race. It got to a point where, if the Democrats were successful, many people felt they would impose their values, or a burden on the white union worker who was going to be hampered by affirmative action in order to make room for a black. To them, it was radically different from what the New Deal was all about. It was a step beyond what most people thought the New Deal was."

Structurally, too, the Democrats seemed to be intentionally distancing themselves from the middle class. Party reforms had diminished the role of elected officials and, in trying to open the party to all its disparate elements, succeeded instead in elevating the influence of relatively small groups of cause-oriented activists and special-interest pleaders.

"They had in mind their own agenda of what needed to be done," Sears says, "and weren't thinking, as Democratic politicians had always done, about what was necessary in order to win. That process resulted in the landslide for Nixon [in 1972 over George

McGovern, the candidate of the anti-war and other liberal activists]. It wasn't a positive endorsement of Nixon. It was just the way Nixon always liked elections—to get people to vote against the other guy."

The political catastrophe of Watergate, in forcing Nixon from office and paving the way two years later for the narrow election of Jimmy Carter over Gerald Ford, also gave the New Deal tradition a temporary reprieve. At the same time, the election of a Democrat to the presidency, even this strange kind of Democrat, lulled many in the party into a false sense of well-being about its hold on the affections and respect of the voters.

Carter, who never would have been the choice of party leaders but who was able to navigate the obstacle course of party activists and special-interest groups by promising the moon to each of them, continued in the basic New Deal tradition. He proceeded, however, on such a modest scale compared to Democratic Presidents who had gone before him that he was twice damned—by Republicans who painted him as just another New Deal giveaway Democrat and by Democratic liberals who saw him as an inadequate heir to the New Deal tradition. Inhibited by rapidly rising inflation and a mounting federal deficit, Carter sought to curb government services and spending in a fashion inadequate to deter traditional Republican attacks but all too effective for the liking of liberal Democrats.

Some younger Democrats did recognize what was happening in the country and tried to sound the alarm. In a speech at the Women's National Democratic Club in Washington in October 1977, Representative Elliott Levitas of Georgia, then in his second term, gave a prescient speech entitled "The New Deal Is Dead; May It Rest in Peace." In it he warned that the New Deal was "being committed to history," and that the Carter administration would likely be judged by the extent to which it "is able to bid farewell to the New Deal, giving it honor but putting it to rest and moving on into a new era."

Carter owed his election the year before, Levitas argued, not solely to the traditional components of the New Deal coalition but to "a broad-based appeal to the average, non-group-identifiable Americans" who saw Carter "as a person not associated with those aspects of Washington government that have proved to be wasteful, oppressive failures. He was perceived as seriously dedicated to fundamentally changing the direction of our federal government. His campaign called for government reorganization, decentralization, tax reform, welfare reform, control over the bureaucracy, less government, more responsive government, and balanced budgets. . . . These themes are the antithesis of the New Deal." They were, in fact, the same themes Ronald Reagan had espoused in his near-upset of Gerald Ford in the 1976 contest for the Republican presidential nomination.[4]

Carter, however, did not prove able to deliver on his promises to get a handle on the Washington that the New Deal had wrought. And to make matters worse, late in his term Carter laid the blame for his domestic problems on the people. In a speech in the summer of 1979, after several days of meetings with dozens of Democratic leaders at Camp David, he warned of a "crisis of confidence" in the land "that strikes at the very heart and soul and spirit of our national will."

This warning came to be known as Carter's "malaise" speech, though he never used that word in it. In any event, voters did not like to have their President passing the buck to them in that way. Nor were they excited by the growing concept within the Democratic Party, most often expressed by Governor Jerry Brown of California but also embraced by Carter, that the country was entering "an era of limits" in which expectations of national accomplishment and individual material consumption had to be lowered.

"In the Democratic Party," Sears says, "what little reasoning was going on about what to do with the country revolved around either the express or tacit statement that 'we've had our better days, and all we've got now are problems. And it's not going to get better. For some it will, if we can lick their problems'—but no statement to the middle class about how they were going to make it. Jerry Brown said, 'Small is good.' Hell, the American people don't believe that. They believe some way or another we can make things bigger, and if we can, everybody will have enough." In the face of such talk, it began to dawn on voters that Republicans like Ronald Reagan, who voiced the old platitudes of an America that could still do anything it set its mind to, were the new "activists."

4. Levitas, after ten years in Congress, was defeated for reelection in 1984, when Reagan at the top of the Republican ticket carried Georgia.

Beyond that, Carter seemed the last straw for millions of Americans disillusioned over what they saw as the disintegrating stature of their country on the world stage. In Nixon's words, the United States had become a "helpless giant" as a result of Vietnam, and Carter had now presided over one of its most humiliating periods in the 444 days of the Iranian hostage crisis—the captivity of fifty-two Americans in the seized American embassy in Tehran. Their countrymen did not feel at all good about themselves—or about their ineffectual President—as the presidential campaign of 1980 unfolded, pitting Carter against the same man who sixteen years earlier had taken to television on behalf of Barry Goldwater to tell them that they had "a rendezvous with destiny."

In the course of that campaign, Reagan picked up where Goldwater had left off, promising the American people that he would get government off their backs at home and make the United States feared and respected once again around the world. He would balance the federal budget in a year or so, he said, get the welfare chiselers off the federal dole, reclaim power from the bureaucrats and "drain the swamp" that was Washington. Unable to run effectively on his own record, Carter countered by trying to frighten the voters about his opponent. He painted Reagan as a dangerous warmonger not to be trusted with his finger on the nuclear button, and as a simplistic throwback to the Republican economic Neanderthals of the past on domestic affairs. And he failed dismally. On the final weekend of the campaign, an eleventh-hour prospect that the American hostages might be released conspicuously fizzled, underscoring in a politically devastating manner Carter's inability to cope with what had come to be a glaring symbol of American paralysis in foreign affairs.

Ronald Reagan's landslide victory over Jimmy Carter was thus in the most obvious sense a rejection of Carter. Just as other political developments occurring since the Goldwater debacle of 1964 had obscured the steady national trend toward conservatism—the civil-rights revolution, Vietnam and Watergate foremost among them—so too did the public disenchantment with Carter mask the maturing of the movement personified by Reagan. But conservatism undoubtedly had arrived. Beyond Reagan's overwhelming election, his party captured twelve Democratic Senate seats, including those of seven of the most liberal Democrats—among them McGovern, the 1972 Democratic presidential nominee. The Republicans thus gained control of the Senate for the first time since Dwight D. Eisenhower had won the presidency in a similar landslide in 1952.

The minute Reagan took office, he served notice that he intended to carry out the classic conservative agenda swiftly. "In the present crisis," he said in his inaugural address, "government is not the solution to our problem; government is the problem. . . . It is my intention to curb the size and influence of the federal establishment. . . . It's not my intention to do away with government. It is rather to make it work—work with us, not over us; to stand by our side, not ride on our back."

It was the same old refrain that Reagan had been singing since the Goldwater campaign, but now he had the chance to act on it, and he did.

Not only his words but events on the day of his inauguration provided an auspicious kickoff. Just as Reagan was sworn in, the American hostages in Tehran were being released—a development in which he had played no role, except in providing a vehicle for a final humiliation of the retiring President. At a White House ceremony honoring the returned hostages one week later and at a subsequent press conference, Reagan vowed that never again would terrorists be permitted to strike with impunity against American citizens.

On the domestic front, the new President moved almost at once to carry out his inaugural pledge. He proposed deep cuts in federal spending and at the same time in federal income taxes as part of a radical plan designed to stimulate economic recovery, to be known in short order as Reaganomics. Reagan's Vice President, George Bush, as a challenger to Reagan for the 1980 Republican presidential nomination had called cutting taxes, increasing military spending and still balancing the budget "voodoo economics," and the Democrats quickly took up the cry. The Reagan budget called for $48.6 billion in cuts below the final budget prepared by Carter, and the gored oxen throughout the federal bureaucracy howled in protest. But Reagan was resolute.

Before Congress could respond, however, a dramatic event occurred that sent shock waves through the nation: yet another shooting of an American President. As Reagan was leaving the Washington Hilton hotel after delivering a speech early on the afternoon of March 30, a young man named John Hinckley, later ruled to have been insane at the time, fired several shots at him with a handgun. Secret Service agents hustled the President into his awaiting limousine and he was rushed to a hospital, where immediate surgery saved his life. A bullet was lodged within an inch of Reagan's heart, but he remained conscious as he was led into the hospital and, aides reported later, in such good spirits that he had cracked to the attending surgeons: "I hope all you fellas are Republicans."

By such remarks were the reputation and popularity of Ronald Reagan reinforced and enhanced even as he lay wounded. Only eleven days after the shooting, he was back at the White House, ready to resume his fight to get the government off the voters' backs.

The capital, and the country, were dazzled by Reagan's display of personal courage and political determination. In the first week in May the House passed his budget proposal over a Democratic alternative, and five days later the Senate followed suit. The final measure called for $695.4 billion in spending in fiscal 1982 and a deficit of $37.6 billion—hardly a balanced budget, but Reagan vowed to be moving in that direction.

As a clear indication that the new administration meant business, Reagan's secretary of health and human services (formerly health, education and welfare), Richard Schweiker, in early May unveiled a proposal to cut Social Security benefits $46 billion over a five-year period. The move caught Congress by surprise and created such an uproar that the scheme was doomed from the start. The Republican-controlled Senate summarily rejected the idea by a resounding vote of 96–0, and Reagan was forced to pull back. The episode reinforced the nagging image of Reagan as a man bent on doing in the system, one way or another. It was an image that would continue to distort and compromise his politics and his policies throughout his presidential tenure.

The primary administration initiative before Congress now was a whopping 30 percent tax cut that the new President sought to achieve over a three-year period. He finally settled for 25 percent—5 the first year and 10 each of the next two; still the largest tax reduction in history. Reagan, riding high in the polls, lobbied hard for the tax bill, even pledging at one point not to campaign in 1982 against Democrats in Congress who would support him on it. By the end of June the historic tax legislation was passed, with some modifications, by six votes in the House, and a month later, after appealing to the public in a televised speech, Reagan won approval in both houses.

The success of his budget package was the centerpiece of a remarkable first year in office for Reagan. There were, to be sure, some clouds on the horizon, the foremost of which were the reports that the federal deficit had risen to $58 billion in fiscal 1981 and that the unemployment rate in October rose to 8 percent—the highest since 1975. The jobless rate went up again in November, to 8.4 percent, and Reagan was obliged to project the fiscal 1982 deficit at $109 billion. His call for a balanced budget had been "a goal, not a promise," he said. Near year's end, however, all seemed to be well, except for a major indiscretion by one of his chief budgetary aides, David Stockman, director of the Office of Management and Budget.

In a remarkable series of interviews in *The Atlantic* with one of the country's most outstanding reporters and political analysts, William Greider, Stockman expressed with a blunt cynicism that was startling his own deep reservations and, indeed, lack of confidence in basic Reaganomics. He talked of the Reagan tax cut, modeled after the legislative proposal of Representative Jack Kemp of New York and Senator William Roth of Delaware, as "a Trojan horse" devised to bring down the top taxation rate. He described the overall supply-side approach as no more than the "trickle-down theory" of Hoover-era infamy. And, most damaging of all, he confessed to having cooked the budget numbers to make the Reagan formula appear more workable than it was proving to be—especially with the skyrocketing deficit.

As Reagan's second year in the White House started, the outlook worsened. The jobless rate for December had climbed again, to 8.9 percent, and for the first time in his presidency, Reagan's approval rating in the Gallup poll slipped below 50 percent. His approval-disapproval rating was 49–41, compared to 54–37 in November, and far below his approval rating of 68 percent the previous May. The budget he submitted in February of $757.6 billion had a deficit of $91.5 billion, and in March the unemployment rate hit 9 percent.

What's more, stories of personal incompetence—always heard about Reagan from the Democrats—began to circulate among Republicans as well. Senator Bob Packwood of Oregon came out of a White House meeting and told of a discussion with the President on the federal deficit in which Reagan had got off "on a totally different track," telling a story about how people were buying vodka with food stamps.

The Democrats, who had rolled over for the Reagan 1981 budget package, were not buying it this time around, as the 1982 congressional elections approached. Attempts at compromise with House Speaker Thomas P. O'Neill, Jr., failed and the danger signs of recession continued to mount. April automobile sales fell 11 percent; the jobless rate hit 9.4 percent in April and 9.5 percent in May, the highest in forty years. Housing foreclosures for the first quarter of 1982 also set a record. And with the federal deficit soaring out of sight, it was clear not only that Reagan's goal of a balanced budget was unattainable for the foreseeable future but also that drastic measures were imperative to combat that deficit. Against Reagan's protests at first, Bob Dole, then the Republican chairman of the Senate Finance Committee, engineered a $99 billion tax increase through the Senate and finally won Reagan's acquiescence on the grounds that most of it was tax "reform" and that, besides, the increase was required to get further spending cuts from Congress.

These developments, however, did not stop Reagan from continuing to seek with great fanfare a constitutional amendment requiring a balanced budget from Congress. He urged its approval just days before his secretary of the treasury at the time, Donald Regan, predicted a fiscal 1983 deficit of as much as $114 billion, itself some $44 billion below the outside figure being forecast by the reliable Congressional Budget Office.[5]

The Reagan tenure that had been launched amid such hopeful rhetoric and had been marked by such remarkable legislative success the year before was now in heavy economic seas. Stories abounded on television and in the press of the hardships inflicted on victims of sharply slashed social welfare programs. The Census Bureau reported in July that families in poverty had risen to 14 percent of the population, the highest in fifteen years. The same

5. Dole was elected Senate majority leader in December 1984, on the eve of the retirement of the incumbent, Howard H. Baker, Jr., of Tennessee. Donald Regan shortly afterward resigned as secretary of the treasury to become the White House chief of staff starting Reagan's second term, in a job swap with James A. Baker III, the chief of staff throughout the first term.

month, joblessness was up to 9.8 percent. The trade deficit also hit a new high, and less than a month before the off-year elections, the unemployment rate reached double figures—10.1 percent, or more than it had been before the United States entered World War II.

Reagan's foreign-policy record was dismal too. No progress had been made on nuclear arms control, and relations with the Soviet Union were getting colder. The Arab-Israeli conflict festered, requiring the dispatch of American troops to Lebanon in a peacekeeping role that was accomplishing nothing. And the President's two ranking foreign-policy subordinates, the tempestuous Secretary of State Alexander Haig and the unimpressive national security adviser Richard Allen, resigned.

Nevertheless, Reagan, campaigning for Republican members of Congress and urging voters to "stay the course" he had set, insisted the country was in better repute abroad than it had been in years and was "recovery-bound" at home in spite of what all the Democratic "crepe-hangers" were saying. "Vote your hopes," he urged his audiences.

In Reagan's terms, however, they didn't. While the Republicans were able to maintain their 54–46 majority in the Senate in the off-year elections, the Democrats picked up twenty-six seats in the House—enough to break the working majority of Republicans and "boll weevil" Democrats who had delivered his major legislative successes in 1981. The Democrats, who had gone into a political coma two years earlier as a result of Reagan's surprise landslide victory over Carter and the even more surprising loss of the Senate, took great heart in the results, in which they also picked up eight more governorships.

Suddenly, the prospects of a Democratic comeback in the presidential election of 1984 appeared to be infinitely brighter. But first the party had to endure the laborious and hazardous business of sorting out the potential candidates without, as had happened so often in the past, severely compromising its chances of winning.

3

Inside Baseball

•

YOU COULD ALMOST FEEL the tide of relief that ran through the Democratic Party when Senator Edward M. Kennedy announced to a crowded press conference on December 1, 1982 that an "overriding obligation" to his three children had led him to decide he could not be a candidate for President in 1984.

Ted Kennedy had become the object of striking ambivalence among Democrats. On the one hand, he was the only party leader of national prominence who evoked any obviously emotional support from traditional Democratic constituencies—most notably in his case blacks, Hispanic-Americans and activist liberals. In twenty years in the Senate he had moved beyond his position as the heir to his brothers' politics to a recognition in his own right as the leading exponent of liberal causes in American politics. And he was clearly the dominant personality in the party.

On the other hand, Kennedy remained a controversial and divisive figure, within his party and with the electorate at large. Many voters saw him as too liberal politically and too self-indulgent personally, and they were not hesitant to express their hostility toward him. The death of Mary Jo Kopechne at Chappaquiddick, although now almost fifteen years in the past, had not been forgotten.

That negative reaction was so pronounced, in fact, that there was serious doubt whether Kennedy could rely for another campaign on many of the political professionals and semi-professionals who had been the mainstays of his challenge to President Jimmy Carter in 1980. Some simply believed it was a hopeless cause in the politics of 1984. Others conceded they had no stomach for the particular stresses of another Kennedy campaign.

One 1980 primary state coordinator told us long after the fact, for example, of listening in on the telephone canvassing lines in campaign headquarters and being stunned by the hostility toward her champion. "I never heard such obscenity," she recalled. "It was a terrible shock."

But, controversial or not, Ted Kennedy had been automatically ranked among the leading possibilities for the 1984 nomination—and his withdrawal changed the political equation significantly. It made Walter F. Mondale the undisputed frontrunner, the man to beat.

The early line had been that Kennedy and Mondale, in that order according to the public-opinion polls, ranked as the leaders and were in a class by themselves. The theory was that all of the other potential candidates would be sparring with one another for the privilege of becoming "the third man" who eventually would be matched against the survivor of Kennedy vs. Mondale at some point during the nominating process.

Thus, Kennedy's withdrawal a full fifteen months before any delegates were to be chosen left an opening in the so-called first tier of candidates. The void was quickly filled by Senator John H. Glenn of Ohio on the basis of nothing more substantial than polling figures showing him on Mondale's heels. Glenn just as quickly demonstrated that he was not yet prepared to play in the major leagues. He rushed into the Senate press gallery and informed the world that because he had been a friend of Robert F. Kennedy he would be a natural heir to Ted Kennedy's support. It was a clumsy gesture that did nothing to improve a relationship between the two that was already barely civil.

Kennedy's decision also seemed to offer some opportunity to other candidates. One was Alan Cranston of California, the Democratic whip in the Senate and, like Kennedy, a leading advocate of a freeze on nuclear weapons. Another was Senator Gary Hart of Colorado, who was not as devoutly liberal as Kennedy but offered some obvious stylistic similarities and was attracting some liberals with his conspicuous devotion to spelling out positions on issues, an approach that liberals always find beguiling.

Indeed, the possibilities seemed so limitless that Representative Morris Udall of Arizona, who had won both respect and affection in the party while running second to Jimmy Carter in the contest for the 1976 nomination, began musing aloud about the possibility he might try again—despite the fact he was suffering from Parkinson's disease. But Udall found the political barriers against a candidate with such a condition too high and announced on February 9 with his usual elan that he would not be a candidate after all.

But the principal beneficiary of the Kennedy withdrawal was obviously Mondale. He could be expected to inherit much of the backing that the liberal from Massachusetts enjoyed among such constituencies of party regulars as labor leaders and local politicians, as well as among blacks and Hispanics. And Mondale was prepared organizationally to begin immediately enlisting those Kennedyites now at loose ends. By contrast, Glenn was in no position even to make the right telephone calls. As William White, his longtime Senate adviser and campaign manager at the time, put it later: "Up to that point the focus had been on Kennedy and Mondale and them going at each other, and nobody was really paying much attention to what Glenn was up to. Mondale and Kennedy had the spotlight and then when Kennedy withdrew, that took him out of the picture and that spotlight all of a sudden shone through on us, [and] we weren't dressed yet."

In fact, however, the campaign had been under way—at least at the political junkie level—for a year or more. Mondale had jumped off to a commanding lead in fund-raising and big-name political support that none of the others could match, and for the next year all the contenders would subject themselves to a bizarre Catch-22. In order to run effectively in 1984 they needed to raise money in 1983. But in order to remain viable as candidates, most of them determined that they had to compete in a series of trial heats that ate up the money they raised, and settled little. As a result, most of them would wonder after the pre-election year was over whether they had accomplished anything at all. And it would be a good question.

Glenn himself had made his first foray into New Hampshire late in 1981, appearing before 600 Democrats at a fund-raising reception at the Sheraton Wayfarer in Bedford for Governor Hugh Gallen. Mondale followed a few weeks later and went Glenn one better by not only raising money for Gallen but also keeping a schedule of coffees and cocktail parties of his own that would have been more appropriate for the middle of a primary campaign than for a weekend two years earlier.[6]

Several other candidates from the "second tier" of the field, as it already was being called, also had been, as the politicians always say, "moving around"—Cranston, Hart, Senator Ernest F. Hollings of South Carolina, former Governor Reubin O'D. Askew of Florida, Senator Dale Bumpers of Arkansas. There was good reason, it seemed, to believe the Democratic nomination would be worth something, even against a politician as obviously imposing as Ronald Reagan.

For one thing, the Democrats were approaching the politics of 1984 without the kind of divisions that had been so destructive to them in the past. There were no moral or even emotional issues to separate them as the debates over civil rights and the war in Vietnam had done in other times. Here, too, Mondale appeared to be in the strongest position as the embodiment of the consensus liberal Democrat in a party in which liberals were still the most aggressive players. And it was probably too soon to expect anyone to worry about how the party could be mobilized without issues with some emotional content. With the memory fresh of the bitter contest between Carter and Kennedy in 1980, there was an obvious priority being given to keeping friction at a minimum. That was apparent from the temper of the party's mid-term conference—the so-called mini-convention—in Philadelphia in June of 1982.

The two previous mid-term meetings had been lively rather than particularly helpful to the image of the Democrats. The first, at Kansas City in 1974, was remembered principally for a brawl over party rules that had put a strain on the talents of even that legendary negotiator, then Democratic national chairman Robert S. Strauss. At the second, in Memphis in 1978, the activist enthusiasm for Ted Kennedy had been an obvious embarrassment to the sitting Democratic President—and putative party leader—Jimmy Carter.

This time, by contrast, party chairman Charles T. Manatt had engineered changes in the rules to minimize the chance of division.

6. Gallen, a widely respected politician, was defeated for reelection to a third term in November of 1982 and died of a particularly virulent bacterial infection several weeks later.

The formula for choosing the 897 official "participants"—they were not to be "delegates"—was written to load the conference with members of the Democratic National Committee, local party leaders and functionaries and public officeholders. No crazies need apply. And the rules for the sessions themselves were written so that any direct conflict on issues would be covered up in the mush of one final statement of principles adopted on a single vote on the final day. One product, for instance, was a plank on the nuclear-freeze issue that managed to combine elements of Kennedy's advocacy and the opposition of Senator Henry M. Jackson of Washington, then the acknowledged leader of the party's conservative wing on national security issues.[7]

Thus obliged by circumstance to be on their good behavior, the Democrats spent most of their weekend in Philadelphia handicapping the potential presidential candidates on their speeches—Mondale and Kennedy probably captured the oratorical prizes—and their ability to draw huge mobs of fellow Democrats to their cocktail parties and hospitality suites. What became clear, however, was that although the Democrats stood together in unusual amity, they didn't stand for anything very new as an alternative to Ronald Reagan and the Republicans in control in Washington. Instead, they limited themselves to the kind of Reagan-bashing that was to become the theme of the 1982 campaign, lustily applauding such sallies as this one from Kennedy: "Ronald Reagan's cheese lines of 1982 are as unacceptable as Herbert Hoover's bread lines of 1932."

But as 1982 came to an end there seemed to be no reason for Democrats to worry. The economy was on the skids, and that was likely to mean Republicans on the skids as well. It was true that Walter Heller, a leading Democratic economist and chairman of the Council of Economic Advisers in the Kennedy administration, had been warning the party since 1981 against relying on the economic cycle as the basis for future campaigns. But right now everything seemed to be coming up Democratic. Shortly before the election the unemployment rate had reached 10.8 percent, the highest level since the Great Depression. Interest rates, business failures, housing starts, farm foreclosures—all the economic indicators were depressed. Reagan was on the defensive on Social

7. Jackson died in September of 1983.

Security. It wasn't going to take some bold new Democratic initiative to prevail in the politics of 1982; the traditional bread-and-butter issues would do the trick.

By the time Ted Kennedy stepped aside, such optimism seemed to have been justified. The Democrats had gained those twenty-six seats in the House of Representatives and eight state governorships. And although they had made no gains in the Senate, they had come close enough in several races to be encouraged about the outlook. The fear of the "Reagan revolution" had been put into a different perspective. Sure, you couldn't deny that the President had moved the ideological center of the country a few degrees—particularly on spending and defense issues. But it was also apparent that the old rules applied when the economy went sour and the party in power took the blame.

There were, to be sure, some small irregularities in the picture that might have been taken as warning signals, but they were quickly explained away. Considering the parlous condition of the economy, the Democratic gain of twenty-six House seats was not that impressive. But it could be argued that unseating congressional incumbents had grown increasingly difficult, whatever the issues in a particular election. Some Democratic professionals found it at least vaguely disquieting that in two industrial states, New York and Michigan, two conventionally liberal Democratic candidates for governor had won by such unimpressive margins over two Republicans from the Far Right of conservatism. But, again, there were easy explanations. Mario Cuomo's narrow victory over Lew Lehrman in New York could surely be attributed to Lehrman's extraordinary personal spending on his campaign. And Republican Richard Headlee's relatively strong showing in Michigan could be attributed at least in part to the blandness of Democrat James Blanchard.

Not everyone was satisfied with these rationalizations, however. Patrick Caddell, the intense young Democratic polling consultant, had noted in 1980 the willingness of so many young urban professionals initially to support independent candidate John B. Anderson and then switch to Ronald Reagan when it became apparent Anderson could not win. Considering the comparative positions of Reagan and Anderson on the issues, this was quite a switch—one that seemed to suggest the one link was an antipathy to Jimmy Carter and, perhaps, the Democratic Party he represented. But whether or not that was the case, there was nothing in the pattern to encourage the Democrats to believe these "baby boom" voters—later to be known as yuppies—represented an especially good target for them. And Caddell noticed that the Republicans were already running generic party advertising in 1981 directed at "baby boomers"—the new voters coming into the pool from that post–World War II generation that had caused such a bulge in the national demographic profile.

The Democrats in search of the 1984 presidential nomination were in no temper, however, to pore over the fine print looking for bad news. After Reagan's remarkable triumph in 1980, the central question had been whether that result was an aberration or the first step in the transformation of American politics. And the answer in the returns of 1982 suggested the former rather than the latter—and that Ronald Reagan might be vulnerable indeed. The opinion polls seemed to support that optimism. A Gallup poll in December of 1982 found Glenn leading Reagan 54 to 39 percent and Mondale ahead of the President, 52–40. Reagan's approval rating dropped to 41 percent, his lowest and a point lower even than that reached by Jimmy Carter at the same juncture in his presidency.

The Democrats were beginning the competition under still another new set of rules governing the selection of delegates for the national convention that would make the nomination. And, like those that had been adopted before the 1972 and 1976 campaigns, the new rules were designed primarily to meet dissatisfaction within the party with the results that had been produced by the old ones.

The rules for 1984 were the product of a commission established in 1981 and chaired by then Governor James B. Hunt, Jr., of North Carolina, a politician moderate enough to have friends across the party's ideological spectrum and savvy enough to understand which way the wind was blowing. In this case, that meant the principal thrust of the Hunt Commission "reforms"—as Democrats always call new rules—was to (1) get the contest for the nomination over as quickly as possible and (2) give more power to the mainstream regulars to prevent the party from producing another George McGovern or Jimmy Carter. As a practical matter, this goal was achieved largely because the controlling forces in the commission were—to no one's surprise—Ted Kennedy, Fritz Mondale and the AFL-CIO.

The commission proposed—and the Democratic National Committee finally approved in 1982—a system with several devices for protecting the power of the permanent establishment and nominating a Kennedy or, once he stepped aside, a Mondale. One provision established a class of "super delegates"—party officials and officeholders—who theoretically would arrive at the convention uncommitted, then use their expertise to temper any excesses of the primary voters that might produce another "outsider" nominee.

"It is the key," an optimistic Hunt told David Broder of the Washington *Post* in an interview, "to the Democrats' appealing to the mainstream of the electorate and to providing the kind of peer review we need to have a winning candidate who can also govern." Although Hunt did not single him out, there was obviously one candidate most likely to benefit from such "peer review"—Fritz Mondale, who had spent years in the political trenches with many of those likely to become super delegates.

Another change—also directed against longshot candidates—raised the minimum amount of the vote, the threshold, a candidate would have to achieve to get a share of the delegates in a state or congressional district. Another, also favoring frontrunners, allowed candidates winning a plurality in some congressional districts to walk away with all that district's delegates.

The change that attracted the most public attention was the effort to compress the delegate-selection process by establishing a thirteen-week period, the "window," in which all caucuses and primaries would have to be held. Because of their history and traditions, Iowa was permitted to schedule its precinct caucuses fifteen days before this official period and New Hampshire its primary seven days before. To no one's surprise, the new rules encouraged states to move their caucuses and primaries to earlier dates in the hope of having some influence on the result. And it was this "frontloading" more than anything else that both Mondale and Big Labor depended upon to produce an early decision and to minimize the internal damage to the party from the contest for the nomination.

The Hunt Commission reforms also had been put forward as

a plan that might shorten the presidential campaign in 1984, thus reversing the trend toward the marathons that had become the rule. But there were several interrelated pressures on the candidates that argued for an early start—and were much more compelling than any reforms.

First, it was imperative for the candidates to make an early beginning because money raised after January 1, 1983—meaning within the year before the presidential election—was eligible for federal matching to finance the primary campaigns. For the outsider candidates, at least, those early contributions would depend heavily on their credibility as candidates. And that credibility, in turn, would depend on where they stood in the national public-opinion polls, which in turn would depend to a large degree on how much press attention they might be able to attract.

Thus, on February 2, 1983, Alan Cranston became the first Democrat officially to announce his candidacy. Gary Hart followed on February 17, Walter Mondale four days later and Reubin Askew two days after that. John Glenn and Fritz Hollings were equally visible, although they delayed their formal announcements until April.

If the candidates were anxious to win some attention, they had ready allies in state Democratic leaders. They had seen their Republican counterparts exploit a similar multi-candidate situation in 1979 to fatten their own party treasuries and, not incidentally, attract the national press. And they had at least tacit allies in the political reporters seeking some basis, however slight, on which to establish a pecking order of the candidates. The product of all these symbiotic relationships was a series of party dinners, conventions, candidate forums and straw votes that ran all through 1983–and had virtually nothing to do with the interests of any voters except that small minority made up of Democratic activists.

The pressure to establish credibility was heightened, too, by another new element in the Democratic equation of 1983—the decision by President Lane Kirkland to swing the AFL-CIO behind a favored candidate during the nominating process. And here again Mondale—once Kennedy was out of the picture—had the obvious advantage of years of identification with union goals.

Big Labor had given favored candidates—Hubert H. Humphrey in 1968 was the best example—intensive support in the past. And some of the most politically effective individual unions—the United

Auto Workers and the International Association of Machinists, to name just two—had worked for various liberal candidates during the caucuses and primaries of the last several campaigns. But under George Meany's leadership the federation itself had delayed any overt and active commitment to one candidate until the Democratic nomination was settled, thus maintaining the fiction of labor neutrality between Republicans and Democrats and mollifying some of the more politically conservative craft unions within his own membership.

But Kirkland had seen enough of the results of that policy of standing aloof in the nominations of George McGovern and Jimmy Carter—and, perhaps most to the point, in the election of Ronald Reagan. Talking with us about the potential of his endorsement plan one afternoon early in 1982, Kirkland gestured with this thumb across Lafayette Park toward the White House and said: "We have the one big issue that certainly unites us."

By May of that year, at Kirkland's behest, the AFL-CIO Executive Council voted to ask constituent unions not to endorse anyone prematurely. And John Perkins, director of the federation's Committee on Political Education, had become a full-fledged player in the Hunt Commission deliberations, making no bones about his goal of producing a system that would assure an early decision. "We hoped," Perkins said long after the fact, "to get the whole thing over by Super Tuesday"—meaning March 13, 1984, the first date within the official delegate-selection period on which several primaries and caucuses would be held simultaneously, yielding a substantial delegate prize.

Kirkland's original plan was to put the decision to the federation's Executive Council at its December 1983 meeting, with a requirement of a two-thirds vote for an endorsement. Once Ted Kennedy had stepped aside, however, there never was any serious question about Fritz Mondale winning the endorsement. All the other candidates, however, were invited to make their cases at one council meeting or another, and most of the member unions made some effort or show of effort to measure rank-and-file sentiment.

Some of the other candidates—Glenn and Cranston in particular—urged the labor leaders to delay the decision in the hope they could sting Mondale early in the primaries and cause some second thoughts in the hierarchy of Big Labor. Instead, at the

August council meeting in Boston, the federation decided to move the endorsement process up to the national convention in October. This decision was cloaked in such good intentions as a desire to allow the endorsement to be made at the most representative level practicable. But the move was clearly part of the Mondale strategy of grinding all the opposition into the dust before the campaign year ever opened.

Lacking among labor politicians and Mondale advisers was any thorough understanding of the hazards of the endorsement and the sharpened picture it might present of the candidate as captive of his own supporters. There had been warnings enough, from the press and elsewhere. On January 18, 1983, Richard Moe, a Washington lawyer who had been Mondale's chief of staff as Vice President, sent the candidate a memorandum on "Getting through 1983" that summarized the endorsement problem cogently:

Handling the traditional constituencies presents a serious dilemma. On the one hand we need their active organizational and financial help to get the nomination. On the other hand being perceived as "captive" of the constituencies can have very damaging consequences. The goal should be to get as much support as possible from these groups while at the same time appearing to be your own man and independent of any special interests.

Recent data show clearly that people increasingly cast their votes as individuals rather than as members of a particular group. (The one major exception to this trend is blacks, who continue to vote primarily on black issues.) While group voting behavior is still identifiable, it is breaking down rapidly. Nowhere was this better illustrated than in Reagan's considerable success with union members in 1980. The reasons for this trend are apparent. As their income levels rise, most people see themselves moving into the great middle class and identify less with whatever labor, ethnic or other group of which they previously saw themselves as a part. Also, they no longer need to rely on organized groups for political information; they now get it directly from television, from which they form their own judgments. Increasingly, members of groups even resent being told how to vote by their institutional leadership. The bottom line is that no one delivers very much any more; an individual's vote for president is increasingly a very personal decision, not to be dictated from above but rather to be cast according to one's own values, goals and priorities.

There's not only a growing mistrust of organizational leadership by the membership but also by the public generally. This is particularly true where presidential politics is involved. People simply don't want their president to be wholly owned by any group or special interest, and they inevitably react negatively to any candidate who is perceived to be so owned. . . .

Most people see special interests as part of the problem, not part of the solution. It follows that they see candidates who pander to these groups for support—saying everything they want to hear, giving them everything they want—as very un-presidential. It really turns them off because they know that's not what the country needs; the country needs someone who has the courage to say no occasionally.

Dick Moe was by no means alone in recognizing the hazards in the labor endorsement. As James Johnson, the chief Mondale strategist, insisted later, the campaign managers had "our eyes wide open" about the pluses and minuses of the labor endorsement but simply considered it well worth the price. The membership and influence of unions had declined markedly, but there were still ninety-six unions representing more than fourteen million workers within the federation. Johnson also doubted that Mondale's competitors were free enough of the taint of their own "special interests" to throw stones at the former Vice President.

"My belief," said Johnson, "was that 'special interest' had some saliency as a press issue but no saliency particularly in the mouth of a candidate." And the AFL-CIO's Perkins saw the threat as one that would come from Ronald Reagan in the fall rather than from other Democrats in the spring. "We thought it would come in the general campaign and it could be overcome," he said later. "You can really thank Glenn and Hart."

As a practical matter, Mondale didn't seem to have much choice—or much chance—of avoiding the perception as the candidate of the power blocs in the Democratic Party. "It wasn't just labor unions or special interests," said one adviser, "but there were a dozen things about Mondale that came together to create that image." These included his longtime identification with Humphrey, his role as Carter's Vice President, twelve years in the Senate, the backing of so many public officials, even the fact that he was considered to be the best organized of the six candidates then in the field. Even if there had been no formal AFL-CIO endorsement, Mondale's managers argued, he would have been seen as having the unions' support—and as being their boy.

Nor did Mondale have much choice about winning everything that might be there for the taking—not if he was to maintain the image as the inevitable candidate that was the foundation of his strategy for winning the nomination. And it was that imperative that dictated Mondale's decision to compete in the series of straw votes that preoccupied the party and the press—but not the voters, as later events made so clear—throughout 1983. Jim Johnson saw the straw polls less as an obstacle than as an opportunity to force Mondale's opponents to spend their limited resources well in advance of the 1984 caucuses and primaries. Mondale already had built such an imposing campaign organization and treasury that it came to be known in political circles as "Mondale Inc."

The first of these candidate "cattle shows" was the California state Democratic convention in Sacramento on January 14–16. And because it was being held on the home turf of one of the candidates, Alan Cranston, there was little pressure in that first test. By most reckonings, Mondale won the prize for steamy political oratory there, and no one was inclined to give much weight to the results of the straw poll. Cranston won with 59 percent of the vote, Mondale ran second with 23 percent and the others trailed far behind the leaders.

Cranston was, of course, a special case at that stage. In his fifteen years in the Senate, the Californian had earned a reputation in Washington as an effective advocate of liberal causes and a reputation in his state as a popular and tenacious politician. But even many of those California Democrats who had played prominent roles in his Senate campaigns were not convinced that he could become a serious player at the presidential level. He was sixty-nine years old and, although extraordinarily fit because of his longtime devotion to running, his baldness and gaunt features made him look older—"like the Shroud of Turin," according to one of the unkinder wisecracks passed over the luncheon tables in Washington. He had never been accused of being an exciting political personality. And many of his old allies in Sacramento were telling reporters privately that they had signed on with Cranston at that early stage as a testament of respect for one of their own—and, in some cases, because he provided a safe hiding place while they waited to see how the competition among the more credible candidates would shake down.

Sergio Bendixen, the able young professional from Florida

managing Cranston's campaign, understood these reservations as well as anyone. He had seized on the straw-vote strategy as one that might give his long-odds candidate the kind of credibility that another unlikely nominee, Jimmy Carter, had earned with an early and tenacious campaign in 1975 or that, on the Republican side, George Bush had earned by exceeding everyone's expectations in similar tests in 1979. So with the credential of California, such as it was, Cranston began to focus heavy attention on the next straw vote scheduled at a Massachusetts state convention in Springfield on April 9.

This question of whether to compete in the straw votes posed an awkward problem for the other candidates in the second or third tier of the Democratic field. On the one hand, they believed they needed some demonstration of strength to impress the party with their potential. On the other, none could claim the kind of identifiable constituency Cranston had isolated by proclaiming himself—in his announcement of candidacy at Saint Anselm's College in New Hampshire—as the candidate most committed to a freeze on nuclear weapons and most devoted to arms control. In point of fact, Cranston had no better claim to be the champion of arms control than several of the others. But the priority he had assigned the freeze issue had been given enough currency to provide a base of activist supporters who could be depended upon to show up for a state party convention. Lacking such a core, most of the other candidates seemed to lurch from one policy to another on the straw votes.

On the face of it, Mondale had some reason to be concerned about Massachusetts. His history as Jimmy Carter's Vice President was hardly an asset there, particularly with politicians who remembered his testy exchanges with Ted Kennedy during the 1980 campaign. And Mondale made things at least marginally more difficult for himself in March by playing the Imperial Candidate, refusing to pose for pictures with his rivals at a Democratic Party "cattle show" dinner in Boston. But Mondale's law partner and senior political adviser, John Reilly, had longstanding connections in Massachusetts politics, and the campaign signed on Paul Tully, a streetwise consultant from Philadelphia who had worked for Ted Kennedy in 1980, to run the operation.

Given Mondale's base with labor and officeholders, these factors were enough to give him a victory in the straw poll with 29 percent of the vote to 17 percent for Cranston, 15 for Glenn and 11 for Hart. Moreover, he won it with most of the union delegates casting a symbolic vote for "jobs" that took second place with 27 percent of the total. Some of the less realistic Mondale strategists imagined that result might help take some of the curse off his position as the establishment and labor candidate. Meanwhile, Cranston was crowing about his second-place finish, insisting it was evidence of his credibility and promising even more intense efforts at other similar events down the road. And in one sense, at least, Cranston was correct as it became clear that even this modest showing was encouraging to the nuclear-freeze advocates who were his base.

Even within the Mondale campaign there was considerable doubt about whether these straw polls were worth the effort and the risk involved. Tully warned that the next major one, in Wisconsin in June, would be more difficult for Mondale because there would be fewer working-class regulars and more political activists among the delegates. Others in the campaign complained about the diversion of resouces. But Jim Johnson was adamant. "From our strategic interests," he said later, "what we wanted was to put as much pressure on as possible and force people to lose." And by so doing, Johnson argued, the Mondale campaign could undermine these rivals' ability to raise money and compete effectively against them in the more serious business of 1984. Johnson's was a strategy, in Paul Tully's phrase, of "beat 'em and bleed 'em."

The stakes in Wisconsin were quickly raised to bizarre levels. Cranston campaigned all over the state and, when convention day arrived, spent $4,000 on 100 Milwaukee hotel rooms to give his supporters a place to sleep and, not incidentally, a greater obligation to stick with him. The aggressive approach spooked at least two of his opponents.

The Hart campaign "allowed ourselves to get stampeded," campaign manager Oliver (Pudge) Henkel said later, in part because Hart had finished so far down the list in Massachusetts. As a result, the campaign spent $120,000 on the Wisconsin straw vote, a preposterous amount in light of how difficult it was for Hart to raise money, and brought William Romjue, the Iowa coordinator, and almost all of his Iowa staff out of Des Moines to concentrate on Wisconsin. And the Hart campaign bought several thousand copies of the candidate's book, *A New Democracy*, so that each delegate and alternate might have a copy. But the deployment of Romjue and his staff was a particular gaffe; it failed with Wisconsin Democrats and sent a signal to Iowa Democrats that they weren't being taken very seriously. "It was probably one of the worst decisions we could have made," Henkel conceded.

But the Mondale campaign wasn't immune, either, to the epidemic of political madness that Sergio Bendixen had started in his effort to make the implausible Cranston appear a credible candidate after all. The Mondale campaign sent top hand Tully into the state three weeks before the vote to organize mailings, telephone canvasses and Mondale's own campaigning. All this activity was undertaken for a poll of some 2,000 Democrats who would gather in Milwaukee to make decisions that would have absolutely no bearing on the Democratic presidential choice in 1984, even in Wisconsin.

The result, however, was a stunner. Cranston won with 39 percent to 36 for Mondale and 22 for Hart—a margin of only sixty-two votes over Mondale but enough to send strong tremors through the frontrunner's operation.

"It was devastating," Martin Kaplan, Mondale's chief speechwriter, recalled long after the fact. "What it did was deflate the entire inevitability strategy. Mondale lost confidence in his field organization, which was supposed to have smelled out what was going on and bused the right people in."

And although—by all accounts—Mondale himself avoided placing blame on individuals, Kaplan recalled "there was a lot of cursing, yelling and anger" inside the campaign. The candidate appeared tight-lipped and shaken when, after some balking on his part, he met with the press in the Pfister Hotel after his defeat had been quantified. "I've had my good days," he said. "This was not one of them."

Gary Hart also was somewhat chastened. He had, he said later, "never felt I'd do well in the straw polls" because he lacked a cadre of regulars. But he had been lured into believing he could succeed in Wisconsin by what he called "some romantic attachment to '72"—meaning to the time when Wisconsin had given a significant primary victory to George McGovern, whose campaign Hart was managing. As it turned out, the best thing that happened to Hart in Wisconsin this time was Cranston's upset victory, which made Mondale's failure the news and relegated Hart's misfortune to the fine print.

At the time, Mondale's managers publicly tried to depict the defeat—"a good kick in the ass," Johnson called it later—as more a product of failed mechanics than anything else. Campaign manager Bob Beckel, who had flown out for the inauspicious occasion, said after the vote, for example, that the problem had been a decision not to charter two more buses to bring voters from outlying communities. Had that been done, said Beckel, things would have been different.

But it was clear there were more basic inferences to be drawn from the upset in Wisconsin. In Tully's view, the first lesson of Wisconsin was that Mondale "didn't resonate" with the voters. Or, as Jim Johnson would put it later, "there was an inadequate level of intensity in some of our supporters."

The questions were more basic than that. The first was simply whether Fritz Mondale had anything to say that would persuade any substantial number of Democrats to help him. And the second was whether Mondale had the kind of personal force that would make any emotional connection with other Democrats. Mondale had come into the campaign back on February 23 by announcing, "I know myself. I am ready." And he had spent the next four months repeating that line and trying to demonstrate through the apparent strength of his organization and breadth of his establishment support that all further resistance by the Gary Harts and John Glenns was a waste of effort. But the "winner argument" is effective in politics only so long as you are winning, and a defeat at the hands of Alan Cranston left Mondale at least temporarily naked.

The Wisconsin defeat made clear that the Mondale campaign could not rest solely or perhaps even largely on the appeal of the candidate. In the Massachusetts straw-vote campaign, Tully had been impressed by Mondale's success in appearing to win converts, but after Wisconsin that success looked very misleading.

"Wisconsin taught me," Tully recalled in the cryptic patois of the political operative, "that for this thing to roll, it's not this giant locomotive, that you just put him out there and get him into the right places and get him a clear shot at people . . . that you've got to have a lot more pieces working for the whole equation to come together and you'll get your win."

But for the moment, it served the campaign better to blame the mechanical failures rather than those of the candidate. "That's the kind of thing," said Tully, "that you have a big interest in keeping internal until you clean up the act."

In the Mondale campaign the Wisconsin result set off another, more intense, round of debate about whether to continue to compete in the straw votes. The campaign field director, Mike Ford, was opposed on the ground that it simply wasn't necessary because if Mondale skipped a straw poll it wouldn't be taken seriously. "If we weren't in it," said Ford, "there wasn't one." The finance director, Tim Finchem, also was opposed to the diversion of resources. But the only staff vote that counted was Johnson's, and he remained convinced that it was essential for Mondale to compete at full speed. The price of being a frontrunner, he argued, was that if you don't show strength, you will be accused of showing weakness. So the policy would not be to duck the straw polls but to be damned sure of winning them—or, as Tully summarized it, "everywhere beat 'em and bleed 'em, only now we got to do it with more resources."

It was a decision that led to some grotesque politics. Shortly after Wisconsin, for example, the Mondale managers got the notion that John Glenn was trying to pull a fast one and line up a lot of delegate strength for the Florida convention in late October—even though that one was supposed to be ceded to the home-state favorite, Rube Askew. So the Mondale campaign dispatched a small army into Florida—sixty or seventy young organizers—to work the county Democratic executive committee meetings at which many of the delegates would be chosen. "We poured people into Florida," Tully said. "We made it a romantic adventure."

But the "must" straw poll for Mondale after the loss to Cranston in Wisconsin became Maine on October 1. The inevitability of Mondale's nomination had to be restored if the whole "early knockout" strategy was to succeed in 1984.

The excess was even more wretched in campaigning for the Maine vote. At one point, the Mondale operation had close to 150 organizers in the state—most of them college students getting fifteen dollars a day walking-around money—preparing for a convention in Augusta in which there would be only 1,817 votes cast. Joe Trippi, one of the young stars of the Mondale staff, was sent in to run things. Mondale himself seemed carried away, racing from one small Maine community to another—more than forty of them in the end—with a message that seemed far out of proportion to the event. The memory is vivid, for example, of the polite but unmistakable puzzlement among the thirty-five Democrats who gathered in the Country Way restaurant in Norway, Maine, one September Sunday. Mondale flew into town in a helicopter, landing on the high school grounds across the street, and then marched into the restaurant with half a dozen aides to tell the group with a straight face: "The world is going to be watching to see what you think. There will be few things you will do in your lifetime that will be more significant than this."

That hyperbole was a symptom of the whole problem for Fritz Mondale and the Democratic Party in 1983. They were playing out their little inside game among themselves—and imagining that it was having some effect on voters who were under the impression the presidential election was still a year or so away and not particularly unhappy about it. The Mondale strategy, Marty Kaplan said later, was always to set up "endless tests of strength" that Mondale would win and his competitors could not.

"We would create a series of hoops and hype their importance," he said, "and then tempt other candidates to match and beat us." But most voters were like those bewildered people who gathered at the Country Way restaurant and couldn't quite see what all the fuss was about.

However hollow the successes, Mondale did dominate the inside game the rest of the year. On October 1 he won the Maine straw poll with 51 percent of the vote to 29 for Cranston, 11 for Fritz Hollings and 6 for John Glenn. And later that same weekend he captured the endorsements of both the AFL-CIO and the National Education Association, possibly the most politically effective union in the country. Later he captured the endorsement of the National Organization for Women, won a straw poll at a party dinner in Iowa and finished a stronger-than-expected second in a straw vote at that Democratic convention in Florida, winning 35 percent of the vote to 45 percent for Askew. As a result, Mondale ended the year rising rapidly in the national public-opinion polls while his opposition seemed to be floundering.

Cranston had proved to be as tenacious as advertised, apparently convinced he could make up for what he lacked in money or political credibility with his physical vigor. He was the candidate, for example, who could be found shortly before noon on Mother's Day of 1983 driving into the Ramada Inn in Concord on the way to a brunch with a dozen young New Hampshire peace activists—the first of four stops that day before he arrived at Hanover that night for a speech at Dartmouth. "I keep saying," said a rival campaign manager, "that there's got to be five of him."

But for all Cranston's energy, the judgment in the political community by year's end was that he was, in the usual formulation, sinking like a stone. Although he had tried to broaden his message, his original emphasis on the nuclear weapons freeze had been translated into a perception of him as a single-issue candidate. And his claim to have given a higher priority to the arms control question had begun to wear thin as more candidate forums made it apparent there were few significant differences among most of the Democrats on the issue. Cranston's goal, he said later, had been to lift himself to the top of the second tier of candidates by the end of 1983. But there was no evidence in the polling data to indicate he had done that, and with the entry of still another liberal—George McGovern, who announced his candidacy in September—the possibility seemed even more remote.

At that, Cranston had fared far better in the preliminaries than some of his colleagues in the second tier. Fritz Hollings had enjoyed a brief vogue, largely because of his talent for colorful and candid speech, and had made an abortive effort to convert some of this interest in him into a decent showing in the Maine straw vote. As it turned out, he came away with a less than stop-the-presses 11 percent and remained an asterisk in the national polls. And along the way that penchant for colorful speech—or what his critics called nasty wisecracks—seemed to discourage some of the fans who earlier had found him so intriguing.

The controversy that developed around Hollings as a political personality obscured to a substantial degree the warnings he was delivering to his party all along about the dangers of playing free-lunch politics in 1984—warnings that might have spared the party some of its subsequent injury. Indeed, the South Carolina Democrat had come into the field after calling for a freeze on federal spending as a device for reducing the budget deficit—an approach that gained many adherents after the 1984 election was all over, but one that was not likely to appeal to many liberal Democrats in 1983.

Asked about that political problem as he began his campaign, Hollings replied with his barking laugh. "You're right," he said, "that's a lunacy platform." In the end, Hollings never became more than one of those, in Paul Tully's phrase, "two-percent candidates," and the rule in American politics seems to be that only the warnings of winners are given any credence.[8]

The other southern candidate, Reubin Askew, marched to a different drummer throughout his campaign. At the mid-term conference in Philadelphia in 1982 he declined to speak because, he said, his organization was not yet equipped to follow through on whatever interest he might evoke. Indeed, during 1982 the former Florida governor and Carter administration trade ambassador traveled constantly but gave speeches rarely. He preferred instead to meet with groups of local Democratic officials in the hope that he might build a consensus on how the country could be governed if he could get himself elected. It was an interesting idea, and Askew had enough of a reputation within the political community so that neither the press nor politicians were disposed to laugh him off. But neither was there any evidence by the end of 1983 that there was any political gold in Askew's unorthodox approach.

Askew's experience was a classic example of how the perception of a politician can be radically altered when he is seen through the prism of presidential politics—and particularly nomination politics. He was one of the members of that celebrated "class of 1970" of southern governors—the others were Jimmy Carter of Georgia, Dale Bumpers of Arkansas and John West of South Carolina—who captured the national fancy because they seemed to represent such a break with the region's hard-line segregationist past. Askew was quickly categorized as very "new breed" indeed after he took positions that were considered liberal by southern standards on, among other things, civil rights and environmental issues. And he attained considerable stature in the

8. Hollings' wife Peatsy was a popular figure and was credited with one of the classic stories of the 1984 campaign: When the telephone rang in their hotel room before seven one morning, she answered, then awakened her husband by asking in a tone that could be heard over the open line: "Hey, Honey, your name Hollings?"

Democratic Party nationally when, in 1972, he stood against an obvious tide in a referendum campaign by defending school busing to achieve racial desegregation.

But the standards of the South were not those the Democratic Party was operating under during 1983. And Askew's history counted for nothing compared to his position against abortion, the nuclear freeze, repeal of right-to-work laws and the "domestic content" bill organized labor had adopted as the prime symbol of protectionism. Although his positions were never extremely conservative on these issues—he did not support, for instance, a constitutional amendment to forbid abortion—Askew did attract, accept and in some instances welcome extremist support. The result, unsurprisingly, was that he was defined by his constituencies—none of which was very influential in the Democratic Party nominating process.

In retrospect, Askew himself could see the problem clearly. "There were a series of very liberal litmus tests set up," he said, "and if you didn't pass those tests, you were really not acceptable as the nominee." Those who passed the tests, he said, "wrote themselves off" with the mainstream of the electorate. "We never got around to appealing to the people on issues without whose support we had no chance to win in November."

Askew had other problems in the Democratic Party of 1984, not the least of which was his superficial similarity as a southern governor to Jimmy Carter. His lack of year-in, year-out experience in dealing with federal concerns hindered him in debates with his rivals, and Askew himself conceded as much in a conversation in his Miami law office months later. "As hard as I worked on preparation on national issues," he said, "it was difficult for me to compete with specificity on some of the national issues."

It was never clear just how much of a burden it was for Hollings and Askew to be the "southern candidates." It was clear, however, that the day had passed when regional pride would give a southern candidate a base across state lines as Carter was given when he had set the precedent in modern politics eight years earlier.

The one candidate from the second tier who might have been counted as marginally better off late in the year was Gary Hart. And that was the case despite a politically disastrous summer and fall. After his folly in Wisconsin, Hart's money dried up, his campaign in Iowa went into a spin and the political speculators began to make book about whether he would withdraw entirely as soon as he received his federal matching money to meet his debts early in January. The bright spot was New Hampshire, where he had a highly skilled organization that had canvassed 25,000 Democratic households and run some radio advertising in October and thus laid a foundation for Hart to build on with his own campaigning. A Boston *Globe* poll of New Hampshire Democrats at year's end offered some slight encouragement—giving Hart 8 percent that placed him a distant third behind Mondale (46 percent) and Glenn (16 percent) but still well ahead of all the other trailing candidates.

By the end of 1983 the focus remained on Glenn as the prime challenger to Mondale, although the conventional wisdom held that Glenn's campaign was in disarray and that he was too ineffectual as a candidate to make a serious race of it. Indeed, everything pointed to Fritz Mondale. He had survived a year as the frontrunner without making any serious missteps, or so it appeared. He had raised almost $10 million, far more than any of his competitors—Glenn was second with $5.7 million—and a reliable indicator of the odds in his favor. He had the support of the AFL-CIO, the NEA, NOW and political leaders from the Congress to the statehouses, courthouses and city halls all across the country. His position in Iowa, where the precinct caucuses on February 20 would offer the first "real" test and start the delegate-selection process, was so dominant that the dreams-while-shaving of his rivals centered on who might be second. In fact, for each of the other candidates the competition had become simply one of trying to establish himself as the prime alternative to Fritz Mondale.

Mondale's position seemed so secure, in fact, that Democratic politicians and the press tended to ignore some of the warning signs of his potential weakness. One, clearly, was his inability to excite much enthusiasm even in the Democratic electorate, as the Wisconsin straw vote had demonstrated, or even to spell out a concise and easily assimilated raison d'être for his candidacy. Long after the fact, Paul Tully recalled a Wisconsin delegate who asked Mondale at a meeting at the Red Carpet Inn near the Milwaukee airport just how he would be different from the other candidates. "He went through the whole laundry list, all of which was right," Tully said, "but on the technical level . . . you can't get it delivered to the people. . . ."

The concern that "something was missing" in the Mondale candidacy was reflected more under the surface than in the public discussion that centered on opinion polls showing him so far ahead. One such indicator, given little real notice at the time, was the flurry of interest earlier in the year at the possibility that Dale Bumpers might become a candidate. In one sense, there was nothing surprising about that interest in light of Bumpers' reputation as one of the most able Democrats in the Senate and as a particularly effective campaigner. But Patrick Caddell, the pollster for George McGovern in 1972 and for Jimmy Carter in 1976 and 1980, was one of those involved in the conversations with the Arkansas senator, and he found that "people were ready to support Bumpers who hardly knew him." In any event, after several meetings to discuss the possibilities with potential campaign operators, Bumpers decided he wasn't interested.[9]

Caddell, however, found a similar vein of essentially unfocused interest later in the year when—at his urging—another Democratic senator, Joe Biden of Delaware, began quietly exploring the possibilities of a late-blooming campaign for the nomination. This interest was apparent in the reaction to some speeches Biden made that spelled out his—and, not incidentally, Caddell's—reservations about the direction of the party. And it was apparent behind the scenes in the interest in finding another Democratic possibility. Seeking assurances of money for such an alternative, Caddell said later, was not that difficult because "they didn't even ask who it is." Biden held a series of meetings with Caddell, Boston media consultant John Marttila and David Doak, who had won a reputation as one of the party's ablest young campaign managers. But indications of support from some leading Democrats in Congress never developed into hard commitments, and by December Biden was ready to give up the idea. It was clear that there were many Democrats privately wringing their hands about the prospect

9. Hart recalled, long after the campaign, running into Bumpers in the Senate one day. Bumpers told him that there were people urging him to run and then remarked that "it must be hard work out there." Hart said that after he agreed it was hard work, Bumpers added he had been told "they could have me home on Friday night and back on the road on Mondays." To which Hart replied: "Tell them they're all fools."

of a Fritz Mondale candidacy, but there is always a distance in politics between whining in private and speaking up in public.

As Caddell recalled later: "Joe said, 'I'm not going to get in this by myself.' " In fact, nonetheless, Biden didn't finally abandon the notion without thinking about it on his Christmas vacation. He embarked on his holiday only after signing and leaving behind with his sister a blank filing form that would have allowed his name to be entered in the New Hampshire primary had he changed his mind.

Not all the problems in a Mondale candidacy were ones that had to be inferred, however. There were more overt indicators of the burden he carried as the putative candidate of the old politics. One was the view that had developed of Mondale as a candidate trying to distance himself from the man he had served as Vice President. This view was founded on Mondale's statements that he had disagreed within "the private councils" of the Carter administration on a variety of a issues, from the grain embargo to the sale of nuclear materials to India to the MX missile. The price he was paying became obvious at an October candidate forum at Harvard when Mondale said he had privately opposed the sale of F-15 fighter planes to Saudi Arabia.

Askew observed somewhat acidly: "I'm still waiting for Fritz Mondale to say what he agrees with Jimmy Carter on, but I guess I'll have to wait." Virtually the entire audience erupted into laughter.

Perhaps a more serious problem was developing with Mondale's image as the candidate of those Democratic constituencies. Late in the fall, just before endorsing Mondale, Governor Mario Cuomo of New York met with him one night and urged him to take the lead in confronting the entitlements question—the runaway spending on programs such as Medicare that was contributing so much to the federal deficit.

"I told him," Cuomo reported the next day, "that he needed to show he could say no to somebody."

"What did he say?" Cuomo was asked.

"He said no to me," Cuomo replied.

A week later Mondale went to dinner with several Washington reporters and we asked about this conversation with Cuomo and then whether he might be willing to say no on any one of a series of other federal spending programs. His answer, again, was a firm negative. He did not intend, he said repeatedly, to turn his back on the people who were supporting him. He was going to dance with the guy who brung him. And that was that.

The chinks in Mondale were, as it turned out, nothing compared to the flaws in the system and the Democratic Party exposed by the long preliminaries of 1983. All of these candidates had spent the entire year jousting with one another for the favors of political activists without realizing that the voters at large were paying very little attention. And, to the degree that they were watching at all, they were seeing the whole exercise as a bidding war in which they were not involved. Most of these candidates had struggled through a series of straw polls, not one of which forecast the primary or caucus winner of 1984. Two full months before the first official delegate selection, the also-ran candidates had spent all of the money they could raise and mortgaged most of their federal matching funds.

For all of this, however, the party was operating on two premises that seemed reasonable to most professionals. The first was that Mondale's strength among party activists was a generally accurate indicator of his potential among rank-and-file primary voters. The second was that the esteem with which Mondale was regarded by Democratic officeholders and labor leaders could be translated into popular support later. That was something Mondale himself believed.

"Always he had a sense of voters coming with leaders," Tully said. "He had a respect for institutions and organizations and the elected leadership in a way that didn't square up with the television age."

What was missing was any message to the electorate at large. Fritz Mondale had opened his campaign by declaring, "I am ready." But Mondale had not offered any clear vision of how the future would be different under his presidency than it would be under four more years of Ronald Reagan. Instead, he and all his challengers had spent the year—and most of their treasure—arguing among themselves about the past, a past with which most of the voters were not preoccupied or even really concerned.

But Mondale had other things to worry about. Not the least of them now was the potential threat to his own candidacy of a new development: the entry into the race in November of an eighth Democratic candidate—the Reverend Jesse Jackson. In those first weeks Jackson's campaign was viewed as an intriguing curiosity with a potential that simply couldn't be measured because there was no precedent for doing so. But on December 29 Jackson and his usual substantial entourage flew off to Damascus, Syria, where Robert O. Goodman, Jr., a young black Navy lieutenant, was being held hostage by the Syrians after being shot down December 4.

To some, it seemed a fool's errand by a politically naive black civil-rights activist out of his depth in international politics. In fact, it was an event that once again radically changed the dynamics of the contest for the Democratic nomination.

4

The New Wine

•

FOR THE REVEREND JESSE L. JACKSON, there was a significant lesson for blacks to draw from their experience in the campaign for mayor of his home city of Chicago early in 1983. After years of increasingly contentious relationships with the regular Cook County Democratic organization—the Daley machine and its heirs—the blacks had decided to run a candidate of their own, an obscure congressman named Harold Washington. But they had encountered a disappointing response from national Democrats. Walter Mondale, the protégé of Hubert H. Humphrey and Vice President under Jimmy Carter, had come into the primary campaign to support Richard M. Daley, the state's attorney and—more to the point—son of the late Mayor Richard J. Daley. And Edward M. Kennedy had come in to support the incumbent, Mayor Jane Byrne.

"That was unprecedented," Jackson recalled much later. "These guys were getting in the middle of a primary election in a city where you've got two Irish people running and a 2 percent Irish population in a city 40 percent black [and] the blacks having been loyal and productive. They were the two most prominent liberals in the party who'd make this move."

In each case, the white politician was paying a debt, but otherwise their situations were quite different.

Jane Byrne had supported Ted Kennedy in his primary challenge to the renomination of President Jimmy Carter in 1980, which is not the kind of thing a Kennedy ever forgets. But there was no immediate way for black leaders, even if so inclined, to register their displeasure against Kennedy for supporting Byrne, because he had taken himself out of the competition for the 1984 Democratic presidential nomination.

The situation with Mondale was obviously touchier. He was delivering on a commitment he had made to Richie Daley two years earlier, also in recognition of past support, but unlike Kennedy he was still a presidential candidate. Both Harold Washington and Jesse Jackson quickly made it clear to him that they saw his backing of Daley as a hostile act that would affect their own calculations on the presidential campaign.

Mondale protested that he had made the commitment to Daley long before Washington entered the picture, and he could not walk away. But Jackson was not convinced.

"I told Mondale," he said, "you should tell him [Daley] that he is setting you up for a difficult situation nationally." And when Mondale cited Daley's loyalty in the 1980 campaign, Jackson said, "I traveled to twenty-nine states and seventy-two cities myself, so Daley didn't support you as much as I did."

Jackson began a campaign of sorts to pressure Mondale, enlisting members of the black caucus in Congress, black mayors and other prominent black leaders to urge him to change his mind. And, he said later, he told Mondale: "You're going to have to fly in the face of all that just for Daley. . . . That's not good mathematics, it seems to me."

But Mondale was adamant. He reminded the blacks of his own flawless record on civil-rights issues, and he assured them of his sympathy for what Harold Washington was trying to accomplish. But he wasn't going to turn his back on a commitment. That wasn't the way the game was played.

Jackson was not persuaded, however. "That, in effect, had the same effect on our political options as the bus driver arresting Rosa Parks or the Woolworth's guy locking up the four students," he said, referring to the seminal civil-rights protests a full generation earlier. "It forced us to consider new options. One option, of course, was to take it. Another option was to withdraw. Another option came to me: Why don't we run somebody in the [presidential] primary?"

In fact, by that point the possibility of a black running for President was a natural step in the evolution of the political militancy that had taken place in the black community since Ronald Reagan was elected President in 1980. Indeed, almost from the moment he entered the White House, Reagan was viewed throughout the black community as an alien, surely uncaring and possibly hostile figure. And this attitude quickly manifested itself—to the surprise of most political professionals in both parties—in an extraordinary turnout of black voters for Democrats in two special elections in 1981 to fill vacancies in Congress, one in Mississippi and one in Ohio, and in the election of Democrat Charles Robb as governor of Virginia.

In the 1982 mid-term congressional and gubernatorial elections, the evidence of this black militancy against Reagan and the Republicans was even more apparent. In Texas, for example, 100,000 new black voters were added to the rolls in and around Houston. They became an important factor in Democrat Mark White's upset over the incumbent Republican governor, William Clements. In Illinois, a similar number of blacks were added, and their solid Democratic vote was one of the reasons Democrat Adlai E. Stevenson III came within a whisker of defeating Republican Governor James Thompson. In several congressional districts in the South, Democrats unseated or turned back Republicans, largely on the strength of enhanced black turnout.

During that campaign, the nation was in the grip of the most serious recession since the Great Depression, and it was striking with particular force in the black community. If things were going to get better for those on the lower end of the economic scale, Ronald Reagan, the rich man's President, had to be turned out of office.

But Jesse Jackson's interest in becoming a candidate had far more to do with the Democratic Party's treatment of blacks than with Reagan and the Republicans. He was not seeking a practical response to the economic conditions that afflicted blacks. Nor was he making any considered judgment that running might make it easier for the Democratic Party to defeat Reagan. Instead, he saw a candidacy as a vehicle for attracting attention to a cause—and if it skewed the Democrats' process in seeking a presidential nominee, so be it.

Even as Harold Washington was running for mayor of Chicago, Jackson had plunged into a voting-rights campaign in the South. He had gone there initially when Reagan, as Jackson put it later, "started to hedge" on extension of the Voting Rights Act. But as he examined the situation more thoroughly, it became clear that many of the problems in trying to increase black political influence in the South were a product of election laws promulgated by Democrats concerned first with their own control of things.

In a public hearing in Jackson, Mississippi, Jackson recalled, "one of the things that came out was, the issue was not just a matter of motivation versus apathy and voter registration. The issue was lack of voter [law] enforcement and reapportionment." He recalled that he and other black leaders—"most of whom lived in the urban North but [originally were] from the South"—had not been aware of such impediments. These included dual registration systems, which required voters to register separately for elections held by different jurisdictions in which they lived, and redistricting carried out just before passage of the 1965 Voting Rights Act to minimize black voter potential.

One particular problem, Jackson discovered, was the widespread use of runoff primaries—or second primaries, as they sometimes were called—in deciding party nominations. In that system, the two candidates who received the highest number of votes would be matched against one another if no candidate managed to receive an absolute majority of the vote.

In most cases, the runoff primary system had been established for reasons that had nothing to do with diluting the black franchise. But that was clearly the effect, to the extent that voting split strictly along racial lines, as it did most often in the South and elsewhere. A black candidate in a legislative district with a 40 percent black population might poll the most votes in a first primary for the Democratic nomination involving more than one white candidate. Then he would find white voters coalescing behind the remaining white candidate in the runoff.

This system, Jackson argued, was both an "impediment" to black political advancement and a "safety net" for the white politicians. For whites, he said, it meant "if we have a second shot at you head to head, we can beat you. That's the real theory behind that."

The most obvious result of these discoveries was a campaign by Jackson for changes in laws and for tougher federal enforcement. It was a campaign that at one point brought even William Bradford Reynolds, the chief of the civil-rights division in the Reagan administration Justice Department, down to Mississippi to help and, not incidentally, serve as living proof of Jesse Jackson's clout. This success led Jackson to commit his base organization in Chicago, People United to Serve Humanity (PUSH), to run a "southern voter crusade" in the summer of 1983 to get more blacks registered into the political process one way or the other.

And, by Jackson's estimate, neither political party was blameless. "The Republicans were not recruiting blacks, and the Democrats were exploiting them," he said later.

In terms of presidential politics, this initiative by Jackson was significant because, for the first time, he became fully involved in questions about the political process and the effects it had on his black constituents. He had formed PUSH—originally People United to Save Humanity—after breaking with the Southern Christian Leadership Conference in 1971 as primarily an operation that focused its attention on winning economic equity for blacks.

But now Jackson was becoming increasingly involved in politics—first in the Harold Washington campaign, now in the burgeoning discussion about a black presidential candidacy.

There had been one previous black candidate. In 1972 Shirley Chisholm, a black congresswoman representing a district in Brooklyn, had declared her candidacy for the Democratic presidential nomination. But Chisholm was not well known, and she ran a limited and totally symbolic campaign that never was even considered likely to reach the stage where she could be a broker for black concerns at a nominating convention. Jesse Jackson, with the experience of years of playing the media game with such consummate skill, was an entirely different matter.

Nor had Chisholm ever had a goad quite like the experience of the Chicago election campaign. Harold Washington won the primary over Byrne and Daley, in that order, on February 22, 1983, and ordinarily would have been assured of winning the general election in a city in which the Republican Party had been a joke for years. But the white backlash against the prospect of Chicago's first black mayor was so pronounced that the Republican nominee, a political novice lawyer named Bernard Epton, suddenly became a serious contender.

The campaign was one of the ugliest in recent political history, dividing the city sharply along racial lines. Washington's campaign ran television advertising with the slogan "It's Our Turn," and the Epton campaign countered with its own, calling for a vote for the Republican nominee "Before It's Too Late."

In Jesse Jackson's view, what made the white backlash particularly significant was the fact that it extended throughout the regular Cook County Democratic organization. Some white leaders simply sat out the election; others defected to the Republican but white Bernard Epton. When the votes were counted, Washington had won but had captured only 19 percent of the white vote against Epton, a candidate whose unsuitability for big-time politics had become crystal clear in the late stages of the campaign.

Jackson, displaying his special talent for hyperbole, called Washington's election "the most important event since Selma"—the civil-rights march that originated in that Alabama city almost twenty years earlier. And, armed with the evidence that white Democratic leaders either would not or could not deliver for black candidates, Jackson began his public move toward becoming a candidate for President of the United States.

At about this same point, a group that became known informally as "the black leadership family" began holding a series of meetings in Atlanta, Chicago and New Orleans to discuss the course they should follow in presidential politics. Although the group was formalized at one point as the "Committee on Election Strategy," there was no genuine structure, and the two or three dozen black leaders—mostly preachers and politicians—who participated varied from meeting to meeting.

Much of their attention, ostensibly at least, was directed at writing what one of their leaders, the Reverend Joseph Lowery, president of the SCLC, called "a people's platform." It was supposed to be a list of black demands and goals by which presidential candidates could be measured at some later stage in the campaign.

But the idea of a black candidate as a general matter, and of Jesse Jackson in particular, quickly became the central issue, not only in those meetings but in what one participant recalled as "endless conversations" among black leaders all over the country. And in the campaign councils of Walter Mondale, the concern was conspicuous. Defeating John Glenn, it seemed to the Mondale advisers, would be difficult under any circumstances; with a diversion of any substantial minority of black votes, it might be impossible.

Jackson fanned the interest and the debate with a quick trip to Iowa in March "to test the climate" in the state that would hold the first precinct caucuses. Then he made another to New

Hampshire to try out among the Democrats who would vote in the first primary. In New Hampshire he spoke to an assembly at the Lakes Region High School, then attended a luncheon arranged by Ed Theobald, a Portsmouth businessman and longtime party activist. There Jackson clearly impressed the liberal Democrats who attended; radical chic had come to New Hampshire, a state with 1,700 blacks.

But among black leaders, and within the Democratic Party as a whole, the argument was intense. Lines were quickly drawn that reflected Jesse Jackson's history in the civil-rights movement and the role he had carved out for himself as the leader of PUSH over the previous decade.

From the outset, Jackson had some strong supporters, the point man clearly being Mayor Richard G. Hatcher of Gary, Indiana, the senior black mayor of a large city. But other politicians resisted, and some of the best known—Mayor Andrew Young of Atlanta, Mayor Coleman Young of Detroit, State Senator Julian Bond of Atlanta, Mayor Tom Bradley of Los Angeles, Mayor Richard Arrington of Birmingham, City Councilman John Lewis of Atlanta—were already either committed to Fritz Mondale or planning to endorse him when the time was ripe for doing so.

There was also a division among blacks—in the South, at least—by generation or, more properly, something less than half a generation. At forty-one, Jesse Jackson was simply too young to have been on the ground floor of the civil-rights movement in the late 1950s. He led his first substantial demonstration while he was a student at North Carolina Agricultural and Technical College in 1963. And he first came to the attention of Martin Luther King, Jr., at Selma, while he was still a student at the Chicago Theological Seminary.

Across the South there were many other young black leaders who were just a few years too young to have had their tickets punched at the very beginning. And they quickly volunteered to lead what was to become the Rainbow Coalition in their own states—people such as Tyrone Brooks of Georgia, a thirty-eight-year-old state legislator and longtime SCLC official, and the Reverend John Nettles of Anniston, Alabama, forty years old and the state leader of SCLC.

There were, of course, many older black politicians who lined up with Jackson—such veteran Democratic leaders as Percy Sutton and Basil Patterson in New York, for instance. And there were black preachers of all ages who quickly came into his camp, including the Reverend T. J. Jemison, chairman of the National Baptist Convention, U.S.A., Inc. But the younger leaders like Brooks and Nettles weren't looking for a candidate for this one campaign so much as they were looking for a new movement that would continue to be a factor in state and local politics after the 1984 election.

"This thing is going to continue on," Brooks would tell reporters who called on him in Atlanta. "It's going to keep right on going."

Although these younger leaders were somewhat hesitant to put it so baldly, it was clear they were also looking at Jesse Jackson as the successor to Martin Luther King, Jr.—a notion that the Julian Bonds and Andy Youngs clearly found difficult to swallow.

To some extent, the reaction against Jackson was simply personal. He had a reputation as a hot dog who would intrude on a situation, make a flamboyant speech for the television cameras, then leave the hard work of voter registration to those who remained behind when he left. Some of those who had been in the civil-rights movement with Martin King from the outset muttered that Jesse had been too quick to grab glory and too slow to take on the hard burdens of the campaign.

These leaders in particular had always resented the claim by Jackson—which he subsequently denied making—that he had been at King's side at the moment of the shooting on the Lorraine Motel balcony in Memphis in 1968, when in fact he was in the courtyard of the motel below. And they would not forgive him for rushing back to Chicago the morning after King's assassination to appear on the *Today* program on NBC and then making a speech wearing a shirt stained with the blood of their fallen leader.

Long before his run for the presidency, Jackson's reputation for exploiting the press was legendary. One of the stories that made the rounds of black leaders had it that Harold Washington had finally found a way to prevent Jackson from forcing his way to the front of every press conference and claiming all the credit for his success. Washington arranged, the story went, to set up some bright lights in a closet. When Jackson rushed in seeking the television cameras, Washington slammed the door behind him.

In most cases, the black leaders seemed determined to keep

their resentment of Jackson among themselves, but there were times it simply burst through. Once, for example, a prominent civil-rights leader was talking with two reporters. They told him how Jackson, rather than campaigning, had antagonized the George McGovern campaign during the California primary of 1972 by spending most of his time lounging around the pool at the Wilshire Hyatt House. The black leader listened, then suggested: "Why haven't you written about that? I haven't seen that in your column."

But, some of the black leaders would concede privately, there was also an element of jealousy in their attitude toward Jackson. He was an extraordinarily exciting speaker, with a particular genius for attracting the television networks that none of them could match. And he had an appeal to young blacks who seemed beyond the reach of most of the more conventional black politicians. Although it was widely accepted that Jesse Jackson wouldn't follow through on his voter-registration rallies, no one could deny the evidence of his eyes when Jackson led students out of a meeting hall to register.[10] Nor could he be denied the credit for the emphasis he put on persuading the young to finish their educations and keep out of trouble.

But there were more substantial concerns about a Jackson candidacy than petty jealousies or old resentments.

In the South most of the black leaders who had started in the civil-rights movement and then gone into politics had learned to deal with the white power structure, in both politics and business, in a way that clearly benefited the blacks they represented. And that was true in terms of their dealings in state and national politics.

Andy Young, for example, had served in Congress and as ambassador to the United Nations before becoming mayor of Atlanta. He was past the point at which protest politics served his purposes. Similarly, in the state capitol building just across the street from City Hall, Julian Bond had been in the Georgia legislature long enough so that he was a Senate committee chairman—and a politician for whom alliances were more important than symbols.

10. Jackson's appeal was directed most often to black students, but it wasn't limited to them. Speaking to those high school students in New Hampshire in March, Jackson had promised to buy them all lunch if they registered to vote. In June, he returned and delivered on the promise after 179 of the 180 students registered. The only exception was one who had not yet turned eighteen years old.

So the argument in those meetings of the "black leadership family" and in those "endless conversations" elsewhere often centered on whether you make a gesture toward Jesse Jackson or an alliance with Fritz Mondale that might bring some practical reward.

One of those who came down for pragmatism was Joe Reed, the leader of the Alabama Democratic Conference, the leading black political organization in the state. At forty-five, Joe Reed was a veteran organizer who had demonstrated more than once that he and the ADC could deliver—to the point that it was the kind of force that white politicians there ignored at their peril. Reed understood Jackson's appeal to blacks, but he also understood its limits.

"The question that one always has to answer as a leader," he said later, "is, do you tell people the truth or do you tell them what they want to hear? We elected to tell the truth, and that was, we didn't think Jesse could get nominated, and if he got the nomination, he couldn't win."

"We all knew Jesse was not running to win," he said. "I don't think Jesse ever expected to win. He was running to run and to make some points. I think he made his point well—in fairness, better than I thought he'd make it."

But at the time Jackson was "testing the winds," Reed was arguing vigorously behind the scenes for Mondale. He was pointing out that many Alabama blacks had put themselves behind Jimmy Carter early in the game eight years earlier and had earned their reward in the form of two liberal federal judges named by Carter.

"Joe would always make it a point," another black leader said, "that these weren't just judges. They were young judges who would be around for a while."

That line of reasoning was at the core of the opposition to Jackson—that blacks could not risk another four years of Ronald Reagan and thus should quickly get behind their best hope among the Democrats, Fritz Mondale. The alternative, they argued, was that split in the vote that might allow Glenn to slip by.

Blacks who took this view and other Mondale agents also argued earnestly that even if you granted Jesse Jackson the good intentions he claimed and accepted the validity of his goals, his candidacy didn't make sense. He couldn't possibly raise enough money, or put together the staff, or campaign in enough primaries, or organize enough states, or win enough delegates to have any bargaining power at the Democratic National Convention. It was a pipe dream, agreed all the experts, black and white.

The flaw in all this reasoning, however, was that the naysayers—again, both black and white—were measuring Jesse Jackson's potential as a candidate by the conventional standards that would be applied to a white candidate thinking about running for President. What they did not see—perhaps could not see—was that Jackson wouldn't need the money and organization conventional candidates require just to get attention.

While Gary Hart, Alan Cranston, Fritz Hollings and Reubin Askew were struggling in obscurity for credibility and some exposure in the press, Jesse Jackson was able to command the attention of the networks simply through the excitement he sent through the black community and the curiosity he inspired among whites.

By late in the spring of 1983, that fact was becoming apparent. Meeting at the O'Hare Hilton outside Chicago, the black leaders endorsed the concept of a black candidate, although not Jackson himself. But, by this time, even the diehards had abandoned the idea that they might persuade someone else. Maynard Jackson, Andrew Young's predecessor as mayor of Atlanta, had been the one most often mentioned, but he had declined and had decided to support Jesse Jackson. And Jackson himself was moving ever closer to the decision to run.

"I kept raising the issue that somebody ought to run," he said later. "After a certain point, the momentum was such that if nobody was going to do it, if I didn't do it, it would look as if I had teased the people in a mischievous way, but I was quite serious.

"But what it did was it created an authentic draft, as opposed to one of those contrived drafts. Somewhere in the course of that mass education came 'Run, Jesse, run.' All that stuff from outside the organized leadership family, and the people began to cry out."

Just what constitutes an "authentic draft" in politics is always open to some dispute. We have certainly never seen a case in which some outsider was dragged kicking and screaming into a candidacy. But Jackson's claim is probably justified in the sense that once he advertised his availability, there was a genuine demand from many people in the black community who called out "Run, Jesse, run" as he went about the business of positioning himself to do just that.

Out on the road, Jackson helped things along by presenting the whole issue in movement terms, using rallies and church meetings to urge other blacks to plunge into politics. Preaching to several thousand Baptist ministers in Memphis that June, for example, Jackson listed the offices available and used a favorite formulation. "If you run, you might lose," he shouted. "If you don't run, I'll guarantee you'll lose. Run!"

"Run!" the audience shouted back.

"If you run, your friends can't take you for granted and your enemies can't write you off. Run!"

"Run!" they shouted again.

"If we go from ten million registered voters to fifteen million registered voters, America will never be the same again. Run!"

"Run!" came the response once more.

"From the outhouse to the statehouse to the White House," shouted Jackson. "All the way!"

The vintage Jackson rhetoric was a combination of rhyme, alliteration, parallel constructions and contrapuntal rhetorical tricks.

"The issue for us is not welfare, it's our share," he would say. "We are not hanging around fighting for charity. We are fighting for parity."

In the Democratic Party, he would say, "we have membership but no proprietorship." Or, over and over again for months, "It's time for the old wineskins to make way for the new wine."

"Hands that once picked cotton can now pick Presidents," he would say. "We are going from the guttermost to the uppermost." Or: "We are going from the slave ship to the championship."

Or, in a speech in Baltimore in late August, he put it like this: "Twenty years ago we were striking for the right to sleep in a downtown hotel or sit in a park. It's not a movement today to share the bathrooms. It is a movement to share the power. It's not a movement from the outside in. It's a movement from the bottom up."

However contrived the rhetoric may have been, it always seemed fresh to the audiences of black Americans electrified by the notion of one of their own having the audacity to run for President. And as the summer wore on, the cries of "Run, Jesse, run" rose up all around him—and all around the other politicians, black and white, involved in the contest for the 1984 Democratic presidential nomination.

By late summer the views of the "black leadership family" were essentially irrelevant. As Ron Brown, a Washington lawyer and deputy chair of the Democratic National Committee, put it later: "Jesse just preempted it."

"Jesse didn't really have the blessing," he said. "He kind of took the blessing and went ahead . . . the momentum of the thing was incredible."

Jackson himself said later he had harbored some reservations about whether he could organize such a campaign.

"I had great anxiety about running," he said. "No fund-raising machinery, no budget, no knowledge of how to rent a plane or how to deal with the Secret Service and the traveling press corps. We learned all that on the job."

Jackson also was being impressed with what he later called "the anxieties" of the black leaders about his campaign, quite beyond the possibility that he might undermine Mondale. Many of them warned him, he said, "If you run out there, you could get killed." (It was not a caution he could take lightly. Before his campaign was over, he said later, there had been 311 death threats made against him, and fourteen people "put in jail because of the quality and proximity of their threats.")

But the most common anxiety among the black leaders was that Jesse Jackson, preacher and social activist but political neophyte, would not be able to present himself credibly in competition with all those white politicians.

"If you run," he recalled them warning, "there's so much involved, it could be embarrassing."

Jackson was also hearing discouraging talk from the Mondale campaign and from blacks allied with Mondale about how difficult it would be for him to do all the things required to compete.

"I met with Fritz several times," he recalled. "All roads led to the disadvantages of running."

By fall, however, there was some new evidence to encourage him—findings in opinion polls that showed him running ahead of several of the white candidates. The data was skewed by the fact that Jackson was getting so much press attention and consequent name recognition, but it could not be ignored.

"The more those type polls came out," Jackson said, "the less rational the arguments about why we should not [run] were."

In September Jackson flew off to Europe in a politically conventional attempt to bolster the foreign-policy credential he would need to be taken seriously as a candidate. It was, as usual, a media event of impressive proportions—Jesse Jackson visiting the scene of racial rioting in Great Britain; standing at the Berlin Wall, calling on President Reagan to meet for arms-control negotiations with then Soviet leader Yuri Andropov; preaching to United States Army troops in West Germany; and, perhaps inevitably, straying into a controversy in Amsterdam.

Jackson had flown to the Netherlands and been granted a seventy-minute private audience with Queen Beatrix. But in an interview with the Associated Press later he quoted the queen as saying that she wanted deployment of U.S. missiles in her country "to be delayed" unless there was success in the arms talks then under way in Geneva. The interview caused a small furor. It seemed to put Beatrix on record contradicting the Dutch government's policy on the missiles. And it seemed to violate the Dutch constitution's prohibition against public policy statements by a queen.

But Jackson quickly issued an apology for what his spokesman called "any error of judgment or interpretation" he had made, and the incident was quickly smoothed over. By the time Jackson returned from Europe, there was no longer any question about whether he would run but only about when he would make it official.

Characteristically, Jackson made his declaration under the most auspicious circumstances—in an appearance October 30 with Mike Wallace on *60 Minutes*, the television program that consistently enjoys the largest audience of any in the nation.

"You measure America's greatness by what America does for the least," he said. "I want to help again measure greatness by how we treat children in the dawn of life, how we treat poor people in the pit of life and how we treat old folk in the sunset of life. That's the America I want to identify with."

The following Thursday, in Washington, he made it official before a crowd of perhaps 3,000 cheering partisans who jammed the D.C. Convention Center for a three-hour event that combined the salient features of a political beginning and a revival meeting.

Reaching the podium more than two hours behind schedule, Jackson declared: "Our time has come." And he seemed to be warning the Democrats in the bluntest possible terms that he intended to be a voice of influence for blacks within the party.

"We can do without the Democratic and Republican parties," he said at one point. "They cannot do without us. We are necessary."

It was, of course, a carefully staged event. There were more than a hundred people crowded onto the platform to make his point that this was truly a rainbow coalition—Hispanics, Asians, Indians, women, farmers, environmentalists, as well as blacks. But the size of the crowd and the intensity of the cries of "Run, Jesse, run" and "Win, Jesse, win" offered a sharp contrast to the tepid response most of the other Democratic candidates were evoking in 1983 as they went about the business of playing their inside games at straw polls.

And for the Mondale campaign, the one with the most reason to be concerned, there were some surprises on that platform. As expected, District of Columbia Mayor Marion Barry was there, standing with Dick Hatcher at Jackson's side. But Walter Fauntroy, the District's delegate to the House of Representatives, was there, too, despite the reservations he had held earlier about a black candidate that had led the Mondale campaign to count him as one of theirs.

Jackson's candidacy sent tremors throughout the Democratic Party. Politicians are always uncomfortable dealing with situations that have no precedents, and clearly this was just such a situation.

All the conventional calculations suggested that Jackson would be unlikely to win more than 200 to 250 convention delegates, obviously far short of the 1,967 needed to be nominated. And although politicians and the press speculate every four years about the possibility of a brokered nominating convention—the kind in which even 200 delegates might be pivotal—it rarely happens. The rise over the years in the proportion of delegates chosen in primaries and caucuses as committed to a particular candidate made it more likely that one candidate would arrive at San Francisco with the nomination apparently assured. That had happened even when the Democratic Party was seriously divided, as in 1968, when Hubert Humphrey was nominated at Chicago, and again in 1972, when George McGovern became the nominee in Miami Beach.

There were obvious chances for Jackson to be an influence on the nominating process, nonetheless. If Mondale were to face close races in the primaries of northern industrial states—New York, Pennsylvania, Illinois and Ohio, for example—he would need the black votes that might be drawn away by Jackson.

At that stage, however, the concern of the Mondale strategists was focused more directly on the South and the so-called Super Tuesday primaries to be held on March 13 in Florida, Georgia and Alabama. This cluster was where they intended for the former Vice President to put the nomination on ice. But it was also where they expected their principal rival, John Glenn, to be strongest—with those white Democrats among whom his patriotic appeal might be most compelling.

Blacks made up less than 14 percent of the population in Florida, but they represented one-fourth of the population in both Alabama and Georgia, and an even greater potential share of the Democratic primary vote. If Glenn was still the prime opposition, Mondale would need support from them to succeed on Super Tuesday.

Just how much of the black vote Jackson might attract was a puzzle, however. Some early polling showed him getting half or less than half of it nationally, with Mondale winning the remainder. But political professionals have learned to have some doubts about the reliability of polls conducted among black voters, north or south. For one thing, fewer blacks have telephones. For another, the interviewers are usually white, which polling experts say causes an inordinately high "undecided" response among blacks.

No one could assess immediately just how much of the enthusiasm for Jackson in the black community, particularly among younger blacks, would be translated into votes when the time came. Nor could anyone forecast with any reliability how many blacks might be susceptible to the practical argument that their self-interest dictated an alliance with their preferred white candidate, simply because he could be nominated and ultimately could satisfy what Joe Reed called "the burning desire to get rid of Ronald Reagan."

For black politicians, the reality of the Jackson candidacy offered awkward choices in many situations. On the one hand, they wanted to be with a winner who might help them out later, and, in many cases, they had those serious doubts about Jackson anyway. On the other hand, they obviously didn't want to risk alienating black constituents now caught up in the excitement of the Jackson campaign. In some states—Georgia was one example—younger blacks supporting Jackson were muttering about taking retribution in local elections later if established black politicians wouldn't go along with them.

Some black leaders simply chose to move quickly to Mondale to make a point of their antipathy toward Jackson. Coleman Young, the mayor of Detroit, was an outspoken example, declaring: "Jesse has no experience, and he has no platform, and he has no chance."

But in Atlanta, another mayor, Andy Young, stayed officially neutral. In a meeting shortly after Jackson's declaration, he introduced Mondale as "the person most prepared to move into the White House and start providing leadership for the country"—but then insisted that the statement was not an endorsement of Mondale for the nomination.

Long after the campaign, Jackson said he understood the ambivalence of those other black leaders. "The idea was so new and it involved so much risk," he said. A certain amount of tension, he said, "is so normal for an intragroup struggle for position."

Thus, for Mondale strategists, for Democratic operatives in general, for black leaders, it was a time of waiting and watching—to see how Jesse Jackson would perform now that he had taken the final step.

What Jackson did was what he had been doing all along and would continue to do: Over the next two months he conducted an essentially non-stop schedule of appearances and press conferences that were catnip for the press and gave him far more attention than the other trailing candidates in the Democratic field. His ability to draw consistently impressive crowds of the enthusiastic—one day in a black church in Selma, another at the University of Texas in Austin—made it impossible to ignore him, even if the press had been so inclined.

He also made obvious to his rivals and party leaders that he was going to be a prickly opponent. At one point, he assailed the endorsement of Mondale by the AFL-CIO as an "undemocratic" decision handed down by union "bosses." At another, he began an assault on the party's delegate-selection rules, labeling the "reforms" written by the Hunt Commission a "throwback" that would "lock out" the poor and members of minorities from equal participation.

The rules challenge was taken most seriously inside the party because there was always an undercurrent of threat in it—the possibility that Jackson might walk out on the Democrats and take his black supporters with him. In fact, however, Jackson—despite his "we are necessary" language when he announced his candidacy—never made any explicit threat he would leave the party, and when pressed, publicly or privately, he denied that he ever intended to do so.

Ron Brown, who sat in on meetings between Jackson and Democratic National Chairman Charles T. Manatt, credited Jackson with good intentions all along. Talk of a walkout "kept getting play," Brown said later, "but . . . I think he did everything reasonable that he could to dispel that."

Jackson objected to several rules, all of which he was persuaded would make his task in the primaries more difficult. One was the provision in some states for so-called bonus delegates to be awarded to the candidate who won the most votes in a congressional district. Another was the system in other states of allowing the candidate with the most votes in a congressional district to win all the delegates. A third was the provision for the seating at San Francisco of 568 so-called super delegates, principally party leaders and public officials.

He also objected—and this was the most significant—to a provision in the Hunt rules for a "threshold" of 20 percent in primaries. This provision meant that for a candidate to get any share of the delegates in a particular jurisdiction, he would have to win at least 20 percent of the vote.[11]

The requirement had been written into the rules, with the blessings of the Kennedy, Mondale and union agents, with the idea of wiping out the minor candidates as early as possible in the competition by requiring them to get a larger share than had been needed in the past.

But what Jesse Jackson saw was the fact that there were only eighty-six congressional districts in the country with a black pop-

11. As a practical matter, the threshold varied somewhat from one congressional district to another, depending on how many delegates were being chosen. But the 20 percent standard applied most widely.

ulation of 20 percent or higher, fifty-seven of those in the South. And for all the talk about rainbows, Jackson and his agents clearly understood that he could not afford to have blacks in lesser concentrations written out of the process.

In fact, there was never any serious possibility that the rules would be rewritten at this stage of the game to accommodate Jackson. As party leaders correctly pointed out, the Hunt Commission had included a disproportionately large number of black members, one of them being Dick Hatcher, now Jackson's prime agent. But Manatt agreed to take the issue to the executive committee of the Democratic National Committee, and Jackson had made his point.

Not everything was going well for Jackson, however. The resistance among black politicians was a particular problem, as two developments in December made clear.

First, Harold Washington, whose election as mayor of Chicago had touched off the idea of a black candidacy, announced that he was thinking of running as a favorite son in the Illinois primary on March 20 in three Chicago congressional districts with predominately black populations. Although few imagined that Jesse Jackson was playing the delegate game, Washington's threat was a clear signal that he was not going to get a free ride, even in the black community.

An even clearer—and ultimately more significant—signal was sent on December 10 in Mobile, when Joe Reed's Alabama Democratic Conference voted more than three to one to endorse Mondale for President despite intense pressure from Jackson and his partisans in the state. The ADC threw Jackson a bone, an endorsement for the vice-presidential nomination. But, again, the only inference that could be drawn was that some black politicians were not ready to toss aside their practical concerns in the interests of a symbolic candidacy.

The attitude was, Joe Reed said, "that we cannot gamble on anyone losing that White House to Ronald Reagan."

But those who may have imagined that Jackson's campaign had stalled on a plateau had not figured on either his restless energy or his daring—at least not until Christmas Day, when Jackson announced he would lead a religious mission to try to rescue Lieutenant Robert O. Goodman from captivity in Syria. Goodman was a black twenty-seven-year-old Navy flyer, a bombardier-navigator, whom the Syrians had been holding since his light bomber was shot down while it was attacking a Syrian position in Lebanon on December 4.

The initiative was greeted with predictable skepticism in Washington, and with a slight from the White House. President Reagan refused to take a telephone call from Jackson. A presidential spokesman told reporters that "diplomatic efforts" to free Goodman were already under way and then added: "History has proven that efforts of this type have a better chance for success when they are not politicized."

In fact, however, it was clear that the Goodman situation was an obvious political problem for Reagan, who had made such a point of blustering about how forcefully—in contrast to his predecessor, Jimmy Carter—he would behave in such a confrontation. In this case, the problem had grown more awkward. The President had said at a news conference a few days earlier that the Goodman question had been "very high on the agenda" when Donald H. Rumsfeld, his special ambassador to the Middle East, had visited Damascus earlier in the month. But the Syrians said the matter of Goodman's fate never came up in Rumsfeld's visit, and then White House officials confirmed that Rumsfeld had been under instructions not to raise the issue, lest it be interpreted as a first step toward bargaining with the Syrians.

In any case, Jackson flew to Damascus at the end of the week, leading a dozen ministers and aides, including a press secretary and staff photographer, and an entourage of reporters and Secret Service agents. The other putative leader of the group was the Reverend M. William Howard, a former president of the National Council of Churches. Also in the entourage was another Jackson associate of some standing, Minister Louis Farrakhan, a prominent Muslim and leader of the Nation of Islam in Chicago.

On the face of it, the political risk for Jackson was enormous, although there were some indications the mission might not be as hopeless as the White House had suggested. Ed Theobald, the New Hampshire Democratic activist who had lined up so early with Jackson, had joined the group in the hope his business connections in Damascus and his own experience there might be some help. And in notes on the mission he wrote later, Theobald said that two days before departure the Syrians had "indicated an apparent willingness beyond expectations on the part of the

Damascus government to further consider a proposal by Jackson to release Lieutenant Goodman."

Nonetheless, it was far from certain that Hafez al-Assad, the president of Syria, would meet with Jackson, let alone free Goodman. He had refused to meet with Rumsfeld, and there was no assurance he would see any American at this point. And if he did not, Jackson could easily be portrayed as a naive neophyte playing games beyond his capacity. That impression could be particularly damaging to a candidate who was running for his first public office.

The group arrived in Damascus late on December 30, and Jackson spent much of the next two days in a series of meetings, first with government officials and then with religious leaders. He was also allowed to meet with Lieutenant Goodman and, most importantly, bring him before the reporters and cameramen. In the meetings with Foreign Minister Abdel Halim Khaddam and the religious leaders alike, Jackson combined political and essentially theological arguments. When Khaddam suggested, for example, that the Syrians might deter the United States from further attacks on their positions by continuing to hold Goodman, Jackson replied that the "hawks" in the United States might take just the opposite view. To which Khaddam replied: "Yes, but we have hawks in our government too."

But Jackson also argued repeatedly, Theobald recalled, that what he called the "circle of pain" in the relationship between the United States and Syria could be broken if the Syrians would only agree to free Robert Goodman. And he repeatedly told the story of Saint Paul, then Saul of Tarsus, being struck by a vision on the road to Damascus and being converted. The suggestion was that even though Goodman had been attacking Syrians when he was brought down, he was not beyond redemption. At one meeting, Theobald wrote, the Syrian officials were clearly impressed when Jackson suggested they adjourn with a prayer—and then turned to Farrakhan, who recited an Islamic prayer in Arabic.

"It was a long glass table," Theobald wrote later, "and with my head bowed but my eyes open, through the reflection from the glass top, I could see the Syrian delegation turning their heads and looking at each other as if saying to themselves, 'Is he with us or them?' It was a stroke of genius on Jesse's part to include

Louis in our delegation, and it greatly increased our standing with our Syrian hosts."

On Monday, after a weekend of tense waiting, Assad met for ninety minutes with Jackson and two other ministers without handing down a decision. But the following morning, Jackson was summoned by government officials once again—and told that Goodman would be freed.

In political terms, Jesse Jackson had scored a ten strike, and he exploited it with all the skill he had developed in almost twenty years of playing the media game as well as any public figure in the world. Goodman was released early enough so that, with the time difference, the story broke on the television networks' morning shows. And as the New York *Daily News* headline trumpeted "Jesse Did It," the entourage flew to a military base in West Germany in time for a round of live appearances on the networks' evening news broadcasts.

Then it was back across the Atlantic and a landing at Andrews Air Force Base, again just in time for live reports on the 7 AM EST programs. And finally there was a trip to the White House, and a greeting by Reagan in the Rose Garden in time for the next news cycle. Faced with the fait acompli, the President was gracious, and all thoughts about politicizing diplomacy were put aside, at least for the moment.

"Reverend Jackson's mission was a personal mission of mercy," said Reagan, "and he has earned our gratitude and admiration."

Just as apparent, however, was that Jesse Jackson now had earned a new credibility in the contest for the Democratic presidential nomination. There was still no reason to believe this black preacher could win the nomination, but it was equally obvious that he could not be brushed aside as a nuisance candidate. At the very least, his astonishing success in Syria had given more serious black voters a better rationale for voting for him. He had played the white man's game and beaten him at it.

The Mondale strategists understood that fact as well as anyone, but they were limited in how they could respond. A few weeks earlier, Richard Arrington, the highly respected black mayor of Birmingham, had told Jim Quackenbush, Mondale's southern coordinator, that he would deliver his endorsement "when you need it the most." So Quackenbush played that card, and Arrington announced his endorsement the day after Jackson's return from Damascus.

But that public commitment was an exception. In contrast to Arrington, some of the Mondale operatives believed that Andy Young, among others, seemed even more reluctant to take the final step and endorse their candidate. And at one meeting of black leaders in Atlanta, there was even some discussion about another way out—running a slate of uncommitted delegates in the predominately black Fifth Congressional District in Atlanta as a device to avoid choosing between Mondale and Jackson.

As the campaign evolved, however, such neutrality became virtually impossible. Jesse Jackson had become a force that could not be ignored.

In a larger sense, however, the Jackson candidacy was still another distortion of the process. He was not offering himself to his fellow Democrats as the candidate best equipped for the presidency and best able to defeat Ronald Reagan in November. Instead, he was using the contest for the Democratic nomination as a forum for expressing black demands for a greater voice in the party—and, quite obviously, as a way of establishing himself as the unquestioned leader of black America.

5

Standing Tall

•

ON THE DAY OF THE 1982 CONGRESSIONAL ELECTIONS, which had brought bad news to the Reagan White House but new hope of a comeback to the Democrats, the President called in his close friend Senator Paul Laxalt of Nevada. He asked Laxalt to take the Republican Party under his wing. A new post of general chairman of the party would be created. He would function as an umbrella leader over the various party units, including the Republican National Committee and the House and Senate campaign committees, and he would provide liaison between the White House and the next presidential campaign operation. Another individual of Laxalt's choice would handle the nitty-gritty direction of the Republican National Committee. Laxalt was cool to the idea.

"I didn't want the job," he recalled later. "I had enough to do around here." But Reagan persisted. Finally, Laxalt told him: "I don't want to get into this thing unless there's some indication you're going to be a horse [candidate]. That's the only reason I'd do this. Are you prepared to commit?"

"No," Reagan replied. "Well, let me put it this way," Laxalt said. "In '76, you asked me to chair the campaign against a sitting Republican President who I liked, and to get out front for an exploratory effort. I asked you to give me a reading, one to ten, where the hell you were, and you gave me an eight. All I ask you about any commitment is, Are you in that range now?"

Reagan's eyes, Laxalt recalled, "twinkled, and he said, 'Yes.' So I figured, hell, he's a horse. It was a go, subject to something happening to make it a no-go."

On that same premise, but with no more explicit intelligence about Reagan's reelection plans, a strategy group in the White

House had been holding periodic meetings ever since 1981 on the political aspects of various policy decisions. After the 1982 elections, the group intensified its focus on a 1984 presidential campaign. The regulars were White House Chief of Staff Jim Baker; Mike Deaver, the shaper and protector of the Reagan image and interests; and two outsiders—Stuart Spencer, the 1980 campaign troubleshooter from California, and Bob Teeter, the pollster-analyst from Detroit.

"It was an ongoing thing," Spencer said later, "but we started addressing it more seriously after the distinct lack of success in the mid-term elections. We as a group felt at that point in time that we maybe had very serious problems on our hands in terms of reelection, based on what had happened there and what was happening in the economy." The losses in the House persuaded him, Spencer said, that a Democrat could win the presidency in 1984. "The recovery hadn't taken hold, and they were nailing him [Reagan] with issues that were his problems—rich versus poor, Social Security, all those things."

To shore up these real or potential presidential vulnerabilities, the White House political group increasingly sought ways to use Reagan and the presidency. "The modern presidency is necessarily a full-time four-year job of political coalition-building," one of the strategy group observed later. "Governing is a full-time electoral exercise." Accordingly, in anticipation of a second Reagan candidacy, "we were consciously moving to the middle," he said.

Special "themes of the week" were conceived and implemented through highly visible, heavily reported presidential trips and speeches. "Blitzes" on specific issues were launched, such as an intense offensive to demonstrate that Reagan, contrary to Democratic harangues, was deeply concerned about the state of public education, which had taken a beating in his earliest budget proposals.

When, for example, the National Commission on Excellence in Education released a report in April 1983 entitled "A Nation at Risk" that was strongly critical of the state of public education and the level of federal aid to it, Reagan grabbed the report and used it as a rationale for his own criticisms.

The Commission judged that an erosion of educational foundations "threatens our very future as a nation and a people" and warned that "a rising tide of mediocrity" was plaguing the schools.

It recommended more high school emphasis on English, mathematics, science, social studies and foreign languages, as well as computer science; longer class days and more homework; merit pay for teachers. It said primary responsibility should remain with local and state government, but the federal share in special education for the gifted, disadvantaged and handicapped should be increased.

Reagan sweepingly labeled the report "a call for an end to federal intrusion" in the schools, and he embraced the cause of merit pay for teachers—strenuously opposed by the National Education Association, the largest teachers' union—and made the NEA a whipping boy. The strategy group, with Deaver as the chief technician, had Reagan visit classrooms to underscore his commitment to education of the nation's young. The same essential formula was used in other areas and for other constituencies in which he was weak—environmentalists, Hispanics, blacks and women. Some of these ventures were more successful than others, but they all came in the context of the improving economy, and Reagan's political fortunes climbed.

Concerning the economy, the administration touted the signs of recovery—steadily declining unemployment and inflation rates—and wished away the rest.

"We quite consciously decided to begin to rationalize the toleration of deficits," one White House policy-maker acknowledged much later.

The remarkably candid observation revealed the readiness of Reagan's key advisers to blur reality for political considerations. It was a willingness that already had come to mark the President's public statements and speeches on issues across the spectrum of administration policy, and would continue through the election of 1984 and beyond.

In 1982 there was ample reason to fudge the economic realities. Unemployment had averaged 9.7 percent, the highest annual figure in forty-one years. On top of that dismal statistic, Reagan's personal approval rating had plummeted to 41 percent, below the low points of predecessors Carter, Nixon, Kennedy and Eisenhower. But with the advent of the new year, the country began to climb out of its deepest post–World War II recession. The monthly jobless rate dropped from 10.8 percent to 10.4 in January, and it fell steadily after that. It was down to 9.3 percent in July and

8.2 percent in October, the same month that registered a 1.2 percent increase in income and spending.

Reagan was making a comeback in the polls as well. In November, Democratic frontrunner Walter Mondale had been beating him, 48 percent to 47, in the Gallup poll. In December, the President shot up to a 51–44 lead over Mondale in the same poll, and held a narrower lead, 49–45, over John Glenn.

Baker, meanwhile, as the undisputed leader of the political strategy group was not awaiting a signed statement of candidacy from Reagan to start building a campaign operation. In establishing a formal Office of Political Affairs in the White House in 1981, first under Lyn Nofziger and then under Ed Rollins, he had long since been contemplating a 1984 reelection campaign. Rollins' deputy, Lee Atwater, a young South Carolinian with a historian's knowledge of southern politics and a politician's understanding of it in contemporary terms, labored long over an electoral strategy anchored by a Sun Belt base as the key to Reagan's reelection.

In April 1983, Atwater wrote a sixty-three-page confidential memo to the political inner circle at the White House. "The balance of power in GOP presidential politics," it said, "has shifted to the region known as the Sun Belt. President Reagan has always been strongest there and the same is certain to be true in 1984. The Sun Belt's bloc of 266 electoral votes must be the centerpiece of our campaign plans." That figure was only four short of what was needed for election.

The memo further made the case that the Sun Belt—thirteen states in the South and eleven in the West, plus Hawaii and Alaska [!]—was a particularly rich electoral-vote lode. In six presidential elections from 1960 through 1980, the memo noted, Republican candidates had won 51 percent of the popular vote in those twenty-six states but had received 63.8 percent of the electoral vote. So, from the start, the Sun Belt offered an obvious target.

In May, Rollins and Atwater were told by Baker that they would be leaving the White House to run the reelection campaign, Rollins as manager, Atwater as his chief deputy, both answering directly to Baker. They made the move in mid-October with Baker's chief personal aide, Margaret Tutwiler, taking over the political office at the White House as liaison with the campaign.

Right after Thanksgiving 1983, the first expanded senior staff campaign strategy meetings were held at a hotel at Los Angeles

International Airport, with Rollins presiding. Also present were Atwater, Spencer and Teeter; Drew Lewis, Reagan's first secretary of transportation, now in private business; Jim Lake, for a time the 1980 campaign press secretary, who was resuming that post; Dick Wirthlin, the campaign pollster; Charlie Black, former executive director of the Republican National Committee, and Lyn Nofziger, Rollins' predecessor in the White House political job. Lake and Black perhaps were best known as the men Reagan campaign manager John Sears had taken over the side with him when Reagan fired him in a losing power struggle with Edwin Meese, later White House counsel in Reagan's first term and attorney general in his second. Both obviously were back in good graces again.

These men represented the cream of the crop of Republican political professionals—not *all* the cream, but a good portion of it. With no primary election opposition in sight and no other political horse to ride, they set out to organize and field what would be the most professional and meticulously planned presidential reelection campaign in history, outdoing even the classic incumbency campaign of Richard Nixon in 1972.

Around this time, Atwater wrote another memo, entitled "Building an Electoral Fortress in 1984," in which he hammered home again the importance of the South and West to a Reagan reelection.

"Jesse Jackson's entry into the race is being portrayed as a major turning point in the 1984 election," he wrote. "I disagree. Jackson will be a minor blip on the big screen, and his registration will be offset by the enthusiasm of conservative Southerners for President Reagan. We have the opportunity to expand beyond our current base in the West. The South is our key to ensuring victory in 1984. We must assume that the election next November will be close. This is prudent, but—we should not foreclose the possibility of a landslide by wasting our resources in securing states that are already ours. Our success in securing the South will mean the difference between a close election and a landslide in 1984."

Without primary opposition, Atwater noted, the Reagan campaign could use its pre-convention money, including the federal subsidy, "to build a strong organization. If we put the money into voter registration, local organizing and some spot media, we can secure our electoral base earlier than any campaign in history. . . . If Ronald Reagan becomes the first Republican to carry a

Solid South for two consecutive elections, we could well leave our party a lasting legacy—no matter what Jesse Jackson does as a Democratic or independent candidate. The Sun Belt coalition—Ronald Reagan's legacy to the party—can become the Republican base for decades to come."

On the home front, both economically and politically, Ronald Reagan appeared to be in good shape. The same, however, could not be said for him in foreign affairs. In spite of the massive military buildup he had promised and delivered, he had made no progress on arms control, and relations with the Soviet Union had become progressively cooler. And in neither of the two most critical areas of unrest, the Middle East and Central America, had he advanced American interests appreciably. Strong talk had marked the Reagan approach from his first days in office. He proclaimed that *he* would not suffer without retaliating the indignities of terrorism inflicted upon his predecessor by Iran. But Reagan's actions had not brought achievement of American objectives on any major foreign-policy front.

In the Middle East, the United States' traditionally strong ties with Israel had suffered almost from the start of the Reagan tenure. In April 1981, the new President dismayed the Israelis by announcing his intention to sell advanced early warning radar aircraft, known as AWACS, to Saudi Arabia, precipitating a bitter fight in Congress. American-Israeli relations slipped further in June when the United States joined in the United Nations' condemnation of the Israelis' bombing of an Iraqi nuclear reactor they said posed a military threat. And in July, the Israelis' intensive bombing of Palestine Liberation Organization strongholds in southern Lebanon and Beirut further underscored the ineffectivensss of American peacemaking policy in the region.

In August, the Reagan administration flexed its military muscle off the coast of Libya when U.S. Navy fighter planes shot down Libyan jets that had challenged them. But the incident raised more questions about Reagan policy and command procedures than it answered; the White House disclosed that the sleeping President was not told of the incident until six hours after it had occurred.

In October, the assassination of Egyptian President Anwar Sadat threatened even greater turmoil in the Middle East, jeopardizing fulfillment of the terms of the Camp David treaty between the Egyptians and Israelis that had been hammered out by President Carter. And in December, another bold Israeli move—the annexation of the Golan Heights—drew yet another United Nations condemnation, with the United States again joining in the opposition to its stalwart ally.

Reagan's second year had been no better on the foreign-policy front. When Argentina invaded the British-held Falkland Islands in April, Reagan's secretary of state, Alexander Haig, plunged into frantic shuttle diplomacy to resolve the crisis. But the administration backed the British in the end. While some governments in Latin America recognized Argentina's folly and understood the United States' position, Washington, by taking it, diminished its credibility with some others. And Israel's invasion of South Lebanon in June to crush the PLO led the next month to Reagan's first deployment of American Marines. They were assigned as part of a multi-national force monitoring the pullout of PLO forces agreed to by the triumphant Israelis.

No sooner had the pullout been achieved, however, and the Americans withdrawn, than all hell broke loose. President Bashir Gemayel of Lebanon was slain, a casualty of the complex internal factionalism in the country. Two days later, brutal raids on two Israeli-guarded Palestinian refugee camps at Sabra and Shatila in South Lebanon by a pro-Gemayel faction killed hundreds, including women and children. Reagan agreed to send the Marines back into Beirut in a resumed peacekeeping role. He vowed that they would remain until all foreign troops had pulled out of Lebanon and the newly reconstructed government under its new President, Amin Gemayel, brother of the slain Bashir, was able to maintain order itself.

On September 30, 1982, the situation came to the doorstep of an American family. Marine Corporal David L. Reagan of Chesapeake, Virginia, was killed by an exploding bomb at the Beirut airport, the first of hundreds of casualties the United States military would suffer in the region over the next two years—without effective response by the tough-talking Ronald Reagan. With the American troops still stationed in Lebanon six months later, a bomb wrecked the American embassy in Beirut, killing forty-six people and injuring ninety-five others. In late August of 1983, two more Marines were killed in Lebanon and another two by mid-October.

By now, American involvement had gone well beyond mere

"peacekeeping." In mid-September, the Reagan administration had authorized Navy ships off the coast of Lebanon to launch artillery and air strikes against positions from which the American Marines were threatened. Senate Democrats, deeply disturbed, moved for invocation of the 1973 War Powers Resolution, which would require specific congressional approval for continued deployment of the Marines in "hostilities." Without such approval, the resolution would oblige Reagan to pull out the Marines within sixty days. But the President sidestepped, saying the Marines "will be needed only for a limited period" and that "there is no intention or expectation that the U.S. armed forces will become involved in hostilities."

U.S. naval fire was authorized, however, and within days began against anti-government positions. But the Marine Corps commandant, General Paul X. Kelley, insisted that intensified fighting was not drawing the Marines into hostilities. It was, he said, no more than jockeying for position in advance of an anticipated cease-fire.

"There is no indication anyone is purposefully taking Marines under fire," he said on a network panel show.

Congress, under pressure from the White House, agreed to a compromise on the War Powers Resolution. It authorized Reagan to keep troops in Lebanon another eighteen months at the same strength and in the same role, with a proviso that "protective measures" could be taken to "ensure the safety of the multinational force." Senate Majority Leader Howard Baker hailed the compromise as "a major milestone, an achievement of a true bipartisan approach."

But many Democrats did not see it that way. Senate Minority Leader Robert Byrd called the proviso "a hole that we can run Amtrak through," and Ted Kennedy said the eighteen-month leeway was "a blank check for far too long a period." Kennedy voted against the compromise, observing: "Some say that Lebanon is not Vietnam. But I reply, we must not give the President the power to turn it into one." Congress, however, quickly approved the compromise.

Then, on October 23, the great disaster struck. A truck laden with high explosives easily ran a casual checkpoint at the main American Marine barracks in Beirut and crashed into it, destroying the building, killing 239 Marines and wounding at least 75 others.

Almost simultaneously, two miles away, another suicide truck crashed into a French paratroop barracks, exploding and killing more than 50 Frenchmen. The American death toll was greater than any suffered in any single action throughout the Vietnam war, and on only one day during that conflict of nearly a decade had more Americans been killed. Immediately the cry went up from Congress—and from a number of the Democratic presidential candidates: How could it have happened?

In Central America, too, Reagan had come off as an ineffective meddler. In his second month in office, he had raised the ante slightly in El Salvador by dispatching twenty more military advisers to join the five Carter had already sent there. He also asked for $25 million more in aid from Congress, to help the regime of President José Napoléon Duarte cope with insurgent forces abetted by the Sandinista government in neighboring Nicaragua. Liberals in Congress protested the aid, as well as the conduct of an American-backed covert war that was going on simultaneously against the Sandinistas. All through 1982 they pressured the Reagan administration to hold the El Salvador regime accountable for the conduct of military-related "death squads" that terrorized the populace with impunity. Thousands of deaths and disappearances of suspected opponents, critics and collaborators with the left-wing insurgents were reported.

In April of 1983, Reagan openly acknowledged American assistance to the anti-Sandinista guerrillas—"Contras," they were called, but he dubbed them "Freedom Fighters." He pressed Congress for more Central American aid, to them and to the El Salvador regime. A House committee voted in May to bar covert aid to the anti-Sandinistas, but Reagan vowed that American help would continue somehow. The administration announced that 100 American advisers would be dispatched to Honduras to train 2,400 Salvadorans for the defense of their country. When congressional criticism continued, Reagan resorted to one of his favorite devices for coping with it—the creation of a study commission, this one headed by former Secretary of State Henry Kissinger, to recommend the course American policy should follow in the region. Meanwhile, the House voted down covert aid—on the same day in July that the administration announced large-scale maneuvers of American forces in and off the coast of Honduras. Suspicions of U.S. intentions multiplied in Congress, and in the region.

Then, on October 25—two days after the Marine barracks in Lebanon had been blown up—Reagan resorted to force himself, but halfway around the globe. Without warning, or even much awareness in the United States that any trouble was brewing, he ordered an invasion of the tiny Caribbean island of Grenada. The ostensible purpose was to rescue 1,100 Americans, most of them students attending medical school there and said by the administration to be in danger of their lives amidst internal repression on the island. At last the vaunted American military that had suffered so many indignities in the recent past struck—and, in short order, won. The students were extricated with an awesome display of firepower, routing more than a thousand Cubans who were in the process of building an airstrip administration sources said was intended to facilitate the transport of arms to the Sandinistas and anti-Salvador guerrillas. Eighteen Americans were killed and 115 wounded in the fighting, compared to 24 Cubans and 45 Grenadans.

Confusion reigned for several days over the purpose of and justification for the invasion—confusion compounded by a strict news blackout and barring of members of the news media from the invasion force and the island. The official line was that the United States had responded to a request from the obscure Organization of Eastern Caribbean States, and had been part of a "multi-national force" that also included "troops" from six tiny Caribbean states barely able to police themselves.

During a press conference announcing the invasion, Reagan said the United States had received an "urgent, formal request" from the OECS to "assist in a joint effort to restore order and democracy" on Grenada after "a brutal group of leftist thugs violently seized power." Reports that American citizens were trying to escape convinced him, he said, that "the United States had no choice but to act strongly and decisively."

A 1981 treaty creating the OECS was cited, which said members could take collective action against external aggression if they acted unanimously. But this action was not unanimously approved, nor was it immediately apparent that the threat was external, though Reagan trotted out the OECS chair, Prime Minister Eugenia Charles of little Dominica, who said she had information that Cuba and the Soviet Union were behind the recent Grenada coup. Subsequently, the Pentagon displayed videotapes said to show six warehouses laden with Soviet-made small arms and ammunition discovered on the island. But because American reporters had not been permitted to accompany the invasion and had been kept off the island as it unfolded, suspicions flourished.

On top of all this confusion, reports came from the invaded island that the medical students had not really been in grave danger at all. But when they were airlifted to the United States a few days later, one of them kissed the American ground in gratitude in front of a battery of network television cameras. The debate as far as the general public was concerned was over. In Congress, however, and from among the same Democratic presidential hopefuls who were asking hard questions about the Marine barracks bombing in Lebanon, Reagan was confronted with demands for an explanation: What had happened, and why was the use of force necessary?

These were two developments, just two months before the start of the presidential election year, that seemed made to order for the Democrats to use against the incumbent Republican President, who by now had approved the formation of a reelection committee. Heavy losses in the Middle East were humiliating evidence of America's futility. And now there was the bullying use of military force in Latin America against a gnat of a foe, in clear violation of international and hemispheric law, and without congressional consultation. Open season on Ronald Reagan appeared to have arrived.

Demands for a second invoking of the War Powers Resolution, this time with no special time extension, sprouted on Capitol Hill. Democratic Senator Daniel Patrick Moynihan of New York demanded that Reagan "explain what legal grounds exist" for his attempting to "restore democracy at the point of a bayonet."

Republicans, too, expressed concern. Representative Olympia Snowe of Maine said the U.S. involvements in Lebanon and Grenada taken together "raise a lot of concerns about exactly what we're doing. To what extent are we involved in so many situations that we could get into a war?"

Democratic Senator Lawton Chiles of Florida put it more bluntly: "Are we looking for a war we can win?"

Of the Democratic presidential candidates, Gary Hart was the first to take concrete action. He introduced almost at once a resolution in the Senate calling for the War Powers Resolution to be invoked on use of force in Grenada. Other longshot candidates, including George McGovern, Alan Cranston and Fritz Hollings, also swiftly condemned the action. John Glenn said that if the mission was undertaken to rescue Americans, they should be evacuated at once. "If there is a larger strategic mission," he said, "then the President should inform the Congress and the American people as to the nature, scope and duration of that mission." Front-runner Fritz Mondale, cautious as always, observed only that congressional leaders should have been consulted.

Reagan, however, had plenty of outright defenders for his Grenadan invasion, including some liberals. But his strongest support came from the far right. Freshman Republican Senator Steve Symms of Idaho proclaimed: "This could be Ronald Reagan's Falkland Islands victory, signaling a welcome change in foreign policy. It is the first time in twenty years that we have tried to enforce the long-neglected Monroe Doctrine." And Representative Phil Gramm of Texas, the one-time Democratic "boll weevil" who had converted to the Republican Party, declared: "We must end the open season on Americans which has been declared by every terrorist and criminal element in the world."

Still, there were those suspicious individuals, mostly liberal Democrats, who wondered whether the disaster in Lebanon had encouraged the action in Grenada, or at least affected its timetable. Reagan took to television to try to justify the American military presence in Lebanon that had now proved so costly, and to defend his decision on Grenada. Concerning Lebanon, he cited "strong circumstantial evidence" that the same terrorists who had destroyed the American embassy in Beirut the previous April had directed the truck bombing of the Marine barracks. And he asked: "If we were to leave Lebanon now, what message would that send to those who foment instability and terrorism? If America were to walk away from Lebanon, what chance would there be for a negotiated settlement producing a unified, democratic Lebanon? If we turned our backs on Lebanon now, what would be the future of Israel? . . . Brave young men have been taken from us. Many others have been grievously wounded. Are we to tell them their sacrifice was wasted? They gave their lives in defense of our national security every bit as much as any man who ever died fighting in a war."

As for Grenada, the President justified the invasion on grounds that the OECS request was legitimate and that the Americans on the island were truly in peril. "I believe our government has a responsibility," he said, "to go to the aid of its citizens if their right to life and liberty is threatened. The nightmare of our hostages in Iran must never be repeated."

Furthermore, he said, Grenada had indeed turned out to be a Cuban base. Some 600 Cubans had been taken prisoner, he said, "and we have discovered a complete base with weapons and communications equipment, which makes it clear a Cuban occupation of the island had been planned. . . . Grenada, we were told, was a friendly island paradise for tourism. Well, it wasn't. It was a Soviet-Cuban colony being readied as a major military bastion to export terror and undermine democracy. We got there just in time."

The television address was heavily sugar-coated. Subsequent testimony revealed that the Marines had received warnings of impending terrorist attacks in Beirut but construction of basic defensive facilities lagged, and that the weapons of the two guards on duty outside the barracks were not loaded at the time of the attack. Yet Reagan said in his speech to the nation there was no way the guards could have known the truck contained explosives, that "their first warning that something was wrong came when the truck crashed through a series of barriers," and that they had "opened fire but it was too late."

As for the Grenada invasion, if the reason for it was to rescue the American students, how was the ex post facto discovery of an arms cache justification for the action? Such questions never seemed to get an answer—nor was there ever much demand for one from the public. In the course of Reagan's presidency, some critics had begun to call him "the Teflon President"—a name coined by Representative Patricia Schroeder of Colorado, a co-chair of the Hart campaign—because nothing damaging ever seemed to stick to him. Once again, his special insulation appeared in both the Lebanon and Grenadan episodes to have protected him from excessive public criticism, even in situations where American lives were at stake.

The few political operatives preparing the groundwork for the President's reelection were concerned, to be sure, about how the two crises might affect Reagan's standing with the voters. But decisions involving Lebanon and Grenada, White House insiders told us later, never included the purely political players. It was true, at the same time, that two of the four charter members of the reelection campaign strategy group, Baker and Deaver, were chin-deep in all policy decisions and were positioned to protect the President's political interests as a matter of course.

In the Lebanon involvement, the most sensitive political consideration was getting the Marines out before the situation developed to a point where the Reagan administration might find itself drawn into "another Vietnam." Ironically, however, Democrats in Congress did Reagan a favor by insisting that the eighteen-month extension on troop deployment also required him to come back to Congress if he wanted to raise the fifteen-hundred-man ceiling imposed on troop strength or change the mission. That requirement was a means of saving the administration from its own excesses; that is, knowing any escalation would have obliged Reagan to get Congress' approval was a strong deterrent against even asking.

As for Grenada, although domestic political considerations were said never to have been factored in before the invasion, the White House had some clear perceptions of the political ramifications once it was over.

"Grenada was an unquestionable plus provided you didn't claim too much for it," one insider said later. Politically, he said, "it was not something terribly important in its own right but a symbol that 'America was back.' And provided that you made clear it was only a first step—we used the term 'a rising tide of freedom.' This was just one little wave, and if you tried to pretend it was a whole ocean, it was implausible with the public, because the public knew it was one little island. If treated as if it was on a level with reversing U.S.-Soviet relations or bringing peace to the Middle East or something like that, that we thought might backfire. So we let it speak for itself, and not claim too much for it." Administration polling, this insider said, indicated that voters, "in foreign-policy terms, didn't think it was any great big deal, although they all loved it."

Indeed they did. If the Lebanon tragedies brought back the feelings of national frustration that had mired the Carter years, the display in Grenada of swift U.S. military muscle and presidential decisiveness did much to wash those feelings away for the average American. And while the insiders at the White House may have felt they were not claiming too much for the invasion, many Democrats were outraged at what they saw as an unbridled milking of public emotions, and they looked to their presidential candidates for effective response.

On the weekend immediately after the Lebanon and Grenada incidents, the seven Democrats then running for the party's nomination debated in New Hampshire at a state party convention. Lebanon and Grenada, naturally, were high on the agenda, and the audience listened to the seven, and particularly to frontrunner Mondale, for clear-cut criticism. But Mondale was his customary cautious self, saying, for example, that he didn't have all the facts on Grenada to make a judgment. And Glenn said only that the invasion was "a question of what the President knew and when he knew it."

Such answers gave the longshot Democratic candidates a clear opportunity to show some leadership in shaping their party's positions on Lebanon and Grenada—and to make Mondale and Glenn look bad in the process. McGovern reiterated his flat demand, made before the barracks bombing, that the American forces be withdrawn from Lebanon. Hart called for congressional reconsideration of the resolution authorizing Reagan to keep the Marines in Lebanon up to eighteen months longer. Even the hawkish Fritz Hollings condemned "macho politics."

But voters were not paying much attention to the longshots, regardless of what they were saying. The polls were casting the Democratic nomination competition as a two-man affair—Mondale against Glenn. The Gallup poll, which had Mondale leading Glenn 40 percent to 21 in October, narrowed Mondale's lead to 34–23 in late November. That circumstance in turn persuaded the Mondale campaign that the former Vice President would have to get off his high horse and deal directly with the challenge from the senator/astronaut from Ohio. The process of "getting Glenn" had in fact already begun, with eventual ramifications for the Democratic competition not remotely anticipated this early in the game.

6

The Wrong Stuff

•

AS EARLY AS MEMORIAL DAY OF 1983, Walter Mondale's campaign strategists had been considering whether they ought to draw a bead on John Glenn's candidacy. Ever since Glenn had entered the race formally on April 21, the astronaut-turned-senator had been climbing in the public-opinion polls, already creating a public perception that the contest for the Democratic presidential nomination was narrowing to a two-man race. At a meeting in the living room of Mondale's home in North Oaks, Minnesota on that holiday weekend, Bob Beckel, the aggressive campaign manager, had argued strenuously for using Mondale's speech before the approaching Wisconsin straw vote to bash Glenn, who had been enjoying a free ride on the wave of his celebrity.

"What's the point of not going after this guy?" Beckel asked, according to another at the meeting. The overall Mondale strategy, after all, was to create what Beckel himself called a "juggernaut" that would roll over all opposition early and leave only Mondale standing after the first few primaries.

The goal in the straw polls had come to be at least 40 percent of the total vote, and, in the words of another of the top strategists, "the mentality around there was, 'Crush people. Crush campaigns. Crush candidates. Crush 'em.' " That remark revealed in its intensity the atmosphere that governed this early stage of the Democratic nomination fight. These preliminary skirmishes always were justified in terms of educating the voters on the candidates' position on key issues of the day. But in reality they were bitter cockfights for political survival, in which the objective was to clear the ring of challengers long before most of the voters would have their say.

fellow Democrats. At least by not rapping them specifically by name.[13]

On the night of Glenn's appearance before the Democratic panel in Syracuse, however, Mario Cuomo posed an immediate dilemma for him. "I think we approach now the time when we have to start drawing distinctions between and among the candidates," Cuomo told the Ohio senator. "I wonder if you would help us by telling us, if you will, what you believe the differences are between you and, let's say, Vice President Mondale . . . [on] the question of industrial policy and the question of education."

But Glenn would not bite. "I've made it a policy throughout the campaign, because I might misstate other people's views, to not specifically set a he-says-this, I-say-that type approach to things," Glenn answered. "I'm very happy to put out my views on these issues and talk about them." And he proceeded to do so.

Cuomo clearly was dissatisfied with the answer, and so informed other New York Democrats.

It so happened that in the audience that night was a Mondale volunteer who taped the exchange. He phoned the substance of it to Mondale headquarters and then dispatched the tape by express mail. Mondale aides were quickly on the phone to Cuomo's office, asking that their man be given a shot at the same comparison question in his forum two days later in Rochester. Cuomo, obviously, would be only too glad to oblige, since he had been pushing Mondale all along to be specific on issue differences.

In advance of the Rochester forum, the Mondale staff carefully crafted the answer—a point-by-point indictment of Glenn as a Reagan in Democratic trappings. The afternoon of the forum, Cuomo said to Mondale:

"On Monday in Syracuse, I asked Senator Glenn what in his opinion were the differences on the issues that distinguished his candidacy from yours. He chose not to answer that question. I put the same question to you."

Mondale replied in a most dispassionate tone, more in sorrow than in anger. "I have tried to make my campaign as positive as I can," he began, "defining specifically what I intend to do, how I see the future and I intend to deal with it."

But then he went on: "There are differences obviously between

13. The eleventh commandment was actually the brainchild of Gaylord Parkinson, the Republican state chairman in California when Reagan first ran for governor in 1966.

Senator Glenn and myself. For example, I strongly supported SALT II [the 1979 arms-control treaty] and he opposed it. I'm opposed to the B-1 bomber, and he favors it. I wrote a letter to the Senate urging that they turn down poison nerve gas, and he voted for it.[14] I believe in real increases in the defense budget, but at a reasonable, manageable pace. The figures he proposes are substantially higher than those that I think are supportable.

"I spent several years opposing what was then known as Kemp-Roth [tax cuts] and opposing the adoption of Reaganomics. I opposed it because I thought it was nuts. And he said the other day he voted for it because he thought it would work."

Cuomo, not surprisingly, was pleased at Mondale's forthright reply and said so. For some time he had been criticizing President Reagan, the former movie actor, as a "celluloid hero," and he began to characterize Glenn, who along with his fellow Mercury astronauts was portrayed in the soon-to-be-released film *The Right Stuff*, as a "celluloid candidate." When Glenn heard about it, he did a slow burn.

Ten days after his appearance at the Syracuse forum, Glenn joined Mondale and the other candidates at Town Hall in Manhattan for the final New York forum. After Cuomo had introduced the candidates, he took a seat in the front row of the audience. And in answer to one of the first questions posed to him, a particularly tasteless one from an supercilious Duke political science professor, James David Barber, Glenn pointedly showed his irritation.

Barber, obviously trying to be clever but falling far short, said: "If I may ask Senator Glenn a question about the right stuff

14. The nerve-gas issue as raised by Mondale particularly irked Glenn. The proposal was to scrap large quantities of existing nerve gas stocks that were considered to be dangerous to populations near storage areas because their chemicals could mix by accident. A new "binary" gas was developed in which the activating chemicals were kept in two separate cannisters and hence were deemed safer in storage. Glenn insisted that a vote for binary gas was not an arms-control issue but a safety issue. Johnson said later Mondale had begun discussing the issue using the term binary gas until his campaign chairman told him at a staff meeting: "There is nothing called binary gas in the minds of the American people. They don't have the slightest idea what you're talking about. It means nothing; it is nothing; you might as well keep your mouth shut as talk about binary gas. They think it's something you go to your gas station for. I said, 'Henceforth, can we agree, and can everyone else in this campaign agree: PNG—poison nerve gas.' From that moment on, Mondale never said anything else." True to that agreement, Mondale did always talk about "poison" nerve gas, presumably as opposed to the nice kind.

to be President . . . All of us applauded your heroism as an astronaut; that you went up in the air and orbited around the world and then that terrifying return when you may or may not have hummed 'The Battle Hymn of the Republic.' But it's reminiscent of Lindbergh going over the Atlantic or Houdini going over Niagara Falls in a barrel or Evel Knievel flying over the Grand Canyon in a motorcycle. But what does that have to do with sitting in the Oval Office and talking to politicians all day long?"

The question, a strong argument for improved screening methods in the choosing of panelists for serious political forums, drew hisses from the audience. But it gave Glenn just the excuse he needed to get something off his chest. Flicking the questioner aside for "your characterization of what we accomplished in those early days," he launched into a long recitation of not only what the space program had achieved but also of what he had done as a businessman, senator and Marine officer, including combat in two wars.

Then, glaring directly at Cuomo in the front row, Glenn took note that he had been called a "celluloid candidate." Recalling that he had run well ahead of Reagan in Ohio in 1980 in being reelected to the Senate, he added: "As far as the 'celluloid' charge, I wasn't doing *Hellcats of the Navy* [a Reagan film] on a movie lot when I went through 149 missions. That wasn't celluloid. That was the real thing. And when I was on top of that booster down there getting ready to go, it wasn't *Star Trek* or *Star Wars*, I can guarantee you that. It was representing the future of this country, and I was very proud to take part in that."[15]

The audience applauded its approval.

Notably, Mondale did not go on the offensive against Glenn that night. But Glenn, in his closing statement, attacked Mondale by inference by asking: "Will we offer a party that can't say no to anyone with a letterhead and a mailing list? Will we offer a party that mouths the words 'strong defense' but opposes every program designed to provide it? . . . Will we offer a party that derides the Reagan policies of the nineteen-twenties and promises

15. After the forum, a New York Democrat asked Glenn if his crack at Cuomo was "personal." Glenn replied heatedly: "Damn right it was personal, because his comments about me were personal. I meant them to be personal." Much later, after the 1984 election, Glenn reflected on the incident and said of Cuomo's remark: "I thought it was grossly unfair—and still do."

to replace them with the programs of the nineteen-sixties? If that's the alternative we offer, I tell you we will meet the same fate in 1984 that we met in 1980."

By this time it was Mondale who was doing a slow burn. Not only Glenn, but the other Democratic hopefuls as well, had been hammering him as the candidate of the special interests—an allegation further fueled by the formal endorsement only five days earlier of the AFL-CIO convention, meeting in Hollywood, Florida.

"Mondale by now had to sit through maybe ten, twelve, fifteen joint appearances," chief speechwriter Marty Kaplan said later. "At all these straw polls, state conventions, cattle shows, he heard himself described as the special-interest candidate [who] promised them anything, and on and on. It was Hollings doing it, and Hart, and Glenn, and Cranston. No one let up. And here was this affable guy listening to it, and he was boiling—just boiling—about it."

Mondale resolved to strike back, and the ideal opportunity came two nights later at the traditional Jefferson-Jackson dinner in Iowa. The event was the recognized kickoff of competition for the state's precinct caucuses in February, at which the first official step anywhere in the country would be taken toward selecting delegates for the 1984 convention. This dinner was the same one that had yanked Jimmy Carter from national obscurity in 1975 when he won the straw poll conducted among the diners. And once again the straw vote was regarded as the first test of political strength for the coming critical first-in-the-nation caucuses.

For several reasons, the Iowa straw poll was deemed vital to Mondale's status as the frontrunner. He was particularly well known in this state bordering on his own Minnesota; he had campaigned there often, especially in 1980 as Carter's chief surrogate against Ted Kennedy; he had most of the Iowa Democratic Party structure and leadership behind him; he had a large and well-financed campaign organization, supplemented by strong, unified labor support. Mondale could not afford a weak showing, either in the straw vote or at the dinner in Des Moines, at which everybody who was anybody in Iowa Democratic politics would be present.

In terms of rival organizational strength, Mondale's chief competitor in the state was clearly Alan Cranston. He had tapped into the same nuclear-freeze lode that had helped him upset Mondale in the Wisconsin straw vote, and he had, in former state party executive director John Law, arguably the best organizer in Iowa.

But Cranston's wings had been clipped in the Maine straw vote, and Mondale had Glenn in his sights as the main threat nationally, particularly after the way Glenn was hitting him on the special-interest issue. The others in the field, including long-shot Gary Hart, did not seem to be going anywhere in Iowa. In advance of the Jefferson-Jackson dinner, in fact, state party chairman David Nagle had pronounced Hart "dead in the water" after he had shipped his Iowa staff to Wisconsin in that earlier futile straw-vote effort and his first Iowa campaign manager, Carter campaign veteran Bill Romjue, had resigned.

By the luck of the draw, which was alphabetical, Mondale was to be the final speaker at the J-J dinner. Flying out to Des Moines in a small plane with Johnson and Kaplan, Mondale decided to let Glenn have it with both barrels.

"All the way in on the little jet, we talked through the special-interest thing," Kaplan recalled, "using the angle that the biggest special-interest boondoggle in history was the Reagan '81 economic tax package. . . . The hogs were really feeding. . . . Mondale rehearsed this thing over and over again on the plane."

As Kaplan frantically took notes, Mondale tried various phrasings, with Johnson and Kaplan making suggestions, until the theme was well honed. On arrival, Kaplan took his notes and worked them into Mondale's text for that night.

"The only thing remaining," Kaplan said, "was would the others do the special-interest thing on him?"

The J-J dinner was a particularly fortuitous opportunity because, Kaplan said later, "Mondale was batting cleanup . . . We knew if he would be seen by an essentially friendly audience to have to endure an evening like that, hearing himself ripped to pieces over and over on the special-interest point," he would come out a winner. "The thing worked like clockwork. Each of the other candidates tore Mondale apart on the special-interest issue."

Mondale thereupon got up, said he had planned to give a speech on something else (which he had never intended to do) but was throwing it away, and launched into the prepared text Kaplan had worked up from the dry run on the flight in.

Without mentioning him by name but making the implication crystal clear, Mondale charged that it was Glenn, in voting for the Reagan tax and budget cuts, who was the candidate of special interests. Mondale called the cuts "the most radical measure of our time" and "the most comprehensive onslaught against social justice in our time."

About those votes on Reaganomics, Mondale said: "Of all the measures in modern political history in which the forces of special interests clashed with the profound public interest of our nation, I cannot recall a single instance where the issues were as clear. Even David Stockman said, when that bill passed, 'The hogs have been fed.' That would have been a good time for a Democrat to stand up against the special interests and vote no."

And on arms control, he said in an obvious reference to another Glenn vote: "I bled my heart out for SALT II. . . . The world needs the ratification of SALT II, and I wish everyone would have voted for it."

Glenn left the stage, Kaplan recalled, "looking absolutely shaken." Mondale meanwhile basked in a very positive reception from the audience, a majority of whom had voted for him in the straw poll. Mondale won a clear victory over runner-up Cranston as well as Glenn, who had not competed aggressively in the essentially stacked vote. The outcome depended on which campaigns bought the most tickets and found bodies to use them. To the embarrassment of the Cranston campaign, it had more tickets than people—the first clear indication that there was less to his candidacy in Iowa than met the eye.

Mondale flew back to Washington that night in a buoyant mood, taking with him as a passenger George McGovern, who had entered the race only weeks before. McGovern had proved to be a sentimental favorite at the dinner with a short, pointed speech telling his party to stand up squarely against Reaganomics at home and what he saw as recklessness abroad. As Mondale sipped a scotch and puffed on one of his favorite cigars, he and McGovern reminisced about their days in the Senate and about their colleagues, including Hart, McGovern's old campaign manager from the 1972 presidential campaign. It was clear that night that neither figured Hart would be a serious factor in the 1984 race.

Indeed, Hart himself said later that his financial situation had become so precarious around this time that he thought he might have to withdraw. Before the end of the year, his Iowa campaign director, Keith Glaser, pleading for money simply to feed and transport volunteers, warned that unless some could be found, Iowa ought to be abandoned.

Right now, though, Mondale's mind was on the perceived chief threat, John Glenn. And back in Des Moines, Glenn was steaming over what he considered a wildly irresponsible attack on his own integrity as a Democrat. In his suite at the Savery Hotel that same night with national staff aides Bill White and Greg Schneiders and Iowa supporters Lieutenant Governor Bob Anderson and former gubernatorial candidate Roxanne Conlin, and in a second meeting the next morning, Glenn sizzled and vowed not to take the attack lying down.

"We were the ones who had to be in the position of defining the relationship," Schneiders said later. "If we allowed what Mondale said in Iowa to stand unchallenged, then basically he was going to define Glenn as the clone of Reagan. So we had to come back at him."

A response was planned that would remind voters that Mondale was a liberal rather than the moderate Glenn saw himself—and the bulk of the electorate—to be, and that would put Glenn back on the offensive. Even before the Iowa dinner, Schneiders recalled later, it had been determined that Glenn was going to have to go after Mondale because Glenn's own initial strength with voters was rapidly ebbing, apparently out of disappointment with him as a candidate.

"He never really had any choice by the time we got to that point in the campaign but to go after Mondale," Schneiders said. "He was fading fast and Mondale was pulling away. . . . We saw the thing slipping away and felt that we had to get more aggressive. Also, we were finding, particularly in the South, that Mondale was being allowed to define himself, and he was defining himself as moderate."

Part of this definition business entailed Glenn casting himself as a sort of non-establishment figure in the Jimmy Carter mold, without the Carter connection. And it followed naturally that Mondale thus would be cast as an establishment figure, which he was. He was a longtime protégé of Hubert Humphrey in Minnesota politics and then in the Senate. And he was selected as Carter's Vice President precisely because he was a needed link to the establishment that outsider Carter lacked.

Polling data had indicated to the Glenn campaign that roughly two-thirds of voters in New Hampshire and in the South identified with a moderate posture independent of party. Schneiders, one of Carter's closest traveling aides during his 1976 longshot trip to the White House, was a believer in the political advantage of the non-establishment posture and of the potency of the special-interest issue against Mondale.

"Greg," said another Glenn insider later, "was the campaign's in-house party-basher and labor-basher."

Glenn thus was primed to carry the fight to Mondale as he left Des Moines and headed South for more campaigning in what was perceived as the most hospitable region to his candidacy. But not planned or foreseen was the manner in which he elected to implement the attack plan.

At the Florida Institute of Technology in Melbourne, Glenn sought to defend himself against Mondale's charges on his Reaganomics votes. Mondale "was making considerable hay with that," Glenn told us later, "and I thought it was time to put that in proper perspective." He and 90 percent of the Senate's Democrats had voted for the tax cuts, Glenn said, because in 1980 "the people had voted their fears . . . that we were going to continue the high inflation and the high interest rates that had occurred during the time Mondale was over there as Vice President, and that's what I pointed out."

In his remarks in Melbourne, Glenn said Mondale was "part of the administration that gave us 21 percent interest rates and 17 percent inflation rates. . . . We tried and tried and tried in the Senate of the United States to make programs that were . . . a change from those disastrous policies, but that were more responsible than Reaganomics. What it came down to was, Were we going to make some changes from those disastrous, failed policies of the past, or were we going to have no change?"

Those words—"the disastrous, failed policies of the past"—would haunt Glenn for the rest of the campaign, because they were immediately reported as a rap not simply at Mondale but also at former President Carter. While Carter was not being nominated for sainthood in the Democratic Party just then, the remark was taken by many Democrats as unnecessarily divisive and helpful to the Republicans.

Asked at a press conference whether he believed the country

was better off with Reaganomics than it would have been had Carter's policies been continued, Glenn replied: "I think that was a good vote at the time."

Glenn insisted he wasn't launching any attack on Mondale. He was only "responding" to Mondale's Iowa remarks, he said. "I hope that what he has initiated is not to become the norm in this campaign. If I am attacked, I'm going to respond, and I'm going to respond hard."

Mondale's blast at him, he said, was "a little like the first mate on the *Titanic* criticizing someone for going for a lifeboat."

Looking back at the incident after the election, Glenn had a possible explanation for why the press made such a to-do about it. "Maybe," he said, "it was just that it was out of character for me to be saying anything about the opposition. It was such a change that maybe it got itself overemphasized."

Thereafter, Glenn always contended he had never started the fights with Mondale, and had never indulged in negative campaigning because what he'd said had always been based on issues and never had been "personal." So say all candidates.

"When Glenn started ad-libbing down in Florida, with the 'failed, disastrous policies of the past,' that was not planned," Schneiders said later. "The response was planned and it was going to be along those lines," he said, but the intent was to make Mondale the target, not Carter, as the remarks came off and were played in the news media.

"The general linking of Mondale to the Carter administration was part of the plan. The only thing that stands out that was not a part of the plan was the 'failed, disastrous policies,' which was seen as harsher than what we had talked about. Our feeling on that was that, except in Iowa where Carter was still fairly popular, he was a liability for Mondale. We had no idea, and to this day still don't understand, why there was the reaction that there was with Glenn appearing to attack Carter. I mean, Kennedy did it all through 1980 when the guy was still the sitting President of his own party. Everybody else of both parties had publicly and privately been disparaging the guy for three years. The idea that saying Mondale has no right to be talking about a vote for Reaganomics because he created the conditions in which Reaganomics passed in the Congress seemed like a fairly mild thing to say relative to much of what had already been said in both parties about Carter."

What the Glenn people did not seem able to grasp was that Glenn's sudden slam at Carter was seen first of all as an act of party disloyalty. No matter what was thought of Jimmy Carter inside the Democratic house, he was one of theirs, and it just wasn't kosher to throw rocks at him in public in the context of a Democratic fight for the party nomination. Carter after all, for reasons infinitely less valid, had already become a sort of Democratic Nixon—a party embarrassment best left unmentioned, like the family eccentric. Beyond that, disparaging Carter as a way of attacking Mondale was seen as hitting below the belt, or at the least a sneak punch that clashed with Glenn's Mr. Nice Guy image.

"For whatever reason," Schneiders said later, "I still doubt in my own mind that that was a major factor with voters initially. But I think it got perceived as a mistake and something a Democrat shouldn't do, and again another example of ineptness. This thing about Glenn being negative got going and just became the conventional wisdom and got repeated over and over. And even though we didn't see that perception among voters, it just became part of the general litany of miscues and missteps in the campaign."

Schneiders was right on that score. The Carter gaffe could not have come at a worse time for Glenn. Three major national polls in the first days of October had shown him slipping badly, a fact that had convinced Glenn strategists that he had to step up the personal confrontation with Mondale.

On top of that, the Mondale campaign had just scored what Bob Beckel referred to as "The Triple"—the AFL-CIO and NEA endorsements and the Maine straw vote—that taken together had emphatically cemented Mondale as the frontrunner. His Iowa blast at Glenn as a Reagan clone was mere icing.

"The whole first ten days of October were a walking disaster," Bill Hamilton, the Glenn pollster, said later.

Glenn, though, had the bit in his teeth. In advance of the Florida straw vote in late October, some Mondale supporters circulated a letter to delegates at the state party convention in Hollywood implying that Glenn, having voted for Reaganomics, was not a "real" Democrat. Glenn was furious. He blistered Mondale in a

"That," said White later, "was the ultimate triumph of form over substance."

Glenn himself observed after the election: "Almost every write-up that went out about me was, 'Glenn on the launching pad,' and 'Will the rocket fizzle?' and all the connotations that kept that in the foreground. The movie came out in the middle of all this, which once again refocused attention in that area, and I think in some respects prevented us from maybe filling in the gaps of information that we should have been able to fill in."

The failure on the public's part to accept astronaut-turned-senator John Glenn as a credible presidential candidate was compounded, Schneiders acknowledged later, by his uneven performance on the stump and seemingly endless trouble within his campaign. What the man in the street knew about Glenn, Schneiders said, was that in addition to him being the astronaut now running for President, "he's doing it badly. He's got a lousy campaign staff in constant turmoil, he can't raise as much money as Mondale, can't get endorsements, can't put things together. And implicit in all that was, [he] can't operate in a political environment, and therefore wouldn't be able to govern."

The impression of a staff in turmoil was a painfully accurate one. In organizing, Glenn had relied initially on Bill White, his longtime chief Senate aide, an amiable man with no national campaign experience. White and others had been with Glenn through his political rise in Ohio, where he was the all-time best vote-getter, and had come to see the celebrity image as something they could take to the political bank. Also, there happened to be the fact that Glenn was a very independent politician, which voters liked, and an extremely conscientious and meticulous legislator. His image as a no-nonsense straight arrow was an entirely valid one that should have appealed to a national constituency, on top of the celebrity factor.

From the start, there was a sense in the campaign that Glenn's best bet was to be seen as a non-establishment figure; a man who marched to his own drummer and had been spectacularly successful in doing so, first as a Marine fighter pilot, then as an astronaut, then as a businessman and finally as a senator. Glenn clearly saw himself that way. While he listened to and accepted much of the counsel of the image-shapers who later joined his campaign, one campaign insider said, "John Glenn believed to the very end that it was a matter totally of personal leadership—that's what he could do, that's what he had been, that's why he should win." Glenn accepted that he had to make accommodations to deal with the new mechanics and technologies of politics and with the changes in the Democratic Party, this insider said, but "down underneath, I think John Glenn thought that the single combat warrior, which he was, was going to out in the end."

At the same time, Glenn believed that a strong pitch by him to American patriotism, pride and self-confidence—of the sort Reagan made so effectively later—could carry the day.

"Glenn would always say Reagan won in 1980 because he described that shining city on a hill," one Glenn strategist recalled. "We'd always say, 'No, that's not why he won.' And he'd say, 'I want to have that kind of vision. That's what my theme ought to be.' He'd say, 'I don't see why America can't be like those Styrofoam fingers at the football game—We're Number One! We're Number One! We're Number One!' Sometimes he'd go on with that line five or six times. But he was essentially right. He knew what people were looking for. He would either get into a specific issue in great detail or the opposite problem—the vision of the future was sort of shibboleth—it was just an empty Styrofoam finger."

Beyond that, another Glenn adviser said later, the man's basic view of his own candidacy, coming out of his military background, was that all that he had to do was demonstrate his qualifications; the voters would immediately recognize that he was the obvious choice over the others who did not have his credentials.

"His view," this adviser said, "was that he had 'made' President. He'd earned the rank." Glenn thought, he said, that people in looking the field over "would realize that Glenn's just a better man, and what we need in the presidency is just a good man, a guy who is just the best all-around man for the office." Glenn, he said, "is not an unintelligent guy. This is a very bright man, but he has a very linear view of things, and he's very military. He says, 'Look, I'm the guy, and why can't they see it?' "

Polling in Iowa well in advance of the February 1984 caucuses by Glenn's pollster, Bill Hamilton, found a public desire for a new kind of candidate who resembled Glenn. But Glenn and his advisers underestimated how difficult it would be to link the former astronaut with the public's vision of that new kind of candidate who could provide presidential leadership. And the advent of *The Right Stuff* only heightened the difficulty of making that linkage.

In any event, as the Glenn campaign advanced and the staff grew, "outsiders" inevitably were brought in who had been around the track and saw the campaign in somewhat more complex terms than did the Senate loyalists. In addition to Schneiders, the Carter veteran who advanced from being Glenn's press secretary to a major political adviser, and Hamilton, these included the following: Joe Grandmaison, the temperamental dynamo from New Hampshire who had cut his teeth in presidential politics as state coordinator there for George McGovern in 1972, who became political director; David Sawyer, the experienced New York television ad producer, and his associate, Scott Miller; and Bob Keefe, the longtime manager of Democratic candidates, often with strong labor ties such as Birch Bayh and Scoop Jackson. They did not constitute a uniformly congenial group, to put it mildly.

Budget priorities always were a source of conflict. Headquarters expenses and "the road show," in the view of the outsiders, ate up an inordinate amount of the campaign treasury, leaving little to be spent for the field operation or paid news media. There was a heated debate, for example, over how to capitalize on the release of *The Right Stuff*. Hamilton recalls that he, Sawyer and Schneiders wanted to do some paid television "to color the glasses one more shade that we wanted them colored as they watched the movie, because the movie wasn't going to do a damn thing for [Glenn's image of] presidential leadership. We were trying to get him placed in that context. . . . In one sense that's not manipulative because that's what he was running for. He wasn't running for the astronaut program again." But no money was freed up for that purpose.

While Glenn was continuing to do verbal battle with Mondale over which of them was the "real" Democrat, the first major staff explosion occurred, with Grandmaison the casualty. There had been an earlier decision, in line with the thinking that John Glenn would be a "national candidate," to run a fifty-state strategy but with only a paper organization in most states and with very little money allocated to Grandmaison for that purpose. Nevertheless, organizations of sorts—"presences," Grandmaison called them—were established in about twenty states, to give the campaign some semblance of credibility.

But instead of Glenn's travels being focused on states targeted politically, where he went and when he went there often resulted from fund-raising possibilities—an opportunity to hold a lucrative dinner here or cocktail party there, even in states where his chances to do well in a primary or caucuses were rated slim. He found himself constantly raising money to pay for his overblown Washington headquarters and for his expensive traveling entourage, as well as for field offices to provide that "presence" in key states. The more money he raised, the more was spent; the more was spent, the more he had to raise.

After the election, reflecting on his dilemma, Glenn said he probably had erred in not getting off that merry-go-round and putting his political house in order.

"When those [problems] first became apparent," he said, "rather than trusting that those things would work out as I did, being in charge, I should have come off the road, cancelled whatever we had for a week or ten days and straightened out any problems we had in the fund-raising and the staffing problems."

The thinness of the field operation was particularly apparent in Iowa, where reporters dutifully trooped from one candidate's campaign headquarters to another's and made the obvious comparisons. On top of that, Grandmaison's personal volatility—he was famous for throwing furniture around the office—clashed with what some called White's virtual somnambulance, and an explosion was inevitable. One of the causes, insiders said, was the failure to have a competitive organization in place in critical Iowa by November. White sent some agents there—they were regarded as "spies" by Grandmaison allies—and they reported little effective organizing had been done.

The problem, Grandmaison said later, was that it was impossible to get any decision about anything from White, and that the musclebound Washington operation was eating up all the resources. Roxanne Conlin, the most recent Democratic gubernatorial candidate in Iowa, signed up with Glenn only after insisting that real resources be put in the state, Grandmaison said.

"We never thought we could win there," Schneiders said later, "but we felt there were enough John Glenn supporters out there that we could come in second if we'd had the organization and the message effectively delivered."

Critics of Grandmaison contended he had relied too heavily

that fact. So strong was this perception, in fact, that survival for Mondale in the Iowa caucuses meant nothing short of victory, and a sizable victory at that. While the Glenn campaign was stumbling along in the state, however, Mondale's was not without its own nagging troubles, both financial and organizational.

For openers, Mondale's first-place finish in the J-J straw poll had come only after a rescue operation from the Washington headquarters. And it had been followed by a major staff shakeup that the Mondale hierarchy sought to masquerade, with considerable success, as little more than a normal ratcheting up of the field operation as the caucuses approached.

The Mondale campaign, like Glenn's, was a beehive of clashes over political approaches, personalities and ambitions. The most serious of these was between the campaign manager, Bob Beckel, a veteran of the Carter campaign of 1980, and the political director in charge of field operations, Mike Ford, a 1980 Kennedy hand. Both were volatile types, and both had their favored subordinates. One of Beckel's was Peter Slone, sent to Iowa as the Mondale state coordinator. One of Ford's was Joe Trippi, a young Californian who had run the successful Maine straw-vote operation and in the process had, with Ford's help, built a team of contemporaries who labeled themselves in their youthful enthusiasm "The Hogs."[18]

In retrospect, Beckel said the Mondale campaign in that Maine straw vote "gave too much leeway in the field to build an organization that we didn't need. It was my fault more than anything else. I let Ford get away with having too much access to money. . . . Before I knew it we had eighty or ninety people up there, all these kids, the infamous Hogs that Ford was putting together for his army, to send them to Iowa."

In any event, in advance of the Iowa straw vote, Paul Tully and Gina Glantz, then a Ford aide, were sent to Iowa and reported back that Slone had not sufficiently mobilized Mondale supporters to assure victory in the straw poll. At that time, the Cranston campaign, led by John Law, was making a major effort to win

18. The name came from a pep talk Ford once gave to a bunch of young recruits he was trying to get to brave wintry chills to go canvassing door-to-door. The difference between involvement and commitment, he said, could be illustrated by a chicken and a hog contributing to an order of bacon and eggs. To a chicken, he told the recruits, the eggs represented involvement. To a hog, the bacon represented commitment. Hence, "The Hogs."

it, so Ford dispatched one of the Maine Hogs, Tom Cosgrove, to Des Moines to rectify the situation.

The problem was a purely mechanical one. David Nagle, the Iowa Democratic chairman, had announced he would make an equal number of dinner tickets available to each of the campaigns. So it was simply a matter of buying them and hustling up enough warm bodies to use them—a dinner ticket being required to vote. What Tully later called "extraordinary resources" were poured into Iowa to win that vote. To keep the Mondale "inevitability" image on track, he said, "we had to win it big. We had to start strong."

Once the dinner was over and Mondale had won the straw vote, pressure built for Slone's replacement. Prominent Iowa Democrats heading the Mondale campaign there, including former state party chairman Ed Campbell and Iowa Senate Majority Leader Lowell Junkins, warned the Washington headquarters that the organization was in disorder. Earlier, in a deft move, Ford had arranged for Junkins and other Mondale supporters in Iowa to go to Maine in advance of the Maine straw vote, held a week before the Iowa dinner, to observe the Mondale preparations there.

"They saw a full-bore, flat-out field operation cooking—and knew what they were involved in back home didn't look like this," Tully said.

Responding to the complaints from Campbell and Junkins, Jim Johnson agreed to Ford's suggestion that Trippi be sent into Iowa to take a look. He interviewed all the staff people and reported back that essentially Campbell's and Junkins' concerns were well founded. He reported he had found no phone-bank operation to speak of, only a small percentage of the required precinct captains in place, and the state of the campaign's computer data a disaster.

At one point, Trippi said later, he opened a closet door "and it was like a comic strip, like one of those cartoons. You open the door and everything in the closet just comes down on you"—all the unprocessed computer cards that were supposed to have been completed, storing full information on 120,000 Iowa Democrats who would be potential Mondale supporters at the approaching caucuses.

Whatever the merits of Trippi's report, the Iowa situation was increasingly perceived within the Mondale campaign as a battle over turf between Beckel and Ford. The pulling and hauling lasted more than a month and was settled temporarily by sending Trippi back to Iowa as Slone's deputy, but with operational control. That arrangement, however, was foredoomed by the circumstances and the temperaments involved.

"I don't want to hear it's not working," Trippi later said Johnson had told both Slone and him. But it wasn't, and it didn't.

Trippi called Ford and told him: "What you've got here is a ship, and it's been hit by a torpedo. There's land on the left side and there's land on the right side. When I'm in charge of the boat, I'm steering to the right. When Slone's in charge of the boat, he's steering to the left. What that is basically is a zig-zag straight line, and we're not getting any closer to land, and we're sinking. So take me out of here, or clarify the situation."

More complaints from Campbell and other Iowans about the turmoil, which they laid at Slone's feet, finally resulted in Slone's transfer back to Washington and Trippi's taking over. But the whole episode left deep scars within the Mondale campaign, particularly between Beckel and Ford. With Trippi in charge, the Mondale campaign in Iowa hunkered down to the assigned task—to make sure Mondale "won big;" meaning at least 40 percent of the caucus vote, and, if possible, 50 percent. That's what the Mondale strategists believed it would take to crush Glenn, the only opponent they really were at all concerned about as they relentlessly pursued their strategy of an early knockout.

Cranston's challenge, inflated by his perceived strength among the nuclear-freeze forces and the reputation of John Law as the state's most effective Democratic organizer, had been somewhat downgraded within the Mondale camp as a result of the straw vote. It was hard to take seriously a campaign that acquired more dinner tickets than bodies it could produce to use them. And on top of that came the candidacy of George McGovern, which Cranston acknowledged afterward had severely cut into his support from nuclear-freeze proponents and liberals in general.

Finally, Cranston was simply a very weak and unpersuasive candidate. His ludicrous attempts at downplaying his age and elderly appearance only underscored the problem. He dyed his eyebrows and the white fringe that encircled the back of his head an obvious orange color. And he came off as a Johnny-one-note on the nuclear freeze, attempting, among other things, to elevate an early association with Albert Einstein into a major credential as the one candidate who cared most about avoiding nuclear holocaust. Law and his capable Iowa associate Karen Kapler labored diligently to bring Cranston in second in the caucuses, but it was a very weak horse they were riding.

Reubin Askew, a fish out of water in Florida, found a small pond in which to swim in the anti-abortion movement in Iowa, which had been credited with helping defeat two liberal Democratic senators, Dick Clark and John Culver. And as the caucuses approached, Askew was obliged to rely heavily on this resource. Embarrassed by Mondale in Askew's too-narrow victory in the straw vote in Florida, Askew had hammered Mondale hard on the special-interest issue at the Des Moines J-J dinner, apparently in hopes of winning support as the Democrat who dared to be different. But his speech ignited no fires among the mostly liberal diners, and he clearly would be no serious factor in the caucuses.

As for McGovern, he was a sentimental favorite who conducted himself admirably in reminding the party of its roots and commitments, but that was all. Two other declared candidates, Fritz Hollings and Jesse Jackson, were taking a pass in Iowa, pointing to the New Hampshire primary eight days after the Iowa caucuses. So that left only Gary Hart, and the Mondale campaign saw no reason to quarrel with Dave Nagle's fall assessment that Hart was "dead in the water" in Iowa.

There was no doubt, Hart acknowledged later, that the Wisconsin adventure—Bill Romjue's taking much of his Iowa staff there for the straw-vote competition in June—and Romjue's subsequent resignation from the Hart campaign, had been damaging. Like Glenn's staff troubles, it fed a perception of failure and disarray. The hiring of Romjue late in 1982 had raised expectations about Hart, since Romjue had been the Jimmy Carter state coordinator in Iowa in Carter's 1980 rout of Ted Kennedy. But Romjue proved to be a mercurial personality in the Hart campaign. When Romjue's immediate successor, Sharon Darlington, also quit, campaign manager Pudge Henkel sent in one of Hart's young Senate aides, Keith Glaser, in the fall of 1983. Glaser was a hard-working loyalist who believed in his candidate and his ability to exceed expectations in Iowa, which by this time had approached rock bottom.

Though it hadn't been planned, the lower expectations for Hart resulting from his earlier 1983 setbacks positioned him well to do what the political prognosticators had said could never be done again after the upsets in Iowa by McGovern in 1972, Carter in 1976 and George Bush on the Republican side in 1980: blindside the process, and the mammoth press corps covering it, with a surprise showing.

Complicating the Hart situation immensely was a severe money shortage. Matters reached such a desperate point, Glaser said later, that he was obliged to lay out four to five thousand dollars of his own money just to feed the staff and buy gas so the campaign workers could get around. Glaser set up his own local fund-raising effort in Des Moines to keep the campaign alive. Finally, just after Thanksgiving, he flew back to Washington to plead his case: "Look, guys," he recalled saying, "we're gonna get our heads handed to us in Iowa if we don't at least get enough resources to live. I'm not looking for a John Glenn or a Walter Mondale type budget, but I need to have enough money to keep my kids from starving and get them on the road. If we don't do something, then I think what we ought to do is just cut our losses and get out. Because we've got to have at least enough to survive."

Glaser seemed the most unlikely type to be delivering an ultimatum. Mild-mannered, polite to the point of deference, and, above all, a Hart team player, he was no head-knocker. He laid his case before Hart and Henkel at a critical time, however, when some others in the campaign were arguing that Hart should pull out of Iowa and concentrate on New Hampshire. Hart himself acknowledged later that the money crunch was so great at this juncture that he thought he might have to quit the race altogether.

"It was the worst time," he said, "because we had to step up activities—salaries, phones, etc., and the money just wasn't there."

Much of the pressure to abandon Iowa came, not surprisingly, from the Hart organizers in New Hampshire. Sue Casey, one of the Hart campaign leaders in New Hampshire, "felt particularly strongly about that," Henkel recalled later. "We had the nucleus of a very strong strong campaign in New Hampshire," he said, "and the people in New Hampshire were afraid that we were going to divert financial resources to Iowa in what was a hopeless cause, from at least their own perception of Iowa."

Hart himself was discouraged, Henkel said, from an apparent lack of interest in his campaign in Iowa. He had reached 9 percent in polls in Iowa but then had fallen back.

"It caused Gary to wonder whether we were really doing the

right thing by staying in Iowa," Henkel recalled. In the end, he said, he recommended to Hart that they stay there, because the only way he could break out of the pack of second-tier candidates was to do well in both Iowa and New Hampshire. Hart agreed, and the money was found to keep going in Iowa.

As longshot candidacies go, Hart's was a classic of guerrilla political warfare in Iowa. One aspect was to try to lure away from Cranston the hearts and minds of the freeze supporters. To this end, when singer Carole King offered to come to the state for a Hart fund-raiser, Glaser—aware it wouldn't raise the kind of money he needed—decided to hold it instead for the benefit of the Iowa freeze campaign. The freezeniks turned out, including Cranston supporters, and some conversions were achieved afterward, especially after Cranston, in a farm forum, dismissed the concept of parity—inviolate in the farm belt—as no longer relevant.

"There was," Hart said later, "a lot of smoke around the Cranston candidacy." The moment McGovern entered the race, he said, "I knew immediately it was the end of Cranston's hopes. I remember telling people, 'There goes Cranston.' In the 1972 election, I said, 'McGovern is really [Gene] McCarthy.' This time, McGovern was the real Cranston. McGovern went right to the left of Cranston."

More important for Hart, though, was a basic decision of his own campaign to carry out a rural strategy in Iowa—in guerrilla terms, to stake out the countryside. Under the party formula for allocation of delegates to county caucuses, the next level in the selection process, minority representation was guaranteed provided a candidate received a specified percentage of the precinct caucus vote.

For example, if you needed 20 percent to get one delegate at a precinct caucus in which five delegates were to be chosen, and twenty people showed up to vote, a candidate needed at least four votes to claim that one delegate. The smaller the caucus turnout, the fewer attendees a candidate needed to pick up a delegate. And inasmuch as the Hart campaign never expected to beat Mondale in Iowa but instead was striving for whatever showing it took to exceed expectations, the objective was to nickel and dime the delegate competition.

"What we did was go back and look at the caucus attendance numbers from 1976 and 1980," Glaser recalled. "We did a very simple computer run so that we could find out how many people we would need to bring into a caucus to get a single delegate from the [precinct] caucus into the county caucuses. Simple targeting. What we had to do was figure out how we could get the biggest bang for a buck, and we knew immediately that in the largest areas, in the cities, you needed to have maybe twenty supporters in a caucus to get one delegate, whereas you could go to some of these rural areas and all you needed was three or four people to get a delegate. So the conclusion was obvious: We've got limited resources. Let's go where we have a better shot at getting as many delegates as possible. Let's maximize the delegates. . . . We had it targeted almost to the precinct. We knew which precincts were going to be more valuable to us than not." In a state with 2,495 precincts, it seemed an ambitious task, but readily manageable even for a guerrilla campaign in the era of the computer. In the end, Henkel said, forty-six rural counties were targeted as prime objectives. Why the other candidates didn't do the same, Glaser said later, left him "astonished."

The rural strategy was, however, more than an antiseptic computer exercise. It proved to be ideal in another way for a candidacy that had little money and whose best resource was the candidate himself. With Iowa's frigid winter approaching, the customary travel by plane from one end of the state to the other—more than three hundred miles—was not only very costly but also very precarious and undependable. Already in November flights were being cancelled or diverted because of bad weather. It made much more sense, especially since Hart would be working the boondocks, to finesse the customary state fly-arounds and focus on one small rural region on each visit, traveling by car.

Into this scenario in a custom van came one Steve Lynch, a bona fide Hart groupie who looked much younger than his thirty-one years. As the Hart campaign mounted, Lynch would take off from his job as an accountant and go all over the Midwest to hear his favorite candidate speak. He bought the van, put a big heart on the back of it and baptized it "Van Force One." Lynch bought the van, Glaser said, so he could drive Hart around in the state.

The vehicle in due course became not only Hart's low-budget ticket around rural Iowa but also a mobile press conference room. The van would drive into a small town, call at the local weekly newspaper, pick up a reporter and take him with Hart to the next town, so he could interview the candidate—and have a beer or two. On arrival, a local volunteer would drive the reporter back to his paper, often a distance of thirty or forty miles. Then another reporter would be picked up, and so on. To start the day, Hart would be flown into what passed for a major media market in Iowa and would hold a press conference at the airport. Then he would climb into the van and make stops in as many as ten small towns during the day, winding up at another major media market, where he would hold yet another press conference. When a local Democrat needed stroking by the candidate, he was brought along in the van, too, and provided with the same shuttle service back home.

"Keith had the formula worked out," Hart said later, "and we had people where nobody else had them. It requires more candidate work—more events, more towns, longer distances. Mondale and Glenn weren't willing to travel such distances. I sort of had the countryside to myself, as I recall. The caravans would go to eight or ten towns a day. I'd make ten speeches a day. . . . We understood the arithmetic. But knowing the theory was one thing; getting the candidate to do it was another. I was just crazy enough to do it."

The system proved to be a press agent's dream. It produced heavy coverage in the weekly newspapers in these smaller towns, papers that often have a longer shelf life in the rural areas than the major city papers. Glaser started sending out short press releases saying when Hart would be in a particular town, and they often were run, too, generating local interest in the visit. In fact, the weekly papers were making such good use of the press releases that Glaser decided to start sending out two-page releases incorporating the substance of the Hart issues brochures and a big glossy photo of Hart.

"Sure enough," Glaser said, "these weekly newspapers would run a huge picture, a huge headline and often the entire press release on the front page." Sometimes the release would be printed without a word changed—and with a local reporter's byline, no less.

The rural strategy also enabled Hart to tap into what proved to be an important resource—what Glaser called "the farm network." It was, he said, "an incredible network. They all talk to each other. You say one thing in one part of the state and everybody knows it within a week. We figured if we could get that network going and start signing up people there, then right before the caucuses we could start concentrating more heavily on the cities"—the standard guerrilla strategy again. Hart, from a farm state himself, knew farm issues and enjoyed and was most effective with small groups.

By this time, a significant development was occurring within the Hart campaign in Washington. Pat Caddell, the pollster with whom Hart had broken into national politics in the first McGovern presidential campaign in 1972 but who was without a candidate up to now, started conferring with Hart. Having failed in his efforts to encourage first Dale Bumpers and then Joe Biden to make the race, on New Year's Eve he gave Hart the long memo based on his survey in Iowa of previous caucus participants. The memo concluded that most Iowa Democrats hadn't made their minds up yet and would support a "Mr. Smith" candidate, who had been modeled on Biden in the Caddell survey but also fit the Hart profile well enough.

"It was clear to me that somebody could come in and roll that thing," Caddell said later. "There were huge numbers of people who weren't participating in caucuses who normally did. It was beyond my wildest imagination." When he showed Hart the data on "Mr. Smith," Caddell said, "his eyes were like saucers, looking at that stuff."

Caddell's findings, Hart said later, "documented empirically what I had felt intuitively in 1982 and 1983. I didn't become Smith. I was Smith."

All at once Caddell was on the team, in a favored role, as he saw it. "It was like Butch Cassidy and the Sundance Kid," he recalled of that time.

Caddell's arrival strengthened Glaser's hand in winning more money and manpower for Iowa in the constant tug-of-war with the Hart effort in New Hampshire and with others in the Washington headquarters who still did not see much opportunity in Iowa. As caucus night, February 20, approached, Caddell and another part-time adviser, Boston political consultant John Marttila, argued that there weren't enough votes in the boondocks for Hart to finish second in Iowa. He had to bring his campaign into the mass media markets with paid television, they said. Henkel said later it had always been the plan to come in from the countryside, as in guerrilla warfare, with television buys in urban Iowa in the closing weeks.

At any rate, there also ensued a discussion on just what would constitute a good showing for Hart in Iowa, and now high the sights should be set. Caddell said later that others, including Henkel, insisted that it would be enough for Hart to move up gradually among the contenders; it would be enough for him to finish fourth in Iowa, then third in New Hampshire and finally "emerge" by winning the Connecticut primary in late March.

Caddell, recalling this discussion, said: "Marttila goes crazy. He says the campaign will be dead [by late March]."

According to Henkel, "Pat was very much for taking all our financial resources and devoting them to Iowa at that point. And the people in New Hampshire were deathly afraid what impact Pat would have on my thinking, because they needed every last dollar they could come by. . . . There was no possibility I was going to pull money out of New Hampshire and give it to Iowa." He had already committed $30,000 to the final days in New Hampshire, Henkel said, but he did come up with $95,000 in two small loans to make television buys possible in Iowa as well.

Caddell, however, wanted a bigger television buy than Henkel had planned and, he said later, went out to California and raised $30,000 himself, making the bigger buy possible. Henkel, though, told us later that the campaign stuck to his original plan and told Caddell "a white lie" about the level of the television buy to pacify him. Actually, according to Ray Strother, the Hart media man, the buy was boosted in the larger Iowa television markets and cut back in the smaller ones to stay within Henkel's budget. That Henkel felt he had to deal with Caddell in this way was an indication of stickier times to come between the two of them in the Hart campaign.

Already Caddell's presence in the Hart campaign and his aggressive manner were rubbing others the wrong way. "It had to do with people feeling we were doing quite well in Iowa and New Hampshire without him," press secretary Kathy Bushkin recalled. "I think there was resentment at that level. People sort of saying, Caddell came in and took credit for what a lot of really hard-working folks had actually done for a year."

At the same time, she said, Caddell's contribution could not

to dislike him a little bit for the fact that he was tarnishing an image that was important to them too."

If there was any beneficiary in Iowa of the Mondale-bashing, then, it was not John Glenn but Gary Hart, whose anti-Mondale observations were overshadowed by Glenn's.[19]

But if there was a sentimental victor in the Des Moines debate, it was McGovern. In a straightforward way, he told viewers that if they supported his positions but thought he couldn't win, the best way to "send a message" to the party's nominee was to cast a vote for him. "Don't throw away your conscience," he said, to enthusiastic applause.

The day before the precinct caucuses, the bottom really fell out for Glenn. The Iowa poll by the Des Moines *Register* showed Mondale leading among 44 percent of Democrats who said they would definitely participate, with Cranston second at 17 percent, Hart third at 14 and Glenn a dismal fourth at 11.

The Glenn camp was livid, for good reason. The newspaper reported in fine print at the end of the poll story that of its full sample of 1,003 interviews—an ample sample taken as a whole—only 66 said they definitely would attend the Democratic caucuses, the category on which the main percentages were based. In other words, Glenn's 11 percent meant the poll found about seven voters who said they intended to vote for him. Whether the results of that poll had any bearing at all on the ultimate results is conjecture. But they did nothing for the reputation of such polls.

These were not happy days for John Glenn. On top of all his other woes, the man who had assumed political control of his campaign, Bob Keefe, gave an interview to a Los Angeles *Times* reporter, Bella Stumbo, that tore it for Glenn. Keefe said among other things that "we've made a lot of progress, but this campaign is still in worse shape than any I've ever seen." That was only for starters. Of his adversary and Glenn's close aide Bill White, he observed: "What White knows about campaigns, he's read in books. He's read more campaign books than anybody I know."

And worse, Stumbo reported Keefe's saying that Glenn's wife,

19. One Glenn ad, prepared by David Sawyer of New York but never aired, was particularly tough. It showed three identical Walter Mondales at a table, in the mode of the old television show *To Tell the Truth.* Three contradictory statements were narrated as the camera panned to each of them. And then the narrator said: "Will the real Walter Mondale please stand up?" After a pause, all three rose.

Annie, was a hit on the campaign trail, "but we can't send her out anywhere that takes more than a few hours because Glenn practically falls apart if she's gone overnight. He gets irritable, out of focus. It's amazing—a real love story."

To top it all off, Keefe said, concerning a Glenn position on gay rights, that "Glenn's even got one in the family. . . . His cousin is president of the Gay Bar Owners Association in San Francisco." As a divorced man with his kids through college and his mortgage paid, Keefe said, "I say exactly what I think. I don't take any crap from Glenn—I don't take any crap from anybody!"

Keefe much later confirmed the accuracy of the quotes. He said Stumbo was sitting at his desk as he made the remarks about John and Annie Glenn on the phone while explaining why Annie could not accept a speaking engagement. But, he acknowledged, the interview "finished me off with the boss."

He was right. Glenn, outraged, wanted to fire Keefe on the spot, and several of Glenn's Senate aides joined the chorus. Cooler heads, aware that the campaign could not afford yet another staff shakeup story, talked him out of it. But Glenn told those closest to him: "Just keep him away from me."

Long after the election, when we asked Glenn how he felt about Keefe's interview in the Los Angeles *Times*, he smiled wanly and said: "I think I'll just give that one the charity of my silence. That said an awful lot about some of the difficulties."

In advance of caucus night, tens of thousands of Iowans found engraved invitations in their mailboxes from the former Vice President of the United States and Mrs. Walter F. Mondale asking them to join in attending their precinct caucus. Some recipients, very impressed, called in to the Mondale headquarters to RSVP. One caller inquired: "Can I bring my wife?"

And that night they came, in one of the purest grass-roots processes remaining in the electing of a President. In the 2,495 precincts around the state, Democrats filed into living rooms, church basements, schools and other neighborhood gathering places to vote. The Second Precinct in Des Moines, which usually casts the largest Democratic vote in the state, held its caucus in a small hall at the Staves Methodist Church. Some 139 voters showed up and in due time broke into groups according to candidate preference. The Mondale supporters, 87 of them, many wearing union windbreakers, clearly dominated, with 63 percent of the total. Cranston backers were second, numbering 17. McGovern had 14, Glenn 7 and Hart 5; the rest were for Jesse Jackson or were uncommitted. Mondale obviously would receive the bulk of the delegates, but for a second candidate to receive one, he had to have 15 percent of the total caucus participants, or 21. None of the others qualified, but under the rules their supporters were allowed to regroup once.

How they did so in this one precinct was an example of how poorly the Glenn campaign had done its job. One of the leaders of the McGovern group said to the others: "Let's send a message to the Mondale people that it's not cut and dried." Thereupon backers of Hart and Jackson joined the McGovern forces in the kitchen and totaled 23, qualifying for one McGovern delegate. Then the Cranston people also threw in with the McGovern forces, qualifying the group for two delegates. A deal was struck that both would go to the county convention formally as McGovern delegates, but one of them would be a Cranston supporter.

Sitting in the hall through all of this, obviously confused, were the seven Glenn supporters. Finally two or three went into the kitchen to join the anti-Mondale coalition. Another came over to us and our colleague Tom Ottenad and asked us what they were supposed to do.

When the results were in from around the state, Fritz Mondale had his sought-after first big victory of 1984—49 percent of the votes cast for selected delegates. Winning just about half the votes in an eight-man field should have been the big story that night, but it wasn't. Actually there were two others—the utter collapse of John Glenn, who finished a weak fourth, and the emergence of Gary Hart, who to nearly everyone's surprise finished second, ahead of George McGovern.

The final percentages were: Mondale 49 percent; Hart 16.5; McGovern 10; uncommitted 9; Cranston 7; Glenn 3.5; Askew 2.5; Jackson 1.5; Hollings, less than 1.

"The thing that became terrifying in the end," Caddell said later, "was McGovern; that he would draw enough from Gary that Cranston would finish second. I always worried that the Mondale people would figure out what we were doing and throw enough to Cranston so he'd finish second." Indeed, had McGovern beaten

Hart out for second place, the Hart balloon may never have gotten off the ground.[20]

In the Iowa caucuses in 1980, George Bush had upset Ronald Reagan on the Republican side by diligently increasing the turnout, to the point that one of the losers, Senator Howard Baker of Tennessee, said the caucuses had become "the functional equivalent of a primary." Four years later, on the Democratic side, Hart had sprung his surprise by deftly working the old caucus system—and its obscure and complicated arithmetic for allocating delegates.[21]

The scene that night in downtown Des Moines was chaotic. Across from the Hotel Savery, where the results were being posted, Mondale held a rally in a new shopping mall. "Tonight," he told his assembled cheering supporters, "you have launched us toward victory. . . . I am ready to be President of the United States."

But across the way in the hotel, the Hart staffers and supporters were the ones behaving more like the big winners. They gathered around a makeshift telephone hookup between Keith Glaser in the hotel ballroom and Gary Hart in New Hamsphire and listened while Glaser fielded questions from reporters and passed them on to Hart. His answers could be heard over a jerry-built loudspeaker. He was confident but not cocky.

"Will money be a problem?" one reporter, looking ahead, wanted to know.

"Not anymore!" Hart shot back with a lilt in his voice. He credited Glaser's rural strategy for much of his success in Iowa and said he thought the results had turned the nomination fight "into a Hart-Mondale race." He could be excused the hyperbole under the circumstances.

Mike Ford, Mondale's national field director, said later the result among the runners-up didn't surprise the Mondale cam-

20. Glenn's fate was foretold by his Iowa press spokesman, Larry Rasky, the morning of the caucuses. About ten hours before the voting, three reporters picked him up at his hotel in Des Moines to play tennis. He came out to the car with his tennis racket—and his bags, for a quick getaway.

21. The delegates chosen at the precinct caucuses were not delegates to the national convention but to the second level of a four-level process, the county conventions. Later steps were congressional district conventions and a state convention, but the shares each candidate received at the precinct level were to be reflected at each of the next three levels.

paign so much, but the news media play certainly did. "We anticipated Glenn would be the story," he said of Glenn's dismal finish. "We weren't surprised Hart got 15 percent. We didn't think it was going to rock like that."

In light of what happened to Glenn in Iowa, an obvious question was whether he might have been better served, since he was already well known in the country, to have delayed his candidacy. What if he had refused all through 1983 to play the conventional game, which proved by early 1984 to be so debilitating to his image and consequently to his standing in the polls, and ultimately with real voters in Iowa? He would have sacrificed time in which to raise money, but then again he would not have needed so much to spend on the ferret's wheel that took him nowhere. The disorganization of his campaign, however, and his own inability to sustain interest in his candidacy, were probably the result of much more than bad timing.

Long afterward, Bill White, Glenn's longtime campaign manager, said of the outcome in Iowa: "The Gary Hart campaign picked up the future-oriented themes of the John Glenn campaign and used them successfully against Mondale, and ended up being what the John Glenn campaign would have been had Glenn been able to stay in the race."

But that was a far-fetched what-might-have-been, considering the self-destructive mechanisms attached to the Glenn campaign. Glenn, along with the rest of the field, moved on to New Hampshire, acknowledging that "we got out-hustled in Iowa" but labeling as "nonsense" the notion that Iowa had finished him as a serious candidate.

Mondale, the winner, was already in New Hampshire campaigning, and so was Hart. A day later, a stream of fifty rented cars carrying Mondale workers headed north out of Des Moines to Minneapolis. The young "Fritz-blitzers" dropped off the cars—charged to the Minnesota spending limit to cut expenses assigned to Iowa—and boarded a chartered jet for Boston, where they would be sent to their next assignment.

A Mondale insider, recounting the exodus from Iowa much later, observed: "They did not want that jet taking off from Des Moines. They didn't want you guys seeing this jet with a bunch of kids flying to New Hampshire while we were saying there's nothing wrong up there."

The "kids" were given their tickets in Minneapolis before boarding the jet, and nobody bothered about who had paid for them—something called a "delegate committee," whatever that was.

7

Brush Fire

•

EATING BREAKFAST in Concord, New Hampshire, with two reporters late in 1983, Susan Casey, the deputy director of Gary Hart's primary campaign there, explained her theory about Walter Mondale. There was no doubt, she conceded, that he could rely on the support of 30 to 35 percent of the Democrats. That much would come to him simply because of his position as a former Vice President and his backing in the establishment—that is, among party officials, public officeholders and union leaders. But, Casey insisted, Mondale had not yet "earned" any votes on his own.

"I've never heard one person say, 'I'm FOR Walter Mondale,' " she said.

It might have been easy to write that comment off as another example of the kind of wishful thinking that is so common among campaign managers. But by that stage, Sue Casey and Jeanne Shaheen, the state coordinator for the Hart campaign, already had built an organizational structure and core of support that gave both Hart and them credibility. Indeed, at thirty-four, Casey herself seemed the quintessential Hart partisan, in the sense that she saw in the Colorado Democrat a chance to recapture the good feeling she could remember from the days of John F. Kennedy, when she was too young to participate in politics.

"All of our experiences had been sour in government during our adolescence and our college years, all the people that were in that generation," she said. "Government was cynical. Government was bad."

Moreover, Casey found that Hart's plodding emphasis on issues appealed to this group more than glibness might have done. "We would laugh," Casey recalled. "We'd say, 'We bored another group in Manchester tonight.' "

Thus, as the 1984 campaign began more or less officially on January 1, there were some small indications that in New Hampshire Hart was at least nominally stronger than such competitors as Alan Cranston, Fritz Hollings and Reubin Askew. He was credited with having the only organization in the same league with Mondale's, and he had seemed a more comfortable personal campaigner in New Hampshire than anywhere else. He had made an effective appearance at that state Democratic convention in Manchester in October, and there appeared to be dividends coming from the door-to-door canvass of some 25,000 Democratic households his campaign had run late in the fall.

It seemed clear, nonetheless, that Walter Mondale held such an imposing lead in the opinion surveys of New Hampshire voters that it was going to take some radical realignment of political thinking for anyone to overtake him. The point Sue Casey was making late in 1983 was that the votes for such a change were indeed "out there" because Mondale had not yet lighted any spark in the electorate at large.

The Mondale managers had received similar warnings of their own. Back in July, Peter Hart, the polling expert for Mondale, had made a detailed survey of 500 likely primary voters and found Mondale and John Glenn essentially in a dead heat, with 37 and 36 percent of the vote, respectively.

"Mondale had a ceiling in that state," campaign manager Bob Beckel said later, "and it scared the living hell out of us from that summer on. Mondale was just not very popular up there."

At that stage, however, none of the candidates other than Mondale and Glenn recorded even as much as 5 percent. There was nothing surprising in those figures because all of the early polling—whether national or concentrated in a particular state—was reflecting the extent to which the voters recognized names rather than any considered preference on their part. More than four of five respondents said they might change their minds later. And that flexibility continued through the preliminaries.

In a year-end survey made for the Boston *Globe*, for example, poll-taker Irwin (Tubby) Harrison found fewer than 20 percent of Mondale and Glenn supporters willing to say there was "no chance at all" they would change their minds by primary day.

Some of the other "internals" in Peter Hart's data suggested there was still work to be done to shore up Mondale's position in New Hampshire. When he used a "feeling thermometer" to measure attitudes toward the candidates, Mondale received ratings 46 percent positive to 25 percent negative—"mezzo," in Hart's judgment—and Glenn 53 percent positive to only 14 percent negative. Without using their names, Hart also had tested the appeal of "Candidate A" and "Candidate B" and so forth by describing the minor candidates' attributes, an exercise that showed Gary Hart clearly ahead of the others in the field.

"You saw the root appeal before he started," Peter Hart said.

In fact, Mondale and his strategists had shown some concern earlier about Gary Hart's potential. Peter Hart and Jim Johnson, Mondale's chief strategist, told us early in 1983 that they considered Gary Hart the longshot who might provide the stiffest opposition to their candidate. And during the summer of 1983, Mondale himself was saying that Hart was probably the rival with the greatest potential. But by the end of the year, it was not surprising that Hart was being taken less seriously. He had made a hash of the straw votes, come close to collapse in the Iowa precinct caucus campaign and found his money drying up as the national opinion polls continued to rank him far back in the field.

From the outset, Hart's campaign had been based on the idea of generational change—his conviction that Democrats were ready for someone with a fresher face than a fifty-six-year-old protégé of Hubert Humphrey and for some "new ideas" that went beyond reheated New Deal and Great Society spending programs. Hart's analysis was correct as far as it went, but defining a situation wasn't enough to constitute a fully rounded presidential candidacy. Clearly needed was some demonstration that the introverted senator from Colorado was capable of making an emotional connection with some segment of the Democratic Party. That wasn't going to be easy, because he was one of those politicians—and there are more of them than you might imagine—who are sometimes restrained by another self standing off to the side, watching and mocking their conduct.

Hart had few conventional assets as the election year began. He had spent every nickel he had raised and had borrowed heavily against the federal matching funds he expected to receive. Although the Shaheen-Casey operation in New Hampshire was getting top marks, Hart's national campaign was thin. The campaign manager, Oliver (Pudge) Henkel, was a Cleveland lawyer who had been Hart's Yale Law School roommate but had never been involved in a campaign. Most of the key slots were filled with bright but politically inexperienced people from Hart's Senate staff—the most capable, by most estimates, being press secretary Kathy Bushkin.

Hart's polling expert, Dotty Lynch, was handicapped because the campaign didn't have the money to pay for polls. His media consultant, veteran Ray Strother, was similarly hamstrung. He had begun preparing a documentary on Hart in June of 1983 but had been forced to suspend operations before it was completed because the cash simply wasn't there. (Strother did salvage something from that early filming when Henkel called for some quick spots in December. Segments of Hart holding forth on various issues were culled from the footage and put together in a turning-page format that disguised their origin.) Late in the fall money was so short that there were staff layoffs, cutbacks in telephone service and even days when the campaign headquarters had no heat.

"I did have to let people go in the fall of '83," Henkel said, "because just having them around meant they were using telephones, and we couldn't afford the telephone expense. We kept taking telephones out."

The reverses Hart suffered all through 1983 had made the task that much more difficult in New Hampshire. Day after day there seemed to be fresh reports of disaster—Hart losing another straw poll, Hart's campaign in Iowa in collapse, Hart's report to the Federal Election Commission documenting his problems raising money.

"Every day you'd look at the paper and know that you had to call ten people to say, 'It's really not that bad,' " Sue Casey recalled. "We would have to do so much work to be believable."

Through all the reverses of 1983, Hart had maintained a public posture of confidence that eventually he would become a player in the Democratic field once the competition grew serious.

"He always viewed 1983 as a positioning year," Henkel said.

But the situation had become so distressing, Hart himself had begun to face the possibility he might have to pack it in. Of an early December meeting with Henkel in his Senate office that continued over lunch in a Senate cafeteria, Henkel said later, "Gary said, 'Pudge, I think we ought to start to develop some contingency plans for winding up the campaign after the first of the year'. . . . This was not a recommendation on Gary's part. It was just Gary raising with me the notion that maybe we'll have to wind this thing up even before New Hampshire."

But Henkel felt "we had gotten along so long on no money" that they could persevere at least through February, meaning the Iowa caucuses and the New Hampshire primary, and no contingency plan for quitting was ever prepared.

If anything, however, Hart's rivals in the field of "second tier" candidates chasing Fritz Mondale were in much worse shape. After enlisting that hard core of support on the nuclear-freeze issue early in 1983, Alan Cranston had been stopped in his tracks and had essentially deserted New Hampshire for Iowa. Indeed, it was becoming increasingly clear that the little credibility left in the Cranston campaign was primarily a function of the regard his rivals and the press had for some of the people working for him—most notably Sergio Bendixen, the young professional from Florida serving as his national campaign manager, and John Law in Iowa.

Fritz Hollings was following a different strategy and ignoring Iowa in favor of New Hampshire, but he was being treated as more of a diversion than a serious contender. Reubin Askew had run out of money and had decided against heavy borrowing, thus dooming his plan to run ten days of intense television advertising in Iowa and New Hampshire just before the caucuses and primary.

Opinion polls showed George McGovern and Jesse Jackson marginally "stronger" than these other candidates—a reflection of the fact they were better known and were being given more free television exposure. But neither was ever considered a potential winner or ultimate nominee.

Stripped down to the essentials, then, it seemed that these long-odds candidates had spent a full year and millions of dollars just to compete for position among three to four thousand Democratic activists in Iowa and a similar number in New Hampshire. And now, as the campaign moved to a broader electorate, they lacked the resources to campaign effectively to overcome the images as also-rans they had acquired so expensively over the previous year.

The only candidate other than Hart entering New Hampshire with even a breath of political life was John Glenn. And even with his famous name, he was a distant second to Mondale before the Iowa caucuses. Glenn had experienced the same kind of organizational failures in New Hampshire as everywhere else. But now Paul Shone, a professional organizer from Boston, had taken over and begun doing at least the basic mechanics of political organizing the Mondale campaign had completed months earlier. The core of the Glenn campaign plan, however, was a series of television and radio advertisements painting Mondale as the liberal captive of the special interests. In a state as determinedly conservative and anti-union as New Hampshire always had been, there was no reason to believe the spots wouldn't strike home, although there was never any corresponding assurance that John Glenn would be seen as a credible enough candidate to become the beneficiary.

So, despite those continuing figures showing a ceiling of about 35 percent on Mondale's support, there was no obvious reason for concern in the camp of the former Vice President. He had four or five times as much support from the party leadership as any other candidate and, at the end, a steering committee larger than Cranston's eventual vote. His personal campaigning in the state, now going back two full years, had been consistently well received.

Mondale's campaign was being run by Charles Campion, a streetwise twenty-eight-year-old organizer who had moved into the state in December of 1982 and had demonstrated that rare ability to come in as a hired gun and win the full acceptance of the locals. And Campion had the help of Cathy Rogers, one of those indigenous New Hampshire operatives—like Shaheen and Casey—with a special skill for scheduling the candidate where he should be. Finally, the campaign was on the way to spending a full million dollars on New Hampshire, more than twice the $404,000 limit for the state set by the federal election law. (The evasion was legal and feasible, however, because only fourteen cents of each dollar spent on Boston television and radio advertising was charged against the New Hampshire limit, an amount ostensibly reflecting the share of the Boston stations' audiences in New Hampshire.)

Still missing in Mondale's case was a rationale for his candidacy beyond his obvious credentials and his insistence that he was going to win the nomination anyway. As Bob Beckel put it long after the fact, "We didn't get a message down beyond 'experience.' "

At the time, however, that shortcoming didn't seem important to the Mondale strategists. Every bit of evidence they had seen pointed to a runaway victory in Iowa and a comfortable one against a divided field in New Hampshire, triumphs they were convinced would wipe away the last vestiges of opposition in the March 13 Super Tuesday primaries and caucuses. And the lack of a message was easy to overlook in a primary situation in which the first imperative was a quick, clean knockout that would set the stage for the challenge to Ronald Reagan. It would be no problem for any good Democrat to find a message to use against him.

As a practical matter, there were no watershed issues—in the usual meaning of that term—by which the Democrats competing in New Hampshire could be sorted out very neatly. All of them except Reubin Askew supported a nuclear-weapons freeze, although there was some variation in the degrees of their enthusiasm for that initiative. Most of them—Askew and later Hart were the dissenters—went along with labor's demand for a "domestic content" bill, meaning legislation to require more assembly of foreign-made automobiles within the United States. Most of them—here Glenn was the exception—had adopted the New England position that the acid-rain problem required federal restrictions on the emissions of industry in the Midwest.

There was some quibbling about whether the defense budget should be increased 4 or 5 or 6 percent after inflation; the only candidates calling for an absolute dollar reduction in the Pentagon budget were McGovern and Jackson, the two whom almost everyone agreed could not be nominated. Each of the Democrats had plans for improving education, strengthening the economy and producing more jobs for American workers. By the time the New Hampshire campaign opened in earnest in January, all or several of the candidates had appeared together on the same platform on enough occasions so that it was clear this was not a choice that offered radically different futures for the nation if one or the other were to be nominated and elected.

So the debate was centered on questions that ordinary voters, although not party activists, might be expected to consider sterile.

There was the usual argument over which candidate would make the strongest nominee in the general election, which is something voters at large—as opposed to party leaders—rarely consider compelling in these primaries. And there was the interminable bickering over the history of the candidates' performance on particular issues—most notably who voted or didn't vote for some element of the Reagan tax and budget program in 1981.

Nor was the press coverage very helpful in making the campaign seem interesting. Another generation of reporters went over the familiar ground of stories about candidates talking to New Hampshire voters in living rooms and diners, touring the Sanders Associates plant near Nashua, shaking hands outside shabby textile mills and along Elm Street in downtown Manchester; speaking on the campus of the University of New Hampshire in Durham or to a rally in Concord or a Rotary Club in Nashua, flying up to Berlin to pay their respects to the paper workers. All the legends were repeated—the most enduring being the story about the New Hampshire voter who can't decide because he hasn't yet met all the candidates personally.

But the first major event of the primary campaign had been scheduled—a three-hour debate from Dartmouth College on January 15 to be televised nationally on public stations. And there was some understandable hope in each campaign headquarters that this confrontation could be the opportunity for "breaking out of the pack." The debate format had some bizarre elements—Phil Donahue was to be the interlocutor for the second half—but simply the fact that it was coming little more than a month from a genuine primary made it more promising than all those shadow-boxing exhibitions in 1983.

Among those who saw the opportunity were Gary Hart and his new if unofficial political adviser Pat Caddell, last seen trying to bring Joe Biden into the campaign. The two had held conversations going back to 1981, and Hart said later he considered Caddell "smart and well motivated," and he wanted his help. At that point, however, Caddell had obvious doubts about whether the cool candidate from Colorado could be effective.

"I didn't think," he said much later, "that he had the ability to emote"—meaning to make the kind of emotional connection with voters that is so important in building a following. But during 1983 Caddell had become increasingly caught up in the Democratic situation while standing apart from it—enough so that he had been involved in those discussions with Dale Bumpers and Biden as the year wore on. He had begun with the view that, despite their gains, "the Democrats had done not as well as they should have" in 1982 and didn't seem to have a plan for running successfully against Reagan in 1984.

To Caddell, as to everyone else thinking about politics then, it was clear that the Democrats' base would be all those groups that had fared poorly as a result of Reagan's "revolution." But, as Caddell put it later, "the question was where do you reach beyond that?"

Caddell's answer was that the key would lie in running a future-oriented campaign that would recognize "the new demographics"—principally the huge population of "baby boomers" who had not yet formed hard allegiances to either side. With this constituency, the campaign against Reagan needed to be based not on criticism of where he had taken the country in his first term but on the contention that, at his age, Reagan "was not going any further."

The corollary was that the Democrats must avoid at all costs letting Reagan define the election of 1984 as a choice between the present (good) and the past (bad) but instead make it a choice between the present (good) and the future (better). Caddell's analysis, detailed in a 150-page memorandum on "The State of American Politics," noted that Reagan in 1982 had less success by urging voters to "stay the course" than he did by asking them if they really wanted to go back to the way things had been under Jimmy Carter.

The essential in 1984, Caddell became convinced, was to deny Reagan the opportunity to frame the choice in those terms again. But, against this imperative, Caddell saw Mondale and Glenn primarily as arguing over whose past record was the more reprehensible. And in the case of Mondale, Caddell saw as destructive not only his connections to Carter but the image that had developed from his endorsement by the AFL-CIO and NEA and the like. The result was that, as Joe Biden resisted and then refused, Caddell began meeting with Hart, first at the senator's home in Washington on New Year's Eve and then with Hart and Henkel in New Hampshire the following weekend.

Henkel, who had never met Caddell before driving him from

Boston up to Concord that weekend, remembers being "extremely enthusiastic" about the new adviser. The campaign and candidate had been dispirited—to the point that Hart was at least musing about quitting. And now there was new data and new blood.

"That's why the entry of Pat Caddell was so important," Henkel said. ". . . It was a real shot in the arm for us and, I think, for a lot of other people who were observing the campaign. And what it did was reiterate for Gary his own sense of the importance of 1984 over 1983."

What Henkel, the political outsider, could not anticipate then was that his own relationship with Caddell would be one conducted largely at sword's point for the rest of the campaign.

As another campaign insider put it: "They had this war and it never stopped."

Among those who knew Caddell, there was nothing surprising about his being involved in a war inside a campaign. Even many of his critics conceded that he was a brilliant political thinker, and even many of his friends conceded that he had a vesuvial temperament. And both groups recognized that if you let Pat Caddell into your campaign, he was going to become a major player.

Although there were all sorts of particular points of contention, there was one underlying basis of the war between Caddell and Pudge Henkel: Caddell wanted Gary Hart to be more aggressive in drawing distinctions between himself and Fritz Mondale, to be more negative and willing to attack Mondale. Among Caddell critics, there was the obvious suspicion that he was trying to use the Hart campaign as a vehicle for a vendetta against Mondale, with whom he had fallen out more or less publicly during the final days of the Carter administration.

"Those of us who were uncomfortable about attacking Mondale . . . always were skeptical about why he had to come down so hard on Mondale," one Hart intimate said later. There was concern that Caddell "just wanted to get Mondale so badly, sometimes he couldn't see what was in Gary's interest."

In the innocence of their beginning, however, Henkel was delighted that Caddell was now going to help Hart prepare for that Dartmouth debate that everyone in the campaign recognized as being so important. Caddell quickly began writing memoranda for Hart that made the case for a debate—and campaign—strategy directed at the future rather than at the arguments of the past.

He recognized there was a strong organization in place for Hart in New Hampshire but was convinced, as he put it later, "there was no case for him . . . no rationale."

That view was one of the instant sore spots within the campaign because Henkel, Kathy Bushkin and issues adviser David Landau, among others, had been making essentially the same arguments as far back as a speech at American University in Washington during the fall. But even those insiders most suspicious of the interloper were willing to concede that Pat Caddell was effective in sharpening Hart's message. And when the debate arrived, Hart's opportunity arrived with it.

The debate was sponsored jointly by Dartmouth and the House Democratic Caucus, which was preparing to choose its own delegates to the Democratic National Convention. The format called for a loosely constructed confrontation in which the candidates would deal with questions from Ted Koppel of ABC News, Donahue, the studio audience and one another. The whole thing was so unstructured, in fact, that at one point Mondale—who had the most to lose from a format that would allow the others to pounce on him—had threatened to refuse to take part, a threat he finally was wise enough to forget.

As it turned out, the format made it possible for Fritz Mondale and John Glenn, still putatively his prime competition, to get into the kind of so's-your-old-man bickering that probably didn't do either of them any good—but offered rich opportunities to the others. At one point, Mondale spelled out his proposals for cutting the federal deficit in half with a combination of spending reductions and a "progressive" tax increase.

"That is the same vague gobbledygook we've been hearing," Glenn interjected. "I'm disgusted and tired of all the vague promises . . . with no figures attached."

Mondale's promises, he said, would add $170 billion to federal deficits and "put more people out of jobs."

"The reason we have $200 billion deficits," Mondale fired back, "is that you and some others voted for Reaganomics."

Then, when Glenn countered with a reference to "the 21 percent interest rates" that prevailed at the end of the Carter administration, Mondale leaped to his feet and shouted: "Point of personal privilege!"

"Who has the floor here?" Mondale demanded. "There's just

been about a six-minute speech, all of it baloney. Mr. Glenn voted to create the $200 billion deficits. He wants to add to them by building the B-1 bomber and new poison nerve-gas weapons. He attacks my specific proposals with voodoo numbers. . . . Those are baloney figures of his, and my position is responsible."

Other candidates jumped in. Reubin Askew observed that "you're both right in what you say about each other." And Jesse Jackson played the role of elder statesman and conciliator, announcing at one point:

"We Democrats have to conduct our affairs in a serious vein."

But Gary Hart was more obviously focused on making his point by characterizing the Mondale-Glenn dispute in terms unfavorable to both.

"Quarrels between you two," Hart said after one encounter, "are not going to enable this party to lead and govern again." At another such point, Hart said: "This party will not gain responsibility as long as leaders of the past debate whose policies of the past are worst."

Unsurprisingly, Hart directed most of his attention at Mondale and touched the particular sore spots—the question of leadership and his identification with the Democratic constituency groups that had become the "special interests." Mondale, he said, "took eighteen days to say anything" about the invasion of Grenada—an example, Hart indicated, of Mondale's penchant for getting "aboard the consensus" rather than taking the lead.

"Fritz," he said at another point on another question, "you cannot lead this country if you have promised everyone everything."

The one point on which all the candidates seemed to agree, however, was in their reaction—during the second ninety minutes—against Donahue. He paced up and down the aisle, alternately relaying questions from the audience and posing his own, making a show of trying to force the candidates into simple answers—as if this were a no more serious exercise than one of his daytime television ventures into pop sociology.

The candidates bristled, and at one point Hart stared unsmilingly at Donahue and said: "Slow down, Mr. Donahue."

At another, Glenn, his tone heavy with sarcasm, said: "Maybe you want to come up here and be a ninth candidate."

Just who "won" the debate and just how much it mattered

was a subject of some disagreement later. In one sense, Mondale and Glenn were the winners because the film clips of their exchanges were shown repeatedly on television news programs Sunday night, Monday morning and then again Monday night. And between the two, Mondale seemed to have the better of it, if you could take seriously the limited polling on the question. But the less well-known candidates often register the greatest profit from such exposure, if only because voters are forming first impressions. And by that standard, the winners of the Dartmouth debate were clearly Jesse Jackson and Gary Hart.

This was a significant test for Jackson—his first time in the arena before a national television audience with all these far more experienced, and white, politicians. As he had done in his mission to Syria, Jackson exceeded at least some expectations in this case simply by presenting himself as credible in that company. In fact, Jackson threw around some figures that didn't seem to bear much relationship to reality, and he showed his familiar penchant for seeing every issue through his own particular prism. But he demonstrated to a larger audience that he was articulate and relaxed enough to act as the peacemaker.

The Dartmouth debate did far more for Gary Hart, however, because it was the first time he reached a relatively large audience with a coherent and pointed message on the rationale for his campaign. With some help from Mondale and Glenn, he had made the point that his opponents were still arguing about the past when the future was the issue.

"Gary was able to wedge himself between Glenn and Mondale," Henkel recalled. He did it well enough, moreover, to substantiate the claims that had been made in his behalf by his New Hampshire organization, and to reinforce the word-of-mouth reports on him that had spread throughout the community of younger activist Democrats on the basis of his earlier, essentially retail campaigning.

Hart "had already built his image as a substantial person," Sue Casey said, but now that image had been impressed on many more voters.

"It was the first time," Henkel said, "we had been able to make a concentrated impact on the minds of people generally as it related to Gary's candidacy."

Perhaps most important about that Sunday in Hanover, however, was that it established Hart in the eyes of the press and political community as at least a serious player in the competition for the Democratic nomination. That was apparent in the newspaper reports on the debate and in the fact that to whatever extent television reports went beyond the arm-waving argument between Mondale and Glenn, they focused on Hart and Jackson. Henkel could feel the difference when he went into the press room immediately after the debate.

"It was the first time I was not treated by the press as having leprosy," he recalled. Instead, he found himself being asked serious questions. "There was great interest in Gary," he said.

Sue Casey agreed. "Reporters were saying, 'You know, maybe this guy has a chance' after that," she said later, "[and] that's all we needed."

Pat Caddell was somewhat less buoyant. In fact, flying down to Boston with three reporters late that night in a bitterly cold NBC News charter, he was almost morose. He was surprised at the favorable press reaction, he said later, because he thought Hart had accomplished only about 30 percent of what they intended in that debate—and he was already thinking of ways to get that other 70 percent into the campaign. He accomplished that goal in the speech Hart delivered in Council Bluffs, Iowa, a few days later.

Meanwhile, Mondale's strategists saw no reason for any particular concern. Their tiger, in their view, had clearly prevailed in the confrontation with Glenn, and, in their view, Glenn was still the candidate to watch. A new opinion poll taken January 18 and 19, three and four days after the debate, reinforced the optimism in the Mondale camp. It showed Mondale with 41 percent of those polled, probably the highest point he ever reached, to Glenn with 17 and Hart with 9.

These findings were taken essentially at face value because the political community had not yet relearned for 1984 the lesson about polls and primaries that is taught in one party or the other every four years. Opinion surveys in these situations can be relied upon only as the most general indicators because so many voters don't really focus on their choice until very late in the campaign.

Mondale also had prevailed in the first competition for real, live delegates to the Democratic convention—the selection during the final week of January of the 164 "super-delegates" from the

Democratic majority in the House of Representatives. This process was a prime example of the way the entire delegate-selection process had been distorted to help Mondale.

The Hunt Commission had decided that 568 of the 3,933 votes at the convention would be placed in the hands of party leaders and public officeholders who would arrive at San Francisco officially uncommitted. Thus they could serve as a balance wheel if the party seemed about to veer off into political madness. Although the plan was never put forward in quite these terms, it was an obvious expression of the fear among senior Democrats that another outsider like Jimmy Carter might use the primary process to nail down the nomination. The 164 delegates assigned to the House Democratic Caucus represented a significant potential increase in the congressional influence at the convention; in 1980 only thirty-seven Democratic House members had been delegates.

But the idea of these senior Democrats serving as a kind of board of review was a joke. By the time the caucus voted February 1 to confirm choices made in subgroups over the previous week, only 58 of the 164, about one-third, were still uncommitted. Richard Moe, Mondale's former chief of staff, had handled the caucus campaign and locked up 67 firm commitments to the former Vice President, more than five times as many as any of Mondale's competitors. And one of his commitments was from Speaker Thomas P. (Tip) O'Neill, Jr.

Thus, rather than serving as a balance wheel, the super-delegates were leaping on the Mondale bandwagon that had gained its impetus from nothing more substantial than public-opinion polls and the meaningless inside games of 1983.

In New Hampshire, meanwhile, the polling numbers being studied by the Mondale strategists suggested an essentially static situation. A survey February 2 and 3 put the breakdown at Mondale 36 percent, Glenn 18 and Hart 5. The figures for the following two weeks leading up to the Iowa caucuses on February 20 were little changed except to show small gains by Hart. But there were some changes in the political dynamics that affected the relative positions of the candidates other than Mondale, whose support remained apparently frozen at about one-third of the Democrats who would vote in New Hampshire.

As Alan Cranston's concentration on Iowa became more apparent, his campaign seemed to melt away. It seemed to become plain, too, that neither Reubin Askew, Fritz Hollings nor George McGovern would be a serious factor in New Hampshire. Hart's strength, as measured by unscientific canvassing and polling, rose for about ten days after Dartmouth, then dipped before increasing slightly again.

But if there was a dramatic change, it was in the relative position of Jesse Jackson. Although there was no reason to believe he could win in a state with a black population of less than 1 percent, he had proven intriguing enough to young people and some New Hampshire liberals that it seemed possible he might poll 10 percent of the vote and perhaps even a little more than that.

One of the reasons, clearly, was that Jackson was being treated with kid gloves by his competitors and, to a large degree, by the press. He was not being pushed, for example, to justify such things as a figure he used in the Dartmouth debate for defense cost overruns that exceeded the entire Pentagon budget. To some extent, this tolerance on the part of the press and his rivals reflected the consensus that he was never going to be on the ticket anyway, so why worry about the details of his positions. But there was also a definite fear that criticism of Jackson might be interpreted as racism. And, quite obviously, none of the other candidates wanted to put himself in the position of being the prime adversary of the one black candidate in the field.

But then Jackson made the kind of mistake that cast his candidacy in an entirely different light and robbed it of much of its protective shield.

Early on the morning of January 25, Jackson arrived at National Airport in Washington for a flight south and stopped in the cafeteria lunchroom at the general aviation terminal for breakfast. When he saw two black reporters then assigned to coverage of his campaign, Milton Coleman of the Washington *Post* and Gerald Boyd of the New York *Times*, coming through the line, he invited them to join him at his table.

Coleman remembers Jackson saying: "Let's talk black talk"—which he translated as "Let's talk as black folks" and interpreted it to mean on "background." In the news business, that understanding ordinarily means the reporter is free to use the material but cannot attribute it directly to the source. In many cases, par-

I was traumatized by the reaction to that and I handled it badly by not handling it quickly enough," he said. "It was not something that happened out of anger or protest. It had no religious or political overtones. . . . It has no meaning about religion or politics."

He was also convinced that the reaction was, as he put it, "amplified because of our position on the Middle East, not because of the name. . . . These land mines were set for me."

There was obviously something in that argument. There had been widespread suspicion of Jackson in the Jewish community long before the "Hymie" episode because of his support for a Palestinian homeland and his public embrace of Yasir Arafat, leader of the Palestine Liberation Organization, in 1979. But Jackson also seemed puzzled by the sensitivity on the whole question, pointing out that many times "I have been called 'nigger' and 'boy' and other kinds of names and moved right on, you know, without there being any emotional damage."

Just how much political damage Jackson suffered is impossible to gauge. Ed Theobald, his chief backer in the state, had been nourishing hopes that the vote for Jackson there could demonstrate graphically the potential for white support and a genuine "rainbow coalition." But, when the primary was over, Theobald believed Jackson had been hurt by the delay in dealing with the issue. "I think the damage was done in the interim," he said.

Meanwhile, however, another candidate, John Glenn, began to show some rare signs of political health during that third week in February, apparently as a result of a change in his advertising strategy.

Early in the campaign the Glenn television spots were largely positive, but there never was any indication they were improving his position relative to Mondale. "It didn't move," said David Sawyer, his media consultant. But then the Glenn campaign began running negative ads identifying Mondale as the candidate of the special interests, and the picture quickly changed. Polls taken by Glenn pollster Bill Hamilton that had been showing Mondale with 42 or 43 percent and Glenn with 15 now showed Mondale with 32, Glenn with 25 and Hart with 8 percent. The "internals" also were favorable, showing a sharp increase in the number of voters who considered Mondale "too beholden" to his supporters in those Democratic constituent groups.

"We were going to win New Hampshire," Sawyer said later.

But everything changed radically the night the returns came in from those Iowa precinct caucuses. All the strategies developed over the previous year were suddenly invalidated, all of the calculations of the previous month suddenly tossed aside. The darkest suspicions about John Glenn's basic weakness as a candidate for President of the United States had been confirmed, or so it seemed, by the rejection he suffered in Iowa. And so had the quixotic nature of the campaigns of all of the trailing candidates other than Gary Hart.

Mondale behaved like a proper winner, flying into Manchester the morning after Iowa to announce to a turbulent lunchtime rally at the Chateau restaurant downtown:

"I am ready to win this nomination. I am ready to defeat Mr. Reagan."

Then, as if offering a sample of his general-election campaign, he added:

"The people of New Hampshire won't settle for government by staff, policy by default, management by alibi and leadership by amnesia."

Perhaps the strangest thing, however, was how little credit accrued to Fritz Mondale from Iowa. The former Vice President had captured almost half the vote in those caucuses and had outdistanced his closest pursuer three to one, a performance that ordinarily would give a leading candidate irresistible momentum. But Mondale's success was treated as no more than what everyone expected, and the attention of much of the press—and inevitably the electorate—turned to Gary Hart, the "new face" who had emerged as the prime challenger.

It was clear now to the professionals that Glenn was finished. Bill Hamilton did another New Hampshire survey the day after Iowa and discovered that in twenty-four hours the numbers had turned around. Mondale was up only slightly, at 34 percent, but Hart now had 25 percent and Glenn only 11.

Glenn's chief advisers got the polling data at the Tara, a hotel outside Nashua.

"We walked in that night after Iowa," Sawyer recalled, "looked at the numbers and said that's it for the campaign. . . . We just looked at that stuff and we said, Holy Christ, we're no longer the alternative. In twenty-four hours."

"We were out of the campaign," Sawyer said. "There had to

be one alternative to Mondale. It was no longer Glenn. It was going to be Hart."

There was little question, however, that Glenn had left his mark on Mondale—and that the Hart strategists had understood that. Sawyer recalled Pat Caddell urging him on with the negative advertising.

"We had conversations with Pat Caddell," Sawyer said later. "He'd say, 'Why don't you get that on the air? We're both in this together.' And I'd say, 'Come on, Pat, I know what you're doing,' and he'd laugh. He knew we were the only ones who had the money to take Mondale out of New Hampshire."

The Mondale campaign was equally aware that the Iowa results had changed the dynamics. Peter Hart, Mondale's polling consultant, conducted a survey February 21 and 22, the two days immediately after the caucuses, and found just how much things had changed. The matchup numbers, when compared to those in a poll just before Iowa, showed the new order but were not particularly dramatic. In the pre-Iowa poll it had been Mondale 34, Glenn 19 and Hart 10. Now it was Mondale up to 38, Glenn down to 12 and Hart up sharply to 17.

But a "feeling thermometer" measure pointed to more serious trouble for Mondale, in several respects. The data showed Glenn fading rapidly and positive attitudes toward Hart rising much faster than his raw support score of 17 percent, which Peter Hart characterized as "just the tip of the iceberg." The polling also showed negative feelings toward Mondale among 15 percent of the total who claimed to be undecided. In short, there were many reasons to believe Hart would continue to close on Mondale in the remaining days of the campaign as more and more New Hampshire voters came to see the contest as a choice between the two men.

"What I saw was 'Hold it, folks, all the positive feelings haven't been translated,' " Peter Hart recalled later.

The Mondale managers had considered the possibility of some other candidate getting some dangerous momentum out of Iowa. They even discussed the possibility of trying to arrange the election schedule so that the New Hampshire primary would be the very next day after the Iowa caucuses—thus leaving the minimum time for anyone else to capitalize on his momentum. In the end, Beckel recalled, they decided it was "too risky" to attempt because the scheme was likely to be revealed to the press and offend voters in both states.

But a distilled two-candidate race in New Hampshire was never the one the Mondale strategists considered the most likely. On the contrary, their planning had been based on the assumption that Mondale's one-third of the vote would be quite adequate if the rest of the vote were splintered. In the last similar multi-candidate Democratic competition, in 1976, Jimmy Carter had won the New Hampshire primary with just under 30 percent to 24 for Morris Udall, 16 for Birch Bayh, 11 for Fred Harris, and 9 for Sargent Shriver. The Mondale campaign expected something roughly similar.

"We were optimistic," Jim Johnson said, "because we thought we would have a seven- or eight-man race in New Hampshire."

There was one critical difference from 1976, however. Carter had ridden into New Hampshire on Iowa momentum that year as well, but there had been five weeks between the two contests. And that relatively long period gave the other candidates some time to revive their campaigns and Carter some time to cool down. By contrast, this time there was only eight days, and Gary Hart was coming toward primary day with his momentum on the rise, as Peter Hart's polling figures demonstrated.

Hart's new stature was evident in a dozen ways. The networks and local television stations in Boston, almost equally important in this situation, vied with one another in putting him on the air live for one interview after another. Newspapermen who had given him little attention suddenly were playing catch-up in droves. And money began to pour into the Hart campaign in quantities that made it possible for the New Hampshire media buy, which had been running a scant $10,000 to $15,000 a week, to reach $100,000 for the final eight days. As is so often the case, the candidate was finally getting the money to buy advertising at just the time his campaign had reached the point where he needed it least because of the news coverage he was getting.

Sue Casey knew things had changed by Thursday when, three days after Iowa, the campaign drove into a hazardous-waste site in Londonderry and found eighty credentialed press—Hart himself remembered it as two hundred—covering this "event" of such dubious newsworthiness. Even a handshaking walk down Manchester's main drag, Elm Street, became a practical impossibility because of the huge throng of reporters and television technicians swarming around the latest fad in American politics.

"It was," Hart recalled much later, "amazing."

Moreover, one stroke of good luck seemed to follow another. Casey had scheduled Hart into a woodsmen's field day in Berlin in northern New Hampshire on the final Saturday of the campaign. She had planned very carefully to limit his participation to a log throw and to pulling one end of a two-man saw. She had specifically ruled out throwing an ax when told that feat took considerable skill.

"We didn't want him in any event where he was going to embarrass himself," she said.

But Hart, who had changed into jeans for the occasion, jumped into the ax-throwing competition on his own. After but a single miss, he hurled the ax into the bullseye—before cameras that recorded it on tape shown repeatedly all through that final weekend.

"That first one was Iowa," an ebullient Hart told the crowd. "The second one was New Hampshire."

Looking back, Casey shuddered at what might have happened if the determined Hart had not succeeded so quickly. "We could have been there for a week," she said.[22]

By Sunday, the extraordinary response was clearly evident to the naked eye. For example, 500 to 600 people arrived in pairs or small family groups to hear Hart speak that afternoon at a church meeting hall in Nashua. It was obviously the kind of crowd created more by spontaneous interest than by efforts of the advance men. And, as such, it was a crowd made up of people genuinely curious about Gary Hart and perhaps predisposed to be enthusiastic.

The Mondale managers were back on their heels.

"I knew Gary got a lot [out of Iowa]," Jim Johnson said later, "but he got a lot more than I thought."

Moreover, Johnson said, the Hart campaign did all the right things to take advantage of the situation. "He had a good schedule,

22. Republican George Romney created one of the enduring legends of New Hampshire primary lore when, in the 1968 campaign, he visited a duckpin bowling alley and tried his luck. He knocked down nine of the ten pins with the first two balls. Then, his teeth gritted and the cameras whirring, he took thirty-four more balls to get that final pin.

he had good events, the TV was good," he said. "I give them credit as a campaign for really rolling the dice financially."

Chuck Campion was also wary. He had been, he said later, elated by Mondale's victory in Iowa, but now he could see Hart's extraordinary ride on the television news, and reporters were telling him that Hart was on a roll.

Mondale himself realized there might be trouble.

"I always thought New Hampshire was going to be tough," he said much later. "You have the state there with the worst newspaper in the Western Hemisphere [the Manchester *Union Leader*] pounding me every day. You have the fact that, in the absence of a Republican fight, the Republicans could pretty easily cross over, or a lot of them can . . . the so-called independents there came over. Our surveys never showed us in a safe position in New Hampshire . . . I never felt that secure.

"When I realized it could be dangerous was after the Iowa caucuses, when I got there. That's when we started hearing, you know, about a lot of erosion in our position. And by the weekend it was clear that the thing was deteriorating."

By late Saturday afternoon, the final Peter Hart poll for Mondale was in, showing him still leading by thirteen percentage points but with all the indicators moving in an unsettling direction. Campaign manager Bob Beckel later recalled somewhat ruefully a meeting with Johnson and Hart in the poll-taker's Washington office.

"Any chance we could lose this thing?" Johnson asked.

"Oh, eighty-twenty," Hart replied, meaning heavily against losing.

"No, a hundred to nothing, no way," said Beckel, raising the ante.

At the Sheraton Wayfarer Sunday morning, Gary Hart had reached the giddy stage when he came to the room of Tom Ottenad of the St. Louis *Post-Dispatch* to have coffee and orange juice with us and three or four other reporters. Hart was stretched out on one of the beds, propped against a headboard, while we asked questions speculating on how close he might come to Mondale.

Then Bob Healy of the Boston *Globe* asked: "What happens if you win here?"

Hart was dumbstruck. He started to answer, then he began

to laugh almost uncontrollably, face red, eyes watering. It was contagious and soon everyone in the room was dissolved in laughter—to the obvious puzzlement of the Secret Service agents posted outside the open door and the staff down the hall who could hear the howls of laughter.

After the fact, Hart said that by that stage of the campaign "we knew that whatever happened, we had won and that I was ahead of my timetable," even if he finished a close second. His laughter, Hart contended, "was partly to avoid answering the question." But what it looked like at the time was a candidate simply carried away by his own unexpected good fortune.[23]

On Sunday night word spread through the Wayfarer that the latest ABC News-Washington *Post* poll was showing the contest narrowing—down to a Mondale lead of seven or eight percentage points, the kind of margin that might be overcome in another day. After John Reilly called Johnson in Washington to pass on the latest piece of grim news, the Mondale managers began preparing for the worst.

They believed, Johnson said, that there was "an enormous importance to the smell of what you did" the day after a primary in conditioning voters' attitudes toward the next contest. In this case, plans already had been made to take Mondale to Georgia and Alabama on Wednesday. Johnson wanted to give a "clear signal" that Mondale intended to compete fully in the southern primaries March 13, the date set by the front-loading strategy for the final elimination of any serious competition for the nomination.

Now, with the bad news in New Hampshire, Johnson added another stop that he hoped would send an instant signal of viability—a handshaking appearance at a Boston subway stop with Massachusetts Governor Michael S. Dukakis the morning after New Hampshire. Reilly and Johnson also began the business of letting the candidate in on the bad news. They telephoned him about 6:30 AM Monday in Boston with those ABC numbers that

23. After the election Hart, George McGovern's old campaign manager, liked to say that he had seen his own New Hampshire victory coming long before anyone else. One night early in January, he told us, he had dinner with Casey, Shaheen and Dan Calegari, another top organizer in the state, and told them: "I think we're going to win this primary." What he didn't recall as well were other occasions, later in the game, when he was far less certain of the outcome.

would be in the morning papers, and alerted him to the possibility the worst might still be ahead.

"We sort of eased into it," Johnson recalled.

The Mondale campaign in New Hampshire ended on an appropriate note early Monday—with still another endorsement of his candidacy by another politician. This one was delivered by Boston Mayor Raymond L. Flynn and, Johnson said, "locked Boston TV into what we wanted" beamed into all those New Hampshire homes on election eve. It was true that Flynn, who had been elected only a few months earlier, was a popular figure whose appeal theoretically might be expected to extend to many of those southern New Hampshire Democrats who worked in Boston or considered themselves de facto Bostonians. But the notion of still another endorsement from a politician stemming the Hart tide was laughable—and, if anything, another subliminal confirmation that Fritz Mondale was the old-fashioned politician Gary Hart had been painting him to be all along.

On primary day, rain, snow and wind-driven sleet swept across New Hampshire. The weather was so bad it held the turnout to 101,000 Democrats where 120,000 had been expected to vote—weather bad enough, according to the conventional wisdom, to help the candidate with the best organization, in this case Fritz Mondale. But by noon reports on the television networks' exit polls were buzzing through the crowds of reporters and politicians gathered at the Wayfarer. Gary Hart was winning and winning big.

A few hours later, it was official. Hart had captured 39 percent to 27 for Mondale, 12 for Glenn, and 5 or less for each of the others.

Chuck Campion, shattered after fifteen months of planning and organizing, raced out to the Manchester airport to meet Mondale, who was arriving to make his concession statement. The motorcade was already pulling away, but Mondale spotted his young coordinator, stopped the car and opened the door so Campion could hop in. Joan Mondale, herself a veteran of months of campaigning at Campion's side, hugged him.

"The first thing I want you to know," Mondale told him, "is that I know that you did everything you could."

"He was very solicitous of me," Campion recalled later. "He was very concerned about me."

At the Chateau downtown, Gary Hart waved a finger in the air and told the cheering crowd and cameras: "I love New Hampshire."

A few miles away, at Peter C's restaurant in Bedford, Mondale told despondent young backers he had been given "a cold shower" but intended to press on.

"They didn't want the debate to end here," he insisted that night. "In a sense, they voted to carry on."

It was a world-class rationalization, but in the Mondale campaign there were no easy answers. They had done everything anyone could reasonably expect either a candidate or organization to do. They had followed all the traditional practices.

"I thought we had done it by New Hampshire's rules and done it perfectly by the rules," said Campion, "and it just didn't matter."

The hard truth—and it was too hard to expect the Mondale organization to accept then—was that there were very definite limits on the number of voters who would support Fritz Mondale when given what appeared to be a reasonable alternative in Gary Hart. An NBC News poll of voters who had just cast their ballots found that Mondale prevailed among those who identified themselves as strong Democrats, but that Hart beat him two to one among other Democrats and three to one among independents.

That night, after Mondale had returned to Boston, most of his leading advisers—Johnson, Beckel, Peter Hart, Tom Donilon, Mike Ford, Roy Spence and one or two others who wandered in and out—met around a dining table in a small frame cottage on the Wayfarer grounds. For several hours, over the ubiquitous cheeseburgers and a few beers, they tried to sort out what had happened and what needed to be done. There was no panic, and those who attended the meeting said Johnson kept focusing on what needed to be done to correct whatever had gone sour in New Hampshire.

"It was typical Johnson," one of the participants said later. "It was a 'What have we got to do now?' mentality."

"We had a smell of the thing coming, so it wasn't that we were surprised that we got knocked off," Beckel said later. "The size of it surprised us. . . . The question then was, What the hell do we do? Where the hell do we try to stop the brushfire?"

The talk went on into the small hours of the morning without any conclusions being reached. The operative question was clearly when and how intensively Mondale should begin attacking Gary Hart. Beckel and Donilon, the bright young delegate-hunter, argued vigorously for—in Beckel's phrase—"taking him on." Johnson and Hart questioned whether "going negative" might not backfire, coming from a candidate who had just been beaten so badly.

"My argument on the other side," Beckel said later, "was if you don't, you're gone."

The meeting finally adjourned without any conclusions about long-range strategy. But it was decided that Beckel, who had worked in Maine for Jimmy Carter in 1980, would move over there the next day to assume command of that campaign. And there was still no evidence Maine would be a problem. "They had no idea about Maine then," Chuck Campion recalled. "I think they felt good about Maine."

In a press briefing in the shabby Mondale headquarters in downtown Manchester the next morning, Beckel, Hart and Ford, the field director, tried manfully to put a good face on the defeat before an extremely skeptical audience.

Mondale had suffered, said Beckel, because all the other candidates had been attacking him throughout the campaign and because so many of them simply folded themselves. The vote wasn't really a "negative referendum" on Mondale, said Peter Hart. His polling showed Mondale to be the second choice of most of the Gary Hart voters and a candidate who evoked positive feelings from the electorate. The real pip, however, was the echo of Mondale from the night before—that the New Hampshire result was "a process vote" showing, said Mike Ford, the voters wanted to "continue the dialogue" because they weren't ready to make up their minds.

In fact, neither Mondale nor his advisers quite knew what to make of this stunning development now that it was there in the hard, cold figures. Mondale himself was, by all accounts, surprised by the size of the Hart margin but convinced they had done everything they could have done. Looking back later, Johnson speculated that if you had assembled forty political experts someone might have come up with a different idea for breaking through that 35 or 40 percent ceiling on Mondale support in New Hampshire. But the Mondale managers themselves had never done so during the campaign.

"We kept asking the question over and over and over and over again," Johnson said, "but we were asking *ourselves*. We were considering traditional strategies."

Meanwhile, the end of the road was at hand for several of the other players. At Concord Alan Cranston announced at an early morning press conference: "I know the difference between reality and dreams. I know when to dream and how to count votes."

About the same time, in the dining room of the Wayfarer eighteen miles to the south, Fritz Hollings was shaking hands with reporters and saying good-by to the campaign. "I've had enough," he said.

Support for his proposal for a one-year budget freeze "was out there," Hollings told us after the election, but he was never as a southerner able to establish enough credibility to be taken seriously. Had the process started in someplace like Louisiana, he said, he might have gotten off to a strong start, but "I tried to do it all in New Hampshire" and just couldn't get going. And to the end, the doors that Glenn's celebrity opened for him rankled Hollings.

"I'm still frustrated," he said. "I walked into the insurance company there in Manchester, and I know how to make shifts and talk to people and politick. I went to fourteen floors with three little reporters straggling from South Carolina. John Glenn pulls in, he's got two busloads. He talks to the executives and leaves. Now that's bad politics for the insurance company but that's wonderful politics in a national race, because that night he had an AP wire story, he was on national TV, 'John Glenn Politicking in New Hampshire Today.' Nothing, nothing, nothing on Hollings. Then along comes Howell Raines [of the New York *Times*] and says, 'Hollings runs a lackluster campaign.' Christ, I didn't see the New York *Times* and Howell Raines. They were lackluster, not me. I was out there hustling. Working my fanny off. But I just couldn't attract them."

As Hollings headed home, his fellow-southerner Reubin Askew was flying south to make his withdrawal statement on home ground, his 1-percent showing having obviously destroyed the credibility of his campaign even in his own state of Florida.

The end was also at hand for John Glenn, although the Democrat from Ohio was not willing to concede without giving those southern primaries a run two weeks down the road. The real meaning of Mondale's defeat, he kept insisting, was the voters were looking for an alternative but not necessarily just Gary Hart.

"I thought it reopened the campaign," Glenn said later, "and I wasn't just blowing smoke."

Bob Keefe had a different concern. He realized Glenn was finished, and all he could see ahead was growing debt and campaign workers bearing the brunt of a fruitless exercise.

"When you get into the final throes of a campaign moneywise," he said later, "you start hurting the wrong people, in my opinion. The staff that can ill afford it gets stiffed . . . they go off salary. They get stiffed on expenses. The Skinner Donahues of the world"—a reference to a respected Boston organizer—"you can love him or hate him, but when he gets into something, he pours himself in it and you shouldn't stiff guys like that."

On primary night Glenn would hear no talk of quitting, however. And although most of his staff agreed in a meeting of their own that, as Keefe put, "John Glenn was not going to be the nominee of his party," no one was willing to bell the cat. The following day Keefe sent a memorandum to Glenn making his point.

"I just told him there was no real hope of winning," he recalled. "It was important to recognize as you go further, you start asking people who are your best friends to do things that hurt them." But Glenn was still convinced the race was wide open.

In fact, as a shocked Mondale campaign and a delighted Hart campaign quickly discovered, the Hart "fire storm" had by no means run its course.

As Mondale did his handshaking in Boston and flew off for a day of showing the flag in Alabama, Beckel drove to Portland to prepare for the Sunday caucuses. From the outset, the Mondale strategists had supported a party rules exemption to allow Maine to hold these early caucuses because they viewed them as an insurance policy—a place to make a quick recovery in the unlikely event Mondale stumbled in New Hampshire. Now it was time to cash in that policy.

"Nobody had any illusions about how big Hart's victory was in New Hampshire," Jim Johnson recalled. "We knew we had to do everything conceivable to win those Maine caucuses."

Thus, over the next five days, the campaign moved 150 people into the state to work for Beckel, pulling every available body out of campaign headquarters and other states.

"We cleaned out Washington," Johnson said, "and we cleaned out New Hampshire"—including the shock troops under Joe Trippi, who had been flown there from Iowa. Without conceding the state publicly, the Mondale managers decided to abandon Vermont, where a presidential preference or "beauty contest" vote was scheduled the following Tuesday. The canvassing there had shown another disaster in the making.

On paper, the situation in Maine seemed hospitable. Hart had only a skeleton organization of young supporters led by a twenty-four-year-old state coordinator, Ron Briggs. Mondale's organization, directed by a state legislator from Lewiston named Greg Nadeau, already had shown its mettle in winning that straw vote back in October—a straw vote, they were quick to note, that Gary Hart had snubbed. And Nadeau had compiled a list of 32,000 supporters in the state. As usual, Mondale also had the backing of the leading and most popular figures in the Democratic Party—Governor Joseph Brennan, Senator George Mitchell, former governor and Democratic National Chairman Kenneth Curtis.

But none of that counted when the time came. The Democratic voters on the Mondale lists had been rated on the usual scale in politics—one to five, in descending order of support for the candidate, meaning that the "ones" are those considered solid backers. But when Mondale workers began telephone canvassing Wednesday night, Joe Trippi said later, they found first 40 percent and later 55 percent of their "ones" defecting to Hart. By Thursday night, new polling figures showed Mondale running ten to fifteen points behind Hart. Beckel responded with some hastily produced radio spots charging Hart had supported a nuclear build-down and a ten-dollar-a-barrel tax on imported oil. Television spots featuring the endorsement of George Mitchell were run, and an endorsement from former Senator Edmund S. Muskie was produced.

Mondale himself flew into Augusta on Friday and did the only thing a conventional politician could do in such circumstances. He dragged out his bona fides—posing for pictures on a stairway in the statehouse with Brennan, Mitchell, Curtis and several dozen state legislators and officials who had endorsed him.

Hart also made a late foray into Maine, but the contrast with Mondale made it clear what was happening. On Saturday, as the newspapers carried the picture from Augusta of what looked like a Mondale politburo, Hart spoke at a rally in a park in Portland.

It was a bright but cold day, and the wind blowing over the park off Casco Bay was biting even in the sunshine. But 300 to 400 people showed up, in groups of twos or threes, many of them waiting more than an hour to see this new political phenomenon.

The returns from the 414 town caucuses confirmed the picture. Hart had 50.7 percent, Mondale 43.7 percent. At the Sheraton Portland, where the results were being tabulated, the politicians who had supported Mondale and the union organizers who had worked for him were equally stunned.

"There was nothing we could do," one labor skate said, gesturing with his glass of scotch. "Our members were telling us they were voting for Hart because Mondale was making too many promises to us—to our own union, for Christ's sake."

The shock was even greater inside the Mondale camp. The candidate himself, his advisers said, was "distraught" as he went through the motions of attending a Massachusetts Democratic Party dinner in Boston while the figures were being compiled. Later Mondale remembered the jolt.

"I always felt better about Maine than New Hampshire, and I expected to do better than we did there," he said. "I think a month before New Hampshire I'd have carried Maine easily, but the spillover from New Hampshire . . . was devastating."[24]

Mondale had thought he had established lasting rapport with those Maine Democrats when he visited those forty-one Maine communities the previous fall. Now he was discovering that effort counted for nothing when matched against the celebrity Gary Hart had achieved from his success in New Hampshire.

By the next morning, the public Mondale was carrying it all off with his characteristic insouciance. "Somebody told me this morning that this is building character," he told reporters. "I think I've got more character already than I can use."

But the show of bravado masked a candidate who, for the first time in fourteen months of active campaigning, had reason to question whether all his careful calculations and elaborate strategies had any validity at all.

"That was the moment," Johnson said later, "at which emo-

24. Hart showed a cutting edge at that dinner when he described Mondale sardonically as "a little-known dark horse struggling to get by on twelve million dollars and the AFL-CIO endorsement." The sally drew hisses and boos from the audience, largely made up of Democratic regulars backing Mondale.

tionally we understood how big the tidal wave was, and we understood there was a real chance that Hart would be the nominee."

But if Fritz Mondale was not prepared for what happened to him in New Hampshire and then in Maine, it was equally true that Gary Hart was not prepared for what lay just ahead.

8

Dodging the Bullet

•

THE NIGHT OF MARCH 6, as Fritz Mondale was losing still another New England primary to Gary Hart in Vermont, he reached a turning point in Florida.

Mondale's situation was desperate—and he knew it.

"That first explosion of the Hart phenomenon was like a hurricane," he recalled. "I couldn't get my feet on the ground."

The Super Tuesday primaries on March 13—once seen as the events in which John Glenn would finally be eliminated—now had become a last chance for Mondale.

"I figured if I got clobbered that Tuesday," he said later, "I was done, and I was prepared to pull out."

But not without a last fling. Walking into the Curtis Hixon Convention Center in Tampa where several hundred supporters had gathered for a rally in the Gasparilla Room, Mondale told Jim Quackenbush, the lawyer from South Carolina who served as coordinator of his campaign in the South:

"I'm going to really give 'em hell out there."

The result was a speech in which Mondale reaffirmed his own definition of what the Democratic Party represented and, by implication, handed down a finding that Gary Hart did not qualify to speak for that party. The speech was, in essence, simply another reprise of the marathon arguments about the past that had been consuming the Democratic candidates for more than a year now—and had almost nothing to do with the direct concerns of the voters who would be choosing a President for the next four years.

"We are about to decide," Mondale told the cheering crowd, "whether we are a generous party and a caring nation or whether we're not. We will determine whether we care about people and average working families who've always been at the core of the Democratic Party or we won't. We will decide whether we will be a party that follows the polls or is led by principle."

Closely examined, this final point was a particularly curious argument coming from a candidate who for more than a year had been telling Democrats that the primary reason to support him was that his nomination was inevitable. Although Mondale himself had publicly disparaged the opinion polls, his case had rested heavily on their evidence that he was the dominant figure in the party all through 1983 and the first two months of 1984—until those polls were exposed as an inaccurate gauge of voter sentiment in New Hampshire, Maine and now Vermont. There Gary Hart was that very day winning 71 percent of the vote in a "beauty contest" presidential preference ballot. Now Mondale was saying, in effect, that even if his nomination was no longer inevitable, it was the principled choice in a contest for "the soul of the Democratic Party." And without mentioning Hart by name, Mondale cast his rival in terms that clearly defined him as beyond the pale.

"Today there's a new argument in the land, a new idea about the Democratic Party and where it should go," he told the Tampa crowd. "This I believe is the essence of the battle we're in. If you fight for values that the party has always believed in, you're supposed to go on a guilt trip, but if you fight against them, you're supposed to be applauded. If you fight for better schools, you're old. But you fight for big oil, you're new. If you fight for civil rights, that's a special interest. But if you buckle to the hospital lobby, that's a new idea.

"If you defend Medicare, you're cautious, but you attack entitlements, you're courageous. If seniors want Social Security, that's the past, but AT&T wants to tack a big bill on your phone for the privilege of using long-distance lines, that's the future. If a worker wants a raise, that's greedy, but if a plant closes down, that's trendy. If you want big corporations to pay their share of taxes, you're old hat. If you want working families to pay more in taxes, that's high tech. I don't accept it."

The speech was not universally admired, even within Mondale's own campaign. Jim Johnson, for one, thought it was too harsh and warned Mondale it might be risky to go that far again. But others were delighted at this evidence of the emergence of "Fighting Fritz" now that their backs were to the wall.

"It was," Quackenbush said much later, "at an absolute low point for us. . . . It [the speech] gave a lot of spirit back to the campaign."

Others in the campaign also were buoyed up by Mondale's aggressive posture. Tom Donilon, for example, believed the key element after New Hampshire was Mondale's "ability to internalize a change of strategy totally, on a dime" and then implement it.

The most important thing, however, was probably what the speech represented in terms of Mondale's own attitude toward his opponent and the political assignment he now confronted. Mondale had been resisting the demands for attacks on Hart that had originated in that "cottage meeting" the night of the New Hampshire primary. And he had rejected as too tough the first version of a speech assailing Hart that Martin Kaplan, his talented chief speechwriter, had prepared.

Like most politicians, Mondale genuinely didn't like cutting up people in his own party. As he put it to us long after the election: "I hate party fights. . . . I was hoping to get the nomination with as little intraparty bloodletting as possible because I always had in mind that I wanted a nomination that was worth something."

But—again like most successful politicians—Mondale could manage to find a justification for taking the offensive when it was required.

"All this time, meanwhile," he said, "Hart was dumping on me, as I guess is to be expected in a situation like that. And so it was clear that I had to join the debate with Gary Hart and I did. . . . After New Hampshire, there was never any alternative."

Mondale seemed to realize that he didn't have a wealth of material for attacks; Hart's voting record was so much like his own on so many issues. He needed a rationale or at least a rationalization, and—lo and behold—one emerged as he struggled for survival. Just as he had decided several months earlier that John Glenn was not a "real" Democrat, Mondale now judged, in effect, that Gary Hart did not qualify because he stood for change. Mondale always put his assaults in terms of "joining the debate" with his younger opponent, but what he was really doing was "going negative" against Hart.

The burden of the argument, with the bark off, was that Hart did not meet the Democratic Party standards for compassion and sensitivity, at least as Mondale understood them. In an interview with Dan Balz of the Washington *Post* after the Tampa speech, he put it this way:

"I think there's always been this neo-liberal approach that disdains what I view to be a fundamental and sacred objective of the Democratic Party, which is to pursue fairness and stand up against interests that are powerful and that only a President can resist effectively."

This view translated during those days into any shred of evidence that might be used to question Hart's bona fides on traditional liberal concerns. Mondale questioned Hart's commitment on civil rights because Hart, after voting thirteen times against lifting the embargo on Rhodesian chrome, had voted on another occasion in favor of a "sense of the Senate" resolution in favor of Rhodesia. ("They were always finding some shitty little vote to use against us," a Hart adviser complained later.) And Mondale made a point of the fact that, as he said repeatedly, Hart had written a book about the nation's problems and "never mentioned civil rights in 180 pages." That accusation was technically correct, that he didn't use those words, but it wasn't true that Hart did not deal with the issue in the book.

And the fact was that Hart's voting record on most liberal litmus-test issues—civil rights, women's rights, arms control, the environment—was every bit as consistent as Mondale's own. And on one of those watershed issues for liberals, the war in Vietnam, Hart's record was clearly stronger than Mondale's.

But this was no time to quibble. In a television interview right after New Hampshire, Mondale had said:

"The American people are asking, 'Who is this Gary Hart? What does he stand for?' "

Hart enjoyed what the politicians like to call "a clean slate"—and to the extent that Hart failed to fill in all the blank spaces himself, Fritz Mondale was going to do it for him and in his own terms.

There already had been one small indication, moreover, that Hart might be vulnerable. Even before the research from Mondale headquarters could be produced, Beckel had come up with those two issues he used in the final days of the Maine campaign. Hart's position on a proposed ten-dollar-a-barrel tax on imported oil, an element of an "energy independence" plan, could be expected to be unpopular in New England, where people relied heavily on fuel oil for heating. And his backing of the nuclear "build-down"—a scheme for destroying two old missiles for every new one built—was something liberals might see as an either/or alternative to support for a nuclear freeze. That issue could be used to especially good effect with Maine Democrats, the Mondale operatives believed, because one of its chief sponsors was a Maine Republican, Senator William Cohen. Beckel wrote the two commercials in his hotel room, then found a local radio announcer to record them and put them on the air—a strategy he believed helped bring some support back to Mondale in the final forty-eight hours before the caucuses.

Hart, however, was still riding the crest of that political tidal wave. He now had a big chartered jet full of reporters. His picture was on the covers of all the magazines. In each new community he would visit, the local television stations would be lined up to bring him to their viewers, live and in living color. He was, in short, enjoying an extraordinary celebrity.

"Hart the winner of the New Hampshire primary," Hart himself told us later, "was not Hart the senator from Colorado. . . . It was a Jekyll-Hyde. I had gone from this dull candidate within twenty-four hours to a candidate with splash, dash and glitter."

There were, nonetheless, serious problems for Hart in this sudden success. It was now necessary to move from a two-state to a fifty-state strategy, and he had neither the money nor the staff to do so very quickly. And although the money began pouring in, as it does to winners in politics, the business of going big time with the campaign was difficult. Inside the operation there was predictable resistance to bringing in more "outsiders" to help—even such acknowledged professionals as Sergio Bendixen, now at liberty after Cranston's collapse, or Phil Wise, the onetime Carter hand who had been helping Askew. If you hadn't been for Gary before New Hampshire, you simply lacked the credential of faith that was essential.

And the tugging and hauling between Pudge Henkel and Pat Caddell had become even more intense as Caddell pressed for a more aggressive posture, which he was convinced could finish off Mondale by the time of the Illinois primary a week after Super Tuesday. The relationship was so bad, in fact, that on more than one occasion Henkel simply misled Caddell to put an end to an argument. In addition to telling him about that media buy in Iowa that was never made, Henkel promised to run an anti-labor commercial in New Hampshire and distributed it to stations with instructions it should be held for release, which was never given. In the aftermath of the New Hampshire primary, there was one period of ten days in which these two senior advisers to Hart weren't even speaking to one another.

But all of these problems behind the scenes couldn't take any of the steam out of Hart's momentum. Opinion polls taken by Peter Hart showed the Mondale campaign just how formidable a task it faced. In Massachusetts, a survey made right after the New Hampshire primary but before the Maine caucuses showed Hart leading Mondale, 45 to 25 percent, the same margin by which Mondale had been leading John Glenn there in mid-January. And on a "feeling thermometer" measure, Hart received 80 percent positive to only 4 percent negative reactions.

"That's how quickly that thing swept," Peter Hart said.

The Gary Hart tide also was apparent in two southern states, Florida and Georgia. In Florida, Mondale was still leading Hart, 36 to 30 percent in polling done for Mondale on March 3, the day before Maine. But further polling four and five days later showed Hart ahead, 41 to 32 percent. In Georgia, Peter Hart's polls showed Mondale leading Hart by 20 percentage points immediately following the New Hampshire primary but the race essentially even by March 6, the night Mondale made that speech in Tampa. Only in Alabama was Mondale still holding a substantial lead over Hart going into the final week before Super Tuesday.

Super Tuesday was the term the politicians and press had coined long before to apply to March 13, the first day of the officially sanctioned delegate-selection period. On that day primaries would be held in those three southern states, Massachusetts and Rhode Island, and caucuses would be held in four others—Washington, Nevada, Oklahoma and Hawaii. Taken together, the nine states offered a prize of 511 of the 1,967 delegates needed to win the nomination at San Francisco.

Although the delegate prize was significant, the campaign was still at the stage at which perceptions and images were paramount—fortunately for Hart. In Florida, he was so unprepared for success he had candidates running in his name for only thirty-four of the eighty-four congressional district slots. Hart solved the problem by enlisting, with Reubin Askew's tacit approval, many of those who were running under the Askew banner. But the real contest was for proof of popular support in the preferential voting. If Gary Hart could win Super Tuesday—whatever that meant—it would be difficult indeed to argue that his success was based on atypical small-state electorates in New England. Nor, conversely, could it then be argued that Mondale's losses in these states were aberrations easily explained away. This time the tests were all over the map.

It was clear, however, that the battleground would be much smaller. Even as the votes were being counted in Maine on March 4, Mondale's leading backer in Massachusetts, Governor Michael S. Dukakis, was telling him privately that the primary there was probably a lost cause.

The next morning, Jim Johnson said later, "we knew that everything was changing. We knew we had to get into the three southern states as soon as possible." So, although they wouldn't concede the fact publicly, the Mondale strategists abandoned Massachusetts and Rhode Island and turned their attention to the South.

This decision meant that the only active opposition to Hart in Massachusetts was coming from George McGovern, who couldn't quit without giving it a whirl in the only state he carried against Richard M. Nixon in 1972. McGovern said he would withdraw if he didn't finish either first or "a strong second" in Massachusetts, but there was no polling data that suggested he was a threat to Hart there. And Rhode Island, by every measure, was prepared to make it a clean sweep of New England for the senator from Colorado.[25]

It was becoming clear to Mondale's managers that their situation was extremely perilous.

Early on March 7, Jim Johnson flew to Atlanta for a meeting with Mondale and John Reilly, his senior adviser, at Hartsfield Airport in Atlanta.

"I gave him a complete, honest report on where we were and

25. Although Gary Hart had been his campaign manager in that 1972 campaign, McGovern made it clear on more than one occasion that his own choice was Mondale. In an interview with Kathy Sawyer of the Washington *Post*, for instance, McGovern said: "I feel more at home listening to Mondale than I do listening to someone who says this is a contest between the past and the future. I really don't know what that means." McGovern finished a weak third in Massachusetts and promptly withdrew.

the possibility that he had one more week to go and had to find something to win," Johnson recalled. "We had to target resources and he had to speak with a level of clarity and emotion."

Long after the fact, Mondale recalled that meeting in even bleaker terms.

"Johnson flew down to the South where I was campaigning to tell me that it was probably over, that the momentum for Hart was so strong that it was doubtful we could turn it around," he said. The campaign was "slipping dramatically," and, "more than that, we weren't being listened to."

The outlook was so disheartening that Mondale had begun to think of this southern campaign swing as a kind of valedictory.

"I said, then, I think we ought to make my case for history about what I felt was important. . . . Those were important speeches and ones that I felt very deeply about. But the genesis of that was that we were probably done and I ought to be saying some things that defined important issues."

There was, however, no fixed standard in Mondale's mind. Although he was ready to withdraw if "clobbered," there was no rigid criterion. "I would say if we'd only won one state, particularly if we won it marginally, it was probably over," he said later.

So Johnson's "something to win" obviously meant at least two of the three southern states. Mondale decided to intensify his schedule there, campaign through the final weekend without ducking home to Washington and forget about planned forays into Oklahoma and Washington state. He would surrender in Massachusetts—the state in which he had taken so much satisfaction from winning one of those straw polls eleven months and a political millennium earlier.

What Johnson did not tell Mondale in that Atlanta meeting, however, was that he and Michael Berman, a lawyer who had been with Mondale longer than anyone else in the campaign, already had begun to discuss between themselves the possibility that Mondale would have to withdraw within a few days. Although both insisted they never actually wrote a draft statement for Mondale, they agreed they wanted to prepare Mondale to, as Johnson put it, "end in a dignified, classy way" if it came to that.

Berman, who had been supervising the fund-raising for the campaign but had a reputation for excellent political instincts, and Johnson had made it a practice to talk on the telephone every morning, usually about seven o'clock. In one of those calls in the final week of the Super Tuesday campaign, Berman recalled, "Jim—I don't remember his exact words—essentially said it could be that we're going to get knocked out . . . and we need to be sure that if that happens, we're prepared to help Mondale go through that period and do it in a way that is consistent with the way he's tried to be in public life his entire life." They made tentative plans for making the withdrawal announcement in Minneapolis and Washington and for notifying the staff, and drew up lists of people for Mondale to telephone in advance or thank for their help. In short, they did what good political staff people are supposed to do and laid the groundwork for their principal.

But it wasn't easy. Berman said:

"I remember vividly that—you have to remember I'm sitting there at that stage nineteen, almost twenty years with Walter Mondale. So I have a fair amount invested in it in time, an extraordinary amount of emotion. I have great feelings of love for him as a person, and that was a morning I could not do a fucking thing the entire day on that issue. I went to sixteen other things. I could not put pencil on paper. . . . One whole day went by and the next day I just sat down and I start writing. Jim and I met on the third day to go over it, in the morning, and he had a couple of ideas and I made some changes and we then had, quote-unquote, a plan for what we would do if the unmentionable occurred."

Even in this plan, however, there was no arbitrary standard set for when to withdraw.

"We knew that we weren't going to decide, or at least I knew that we weren't going to decide," Berman said. "You all [the press] were going to decide," and when that point was reached, Mondale "would know."

By now the campaign had changed in nature as well as locale. Mondale had core organizations in the three southern states but nothing even remotely comparable to those in Iowa and New Hampshire. And Hart had nothing beyond a few prominent supporters here and there and not enough time to put anything more formal together. Each candidate had about $400,000 in the three states—enough for a television advertising presence but clearly not for saturation coverage. But by this point the advertising was less important than the free media coverage, particularly on network and local television news programs. Each of the two leaders also had some obvious concern about the possibility of critical votes being diverted—in Hart's case, to John Glenn; in Mondale's case, to Jesse Jackson.

Glenn's personal campaigning had come down to what seemed to be just one airport rally and press conference after another in one Georgia or Alabama city after another. But he was also running television commercials that played unabashedly on patriotism and, for the first time, obviously on his special celebrity as a national hero.

One thirty-second spot ended with the announcer saying: "The right stuff? You'd better believe it."

Another showed Glenn and his wife Annie before an American flag, with Glenn saying: "We believe in America, and the red, white and blue values that make America great."

But the press was treating the campaign as a two-man race, and Glenn, despite his complaints about the "politics of stampede," was being cast as a minor player in a way that was almost impossible to overcome after a string of losses. The hazard for Hart lay in the possibility that Glenn still would attract some anti-Mondale votes that otherwise might come his way.

Jesse Jackson was a far more obvious threat to Mondale in both Georgia and Alabama, states in which blacks might easily cast more than one-third of the primary vote. Most of the black leaders in the political establishment of these states were either publicly or tacitly in Mondale's camp. And he also had that endorsement valued so highly in Alabama from the Alabama Democratic Conference, the black political organization run by Joe Reed. But Jackson had enlisted many of those younger politicians, and he had the support of preachers of several generations. He had enough strength so there were fears in the Mondale campaign that, depending on the turnout, Jackson could capture 25 percent of the total vote and make Mondale vulnerable to Hart. And Jackson was clearly quite at home playing the game on the "free media," because he had never had the money to play it any other way.

As the campaign went into its final days, the free media—particularly television news—was playing an influential, perhaps even decisive, role in the whole Super Tuesday story. It was on television that what passed for order could be imposed on the alarums and excursions of the candidates striving so desperately for a little attention. In retrospect, two events late in the campaign seemed especially important.

The first was the decision by Mondale to go to Plains, Georgia, on the final Saturday to appear with the man he had served as Vice President, Jimmy Carter.

Under ordinary circumstances, such an appearance might have seemed the expected thing. But Carter had left office after having committed what was, by political standards, the cardinal sin of losing the White House as an incumbent. Beyond that, for reasons that were not entirely clear, he had inspired a kind of enduring personal enmity in the electorate that went beyond the normal bounds. At Democratic functions, he was considered a kind of non-person, rarely mentioned except in the obligatory way.

Mondale had enjoyed Carter's support all along, and the former President had delivered a specific endorsement in August of 1983. That declaration, written out by Carter in longhand and then read to reporters who came with Mondale to Carter's North Georgia cabin, went beyond the perfunctory; it made a point of freeing Mondale of any responsibility for unpopular policies of the administration of which he had been a part for four years. The statement was a remarkably generous one on Carter's part, but—given the low esteem in which he still was held by the electorate—there were still questions in the Mondale campaign about whether Mondale should maintain some distance.

In the case of the visit to Plains, the argument within the campaign was hot and heavy, splitting one meeting of advisers right down the middle. Jim Quackenbush, the southern coordinator, thought the trip essential because he considered it vital for Mondale to carry Georgia as well as Alabama on Super Tuesday. And that meant he needed the help of Carter partisans.

"We had to get the Peanut Brigade [the Georgians who had worked for Carter first in 1976 and then again in 1980] and those people fired up," he said. "Not to do it would be a slap in Carter's face."

But Peter Hart, looking at his polling results, was opposed.

"The problem," he said, "was that Mondale was getting the Carter leadership qualities grafted onto him." And Hart foresaw "the Sunday papers with a big picture of the two of them together."

As matters turned out, the argument within the staff was pointless. When one of the group called Jim Johnson to tell him of the dispute, Johnson replied that they were wasting their time because, as Peter Hart said, "Fritz was dead set on doing it."

After the fact, Mondale himself described his decision as another product of the fatalistic attitude he had developed about his position in the campaign.

"I wanted to do it," he said. "It was a part of the same thing. . . . I didn't know if I was going to be around and I wanted to demonstrate my affection for the President. I wanted to make it clear that I admired him and appreciated his support."

The result, on the Saturday before the primaries, was what was variously advertised as a "picnic" or a "barbecue" but was really a bit of ersatz Americana manufactured for gullible newspaper reporters and, more to the point, the uncritical eye of the television cameras. The event was held next to the railroad depot in downtown Plains, that single block of stores that had become so familiar during the Carter years. A thousand people were there, perhaps more, but the crowd was in no sense made up of Jimmy Carter's neighbors. On the contrary, most of the "guests" were representing labor unions, many of them in their locals' caps and jackets, and they had driven in or been bused in from Albany or Columbus or some other city within shouting range to serve as props. Carter and Mondale, Rosalynn Carter and Joan Mondale walked the few blocks from the Carter house on Woodland Drive to the center of town, striding down the middle of the street for the benefit of the cameras.

Downtown, while the barbecue waited on wooden tables, Carter and Mondale talked from a railroad flatcar. At one point, just a hint of the former President's sensitivity about his reputation seemed to filter through, when he said Mondale's experience "has been twisted by the press and some of his opponents to be a detriment and not an asset." Mondale unburdened himself of what had become—for the time being, at least—his standard speech, a contrast by implication of his own sterling qualities with the nouveau Gary Hart.

"I am a people's Democrat," he said. "Nothing fancy. No new hair spray. What you see is what you get. I'm a down-home Democrat who believes in fighting for people."

The speech was another version of those Mondale had been giving suggesting that Hart was the candidate of "media and tinsel" rather than substance. But beyond presenting himself as the distillation of the old virtues and, as at Tampa, the old commitments of the Democratic Party, Mondale was offering nothing that might be used for a theme in appealing to the electorate at large. The Mondale advisers argued about how vigorously to attack Gary Hart but were still at a loss for a "message" of their own.

Or, as Peter Hart put it later, "Gary Hart existed in part because we failed to establish ourselves."

But that afternoon after the potemkinesque picnic at Plains, Mondale did find a gimmick that served for a time. Mondale and his entourage left Plains early in the afternoon and drove to Columbus, Georgia, where they would spend the night resting and preparing for the Super Tuesday debate, scheduled late the following afternoon at the Fox Theatre in Atlanta. And when they checked into the hotel, there was Bob Beckel, newly arrived from Washington and bursting with a better idea.

It seemed that Beckel and a friend, Mary Goehring, had been watching television and it had occurred to her that a spot for Wendy's fast food—actress Clara Peller demanding to know "Where's the beef?"—could be applied politically to Gary Hart's new ideas.

So, meeting with Mondale and the debate team, Beckel described his idea.

"I got it," he told them. "I've got the answer—'Where's the beef?' "

"I don't have the slightest idea what you're talking about," Mondale replied. It seemed that neither the candidate nor his chief strategist Johnson had ever seen the commercial. But Beckel was not deterred. Johnson recalled it this way:

"Beckel started describing this woman and what she looked like and what she sounded like and what the settings were and what the point was. He really took it from A to Z. Beckel kept getting more and more animated. At one point he was down on the floor trying to do the size of this woman, on his knees with his hands waving." Considering the dimensions of the burly Beckel, it must have been a memorable spectacle.

Mondale was intrigued but not immediately convinced. He had been irked by all the talk about Gary Hart's "new ideas" and at a loss for a way to make his point that they weren't all that different.

"It was frustrating to us all the time," Mondale said later. So Mondale and Johnson agreed to think about Beckel's idea, and it obviously began to grow in appeal to Mondale.

The next morning Beckel was leaving the hotel, preparing to drive back to the Atlanta airport, just as Mondale returned from church. Beckel was notorious for being a white-knuckle flyer and Mondale called out a gibe about his impending flight to Washington.

"I said a prayer for you," he said.

Beckel laughed and replied:

"Kick the hell out of him tonight."

"Where's the beef?" said Mondale, grinning broadly.

That afternoon in Atlanta, when Hart was outlining his proposals for improving the economy, Mondale quickly found an opening.

"You know, when I hear your ideas," he said, looking directly at Hart, "I'm reminded of that ad, 'Where's the beef?' "

As laughter ran through the audience, Hart tried to respond and turn the argument back against Mondale. But his reply was flat, convoluted—and too serious for the moment.

"Fritz, if you'd listen just a minute," Hart said, "I think you'd hear. One of the other differences, by the way, is if a President goes back into office—and one of us must, I think, to save this country—you cannot go back so committed to a handful of constituency groups that you cannot make this economy grow again. And that's again a major difference, I think, between myself and Walter Mondale."

It was a game try, but the Mondale thrust was surefire for the television news coverage of the debate. And although Hart tried to counter late the following day by displaying a copy of his book—the beef—sandwiched in an oversized hamburger bun, it was too late to save the situation.

The incident was a classic case of the mindlessness of the campaign of 1984, one of many occasions when an event and the perception of candidates seemed to turn on some trivial and not necessarily accurate accusation. Of all the Democratic candidates for President, none had gone further than Hart in laying out for anyone who was interested his views on every imaginable issue. Not all of his ideas were either "new" or solely his own—and to the extent his campaign presented them that way, Hart invited trouble. But the suggestion that there might be any genuine reason to question where he stood was palpably absurd. As one political consultant not aligned with either man put it:

"Gary Hart spent a year and a half putting out these lengthy position papers—nothing but beef. It's like a six-thousand-pound meatloaf of beef."

The critical thing, however, was that first Bob Beckel and then Fritz Mondale had the political savvy to see how the slogan could be used to distill the point they were trying to make in a moment irresistible to television.

In fact, Hart's own performance that night was clearly lacking. He had been advised, he said later, "to be lighthearted" and "to let the people see the other side of you." But there was little evidence of that—and one gaffe that made him a target for ridicule.

The moderator, John Chancellor of NBC News, asked one of those theoretical questions that had become all the rage in the debates of the 1983 and 1984 campaign. What would each candidate do, he asked, if as President he were notified that a Czech airliner full of people was flying toward the North American Air Defense Command headquarters and ignoring warnings from U.S. fighter pilots? The pilots had reported that "the lights are on and it's full of people."

Hart had the misfortune to be the first in line but not the wit to see the folly of trying to answer.

"If the people they looked in and saw had uniforms on, I'd shoot the aircraft down," he replied. "If they were civilians, I'd just let it keep going."

John Glenn, obviously itching for a chance to take a dig at Hart, leaped in.

"Let me say first," he said, "there's such a fundamental lack of understanding by saying we're going to go up and peek in the window on this thing and see whether they have military uniforms on."

"That was Chancellor's," Hart protested. "He said you look in there and see people."

"You said you're going to peek in," Glenn insisted.

"Don't you know, that's what he [Chancellor] said. That's what he said."

"I've been in these airplanes," said Glenn, "and you don't go up peeking in the windows."

The other candidates were wise enough to recognize the trap.

"I think that's a wonderful hypothetical but it's ridiculous," Mondale scoffed.

Said Jesse Jackson: "I wish we could get on to something real. I think the answer to that question was Fritz's finest hour in three weeks."

Hart insisted later that he was trying to make a joke out of a "very ridiculous question." But on the nineteen-inch screen, it didn't look that way. And sitting in the front row in the old theater, Mondale coordinator Jim Quackenbush was delighted.

"I thought we were going to kill him on the Czech airliner," he said later.

Instead, they "killed" him on both the beef and the airliner. Although the Atlanta debate earned a small audience across the South that Sunday, those exchanges were shown repeatedly on television in the thirty-six hours before the Super Tuesday voting.

In one sense, it was not surprising that Hart had a bad night in Atlanta. In the three weeks since the Iowa caucuses had lifted him out of the pack, he had been in perpetual motion—racing from airport to airport to milk the last drop out of his instant celebrity. There had been no time for thoughtful campaign planning; instead, it seemed to be motion for its own sake. In his first rush to the South he had suddenly begun attacking President Reagan, on the theory this tactic would convey the image of the candidate in the lead showing Democrats how he would perform in the fall. But Caddell pointed out that Hart's market in the South would be almost exclusively white voters, and that Reagan had an approval rating of 60 percent or higher among them. So Hart turned his attention back to Mondale—and the theme that had put him where he was.

"The Washington insiders and special interests have handpicked their candidate for President," Hart said in a stinging television commercial, "but I offer our party and our country a choice. This election is about the failure of the past and the promise of the future."

The pace was so frenetic, however, that Hart went into the Atlanta debate with only perfunctory preparation and a nagging bronchial infection that had left him exhausted. That night, after the debate, he sat in a restaurant at the Hyatt Regency with several reporters and, sipping an Irish whiskey on the rocks, delivered a couple of one-liners aimed at Mondale.

"Why didn't you use those in the debate?" we asked.

"I meant to," he replied, "but I could never get them in."

This debate was, as it turned out, only the first of a series in which Hart had problems dealing with Mondale in that format. Although both men insisted all through the campaign and thereafter that they were uncomfortable with attack politics, Mondale found himself able to attack when the occasion demanded—and Gary Hart did not. As Peter Hart, Mondale's polling consultant, put it later:

"Gary Hart could not sit on the same platform with Walter Mondale and give it to Walter Mondale. And Walter Mondale, to his credit, sensed that in Gary Hart."

The underlying problem for Hart, however, was that he had burst on the scene with such force that people had not had much chance to get to know him. And in the days leading up to the Super Tuesday voting, the press began to pursue him on a whole series of questions that would not have been important had he been a long-established public figure.

Even before Hart emerged from the pack in those Iowa caucuses, George Lardner of the Washington *Post* had written a profile of the Colorado Democrat that contained some intriguing revelations. One was that as a young man he had changed his name from Hartpence to Hart. The other was that although he had listed his age in his official and campaign biographies as forty-six years old, he was in fact forty-seven. Neither of these disclosures qualified as earthshaking, but the manner in which Hart handled them stimulated further interest and speculation.

He pictured the change of name as one the family had decided on, but relatives in Kansas said Gary himself arranged the switch. And the court records supported that recollection by showing him as the petitioner. The speculation was that he had made the change because he was already planning a political career and considered "Hart" a more salable name than "Hartpence." That action, in itself, might have been passed over lightly because everyone in politics knew politicians who had changed their names, for one reason or another. But the age question was more baffling. There was never any question about the legitimacy of Hart's birth, never any year-long gap in his life, never any suggestion that he had made the change as a young man to avoid the draft. But Hart simply refused to explain, contending at one point that he couldn't be responsible for everything some staff member put down in a biography.

Asked in a television interview program about the discrepancy, Hart replied:

"It's no big deal. It's whatever the records say."

And the records said he had been born November 28, 1936, rather than November 28, 1937.

Finally, Hart did say that the whole thing had to do with a family joke involving his mother and one of her sisters, but that was all he planned to say about it. Privately, he was just as determined to maintain his silence. A close friend recalled pressing him to offer an explanation and take the question out of the political arena.

"It has to do with my mother, for God's sake," the friend recalled Hart replying. "And she's dead and I'm just not going to do it."

The friend dropped the subject. "It was so genuine," he said, "I knew I'd intruded on something."

Hart was correct that the mystery was "no big deal"—at least not intrinsically. But when a man has just come from obscurity to a position in which he might become President of the United States, everything about him is a big deal. And the press was now in full cry, discovering one day that Hart also had changed his signature and another that after he had come to the Senate he had obtained a special age waiver so he could be granted a Naval Reserve commission. All of these little mysteries became hot topics for the news media—and during the final days of the Super Tuesday campaign, for the television networks in particular. And although the age question might have been old stuff for readers of the Washington *Post*, it was very new stuff for most voters taking their first hard look at this political phenomenon.

In the political community, it became an established legend that the networks "savaged" Gary Hart in the last few days before Super Tuesday, just at the time most primary voters were paying the greatest attention. As Jim Johnson put it much later: "The goddamned networks turned like a firing squad on Gary Hart." There was, moreover, clear evidence in exit polls that Hart had a lot less support from voters who made up their minds over that final weekend than he did from those who had done so earlier.

In fact, what the politicians considered "savaging" by the networks was the networks catching up on a story they probably should have covered earlier, and telling people whatever they could find out about Gary Hart. Some of the television stories were tough, but there was never the kind of mass attack on Hart perceived by either his advisers or Mondale's.

There was, however, a totally predictable common element in the three networks' approach—and it played directly into "Where's the beef?" and Fritz Mondale's insistence that nobody knew much about Gary Hart—but would find out now that "the debate" had been started.

Thus, on March 8, Dan Rather introduced a story about Hart on the CBS *Evening News* this way:

"Who is this man, this Gary Hart, who in little more than a week has forced Mondale into such an uncomfortable and politically dangerous corner?"

The following night, on the NBC *Nightly News*, an announcer gave this tease:

"Next, how old is Gary Hart? Why did he change his name? Roger Mudd tries to find out."

The following night, also on NBC, Connie Chung began a story this way:

"Who is Gary Hart? Many who vote for him admit they have little or no idea what he stands for."

And two nights later, on the eve of Super Tuesday, John Dancy of NBC began a report:

"Who is Gary Hart, anyway, and what does he believe?"

The same approach ran through many of the stories. In answer to Dan Rather's question of March 8, Bruce Morton's story began this way:

A film clip of Hart saying to voters, "I'm Gary Hart. Good to see you, need your help."

Morton: "He is not a shoulder-squeezer, not an elbow-grabber. He sees a baby in the crowd but doesn't kiss it."

Another clip of Hart saying: "I think, frankly, I'm basically a shy person. I don't . . . move into a room and take it over. But clearly the voters of Colorado haven't been bothered by that, and the voters of New Hampshire either."

Morton: "Gary Hart is the hottest political property around, at least this week. But who is he?"

Mondale helped the process along. On CBS the following night he was shown saying:

"In an age of Cabbage Patch dolls, no wonder you are suspected of being addicted to novelty. The fact of it is that up until now, Americans do not know what Mr. Hart believes and who he is."

But it was the raw material that made the stories, not some television cabal. Thus, on primary eve, Jack Smith of ABC did a long piece on Hart that included this observation:

"Like many politicians Hart's moves have sometimes appeared calculated. In 1980 when Ronald Reagan swept the country, Hart was nearly defeated in Colorado. A month later Hart acquired the military record missing from his résumé. He got the Pentagon to waive his age and make him an officer in the Naval Reserve. Hart and his wife Lee have been separated twice. Just a few months before he announced though, they were reconciled. Hart also changed his religion from evangelical Methodism to Presbyterian, changed his signature from this [sample shown on screen] to this [another sample]. He has changed his name. He was born Gary Hartpence and he's even fudged the year of birth, 1936, but for years Hart has listed it, a family joke he says, as 1937."

Whatever doubts may have been raised about Hart—and the poll figures on the late-deciding voters suggested there were some—they were not substantial enough to deny him an impressive victory when the votes were counted on Super Tuesday. Or, at least, the results should have been seen as an impressive victory.

In Florida, the largest state holding a primary, Hart defeated Mondale with 39 percent of the vote to 36 percent. In Massachusetts, it was Hart 39 percent and Mondale 26. In Rhode Island, Hart won 45 percent to Mondale's 35. Hart also won the caucuses in Washington, Oklahoma and Nevada. And in Hawaii an uncommitted slate defeated the Mondale delegates in a result that was viewed there as either a standoff or a triumph for Hart, who had no delegate candidates of his own there.

Mondale won only two of the nine events. On the strength of heavy backing from black voters, he won Alabama with 34 percent to 21 each for Hart and Glenn and 19 for Jesse Jackson. In Georgia, Mondale squeaked by with 30 percent to 27 percent for Hart, 21 for Jackson, 18 for Glenn. In that case, the Mondale gamble in going to Plains had paid dividends as he won widely in southwest Georgia.

"It was probably worth the margin," Beckel said.

It seemed to us and to many other political reporters and professional operatives that night that Mondale had done no more than, as Mondale adviser Peter Hart put it in a memorandum the next day, "dodged the bullet."

In *The Washington Post* the following morning, David S. Broder began his report:

"Sen. Gary Hart (D-Colo.) planted his campaign flag in the South yesterday and kept his New England bandwagon rolling on the biggest voting day of the race for the Democratic presidential nomination.

"Hart, who burst to the front with an upset victory in New Hampshire just two weeks ago, won the biggest states of 'Super Tuesday,' Florida and Massachusetts, with the largest percentages of the day, while his leading rival, Walter F. Mondale, broke his losing streak with smaller victories in the Georgia and Alabama primaries."

In a column that night, we wrote: "For Fritz Mondale, Super Tuesday was better than a poke in the eye with a sharp stick. But not much better."

Two weeks earlier, Gary Hart had been naked in the South; now he had won the largest prize in Florida and come very close to taking Georgia from Mondale. But the television networks viewed the results differently—and demonstrated once again the extraordinary power they have to set the agenda and define the results in modern political campaigns.

In every primary situation all the candidates and their advisers play "the expectations game." They try to persuade the press and, through the press, the public that a particular result should be accepted as a success. And as a campaign evolves a level of expectations does indeed develop through some mysterious process that distills the competing propaganda, often in saloons late at night, to the point of a rough consensus.

In this case, the Mondale operatives made a point of helping the process—selling hard the idea that winning two states in the South would be a bonanza for them. Privately, they were convinced they needed to win two of the southern primaries and the Oklahoma caucuses just to keep the campaign even breathing. But in both their public pronouncements and in the sotto voce "inside" dope they passed on to reporters, they depicted such an accomplishment as probably beyond their reach.

"We worked at it," Beckel said. "It was a conscious decision. We were trying to set up Hart and the press. We knew if we could come back in a couple of states, there would be an inclination in the press to keep the thing going, that they weren't going to hand it over to Hart."

In this pre-conditioning the Mondale campaign was helped enormously by the great expectations set for Hart. He had won three states in New England and Wyoming on the Saturday before Super Tuesday. And although the votes were still to be cast, Massachusetts and Rhode Island were already being counted in his column because Mondale had surrendered there. Thus, the focus on the three southern states was more intense than the situation might have merited.

Then, when primary night arrived, the Mondale managers were ready with a detailed plan to make the most out of whatever they received.

"With a little bit of luck and a lot of planning," Marty Kaplan said later, "you can create the appearance of strength and victory. We planned every one of our primary election nights very carefully."

In this case, the first element of the plan was to get Mondale back to Washington so, as Kaplan put it, "we wouldn't run the risk of losing the state he was standing in." Then they made a point, Johnson recalled, of assuring "a show of enthusiasm" by filling the ballroom at the Capital Hilton Hotel with everyone in Washington who could be counted in the Mondale camp, from leading figures in Congress down to gofers from the campaign headquarters on Wisconsin Avenue.

"We packed the room with supporters," Kaplan recalled, "and that was easy to do and do it with genuine electricity and excitement." Up to this point, he noted, all the campaign action for over a year had taken place outside Washington, "so no one had any way to play if they weren't on the road. . . . It was a great night for the Mondale supporters . . . to let out their pent-up enthusiasm. So we had the atmospherics of a victory in place."

Kaplan also had prepared a script for Mondale of "hoped-for news bites . . . all on the order of 'I have now turned this race into a marathon.' So that we tried to set up the legitimacy of a long, long road ahead. We were back in it."

On the evening news programs early that night, all this conditioning didn't seem to be much help. On CBS, Dan Rather made a point of noting that, on the basis of exit polls, Gary Hart was even winning the union vote in Massachusetts. On NBC, Tom

Brokaw said it "looks like a super night for Senator Gary Hart and probably a good enough night for Walter Mondale."

But the Mondale operatives were optimistic, although the candidate himself, said one of those with him, "was very, very downbeat watching the results, very downbeat, angry, shaken."

"Then as we watched the early network play," Kaplan said, "we believed that our game plan had the potential to succeed—namely that by claiming victory, by characterizing the race as 'now we're back in it' as opposed to 'now it's over' or that 'we're on our last leg,' that we had a chance to get that across."

The first hard evidence of success came at 10:00 PM when NBC News, which had elected to do its special coverage in prime time, came on the air with Tom Brokaw presiding. The network immediately went live to that packed ballroom in the Capital Hilton where Fritz Mondale was thanking everyone and the crowd was cheering without restraint.

"Walter Mondale, alive and well tonight," declared Brokaw, "in this race for the Democratic presidential nomination, thanking, as he put it, his friends in the South. And well he might, because they have kept him in this race tonight."

The NBC anchorman then began recapitulating the results. NBC was "declaring" Mondale a winner in Georgia. Hart had won in Florida, Massachusetts and, "as expected," in Rhode Island. Mondale had won "a big victory" in Alabama.

"So tonight," Brokaw summed up, "Gary Hart wins three states. Walter Mondale wins two—two of the big southern states that he had to have to stay in this race."

Then it was back live to Mondale headquarters and reporter Lisa Myers, who announced:

"They are euphoric. You'd think they locked up the nomination."

Then she added:

"Actually, they were, a week ago, they were looking at being swept in the South by Hart, so they're delighted to escape with Alabama and Georgia."

In fact, the Mondale strategists had known from the outset of the Super Tuesday campaign that they were far ahead in Alabama. But what mattered was that these two primary victories were now being presented as something more than "dodging the bullet."

A few minutes later came what might have been the high point of the night for Mondale and what was clearly the low point for Hart—an interview of Hart by Roger Mudd. The interview was extraordinary in light of the fact that Hart had just won three of five primaries, including those in the two largest states at stake.

MUDD: Senator, not to take anything away from your victory this evening, but it appears your principal opponent, Walter Mondale, is on his way back. Is that correct?
HART: Well, I'm not quite sure. Back from where? He was the frontrunner in this race for a year and a half, and he, as you will remember, two weeks ago challenged me to come to the South and campaign, which I did, and campaigned all across this country . . . this campaign was the only one who was campaigning nationally. He was concentrating on the South, as was Senator Glenn. And so we combined a campaign in New England and the West with a campaign in the South, and I think we've won at least one state [in the South] and for practical purposes won another one [Georgia].
MUDD: Well, he was in danger, everyone thought, of really slipping through the ropes today, and he's not done that. Apparently, he's won in Georgia and Alabama. So you have not got rid of him. When are you going to get rid of him?
HART: Well, I don't—it's first of all not my task. I am going to continue to campaign. We won Massachusetts, we won Florida—the two largest states. There are three western caucus states still to be heard from. We may do very well out there. We stood off Vice President Mondale in the home state of the President he served with. And I think all of those represent major victories.
MUDD: But you didn't win in Georgia and you didn't win in Alabama. So really all you won was Florida, which isn't a true southern state. So you're really not a national candidate yet, are you?
HART: Well, Mr. Mudd, please. We won two New England primaries today. We won the largest southern state. You may think that Florida is not a southern state, but Floridians may quarrel with that. As I say, we stood off the Vice President in the President's own state, and I think that was a major victory, and we'll do well in the western caucuses. I think this was a major boost for our campaign nationally.

Then, after a couple of questions about future primaries, Mudd asked:

"A lot of people want to know, Senator, why do you imitate John Kennedy so much?"

That led to an even more bizarre exchange over whether Hart imitated John Kennedy and whether politicians were phony.

"And a final question," said Mudd. "Would you do your Teddy Kennedy imitation for me now?"

HART: No.
MUDD: I've heard it's hilarious.
HART: I don't think it is.

By the time the other networks weighed in with their special reports at 11:30 PM EST, they had the benefit of another result, Gary Hart's victory in the Oklahoma caucuses. And neither CBS nor ABC would match either Roger Mudd's interview or the "two big winners" thesis of NBC. On CBS, in fact, Dan Rather asked Mondale at one stage if the truth was not that "if your candidacy is still alive, it's hanging on the ropes."

But Mondale was doggedly delivering his own line at every opportunity.

On CBS: "It looked like Mondale doing a hundred-yard dash. Then it looked like Hart doing a hundred-yard dash. But tonight, that's all changed. It's going to be a marathon all the way to California."

On NBC: "Now what we've got is a marathon and that guarantees the American people what they're entitled to—a debate about what the difference is, who is Gary Hart, where would he take the country, how experienced is he, what are the differences, who would make the best President . . ."

On ABC: "It's now clear that what looked like it might be a hundred-yard dash—first for me, then for Senator Hart—is now going to be a marathon, maybe right into the San Francisco convention."

The best summation of the whole process that night may have come from Peter Jennings of ABC:

"I was just thinking . . . that if you'd arrived in this country tonight from outer space, you would have thought Hart was the big winner. Two states, two biggest states, Massachusetts and

Florida. But because Walter Mondale set so many of the expectations for the South tonight it looks, as I think we're pretty well describing it, as pretty much of a standoff."

In fact, it was not a standoff by any objective measure. But none of the networks had ruled that Gary Hart had won another "big" victory and, because they didn't, Mondale escaped with far more of a lift than the results justified. To some extent, it may have been a result of the time element—the fact that the news of Hart's success in Washington, Oklahoma and Nevada did not arrive in time to be factored into the judgment. But it also seemed clear that the Mondale con artists had been extraordinarily successful in selling the notion that "dodging a bullet" was a great success.

The Mondale men were clearly delighted. Jim Johnson recalled watching in amazement and asking himself: "How could they be doing this for us. . . . If you turned off the sound and blotted out the numbers, you would have watched and said Mondale was the big victor."

"TV basically declared us a winner after winning two of five primaries, and it changed the whole psychology of the campaign," Peter Hart said.

Said Beckel: "The whole mood of our operation turned around."

Or, as Tom Donilon put it in the vernacular: "We got the spin on it."

Mondale himself defended the networks later.

"We knew we were fighting for our lives. We tried to put the best face on," he said. "But, in fact, psychologically, I think the nets were right. This was a comeback. We did carry Alabama and Georgia, and while we lost Florida, we were clearly coming back there, and I think they saw there was a psychological turn there."

But Mondale got more than the spin from television out of the Super Tuesday campaign. He got an insight into how he might bring Gary Hart down in the primaries ahead.

On March 6, a week after New Hampshire and a week before Super Tuesday, Peter Hart had assembled a "focus group" of fifteen people in Atlanta. Such small panels are obviously of no help to a poll-taker in measuring where a candidate stands in a particular campaign. But the give and take among the panelists sometimes can reveal popular attitudes.

In this case, Peter Hart found the voters in the focus group investing Gary Hart with all sorts of surprising qualifications. When they were asked, for instance, which candidate might do the most to provide more jobs for American workers, most of them said Gary Hart—an unsettling finding in view of the emphasis Mondale had placed on that issue. The same pattern appeared on other questions: Gary Hart clearly could do no wrong. But then Peter Hart asked his panelists who they would rather have in the White House if a foreign-policy crisis developed.

"Fifteen hands went up for Walter Mondale, and I said, 'Bingo,' " Hart recalled.

Hart rushed to the Hartsfield airport and called Beckel in Washington and media consultant Roy Spence at his base in Austin, Texas, to pass on his findings. The voters might be ready to believe that Fritz Mondale was the better man in a crisis, that he was steady, that he knew what he was doing.

Beckel and Spence had been trying to find a way to make a political asset out of the fact Fritz Mondale had been around so long. Now they had what appeared to be confirmation that his experience could be exploited on what is always the most primal issue in American presidential politics—whether a candidate is "safe" enough to entrust with the "button" that could trigger nuclear war.

The result was "the red telephone" ad—a television spot that Peter Hart said later "was probably the longest-running political commercial in the history of American politics."

The first version was cobbled together by Beckel and didn't show any telephone at all. It was built around some old footage of the Oval Office in the White House borrowed from Gerald Rafshoon, Jimmy Carter's media consultant. That version ran the last few days of the Florida primary campaign, and it seemed to take some of the steam out of Gary Hart there.

Meanwhile, Roy Spence was preparing the finished product—the red telephone ringing in the Oval Office, the light flashing, the warning against an "untested" man at the helm in a world full of peril.

"The most awesome, powerful responsibility in the world," the somber voice said, "lies in the hand that picks up this phone. The idea of an unsure, unsteady, untested hand is something to really think about. This is the issue of our times, . . . Vote as if the future of the world is at stake, because it is. Mondale. This

President will know what he's doing, and that's the difference."

The question now, as the campaign moved on to the big industrial states of the Midwest and Northeast, was whether Gary Hart could reassure the Democrats who had been signaling so clearly that they wanted an alternative to Fritz Mondale.

9

Turning Point

•

IF THE TELEVISION NETWORKS' treatment of the Super Tuesday results—six victories for Gary Hart, two for Fritz Mondale in eight contested states—were a triumph of hype and salesmanship by the Mondale campaign, it was a bewildering and disorienting jolt for Hart's.

"We were trying very hard not to be frontrunners," Hart press secretary Kathy Bushkin recalled later. "Gary kept saying so. But there was a sense afterward that we let Mondale get away with too much." His campaign did a much better job exploiting his limited success on Super Tuesday, she said, "and we never thought of it. We were still naming him as the frontrunner, and we hadn't thought about how desperately they'd behave."

Billy Shore, Hart's young political director, agreed. "We didn't do enough saying that if Gary Hart does this, this and this, it will be more amazing than what we did in New Hampshire. Reporters on our plane were saying, 'You have nothing in Florida, you have no money, and now that you're here in the South, how are you going to keep going?' "

Such questions had presented the Hart forces with a clear opportunity to poor-mouth, to lower expectations and then declare a huge victory in winning one of the three major southern primaries on Super Tuesday, plus Massachusetts, Rhode Island and the caucuses in the three other contested states. But they blew it.

"Everything is perception," Hart said later. "If there was overreaction to my second place in Iowa, which was not a strong second, there was even more overreaction to Super Tuesday. It was seven to two, but the question was, Why didn't you win in

Georgia and Alabama? Obviously we would have been better off if the stories had said, 'Mondale Barely Survives.' Clearly, if he hadn't won those two primaries, he would have been gone."[26]

To Bushkin, part of the problem was the news media's way of looking at a campaign. "You can only have one underdog," she said later, "and Mondale had been the underdog. You can't have two candidates with insurmountable advantages, and we were supposed to have momentum on our side."

That is, the price Hart had paid for his lightning successes in New Hampshire and Maine had been the raising of his expectations so high, and the lowering of Mondale's so low, that Hart had been the candidate who "needed" stopping in the interest of the press, wittingly or not, to see the "horse race" continue.

The Hart strategists were convinced that reporters covering the campaign, particularly the network anchormen, had a professional interest in seeing the contest for the Democratic nomination continue—to keep alive the story in which they had invested so much time and, in the case of the networks especially, so much money. The Hart people did not deny, when pressed to examine their theory later, that had the Super Tuesday results been perceived by the news media as another Hart victory, and possibly forced the withdrawal of Mondale, it would have made for a much bigger story at the time. But they could not be disputed, either, in their contention that the air might have quickly gone out of the nomination story thereafter, unless a new challenger to Hart, then nowhere in sight, were to have emerged.

"It may not have been consciously that the media built somebody up and then ganged up on him to bring him down," Bushkin reflected. "But all the stories up to Super Tuesday were about the demise of the Mondale campaign and about Hart's phenomenal rise." Then, she said, the attention all at once switched to "Fighting Fritz" and his comeback.

Hart himself realized that the way Super Tuesday's results had been interpreted by the networks added up to a missed opportunity for him at a time he could least afford it. He was heading now into the Midwest, where caucuses in Michigan four days later led the list of four Democratic contests around the country

26. Hart's reference to seven victories included the victory of an uncommitted slate in Hawaii, where he did not run but where he urged his supporters to vote uncommitted.

lumped together as Super Saturday, and where the next major primary, in Illinois, was scheduled three days after that.

"The calendar began working for Mondale," Hart said. The race was heading into northern industrial states—New York and Pennsylvania hard on the heels of Michigan and Illinois—where Mondale had strong party and labor support.

In Michigan and Illinois, two strong United Auto Workers states, Mondale and his campaign started using "the Chrysler issue" against Hart—the fact that he had opposed the federal loan guarantee, the "bailout" in the vernacular, that had rescued Lee Iacocca's beleaguered auto firm. Also, Mondale had full delegate slates filed in Illinois and a resource the Hart campaign did not yet know about: Mondale "delegate committees." In due time, however, they would become the grounds for a major controversy in the campaign, touching not only on legality but also ethics in Mondale's pursuit of the nomination.

In the methodical manner of campaign chairman Jim Johnson, the Mondale forces went into the Midwest after Super Tuesday prepared for the worst. As a hedge against a major setback in the South, they in effect had taken out an insurance policy in Michigan. Back in the spring of 1983, Johnson and Bob Beckel had gone to one of Mondale's most conscientious backers among the Democratic governors, James Blanchard, and persuaded him to have the date of the Michigan caucuses, then tentatively scheduled for May, moved forward.

"Beckel and I personally went out and pleaded with Blanchard," Johnson said later. "We spent two weeks moving Michigan, because we wanted Michigan the Saturday after the South, in case Glenn [then perceived as the main opposition] had a good southern day. We were constructing the calendar. We were trying to make sure we had insurance as we were going through."

Immediately after Mondale's defeat in the Maine caucuses, which also had been looked upon as an early insurance policy but had failed to pay the expected dividend, Johnson had begun to look down the road, not only to Super Tuesday but beyond.

"We spent another day or so focusing on Michigan," he said, "thinking once again that if we were still alive, but barely alive, out of Super Tuesday that we had to have a Maine that would work. So we sent some more people out there. . . . I had some quite substantial faith in Michigan. Talk about an insurance state, that's a quality insurance state, with their system. We had the kind of caucus, the kind of organization, the depth of commitment by the governor and the UAW and Coleman Young [the mayor of Detroit]. If you were designing an insurance policy, I was not aware of one that could have been designed better."

Hart, however, was well aware of the advantages Mondale had in Michigan. In fact, he was under the impression that the advantages were even greater than they were. He believed, for example, that many or even most of the three-hundred-odd caucus sites would be in labor union halls, and his staff trumpeted that notion, implying there might be intimidation of union voters who might otherwise vote for Hart. In fact, fewer than 10 percent of the sites were in such halls.

Nevertheless, Hart came out of Super Tuesday focused on Illinois, where he believed the primary would be a more congenial process to him than Michigan's caucuses. He also had some organization in place in Illinois, and polls there indicated the effects of his New England tidal wave were still having impact on voters. Pat Caddell said later that Hart was about two percentage points ahead going into Illinois, and Peter Hart, Mondale's pollster, had the Coloradan leading there by a whopping thirteen points. If Gary Hart could beat Mondale in Illinois after a setback in Michigan that could be dismissed as a stacked contest, that Illinois victory might well put what had happened on Super Tuesday in more realistic perspective. And Mondale might be forced to consider withdrawing from the race.

Mondale by now was playing the "Fighting Fritz" role to the hilt, contending that his Super Tuesday "victory" had put him solidly back into contention. He was hitting Hart hard, questioning directly or by implication his maturity and decisiveness with the red phone ad. The "Where's the beef?" gimmick had pretty much worn thin, but Hart's quick rise to prominence by now had put him under much more intensive press scrutiny than he had faced before. The questions about his age, his name and other matters that had surfaced earlier continued to come up, and Hart's evasiveness and vagueness only guaranteed that they would linger. Those responses in turn fed in an indirect way the Mondale effort to undermine Hart's general credibility—"the steadiness factor," Beckel called it.

In advance of the Illinois primary, the Mondale media team videotaped man-in-the-street interviews in Illinois in which voters made negative comments about Hart that conveyed an unsureness and an uneasiness about him among some voters. He had burst upon the scene so quickly that he was bound to be somewhat of a mystery man, and his personal aloofness further raised curiosity—and doubts—about him.

According to Frank Greer, one of the members of the Mondale media team, the videotapes were reviewed by Beckel and Roy Spence, head of the team, and a debate ensued about whether to use them. But because the red phone ad already was raising "the steadiness factor" effectively, Greer said later, and because there was always a danger of a backlash from negative advertising overkill, it was decided not to use the anti-Hart street interviews in any commercial.

Nevertheless, there occurred in the wake of these events two related developments in Illinois that had a profound influence on Hart's candidacy—and on Mondale's ability to make a real comeback, as opposed to the essentially ersatz one created by the network anchormen's Super Tuesday generosity.

Two days after Super Tuesday, as Hart campaigned in Illinois, campaign manager Pudge Henkel met at Hart headquarters in Washington with the campaign's outside advisers and senior staff members to consider, among other things, how to cope with Mondale's negative campaigning. The meeting proved to be a fateful one for Hart.

According to Henkel, Mondale's tactics were already throwing Hart off stride. A special counsel to the campaign, Ken Guido, reported he had been told that an opposition radio ad was being prepared in New York that transparently raised the matter of the candidate's earlier name change from Hartpence to Hart. Reading from notes he had jotted down from his conversation with his informant, Guido said the narrator in the ad observed that one man in politics had always stood for certain things, had always been constant, and his name had always been the same—Walter Mondale. Also, Keith Glaser, the state coordinator in Iowa now back in Washington, reported that word had come in from the field that the Mondale campaign had produced and was running a commercial that talked about Hart's name and age.

"Nobody challenged it," Henkel said later, or asked whether

Glaser knew the ad was running. But the idea that Mondale would try overtly to exploit personal issues against Hart angered the Hart staffers. One of the senior issues advisers at the meeting, John Holum, who had worked with Hart in the 1972 McGovern campaign, wrote down a few lines for Hart to use in response to the reported ad.

In any event, around this time Kathy Bushkin called in from Arkansas, where the Hart entourage had arrived. It so happened that Hart and his traveling aides were already concerned about the way negative campaigning had been dominating the dialogue, crowding out Hart's positive "new ideas" message. Hart decided to make a direct public appeal to Mondale to join him on a higher road of positive campaigning, and Bushkin was calling in to discuss the planned statement with David Landau, the chief campaign issues man. He informed her of the alleged ad, and then he read her the lines Holum had just written. Bushkin took them down and shortly afterward gave them to Hart as the campaign plane headed for Springfield, Illinois, where he had a scheduled press conference. On arrival, he issued the challenge to Mondale, rewriting and adding Holum's words about the alleged radio ads.

"I have spoken of new ideas for the future," Hart said, "and for some reason former Vice President Walter Mondale wants to talk about my handwriting. I propose new ways to make this economy grow again and to create real social justice in the 1980s, and for some reason Vice President Mondale proposes to talk about what my birthday is. I've spoken about a new generation of leadership for this country, and for some reason Vice President Mondale wants to talk about my family name."

Hart concluded: "In politics and in life, there is a fine line between desire for office and inordinate need for power. There is a line between legitimate ambition and blind ambition. There's a line between constructive criticism and destructive assault, and that line is called personal integrity. . . . I believe Walter Mondale knows where that line is. I hope for his sake and his country's sake that he does not cross it."

Reporters traveling with Hart called the Mondale campaign. They were told no such ads existed. Mondale, for his part, recognized at once an opening to fan the "unsteadiness" issue against Hart. "I think there's a lot of evidence," he said, "that my opponent's getting unnerved."

The reporters went back to Hart and asked him about the "phantom" ads. Bushkin checked back with the headquarters, triggering a frantic search for the ads or any evidence of their existence. Henkel called Ray Strother, the Hart ad-maker, asking him to try to locate them. Strother called all the radio and television stations in the Chicago area, to no avail.

"We spent two hundred to three hundred dollars on telephone calls trying to find that spot," Strother recalled. "It didn't exist." So after Hart had made a federal case of accusing Mondale of hitting him below the belt, he was left hanging out to dry.

Bushkin, armed with several excuses Hart could use, went to him with the bad news. He rejected all of them. "Settle down," he told her. "We made a mistake."

Hart went out and publicly apologized to Mondale before the television cameras, saying he had been in error about the ads being used.

Rather than waiting to see whether they might yet turn up, Bushkin said, "my gut told me they were not going to find those ads," and as the campaign moved into the next news cycle, the story would only grow bigger and more damaging. "My judgment was that it was wrong to keep the story alive; that it was better to cut our losses."

She may have been right, had the episode occurred in isolation. But it didn't. The fact that Hart had made an accusation that he then had to retract played directly into the hands of Mondale, who had been relentlessly telling the voters that they didn't know this Gary Hart; that he was simply too unsteady to be trusted with the White House and, it was implied by the red phone ad, the nuclear button. Nothing further had to be said by Mondale. His point had been made by Hart's gaffe better than he could make it himself.

Later, Hart and his ranking aides attributed the fiasco to fatigue and lack of adequate staffing resulting from the pressures generated by his swift emergence as a serious candidate. The incredibly demanding primary and caucus schedule in those first weeks of the front-loaded process were taking their toll.

Landau himself said afterward: "Signals got confused between the plane and the ground. I probably never should have read Holum's lines to Kathy. They [the staffers on the plane] were so tired, not able to make judgments, and we were telling them to go negative. It was probably more our responsibility than theirs. But the hours they were working . . ."

Of the episode, Hart said later: "It came at exactly the wrong time, because I by that time had gotten raw nerves about this thirty days' attacks [by Mondale]. I began to feel very deeply about this in terms of character—mine and his, and I had been drafting a statement, handwritten, that I was going to read when I got to our Springfield headquarters. When this information came along, I just added another page or two saying that the fact that my opponent had prepared ads to question my background and character is further proof of what I'm saying. That there's something more important in politics than winning. That there is a point beyond which you sacrifice, in attacking your opponent and running a negative campaign, that you erode your own character."

When he was confronted with the Mondale campaign's denial, Hart said, and he checked back with his own people, they still contended there were such ads but hadn't been able to establish that they had been run.

"That's when I said, 'Wait a minute. Having ads is not the same as running them.' I went out and apologized. I said I made a mistake. But I also said, 'The bulk of that statement still stands.' But by then the whole question was, Hart can't get his information straight." (He added: "I still think they had them.")

What actually happened was a tribute to the famous Washington rumor mill. Right after Super Tuesday, Bob Beckel had talked to an old friend from New York, Joe White, a specialist in negative political radio ads. According to White, Beckel said he thought the time had come to do some negative ads against Hart and asked him to come up with some ideas.

The next day, White said, he got a phone call from Charlie Scalera, an aide to Representative Peter Rodino of New Jersey, who was a White client. "There's a rumor going all over Capitol Hill that you're doing negative ads against Gary Hart for Mondale," White said Scalera told him.

The report made White laugh, because he had only begun to think of some ideas, and the Washington rumor mill had picked up on the ads even before he had gotten them out of his head. As he and Scalera talked, Scalera reminded White of an ad he had done for Rodino in one of his reelection campaigns. It went, White said, something like this: "There are a lot of names listed when you go into the voting booth, but one name has always stood for integrity, one name has always stood for honesty, one name has always stood for experience, and that name is Peter Rodino."

Why not something like that, Scalera suggested, to play on Hart's name change? White liked the idea, and he and Scalera kicked it around on the phone, White said, until he came up with the right formulation—one that would get the point across, but subtly. He suggested, White said, something like this: "One name has always stood for civil rights; one name has always stood for the working man; one name has always stood for arms control—and that name is *still* Walter Mondale."

The best negative ad, White said later, is one that isn't overtly negative but that makes the point in saying something positive about your own candidate. After his conversation with Scalera, he said, he hung up and started making some notes on the idea. But, he swore, he never produced a script.

A night or two later, he said, he was watching the evening news and there was Gary Hart apologizing for accusing Mondale of running an ad raising the issue of his name and age—an ad, he said, that was still only an idea, not even a script.

Both White and Scalera told us they had no idea how the story grew into a full-blown report of an ad that not only was produced but, by some accounts, already on the air. Apparently, though, somebody heard about the idea, phoned a friend in the Hart campaign, and the rumor was off and running. So it was not so much that it was flat wrong; it was just premature—to the misfortune of Gary Hart and the good fortune of Fritz Mondale. By such twists of fate are presidential campaigns sometimes shaped, for all the millions and millions of dollars spent on carefully concocted stratagems by high-salaried political braintrusters and media wizards.[27]

It was now Thursday, five days before the Illinois primary, and Caddell had an idea of how it could still be swung decisively for Hart. A year earlier, Caddell had been involved in the bitter primary race for the Democratic mayoral nomination, handling polling and political advice for the eventual winner, Harold Washington. His candidate had won the primary over incumbent Mayor Jane Byrne by maximizing black support and running hard against

27. White said later that in making presentations to prospective clients, he began to tell the story, adding that he now charged two prices: one if he produced an ad, and one only slightly less if he only threatened to produce it.

entrenched machine politics, represented and best symbolized by Byrne's most influential backer, Cook County Democratic Chairman and leader of the Chicago City Council, Alderman Edward Vrdolyak.

Vrdolyak was the classic "Fast Eddie"—a political swifty right out of Central Casting, smooth and polished but with the street-smarts clearly showing through. Washington, seeking to become Chicago's first black mayor, had run not only against Byrne but also against Vrdolyak, the hero of Chicago's white ethnics, intentionally polarizing the contest by race. With a second strong white candidate running, State's Attorney Richard M. Daley, son of the late Mayor Richard J. Daley, the white vote split and Washington squeezed through. Now Vrdolyak was supporting Mondale. Why not, Caddell reasoned, run against "Fast Eddie" again?

In Ray Strother, the Hart ad-maker, Caddell had an obvious and willing ally. Strother had worked for Daley, one of Vrdolyak's political arch-enemies, in the same primary campaign.

"We both came to the same conclusion," Strother said later, "that the association with Vrdolyak was deadly."

They agreed that the thing to do was prepare and run an ad for the Illinois primary putting "Fast Eddie" right on Mondale's back.

Caddell, in fact, had been peddling Vrdolyak as a prime whipping boy for some time. Much earlier, he had advised the Glenn campaign to send the astronaut/candidate into Chicago to blast Vrdolyak's endorsement of Mondale. And in advance of Super Tuesday, Caddell, now as a Hart agent, had gone to see Washington and then brought Hart in to meet him, hoping to encourage Hart to take on Vrdolyak and in the process persuade Washington to endorse Hart. Caddell told Hart that polling data showed Vrdolyak to have a 60 percent or more negative rating statewide—a figure that included white ethnics in Chicago.

"I said," Caddell recalled later, " 'This is what we're going to do. We're going to hang Eddie Vrdolyak around Walter Mondale's neck. Very simple. Nothing cruel, nothing mean. There was no reason to anger Vrdolyak by attacking him. You don't have to say anything. You just put them together.' Gary said, 'That's good.' He signed off on that."

Right after Super Tuesday, Caddell and Strother put their heads together and Strother prepared a couple of anti-Vrdolyak scripts.

One, for use in the Chicago–Cook County area, mentioned Vrdolyak by name as having endorsed Mondale. The other, for use downstate, referred only to "Chicago political bosses" backing Mondale. Strother showed the scripts to Caddell and to Senator Christopher Dodd of Connecticut, a major Hart supporter and associate, and when both thought they weren't tough enough, he strengthened them.

On the Thursday morning before the Illinois primary, when the Hart senior staff met at the Washington headquarters, Strother presented the scripts. As he recalls the meeting, there was no consensus on them, and Henkel, as usual, said he was opposed to negative ads. But Strother denies he was ever told not to make the commercials.

As Caddell recalled the episode, Dodd took the ads to Henkel who, Caddell said, was "in agreement we do the ad. . . . For the first time in the campaign, there's consensus because the numbers [in the polls] scared hell out of everybody."

But Landau had a sharply different recollection. "There was a unanimous decision that the ads were bad," he recalled. "Everybody kind of rolled their eyes upward. What did Eddie Vrdolyak have to do with the Illinois primary?" Strother was told, Landau insisted later, "if you want to prepare an anti-boss ad, just don't use Vrdolyak's name."

(Henkel could not recall, however, that Strother was told specifically to cut Vrdolyak's name, but rather he thought Strother was instructed to make the ad less negative toward Mondale. "The Vrdolyak name problem," he said afterward, "was Gary's problem. . . . The fact that we were naming Vrdolyak was not, as I recall that meeting, a point of attention. It was more, this is really kind of slimy. Somehow you felt dirty about being in the middle of Cook County politics, Chicago politics, when this is a presidential campaign.")

In any event, Strother prepared the ads, one with Vrdolyak's name and picture, the other without either. The Chicago version said: "Eddie Vrdolyak has decided Walter Mondale will be your candidate for President. Gary Hart and a lot of people who think for themselves stand in the way."

That afternoon, as Strother worked, Henkel called him and reminded him: "Whatever you do, Gary has to approve all the spots."

It so happened that Dodd was going out to Chicago that night to see Hart and he agreed to take the scripts to him. Strother also took copies to Henkel late that night. Henkel was on the phone, so Strother left the scripts and departed.

"I read the commercials and did not like them," Henkel said later. "Again, for the same reason. They were unbecoming to a presidential campaign. But Ray knew that we were not to run any commercials until Gary and I had signed off on them. It was a point of continuing tension that used to drive Pat up the wall, that Gary was involved in okaying scripts for commercials, because he didn't think the candidate had time to do that."

Twice that night and early morning Strother checked with Caddell to determine if he had heard whether Dodd had delivered the scripts and obtained Hart's approval. Caddell had not heard from Dodd by 2:30 AM, and Strother was worried; he knew he had only until nine o'clock the next morning to kill the ads before the Illinois stations moved into their weekend cycle.

Dodd, meanwhile, had spent the day campaigning for Hart in Michigan and had flown into Chicago late that night. He caught up with Hart at a fund-raising reception at which Hart's friend, actor Robert Redford, was the drawing card. Bad weather had forced Hart's plane to land at South Bend, Indiana, and the entourage was obliged to motor the eighty-odd miles into Chicago. Redford filled time before the restless crowd at the reception until Hart finally appeared, looking utterly exhausted. This was the same day, remember, in which he had gone through the attack on Mondale for allegedly running the name-and-age ads against him, and subsequently had apologized.

After the reception, Hart, Dodd and Redford had a late dinner in Redford's hotel suite, and Hart, according to Dodd, was barely able to function.

"Gary was absolutely a zombie," Dodd recalled. "He was completely wiped out. He could hardly keep his eyes open."

As they sat at the dinner table, Dodd pulled out an envelope. "I've got that script here," he said to Hart. "Want to see it?"

"No," Hart replied, as Dodd remembered it.[28]

Before going to bed, Dodd phoned Caddell in Washington and

28. Hart told us later that as he recalled the matter, he had seen two versions, one that mentioned Vrdolyak and one that didn't. "I approved the one that didn't," he said at one point, while acknowledging that his memory was hazy about that trying night.

told him that Hart was tired and hadn't wanted to look at the scripts at all. It was then about 3:00 AM in the East, Caddell said.

Early the next morning, Strother and Caddell met at National Airport in Washington to catch a flight to Raleigh, where both were working on the North Carolina Democratic gubernatorial campaign of Rufus Edmisten.

"I walked up to Pat," Strother said later, "and I asked him: 'Pat, have you heard from Chris?' He said, 'The spots are okay. Release them.' " Strother called his man in Chicago, who then did so.

Meanwhile, that same Friday morning, Hart told Chicago *Sun-Times* reporter Robert Hillman in an interview aboard the campaign plane that he was not going to get involved in local Chicago politics in the course of the Illinois primary campaign. But Hillman, checking in with his office at the next stop, was informed by the *Sun-Times*' chief political writer, Basil Talbott, that a new Hart ad rapping Vrdolyak was being aired. Hillman, feeling he had been lied to, sought out Bushkin for a clarification, but she was in the dark.[29]

Back in Washington, Henkel was still trying to find out whether Hart had seen the script and had approved it. But Hart was out campaigning and hence out of pocket. Finally, at about four o'clock in the afternoon, Washington time, Henkel got Hart on the phone and read him the ad.

"Pudge," Henkel recalled Hart saying, "I don't like it. I don't want to use a commercial that uses somebody else's name."

Hart, Henkel said, "was the one who focused on the name Vrdolyak. He was willing to go with the generic ad. [But] he did that reluctantly, because of the negative aspects of the commercial."

Henkel went on: "While I was talking to Gary, I wrote on the script, 'Make sure that this commercial is not running.' I handed the script to David Landau. I completed the conversation with Gary and about thirty minutes after that, David Landau came in."

"Pudge," he said, "I've got bad news. That commercial is running. It's on the air."

Henkel, realizing how strongly Hart felt, was—as he put it himself later—very "exercised," and he tried to reach Strother to

29. Hillman left the *Sun-Times* in April 1984 and joined the staff of the Dallas *Morning News*.

find out what had happened, and to get the ad pulled. But Strother, too, was out of pocket. He was flying from North Carolina to Arkansas, where he had another candidate-client. And besides, getting the ad off the air would be a major task under any circumstances at this hour. The managers of most of the stations involved had gone home for the weekend, with the weekend programming locked into computer-controlled systems. Unless something extraordinary was done, removing the ads would have to wait until Monday, and Henkel still had not even reached Strother.

To Landau, it had all been a cute Caddell ploy. "Caddell was to blame for the Vrdolyak ads," he said later. "No one else could have been responsible." He insisted that Hart had never approved their use as Caddell had said.

Whatever the case, Caddell had no reservations about the political wisdom of running the ads. "This spot hit the air," he said afterward, "and twenty-four hours later we are twelve or thirteen points ahead. This thing blew the suburbs of Chicago. All the undecideds we were having in our data, this thing just blew wide open; I mean, blew wide open. . . . It was the first comeback on Mondale."

In other words, the anti-Vrdolyak ads, for all the reservations about taking him on directly, according to Caddell were virtually assuring a victory for Hart in Illinois, three short days before the balloting. All he had to do was hold on.

Mondale's polling confirmed the same sudden turnaround. "We were scared to death," a Mondale aide recalled.

And then Hart made his second major mistake involving television advertising, imagined or real, in two days. After having apologized to Mondale for having charged him, without proof, of preparing to run unfair ads, Hart now said his own campaign had erred again in running the anti-Vrdolyak ads. They would be pulled off the air at once, he told reporters who were now hounding him about their use.

"The difference between me and Walter Mondale was that he was the candidate of the organization," Hart said later in explanation. "It was the fact that it [the ad] personalized Vrdolyak. I had no quarrel with Vrdolyak. I disagreed with his politics a lot, but I wasn't running against Vrdolyak. We had gone to great lengths not to get involved in Chicago politics. I felt if I was the nominee I was going to have to go back in there. I needed everybody's help."[30]

How Hart felt about Eddie Vrdolyak, however, was not the point now. The point was that Hart, or his campaign for which he was ultimately responsible, had goofed again. As every hour passed and the ads continued to appear, even as he insisted he was trying to get them off the air, the incident was playing directly and dramatically into Mondale's hands. A candidate must be "surefooted," Mondale was saying now, and he didn't have to elaborate.

At about ten o'clock that night, as the situation festered in Illinois, Strother arrived at his hotel in Little Rock. The phone was ringing as he entered his room.

"It was Henkel," he reported later, "weeping on the telephone. He was actually crying. He said, 'Why have you done this?' I said, 'What have I done?' He said, 'Those ads went on the air without Gary's approval.' I said, 'No. I had Gary's approval. Check with Chris Dodd. Check with Pat Caddell.' He said, 'Gary wants those ads off the air.' "

Strother explained that with the computerized system of programming at major city stations, the ads could not be lifted until Monday. He suggested that they say nothing and let the ads run the four or five times they were scheduled over the weekend and they could be yanked Monday morning without fanfare. Joe Mercurio, who was involved in the time-buying, had told Henkel the same thing.

"I didn't understand that," Henkel said later, "but I took them at face value. They said, 'You're gonna make a big fuss over getting it off the air and not going to be able to do it. So forget it. Let us play it, because we're only going to play it through the weekend anyhow, and then move to other commercials on Monday."

Henkel tracked Hart down at Eugene's, an elegant small restaurant a few blocks off the lakefront in Chicago. It was now about eleven o'clock. "Gary, it's [still] running," Henkel told his candidate.

Hart was adamant. "I want it taken off the air," he told Henkel.

30. Hart did, however, defend the use of the anti-Vrdolyak ad for a brief time. He told reporters who questioned him that night at the University of Illinois: "People have a right to know who is supporting which candidate, and make their decisions based on that."

When Henkel related Strother's explanation of why it was impossible to do so, Hart replied: "I don't care what it takes. I want those commercials taken off the air."

Henkel, still agitated, called Strother again. "Gary wants the ads off this minute," he said. Henkel, Strother recalled, "would not take no for an answer."

Strother then began a frantic but largely futile effort to locate station managers by phone in the middle of the night, get them out of bed, endure their irritated explanations about why the ads couldn't be killed, and try to persuade them to go into the station to do so.

"We did everything in our power to get that done [get the ads pulled]," Henkel said later, "but we were successful in only one or two cases. We ended up on Monday morning sending telegrams out to every station where we had sold that commercial."

The affair became such a fiasco, he said, that one Chicago television station received the telegram shortly after nine o'clock Monday morning and at about eleven, Henkel got a phone call from Howell Raines, the New York *Times* political reporter, covering the primary in Chicago.

"Pudge," he said, according to Henkel, "I thought these were supposed to go off the air. I'm sitting here in my hotel room and I've just seen another one." Henkel told him of the efforts made to pull the ads, but skepticism was rampant by now, with obvious reason.

"It was so bad," Henkel recalled, "that that same channel . . . editorialized that night about our apparent lack of sincerity," when it had itself received the "kill" telegram. "That kind of epitomizes how the Illinois campaign fell apart in a tactical way."

"At this point," Strother said, "the message became, 'Why can't Gary Hart pull the ads?' Just what I predicted would happen happened. Mondale said, 'How can a man run the country if he can't run his own campaign?' At that point, the campaign changed direction. It wasn't necessarily lost, but it lost all its steam built up in New Hampshire and Florida."

Caddell agreed. "I've been in campaigns where it's happened before," he said later. "The one drill is that the candidate doesn't say anything about it [the unwanted ad]."

Because Hart wasn't able to get the ad off the air after saying he would, Caddell said, he suddenly plunged from being ahead of Mondale by twelve or thirteen percentage points to falling 9 percent behind. "I've never seen anything like this," Caddell lamented.

Henkel later disputed Caddell's reading. There actually were two public-opinion samplings after the incident, he said, the first of which included no minority voters. This one showed Hart artificially high, he said, and when the minorities were factored in, Mondale went up and Hart down. It was that factor, rather than the content of the commercial, that gave the appearance of a precipitous Hart drop in the wake of the Vrdolyak ad, he insisted.

In any event, the episode clearly hurt Hart. Why he was so insistent on pulling the ads has remained a matter of conjecture among his closest aides and supporters. Most believed that once the ads ran it would have been much better to leave them on, at least over the weekend, particularly since Hart had been obliged just the day before to backtrack on the Mondale ads that never ran. Moreover, there was an obvious justification for running them in the first place. Mondale had been trumpeting his endorsements for a year. So how could he complain about having one of them hung around his neck?

One reason Hart was so adamant may have been that after the fiasco on the "phantom" ads, Hart felt he had to reassert authority over his campaign. It was then in the throes of what one of the participants later called "a fight over message control" involving Henkel, Landau and pollster Dotty Lynch on one hand and Caddell on the other.

Exasperation and exhaustion may well have played a part, too, Henkel acknowledged. The gaffes "came so closely on the heels of one another, and I'm sure at this point, Gary was exhausted having just come through Super Tuesday and all the strain that put on him. In one and a half days, all of this problem with communications and media—What in the hell is going on? I'm sure that played a part in his reaction: 'I don't care how tough it is, take it off the air.' "

At any rate, trying to pull the ads proved to be a politically disastrous action—and a commentary on the hazards of inadequate or harried staffing in the insane, pell-mell exercise of "front-loading" the delegate-selection process.

Before Illinois Democrats went to the polls, however, Mondale had his "insurance policy" in Michigan to cash in. And for a time early on Super Saturday—with tests also in Arkansas, Mississippi and South Carolina—the former Vice President had a major scare.

The Michigan caucuses were supposedly made to order for Mondale. The process was not as open as a primary; there were not as many voting sites as there would be in a primary, and their special locations were unfamiliar to many voters. All these factors were viewed in advance as advantages to Mondale because they seemed to dictate a limited, calculable turnout hospitable to his superior organizational support in the state.

The combination of forces in Mondale's corner was formidable: Blanchard's state party and personal campaign team, the United Auto Workers and other AFL-CIO affiliates in this heavily organized state, and the support of Mayor Coleman Young of Detroit, who was openly hostile to Jesse Jackson and was determined to deliver the black vote to Mondale. By contrast, Hart had only a ragtag, makeshift operation centered in Ann Arbor to try to capitalize on his ebbing early New England momentum.

If the Mondale forces could deliver the voters they had identified as dependable for him—about 25,000 of them—it was calculated they would be enough to assure him a solid victory. The total turnout in the 1980 Michigan caucuses, after all, had been only 16,000.

For all these reasons, however, Marty Kaplan said later, "Michigan was more of a problem for us because expectations were so high."

For a time on Saturday, those expectations, in fact, threatened to do Mondale in. Something never anticipated happened. Michigan Democrats around the state started coming out of the woodwork to vote in numbers that suggested the possibility of another Hart "tidal wave."

Mondale, marching in a St. Patrick's Day parade in frigid Waukegan, Illinois, in the early afternoon, had his mind on the Michigan caucuses but knew nothing about this unexpected phenomenon.

Tom Donilon, his chief delegate-hunter, recalled the scene: "Mondale grabs me in the parade and he says, 'Call Michigan and find out what's going on.' So I go to a telephone booth and call Ellen Globokar, the state coordinator. Globokar says turnout is twice what we expected. At that point, it was no way; Hart had brought another hundred thousand new voters into this thing, and we were dead meat. I got in the car with Mondale, it was cold as hell, and he says, 'What's going on in Michigan?' I said, 'It's going to be a hundred and fifty thousand participants.' Mondale goes, 'That's it. We're gonna get our ass kicked."

Mondale told us later that for all the supposed advantages he had in Michigan, he was still worried that morning. "I was still traumatized by Maine, which was also a caucus state," he said. "I thought we'd do okay in Michigan, but we were still fighting back."

The Mondale party returned to a conference center where he was supposed to be preparing for another debate with Hart and Jackson in Chicago the next night. But he was now consumed with what seemingly was shaping up as a disaster in Michigan.

"He was nervous all afternoon," Kaplan recalled, "and we spent the better part of the day sitting in his suite on the phone with virtually an open line to Ellen Globokar getting accounts of what was happening. He was relentless in wanting to know the latest scrap of information. Walk-ins in a caucus state are just what you don't want."

Jim Johnson, the campaign chairman, said later: "It was clear that if it was a test of organization, we were in trouble."

As matters evolved, the Michigan turnout was about 140,000, dwarfing the 25,000 Democrats Mondale's organization had identified and was geared to bring out for him.

"The turnout was fantastic," Mondale recalled, "and it turns out they were for me."

That the walk-ins in Michigan were heavily for Mondale—the Democrat alleged to have no charisma—in fact gave him and his strategists their biggest psychological boost since television had bestowed the Super Tuesday "victory" on the candidate.

"A lot of people came who weren't organized," Donilon said later. "In Maine, people we'd never seen were coming to the caucuses, and when that happened we were dead. It changed that day in Michigan. That was the first real smell we had that there was a new dynamic out there. The strategy was working—the contrast and comparison with Hart over a sustained number of days was hurting, and Mondale was starting to become more attractive."

Whether that latter judgment was accurate was debatable. But it was clear that at least some of the air was going out of the Hart balloon.

Mondale's victory in Michigan did not yield the news-media boon the campaign had hoped for, simply because Mondale had been expected to win. But it did generate a very substantial delegate prize for him—79 out of 136 at stake that day and the single largest number from any state up to that point—at a time delegate-accumulation had begun to take on more significance.

"We were disappointed about the spin we got out of it," Donilon said, "but from our own point of view we thought it was a big turning point."

Mondale wound up with just under 50 percent of the Michigan vote to about 32 percent for Hart and 18 percent for Jackson, and Mondale also won in Arkansas, enabling him to claim that he really was on the comeback trail after Super Tuesday.

"This has been a good national win for me," he said. "We did well on Super Tuesday, we did better today. We're fighting back."

Hart contented himself with claiming "an extraordinary achievement" in a state "where the process was stacked against us."

The national focus, however, remained on Illinois, where Hart's gaffes were doing him in. His inability to get the anti-Vrdolyak ads off the air had by this time become as much a subject of discussion as any of the issues separating the candidates, and the diversion made it impossible for Hart to get back on track. Chicago's newspapers and television stations were inundating the voters with coverage of the primary fight—especially now that it had embroiled "Fast Eddie" Vrdolyak, who by now also was taking swings at Hart.

From Michigan, Kaplan said, "we went to Illinois with several things going for us. Hart played into precisely the set of mistakes which we defined as a test. What we had managed to do through the red phone ad and this pattern of attack was to allow the public to conclude about someone that if he couldn't pull an ad off the screen, he was the wrong person to deal with nuclear war. That's a hell of a leap, but somehow it all worked because we had been pounding away at it so relentlessly and Hart provided two major opportunities for him to be seen in that context."

On primary night, Mondale, in spite of a heavy black vote for

Jackson, beat Hart by five percentage points in a state in which he had trailed by more than twice that much in some polls only a few days earlier. The Illinois result served to validate politically the very generous network reading for Mondale of the Super Tuesday voting, and to restore Mondale as the frontrunner.

"It sealed the marathon theory," Kaplan said, referring to the Mondale argument at this point that the race would go on all through the primaries. "People were catching up to the Super Tuesday results. The hindsight began to show what was and was not accomplished that night, and essentially that what we had done prior to the Illinois primary was to get back into the race. People allowed us to be thought of as a contender. The question was, Could someone rehabilitated after such serious damage possibly be strong enough to go on and really be a winner?" Illinois provided an affirmative answer, he said.

Johnson agreed. "If Hart had won Illinois," he said later, "it would have exposed the fragility of Super Tuesday. Illinois was the crucial point."

And Bob Beckel, the campaign manager, acknowledged that Mondale could very well have lost Illinois "if Hart hadn't had that screwup" on the Vrdolyak ads. Instead, Mondale went on to the New York primary with his image considerably restored and his delegate total building, leaving a dazed and wounded Hart limping behind him.

Mondale himself said later that "if Illinois had gone down it would have been very difficult to carry on." Illinois, he said, was the turning point for him.

After the Hart upsets in New England had hit him "like a hurricane," knocking his feet from under him, Mondale said, now at last he was able to get a foothold. "I'd found ground again," he said.

But what the voting public had gained from the week-to-week, sometimes even day-to-day, skirmishing across the map of America was another matter. The "debate" that Mondale bragged he had forced on Hart had now been elevated to such lofty questions as whether or not Mondale had tried to make capital of Hart's name change, and whether or not Hart could withdraw television ads his staff had aired against his wishes. Neither of these "issues" was helping the voters to assess the candidates in terms of the truly pressing problems of the day, such as the state of the economy or arms control. Even in the more partisan terms of helping Democratic voters identify issues that held promise of posing a serious challenge to Ronald Reagan in the fall, the "dialogue" was weighted down in negativism and trivia. As an educational process, the campaign was leaving a great deal to be desired.

As for the sheer politics, the front-loading of the nomination process—which Hart unexpectedly had turned to his advantage with his momentum-building surprises in Iowa, New England and Florida—was at last catching up with him. His own energies and those of his undermanned, overextended and inexperienced staff had been taxed to the breaking point by the pressures of the political tidal wave on which he had been riding through nineteen primaries and caucuses in the solitary month since the process had begun. Just as suddenly as fortune had smiled on Hart, it was now leering as he struggled to remain in a race that moved toward other northern industrial states—New York and Pennsylvania—of Mondale organizational and labor strength.

What Hart needed now was an issue to cool off Mondale the way his own two gaffes in Illinois had brought him back within Mondale's sights. But the Mondale campaign, unlike Hart's, was made of up old pros in the political game who were too smart, and too careful, to hand Hart any such opportunity. Or so it was generally thought.

10

The Delegate-Committee Thing

•

AS WALTER MONDALE moved East to the next two major primaries in New York and Pennsylvania, all was not as rosy in his campaign as might have seemed from his comeback victory in Illinois. His candidacy was back on track, to be sure. But unknown to most outsiders was the fact that Mondale Inc., as the high-powered campaign had come to be called, had very little money left, after the failure of its expensive "early knockout" strategy, to continue waging the nomination fight.

Many of Mondale's dependable contributors had already given his campaign the maximum $1,000 permissible under the federal election finance laws. And the campaign itself was fast approaching the spending ceiling of about $20.4 million under those laws for the pre-convention period. Meanwhile Gary Hart, though beaten in Illinois, was now raising ample funds to challenge Mondale in the key tests ahead.

Ways had to be found to enable Mondale to persevere. It so happened that the general counsel of the Mondale organization, a young lawyer named David Ifshin who specialized in the federal campaign finance laws, had already located an answer. In the spring of 1983, campaign manager Bob Beckel recalled later, he had instructed Ifshin "to go through every regulation the Federal Election Commission had, and every finance law. I wanted to be sure that we knew every legal avenue open to us. . . . Was there anything new that we could take advantage of? I thought it was my responsibility to get every resource I could figure out to get into that campaign. The delegate-committee thing came back. It was perfectly legal. . . . It was going to be just another avenue for us to have funds to try to knock the thing out early."

What Beckel called "the delegate-committee thing" was a vehicle authorized by the FEC in 1980 to elect individuals running in the primaries for national party convention delegate. The device had been uncovered by Ifshin's legal staff while preparing a manual on the federal campaign finance laws for the guidance of Mondale campaign workers.

"When it came back to me," Ifshin said later, "I was astonished at the size of the potential loophole. It was pretty clear that the regulations were not carefully drawn or well thought through."

In the 1976 campaign for the Republican presidential nomination, the strategists for President Gerald R. Ford had created such committees, but they were barred afterward by the Federal Election Commission on grounds they were not sufficiently accountable under existing FEC guidelines. However, amid complaints that highly centralized national campaigns, with their heavy preference for television advertising, were killing grass-roots politics, the FEC rewrote the regulations in 1980. They now specified that local delegate-candidates could, as individuals or with committees, raise and spend money to advance their own election as delegates, provided they limited their activities to basic grass-roots activities. They could buy brochures, buttons and bumper-stickers, for example, but not mass-media activities such as newspaper, radio or television advertisements.

Ifshin immediately saw the new regulations as a way to put grass-roots politics back into the Mondale campaign. He noted that the FEC rules specified that such delegate committees had to be autonomous—that is, that they could neither be established nor directed by the campaign of the presidential candidate. But he noted also that the regulations provided that a presidential campaign could give candidates for delegate advice and assistance in establishing such committees on their own, and in complying with FEC financial reporting requirements. The committees just had to take care to remain separate entities. From all accounts, Ifshin bent over backwards at this juncture to emphasize that the division of function and control remain clear, in both appearance and reality.

"Out of an abundance of caution," he said later, "we cautioned people to be absolutely careful that we did not control the committees."

The formula seemed simple enough. With the national campaign raising and spending money on such big-ticket, nationally focused items as television advertising, massive direct mail, headquarters operations and candidate travel, there was a vacuum of activity, including non-competitive fund-raising, at the local level. And who would be better to fill it than delegates working in their own behalf to go to the national convention? In advancing their own cause, as Mondale delegates they would at the same time be working for him in the primaries.

At 34, David Ifshin was an expert in campaign finance law. A graduate of Syracuse University and the Stanford Law School, he had written a lengthy tract on the impact of the Federal Election Campaign Act on the 1976 Democratic presidential nomination contest that was published in the Santa Clara Law Review. After graduation from Stanford and admission to the California Bar, he had plunged into campaign finance law in Washington, handling cases for both the Republicans and the Democrats, and for private corporations challenging union political contributions. He had also worked on Capitol Hill for Senator Howard Metzenbaum of Ohio and others and lectured part-time at the Yale Law School. In other words, he was already steeped in campaign finance when the Mondale campaign made him their in-house specialist.

But Ifshin was more than your run-of-the-mill campaign finance lawyer. He was a political animal as well, having worked as an organizer in Michigan and elsewhere, and on top of that he was involved in Jewish political affairs. In fact, he wore two hats in the Mondale campaign, also giving advice to the candidate on Jewish matters, especially regarding Israel and the Middle East.

Above all, David Ifshin was the classic young man in a hurry. Lean and frenetic in speech and movement, with a black beard that would have made him look menacing except for a confident openness about him, he was not one to hide his light under a bushel basket. Ask him his name and you would get not only his rank and serial number, but also a synopsis of all his legal and political credits going back to the cradle. Talking to him only a few minutes revealed a man with an intense desire and determination to be an important player in the Mondale campaign.

Ifshin took his idea for Mondale delegate committees to his superiors, presenting it as a supplementary campaign tool at a long meeting in May 1983 at Jim Johnson's farm in Virginia, and they bought it. Mondale, from all accounts, knew nothing of the idea at the time, nor for many months to come. Ifshin and his associates wrote a forty-three page memo to the campaign staff that spelled out what could and couldn't be done under the regulations. The approach, he said, was "not going to decide the campaign" but would help to put it back on Main Street.

Mike Ford, the campaign's political director, remembered later, however, that Ifshin in the fall handed him a heavy document and said: "We've got a loophole big enough to drive a truck through."

In two subsequent meetings in the fall, the scheme was discussed and developed further. Subsequently, another memo on the subject was prepared for Mondale delegate-candidates by the campaign's chief delegate-slater, Elaine Kamarck, in consultation with Ifshin and Beckel.

That memo, finally dated January 12, 1984, later became a centerpiece of a lively controversy inside and outside the Mondale campaign, because it specifically drew another critical point. Mondale earlier had made much of a decision of his that as a presidential candidate he would not accept political action committee (PAC) money. He had been an outspoken critic of the corrupting influence of PAC money on the political process, and as far back as the California state convention in Sacramento in January of 1983 he had said:

> The first thing we must do as Democrats is to restore the trust of the American people in their government. It's not just that Ronald Reagan is abusing that trust. There is a reason why over half of the American people don't even bother to vote anymore. . . . That is the rising, growing, exploding power of special-interest money in American politics.
>
> Last year, the Republicans spent $150 million more than we did, but that's not my point. This problem affects both our parties. You and I know that these rivers and oceans of special-interest money are pressing and compromising our government—shattering public trust and paralyzing the capacity of the American people to serve the public interest.
>
> I say it's time, fellow Democrats, that we declare war on special-interest money in American politics. Let's put a cap on campaign spending. Let's plant controls on these PACs. Let's end the loopholes of so-called independent committees. . . . And in these next two years, let us say again that the government of the United States is not up for sale. It belongs to the American people, and we want it back.

Kamarck's memo reminded the Mondale delegates of their candidate's position against accepting PAC money. But at the same time, it informed them that it was legal to do so—and that each delegate committee was free to decide whether or not to accept it.

The memo stated: "Contributions by corporations, labor unions, foreign nationals and federal contractors are not permitted. But contributions from Political Action Committees of issue groups or labor unions are permitted. Individuals and Political Action Committees can contribute up to five thousand dollars to a delegate committee. Walter Mondale has made a decision not to accept money from PACs for his campaign. Each delegate committee may make their own decision regarding PAC money."

Jim Johnson said later in an interview that Kamarck's memo, though written "in an effort to be helpful to people," had been "totally unauthorized." In fact, its wording was carefully reviewed by both Ifshin and Beckel, as witnessed by notations each made in the margin of her draft copy before it went out.

Johnson said subsequently that as a result of the Kamarck memo, he told Beckel "we've got to get square" on the matter and instructed him to send another letter to the delegates laying out the policy on PAC money. Beckel indeed did write such a letter—dated the very same day as Kamarck's.

"It is the policy of the Mondale Campaign," it said, "not to accept money from organized Political Action Committees. This policy was announced prior to the start of the campaign. It is our sincere hope that Delegate Expenditure Committees will follow suit and decline to accept Political Action Committee contributions."

One campaign insider later described Beckel's letter as "a cover-your-ass memo, a memo for the file. It was clear," this insider said, "that a good deal of money was going into the campaign from PACs, inconsistent with what Mondale was saying. So it was important that there was paper."

Significantly, from all accounts there was little thought given to the approach of telling the Mondale delegates in a single letter that while PAC money could legally be accepted, Mondale was against doing so and that he urged his delegate committees to abide by his wishes. Instead, it was rationalized that to make any such direct observation would constitute evidence of control over, or affiliation with, the committees, in violation of the FEC regulations.

"We had said at the outset," Ifshin said later, "that Mondale had a policy of taking no PAC contributions, [but] delegate committees did not have that restriction. If we were simply to impose on the committees and say, 'You've got to follow Mondale's personal preferences—not what the law is—because Mondale believes PAC contributions shouldn't be given, you've got to follow his rules,' that's an indication of affiliation. So I felt, listen, the worst thing you can do is go out and tell these committees that you've got to follow Walter Mondale's personal views as opposed to the law."

Such reasoning, obviously, was a dodge; the Mondale strategists wanted labor money, but they couldn't get their hands on it directly without violating Mondale's edict. Here was a way to get that money into the campaign through a back door conveniently provided by the delegate-committee device.

Beckel himself said afterward: "That's exactly one of the things you don't talk about. I knew we were going to take PAC money. Mondale didn't know we were going to take PAC money. Only a couple of us knew we were going to take PAC money, and that's the way it should have been."

Still another memo was written by the campaign finance chairman, Tim Finchem, dated January 30. It instructed the state coordinators in Florida, Illinois and Pennsylvania to "urge our delegate committees to raise money from only those people who have maxed out to the Mondale campaign." Finchem sent along lists of "maxed-out" contributors in each state—those who had already given the maximum allowable $1,000 to the Mondale campaign. He did not want competition in fund-raising from the new entities.

Long before the first delegate-selecting primaries, Ifshin and other Mondale Inc. lawyers busied themselves informing Mondale state coordinators in key states about the delegate-committee scheme. It seemed particularly applicable in those states where party rules stipulated that delegates' names appear directly on the ballot, rather than only the presidential candidates they supported.

One such state was Illinois, where state law required a very early deadline for filing delegate slates. Although Johnson said in an interview after the campaign that "we didn't have delegate committees in Illinois to speak of," the fact was that in due course some twenty-one delegate committees were established in the state, without fanfare and apparently within the FEC regulations. Delegates were properly slated and, from all indications, ran their own committees as the regulations specified. The Mondale state coordinator, a conscientious young man named Jim Margolis from Michigan, proceeded cautiously, uneasy about the legality of the procedure. He even asked Ifshin to come into the state to satisfy him on the matter and explain its workings to his staff, which Ifshin enthusiastically did.

Weeks in advance of the Illinois primary, however, delegate committees were being established in other states that did not clearly meet the criterion of delegates running directly on the ballot for their own election. One was New Hampshire. The prime reason there for such committees was not to help elect individual Mondale delegates, but rather to help the Mondale campaign in the state skirt the federal spending ceiling, which, based on the voting-age population, was about $404,000. The campaign was approaching the ceiling—it eventually exceeded it in violation of the law—and the "independent" delegate committees became a way to funnel money into the state that would not be counted against the campaign limit.

As disclosed later in the Washington *Post*, Mondale agents in New Hampshire began setting up the first delegate committee there one day after the date of Elaine Kamarck's memo informing delegates of the device, the procedure and the legality of taking PAC money. It was, at the least, a tribute to the incredible speed on this one occasion of the much-maligned U.S. Postal Service. Somehow, frequent givers to Democratic Party causes from as far away as New Jersey, Maryland, Florida and California learned that the new and presumably obscure "New Hampshire Second District Delegates for Mondale" committee was in need of funds, and that contributions could be mailed to the committee's treasurer, one Anthony Redington, at 4 Neil Drive in Allenstown, New Hampshire.

None of the givers contacted by the *Post* reporter seemed able, however, to recall how he or she had learned about the delegate committee or where to send money to it. Nor would Redington tell the *Post* at the time who had advised him to establish the committee. He acknowledged that more than $14,000 raised went for subsistence for Mondale workers who had somehow found their way to New Hampshire from as far away as Minnesota, Michigan and Alabama. At least ten of them who got delegate-committee subsistence checks turned up on the Mondale Inc. payroll a week later. After the election, Redington told us a Mondale staff representative had met with the delegates and advised them on formation of the committee in accordance with the law.

That mysterious chartered jet that flew from Minneapolis to Boston two days after the Iowa caucuses, transporting about sixty-five young Mondale campaign workers to New Hampshire, was financed almost entirely with funds from delegate committees. The purchase and allocation of their plane tickets, obviously, were not accomplished without the sort of collaboration between the main campaign and the delegate committees that was specifically prohibited by the FEC regulations. Finchem, in yet another internal staff memo, explicitly assigned a priority to "encouragement of fund-raising for the New Hampshire delegate committees."

Later reports to the FEC showed that all fifty-one individual contributors to delegate committees in New Hampshire were from out-of-state, that forty-two of them had given $1,000 or more, and that thirty-one of them had given a like amount to the Mondale-for-President Committee.

Because the Mondale campaign had front-loaded its spending in pursuit of an early knockout of the other Democratic contenders, money became a problem as the campaign dragged on. That condition in turn soon converted the delegate committees from convenient helpmates to essential sources of money and manpower. And in the process, one insider said later, the device "turned into a monster." Before the controversy was over, some 134 delegate committees had been established, raising and spending more than $700,000—often in ways in violation of or at least flirting with violation of, the law, and in conflict with Mondale's professed wishes about PAC money.

"These things began to multiply like rabbits," another insider recalled.

In spite of Beckel's letter urging delegate committees to adhere to Mondale's policy against taking such money, labor union PACs quickly became major contributors to them. The reasons were simple.

First, since Mondale had expressly prohibited receipt of PAC funds in his own national campaign, unions that had endorsed his candidacy had to find other channels for their support, and delegate committees were obvious ones.

Second, unions that were backing Mondale sought to have their members elected as Mondale delegates. They saw no reason why they could not, or should not, direct their PAC resources into the election of their own people as delegates. If Mondale were to fail as a candidate, if for no other reason, the unions still wanted their people at the Democratic convention to vote labor's interests.

"We were slating enormous numbers of labor delegates," Kamarck recalled. "One of the reasons so much labor money ended going there [to the delegate committees] was that the AFL-CIO made a very strong policy that their people were to run only as Mondale delegates. When we lost the New Hampshire primary, the AFL-CIO was in the position of having a candidate looking like he was going down the tubes but having every single labor delegate already on ballot pledged to Walter Mondale."

This fact, she said, gave labor unions an extremely strong motivation to raise and pump money into the delegate committees on which so many labor people were slated. The AFL-CIO's political operatives needed no advice from anyone to look ahead and see where their best interest lay in the event of a Mondale collapse.

Florida, as Finchem's memo suggested, was another place where the delegate-committee gimmick was heavily utilized by the Mondale campaign. Ifshin assumed that the Hart campaign had also discovered the FEC loophole and, as the Mondale campaign was now doing, was preparing to drive a truck through it. By this time, former Governor Reubin Askew's presidential campaign had collapsed, and Hart, who had not adequately slated delegates of his own for the Florida primary, sought to "adopt" some of the Askew slated delegates. To this end, the Hart campaign ran newspaper ads urging voters to back the Askew delegates as Hart delegate stand-ins in certain congressional districts (CDs). Ifshin concluded that the advertising was being done under the delegate-committee rubric and hence was illegal. He called Jack Quinn, counsel for the Hart campaign, and told him some of his people in Florida were running newspaper ads on delegate committees. According to Ifshin, Quinn replied: "Delegate committees? What are delegate committees?"

It was a great little story, but Quinn said it never happened. "That is just pure fiction," he told us later. He got a phone call from Ifshin all right, he said, but "we knew all about the regulations governing delegates. The problem was, the regulations he was using didn't apply to delegate committees," Quinn insisted.

As the money crunch got worse for the Mondale campaign, the delegate-committee scheme spread not only to primary states where delegates actually ran on the ballot but also to those primary states where they didn't or where some were chosen at-large after the primary election. Soon they were being created even in caucus states in which there never was a normal ballot procedure. From their original status as complementary appendages to Mondale Inc., delegate committees in some states were becoming the whole Mondale field operation—with Ifshin by this time aggressively selling his "baby" as the savior of the financially beleaguered campaign.

"Money was needed too badly to keep the field running," one insider said later. "The thing was a creeping cancer. When it was originally thought of, nobody ever anticipated that the entire campaign in states would be run on delegate committees."

When the campaign got into financial trouble in losing New Hampshire, this insider said, "every single penny had to go into media costs and travel costs for Super Tuesday. There was no other way to run the field operation. And so what you had was this interaction between Ifshin and the field people in the campaign. The delegate committees became a way to keep the field organization going, to keep all these organizers on payroll. Somewhat because he was under pressure and somewhat because he wanted to help, Ifshin's legal opinion evolved."

This same Mondale campaign insider later gave this version of Ifshin's role in the expanding function of the delegate committees: "A good election lawyer lawyers, and keeps the blinders on. A good election lawyer is always giving you the most conservative opinion and then letting you decide whether or not you want to go one step further. Ifshin was very, very insecure. He desperately, desperately wanted to be part of the inner circle and part of the decision-making. This delegate-committee thing allowed him to play with the big boys. . . . When he started getting into things like at-large delegate committees (when no at-large delegates were actually running) and delegate committees in caucus states, that was just ridiculous. That was really stretching it. But it was Ifshin's personal desire to be a big player. And the campaign needed these things too badly. Your lawyer tells you something, and you want to believe it, and you don't second-guess your lawyer. . . . Once you got into trouble, the delegate committees got too important to the running of the campaign."

A very personal element also entered into the growth of the "creeping cancer" of delegate committees. Their use became, in addition to a means to give the Mondale campaign a local presence in the field, a vehicle—eventually the only vehicle—for keeping scores of young Mondale loyalists in the campaign—and eating.

After the Iowa caucuses, when many of these young and enthusiastic foot soldiers were brought into New Hampshire with delegate-committee money, their assignment to delegate-committee payrolls threatened to shatter any pretense that the committees were not directly controlled by Mondale Inc. So the solution simply was to drop them from the official Mondale campaign staff and insist they were free agents who drifted from one state to another seeking out and working for local delegate committees, in the manner of migrants finding seasonal work in farm country. It was not, in fact, an entirely inaccurate description of what happened.

At least as far back as the Gene McCarthy campaign of 1968, presidential campaigns had become an irresistible magnet for hundreds of young men and women, a great many of them college students. Previously, many of them had plunged into politics in the great civil-rights revolution in the South in the early 1960s. Then they had turned to elective politics as a means to advance the ideals that motivated them or to try to bring an end to American involvement in the war in Vietnam. In 1968, although they were monumentally frustrated by a year that saw the defeat of McCarthy, the assassinations of Martin Luther King and Robert Kennedy and the election of Richard Nixon, many retained faith in the system as a promising avenue for social and political change.

Many others were attracted by the sheer glamour of a presidential campaign, by the sense of importance participating in it gave them, and by the camaraderie that quickly developed among the young participants of both sexes. For whatever reason, there grew up a very sizable community of young political activists whose energy, commitment and innovative talents became a valuable resource for any campaign. Fritz Mondale, for all his reputation as a tired old warhorse representing the politics of the past, was able to attract a considerable cadre of these eager beavers. They were ready, willing and able to bop about the country, living on a shoestring per-diem allowance of fifteen or eighteen dollars for the joy of being a player in the great quadrennial political drama.

Out of this community there also developed leaders—young political organizers who, very like migrant workers, labored in the rhythm of the political cycle, going from one campaign at one level to another in the "off-season"—the three years between presidential election years. They sustained themselves, if they were lucky and good, as political consultants or public-relations hirelings, or even in the usual odd jobs behind a bar or on a construction crew until another campaign came around. The men and women who ran national and statewide campaigns came to know who these young leaders were, and they competed for them at the time campaign organizations were being assembled.

In the Glenn campaign already examined, to take one example, Joe Grandmaison was one of these sought-after young leaders; in the Mondale campaign, Paul Tully and Mike Ford and, on a lower level, Joe Trippi were in this same category. They were, in the description of one Mondale insider, political "gypsies," and the young legions who answered their call were "camp followers" who drifted from one state to another just to remain in the action.

These were the personalities and the dynamics that played into the delegate-committee phenomenon in the Mondale campaign. After the Iowa caucuses, when the young organizers on the Mondale staff payroll were told there would be a jet in Minneapolis waiting to take them east to another state assignment if they wanted to go, they didn't waste time asking who was going to pay their way or who would pay them when they got there. Trippi said later that none of those who drove rented cars back to Minneapolis and boarded the jet as part of the transfer east of "the Fritz-blitzers" knew or cared about the fine print.

A memo from Ford's field operations office in Washington went to the Mondale state coordinators in Iowa and New Hampshire on the eve of the Iowa caucuses, when the campaign was beginning to recognize it had a fight on its hands in New Hampshire. It listed sixty-six staff and per-diem workers in Iowa who were to be asked on a last-minute basis whether they would go to New Hampshire. The movement was code-named "Fritzkrieg" in the memo, and it concluded: "These 66 will be asked Monday nite/Tuesday morning. We expect some dropoff. Please replace so that we do in fact have 64 people coming into New Hampshire."

Ford later said it was his understanding that the letter of the law was spelled out to the young loyalists, but all they wanted to do was get on with the campaign, which after Iowa seemed to be soaring.

"A delegate-committee network built up," he recalled. "In Iowa, the first movement of people, it was explained I think that 'you're no longer employed by the Mondale campaign. You're going to have a chance if you want to be employed by delegate committees. Their function is to elect delegates, and that obviously benefits Walter Mondale.' And they all said, 'Yeah, yeah, yeah, let's go.' And they got on a plane and went."

As for the staffers who were running the Mondale field operation, the delegate committees were a welcome resource at a time of real need.

"One thing that happens in the field," Ford said, "it's just like any infantry. Anything you can get—you take. If you get five bucks, that's great. You can buy a P-and-J [peanut-butter-and-jelly sandwich]."

Ifshin himself recognized this reality. In cautioning field organizers about the proper role of delegate committees, he said later, "you were talking to people who are political operatives running a campaign. This was not General Motors, where you've got people sitting around big offices and can bring the lawyers in every five minutes. People understood the nature of control and did their best to comply, in my judgment."

The movement of the young organizers from the Mondale staff in Iowa and elsewhere to delegate committees in New Hampshire, however, raised a red flag with Ifshin and the legal staff. After the New Hampshire loss, Ford planned routinely to move those imports on to Maine, where Trippi had gone to try to put out the Hart fire storm there. They would be placed on the Maine payroll for the few days left to go before the Maine caucuses. Ifshin said no.

"The legal staff," Trippi explained later, "had decided it was okay to move off national staff to a delegate committee, but it was illegal to move back to the Mondale staff, because that would show coordination. So what that meant was these legal geniuses had just shot their best organizing team. They had just killed the Iowa state organizers, because they could never again work for Mondale-for-President."

Beckel, according to Trippi, told him to send home all these crossover workers thus "tainted" by the delegate-committee connection. That idea caused an uproar among the foot soldiers. They had unwittingly got themselves into this bind through no misstep of their own but through the hotshot scheme of setting up the delegate committees in the first place, and then the exploiting of it out of expedience.

It became, Trippi said, "more a fight to keep the people, not the committees. We ended up arguing to keep the committees," he said, but it was more a "save-the-kids program."

After the Maine defeat, the need to maintain a field operation on the cheap through the delegate committees became even greater. So the solution was to start moving "the kids" from delegate committees in one state to delegate committees in the next holding a primary or even, in some cases, caucuses. With all the money the national staff could raise now going desperately for media buys and candidate travel, delegate committees in states like New Hampshire that had concluded their primaries started sending surplus funds on to those in states with their primaries or caucuses still to come. Through all this, Mondale Inc. took the pose of innocent bystander. It became abundantly clear later, however, that it had played a considerable if sometimes indirect role in routing both money and manpower.

"There may have been specific cases," Ifshin said afterward, "where people may have been told, 'There's a job. If you go up to that committee, they may hire you.' If you're John Jones, a twenty-year-old kid who has worked in the campaign since the Maine straw poll, the Wisconsin straw poll, and I'm telling him he's fired because there's no more money after New Hampshire, he says, 'I've worked for a year for you, the fight's just beginning, and we're off to Wisconsin. I don't care about my twenty-five dollars a week. I just want to be in the war. Where do I go?' I might say, 'Well, there's a delegate committee out there. Go talk to the delegate committttee. They're going to have some leaflets to pass out and do some stuff.' "

What was happening, however, was much less casual than that mild and innocent scenario. In the pattern of the Iowa "Fritz-krieg," although perhaps not as massively, the young organizers were being shuttled from state to state as the need arose for cheap field hands. All through Super Tuesday and into the Illinois primary, the delegate-committee scheme functioned in secret outside the Mondale Inc. hierarchy.

Then, however, two days before the Illinois primary, a Chicago television reporter broke part of the story in the course of exposing an infiltration of the Mondale Illinois headquarters by private eyes hired by the strongly anti-union National Right to Work Committee, which was seeking evidence of organized labor's role in the campaign. Two of the "spies" were interviewed, and their client subsequently charged in a complaint to the FEC that the Mondale delegate committees in Illinois existed "to launder Big Labor's political contributions and to circumvent federal spending limits." The complaint called the delegate committees "a sham" and "simply branch offices of the Mondale campaign," whose fund-raising should have been included in calculations of the FEC limit for Illinois.

When the Mondale campaign learned its headquarters had been infiltrated, Ifshin wrote to the FEC, asking that the right-to-workers' complaint be thrown out because it was "the product of unlawful conduct which should not be sanctioned by the Commission." One of the hired "spies" told the Chicago television reporter prior to the Illinois primary that he had gained access to the campaign's computer records, and Ifshin in his counter-complaint to the FEC deplored the conduct as "not only egregious and dishonest, it is also unlawful."

The admissions of the two "spies," Ifshin wrote, "are truly shocking and revive memories of the Watergate era when campaign infiltration was unfortunately a commonplace occurrence." He went on: "Infiltration of a political association, by self-appointed police, solely to see if information might constitute some form of wrongdoing, serves no valid public purposes. This sort of vigilante activity cannot be tolerated in any context—and certainly not where freedom of political association is at stake."

The Commission, Ifshin said, "must send a strong signal that these sorts of dirty tricks, which are directly contrary to the purposes and spirit of the Federal Election Campaign Act, will not be tolerated." It was an admonition that would take on a certain irony in light of later events concerning the delegate-committee operation in another state—Pennsylvania.

Interestingly, Mondale was told by a questioner in a debate televised statewide from Chicago on the Sunday night before the primary that a local channel was about to broadcast "a right-wing spy's plot to secretly infiltrate" his campaign. Mondale brushed the report off by observing that "in every campaign we have these cheap Segretti-type tricks"—an obvious reference to Donald Segretti, the confessed dirty-tricks artist in the Watergate scandal. Nothing was mentioned, however, about delegate committees.

The report that subsequently was televised in Chicago did not attract much attention elsewhere, and it was considered suspect anyway because the National Right to Work Committee had such a strong reputation as a labor-baiter.

It was not until about a week later, when Mondale's New York campaign chairman, state Democratic chairman Bill Hennessy, hand-picked by Governor Mario Cuomo, openly talked about the delegate committees in his own state to a Washington *Post* reporter, that their existence surfaced.

"Mondale says he can't take any PAC money," Hennessy said, "but these delegate committees can, and they are taking PAC money. They will get a lot of their money from PACs—both unions and others."

Mondale, campaigning for the New York primary the following Tuesday, hit the ceiling when he found out. Although the matter of the delegate committees had been under discussion at the top levels of the Mondale campaign for about ten months now, every member of the Mondale Inc. hierarchy vowed later that the candidate knew little or nothing about them. And they swore he knew absolutely nothing about their accepting PAC money in contravention of his own declared policy.

At the outset, according to Johnson, the committees were not considered important enough to bother Mondale about. "If I felt in my judgment that there was a strategic importance to a decision about money where he should be asked," Johnson said later, "I would ask him. On the other hand, if there was some reason, even in the primaries, why I was going to spend a million dollars one place and not another place, there was in no sense that he was signing off on that decision. He left that to us."

Johnson said Mondale "must have known" about the committees when Mondale workers from Iowa showed up in New

Hampshire and reporters questioned him about the campaign's approaching the New Hampshire spending limit. But it was of no particular concern to Mondale, he said, until it became public that these committees were taking PAC money.

Mondale himself, however, told us after the election that he knew in advance of the Iowa caucuses—perhaps as early as November or December of 1983—not only that the delegate committees were being established but also that they would be receiving PAC money. At that early juncture, he said, "I said I was very much opposed to it, that it wouldn't be understood, and although the delegate committees were probably legal, and as a matter of fact most of them were legal, and the PAC money was legal, because of my pledge I wanted that pledge kept. I said I wanted it stopped. . . . I said I didn't want it done because I didn't see how I could justify that with what I said I wouldn't do."

But regardless of what Mondale knew and said, his campaign managers went ahead and established the delegate-committee network, financed overwhelmingly in industrial states with labor PAC money.

"Everybody knew that if PAC money filtered in," Ford said later, "Walter Mondale would be very angry."

That, it turned out, was the understatement of the year. At a dinner with his chief aides at the home of wealthy New York backer Arthur Krim the night he found out, Mondale exploded at Johnson and Beckel.

"He was," said one of the participants, "absolutely batshit about the PAC money. Mondale just went crazy. He really got angry. He said, 'I told you guys not to do that. Who made this decision?' "

What irritated Mondale most, his chief delegate-counter, Tom Donilon, recalled, was that the use of PAC money indicated he was welching on a pledge.

"He had made a promise not to use PAC money, and he was going to be damned if they were going to do it some other way," Donilon said. "He said, 'It goes to character. It goes to my ability to make decisions, to my ability to be President. If we flip-flop on a promise is the thing that's going to kill me, and I'm not going to allow it.' Mondale takes these things more seriously than anybody I've ever met, which is why this delegate-committee thing really tore him apart. It really ate at him because of the ethical standards he held himself to. That issue bothered him as much as any attack Hart made on him."

Nevertheless, it took Mondale an inordinately long time to translate his high ethical standards into action, as events and his public pronouncements over the next month amply demonstrated. At first he sought to dismiss the growing allegations of impropriety or worse as ill founded or overdrawn. Then for a time he tried to stem criticism by saying there was nothing he could do about the use of PAC money even though he didn't like it, or that the delegate committees were winding down. But in fact they were taking over virtually his whole field operation.

The surfacing of the delegate-committee controversy, and Hart's attempt to exploit it, did not prevent Mondale from scoring a rousing seventeen-point victory over Hart in the New York primary. But that success stemmed largely from two more tactical errors on Hart's part. The first was challenging Mondale for the Jewish vote, a constituency—in New York particularly—that Mondale had courted effectively over many years and was unshakably for him. The second was Hart's overplaying his hand in a television ad and in stump speeches attacking Mondale as, in effect, no better than Ronald Reagan in advocating reckless policies in Central America.

Both these missteps by Hart had their genesis during the same Illinois primary that witnessed his self-inflicted wounds regarding the "phantom" Mondale ads and his own anti-Vrdolyak ad. In the Chicago debate with Mondale and Jesse Jackson, Hart appeared to have switched positions on an issue of some special interest to American Jews: pressure to move the American embassy in Israel from Tel Aviv to Jerusalem. Mondale had long supported the move, but Hart's staff earlier had sent a letter to a Jewish group indicating that Hart did not.

"I remember being jubilant," Mondale speechwriter Marty Kaplan said later, "when Hart flip-flopped on Jerusalem." Kaplan said he was aware of the letter, and in the press room after the Chicago debate, the customary Mondale "spin patrol" assigned to influence the "spin" the news media put on the candidates' performances—"did some pouncing on it." At that stage, Kaplan said, "we instantly knew we had something for New York. It was the flip-flop, inconsistency, unsteady, untested thing which was happening in Illinois. And so we had another example for it, with relevance to an important group in New York, to now take to that state." Kaplan immediately called David Garth, who at Mario Cuomo's insistence was handling Mondale's television ads for the New York primary, and told the New York media expert about it.

Hart insisted later that the letter in question had not been seen by him and had been sent out by a campaign aide without authorization. It did not represent his position on the embassy move, he said, and in fact he had favored the move "for the better part of two years." He was in agreement, he said, with the official position of the Democratic Party platform since at least 1980 that the embassy ought to be in Jerusalem as the legitimate capital of Israel.

"The only issue," he said, "was timing. In one or two instances [before Jewish leaders in New York], I said this decision to move the embassy could be part of an overall peace settlement in the Middle East—the United States' contribution."

Subsequently, Hart appeared before the Conference of Presidents of Major Jewish Organizations in New York to explain. But with Mondale charging flip-flop, his attempt came off as pandering—exactly what he had been accusing Mondale of doing toward labor and other special-interest support groups.

"What that issue did, because it got portrayed as a pandering issue to get Jewish votes," Hart said afterward, "was to further move me into the more political mold." He was right; whenever Mondale was able to make it appear that Hart was just another politician, it undermined his own criticism of Mondale for being just that.

Also, Mondale was only too willing to have Hart try to compete with him for the Jewish vote, which had always been solidly in his corner. Johnson recalls him saying when he learned of Hart's obvious bid for the Jewish vote: "Gary Hart is going to regret ever raising this issue."

Hart said later the reason he had gotten into it in the first place was that two of his strongest supporters in New York, Representatives Charles Schumer and James Scheuer, had told him the embassy move was the only one that Jewish voters really cared about at that time—a highly questionable contention. Others in the campaign said there was great pressure on Hart from Jewish contributors in California and that Pat Caddell pushed hard for him to make clear an unequivocal position on the embassy move.

One insider insisted, in fact, that the letter in question did fairly reflect Hart's position at the time; that right after Super Tuesday, with Illinois and New York and their influential Jewish constituencies looming ahead, it was decided Hart would have to change his position publicly. Some in the campaign, including issues coordinator David Landau, argued that it was a mistake for Hart to seem to be courting the Jewish vote so ardently, and that instead he should have worked areas of high unemployment in Rust Belt cities upstate like Buffalo. In any event, Hart had stumbled again, and he paid for it in New York.[31]

The other issue that diverted attention from the delegate-committee matter and hurt Hart in New York was his attack on Mondale on his Central America policies. In speeches before the Council on Foreign Relations in Chicago in the last days before the Illinois primary, Mondale and Hart appeared to differ on retention of American troops in Central America. Hart took a more categorical position about getting them out; Mondale seemed to be suggesting that some American troops ought to be left there as a bargaining chip with Nicaragua, to get the Sandinista regime to desist in its alleged attempts to overthrow the anti-Sandinista government of El Salvador.

Hart, champing at what he regarded as blatant misrepresentations by Mondale of his own positions on everything from arms control to civil rights, elected to attack Mondale with heavily negative ads on Central America. His campaign in New York began to run what came to be known as "the fuse ad," showing a bomb with a lighted fuse, as a narrator said: "When President Reagan sent men to Central America he called them advisers. Remember Vietnam? Our troops now serve as bodyguards to dictators, and are a slow-burning fuse to war. Vice President

31. Ray Strother, Hart's media consultant, said later that another gaffe that would have fed the "unsteadiness factor" was averted in New York when he talked Hart out of withdrawing a television ad on the embassy question that Hart belatedly didn't like. "I told Gary at that point," Strother said, " 'Gary, if you go through this again like you did in Chicago, you can write it off.' " Again, as in Chicago, it was a weekend night, and Strother told Hart the ad could be pulled off the air quietly on Monday morning. Hart agreed, and it was, and nothing was ever said or written about it.

Mondale agrees with President Reagan and said he too would leave some of the troops there as bargaining chips with Nicaragua. And he attacks Gary Hart for forcefully saying, 'Get them out.' Our sons as bargaining chips . . . Will we never learn?"

One purpose of this tack, Kathy Bushkin said later, was to get Hart back on his generational theme—that he represented the generation that had learned from Vietnam the folly of American overextension in areas of foreign policy in which U.S. interests were questionable.

The ad outraged Mondale and probably made Hart look like just another hack politician, as did his appearance of pandering on the embassy question. Mondale adopted a centrist position in his foreign-policy speeches and very effectively played the irate, wronged victim in a televised debate at Columbia University with Hart and Jackson a few days before the New York vote.

"The ad was infuriating to Mondale," Kaplan said. "It just made him livid every time he watched it. I remember watching Mondale watch in Arthur Krim's study. He said something on the order of, 'How can he say that about me?'—pounding his fist against his palm."

In the debate, Mondale and Hart glared at each other in open bitterness.

"Why do you run those ads that suggest I'm out trying to kill kids when you know better?" Mondale barked. "All my life I have fought for peace. . . . To run ads as you suggest, that there's something in my policies that will lead to the death of American boys, I think you ought to pull those ads down tonight."

Hart seemed shaken by the intensity and directness of Mondale's charges, and he countered weakly that Mondale had misrepresented his views.

"Why have you questioned my commitment to arms control and civil rights," he asked, with less passion, "when you know I have just as much commitment to both of those as you do?"

Caddell, who had been pushing Hart for weeks now to paint Mondale as indecisive on foreign policy and to remind voters that he had been a continuing supporter of the American involvement in Vietnam, was stunned by Hart's relatively mild reply.

"He gets into the debate and lets Mondale beat up on him," Caddell said later. "I can't believe it. I came out of my seat. I said, 'Vietnam, Vietnam! Fritz, it's not that you want to kill people. People don't kill people, policies kill people. Vietnam is an example of it.' This is a place he can destroy Walter Mondale. Mondale has left himself with his chin out and Gary can only sit there and shake at him. Strange. Strange."

The bitterness evident on both sides in that debate did not subside. Mondale and Hart, as is often the case with candidates in the heat of battle, insisted all the negative campaigning was on the other side. Later, in an interview, when we told Hart that Mondale and his aides were pretty bitter about his negative campaign remarks about the former Vice President, Hart said animatedly: "They were bitter? They were bitter? Why were they bitter?" Reminded of the "fuse ad" on Central America, Hart retorted by recalling the Mondale "red phone" ad, adding: "I will show an impartial jury my ads and my speeches up against Mondale's positions and let people decide whether they were unfair or not. I think the whole 'Where's the beef?' line in my judgment was unfair. And attacking my civil-rights record, environmental record, compassion and all that was unfair. It just did not comport with the facts. That's the difference. It anyone wants to read the Mondale speech to the Council on Foreign Relations in Chicago and then look at the ad and decide that ad was unfair, I'll eat my hat."

Of the New York debate, specifically, Hart said of his obvious anger: "That was after three or four weeks of persistently mischaracterizing my record. He knew what he was doing. I would have been inhuman if I hadn't been sore at that point. But I would defy anybody in the Mondale campaign to find one instance where I had mischaracterized his record. Of course I was critical of him—on Lebanon, Vietnam, Grenada, Central America, but it was based on what he had said and done. He was saying things about my record that I had not said or done. He was saying I was weak on civil rights. I had a hundred percent voting record on civil rights, a leadership role. I think there was a qualitative difference in it."

Mondale, for his part, was more philosophical about the whole business after the election. "That is one of the big problems that confronts the Democratic Party and maybe the presidential selection process," he told us. "These primaries of the kind we went through, the nominating process, are very much like the Christians and the lions in Rome. You know, you throw good friends in there, and the first thing you know it starts unraveling. After the lion takes the first bite, it gets worse and worse, and little things get exaggerated, and people become desperate and tired, and they go further and further.

"You know," he went on, "Hart and I were good friends when this started, and I think we're friends again, after we both got some sleep. But it is too bad. Things unravel, and when people get desperate their minds do funny things. I guess there's no way around that, but I have no doubt that that roughly year and a half of fighting leading up to the nomination left scars that were very damaging to my campaign, even though I think Hart tried very hard afterwards to elect me."

As for Hart's contention that he attacked Mondale only on the facts but that Mondale hit him with allegations about his record that weren't true, Mondale said, smiling: "I used to say, nothing will help more with an argument like that than a good night's sleep."

The personal bitterness aside, the New York defeat on April 3 left Hart reeling, but Mondale was far from out of the woods as they moved into Pennsylvania for the primary there a week later. The flaps over the embassy move and Central America had diverted attention from Mondale's internal troubles but they had not diminished them. The Mondale campaign was now in a second "knockout" mode; the objective was to capitalize on its earlier large industrial-state victories by winning in Pennsylvania, then force Hart out of the race by defeating him again in Texas and Ohio in early May. But the delegate-committee controversy was not over. Far from it.

11

Just a Beltway Issue

WITH THE Democratic nomination fight now dominating the news going into the Pennsylvania primary, the Mondale strategists decided to put virtually all their financial resources into two areas—news-media advertising and "the road show"—Mondale's own travels, which would generate free press, radio and television coverage, both local and national. But because the campaign in Pennsylvania needed some on-the-ground visibility, some presence to keep local politicians and volunteers happy and engaged, some field operation was required. The answer was obvious: delegate committees.

The young "camp followers" who had been shuttling from one state to another, magically finding out where delegate committees were operating and getting jobs with them, just as magically showed up in Pennsylvania. As a matter of fact, it came to pass that there was no other Mondale field operation in the state other than the delegate committees in twenty-four congressional districts and an at-large delegate committee with offices in Philadelphia and Pittsburgh. And it didn't seem to matter a whit that no at-large delegates would actually be elected in the primary. As in New York, they would be selected *after* the primary.

Joe Trippi, late of Iowa and Maine, was moved in to be *the* official Mondale campaign. Trippi holed up in a fourteenth-floor room of the Bellevue Stratford Hotel in Philadelphia and from there functioned as an intelligence-gatherer for the road show. He tracked nightly polling in the state to determine what issues were cutting and where. He massaged party officials, and passed on the information for the top-level strategists who decided when and where to use specific commercials and to schedule the candidate.

Next door to the hotel, in a small storefront office that in campaign after campaign seems always available for rental to candidates, the Pennsylvania Delegates At-Large Committee for Mondale held forth. If you wanted to find out anything about Mondale or wanted to work for him, this is where you went. Droppers-by who might have been in other states for other primaries and caucuses, such as newspaper reporters, might recognize more than a few faces working there. This committee, and the twenty-four in congressional districts around the state, did everything—beyond Trippi's limited tasks—that needed doing to win Pennsylvania for Mondale.

In charge of the at-large committee was Edward Rendell, the Democratic district attorney of Philadelphia (later, in 1985, to become a candidate for governor). Rendell was a Mondale loyalist with an easy manner and extensive political contacts in the state, and for some time he had been worried about the Mondale campaign in Pennsylvania. Although full delegate slates had been filed early under the "early knockout" strategy, the Mondale strategists had figured the nomination fight would be all over by the time the Illinois primary was concluded. And so they didn't pay a lot of attention to the Keystone State.

Another factor in the low-priority treatment was Wilson Goode, Philadelphia's first black mayor. He took a long time deciding to support Mondale, what with Jesse Jackson on the ballot, and hence so did other black leaders. Mondale, not wanting an all-white campaign committee, waited to organize his Pennsylvania leadership committee until Goode came around. At the same time, John Glenn—an Ohio neighbor popular in rural western Pennsylvania—had been building an impressive organization in the state, and it concerned Rendell. It was not until Glenn folded just before the Illinois primary that Rendell breathed easier. But then along came Hart, and although he didn't have much going for him in Pennsylvania, he was a threat of uncertain dimensions.

Into this situation came the delegate committees and the "kids" to staff them. Although no at-large delegates were on the ballot, Rendell said, his at-large committee began raising and spending money "on the theory that our efforts were in behalf of all the Mondale delegates." In the course of the primary, the at-large committee raised and spent about $57,000. If the Mondale delegates didn't win a certain percentage of the vote in the congressional districts, he noted, Mondale would not have qualified for at-large delegates.

The former Mondale staffers now assigned to the Pennsylvania delegate committees worked for him, Rendell said, not for Trippi, an arrangement that caused considerable personal strain, inasmuch as Trippi himself was a "kid"—twenty-seven years old at the time—who had trained and palled around with many of the others back in Maine and Iowa. John O'Leary, a young Pittsburgh Democrat who worked for Mayor Richard Caliguiri, a co-chairman of the Mondale At-Large Delegate Committee, ran the committee's Pittsburgh office. He was a buddy of Trippi's, but when he phoned him in Philadelphia, O'Leary said later, Trippi told him they couldn't talk. Trippi and all the young ex-staffers vowed, for the record, that they meticulously abided by the separation requirement in this way. But to believe them would have also required belief in the tooth fairy. Nevertheless, by this time "the kids felt totally abandoned," one of their champions within the campaign said.

Both Trippi and Mike Ford, the field director, neither of them a favorite of Jim Johnson or Bob Beckel, came under fire within the campaign for the looseness and excesses of the delegate-committee operation in Pennsylvania, which by now had become a lifeline for both the campaign in the state and for the "gypsies" who were trying to stay involved. Beckel, a Carter state campaign coordinator in 1980, and Ford, a Kennedy state coordinator the same year, had no love for each other. And general counsel David Ifshin, according to insiders, blamed Ford for taking the ball and running with it—that is, for not being duly concerned about the line between the two campaign entities in Pennsylvania. That posture, to some, was easy scapegoating for Ifshin, the godfather of the now increasingly beleaguered delegate-committee scheme, as well as for Beckel and Johnson, who sat where the buck supposedly stopped.

Rendell acknowledged freely after the election that he had learned of the availability of the Mondale camp followers from the Mondale-for-President Committee in Washington.

"There was no question that they didn't show up and apply for jobs from me," he told us. "There was no question that the Mondale campaign asked them to come to Pennsylvania and asked them if they would work for Mondale at-large delegate committees."

But, Rendell said, they took their orders from him. "Trippi obviously talked to some of the staffers on the delegate committee, but I made it pretty clear once I read the law that I made the decisions on how we spent money and things like that, and Trippi didn't. And Trippi and I were pretty careful not to talk." Once, Rendell was called to a meeting of Jewish leaders for Mondale at a bar in the Bellevue and Trippi was there, "but we were very careful not to have much contact."

Another very sensitive matter in the circumstances was the fact that to nobody's surprise, labor PACs were very heavily involved in financing the Mondale delegate committees in Pennsylvania. The state was known to have one of the most politically active labor structures in the country, though not always successful in its undertakings. In the 1976 Democratic presidential primary, for example, it failed to deliver the state for one of labor's heroes, Senator Henry Jackson. But this year it was not just a matter of who the labor candidate was; members of Pennsylvania's AFL-CIO unions were running for delegate only on Mondale slates. Hence, contributing to the Mondale delegate committees was a virtual necessity for labor to take care of its own.

To coordinate activities with Mondale's labor supporters, the Mondale campaign early on had hired Paul Jensen, executive assistant to Secretary of Labor Ray Marshall in the Carter administration. Jensen, an affable and very conscientious political operative, had successfully courted major unions in connection with the AFL-CIO's eventual endorsement of Mondale, and thereafter became the campaign's chief liaison with organized labor. In Pennsylvania, that was the case as well, especially because labor unions were now carrying the financial brunt of the field operations, either in their own grass-roots membership political "education" or through the delegate committees.

"When they became an apparatus to promote our field activities," Jensen said later, "they were already creatures known, and in fact already partially funded in some cases, by labor."

As an early member of the Mondale campaign staff, Jensen was aware of the delegate-committee operation well before it became a financial crutch for the field effort. When the money bind came, he understood the legal requirement against affiliation and, he told us, he made every effort to observe it while being helpful to the unions with which he worked so closely. Independent of the Mondale campaign, he said, John Perkins, director of the AFL-CIO's political arm, the Committee on Political Education (COPE), had discovered the delegate-committee device and readily saw it as a means for supporting labor delegate-candidates, all of whom were for Mondale by nature of the AFL-CIO's binding endorsement.

Channeling labor PAC money into the delegate committees that needed it most and in the most timely fashion, Jensen said, "wasn't that complicated. It was fairly straightforward. Most of the affiliated unions had organizers in every congressional district." By the time the campaign got down to New York and Pennsylvania, two strong labor states, it was natural and not difficult for labor to concentrate its efforts and money on them, he said.

To the extent that the Mondale campaign did encourage the delegate committees and the flow of labor PAC money to them, the Mondale campaign always insisted that such activities "had to be done in an absolutely legal way." The campaign was already well aware of legal pitfalls in the use of labor money and facilities as a result of a court challenge by the Glenn campaign in Iowa. There, the Glenn campaign had alleged that Mondale got major financial help in the leasing at cut rates of phones and office space from labor unions using them primarily to do their own in-kind and "soft money" political activity in Mondale's behalf among their rank-and-file.

Thereafter, Jensen said, the Mondale campaign "had to go back to all organizers, all of the unions, and indicate that where there were leased arrangements for space, for phones, we had to be sure that the lease agreements had all been signed and sent to Washington. . . . It was amazing for a campaign. It was probably the best legally run campaign in the history of American politics."

At the same time, Jensen said, the Mondale campaign was aware of the dynamics that often ruled in the field, especially when money was tight.

"Organizers were in there," he said. "Like all organizers, all they care about is resources. Once they get resources they don't particularly care about all of the details of reporting of the funds and so forth. I mean, if you're on the ground there's an enormous amount of pressure, and what we were concerned about was that it all be conducted in a manner that was legal and defensible. And obviously what ultimately happened is it became a political issue [and] the potential damage to us far outweighed the benefits we were acquiring from the delegate committees."

Jensen did acknowledge, however, that he did serve as an informational conduit on occasion between a delegate committee that was expecting labor PAC money and a union that had promised to send it.

"There would be people [in delegate committees]," he said, "who would call and say they had just talked to the CWA, and CWA said they were going to send $5,000 to the Eleventh Congressional District of Pennsylvania. They had not yet received it." He would then call the union, Jensen said, and "I would say, 'We got that call. They were trying to reach you to find out if it had been sent. Would you call them back and let them know?' I had to be again as careful as I possibly could, knowing full well that if there were any legal questions around that I'd be spending two or three years of my life giving depositions, which was not something I had in mind. . . .

"It didn't happen that often, but if people ended up getting remarkably pinched and could not make the union contact themselves, the chances are I would have gotten a call, probably not from the delegate committee but probably from whoever was the Mondale state coordinator in the state, or it would have come through our regional desk. And they would have said, 'We understand there was $15,000 that was supposed to be sent by AFT to this congressional district . . . and they don't have any record of having received it, and can you find out if that has occurred?' And I would say I'd rather not, but if the delegate committee itself could not make contact with the union, that I would at least check."

In such cases, Jensen said, he would ask the union to send the money by Federal Express—an indication of the urgency with which labor funds then were needed by particular delegate committees.

The conscientious Jensen was scrupulously careful to observe all the legal niceties of the situation. And a Mondale campaign official playing this kind of role as an unofficial traffic cop in the flow of labor PAC money to the delegate committees might not have seemed to an outsider much of a breach of the "no coordination" regulation. But in a campaign whose chief operatives were now feeling heat, not only in the press but from their very irritated candidate, about the whole matter of labor money in the campaign, it could have raised questions. And if any indication at all of a link between the Mondale campaign and delegate committees in Pennsylvania receiving labor PAC money had been put in writing anywhere, so much more would that have been the case.

Any such evidence would have been seized by the Hart campaign, in the words of one Mondale insider later, as "empirical evidence of the big connectiveness in the sky"—proof that the Mondale campaign was working hand-in-hand with the delegate committees. And it would make matters all the worse if the link—"the smoking gun," as another insider put it—involved PAC money, the one thing Mondale had vowed would not sully his campaign.

This whole farcical fandango, encouraged by Beckel and Ifshin back at Mondale Inc. headquarters, muddled through in Pennsylvania as it had in New York, and Mondale won the primary by about 12 percent. But there occurred before the primary a bizarre episode that, had it come to light at that time, or even later before the Democratic convention, might have given Hart the ammunition he needed to stall Mondale's comeback. Disclosure of the incident would have thrown Mondale even more on the defensive on an issue that already was a considerable embarrassment to him as a self-proclaimed candidate of unimpeachable integrity, and would have raised in much higher profile questions of his ability to control his own campaign.

Among the former Mondale campaign staffers who came to Pennsylvania to work for Rendell's at-large delegate committee was a young Washington lawyer named Diane Thompson. She had run a local Mondale office in New Hampshire and was now installed as executive director of the committee. She was known to have a passion for accuracy and thoroughness and, well aware of the FEC regulations concerning delegate committees, was determined to comply with the letter of the law.

Accordingly, she began keeping meticulous records of the contributions to and spending by the at-large committee, as well as its dealings with the other twenty-four delegate committees in the congressional districts around the state. She talked to treasurers of the other committees regularly and kept information and data on various financial transactions in a large loose-leaf notebook.

She received checks from delegate-committee contributors, including labor PACs, and wrote and disbursed checks in payment of various delegate-committee bills, including the printing of brochures and other routine campaign paraphernalia.

Also, according to some sources close to the campaign, Thompson assisted in moving funds among the various delegate committees according to need. All these functions presumably were allowable within the FEC regulations. But because the delegate committees had now taken over the full field operations for the Mondale campaign in Pennsylvania, and because the overwhelming source of funds for them was labor PACs, how Thompson was recording the money transactions, and in what detail, came to be of extraordinary interest to some in the Washington campaign headquarters.

There was concern that the people in the field—many of them former Mondale staffers "exiled" for legal and fiscal reasons to the delegate committees—were, in their organizing zeal, finessing the legal niceties of separation between the Mondale campaign and the delegate committees. And the fact that labor money was almost entirely bankrolling "field" in Pennsylvania was information guaranteed to drive Mondale berserk if he found out.

Even in the absence of any clear connection between the Mondale campaign and the routing of labor PAC money to the delegate committees, there was plenty of reason to conclude that the delegate-committee apparatus in Pennsylvania was, at the very least, a stepchild of Mondale Inc. Ford and Trippi were up there representing the national campaign, and many of their old troops were spread around the state in various delegate committees. It was not unnatural to expect that Ford was looking out for them, and that they were keeping in touch with their old leaders. And, not the least of it, the at-large committee was being run by Thompson, herself a former Mondale national staffer, and she was not only talking to the other delegate committees in the state but, reportedly, keeping records concerning them.

So when, about week before the Pennsylvania primary, a thirty-two-year-old Washington lawyer named Rich Goodstein, who was a volunteer on Ifshin's Mondale legal staff, decided to go up to his home town of Philadelphia to work for Mondale, Ifshin was interested. As Goodstein remembered it later, Ifshin told him: "Look, we don't want to take any chances. Let me know if you see something that shouldn't be going on."

Also, Goodstein said, the campaign's deputy general counsel, Lyn Oliphant, told him to instruct those running the delegate committee in Philadelphia what they were supposed to do to comply with the law. The first stories about the delegate committees, and their taking PAC money, had just broken in New York, and the campaign was uptight.

Goodstein, a tall, bald, sturdy-looking man, had an open and friendly if somewhat straitlaced manner. A graduate of Wesleyan University and Georgetown Law School, he had run Senator Abraham Ribicoff's field campaign for reelection in 1974 and later was a legislative assistant for Ribicoff. After graduation from Georgetown he had clerked for the Chief Judge of the United States District Court in Washington and was now a lawyer in the firm of Wilmer, Cutler and Pickering. As a field organizer in Connecticut he had once worked under Beckel. But he was going up to Philadelphia strictly as a volunteer, he said, so he didn't bother contacting Beckel or anyone in the Washington field section. Instead, he simply phoned the at-large committee and said he was coming up. On the Monday a week before the primary, he "came in off the street," in the words of one of those present, and was put to work doing very routine office chores in the at-large committee storefront.

Almost at once, he told us later, he saw things going on that he, as a lawyer who had been working in the Mondale campaign, didn't think were proper for a delegate committee to be doing. Literature was being handed out, he said, that had Mondale's name on it and, as he recalled, nothing about electing delegates.

Also, he said, the few national staff people in the state seemed to be "shuttling" between the hotel next door and the delegate-committee storefront. In casual conversations with Diane Thompson and others in the office, he said, he found out that they had worked "with Mondale Inc. in other states." When he expressed his concern to them that they seemed in his view to be overstepping the legal limitations and reminded them that delegate committees were only supposed to elect delegates, they looked incredulously at him.

"They thought I was a stick-in-the-mud," he recalled.

If an advance man from the national campaign staff came into town, he said, he would have no hesitation about coming into the at-large committee storefront—the only Mondale entity in town—to use the phones, which from Goodstein's legal perspective was off base.

That first day or the next, Goodstein recalled, he was sufficiently disturbed that he called Oliphant and told her what he had seen. On Wednesday, according to Goodstein, he got a phone call from Ifshin, who had just returned to Washington after the New York primary. Goodstein told him of his concerns, and Ifshin said he would be up to Philadelphia the next morning.

They met there the next day and together went to see Ford and Trippi at the Mondale campaign's one-room command post on the fourteenth floor of the Bellevue Stratford. According to Goodstein, Ifshin "laid down the law" to them about being sure to keep national campaign and delegate-committee activities separate. The caution, he said, "seemed to register" on Trippi but Ford's attitude was that he had responsibilities to the people in the field. I can't let them down. Goodstein was telling him what the law was, and Ford was insisting he had his commitment.

Ifshin told Ford and Trippi that Goodstein was "my agent," Goodstein recalled. "I'm telling you what we want in Washington." But he knew, Goodstein said, that Ifshin might as well have saved his breath, for all that Trippi and Ford would listen to him.

From there, Goodstein said, he and Ifshin went to the at-large committee storefront to see Thompson. It was then early afternoon. Their joint appearance apparently was the first indication to those at the committee that Ifshin and Goodstein knew each other. After some brief conversation, the three of them—Ifshin, Goodstein and Thompson—repaired to a nearby bakery-coffee shop to talk.

Again, according to Goodstein, Ifshin played the prosecuting attorney with Thompson, asking her what she was doing, how the at-large committee was structured, who was on it, how much money it had, who was being paid expenses. She responded nervously, Goodstein recalled, as Ifshin emphasized the seriousness involved, telling her that "Walter Mondale's got a lot at stake here and we don't want to screw around with it."

Apparently concerned that through Thompson the at-large committee was functioning as a general Mondale clearinghouse in the state, dealing with all the congressional district delegate committees, Ifshin explained to her, in Goodstein's recollection, that "the at-large committee can't be anything like an octopus, with an arm here and an arm there."

In the course of the conversation, Goodstein said, "the question came up: 'How did you keep track of these things?' Answer: Notebook. She made entries in a loose-leaf notebook."

Ifshin, as Goodstein recalled, shook his head and said, "Look, don't do that," or something to that effect. "The impression was, 'Look, you ought to stop it, because I would just advise you not to be doing that type of thing.' "

Ifshin then suggested, according to Goodstein, that he, Goodstein, talk to Rendell, the head of the at-large committee, to make sure he stayed "on top of things" and kept the committee within proper bounds. After attending another unrelated meeting, Goodstein took Ifshin to the train station, and the campaign general counsel went back to Washington.

On Friday, Goodstein and Thompson met with Rendell and talked generally about the legal guidelines the at-large committee had to follow, without getting into any reference to Thompson's record-keeping or activities involving any of the other delegate committees in the state.

After the meeting in Rendell's office, Thompson went about her business, and Goodstein, by now feeling—in his words—"persona non grata" and "concerned people would be listening in to my phone conversations while I was at the at-large committee," went to the nearby office of a lawyer friend. There he checked in by phone with Ifshin, who, Goodstein said, continued to be worried and frustrated about how the delegate-committee device was being carried out in Pennsylvania. Then, according to Goodstein, something approximating this conversation took place over the phone:

IFSHIN: Look . . . if they're not going to keep things as separate as I think they should, get your hands on that notebook.
GOODSTEIN: Well, what do you mean?
IFSHIN: I want to see that book.
GOODSTEIN: Well, I don't think they're gonna give it to me if I ask.
IFSHIN: Well, just get it. Take it.

Goodstein said he told Ifshin that before he took such a step, he wanted to hear the instructions from Mike Berman, the campaign treasurer, or somebody at that level. A few hours later, Goodstein was back at the storefront. Nobody else who in his view was concerned with the matter was around, so he talked to Ifshin by phone again right there. According to Goodstein, Ifshin told him:

"Look, I've discussed this whole situation of what's going on with the delegate committees with Mike, and he said to get the book and bring it to Washington. . . . I'm telling you, Mike says it. It's the only way we can get them to stop doing what we think they should stop doing."

"So," Goodstein told us, "I knew Mike. We weren't fast friends, we didn't socialize, but I knew him in the course of campaigns and I had a tremendous amount of respect for him. I figured if he said it, recognizing all that was going to fall on me, the difficulty I had in doing it. They didn't give it to me, so I had to take it."

He didn't insist on talking to Berman, Goodstein said, because he thought he heard Berman's voice in the background as he spoke with Ifshin, and that was good enough for him. And so, Rich Goodstein simply took the committee's records.

The black loose-leaf notebook, which he had seen Diane Thompson carrying in the office, was sitting on a shelf. Other workers were in the storefront, but not Thompson.

"I opened it," Goodstein told us. "I saw sort of ledger sheets, names of either CDs or what have you, and I realized that was it. I looked through it other than to determine as best I could that was it."

With the notebook in hand, Goodstein left the at-large headquarters, got in his car and drove back to Washington.

"I felt lousy about it," he said, "because that's not my style—by a long shot. I remember just feeling horrible about it."

Goodstein took the book home and told his wife, and the next morning he dropped the book off at the campaign general counsel's office. To others, the episode may have seemed a clear matter of theft, but to him, he said, "it was your classic moral dilemma. Here somebody who you respect and is in a position of authority, and is concerned about the national campaign, is saying, 'Look we're not real keen on what they're doing. We want to stop it.

And the only way we know to stop it is to take this notebook.' So I was satisfied it was their decision. I would certainly never have done anything like that unilaterally—no way."

He was, as they say, just following orders.

In taking the notebook and returning to Washington, Goodstein said later, he was obliged to miss a scheduled meeting the next day with Rendell, the head of the committee. So he wrote Rendell a letter apologizing, not for taking the notebook belonging to his committee, but for having missed the meeting!

As Goodstein recalled the note, "I said, 'Sorry I couldn't make the meeting, but I had to get back to Washington.' " As for taking the notebook, Goldstein said, "I sort of made some veiled reference. . . . I said, 'You know, lawyers end up having to do things in the course of a campaign that field people don't like,' I continued, 'and I found myself in that position. You're a lawyer. You'll understand.' "

What he meant, Goodstein explained to us, was that as a lawyer he had an obligation to his "client"—the Mondale campaign—to see that the delegate committee in Pennsylvania stopped doing what it should not have been doing. He compared himself to a lawyer for a parent company who finds that a subsidiary is doing something harmful to the parent company. "By virtue of your powers of persuasion," he said, "you can't get them to do what you think is right. Do you let them keep doing it? Or do you step in?"

The whole point, however, was that under the FEC regulations the delegate committees were supposed to be completely independent of the Mondale campaign. A parent company-subsidiary relationship would have been a violation. So Goodstein's action as a Mondale lawyer either established that the committee and the campaign were affiliated, or he was intruding on an independent group's affairs. Wasn't the situation a classic Catch-22?

"I guess," Goodstein said, "but I mean it's not unique in the annals of lawyering. . . . Lawyers can basically do, in the interest of law-abidingness and urging their clients to toe the line, what non-lawyers can't. . . . The advice I was giving was spurned. So where does that leave you? Do you just throw up your hands? . . . The judgment was, you've got to step in. You're lawyers, you're acting responsibly. It's not like you're acting venally. It's a little drastic, admittedly, but it was a tough situation. It was a hot issue.

Hart was trying to make a lot of it. . . . He thought he had a good issue, and you're in a campaign. You try to seize what you can. I feel comfortable that what I did was appropriate. . . . If I had to guess . . . the FEC would tell you that they would encourage a lawyer to take the steps that the campaign ultimately took with respect to the delegate committees, recognizing there was supposed to be the separation."

Regarding all of the above, Ifshin acknowledged to us that he had gone to Philadelphia and was concerned that Thompson's records might show too close an affiliation between the Mondale national campaign and the delegate committees, and that she herself as a former Mondale campaign staffer running the at-large committee would be strong evidence of that affiliation. He insisted that although it could be defended legally, he was concerned about the "perception" in political terms in the midst of a tough campaign.

Asked why he wanted to get Thompson's records, Ifshin said: " 'Getting the records' is not correct. It was a perception in their minds we wanted the records themselves. We wanted to make sure that whatever bookkeeping was going on, was being done by the committees themselves and was not an effort to exert undue control over any of the functions of those committees by our campaign."

Although Thompson was working for the at-large committee, he said, the fact that "she worked for us before" could have required some explaining, especially if her books suggested "affiliation." Unlike the young organizers who moved from state to state to work on delegate committees as volunteers on a per-diem basis, Ifshin said, the fact that Thompson had come in at a higher level as a director could have been perceived as control by the Mondale campaign.

Also, he said, "my concern was that she was keeping records for more than the at-large committee. Matter of fact, I know she was. I saw her do it. I walked in the office and she was doing it."

Well, did he send Goodstein up to Philadelphia and tell him to take the records?

"I don't know how much of a difference it makes whether he was already there or I asked him to go up," Ifshin said. "When he was there, I asked him to help. And anything he did, he did at my direction. Any acts he took were at my request or Mike Berman's request."

Berman, too, confirmed that Goodstein had taken the book at his instruction. "I wanted to know what was going on, very simply," he said. "I thought better about it afterwards, frankly, but at the time I wanted to make sure our people weren't engaged in anything that was inappropriate. There was communication going back and forth. . . . We were always trying to be very careful that there wasn't crossover between our people and their people. . . . I wanted to make sure whoever was getting paid were people on their payroll and not on our payroll, that expenses weren't getting picked up for our campaign by the delegate committees and those kinds of things."

Berman concluded: "Obviously we were trying to avoid anything that wasn't appropriate. That's always been our posture."

Meanwhile, back in Philadelphia, when Diane Thompson returned to her office, it didn't take her long to realize her notebook was gone. She customarily kept it on or in her desk in a small area partitioned off from the main room at the rear of the storefront office, and it was nowhere to be found. She checked with others with whom she had worked since her meeting with Ifshin and Goodstein, but to no avail. She was livid. She went to Rendell and told him what had happened.

After all that had occurred in American politics as a result of Watergate—including the establishment of the watchdog Federal Election Commission itself—it was almost unbelievable: A Mondale campaign lawyer had all but functioned as a spy in the headquarters of the Mondale at-large committee and then—had taken Thompson's book of financial records.

"She was a real heroine," Rendell said of Thompson later. "She put her foot down and said, 'I'm not going to be a party to this and I don't want Walter Mondale to be a party to it. . . . If you don't do something about it, I'm going to make a complaint.' "

To which Rendell, the district attorney, laughing about it later, said he replied: "Who are you going to complain to? Me?"

Rendell, who believed the at-large committee had operated legally and had nothing to hide, was furious at the act and appalled at its stupidity. And, as he put it afterward, "aside from everything else, I wasn't going to get my ass in a wringer. A), I'm the district attorney, and the last thing I want to do is be involved in consciously disregarding the law. And B), I took it seriously, that we were an independent committee and I was in charge of it."

Rendell picked up his phone and called Ifshin. "Listen," he said he told the campaign's general counsel, "it's my belief that one of your guys took some of our records. We happen to have Xeroxes of them anyway. I want those records back here tomorrow. . . . Get this goddamn thing back and let's put an end to all this stuff."

Rendell also called Berman. "I didn't use the word 'stolen,'" he recalled, "but I was pretty sure this guy had taken the papers."

The upshot of it all was that Diane Thompson's notebook of financial records, which had so mysteriously disappeared, arrived back on Rendell's desk in Philadelphia—not so mysteriously—by Federal Express the next morning.

Both Ifshin and Berman said later, making no reference to Rendell's urgent calls, that they had sent the book back to Rendell—without bothering to look at it, if you can believe that.

"The idea was to re-establish that distance, to make sure that no link was there," Ifshin said. But if that was the objective, going to the trouble of taking the notebook, having it brought to Washington from Philadelphia and then mailing it back was certainly a roundabout way to do that.

Berman said he sent the book back because by that time it was clear that there was a lot going on involving the FEC "and it just didn't make any sense. I didn't want any idea or any suggestion that we ever manipulated the records."

Well, he was asked, why get them in the first place, then?

"Well, between the time that we originally talked about it and the time they came down," he said, "I changed my point of view."

Translation: A phone call from an angry district attorney can marvelously clear the mind.

"They were overreacting, they were panicking," Rendell said later. In his judgment and that of the at-large committee's lawyer, he said, "we were on safe grounds—not the best grounds to be on, but safe grounds. We hadn't done anything wrong."

But Rendell in so saying was not focusing on the possible "smoking gun" or at least the evidence of the PAC money involvement that concerned the Mondale campaign hierarchy now; its members knew how worked up Mondale was about it—and about how his chief aides had let it continue. It was now about a week after Mondale's explosion against Johnson and Beckel at Arthur Krim's, and the PAC money was still coming in.

When the story of the delegate committees had first broken, Berman had denied any connection whatever with them in a television interview with Ken Bode of NBC News. In the view of another Mondale insider, Berman and Johnson for all their long experience with Mondale, as well as newcomer Beckel, all were afraid of the candidate and his temper, which could be monumental when he was aroused. So they first tried to deny that there was anything untoward in the delegate committees and their acceptance of PAC money.

"They were trying to hide it from Mondale," in this insider's view, and as the controversy continued and deepened and the candidate was getting angrier, "they were covering their asses with Mondale."

But Rendell realized the folly to which panic at the top was bringing the campaign. "At one point I got a little exacerbated [sic] myself," he recalled, "and I screamed at Ifshin or Berman. I said, 'You guys are crazy. We've got this thing won.' I didn't mean just Pennsylvania. I said, 'It's over with, and you guys are futzing with something that could be construed to be another Watergate. You guys are absolutely crazy.' "

The less than $60,000 that was spent by delegate committees in the Pennsylvania primary was chicken feed for a presidential election, Rendell said, and to suggest that the committees were the critical factor in a primary Mondale eventually won by 12 percent was ludicrous.

"The thing that got me so upset when I realized what was going on," he said, "was that for something that meant very little in terms of changing votes in Pennsylvania, people were overreacting and creating a situation where if the media wanted to, if that ever came out . . . it could have crushed Mondale's chances of getting the nomination."

If the press had found out and had written that the matter was rectified in twenty-four hours, as it was, it would probably have caused "only a ripple," he said. "But if the media wanted to play 'Attempted Watergate Cover-up,' " it might have been another matter entirely, he said.

Whether that judgment was valid or not, disclosure of the episode then certainly would have given Mondale a lot to explain.

And it would have given Hart a whole new avenue to pursue—not simply concerning the incident itself, but what it said about Mondale's control over his own campaign at a time Hart himself was still fending off Mondale's suggestions that he was too unsteady, too indecisive, too unreliable to be President.

Also, had this episode come to light then, Ifshin's earlier declaration of indignation in his brief to the FEC about the National Right to Work Committee's "egregious, dishonest and unlawful" infiltration of the Illinois Mondale headquarters might have taken on a somewhat hollow ring.

The Mondale hierarchy, defensively, tried later to disparage the importance of having the delegate committees in Pennsylvania. Johnson, Beckel and campaign treasurer Mike Berman all argued that by the time the fight for the nomination had reached that state, the campaign was being waged almost entirely in the news media, and especially on network television, and that fact required diverting available resources into advertising and candidate travel.

In assessing the importance of the delegate committees, Berman said, "That depends on whether you decide whether the stuff that the delegate committees did, actually did make any difference. My own belief is that by the time we were doing New York and Pennsylvania, we weren't dealing with whether or not you put out palm cards or x-number pieces of literature. We were dealing on what was the political climate and what was happening. You were on television every single day and every edition of every newspaper was doing it. . . . Your field organization [always] wants to have field, and we weren't prepared to commit money to field, that's for sure. I don't believe in that stuff. The campaign was being waged on a wholly different level."

Beckel agreed. "If we hadn't won New York," he said, "ten thousand delegate committees in Pennsylvania wouldn't have mattered." Media was the answer thereafter, he said, "so delegate committees in a sense didn't have an impact on votes either negatively or positively . . ."

Others, however, saw it differently. John Perkins, the AFL-CIO COPE director, insisted that the labor money that was poured into the delegate committees, as well as labor's independent effort, was critical to Mondale in both New York and Pennsylvania.

"I don't know whether I'd agree that it was a media campaign. Other people were providing the grass-roots effort," he said. ABC

News' exit polls later indicated 52 percent of union households in the three-candidate race, with particular strength in coal and steel counties in the western part of the state where union money fueled the delegate committees, supported Mondale.

Jensen, while terming "inconsequential" the impact of the PAC money going to Pennsylvania delegate committees, said other "soft money" from the unions in pushing Mondale's candidacy among their members was the crucial element in his nomination. Jensen also cited the evidence of exit polls. "We would have lost Pennsylvania," he said, without labor's activity in Mondale's behalf. Although the political accomplishments of organized labor were disparaged by others in the Mondale campaign, he said, "they did more in this presidential election than they have ever done, even exceeding the effort in behalf of Humphrey in 1968."

The CBS News-New York *Times* polls appeared to bear out Jensen's view. They suggested clearly that had it not been for the AFL-CIO endorsement, Mondale would have lost most of the key northern industrial-state primaries and those in Georgia and Alabama as well. He won the union vote in Georgia by 36 percent to 22 percent for Hart, the exit polls indicated, while winning the state by only 3 percent. And a whopping 49–15 margin in the union vote over Hart in Alabama was critical to his victory by 13 percent there. In Illinois he won the labor vote by 48–32 in carrying the state by 6 percent; in New York, labor backed him 48–22 and in Pennsylvania 49–32, according to the exit polls.

Ford, in defense of the field operation such as it was, observed that any credible campaign must fulfill "obligations to the institutional party and obligations to offer certain symbols that everybody believes are part of a good campaign. It hurts if you don't do them. If there's no visibility for Walter Mondale in Pennsylvania, then there's no campaign. It's probable that those things have nothing to do with moving an electorate, but it's meeting expectations."

Whatever the ultimate importance of the delegate committees to the Mondale campaign, the Hart campaign did its best to damage Mondale with the delegate-committee and PAC money issues, even without knowledge of the bizarre "stolen records" episode. As soon as the first Washington *Post* stories had appeared, Jack Quinn, the legal counsel for the Hart campaign, dispatched paralegal aides to the FEC to check the financial reports. They quickly established the broadening scope of the committees' existence, the transfer of Mondale staffers to them, the receipt of PAC money and evidence of more than simple legal advice from the Mondale campaign to them. Quinn on April 6, four days before the Pennsylvania primary, filed a formal complaint with the FEC, demanding that the Mondale campaign be ordered to stop what the Hart campaign charged was circumvention of the regulations on delegate committees.

Hart's campaign manager, Pudge Henkel, after a strategy meeting to shape an intensified attack on the issue, declared: "We strongly feel that the committees are wrong morally, wrong ethically and wrong legally. We've had Watergate, debategate [charges that the Reagan campaign had stolen Jimmy Carter's debate briefing papers in 1980] and now we've got delegate."

On April 18, eight days after the Pennsylvania primary, the Hart campaign again asked the FEC to intervene. But procedural red tape—specifically the right to reply to the initial complaint, which Mondale Inc. took its sweet time doing—barred any immediate action.

Ifshin continued to defend his "baby" inside the campaign and outside it. To Hart's complaints, he recalled later, "We said, 'PAC money, schmac money, it's not illegal.' "

By this time, however, the Elaine Kamarck memo of January 12 specifically informing delegate committees that taking PAC money was legal had surfaced, and the Mondale lieutenants were diving for cover. Beckel and Berman went to her, she said later, and told her: "Look, this is going to be tough."

"How mad is Mondale?" she asked Berman at one point.

"Well," she remembered him replying, "he's already at a slow boil on the labor money. You increased the temperature, Elaine."

Apparently neither Beckel nor Ifshin, whose handwritten notations on the original draft of her memo confirmed their involvement, volunteered to share the heat.

Mondale at first, for all that his aides and he himself said regarding his concern about keeping his promise not to take PAC money, was notably slow and evasive about dealing with the issue. He reported that he had written to all the Mondale delegate committees urging them to cease accepting PAC funds, and to union presidents asking that they stop offering them. However, it was not until April 23, nearly two weeks after the Pennsylvania primary, that he personally phoned AFL-CIO President Lane Kirkland and made the same request. Kirkland acceded, while noting he believed it was perfectly proper for labor PACs to contribute toward the election of labor delegates. As he said later, labor had its people trying to become delegates, "irrespective of the Mondale candidacy. We had legitimate grounds for wanting to help them. We had no misgivings about the candidate. We wanted a significant presence at the convention." Labor felt it was important to be there to play a role in "the direction of party programs, the thrust in respect to issues," Kirkland said.

As the campaign moved South again for contests in Tennessee and Texas among other states, Mondale now reported that "almost all" PAC contributions to the delegate committees had stopped. He insisted that "there's no games being played," but he continued to defend the legality and existence of the committees. And he called Hart's intensified attacks the acts of a "desperate candidate who is saying things that won't stand analysis."

Meanwhile, new delegate committees continued to blossom in approaching primary states. Johnson publicly expressed surprise, adding:

"At least no one can say we're organizing and controlling what those committees are doing."

Hart, in fact, continued saying just that, as evidence mounted concerning his charges that the delegate committees were coordinated by the Mondale campaign, specifically including the transfer of money and manpower from one to another along the campaign route. By now, 124 Mondale delegate committees had registered with the FEC, the Washington *Post* reported in another well-documented story on the linkage.

Berman, even at this late date, was clinging to deniability. Evidence of Mondale staff members showing up on delegate-committee payrolls, he said, "suggests we laid them off and they may have gone someplace else. I don't think that is any evidence that we coordinated. . . ." It was the magic carpet theory again.

But Mondale was now feeling the heat in ways a politician cannot easily tolerate. He made what he regarded as a major speech at Case Western Reserve University in Cleveland, sharply attacking President Reagan's "Star Wars" space defense concept and calling for a "space freeze," but all he was asked about by the press the rest of the day was delegate committees.

After a particularly contentious press conference in Nashville, Mondale returned to his hotel suite and, ordering most of his entourage out, turned to senior adviser John Reilly. He told Reilly that he'd had it with the distraction the committees were causing.

"We've got to get rid of it," he said. Then he phoned Johnson in Washington. "How can we possibly make progress if, when I give a major speech on arms control," he complained, "the only story for the day is delegate committees? We've got to do something to get this over with."

The next day, in Chattanooga, Mondale bit the bullet—or a part of it, anyway. He announced that he was asking his delegates to disband all the delegate committees, not because there was anything wrong with them, but because they were "undermining my capacity to carry on a campaign on matters that count." At this late date, with all that had now been published, he had no qualms in saying:

"These committees are operating on their own, making their own judgments. And even though I don't know a thing about it, haven't been involved in it, don't know what they're doing, I find that I have to answer the questions and somehow try to find out. I don't want to do that. So rather than keep answering questions, I said, 'Let's just get rid of these committees to the fullest extent possible.' "

The statement was hardly a ringing reassurance of Mondale's knowledge of and control over what had been going on in his own campaign for months—or, for that matter, of his candor either. And when he was asked whether the money raised by the delegate committees, reported at about $250,000 by now, ought to be counted against his federal spending limit, he replied:

"I don't think that's necessary or appropriate."

But Gary Hart definitely thought it was. He was riding the issue hard as a matter of Mondale's personal integrity, and he now took the dispute another step. To an approving, cheering crowd at Vanderbilt University in Nashville he demanded:

"Give the money back, Walter. That's the way to solve the problem. Just give the money back."

Mondale, although he later stoutly insisted he had agreed to return the PAC money as soon as he learned about its involvement in his campaign, said when first asked about Hart's suggestion, that the money was used "at the local level for delegate selection

. . . so the advice is rejected." He was still on his high horse about the matter.

Even shutting down the delegate committees proved not to be as easy as it sounded, partly because a number of them truly had been acting independently, and they resisted instruction from the Mondale campaign on what they could or couldn't do. Also, there was the matter of keeping up the charade that the Mondale campaign was totally uninvolved in the committees. Influential Democrats in a state, such as a friendly member of Congress, could call the committee chairmen and ask them to lay off.

Some Mondale field organizers said later, however, that some committees were not shut down right away, and PAC money was not turned down, because one or more of Mondale's top managers, struggling to keep the campaign afloat financially, didn't want either to happen. One of the field hands told us that when he was asked for guidance from a delegate committee, he phoned Washington. "I said, 'Hey, I just saw Mondale on television saying don't take any more money.' " What was he supposed to tell the delegate committees that asked him about it? He was told, he said, "You don't work for them [the delegate committees]." The inference he drew, he said, was, "You work for us and we're telling you to keep going. We'll take care of the old man. Don't worry about it."

All this time, Hart was keeping the pressure on. The day after Mondale asked his delegate committees to disband, the Hart campaign again petitioned the FEC to take action. There was no reason to think that Mondale's announcement "will end the matter any more than Mr. Mondale's announcement earlier in April stopped the flow of PAC money into the committees," the brief said.

Referring to Johnson's statement of surprise about the proliferation of the committees, the brief went on: "The Mondale campaign cannot insulate itself from the consequences of its own acts by professing 'surprise' that its own program was working. Nor should the Commission hesitate to take action simply because the Mondale campaign has announced that it will stop the activities of the delegate committees which it fostered and encouraged to proliferate." The FEC, however, did no more than continue its slow investigative procedure.

The same day, though, Mondale finally threw in the towel. "Mondale still felt he was not being leveled with," Reilly said later.

Accordingly, Reilly spent several hours on the phone with Johnson, going over every detail of the situation. Then, in Mondale's hotel suite in El Paso, where he was campaigning for the Texas caucuses, Reilly spent six grueling hours with the candidate, considering every aspect.

Chief delegate-tracker Tom Donilon, who was also there, said Mondale finally concluded "that the standards set down in the regulations and the law were totally unworkable and ambiguous, and that there were hundreds of people [involved] all over the country who could not meet these vague standards," and that he could not insure that his own standards would be met. "So the best thing was to shut it down and protect his integrity at all costs."

To do that, it was decided, Mondale would have to pay the cost that Hart was demanding—give the money back. Not only that, to demonstrate that he was going the extra mile to preserve his integrity, Mondale would also accept the money raised and spent by the delegate committees under his own federal spending limit, while still holding there had been no illegal coordination. Mondale agreed to put $400,000 in escrow for repayment until details of who got how much were worked out.

Mondale, explaining his decision after the election, said that in looking into the whole delegate-committee situation "what I found was a total swamp. The regulations did not define what was or was not illegal, so there was no way to defend myself. And so I tried as rapidly as I could to define what my position was, to tell my staff what my position was, and to try to restore public trust in the integrity of my commitment by returning all the PAC money."

He refused to blame his campaign chiefs and attributed the whole matter to the pressures of a campaign in financial distress.

"My opinion was, and still is, that the decision was made [to take PAC money] in the depths of our campaign, when things were going badly, and they went ahead anyway. These are all my closest friends. They were doing what they thought was best. I forced a reversal of the decision and repayment of funds. It's hard to explain how those things happen, but I thought I had to do what I did to make it clear what my personal view is."

The fact was, though, that the delegate-committee scheme had begun long before the Mondale campaign had reached "the depths," but rather while it was still pursuing its "early knockout" strategy, as witnessed by the creation of the first delegate committees in New Hampshire before that state's kickoff primary.

Hart, asked whether he was satisfied with Mondale's decision to repay the money, observed: "Whether he would have made it on his own without public pressure, without the scrutiny that has gone on in the last couple of weeks, is a question that remains open." Hart said the primary victories Mondale had won with the help of delegate committees were "tainted," and he observed that "whether he ought to give back the delegates is something perhaps the party wants to consider."

The Hart campaign calculated that there were more than 500 Mondale delegates elected in the state primaries and caucuses in which the committees had functioned, and the threat to challenge them was one that could have imperiled Mondale's nomination. Many in the Hart campaign wanted to do so, and Hart held out the possibility almost to the convention, though he said the matter was one for the party to press and resolve. If the FEC were to rule against Mondale on the matter or if the Justice Department decided to investigate it, Hart warned, there would be a "tremendous cloud" over Mondale as the Democratic nominee that would give the Republicans "a ready-made issue." In retrospect, had Hart known about the "stolen records" in Pennsylvania, he might well have mounted the challenge, with more success than the situation at that juncture seemed to offer.

Mondale, on a television panel show, was not content with extricating himself from the mess. He sought to pin a rose on himself for doing what his campaign's chicanery and his own foot-dragging finally had forced him to do to salvage the political situation.

"I've gone clear beyond anything that's necessary," he said in an ABC News interview, "and I do that to demonstrate what I think is the responsibility of a President—not just to deal technically with the law, but to deal with the ethical posture and clarity that the American people must expect from the position, which as Roosevelt once said is pre-eminently a position of moral leadership."

He was going beyond what the law required of him, including accepting the delegate-committee money under his own campaign's spending limit, Mondale said, "to make clear that I, personally, take the responsibility of establishing an ethical, not just a legal, but an ethical standard for which I take personal responsibility."

Although it was legal to accept PAC money, he emphasized, he was against it, and therefore "as soon as I found out PAC money was being used, I asked it be returned."

But that had hardly been the case. When Hart had made his memorable "Give the money back, Walter" suggestion at Vanderbilt, Mondale had said the demand was not "appropriate" because the PAC money was for the purposes of electing his delegates, not him, and "so the advice is rejected." It was only after the heat had built to a politically unbearable temperature that he did the noble thing.

At that, it was revealed later, Mondale had acted in the nick of time. The FEC, in its investigation kept secret by law until after the November election, found on May 5—just nine days after Mondale had ordered the delegate committees disbanded—"reason to believe" that the Mondale for President Committee had violated the law by its dealings with them. It found sufficient evidence to suggest that the delegate committees were indeed affiliated with the Mondale campaign, and hence that the campaign had accepted "excessive contributions" and had made "excessive expenditures" under the law.

The "reason to believe" finding, a procedural step necessary before a full investigaion could be launched, was itself not made public at the time, and the Mondale campaign was given time to respond. The Mondale campaign committee moved to enter into a conciliation on the issue, another procedure that guaranteed secrecy for, as it turned out, the duration of the presidential campaign.

It was not until November 27, three weeks after Mondale had been swamped by President Reagan, that the FEC disclosed a conciliation agreement had been reached, and at the same time made public the May 7 finding. In the settlement, the Mondale committee agreed to treat the delegate committees as affiliated for the sake of disposing of the matter, without conceding the point. The agreement was determined to have put the Mondale campaign over federal limits on PAC contributions received "by at least $299,215" and on individual contributions "by at least

$47,402," and to have exceeded spending limits "by approximately $92,975.73." The Mondale campaign agreed to pay $350,000 to the Treasurer of the United States, plus $29,640 for exceeding the $404,000 limit in New Hampshire as a result of delegate-committee spending there, plus a civil penalty of $18,500.

When the reconciliation agreement was released, the Hart campaign lawyers were irate to learn that the FEC had found as early as May 7 "reason to believe" the Mondale campaign had violated the law. Had voters in the primaries after that date known, Jack Quinn said, they might have rejected Mondale.

"Primary voters in the states after May 7 had an interest in knowing," he said. "And certainly delegates at the convention did. This could have blocked the nomination." The whole matter "didn't become a big deal because we didn't have any official government pronouncement that it was really illegal," the Hart lawyer said. He questioned why Uncle Sam got most of the money instead of the contributors to the delegate committees, and he lamented that "now we'll never know how much money was raised" by the delegate-committee device that "kept the Mondale campaign afloat."

Pudge Henkel, Hart's campaign manager, agreed. "The bottom line," he said, "is we needed the FEC to make an early judgment that it was illegal, because people were not willing to believe it was in fact until the FEC so ruled." When the FEC finally did, he said, it didn't matter, "and that's not right because it impacted on the campaign. It was the thing that enabled [Mondale] to overspend in New Hampshire and to allow PAC money, particularly labor money, to come in the back door through labor's PACs, and to prop up that whole campaign at a time they had real financial problems."

David Landau, Hart's issues director, said later that the press, which had moved the story along to a point, had given up too soon. "It had a potential for being a real Watergate," he said, not knowing when he said it about the "stolen records" in Pennsylvania. "We all believed at the time this was the issue that could turn it around. It was so much the old politics. But the issue died. I blamed it partly on the press. In 1972 [the year of Watergate] they would have been all over the FEC [not created until 1974]."

Landau said that as the controversy grew, most reporters "didn't want to do the work" required to make a stronger case that the

Mondale campaign was violating the law. "They wanted us to find the smoking gun," he said, and the Hart campaign didn't. Even after Mondale said he would give the money back, Landau said, the press failed to pressure him to do so, and Mondale never did until the conciliation agreement came in.

Hart told us later that if it could be established that as much as one million dollars had flowed into the Mondale effort through the delegate-committee device, it could be said they were "crucial" to the outcome of the nomination fight, because Mondale was so strapped for funds toward the end. In any event, he said, the device was very helpful to Mondale in such things as "opening offices, putting in phone banks and putting people out on the street under the rubric of delegate committees. The so-called Mondale organization was top-heavy in Washington and didn't have very much going for it at the grass-roots level. Those delegate committees turned out not only to be a funnel for money but also a means by which constituency groups could provide a grass-roots base."

The Mondale strategists, not surprisingly, saw the delegate-committees controversy as vastly overblown. "I always believed it was a Beltway issue if there ever was a Beltway issue," Beckel said, meaning it was of interest only to political junkies inside the Washington Beltway. "I told Mondale it didn't matter, that it wasn't a voting issue," he said. ". . . I believe we never should have shut down the committees."

Johnson, for his part, was critical of the press, but not for the same reasons Landau was. "I thought the coverage of the delegate committees," he said, "was the most irresponsible part of the coverage of the entire presidential race of 1984. Things like offering legal advice to these committees were explicitly provided for in the regulations as an acceptable campaign practice. Things that were being found and put into screaming language were in many cases totally all right. It may be that the whole thing was totally all right still. It was the point in the campaign where I thought the press did the worst job in terms of taking the time to learn the law, or to give us a fair shake about the fact that there was an enormous disagreement about what the law and regulations said."

As for David Ifshin, the Mondale campaign lawyer who ferreted out the FEC delegate-committee "loophole," asked if there ever was anything touching on a criminal matter concerning the delegate committees, he replied: "Criminal? Jesus . . . Barring some fact I never knew about . . . I can look anybody in the eye—reporter, judge, lawyer, bailiff—and say the Mondale campaign . . . executed as well as can be done by a campaign for President. . . . Given the nature around a campaign, no one could have executed the regulations written by the FEC, and their intent, better than we did."

One key question remained, however. What would have happened had the episode of the spy in the Pennsylvania at-large committee and the stolen financial records been known at the time? Maybe nothing. But already the course of the 1984 campaign had been affected in a major way by more trivial matters such as "Where's the beef?" and the "phantom" and anti-Vrdolyak ads. In this fiasco of a campaign, the pendulum had swung on matters of far less substance than the questions of political ethics, if not legality, raised by that incident in Philadelphia and the whole delegate-committee scheme it highlighted.

Fritz Mondale came out of Pennsylvania apparently in very good shape. But as subsequent events were to prove, Gary Hart was not finished yet, and Mondale was not home free. Approaching primaries in key states like Ohio and California would demonstrate there was no Mondale stampede building as a result of his earlier primary and caucus victories. It is not inconceivable, therefore, that disclosure of the mischief that was made on his behalf in Pennsylvania might at the very least have thrown the Democratic nomination race wide open again.

As it was, Mondale still had cause to worry from another quarter, not in the sense of threatening his nomination, but in terms of whether the nomination would be worth much once he had won it. That cause for concern was named Jesse Jackson.

12

Our Time Has Come!

•

THE WAY Jesse Jackson preached it that winter night at the Vermont Avenue Baptist Church in Washington, he was David and Ronald Reagan was Goliath. The stones for David to use as weapons were unregistered black voters.

"I think about David picking up his rocks, using what he's got," he told the rapt congregation.

"Illinois—Reagan won by 376,000; 700,000 unregistered blacks, 500,000 unregistered Hispanics. Rocks—just layin' around.

"New York—Reagan won by 165,000; 900,000 unregistered blacks, 600,000 unregistered Hispanics. Rocks—just layin' around."

Jackson went on, voice rising, naming one state after another in which unregistered blacks and Hispanics might have made a difference in the election of 1980.

Then, typically, he reached a crescendo, and his listeners shouted back at him.

"Little David!" he cried. "Dry your eyes!"

"Yeah!"

"Little David! Throw your chest out! Don't feel inadequate anymore!"

"Go on!"

"Little David! Use what you got! Use your slingshot!"

"Talk!"

"Pick up your rocks! Jesse Jackson is coming! Now!"

Jackson's performance at that Washington church was no different from those he was giving almost every day in one city after another through the winter. But in this case he was using a theme that went to the heart of the Democratic Party's strategy for 1984—and his own place in it.

From the outset, the party's hopes for mounting a serious challenge to President Reagan had rested on the premise that the universe of voters would have to be enlarged significantly in 1984. If the party had no truly compelling program to present—and it didn't—it would rely on the reaction against Reagan among those who had suffered what Tip O'Neill called "the hurts" of the budget reductions of the previous three years.

On paper, this mechanistic theory sounded reasonable. The black vote had increased dramatically in the state and congressional elections since Ronald Reagan had entered the White House. And blacks could be relied upon to divide at least nine to one for Democratic candidates. Moreover, there were still huge pools of voting-age blacks unregistered, the "rocks—layin' around" Jackson had cited.

The registration of Hispanic-Americans also had been increasing at a steady, if less spectacular, pace. Except for the politically conservative Cuban-Americans in south Florida, the Hispanics usually split at least seven to three for Democrats. They, too, were concentrated most heavily in states that would be pivotal—Texas, New York and Illinois being the most obvious.

There also seemed to be great promise in the so-called gender gap, the pattern of women preferring Democrats that was apparent in election returns and opinion-poll results. The political professionals were convinced that this phenomenon had far less to do with "women's issues" per se—such concerns as abortion rights and the Equal Rights Amendment—than it did with broader issues. Working women, particularly those with children but no husband, were considered an especially good target because they had felt more directly the brunt of reductions in government social programs under the Reagan administration. It seemed that every cocktail waitress in the country had two kids at home, a husband on the lam and child-care problems.

But the prime target was clearly the black vote. And it was here that Jesse Jackson seemed to represent both a potentially rich opportunity and a potentially destructive hazard. At root, the operative question for the Democratic Party about Jackson's candidacy was whether the rewards it might bring would be worth the price if it caused a significant backlash among whites.

For Fritz Mondale, however, the problem was more immediate. The question was simply whether he could make it through the primaries to the presidential nomination without wrecking the coalition he would need to have a chance against President Reagan in the November election.

On the one hand, Mondale was obliged to deal with Jesse Jackson in a way that would keep him in the Democratic tent and perhaps even make him useful in the general election. On the other, Mondale had to concern himself with the attitudes of the black leaders who had chosen to support him rather than Jackson, the conservative white Democrats put off by Jackson and the important Jewish voters—and contributors—who considered Jackson blatantly anti-Semitic.

The guidelines for dealing with all those dilemmas could not be established, however, until some reading could be taken on whether Jesse Jackson was going to be a formidable influence in the primaries or just so much rhetoric.

Heading South after the first primaries in New England, Jackson was somewhat chastened by the furor over the "Hymie" incident. Early in the New Hampshire primary campaign, not long after Jackson's triumphal return from Syria with Robert Goodman, a poll made for the Boston *Globe* had shown him with 16 percent of the vote and in third place behind only Mondale and John Glenn. He was the candidate running the different campaign, and even white voters were intrigued.

But on primary day, Jackson had received only 5 percent, leaving him down in the field of also-rans. He had managed a slightly better showing—8 percent—in the Vermont primary. But it was plain that the initial flush of white liberal enthusiasm for Jackson had been tempered by the controversy over anti-Semitism.

On the face of it, the southern primaries seemed to offer Jackson fertile ground. His potential in Florida was limited because less than 15 percent of the population there was black. But in both Alabama and Georgia, blacks made up one-fourth of the population and might easily cast one-third of the vote in a Democratic primary—particularly if white participation was limited. And in both states Jackson was supported by an extensive network of younger political leaders and preachers of all ages, particularly in rural areas.

But these were also states in which Jackson was confronting the opposition of important black political leaders advising their constituents not to waste their votes on symbolism. In Alabama, the key figures for Mondale were Richard Arrington, the mayor of Birmingham, and Joe Reed, head of the Alabama Democratic Conference. In Georgia, Mondale had the support, open or tacit, of Mayor Andrew Young of Atlanta, Julian Bond, John Lewis and Coretta Scott King.

Striving for credibility, Jackson directed his fire at both of the leading candidates, now Gary Hart and Fritz Mondale. His campaign, he told the southern black audiences, carried their cause a step further than either of the white candidates.

"Hart and Mondale represent advocacy. I represent action," he said. "At best, they represent liberalism. I represent liberation. Both are talking forward and moving backward."

In New England, Jackson said later, "we were surviving in the Valley of the Giants, in, quote-unquote, alien territory," because the voters were so overwhelmingly white. By contrast, he contended, he could have won in the South if the vote had been divided among a greater number of credible white candidates, if both John Glenn and Fritz Hollings had survived as genuine players in those Super Tuesday primaries.

But earning credibility for himself, even among blacks, was difficult, he said, because the whole idea of a black candidacy "was so new to the people there."

Jackson persevered, flying around the South in an old Lockheed Electra—quickly dubbed "The Rainbow Express"—chartered from the Rex Humbard Foundation. He lacked the money for a television advertising campaign, but he was accompanied by a front-runner-sized press corps known as "the Soul Patrol." And the news coverage was extensive and intensive. The first "serious" black candidate for the presidency was going to be big news everywhere, at least the first time around.

In fact, Jackson's candidacy caused some problems for the press quite different from those normally encountered in a campaign. Many news organizations chose to assign black reporters with little or no experience in politics to cover Jackson on the theory that black reporters would have a special insight—and perhaps special access to the candidate. This idea may have been correct on the occasions when Jackson wanted to "talk black talk"—as with Milton Coleman in the "Hymie" conversation. But some of the black reporters came to believe that Jackson "saved" his best material for white reporters because he thought that would give him the greatest exposure. Some blacks were irked, for example, when Jackson used *60 Minutes* and Mike Wallace as the vehicle for declaring his candidacy. Only a few days earlier, Jackson had met with the black reporters and had left them with the impression that they would have the story first.

Jackson believed, he said after the campaign, that because of "politics in the main office"—meaning news executives' decisions—stories done by white reporters were treated better than those done by black reporters because it was "assumed" the white reporters were fair. He cited one case in which a black correspondent for a television network had a serious problem getting stories on the air in comparison with a white colleague who replaced him on the assignment.

The result was a pressure on some of the black reporters. As Jackson said later, "They knew they had to prove themselves." And the pressure seemed to be reflected in a coolness toward Milton Coleman that bordered on hostility in one or two cases. Some black reporters complained to other reporters that Coleman had violated an off-the-record understanding in quoting Jackson in that incident. But there was also the question of whether that story had not raised doubts in their editors' minds about their own access to the candidate—and whether they might be protecting Jackson because they saw themselves first as blacks rather than reporters. In fact, there never was any problem of access to Jesse Jackson for reporters, black or white; in many respects, his campaign was one big rolling press conference.

There were many reasons for tempers to become frayed in the Jackson campaign, however. The candidate's schedule was seldom ready in advance and often subject to last-minute revisions. There was often no time built into the schedule for reporters to file their stories. The problems with the airplane were so serious that at one point the networks and several of the major newspapers chartered their own plane separately rather than travel with Jackson. On more than one occasion, the press corps would land at an airport to find no one had arranged for buses for them to follow Jackson. On others, they would arrive at a hotel at 1:00 AM or some such hour, with time for only four or five hours sleep before the next campaign day was to begin, only to discover hotel rooms had not been reserved for them. It was, all in all, a very different campaign.

The results on Super Tuesday were a mixed bag for Jackson.

In Alabama, Dick Arrington and Joe Reed had delivered well enough for Mondale that he received 47 percent of the black vote to Jackson's 50. In Birmingham, blacks voted two to one for Mondale. The result statewide was 19 percent for Jackson—fourth place.

But in Georgia, he polled 21 percent for third place, ahead of John Glenn. That figure was particularly significant; first, because Jackson needed a share of 20 percent or higher in at least one primary that day to remain eligible for federal matching funds for his campaign. But the result also was significant because Jackson's 21 percent was founded on his having captured about 60 percent of the black vote, to roughly 35 for Mondale, in the face of all those established black leaders' opposition.

"We came out of that period with at least our self-respect intact," Jackson said later.

Over the next few weeks, however, the Jackson phenomenon would reach a new level that was qualitatively different. In Illinois on March 20, he won 77 or 79 percent, depending on which poll you accepted as accurate, of the black vote. In New York two weeks later Jackson captured 87 percent of the blacks, and in Pennsylvania a week after that, 75 percent.

In each case, the black vote also was so substantial that Jackson won respectable shares of the total vote—21 percent in Illinois, 25 in New York—just below Hart's 27—and 17 in Pennsylvania. The message—for black and white politicians alike—was that Jesse Jackson had become an important element in the equation. There was still no reason for anyone of political sophistication to believe that he was going to be on the Democratic ticket in San Francisco. But it was apparent he had ignited something in the black community that Fritz Mondale—once again the frontrunner after three straight victories in these industrial states—would be obliged to consider.

The direct effect on Mondale's campaign up to this stage could only be a subject of conjecture. If the opinion polls were correct, it was reasonable to suppose that Mondale would have taken most of the black vote in all these states had there been no Jesse Jackson running. On the other hand, in that critical test in Georgia, you could make a case that Jackson rescued Mondale. Apparently because of the intensity of the campaigning in the black community—and particularly in Atlanta—the black vote in Georgia was twice what it had been in the presidential primary four years earlier. The result was that Mondale received about 100,000 votes from black Georgians in a primary in which he defeated Gary Hart by only 22,000 votes.

That primary was one of many occasions when Hart might have regretted his total failure to compete for the black vote. At first blush, it might appear that such an effort would have been wasted in view of Jackson's and Mondale's claims. But Hart had a civil-rights record strong enough to enable him to enlist some of the younger black leaders and at least a respectable share of the vote. In fact, he had almost no identifiable black support—the prime exception being the backing in Atlanta of Michael Lomax, chairman of the Fulton County board of commissioners. Quite beyond whatever dividends an effort by Hart among blacks might have paid in black support, however, it could have been expected to strengthen his case with some liberal whites. After the campaign, Hart and his advisers contended that they always intended to make more of an appeal in the black community. But they pictured themselves as having been thwarted by circumstances beyond their control, such as a campaign plane breakdown when they had scheduled an appearance before a black group. It was a lame story, at best.

The growing share of the vote Jackson received in Illinois, New York and Pennsylvania seemed directly related to his performance in the nationally televised debates that were held over the period of the primaries in Atlanta, Chicago, New York, Pittsburgh and Dallas.

Jackson had demonstrated he could "play with the big boys" in that first televised debate at Dartmouth back in January. Now, with the field narrowed to three candidates after Super Tuesday, he was at the top of his form in these sessions. He was still sometimes vague on specifics, but he was also still insulated against any serious challenge from his opponents on those specifics. Neither Mondale nor Hart wanted to be the first to put down a black candidate. On several occasions, Jackson played the role of peacemaker—chiding the other candidates in an avuncular manner for their attacks on one another.

In the New York debate, for instance, Mondale and Hart fell to bickering between themselves about charges they had made against each other in commercials and speeches. Jackson said: "Tomorrow the issue will be this rat-a-tat-tat, without dealing with directions. The fact is the reason why they are having this kinship struggle is that there is such similarity in policies. It's a matter of both going in the same direction, just a little slower. That's all it is."

The result of Jackson's performance in the debates was an extraordinary pride in the black community. Jesse Jackson was proving not only that he could run for President but that he could hold his own.

Jackson himself recognized the significance of the credibility he gained from those confrontations—and the risk he had taken.

"Suppose I had made big, classical errors in the debates," he told us later. "It would have embarrassed my people. They would have said, 'You know, I told you we were not ready.' It salvaged the ego investment of blacks, gave us a new sense of confidence that we can debate foreign policy, we can debate domestic policy. We can engage in hard exchange with the best the party has to offer. It began to strengthen the ego resolve of blacks and again to broaden the respect base among whites."

Jackson was clearly impressed by the impact he was having on other black Americans. After the campaign he enjoyed recalling those who told him of the doors he had opened for other blacks, such as one young woman in Selma, Alabama:

"She said, 'If Reverend Jackson can run for President, I can run for tax assessor,' and everybody laughed. She ran for tax assessor and won."[32]

"For blacks," Jackson said, "it became a great confidence-builder around the country."

The white reaction was ambivalent. An opinion survey taken by the Mondale campaign right after the New York debate found that more voters thought Jackson had "won" than either Mondale or Hart. Jackson was demonstrating that it was not necessary to have all the elaborate campaign machinery of the more conventional candidates to become a significant factor in the competition. Where Mondale had organizations of labor leaders and public officials, Jackson had the huge network of black preachers. Where Hart had a media consultant designing television commercials,

32. The young woman was Jackie Walker, and she was elected Dallas County tax collector in October of 1984. She was killed in an automobile accident on an icy highway in February of 1985.

Jackson had the "free media" coverage that came with being a novelty.

But this fascination with Jackson was not by any means being translated into a genuine rainbow coalition. If the exit polls were accurate, Jackson failed to win as much as 10 percent of the white vote in any of these primaries in which he was making such a strong showing. And a Gallup poll found 18 percent of white voters who said they would not be willing to vote for a black nominee for President, a figure that probably understated the resistance to a black. Other surveys over the years had revealed a reluctance among whites to say they wouldn't vote for a black simply because he was black. Jackson did have some support among Hispanic-Americans, but in many states the relationships between blacks and Hispanics were far from congenial, so there were clear limits on that détente.

Jackson was defensive about his monochromatic support. At one point, he told reporters in Richmond there was "a general disregard" for blacks among white voters and news media alike.

"It's not my fault that whites haven't developed a high regard for the intelligence and achievements of blacks," he said.

But Jackson clearly had several problems with white voters that put a ceiling on his potential as a candidate. For a few issue-oriented voters, at least, Jackson's agenda was simply too radical. He was the only candidate still in the field urging an absolute reduction in the defense budget and a tax surcharge on upper-income taxpayers to finance expanded social programs.

Jackson also seemed to be a candidate constantly involved in controversy in an election year in which the first imperative seemed to be not to rock the boat. He was forever complaining about the Democratic Party's delegate-selection rules. And he often seemed to be threatening to walk out on the party, although he kept insisting that notion was a perception in the eye of the beholder.

"I have no record of walking out of conventions," he said during the New York campaign. "I've spent all my time trying to break in them."

For other whites, the questions about Jackson grew out of his style. Here was this big, handsome black man in the fancy clothes who was not acting like any preacher they had ever seen, unless it was Adam Clayton Powell. At best he was a demagogue, at worst a charlatan taking the press and his own people over the jumps. It was obvious that many black leaders, who presumably knew him better, also held that unsympathetic view of him.

But the most basic problem for whites was simply cultural. When Jackson would appear on television telling a black audience, "Our time has come," that declaration would seem far more threatening than it really was. Except for the youngest voters, the memories of the racial strife of the 1960s were vivid. The country had reacted against protest politics, and even many erstwhile liberals were backing away from black demands. And here was another black man who seemed to be preaching revolt against the established order.

In fact, Jackson's rhetoric with black audiences was neither hostile to whites nor inflammatory to blacks. His style had always been confrontational. But his message was often conciliatory and almost always directed at evoking black pride. A typical peroration at a rally in West Virginia makes the point.

"We as a people and as a nation, we've come a mighty long way," he began.

When a cheer went up from the audience, he said:

"I see black people and white people coming across lines of race and religion and region, working on a common existence. We've come a long way."

More cheers and applause.

"When I see us bury the hatchet in the ground and not in each other, we've come a long way."

A rising tide of cheers and applause.

"We have moved from racial battleground to economic common ground and survival and moral higher ground."

Jackson clearly reveled in these exchanges with his audiences, and particularly with the throngs of young people who would shout the responses that had become so familiar.

"I am—" he would shout, sweat running down his neck.

"I am—" they would respond.

"—some-body!"

"—some-body!"

Or he would say, "We're not asking for welfare, we're asking for our share." Then he would lead another shouted colloquy.

"Not welfare!"

"Not welfare!"

"Our share!"

"Our share!"

For many whites, much of what they knew about the Jackson campaign came from televised reports of such meetings in a world they had never experienced. And unless they were there, they could not see how Jackson, whatever his motives, evoked a pride in other blacks that didn't have to include racial hostility. One of us encountered a middle-aged black man named Harley Williams in northeast Philadelphia a few days before the Pennsylvania primary.

"What do you think of Jesse Jackson?" we asked.

"He's telling it like it should be told," he replied. "We can all hold our heads up now."

"What can he really do for you?"

"He doesn't have to do something for me, man," said Williams. "He's already done it, just being there."

And if anyone missed the point, Jackson reminded them. Speaking to a rally of his own group, Operation PUSH, in Chicago a few days before the Illinois primary, he summed it up this way:

"We're moving on up. At the '72 convention, George McGovern was the nominee . . . Reubin Askew was the keynoter . . . I was just fighting for a seat in the hall . . . and I beat 'em in New Hampshire.

"Moving on up! Alan Cranston, a powerful senator from California, and I beat him. Fritz Hollings . . . When he was governor of South Carolina, I couldn't use the bathroom in the state capitol. I beat Fritz Hollings!

"We're moving on up! John Glenn was up there orbiting the earth when I was scuffling for dimes down here. Now he's gone and I'm still in the race. We're moving on up!"

Perhaps the central irony in Jackson's campaign was the one campaign of the recent past it most closely paralleled was that of George Corley Wallace when he was running for President in 1964, 1968 and 1972. Wallace's campaign, too, was aimed at a particular voter—the one he liked to call "the average citizen" and described most often as a beautician or a steelworker. And Wallace liked to make the point that he was bringing attention to his constituents back home that, he implied, would pay some dividend sometime in the future. He loved to talk about how "they called the name of Alabama" in Boston and New York and Los Angeles when he ran there.

But there was a crucial difference. Wallace played on the resentments and angers of the working people whose support he sought—their disgust with "pointy-headed bureaucrats who couldn't park a bicycle straight." By contrast, Jesse Jackson played on the pride of American blacks. He was the example they could all hope to follow.

Harley Williams, talking in northeast Philadelphia that day, put it like this:

"I see Jesse on TV with all those big people, and I just puff up. I know he's not going to be President, but he could be."

Or, as a young black student in Pine Bluff, Arkansas, said after a Jackson rally months later: "He makes me feel soooo good."

Jackson was not making Fritz Mondale or the white power structure of the Democratic Party feel so good, however. On the contrary, he was proving every bit as prickly as they had expected and feared. And on one issue in particular—his relationship with Louis Farrakhan—he was threatening directly the hopes for a united party that might have some chance against Ronald Reagan.

Farrakhan, then fifty years old, was the leader of the Chicago-based Nation of Islam, one of the Black Muslim factions that had developed out of the split in the original Nation of Islam after the death of Elijah Muhammad in 1975. Minister Farrakhan, as he was called, was a protégé of Muhammad and preached the same doctrine of black self-reliance, superiority and separatism. He had always stood apart from conventional politics and encouraged his followers to do the same.

But the Jackson campaign changed all that. Farrakhan was close enough to Jackson to have been part of the official delegation that had gone to Syria to rescue Robert Goodman at the end of 1983. Until Jackson received protection from Secret Service agents, Farrakhan had provided bodyguards for him from his own security force, the Fruit of Islam. A riveting speaker, he also served as the warm-up to Jackson at some of his rallies and held rallies of his own followers in Jackson's behalf. He also regularly made radio broadcasts and in one of them, on March 11, he made statements that—when they came to press attention two weeks later—ignited a searing controversy.

In the broadcast Farrakhan attacked Milton Coleman, the black reporter for the Washington *Post* who had originally reported Jackson's use of the term "Hymie" to describe Jews and "Hymietown" to describe New York. Coleman, Farrakhan said, was a "traitor" and a "Judas" and an "Uncle Tom."

"We're going to make an example of Milton Coleman," Farrakhan said.

He said he would urge churches in Washington, D.C., where Coleman lived, to bar the reporter, to "tell him he's not wanted" and to tell his wife she could enter only if she left him.

"If she won't leave him," he went on, "then you go to hell with your husband. If he is a traitor of your people, then the same punishment that's due that no-good filthy traitor, you'll get it yourself as his wife."

At one point in the broadcast Farrakhan specified that there would be "at this point, no physical harm" to the reporter. But at another he said:

"One day soon we will punish you with death. You're saying when is that? In sufficient time, we will come to power right inside this country—one day soon."

And later he added:

"This is fitting punishment for such dogs. He's a dog. We don't give the bread of Jesus to dogs. We just throw him out with the rest of the dogs."

Some blacks familiar with Farrakhan's militant rhetoric contended that the threat to Coleman shouldn't have been taken literally—that it was intended metaphorically. But Farrakhan was a man who called whites "devils" and "demons" and once referred to Adolf Hitler as "a very great man" albeit "wickedly great."

So the threat against Coleman was taken quite literally in the press—and left Jackson in an untenable position he soon made much worse for himself.

Jackson quickly responded that "the threat was wrong." But then, just as quickly, he tried to depict it as something that had nothing to do with him and might even be a political effort to discredit him.

"It does not fall on my shoulders," he said in an interview with the Washington *Post*. "It falls on the shoulders of the man who said it. Of course, I might add that this speech was given two weeks ago. For this to surface on the eve of the New York primary makes me very suspicious."

Over the next several days, Jackson kept insisting that Farrakhan had no "official" position in his campaign and that he was in no position "to muzzle surrogates" who maintained their independence while supporting him.

But Jackson was being disingenuous to a fault. His relationship with Farrakhan was too well established to be dismissed. And the Black Muslim's rhetoric had been so outlandish—at least in conventional terms—that his Democratic rivals felt compelled to violate their usual policy toward him of ignoring his candidacy. Gary Hart said that if he were Jackson, "I would repudiate the support of Mr. Farrakhan." Fritz Mondale called the threat to Coleman "an outrage" and added:

"I think Jesse should use his influence to seek an apology or a retraction from Reverend Farrakhan to see that this is cleared up."

Nor did the Republicans miss an opportunity to rub a little salt into the wound. Vice President George Bush piously demanded that the other Democratic candidates speak out "loudly and clearly" in condemnation, then added:

"I tell you here and now for the President and the entire administration that we denounce the intrusion of anti-Semitism into the American political process."

But Jackson steadfastly refused to repudiate his Black Muslim ally. So the controversy boiled through the next ten days and the Pennsylvania primary. Farrakhan himself helped it along by coming into Philadelphia three days before that vote and telling a rally that white America "has always tried to pit nigger against nigger" and that the press was playing the game with him and Jesse Jackson.

What gave the whole controversy such a dangerous political dimension for the Democrats was Farrakhan's well-established history of hostility to Jews—and the suspicions that Jesse Jackson also was anti-Semitic. He had embraced Yasir Arafat and the Palestine Liberation Organization, after all, and there was the "Hymie" incident. Farrakhan brought the issue into sharp focus. In that same radio attack on Milton Coleman, he had said rhetorically to black reporters:

"You already know what you want to write of me so it doesn't really make any difference what I say. You already have a picture. Your editors have a picture of what they want Farrakhan to look like, especially your Jewish editors and Jewish writers."

Talking about the episode after the campaign, Jackson insisted the press had "magnified" Farrakhan's statements and that the Black Muslim leader "was not an official in our campaign" but nonetheless represented "a definite school of thought within the black community."

In running for office, Jackson said, "you try to reach out to as many people as you can. . . . When I talked with him about positions that were different from my positions, I thought that was enough."

He pointed out that the white candidates had not denounced Mayor Edward Koch of New York when he threatened to disavow the Democratic ticket if Jackson had a place on it.

"I never felt it was fair," he said.

Nor did he believe he deserved to be tarred with the "theological and philosophical positions about Zionism" held by Farrakhan.

"That was all religious persuasion," he said. "I'm a Protestant. My religious persuasion and dogma is different from that."

"I'm a firm believer that no man is beyond repair," Jackson said. "Look at the people I have been asked to forgive. It's almost noble to forgive white people . . ."

He pointed out that Ernest Hollings had been governor of South Carolina while racial segregation was still in force there.

"Yet I have no lingering bitterness toward him. I am redemptive toward him," Jackson said. "If I can be expected to relate to Fritz Hollings on new terms or Bert Lance or Jimmy Carter or the Mississippi Democrats or the Louisiana Democrats, I would expect whites to be at least as . . . redemptive toward blacks."

But the political question never had anything to do with whether whites might be redemptive toward Louis Farrakhan or Jesse Jackson. The point was that American Jews considered Jackson a hostile force and were waiting to see Fritz Mondale reflect their attitude.

Jewish voters represent only about 2 percent of the electorate, but they cast about 3 percent of the vote nationally and a great deal more than that in Democratic Party primaries in some states. Moreover, they are a significant force in the party as contributors and as political activists and liberal leaders. In the general election, their support was essential to the Democrats because they represented an important bloc in states the Democrats needed—New York, Pennsylvania and Illinois, most notably.

In most presidential elections, that backing had been forthcoming. But in 1980, Jewish voters had given Jimmy Carter only about 45 percent of their vote, independent John B. Anderson 15 percent and Ronald Reagan a surprising 40 percent. Those were figures very much in the minds of the Mondale strategists as they looked down the political road.

The Jewish case against Jackson was founded on more than simply Farrakhan or the Hymie incident, however, and on more than that embrace of Arafat in 1979. The Jewish concern was not simply that Jackson was sympathetic to the Arab cause or that his organization, PUSH, had received money from Arab sources. Instead, the antipathy was based on a long history of incidents and remarks that Jews found frightening. Jackson, as might be expected, always had an explanation.

In a *Playboy* magazine interview that spring, Jackson was asked by Robert Scheer of the Los Angeles *Times* about the time he had said he was "tired" of hearing about the Jewish holocaust. Jackson replied:

> It was a statement taken completely out of context. In 1971 or 1972 I was in Africa with my wife and the Staple sisters and Roberta Flack. We decided to go see where the slaves had been kept. We were taken to some caves. They were damp and ugly, and what had started out as a tourist visit became quietness and then singing and prayers and tears. By the time we got out at the other end, there was kind of anger, a real resentment among us. But then I said to my wife, "You know, if we rehearsed this slavery ritual every day, or often, we could develop the kind of resentment toward the blacks who sold us and the whites who captured and then enslaved us that would never lend itself to human progress. I would just be so bitter."
>
> Later, in a private talk with two guys, I referred to the Jewish holocaust in that context. We had seen several references to the holocaust on television that year, and I said that while I appreciated the memory of it as a basis for saying, "Never again," we really had to move beyond that and not linger at graveside. That was analogous to our own experience, having come through the holocaust of slavery, having lost thirty million or forty million people in slavery. My remark was one of personal experience, not one that was designed to be negative or hostile.
>
> That was the context of that statement, because I, too, am a member

of a race that has known a holocaust and has known subjugation in this land, not as a matter of history but as a matter of personal experience. I look at those striped uniforms that the Jews wore in those Nazi camps and I recall that I grew up watching the police act like Nazis every weekend and lock up blacks, charging them with vagrancy, making them wear striped uniforms and putting chains on their ankles. What they really were looking for were street cleaners they wouldn't have to pay, and they'd sentence a black to ten days in prison for being drunk on his own porch and stuff like that. So it wasn't the first time I had seen those striped uniforms.

But Jackson's explanations had never been persuasive to American Jewish leaders, and there was a drumfire of demand for Mondale to set himself apart from the black leader.

The truth of the matter, however, was that neither Mondale nor his campaign advisers had found any formula for dealing with Jesse Jackson. He was not a conventional opponent who might have visions of a Cabinet post in a Mondale administration and thus might mute his criticism. He was not concerned with paying his campaign debt. His goal clearly was to establish himself as the dominant black voice in American life, and that objective wasn't going to be achieved by playing orthodox politics. But just what he wanted was difficult to define.

One obvious goal was the fair share of the convention delegates that Jackson was convinced he was being denied by those rules setting thresholds and providing bonus delegates to primary winners. Shortly after the Pennsylvania primary, a compilation showed that up to that point in this convoluted Democratic Party process, Mondale had won 39.4 percent of the popular vote in primaries to 34.5 percent for Gary Hart and 16.8 percent for Jackson. Yet Mondale had captured 672 delegates—just under 60 percent of the total—to 372 for Hart and only 86 for Jackson. So, while insisting that "we're not going anyplace," Jackson kept pressing for after-the-fact changes in the rules that would give him greater representation at San Francisco. There was never any realistic possibility the formula would be rewritten at this stage, but the complaints made Jackson's point—that he and his followers were not being given the voice they deserved in the party's deliberations.

Inside the Mondale campaign the hints of a possible walkout were being taken quite seriously. But so was the reaction of Jewish supporters.

"We had a lot of pressure on us to back off from talking to Jackson at all," one Mondale adviser said later. "But after New Hampshire we didn't have the luxury of letting Jackson walk out."

Mondale himself clearly found dealing with Jackson extremely awkward. From the outset, he had understood that the stakes were high and the risks great. Having a drink with him in New Hampshire one night late in 1983, one of us asked him:

"How are you going to handle Jesse?"

Mondale puffed on his cigar and laughed.

"Veerry carefully," he replied.

At that time, however, there was no reason for Mondale to expect that Jackson might be as prickly as he became. Mondale was accustomed to bargaining with black political leaders under essentially the same rules that applied with white political leaders. But Jackson might seem conciliatory in a private conversation, then hold a press conference in which he would make a point of being angry and confrontational.

It seemed to us at the time that Fritz Mondale might be suffering "the liberal guilt." He was a member of that generation of liberals who had come into politics while blacks were struggling for their rights and who had supported that struggle with commitment and emotion. Now many members of that generation seemed to find themselves inhibited by that history when they felt anger at blacks for what they considered excesses. And, as a result, they would not rebuke a black as quickly as they might a white. But after the campaign, Mondale insisted that was an inaccurate picture of him.

"I don't think it's fair," he said. "I don't have any guilt. A lot of my career has been in the civil-rights movement and I'm very proud of it."

He pointed out that he disagreed strongly with Jackson on the Middle East and didn't hesitate to make that apparent.

"What I decided to do," he said, "was to disagree in a dignified way with Jesse Jackson when I disagreed with him . . . and try to give him the dignity and respect he deserved as a candidate for President, to recognize the profound nature of this new effort by a black in America and what it meant to millions of black Americans and others who agreed with it, while making clear to the American people where I stood. That's what I did."

But the relationship between the two men was never easy.

As one insider put it later, "The best they would ever be is colleagues. They would never be friends."

Most of the burden of dealing with Jackson fell to campaign manager Bob Beckel. He met and talked repeatedly with Jackson's chief advisers and, on occasion, slipped over to the Howard Inn in Washington to meet with Jackson himself. The relationship was a complex one. The two men got along, but Jackson sometimes chafed at dealing with anyone below the level of the candidate himself. And some black politicians in the Mondale camp seemed irked that Beckel had become the emissary and sniped at him for being what one called "on an ego trip" as the prime connection to Jackson.

The Mondale campaign also got some help here from Bert Lance, who had developed a rapport with Jackson in the arguments earlier in the year over such things as the runoff primary system in the South. Although they had been "on opposite ends" on those issues, Lance said later, "we had developed a mutual respect and trust for each other." So the two men talked frequently on the telephone, and Lance came to Washington often to join Beckel, a well-regarded friend, in meeting with Jackson in Mondale's behalf.

"I don't think the Mondale insider group ever really understood Jackson," Lance said later. "I did and could communicate with him and I understood what he was about. I knew what Jesse wanted, which was simply self-respect. They never did understand that and I don't think they really made any great effort to understand it."

The Mondale strategists clearly did understand, however, that Jackson was doing them serious political damage with his constant demands and his relationship with Louis Farrakhan. And they were also convinced they could not afford to tell Jackson to pack it in because he truly did have a constituency.

"If you didn't have to deal with the guy, if it was a complete charade," one Mondale adviser said, "it would be easy enough to deal with him. But he had support."

Beckel himself once had first-hand experience with that fact. One night in Kansas City, Jackson took him to eat some ribs at a place in a black neighborhood, and they took a table near the front window. When they started eating there were perhaps a dozen black youngsters outside who recognized Jackson; by the time they finished there was a crowd of 3,000 waiting to catch a glimpse of him.

But inside the Mondale campaign there was a constant debate about what to do—and some feeling that they might be overreacting in their concern with the black vote.

"Mondale lost his patience with Jackson many times," one campaign operative said later. But everyone agreed, he added, "we couldn't blast the guy out of the party."

"If you thought by blasting Jackson," one insider said, "you'd handle all our special-interest problems at one time, I didn't think that would work."

The threat to Mondale went beyond "the Jewish problem" to the perception of him as an old-fashioned liberal caving in to black demands. No one was more aware of that problem than the candidate himself.

"To this day," he told us long after the campaign, "I don't believe Reverend Jackson understood how that played out with the total electorate. But that's part of the learning process and it's just a burden I had to bear, that's all.

"I didn't give in on anything I believed in. I didn't come up with any big spending program because I didn't think I could be elected if I did. I didn't bend at all on these various flaps that occurred. . . . I wanted the public to see I was my own man."

And "blasting" Jackson out of the party was clearly beyond Mondale.

"The line I drew was the one I felt was the best," he said. "I didn't want to go beyond where I was to the point that I would appear to be deprecating the right of a black to seek the presidency. . . . I still think that was the best line to draw."

After the Pennsylvania primary, with the nomination apparently assured, the Mondale campaign began to seek a way to minimize the danger of a damaging explosion at the convention in San Francisco. The answer, Beckel and Jim Johnson figured, might be a "unity task force" that would function outside the Mondale campaign and outside the Democratic National Committee. The idea would be to find a formula that would give Jackson that undefined "self-respect" he was seeking and still keep him on the reservation at the convention.

Beckel took the plan to Jackson and suggested that Bob Strauss, the party's senior negotiator, might be the right person to head such a group. Jackson, who had always gotten along with Strauss, agreed it was an idea worth discussing, although he was wary about anything that would exclude Gary Hart.

"I did not want to see my role as being divisive," he said later. "I see my role as being that of healer."

So, he said, he continued to keep in touch with Hart as well as with Mondale.

"I chose to keep good relations with both because I knew at some point after the convention that the issue would shift from the intra-league struggle with Democrats to an inter-league struggle with Reagan," he said.

Jackson agreed, nonetheless, to a meeting with Mondale and Strauss at a hotel near the Dallas-Forth Worth Airport when the candidates arrived there in early May for another League of Women Voters debate shortly before the Texas caucuses and the primaries in Ohio, Indiana, Maryland and North Carolina. But things did not go as smoothly as the Mondale strategists had hoped.

Strauss, according to one of those in the room, immediately confronted Jackson.

"You've got to do something about Farrakhan," Strauss told him. "You can't let this hang out there. This thing is killing us."

And Strauss told Jackson in equally blunt terms, the argument he was making about having no control over Farrakhan "just won't wash."

The meeting broke up in less than an half hour with nothing settled—and Jackson obviously having second thoughts. That night he called Beckel and suggested that maybe this "unity task force" should have three co-chairmen—Strauss, George McGovern and Maynard Jackson, the former mayor of Atlanta who was one of Jackson's most respected supporters.

As a practical matter, the whole plan became academic just a few days later when Gary Hart won both the Ohio and Indiana primaries. Mondale was no longer in a position to be making plans for a placid convention; he was still trying to nail down the nomination.

And for all his talk about "healing," Jackson continued to be a problem for Mondale and the Democratic Party. In fact, during the final stage of the primary campaigns in California and New Jersey, Jackson seemed to grow increasingly strident. His successes in the primaries had become old stuff now, and the television reporters traveling with him were finding it more difficult to get stories about him on the air. So Jackson was providing more red meat—and sending chills of apprehension through the Mondale apparatus.

In late May he made a point of refusing to attend a fund-raiser arranged in California with Mondale's and Hart's blessings to help retire the campaign debt of George McGovern. It was true that McGovern had been the only other candidate to demand an absolute dollar reduction in the defense budget. But now McGovern was supporting Mondale, and Jesse Jackson was not about to go along quietly with something that suggested a black candidate was not being taken with enough seriousness by a white candidate who ostensibly shared his views.

Shortly before the final round of primaries on June 5, Jackson also caused a stir by announcing he would be accepting an invitation from Fidel Castro to visit Cuba. The trip clearly would reinforce the image of Jackson as a radical more interested in racing around the Third World than in the mundane business of quibbling over delegates. And in Washington there were the predictable cries about him interfering in serious diplomacy. But Jackson, back on page one, was not contrite.

"The issue of expanding the dialogue between the United States and Cuba and easing tension in Central America is a moral imperative," he told reporters. "Surely a superpower must consult with all nations, friends and foes. If we can talk with China and have diplomatic relations with the Soviet Union, we can do likewise with Cuba."

That Cuba trip was another example of just how different Jesse Jackson was from the candidates who had some genuine prospect of winning the Democratic Party's nomination for President. Serious American politicians don't throw themselves into the embrace of Fidel Castro, no matter how much they may privately question U.S. policy on Cuba.

But Jackson had the luxury of doing almost anything he pleased. The dimensions of his support from an essential Democratic constituency had been demonstrated time and again. And it was clear to anyone who bothered to inquire that Jackson had a blank check from those black voters. They recognized his campaign for what it was, a demand for a better place at the table that blacks could achieve only by using their leverage in the polling booth.

So Jackson was following what the politicians like to call "his own agenda." And if it caused damage to Fritz Mondale and the Democratic Party, that was their problem.

No one understood this attitude any better than Mondale and his political advisers. But they had a much more immediate problem—eliminating the nagging threat from Gary Hart.

13

11:59 or Bust

•

As Jesse Jackson so effectively blitzed the northern urban centers of black America, somewhat overlooked was the fact that Fritz Mondale was proving at the same time that he could win without this major element of the traditional Democratic constituency. Jackson's huge black majorities in Chicago, New York City and Philadelphia had not prevented Mondale from sweeping the key states of Illinois, New York and Pennsylvania. Although Mondale was, in the words of field director Mike Ford, "playing hurt without a sizable portion of his natural base," he was still winning.

That performance encouraged the Mondale strategists to embark on a second "knockout strategy" against Gary Hart. The first had failed because, after Iowa, the calendar had taken the campaign into a string of primary and caucus states in which other elements of the Mondale constituency, most notably organized labor, were not strongly enough represented to counter the phenomenon of a fresh and—temporarily anyway—intriguing alternative in Hart. Now, as the campaign trail led into the border states, Texas and back into the industrial Midwest, the Mondale brainstormers figured their man was poised to put Hart on the canvas for good.

Hart, for his part, was reeling from the pasting he had taken across the Rust Belt and from what he felt was a barrage of intemperate and dishonest attacks on his record by Mondale. And after the tidal wave that had carried him through New England and, though not favorably reported, through Super Tuesday as well, the realities of Hart's organizational shortcomings had caught up with him.

The imperative organizational concentration on Iowa and New

Hampshire had left him short-suited in such vital areas as slating of delegates in the key states across the industrial belt. That fact was making it easier for Mondale to build up his delegate total toward the majority required for nomination and was mortgaging Hart's chances in the process.

It was the Hart campaign's inability to slate delegates in Illinois, New York and Pennsylvania, campaign manager Pudge Henkel said later, "that had a very detrimental effect on the outcome in those three states, and ultimately those were the states that turned this nomination campaign around." In each of them, he noted, "the slates had to be filled . . . before we had had the opportunity to build the momentum we began to gather after the Dartmouth debate."

It was not, Henkel said, that the Hart campaign hadn't looked ahead to the need for slating and made the effort. Rather, he said, it was Hart's relative anonymity at the time.

"We worked endlessly," Henkel said. "But nobody knew Gary Hart, and we didn't have campaign organizations in those states that allowed us the luxury of people to fall back on."

(Pat Caddell later observed that both Alan Cranston and Reubin Askew had been able to put together full delegate slates in Illinois and Pennsylvania. "If Reubin Askew could get slated," he said, "don't tell me Gary Hart couldn't get slated.")

On top of the slating problem, the Hart campaign organization, its thinness and inexperience laid bare by a string of defeats punctuated with gaffes, was in turmoil.

For openers, the Pudge Henkel–Pat Caddell feud that had been boiling ever since Caddell, in his inimitable style, had moved in had not let up. Caddell had been pressing the case that Hart had to attack Mondale or be buried, and Henkel counseled that Hart ought not to be diverted from his own positive issues.

Back in New York the night Hart lost that primary, a large staff meeting had been held, chaired by Mark Hogan, the former lieutenant governor of Colorado, to act on Hart's request that the squabbling stop and a staff consensus on a course of action be pounded out. As Henkel remembered the meeting later, Caddell after a long period of brooding had been persuaded by Hart supporter and friend Warren Beatty, the actor, to come out of the adjoining bedroom and present his case of going after Mondale much more directly. He was so compelling, Henkel acknowledged, that "there was unanimous agreement that Pat was correct," including himself in that view.

Henkel wrote a longhand memo to Hart right after the meeting attempting to present the consensus of the group and gave it to the candidate the next morning.

"Gary didn't buy it," he recalled. "He said, 'In no way am I going to be a negative campaigner.' " Hart's own definition of negative campaigning, however, seemed to depend on who was doing it, himself or Mondale.

Frank Mankiewicz, recruited at that time as a senior adviser to the campaign, remembered the outcome of the meeting somewhat differently. Between the Caddell position of attacking Mondale and Henkel's of staying on the issues high road, he said, he felt the consensus recommendation to Hart was that he "do Hamlet without the prince—to do Caddell's idea without attacking Mondale. In other words, to stress new versus old, unfettered versus fettered, general interest versus special interest, but without saying anything about Mondale."

To Mankiewicz, a colleague of Hart's in the 1972 McGovern campaign, the Caddell-Henkel fight should not have amounted to so much simply because, beyond all the rhetoric, there was not that much difference between Hart and Mondale on key issues. What had put Hart on the wave in the first place, in Mankiewicz's view, was "that people really did not want Mondale."

Accordingly, Mankiewicz said, "I thought it was a rather sterile argument. . . . What were the issues? Suppose you said, 'Okay, Pudge, you're right. We're not gonna talk about Mondale and we're not gonna use Caddell's formulations about 'the voices of the past and the candidate of the past and the tired old ideas' and so forth. What are you gonna talk about? Once you talk about individual training accounts [a pet Hart job-training proposal] and fire the prairies with that one, then what?"

One of the things that frustrated Caddell, he said later, was that after the group had given Hart its advice, the candidate would not implement it. Of Pennsylvania, Caddell said: "Here's a state that's been savaged by the economy; the place to raise the Carter-Mondale record. 'Do you want to go back to this?' " But Hart would not go on the attack. As a result, Caddell argued, Hart lost a state he could have won, and Caddell took a walk—temporarily.

Henkel was also at loggerheads with Kathy Bushkin, who as

press secretary was winning plaudits from the traveling press corps as a paragon of efficiency, dependability and candor. Henkel later said the problem was poor communications between the Washington headquarters and the plane, of the sort that led to the snafus over the "phantom" and anti-Vrdolyak ads during the Illinois primary. He said he considered pulling Bushkin off the road "to give her a breather." But he never did so out of recognition, he said, of how valuable she was to Hart in the campaign.

To shore up what Mankiewicz called Hart's "short bench," a veteran of the 1972 Ed Muskie campaign, John McEvoy, was brought in to take a hand in administration of the staff, and an "executive committee" was created that included McEvoy, Henkel and Caddell among others. At the same time, Hart, frustrated by the disorganization, began to take more of a hand in things himself. After the television ad snafus in Illinois, he insisted on approving all scripts before they were aired. That insistence, in fact, was one of the reasons Caddell walked out at one point, Hart said later.

"He said, 'I can't do this job if you insist on seeing everything I put on the air,' " Hart recalled. "He said Jimmy Carter in 1976 had never laid down that requirement. I said, 'Pat, I'm not prepared to do that with anyone.' "

Increasingly, in the words of David Landau, "the plane became the campaign manager"—that is, strategy was being handled by Hart himself and the staffers who were aboard.

Yet another staff meeting was held, however, as the campaign moved toward the Tennessee primary on May 1 and the Texas caucuses on May 5. Apparently, in keeping with the plan to "do Hamlet without the prince," it was decided Hart would continue his new-versus-old, past-versus-future theme; but he would also go on the attack against Mondale on the delegate-committee controversy and on the Chrysler bailout issue, with which Mondale had bloodied him directly or indirectly in Michigan, New York and Pennsylvania.

Hart researchers had dug out the fact that for all of Mondale's stout defense of the Chrysler bailout, Mondale himself had opposed not only a similar federal loan guarantee arrangement for the Lockheed Aircraft Corporation but the general idea of such individual corporate bailouts. Hart, according to Henkel and Caddell, earlier in Pennsylvania had balked at using the Lockheed material on grounds it was too negative. Now, in two speeches in Ohio,

Hart unveiled the new ammunition and the new strategy. Citing Mondale's position on the Lockheed loan, Hart said the Chrysler bailout had actually cost jobs, not saved them. And before a steel plant in Youngstown that had been closed for more than two years, Hart observed:

"The Carter-Mondale administration had four years to put this industry back on its feet and it didn't do so."[33]

In Texas, Hart also rapped Mondale's support for domestic-content legislation favored by organized labor and, reminiscent of John Glenn earlier, he asked:

"Do we really want to offer the voters a referendum on the politics which they rejected in 1980? If we do, then they'll decide in 1984 that the policies which did not work for Carter-Mondale will not work for Walter Mondale."

This argument really was, in a sense, what the fight for the Democratic nomination—and the Democratic Party—was all about in 1984. Mondale not only had the "Carter connection," but he had the "Humphrey connection." He was the epitome of a New Deal Democrat at a time the bottom was falling out of the old New Deal appeal.

Hart recognized this fact and addressed it politically with his courtship of the growing middle class of voters—not only the so-called yuppies crowding into high-tech and other white-collar jobs but also the young blue-collar workers whose affluence was enabling them to move to suburbia. Both groups were removed generationally from rock-bottom economic need and, consequently, from the concept of government as provider. Mondale with his classic New Deal pitch was leading the party over a cliff, and Hart knew it. But he seemed almost constitutionally unable to maintain an attack mode day in and day out.

Even when Hart appeared to be going for the jugular, he backed off. In a speech at Texas A&M, he recalled "the days of shame we all lived through four years ago," and "an America held hostage to the ayatollahs of the world," referring to the Iranian hostage crisis and the aborted rescue mission that embarrassed the Carter administration and the country, and cost American lives.

The assault stunned Hart's Texas backers. They recognized that Carter had been unpopular in Texas at the time of the 1980

33. The observation was considered such a good political point that the Reagan campaign used a clip of Hart making it in one of their few anti-Mondale ads in the fall campaign.

campaign, when Reagan buried him. But they also believed the "days of shame" formulation went beyond the bounds of good taste, even in the rough-and-tumble of Texas politics.

After having used the strong words, though, Hart in a debate in the state two days later said he did not mean to charge Mondale with "dereliction of duty" but meant only to emphasize the importance of military preparedness.

Such behavior seriously undercut Hart's credibility as well as his protests that he was the innocent victim of a vicious negative campaign by Mondale. Inevitably, Caddell's foes in the Hart campaign, by now legion, were quick to lay the "days of shame" line at his feet. He denied being the author, noting he was involved in another project at the time, but that did not persuade his critics. Whoever actually wrote the lines, the fact was that Hart delivered them.

Although the Texas caucuses had shaped up as a major battleground and Hart spent considerable time there, Mondale had the advantage of a very strong state party organization in his corner in a very complicated voting procedure.

"Hart made the mistake," Marty Kaplan argued later, "of allowing Texas to be seen as a useful test of Mondale versus Hart." But because it was a caucus state with a complicated system requiring persons to vote in a primary before participating in the caucuses the same night, he said, "it resembled Michigan, and then some." Also, Mondale had cultivated the state party and labor there for several years. And on primary and caucus day, that strength was apparent when Mondale routed Hart, winning more than 100 of the 169 Texas delegates at stake that day.

For all practical purposes, Hart looked to be a goner. But he vowed he would stay in the race as the campaign moved toward another big voting day three days later, on May 8, when four states—Ohio, Indiana, North Carolina and Maryland—were holding primaries.

"We had basically a four-cushion shot," Jim Johnson said, and if Mondale could win all four, the nomination fight would be over. That result, Johnson said, was devoutly desired, so that Mondale could turn his attentions and energies to the convention and to the challenge to Reagan beyond.

It turned out, he said, that the impact of the Texas rout was diminished nationally because the caucuses were held on a Saturday night, when network news cycles and Sunday newspaper deadlines were missed.

"There was no Texas caucus," Johnson said. "Texas didn't happen in the rest of the country."

Still, to all the players in the nomination game who followed the returns studiously, Hart seemed ready for the showers, and even the loss of a single state the next Tuesday, if that state was Ohio, would almost certainly send him there. And what reason, after he had lost Illinois, Michigan, New York and Pennsylvania, was there to think he wouldn't lose Ohio?

The same thinking governed the Mondale strategy as the candidate went into Cleveland for his major speech at Case Western Reserve University attacking Reagan's "Star Wars" concept. Mondale was well aware that he had a large gap to close in the polls against the President, and he wanted to get on with it. As he had mistakenly done in New Hampshire, he was starting to run against Reagan again, before the last nail had been driven into Gary Hart's political coffin. Mondale did also deliver a lofty speech in Cincinnati on his vision of the year 2000, to demonstrate that Hart had no monopoly on ideas for the future. But he was not getting down into the trenches against him the way he had done successfully in his own post–New England comeback.

"We had a mixed message," Bob Beckel said. "It wasn't all 'hit Hart.' We were trying to get ourselves set for a race against Reagan. . . . That early knockout punch to [enable us] to take Reagan on was critically important to us. It was a roll of the dice that [first] backfired because of New Hampshire. But it wasn't in my mind the wrong decision because a bloody battle through the primary season could only hurt Mondale. And not being able to begin to develop a case against Reagan early enough so that it sunk into people's mind was going to make the race damn near impossible. . . . We decided, since we had beaten him [Hart] as bad as we did in Pennsylvania, we could begin our case against Reagan."

But, Beckel acknowledged, the Mondale campaign was stretched too thin trying to sweep Texas and all four primaries on May 8.

What was most surprising, and frustrating to Ohio Democrats from Governor Dick Celeste on down, was that Ohio seemed a state made to order to continue the attack on Hart as the anti-

Chrysler bailout candidate more comfortable with the young suburban yuppies than with the blue-collar six-pack set.

Celeste held several conversations with Mondale and with Jim Johnson urging that ads aimed specifically at Ohio's large constituency of steel, rubber and auto workers be made and shown. His own television ad-maker, a volatile but imaginative New Yorker named Jerry Austin, who had run the Carter-Mondale campaigns in the state, was a specialist in pitching for the blue-collar vote. Austin had a professional actor in tow who was right out of Central Casting as Joe Sixpack. Austin's work on Celeste's behalf had been very effective in his campaign for governor in 1982. But the Mondale campaign declined to give Austin a real piece of the action in his own state. The Chrysler ad was used with a Celeste insert, but no other special blue-collar ads were introduced for Ohio.

The Hart campaign, on the other hand, at last pulled up its socks in Ohio. For the first time in weeks, under the new management, Hart's messages on the stump and on television were effectively synchronized, with Boston political consultant John Marttila playing a major coordinating role. Together with the direct responses to Mondale's "Chrysler" strategy, Hart pointedly tied Mondale to Carter's failure over four years to rescue the faltering steel industry, as in his dramatic speech to unemployed steelworkers outside the shutdown Youngstown Sheet and Tube plant. Ray Strother, working with Caddell's associate Paul Maslin, taped this event and turned out ads that complemented what Hart was saying around the state.

"It becomes the seamless campaign," Caddell said. "What was supposed to be done in Pennsylvania becomes Ohio."

Also, Kathy Bushkin noted, for once there were no self-ignited "brushfires" to engulf Hart's message.

The television ads made heavy use of the jobless steelworkers talking with Hart.

"A good many of us in this valley gave Reagan a chance," one of them said in one ad, "because we were so disillusioned with Carter and Mondale." And another: "He's still the same Fritz Mondale. We do need somebody new." And still another: "We lost with Mondale before. He had his chance. He got up to bat. He struck out. Now he wants another turn. You know, he hasn't been out to the field yet."

And Hart in the ad said: "Ronald Reagan represents the past. I think the last administration and Mr. Mondale represent the past. We've got to have new leadership. We've got to have somebody with a vision for this country's future, who has an idea, not only of how to modernize steel mills so that we are competitive in the world, but also to diversify and bring in new industries and put the old industries and the new industries together and offer this country hope."

The upshot of Hart's well-coordinated campaign in Ohio, and Mondale's split resources and split focus, was an upset that in some ways was as surprising as Hart's initial breakthrough in Iowa and New Hampshire. Hart also squeezed through in neighboring Indiana, while Mondale won the Maryland and North Carolina primaries. The two Hart victories, however, were enough to take the air out of the Mondale campaign again and assure that the race would now run its course to the final Tuesday of primaries, on June 5, when five states including California and New Jersey would elect delegates.

The ads in Ohio, Hart himself said later, were particularly effective because people in industrial northeastern Ohio "didn't want somebody from the Carter-Mondale era" and because "at that point they were being told that Mondale had it locked up" and this primary perhaps seemed a last chance to head off that outcome. Johnson, too, attributed much of Hart's upset to the steelworker ads, plus a residue of anti-Mondale sentiment in the state from Mondale's earlier rough treatment of native son John Glenn.[34]

Of his Ohio and Indiana upsets, Hart later said:

"I think that was really the most amazing part of the campaign to me. The early breakout turned out to be easier in some curious ways than any of us thought. I had always felt the field would have to narrow before I could win a victory. I had thought the chances were highly unlikely that I would have an early victory with a broad field, because I thought I had to pick up support from other candidates after they had dropped out and it became a two-way race. But that turned out to be easier in retrospect than the comeback. . . .

"It was both positive and negative. There seemed to be some

34. Glenn, after withdrawing from the race, declined to endorse any of the surviving candidates.

built-in resistance to Mondale, and everytime he looked inevitable was when the deciding votes in the party shifted against him and would move back our way. It was a combination. In the early states I had to prove that I was a serious candidate. In the later states, the issue became electability; new leadership–old leadership and who has the best chance of winning."

In between, however, were those big middle primaries across the Rust Belt where state party organization, labor or both scored heavily for Mondale—and where Hart's own gaffes and those of his staff, bred of exhaustion, overextension and inexperience, had helped do him in.

Hart also contended after the election that his comeback in Ohio and thereafter resulted in part from public weariness with Mondale's negative campaigning, which began right after the New Hampshire and Maine upsets with "Where's the beef?" and carried through the industrial states with what Hart regarded bitterly as knowingly false criticism of his civil-rights, arms-control and energy-policy positions.

"You cannot sustain a negative campaign," he said, "which was essentially the Mondale campaign—an attack on me all the time. If that strategy had occurred let us say in April, you could sustain it through June. But you can't sustain it from February through June, and I think people just got tired from Ohio on of hearing attack, attack, attack. And the final factor was that I just decided at that point to quit responding to Mondale. By that time I'd felt I'd answered all the charges about my record on the environment, women's rights, civil rights, foreign policy, and now I'd go back to my own positive things. That was a very conscious campaign decision. We had two or three meetings and I just said, 'All right, whether it works or not, I'm tired of this dogfight. I'm just going to go back on the positive themes.' . . . And the calendar, the geography, shifted to our favor. We went west."

Mondale and his inner circle took the Ohio-Indiana setback hard. Looking for that early May sweep that was going to knock Hart out, "we essentially lost the last link in the chain," Johnson said later, and the Mondale strategists knew the fight would now go the full route through the last primaries. Again the drawn-out process was exacting its price. Beyond the factor of personal exhaustion, Mondale was losing valuable time in bringing the fight to Reagan, and his political vulnerability was being exposed anew.

The night of the Ohio-Indiana defeat, a big Mondale victory celebration had been laid on at the Sheraton-Washington Hotel in anticipation that the windup was at hand. Marty Kaplan recalled the scene:

"A lot of people had come in from around the country, supporters and fund-raisers, because there was this feeling this could be it now, tonight. It was a real downer to watch the results come in. Ohio came in real late, and among other things it meant this unbelievable slog that we'd been going through would have to continue. Everybody was dead tired. We'd been beaten and rammed and we pulled ourselves back into the ring. And to be told you were down again and you gotta get up again was psychologically very hard news to take."

For Mondale particularly, said Kaplan, who was with him that night, "it was a helluva blow. He was being asked to do the same thing the rest of us were, only in spades, because he was the candidate; namely, pump up and start again. But he had been running on empty for months by this stage, and now he was told he had to keep doing it, and his dream of an early unified party, a convention that looked great, starting the run against Reagan, once again was taken away from him."

Now Mondale was faced with what Beckel later called "a two-ocean war." The two main closing primaries were on either coastline, New Jersey on the Atlantic and California on the Pacific on the same day, June 5, with West Virginia, South Dakota and New Mexico thrown in—and some others in Hart's natural western base in the month before then. And it was not only the physically wearing road ahead; Mondale was plagued now with why at this juncture he had lost in Ohio. The consensus was that Mondale had let Hart get on top of the issues.

"We had to draw a new bead on Hart somehow," Kaplan said, which in the Mondale campaign meant—without any agonizing—more negative campaigning.

But Hart, now in the West, vowed to stay on the high road as he campaigned in more familiar territory. In Oregon, while adhering to his declared determination to get off negative campaigning, he did seem to go out of his way to suggest to reporters that he would have had the nomination locked up by then had Mondale not misrepresented his positions.

On May 15, he won the primaries in his native state of Nebraska and in Oregon, each by better than a two-to-one margin. Nebraska was a classic illustration of how the political context had changed. Mondale's protectionist arguments for the auto industry were poison in a state in which farmers depended on foreign sales and feared trade reprisals. Hart was also in the rare position of being the favorite of much of the political establishment in Nebraska, including popular Governor Robert Kerrey.

The Mondale campaign, however, was not so much interested in primaries won as in delegates accumulated.

"The day after Ohio," Johnson recalled, "I became totally preoccupied at that point with the importance of delegates, because it was my belief if we had it, even with a mixed result, on June fifth [the date of the last primaries], if we could say, 'Mondale is the nominee,' that would just make an enormous difference."

Tom Donilon, the young delegate-hunter who had honed his tools in the Carter campaigns, was pulled off the traveling party to oversee around the clock his sixteen-member delegate-tracking team.

"We could withstand almost anything on the fifth of June if we had the numbers," Johnson said. But if there was "an ambiguous result, and we were a hundred or a hundred and fifty votes short," he said, there would be plenty of factors to cause trouble—"Jackson, Hart, credentials, rules, platform; everything would go berserk."

At the same time, Johnson started calling political leaders around the country who could put heat on delegates, urging them to do so. And on that same day, Johnson took it upon himself to announce flatly "that on the fourth of June Mondale will have 1,750 delegates, and on the sixth of June he will have more than 1,967 [a majority] and we'll be the nominee."

("Talk about boldness in this campaign!" said the manager of the candidate who "dared to be cautious." Several days later, when Mondale was asked about Johnson's bold prediction, he would say only that he expected to win both the California and New Jersey primaries "and I believe I'll have the delegates I need by the time the convention convenes"—which would be five weeks later.)

Mondale then had about 1,510 delegates signed on. Johnson said he set the public goal, because "I wanted to make absolutely certain that there was a clear signal that it wasn't coming apart because of the Ohio-Indiana loss, and I believed it was something we could do. I believed that the goal would once again shake the organization up, to the point that they'd realize that there was a do-or-die element here. We knew somewhere along the line delegates would start being important, and that was a big bid to get everybody preoccupied with delegates."

Up to this time, he said, although rival candidates talked about the Mondale strategy of inevitability, "we never used the word inevitability. But this was a point where we were making the argument of inevitability . . . we moved an enormous number of delegates in that month."

Because Mondale now claimed that he would go over the top by convention time, the press corps traveling with him began to press him for a more precise prediction. He tried to stick to his standard line that "I'm confident I'll be nominated and elected," but at one stop after the Ohio defeat, when asked again, he tossed out what Marty Kaplan called "a throw-away line." Mondale answered: "By noon on June fifth." That was the date of the primary, not the day after, so it had to be corrected to June sixth, and somehow the prediction ultimately got refined to exactly 11:59 AM.

As these things seem to happen in campaigns populated with young enthusiasts, noontime on June sixth soon got to be a rallying cry. Lapel stickers materialized that said "Is It Noon Yet?" and T-shirts blossomed bearing "11:59." Kaplan observed:

"It became a symbol for, 'Thank God the primaries are over.' It was also the Mondale boast. Fightin' Fritz was making a claim." Painters of Mondale's image as a fighter obviously had to make the most of whatever they could find.

Some in the campaign were not wildly enthusiastic about the 11:59 target. Tom Donilon, in charge of the elaborate delegate-tracking operation, was among them.

"I remember," he said, "when I got down to the end, saying to myself, 'Who the hell came up with this thing?' "

While thus focused on the delegate count, the Mondale campaign was far from free of continued money problems. By late May it had spent more than $17 million, or about 85 percent of the $20.4 million federal limit on pre-convention spending. In addition, Mondale's decision to pay back the money given to his delegate committees required placing some $400,000 in escrow against that pledge. As a result, he was obliged to hit the fund-raising trail as well as campaigning for delegates. Aides said he raised an estimated $425,000 in two stops, in Chicago and Dallas, in late May.

Hart meanwhile won another small primary on May 22 in Idaho—he finally won all eight west of the Mississippi—and moved on to California, where he hoped to construct the major element of his design to stop Mondale at the end of the long delegate hunt. California would sent 345 delegates to the convention, the largest single bloc, of which 306 were to be picked in the primary, most of them in the state's forty-five congressional districts.

The Hart campaign, under a young Los Angeles lawyer named John Emerson, was organizing aggressively in most of the districts. Meanwhile, the Mondale campaign, headed by Mickey Kantor, from the same law firm as Emerson and a veteran who had run the 1976 Jerry Brown campaign and Jimmy Carter's California campaigns, mounted an essentially free-media campaign in the state, as California's size and population seemed to dictate. The Hart campaign was confident here, considering the state's laid-back lifestyle reputation.

"If ever there was a state that would look at Gary Hart and Walter Mondale and make up its mind," Hart political aide Billy Shore judged, "it was California."

Mondale naturally wanted to win both major June 5 primaries in California and New Jersey, but, as Johnson noted, the main focus now was on delegate accumulation. After a lively debate within the campaign hierarchy, Mondale's strategists decided to make an effort in California, chiefly with the candidate's presence, but to concentrate organization and money on New Jersey, on grounds Mondale could afford a split but not a double loss. Major California contributors wanted some of their money spent in their own state, and that factor figured too in the resource allocation.

The solution was to have Mondale put a lot of his own time in California to soak up free media coverage, and to send senior staff aides including Bob Beckel, Paul Tully and Gina Glantz into New Jersey along with popular Democratic surrogate candidates. Former New Jersey state treasurer Richard Leone, an old Princeton schoolmate of Johnson's, played a key role as strategist in the New

Jersey campaign, alerting Johnson and others that the state had a considerable suburban mix beyond its smokestack image. The campaign was shaped to accommodate that perspective.

The decision to compete in California chiefly with a candidate who could get himself on the evening television news, and not to organize in the field or buy extensive television advertising, was a simple one, Johnson said later.

"The one thing that prevents you from running forty-five separate races," he said, "is no money and no staff."

Simple decision or not, it was one that contributed to the considerable discomfort Mondale and his inner circle endured soon afterward.

As the final Tuesday of primaries approached, Hart and his wife Lee split the campaigning in the two major states. She worked California and he stumped New Jersey, and then on the weekend of May 25 he joined her on the West Coast. She met his plane at the Los Angeles airport and together they went to a fund-raising cocktail party in the exclusive Bel Air section of Los Angeles, at the sumptuous home of Shelly Andelson, a prominent real estate developer. The house has a magnificent broad patio looking out over Beverly Hills, and Hart took the occasion to have a little fun. Speaking to the guests, with Lee at his side, he told about how they split campaign chores.

"The deal is we campaign separately," Hart said. "That's the bad news. The good news for her is she campaigns in California and I campaign in New Jersey."

Amid the laughter, Lee broke in to say that while campaigning in California she got to hold a koala bear. To which her husband observed: "I won't tell you what I got to hold—samples from a toxic dump."

It was quite funny—in California. But it was not so funny in New Jersey, where people are tired of hearing jokes about their state, its industrial odors, waste materials and dumps so visible in the Newark area and Meadowlands approaching the tunnels into Manhattan.

Billy Shore, who was inside the house at the time and hadn't heard the crack, was approached by Bob Kur of NBC News. Kur read the exchange to him and asked what he was going to do about it.

"Is it that big a deal?" Shore said he asked Kur. "Everyone will understand it was a joke."

After the fund-raiser, Hart gave a speech at a Los Angeles synagogue and then returned to the Beverly Wilshire Hotel for the night. Going up in the elevator with Hart and his Secret Service agents, Shore said to his candidate:

"I just want you to know what may come up tomorrow."

"What?" Hart asked.

"Your remark about New Jersey."

"What did I say about New Jersey?"

Shore reminded his candidate.

"He kind of gave me a look," Shore recalled, "like, 'Come on, Billy, we have bigger things to worry about than that.' "

After a few hours' sleep, Shore phoned Hart's manager in New Jersey, Paul Bograd, and told him the bad news. Bograd thus was ready for the worst, and he got it.

The joke had a devastating impact in New Jersey. In the first week of what was essentially a two-week campaign in the two major states, Hart seemed to have achieved that ultimate goal—what Caddell called "the seamless campaign." The message Hart was delivering in his television advertising, on the New York and Philadelphia stations carried in New Jersey, and in his personal appearances dovetailed perfectly. His commercials used the new Meadowlands sports complex as a background and appealed to the pride of Jerseyites in the success they had achieved in industrial development. And his speeches were aimed directly at the many voters who worked in the hi-tech businesses that now line the state's Route 9.

Hart's opposition to protectionism was certain to go down well in a state building its economy on trade. At the end of that first week of campaigning there, Peter Hart's polling for Mondale showed his man ahead in New Jersey, but the Mondale politicians on the ground—Beckel and Tully—were far from comfortable about his lead.

The "Jersey joke" became the lead story two days running in the Newark *Star-Ledger*, the single most important news outlet in the state. And the press in general leaped on Hart's clumsy explanation that all he was trying to say was that he wished he could spend more time with his wife.

Perhaps the greatest damage was done, however, in the way the new context made those commercials on how great New Jersey was appear to be an apology. And the ads only reminded viewers repeatedly of the gaffe.

"They started working against us," Hart media man Ray Strother recalled. "In retrospect, we should have pulled them."

"It was very similar to the foul-up in Illinois," Beckel said. "Whenever you could raise questions about Hart's integrity, his levelheadedness, all of that, you had him. . . . There was a built-in question about him from all that publicity he took about his name and his age and all that stuff. . . . Then he came off the wall with a crack like that. Part of it was New Jersey pride, but the other was, 'Why does the guy do it? It doesn't make sense. He wants to be President of the United States.' "

Mondale had a simple observation about it all. Campaigning in northern California, he observed: "I love New Jersey." Hart, he added in all his righteousness, ought to apologize to the Garden State. Hart for his part tried to ignore the flap, saying Mondale was throwing up "trivialities" to undercut his campaign, and he continued to tour New Jersey. But the press in the state would not let the matter die, and it plagued him right up to primary day.

With the two chief primaries on June 5 taking place on opposite ends of the American mainland, the differences in time zones became a major factor in the drama that played itself out over that night and the following morning. According to Donilon, Mondale went into this final primary day with 1,775 delegates signed on, or 192 short of a majority. The returns were in first from New Jersey and West Virginia in the eastern time zone, and Mondale easily won by about 16 percent over Hart in both states.

Not only that, Mondale routed Hart in delegates in New Jersey, shutting him out completely, 117–0. Beckel phoned the traveling party at the Radisson Plaza Hotel in St. Paul before all the results were in.

"I got you eighty, maybe better than that," he told Johnson. The even bigger eventual drubbing proved to be critical in light of what was happening in California that same night.

There, as the popular vote came in, Hart and Mondale appeared to be running close—close enough for the Mondale forces to assume that while they might not carry the state they would surely pry enough delegates out of it, together with the New Jersey sweep and West Virginia, to make up the 192-delegate shortfall and enable Mondale to go over the magic number of 1,967.

Indeed, appearing before another victory rally back home in St. Paul, Mondale reminded the crowd that he had predicted "this would be a marathon," but that even in a long, hard race there was always a finish line and a winner.

"This is it," he proclaimed, "and here I am."

Before Mondale went to bed, Donilon told him he expected he would get 110 to 120 delegates out of California.

There still remained the formality, as the Mondale campaign managers saw it that night, of fulfilling Mondale's boast that he would produce evidence of enough delegates to claim the nomination by 11:59 AM the day after the last primaries. The candidate and his chief aides in Minnesota and Washington retired for the night assured in their own minds that they could sleep in and go through that formality routinely and blissfully the next morning.

"We figured we had a good cushion," Johnson said.

But they figured wrong.

The problem was that although the popular vote was close in California—calculated later at 41.2 percent for Hart, 37.4 percent for Mondale, with 19.6 percent for Jackson—the delegate allocation was by congressional district, and Hart had clearly out-organized and out-hustled Mondale on that level. As a result, as the night advanced in the Pacific Coast time zone—after the network news shows had shut down for the night—it became clear that Hart was pulling off a rout in delegates that was comparable to the one Mondale had managed over Hart in New Jersey.

The fair share of delegates that the Mondale strategists assumed from the popular vote their man would receive simply was not coming through. Ultimately, Hart won 205 delegates in California to only 72 for Mondale and 29 for Jackson. But none of this information was known in St. Paul, nor in most of the rest of the country for that matter, through the night.[35]

Donilon, before going to bed in St. Paul, called the Washington headquarters and instructed all his delegate trackers to be at their desks at seven o'clock the next morning, ready to launch a general

35. There was no direct popular vote for President in the Democratic primary in California. The percentages later were calculated by taking the vote for each candidate's strongest delegate in each congressional district and totaling those votes.

roundup of prospective Mondale delegates who hadn't yet come aboard. But the idea then was to do the exercise as a unity move now that the nomination was clinched. At about 3:00 AM St. Paul time, Donilon got a call from Tad Devine, one of his chief deputies in the delegate-tracking operation in Washington.

"We're flirting with threshold in California," he said.

Donilon, fluent in the political jargon, needed no translation. If a candidate in California failed to win 20 percent of the 306 delegates at stake in the primary, or 61, the state party's delegate-selection rules stipulated that he would not get any share of 97 pledged at-large delegates to be allocated. Hart had failed to reach the same kind of delegate threshold in New Jersey and hence had been shut out.

Donilon didn't need to be told, either, what such an outcome would mean—that Mondale's chances of going over the top would be shattered. Even if Mondale made the threshold in California, Donilon knew now, Hart's showing was so strong that the estimate of 110 to 120 delegates out of California was a pipe dream. Mondale was going to wake up in a few hours well short of the 1,967 magic number for a clinching majority.

"Are you sure?" he asked Devine.

His aide said he had just checked with the California secretary of state and with Joe Trippi, now running the California Mondale campaign, and was assured it was so. A few minutes later, one of the country's best political reporters, Dan Balz of the Washington *Post*, called Donilon.

"You're in trouble in California," Balz told him.

"I know," Donilon said.

"Are you going to make it tomorrow?" Balz asked.

"Yes," Donilon said without hesitation, though he confided later he hadn't been that sure.

At about 5:30 eastern time, the phone rang in Beckel's New York hotel room. It was Donilon.

"We may be going down the tubes in California," he told the campaign manager.

"What do you mean? What happened?"

"We're losing delegates hourly from our projections," Donilon told him. "We're going to have to start corralling every delegate we can get."

Beckel said later he wasn't afraid the nomination was in jeopardy, "but this had been the last mark we had put up—this 11:59. Now we're going to go over it, there's no argument, this thing's over, this is the last knockout punch. The idea of withstanding another knockout punch scenario for another thirty days—I couldn't have done it. It was just too much."

About the same time in St. Paul, Johnson got up and turned on the television set in his hotel room and heard the bad news about California. He was due very shortly on ABC's *Good Morning America*, and he got a call from a Mondale press aide, Joe Lockhart, informing him that the network intended to put Hart's manager, Henkel, on first—another indication of the fickle turn in fortunes. Johnson went ahead with his television appearance, putting on the best face he could in the situation, still claiming Mondale was over the top. By the time he got back to his room, John Reilly was there, and then Donilon came in.

"How short are we?" Johnson asked Donilon.

"About forty to make it comfortably in our own count," he was told.

Donilon sat on the side of the bed, phone in hand to Washington, and proceeded to make a list of priority delegates to be called, and in what order, by Mondale. As he did, Johnson watched President Reagan on television from Normandy at the fortieth-anniversary observation of the D-Day invasion—and erupted. Here it was the end of the long primary trail, and Reagan, who had not had to endure any of it, was grabbing all the coverage.

"Johnson's walking around the room," Donilon recalled. "The nomination's on the line and Johnson's saying, 'Twenty-seven minutes! Are you watching this shit? Twenty-seven minutes! . . . Thirty-six minutes!' I'm going, 'Jim, come on, we've got to . . .' He says, 'Look at this shit! I'm gonna talk to somebody at NBC!' "

About now, Mike Berman came into the room. He was elected to go tell Mondale. It was now about seven o'clock. He went across the hall to the Mondales' suite and knocked on the door. When he heard a voice of recognition from inside, he called in through the door:

"We've got a little bit of a problem."

Joan Mondale came to the door and let him in. Mondale was still in bed.

"I told him," Berman recalled, " 'We've got a little bit of work to do.' He asked why and I explained. He issued an expletive."

Mondale hurriedly dressed in a T-shirt, faded jeans and white sweat socks and walked out into the living room of his suite, where Johnson, Reilly and Donilon had now assembled, armed with Donilon's call list. Donilon by now was in touch with his tracking team in Washington, which had already determined the day's whereabouts of the important priority delegates to be called, to be sure they could be reached. The trackers were already phoning, telling the delegates, their spouses or their secretaries to expect a phone call from Mondale shortly. The traveling party always carried a set of what were called "Merlin phones," which with a special control box could be set up in a room in a matter of minutes, without the need to lay extra phone lines. The system was plugged in and about six phones were ready on a table in the living room.

Mondale sat down and asked Donilon what the situation was.

"We're some delegates short," the chief headhunter said. "We've got a lot of work to do this morning."

Mondale grimaced.

"Son of a bitch, bitch, bitch!" he barked. "When will this ever end?"

The phone calling started. Mondale phoned the top names on Donilon's list, and Johnson, Reilly and Berman started working other Democratic figures in position to move other delegates. Marty Kaplan was also there by now, and Joan Mondale took a set of call cards into the bedroom and started making her way through the numbers on the phone there. Presently she came running out into the living room yelling proudly:

"I got one! I got one!"

The pressure built as the calls went out. According to Johnson, Mondale at one point asked:

"Do you have any idea what's gonna happen if we're not over the top by 11:59?"

He had pinned his own credibility, and that of the elaborate Donilon tracking operation, on making that deadline, and everybody in the room knew it.

As Mondale made his calls, however, as best Kaplan could remember, he never played that card directly, asking delegates to save his skin. Rather, he let them think he had the magic number and was appealing to them in the name of party unity.

"Hi, this is Fritz Mondale. I really need your help. We've got to have a great convention," was the way the pitch usually went—never, "I'm forty delegates short," which would have changed the whole psychology.

"We picked up a tremendous amount in those three hours of phone calls, " Kaplan said later, "because no one knew it wasn't coming our way. It was a question of getting to them before they knew. We had a window of a few hours before the news traveled that we'd lost California. . . . There was a sense of racing with the news. Television coverage the night before had essentially given it to Mondale. It closed before California was announced, and so most people went to bed, even on the West Coast, certainly on the East Coast, thinking it was Mondale's. So in many cases, the people who got calls from Mondale the next morning thought they were getting courtesy calls, and being given one last chance to get on the train, even after it had left the station. I think the premise that he based his calls on was that the person getting the calls believed that Mondale was the nominee."

As soon as Mondale would get a delegate's permission to go public with his name, Donilon would call Devine back in Washington, who in turn would have a tracker phone the delegate and confirm his standing. The delegate then would be told to expect a phone call from a young reporter at United Press International named David Lawsky, who was assigned all through the primary period to keep the delegate count for his wire service.

As a wire service, UPI had nearly always been considered a poor relation to the Associated Press and had been known more for its speed than its accuracy. But Lawsky did such an outstanding job of tracking delegate claims and declarations that his UPI numbers soon became the gospel for at least the print reporters in the trade. Devine would phone Lawsky the name of the delegate and his phone number so that Lawsky could check for himself whether the delegate really had signed on with Mondale.

"My nightmare," Donilon said later, "was that we would get to June fifth and I'd be telling Mondale he was nominated, and nobody in America would believe it because the delegate counts were disparate." Other news organizations were all over the lot on the delegate count, as is usually the case, but "David Lawsky was a one-man machine," Donilon said. "His numbers were in fact the best. He knew every human being's predilections in every state in the country. Down at the end, when it was that morning of June sixth in the hotel suite in St. Paul, that was the yardstick by which we measured whether we could go downstairs. We knew we couldn't go downstairs until Lawsky ran the one-line release that Walter Mondale had just crossed the 1,967."

In the course of three hours Mondale—chewing on a cigar, a private enjoyment he didn't allow himself in public—talked to forty or more priority Democrats. Among them were Governor George Wallace of Alabama, who came aboard, and Senator Howard Metzenbaum of Ohio. When Metzenbaum apparently started to weigh in with some of his ideas about what Mondale ought to do, Mondale told him, according to others in the room:

"Howard, I don't need your advice. I need your help."

In cases where delegates raised new issues of concern with Mondale, he would tell them he would check and get back to them, and then Reilly or someone else would concentrate on solving the delegate's problem. Through all this, Kaplan said, "Mondale was stoic. The clock was ticking. There was a sense of, 'How did I wind up in this predicament?' But at least it was something you could do something about. You didn't just sit there and watch totals get racked up the way you do on primary night."

Not everything went smoothly. John Perkins, the AFL-CIO political director, was asked to go to National Airport in Washington and intercept incoming Senator James Sasser of Tennessee for his commitment on the spot. Sasser was not amused and he balked. He did come on board, but not until later. House Majority Leader Jim Wright was asked to track down three Texas House Democrats and put the arm on them. And Johnson phoned Mayor Dick Fulton of Nashville, who had agreed privately but was holding off publicly because he was chairman of the U.S. Conference of Mayors, and Johnson told him:

"We're going with you."

A very critical delegate psychologically, because he was so well respected in the House and because he was trying to play his role as a "super-delegate" with the independence intended when that category was established, was House Democratic Caucus Chairman Gillis Long of Louisiana. Former national party chairman Bob Strauss was enlisted to get Long aboard, and he did so. Long finally agreed to commit to Mondale on the condition that a statement from him be released with the announcement.[36]

Other party leaders elsewhere pitched in. When Mondale failed to budge Dick Koster in Panama, the senior member of the Democratic National Committee in terms of service, the candidate enlisted Democratic National Chairman Chuck Manatt, supposedly neutral, to persuade him. Koster wanted Mondale to pledge that he would make no change in the party leadership until after the election, and when Mondale told him he could not do that, Koster refused to sign on and hung up.

Shortly afterward, Manatt called and asked Koster not to insist on that condition. A few minutes later, moments before the 11:59 deadline, Mondale called Koster again. This time Koster asked only that Mondale consult with party leaders on any change, and according to Koster later, Mondale agreed. Koster then said he would declare for Mondale. In another few minutes, Lawsky was on the phone to Koster verifying whether he had indeed done so. When Koster said he had, Lawsky informed him that he was the 1,967th Mondale delegate—that Koster had put Mondale over the top.

The matter of Mondale's pledge to Koster, a minor detail in the clinching of the Democratic nomination, was to become a sticking point for both men later on, in another context at the national convention.

With only a few minutes to spare before the 11:59 deadline, Donilon finally concluded Mondale was over the top with a margin for error. Some forty-seven delegates had been bagged in the telephonic all-court press, and Mondale was able to go downstairs to the hotel ballroom where the press, and a banner behind the podium proclaiming "11:59," awaited him. He waited for the precise moment of 11:59 to make his entrance.

For Berman, still up in the suite, the ordeal wasn't over. He was assigned to take Gillis Long's statement, type it out and get it downstairs to Mondale before he began the press conference. Berman, a man of distinctly impressive girth, finished the statement, snatched the statement from the typewriter and ran for the ballroom below.

36. Representative Gillis W. Long died on January 20, 1985. President Reagan, before beginning his Second Inaugural Address in the rotunda of the U.S. Capitol the next day, requested a moment of silence in his memory.

"I damn near thought I was gonna die," he recalled, "because by the time I got to the door, I was so out of breath that I handed it off to somebody and I simply sank down onto the floor and sat there."

Mondale thereupon announced Long's pledge, along with those of a dozen or so other heavy hitters.

"Yesterday the primary season came to a close," he said, "and I congratulate Gary Hart and Reverend Jackson for the campaigns they have run. But today I am pleased to claim victory. As of 11:59 this morning, over 2,008 delegates had pledged their support to me. The race for the majority is over."

Mondale actually claimed 2,008 delegates, so that, as Kaplan put it, "we did not look as if we had dragged our ass across the line."

Once again, as on the night of Super Tuesday, Hart had been victimized by inaccurate reporting or interpretation of primary results.

"California was very much underreported," Beckel said later, "because Jersey was so big and everybody wanted to write, 'This story's over, it's done now. Who's the Vice President going to be? And is Jesse gonna walk out of the convention?' And also, because it was late coming. The story didn't really get to be a story until eleven or twelve o'clock [in the East] the next day, when the full impact of what had happened in California came through. And by that time we'd had the 11:59 statement of Mondale claiming victory. So it was hard for Hart to get any kind of initiative on it. If we had been wiped out [in California] we wouldn't have had enough delegates to claim that we had gone over the top."

Johnson contended later that had Mondale missed by 11:59, he still would have reached the magic number the next Saturday, when caucuses were being held in several states congenial to him. But had the Hart campaign in California been able to keep Mondale under the threshold and thus shut him out of a share of the ninety-seven at-large delegates, it may have been another story. As it was, Mondale won only 25 of the at-large delegates. Eli Segal, another veteran of the 1972 McGovern campaign from New York who was now chief of staff for the Hart campaign and a key operative in the California primary effort, calculated later that had Mondale been short only a few hundred votes in a handful of congressional districts there, Hart would have won those 25 at-large delegates too—and caused Mondale great embarrassment as 11:59 passed the next morning in St. Paul.

Whether failing to go over the top at the appointed hour would have put Mondale on the skids was obviously conjectural. But even when he was leaving the impression in those phone calls from his suite that morning that he had the nomination wrapped up, many delegates came aboard with limited enthusiasm. Hart said later he believed Mondale would have claimed he had 1,967 delegates at 11:59 on June 6 whether or not he did have them, because he and his campaign were back selling inevitability.

"They were mounting up delegates, whatever happened in the primaries," Hart said. "They were going to announce victory if I'd won New Jersey and shut them out in California, and then let everybody scramble around and prove them wrong."

Inevitably, the heat was now on Hart to bow out of the race in the name of party unity. But he insisted that the contest was not over, because, for one thing, there were all those "super-delegates" who were supposed to wait until the primaries and caucuses had run their course before definitely committing themselves. Mondale, however, had already moved very effectively, in the effort directed by his old chief of staff Dick Moe, to put the bulk of them on ice.

"Their whole strategy after that last primary day," Hart observed, "was to conduct themselves as the nominee."

But Hart was not going to surrender to that strategy. As Mondale in St. Paul was claiming that he had ended the game in regulation time, Hart opened a press conference in Los Angeles by serving notice he was still playing.

"Welcome to overtime," he said.

14

Spring '84 in America

•

AT ABOUT TEN O'CLOCK one night in January 1983, Lee Atwater, then the deputy director of the White House office of political affairs, and Roger Stone, a young Republican political consultant, knocked on the door of a room in the Carolina Inn, an unimposing motel a few blocks from the state capitol in Columbia, South Carolina. In a moment, Richard Milhous Nixon, former President of the United States, opened the door and let them in.

For the next three and a half hours, Atwater and Stone discussed with Nixon the one subject closest to his heart—politics. Atwater came away remembering three things: Nixon's deep appreciation of the political significance of the so-called Sun Belt states, his thorough knowledge of the arithmetic of the electoral college, and his emphasis on the value of seeking reelection without primary competition.

Atwater, a strong advocate of a Sun Belt strategy for Ronald Reagan's expected bid for a second term, listened with a warm feeling as Nixon laid out the same strategy, with heavy emphasis on the South and its electoral vote. While the former President was not in any sense the author of that strategy for Reagan's reelection, Atwater said later he had provided strong reinforcement for it.

Nixon knew the electoral college, Atwater recalled of that late-night meeting, "like the average person knows the back of his hand. . . . He independently made observations that were right in line with what we were thinking about the Sun Belt."

What made at least an equal impression on Atwater that night in Columbia, however, was Nixon's opinion that the single greatest advantage a President seeking reelection could have was the absence of primary opposition. Not since he had run for reelection as Vice President with Dwight D. Eisenhower in 1956 had an incumbent President been free of some challenge to his renomination, and, Nixon said, the burden was at the very least a pesky one.

Nixon recalled that in 1972 two Republican congressmen, Paul (Pete) McCloskey of California on his left and John Ashbrook of Ohio on his right, had challenged his renomination.

"Those two guys," Nixon said, "were two gnats on my ass."

Because they were congressmen, he said, their challenges for a time denied him the resources of the Republican National Committee, which was supposed to be neutral in any nomination fight, and they drained off other resources as well.

Atwater did not forget the advice and the cautions he and Stone received that night from Nixon. When, nine months later, he and Ed Rollins left their prestigious White House jobs to give daily direction to the Reagan reelection campaign, Nixon's observations remained much in his mind. Although, publicly, the former President was as welcome as a bad case of measles around the Reagan campaign, Rollins and Atwater had been picking his brains occasionally since 1981, going up to New York to keep him apprised of political developments. After the long late-night talk in Columbia, Rollins and others in the campaign conferred with him about campaign strategy from time to time, without fanfare, throughout the election year.

The Sun Belt strategy became an immediate part of the reelection plan. And not having any "gnats" buzzing around the President throughout the winter-spring period of presidential primaries and caucuses proved, as Nixon's recollections suggested, a major bonanza.

"The number-one way an incumbent gets beat," Atwater agreed, "is to have a big primary challenge. What does that do? Even if it's a nice polite challenge, [it questions] leadership. You have a guy standing up saying, 'My President of my party is not capable of leading not only my country but even my party.' "

In other conversations Atwater had with Dick Cheney, Gerald Ford's White House chief of staff, and Jody Powell, Jimmy Carter's press secretary, he got more testimony to corroborate Nixon's warning about the perils of a challenge to an incumbent President. The Reagan political operatives invited Cheney to the White House one day and Atwater asked what was the single biggest problem the Ford campaign had in 1976. Cheney pointed at Atwater and said: "You guys"—meaning the Reagan challenge for the Republican nomination.

A month or so later, at a dinner, Atwater sat next to Powell and asked him the same question about the Carter reelection campaign. Powell replied:

"No question about it. The Kennedy challenge"—Ted Kennedy's bid to wrest the Democratic nomination from the incumbent in 1980.

Carter himself, in fact, publicly attributed his defeat to Reagan at least in part to the damage his campaign suffered in that divisive and expensive challenge.

Stuart Spencer, who was coming into Washington periodically from California for Reagan campaign strategy meetings with Baker, Mike Deaver and Bob Teeter, saw the absence of a primary fight as a boon in another way. It let Reagan be seen conspicuously doing his job in the Oval Office rather than having to get into the political trenches through the first half of 1984.

"It was very helpful for the President to be President for as long as he could," said Spencer, who as one of Ford's chief strategists in 1976 also well understood the destructive nature of a primary contest. "The perception of the public is that if he's not campaigning, he's being President."

With surprising candor, even for the straightforward Spencer, he specified another advantage. Reagan, he said, "was able to conserve his energies. The man was seventy-three years old. He's got great stamina and all that, but you and I get tired as hell going through that process, and we ain't that old. It sure as hell showed to me in Mondale, going through that terrible grueling process he went through."

The absence of a primary challenge also allowed Reagan to delay a formal announcement of his candidacy until a month into the presidential election year. As is the usual practice with Presidents who seek a second term, he told a national television audience on the night of January 29 that "our work is not finished," but that the tasks he had set out three years earlier were well on their way toward fruition.

"America is back and standing tall," he said. It was a theme that voters would hear repeatedly throughout 1984 as he deftly strummed the nation's strings of pride and patriotism, unstirred for so long during the downbeat Carter years and even before.

Not having to ward off any political gnats did more, however, than free Reagan from undue exertion and enable him to campaign from behind his desk at the White House. The situation provided his campaign managers a vast amount of tranquil time to plan and implement an elaborate state-by-state reelection organization—with millions in federal funds to pay for it.

From January through July, while Walter Mondale had his hands full beating off seven opposing Democratic candidates and then dealing with post-primary threats to a unified convention from Gary Hart and Jesse Jackson, Reagan's political managers had a waltz. They spent their time methodically planning strategy, ironing out internal squabbles in the states, building Reagan campaign platoons from Maine to Hawaii and swelling voter registration rolls with new Republicans.

And while Mondale was so strapped for money, and so constrained by legal spending limits, that his staff had to tiptoe through the shady alleyways of the delegate committees just to survive, the Reagan team had more than $20 million, nearly half of it in federal funds, to devote to general-election preparations. Although no Republican was opposing Reagan in the primaries, he received the full federal subsidy just as if he were in a do-or-die nomination fight. The fact that Reagan had always been a critic of public funding of political campaigns never deterred him from taking the money.

The Reagan campaign benefited also from tight and smooth lines of authority. Jim Baker, while holding down the fort as White House chief of staff, was undisputed boss of the reelection campaign. He chaired the meetings of the early campaign strategy foursome—Mike Deaver, Bob Teeter, Spencer and Baker—and supervised the activities of his two deputies at the campaign headquarters, Rollins and Atwater. In some other reelection campaigns, rival power centers had been permitted to exist; this time there never was any question that Baker's desk was the ultimate command post. Rollins and Atwater went to the campaign knowing they were Baker's men and never forgot it.

Indeed, the history of reelection campaign managers who did forget where the power lay, and were swiftly replaced, was not lost on these two, nor were they allowed to forget. In early meetings, members of the strategy group would kid Rollins and Atwater that, in the words of one of the strategists, "the history of the first wave on the beach in incumbent presidential campaigns was not good." Another ribbed Rollins:

"You know, we go through two or three campaign managers, Ed, before we get to the end. You're the first one."

But the same veteran strategist called the campaign teamwork under Rollins "the best I've ever seen."

For the first six months Rollins and Atwater were at the committee, Atwater recalled, they kept uppermost in their minds the necessity of maintaining the confidence of the White House—meaning Baker and Deaver. Notably, the President himself never seemed to enter into any of the deliberations. He was the performer; the others were the producers, the directors, the choreographers, the prop men. As in the most effective campaigns, "the principal," as the professional politicians often call the candidate, was not burdened with the nitty-gritty. In Reagan's case, though, he did not seem even to be particularly interested in the whys and wherefores.

When a Fritz Mondale, an old political trench fighter, didn't know labor money was flowing into his campaign through delegate committees, that fact was startling. Had a comparable thing happened in the Reagan campaign without him knowing it, not an eyebrow would have been raised. But having a principal who wasn't forever looking over his campaign managers' shoulders made their jobs all that easier.

"He's a laissez-faire candidate," Paul Laxalt said later. "He's a dream candidate for a campaign manager."

When Rollins and Atwater were sent over to set up the campaign organization—in lush quarters off Capitol Hill that looked more like a thriving insurance company than your basic down-at-the-heels campaign headquarters—they were to be the advance guard of a "heavier" leadership. The expectation was that Drew Lewis, who had resigned as Reagan's first secretary of transportation to become head of Warner Amex Cable Communications, Inc. in New York, would take over later on. But they put their heads down and worked and stayed in place. Much later, at a senior advisers' meeting that included Lewis, he volunteered:

"This thing is going well. You don't need another boss."

And that was that.

One factor that made things work so smoothly between the White House and the campaign was Baker's making clear to others at the White House to keep their noses out of the campaign. Until the general campaign started, Rollins and Atwater had regular meetings with Baker and Deaver at which they reviewed their progress and problems. And that was the extent of their supervision.

At the same time, one campaign insider said, Rollins took great pains to mollify everybody who felt entitled to some piece of the action.

"He got everybody taken care of," this insider said. "You take all the heavyweight professionals in our party, and they were in our campaign. Not one of them was out short-sheeting us, nobody was out screwing us. Ed Rollins gave everybody something they could go to the bank on. . . . He made them all inside, and as a result, you had a very, very limited amount of back-biting and undercutting between us and the White House or within the campaign."

Rollins' dealings with Senator Laxalt, the President's friend and the official campaign chairman, were illustrative. Laxalt, as we have noted, took on the special job of general chairman of the Republican Party only because Reagan had asked him to do it, and only because it was sold to him on the grounds that it was important to Reagan's reelection. Laxalt felt he had plenty to do in the Senate, but he wanted to be in a position to look out for the well-being of his buddy, the President. And as an old Reagan loyalist, Laxalt naturally became a pressure point for other old Reaganites, many of whom had played important roles in the 1980 election campaign and wanted the same or a bigger slice of the action this time around.

"That was a mine field for me," Laxalt said later. "We had any number of tested and loyal Reagan workers out there who quite frankly wanted to be [state] chairmen. It was apparent to us we were talking about a general-election mode rather than primaries, so the criterion was different."

In other words, political considerations other than who might be the best operative in a state entered the equation.

The most obvious case was Illinois, where former state senator Don Totten, who ran the Reagan campaign in the 1976 and 1980 primaries in that state, wanted to be chairman again. But so did the governor of Illinois, James Thompson, who happened to be a political arch-foe of Totten's. Another thorny situation was in Texas, where Senator John Tower wanted to be chairman. Many Texas Reaganites, Laxalt said, "went up in smoke because Tower in their estimation had really done a number on the President in the Ford campaign in '76."

Laxalt, with Rollins doing much of the spadework but keeping a low profile, smoothed over the ruffled feathers, gave the jobs to Thompson and Tower and still kept the losers working for Reagan in other capacities. Loyalist Lyn Nofziger also used his credentials with the old Reaganites to help work out such problems.

Rollins' dealings with Laxalt in these and other decisions over the selection of the fifty Reagan state chairmen were credited by other insiders with assuring campaign harmony.

"Rollins paid a lot of attention to Paul Laxalt," one insider said. "He called him and briefed him and consulted with him every day. By the time the first month was over, Paul Laxalt didn't care anymore. He knew he had his guy Rollins who was going to take care of him, consider his opinions, call him and brief him whenever anything came up."

Rollins and Atwater also made sure, with press secretary Jim Lake holding affairs on a tight leash, that there were no serious leaks concerning any matters regarding White House–campaign relations.

"We had two meetings a week with the White House people and none of it ever got out," Atwater said later. While the competing Democrats were running up horrendous campaign debts, Rollins kept the reelection effort carefully within budget, and at the same time kept the state organizations, who had no fight to fight, occupied and reasonably content.

"April and May," Atwater said, "are lynch-mob months in a campaign." So to ward off intramural bickering, Rollins conducted a series of regional workshops around the country at which he, Atwater, Drew Lewis, Charlie Black, Dick Wirthlin and Lyn Nofziger briefed groups of 200 or more Reagan campaign workers and loyalists on what the campaign was doing. Some $25,000 went into an elaborate slide-projection presentation and a taped message from the President. At the same time, the customary massaging was done; all campaign state chairmen were brought to the White

House for the announcement of their appointments and to have their pictures taken with Reagan. None of this activity had much of anything to do with informing the voters of where Ronald Reagan stood on the issues the Democrats, rather forlornly, were attempting to raise against him in the campaign.

The campaign also launched an extensive voter-registration drive under a wizard in the field named Helen Cameron, with a goal of putting two million more Reagan voters on the rolls. The Reaganites were well aware that organized labor was working the same side of the street for Mondale. And, of even more concern to them, Jesse Jackson was talking about signing up and qualifying as many as four million new black voters. An achievement of such dimensions, focused as it was on the South, could rip a sizable hole in the Reagan Sun Belt strategy. That strategy called for, in Atwater's memo, a coalition of "country club" Republicans and "populist" or lower-income whites to deliver Dixie to the President, as they had done in 1980. In the end, Jackson's drive fell far short of its objective, and the Reagan campaign claimed to have more than doubled its goal by identifying 4.4 million voters registered through Republican efforts.

Finally, the campaign set itself a special project to combat the much-discussed "gender gap"—polls indicating women supported Reagan in much fewer numbers than did men. The appointments of Sandra Day O'Connor to the Supreme Court and Elizabeth Dole and Margaret Heckler to the Reagan Cabinet were the most conspicuous moves by the President himself. Rollins and Atwater set themselves a target of having women constitute half of all the delegates to the Republican National Convention in Dallas in August. They nearly made it—44 percent, a quantum jump from the 24 percent of 1980.

All this efficiency did not mean that there were no problems in the Reagan organization. As in most, there were egos to be massaged. One belonged to Wirthlin, the pollster, who all hands agreed produced solid data but who, some felt, was not the most perceptive analyst of the numbers. Others saw him as too self-aggrandizing.

"He felt the gathering of information is power," one critic high in the campaign said, "and he used it accordingly."

Another said that had the decision been his, Teeter, not Wirthlin, would have been the campaign pollster. But Wirthlin's ties to Reagan went back to California, this insider said, and "the personal history" assured his role.

Another sometimes problem child was Dick Darman, Baker's chief deputy at the White House who had heavy credentials as a policy implementer and bureaucratic maneuverer but none as a presidential campaign operative. That fact did not stop him from pressing for a piece of the action, however, just as he was accustomed to doing in White House matters, with considerable success.

"Darman was pushing hard," said one insider. "This was a new game for him, and he's a guy who understands power vacuums very, very well."

At this time, Stu Spencer was still commuting from California, and on one of his trips he noticed that Darman's elbows were getting too big and too troublesome. He went to Baker, this insider said, and advised him "to get Darman back in line," and it was done. All was well, he went on, "once Darman realized that Spencer was not someone he could look down his nose at, even though intellectually he may be twenty IQ points smarter, which is his normal measurement of everybody. [He realized] that this guy is street-smart and he's a player because of his role with Baker."

Spencer himself remained high on Darman.

"Darman was a tremendous asset," he said later in his typically direct way. "Not because of his political expertise, because he hasn't got any. Dick Darman was the one guy in that White House who knew where everything was. He knew what was in the pipeline and he knew what potential problems could be coming down the road."

In attempting to anticipate political pitfalls, Spencer said, "he was the source. . . . Without him, we'd have been in trouble. Now, he'd always tell us all these things that were happening, and then he'd have his own ideas about what we should do about them. At that point in time, we'd say, 'Thanks, Dick, you're going to have your opportunity for your input, but don't think you're going to be the last word.' Dick was good for us . . . he made a hell of a contribution. We'd stomp all over him and he'd take it as a man."

Eventually, when the original four-man campaign strategy group of Baker, Deaver, Spencer and Teeter was enlarged, Darman was brought in. Then, Spencer said, "he was a hell of a lot easier to deal with, because he was part of the decision-making process."

The other members of the expanded campaign strategy group at this juncture were Rollins, Atwater, Wirthlin, Margaret Tutwiler, the White House liaison with the campaign, and David Stockman, the budget director. As a key policy man, Spencer reasoned, Stockman had be be brought in.

"The guy who had the handle on things was Stockman," he said. "I went to the other guys and said, 'Hey,we've got to bring Stockman inside the tent. He'll be easier to handle inside the tent than outside, pissing in.' They kind of fought me, but it sure worked out good. He is a smart son of a bitch, and when you make him a part of the conspiracy he starts thinking better."

As the Reagan campaign team methodically went about its business, its strategists were more concerned politically about what was happening in the world than in the Democratic Party.

"It was irrelevant," Atwater said later, "who the Democratic nominee was if we could develop our Sun Belt base."

But there was always the danger, clearly demonstrated in Jimmy Carter's hostage nightmare in Iran, that a foreign-policy crisis could upset the applecart. An article of political faith among the professionals preached that a crisis, when it first broke, would rally the country around the President. That was, in fact, what happened when the hostage crisis flared in November 1979, severely undercutting Ted Kennedy's challenge to President Carter. But the crisis dragged on so long that Carter's inability to solve it marked him as weak and ineffectual. Reagan could afford no such impasse.

The President's luck, though, was holding out. As he began the last year of his first term, he cooled his rhetoric toward the Soviet Union and pulled the Marines out of Beirut without serious incident or criticism. He even weathered a squall that met the disclosure in April that the CIA had been involved in the mining of Nicaraguan ports. He made well-publicized, well-photographed and well-filmed trips to China and Ireland, the land of his ancestors. And he was the featured television performer in the networks' heavy coverage of the fortieth anniversary of the D-Day invasion of Normandy that so infuriated Jim Johnson that morning in his St. Paul hotel room. There were no foreign-policy clouds on the reelection horizon. Even the decision of the Soviet Union in June to boycott the Summer Olympic Games in Los Angeles seemed to work in Reagan's favor, confirming to many the validity of his view that the Russians were an impossibly intransigent lot.

On the political front, Fritz Mondale by this time had staggered through the delegate-selection period, claiming the nomination, and Reagan in short order said he would be happy to debate him. All along the Reagan political strategists had expected that Mondale would be the Democratic nominee, with only the briefest of doubts when Gary Hart's comet rose out of Iowa and flashed across New Hampshire and Maine. In fact, they looked with relish to the prospect of running against Mondale.

"Initially we all thought Mondale was the dream candidate," Laxalt said. "We all prayed he'd be the nominee."

Teeter agreed. "I thought all the way through 1983 that Mondale would be the nominee," he recalled. "I thought that Reagan, if he had a chance to run against the New Deal, that was good. Mondale was just a kind of classic New Deal Democrat, the kind Reagan had run against all his life. He was predictable; he wouldn't change. He was the consummate DFL [Democratic-Farmer-Labor] Minnesota politician, and that was good for us."

The Democrat the Reagan campaign had been most worried about, Rollins said afterward, was John Glenn.

"The only guy we were scared of," he said, "was Glenn. When we opened the doors in October, we always assumed that Mondale would wrap it up early, or Glenn would be our opponent. Glenn was the strongest guy against us."

Before the fall of 1983, he said, he and Atwater thought Gary Hart might be the dark horse. But he didn't seem to be moving, so he wasn't factored into the Reagan campaign polls by the end of the year.

"My sense was always that Mondale had a soft underbelly," Rollins said, "but a very strong organizational effort and the leadership of constituencies who were there to put together a primary win."

He was concerned about Glenn, Rollins said, because the polls showed that "Reagan's strength qualities—patriotism, family values, those kinds of things"—were also qualities Glenn offered.

Those were the themes, in fact, on which the Reagan campaign based almost its entire paid media campaign through the spring. The idea then was simply to contrast the Democratic catfight that was going on with a placid, rosy view of life in Ronald Reagan's America. The President had no primary competition to drain away money or require any specific defense of the Reagan record in the White House. And the Democratic candidates were doing such a good job of tearing each other down—Mondale in particular—that the Reagan campaign had the luxury of using television ads simply to create a positive aura around the President.

The result was a collection of the slickest, smoothest, most professional television commercials ever aired in a presidential campaign—and the most trite. In keeping with Reagan's proclamation that "America is back," the ads showed a country of happy faces and white picket fences. They were scenes that could have made the grade in one of those upbeat thirty-second spots that suggest that the right soft drink or beer can bring health, romance and success. And it was no wonder, because the makers of the Reagan ads were the same wonderful people who brought you those life-is-beautiful commercials.

As with most matters concerning the public image of Ronald Reagan and his administration, Mike Deaver was the critical figure. Early in the year, while Deaver was in China advancing Reagan's trip there, Paul Laxalt had gone ahead and made a deal with Peter Dailey, the Los Angeles ad-maker who had done the Reagan campaign commercials in 1980 and was a loyalist. Deaver—and, importantly, Nancy Reagan—had not been satisfied with the Reagan ads in that campaign, and Deaver balked in no uncertain terms.

In what some said was the only major blowup between the key White House advisers and any senior member of the campaign operation, there was a showdown in Baker's office, with Deaver and Laxalt among the senior players present. Deaver asked:

"Does anybody in this room think Peter Dailey is the best we can get?"

Nobody did. Laxalt, knowing Deaver's close connection with Mrs. Reagan, did not need to have a picture drawn for him.

"I could see where that was going," he said later. "I could have forced it, but it was apparent to me that what we had was a clear personality conflict."

Thereupon Laxalt volunteered that he would not try to impose his view on the others or stand in the way if the group wanted somebody else. To Deaver he said:

"Why don't you get somebody?"

Deaver wasted no time taking up the offer. Inasmuch as his "client" was the President of the United States, and his objective was to elect his client to the most powerful job in the country, why not go for the best? He struck on the idea that with all that creative talent on Madison Avenue, why not try to collar the cream of it to sell Ronald Reagan?

Deaver called Jim Lake, who happened to be a friend of one of the top creative people in the television advertising business—Phil Dusenberry—and Lake approached him. Dusenberry was the vice president and chief creative director at Batten, Barton, Durstine and Osborn, one of the most prestigious advertising agencies in the country. He personally held the accounts of Pepsi-Cola, Gillette razors and General Electric. He had launched the immensely successful "Pepsi Generation" ad campaign and "GE—We Bring Good Things to Life."

Dusenberry had helped out in the 1976 and 1980 Reagan campaigns and was willing enough, but he felt he couldn't afford to go public. He had some prominent Democratic clients, and the major New York agencies frowned on their stars working in politics. Dusenberry extracted a pledge of anonymity from Deaver and Lake, but word leaked out on Madison Avenue anyway. Dusenberry was dismayed, but he recommended that another advertising star, Jerry Della Femina, take over. Lake and Deaver's deputy, Mike McManus, met with Della Femina, and he agreed to tackle the job. But that connection leaked out too, and, besides, Della Femina had recently given an interview to one of the upscale girlie magazines. He had made some lifestyle observations that did not necessarily square with the image the Reagan campaign wanted to project.

When a story about the matter ran in the New York *Times* the Reagan campaign suddenly was inundated with phone calls from Republican ad men on Madison Avenue offering their services. Dusenberry had another idea. Why not put together an all-star team from various agencies? The president of the Della Femina agency, James Travis, agreed to take on the job, and a group of the best creative talents volunteered to work part-time for a special agency Travis set up, complete with full-time marketing, traffic, time-buying and other advertising specialists. Thus was born, after great labor pains, the "Tuesday Team."

The idea did not exactly meet with wild enthusiasm among

some of the old political pros in the campaign, chiefly Spencer.

"I lost that war," he said later. "My position was that we hire an advertising person of political background and go with that person, and he bring in any expertise we might need from Madison Avenue. It wasn't worth fighting over."

That proven approach was rejected, Spencer said, "because there's always this myth, every four years, that all this great talent exists on Madison Avenue, and we want to do something a little bit different. We've got to get hold of that talent and use that talent. It is a myth. There is a lot of talent there, but in the end somebody who's got some political background has got to give them direction."

Spencer turned out to be right, and in due time Bob Teeter was dispatched as political overseer of the Tuesday Team. A California transplant, Doug Watts, former director of communications for Governor George Deukmejian, was brought in as the daily liaison with the team, but it was Teeter's job to give its work the proper political focus. The creative people were excellent once they got the picture. But sometimes ideas had to be bounced back and forth several times before the finished product conveyed the political message the campaign strategists wanted. On one visit to the White House, they were introduced to Reagan, who broke them up with the line:

"I understand you guys are in charge of selling the soap. I thought you ought to see the bar."

There was more truth than poetry in the wisecrack. The first flight of commercials, for use while the Democrats were beating each other's brains out, was called "Spring '84 in America." And the ads told the voters about as much about Reagan's positions on the critical issues of the day as one of Dusenberry's best Pepsi commercials.

The principal ad opened with a scene of a peaceful countryside, dotted with bright yellow flowers, and a cozy white farmhouse beyond. The camera panned to an air view of the majestic Grand Canyon, then showed little children frolicking in the fields, old folks walking hand-in-hand, young boys playing basketball, factory hands at work, and a man in a space vehicle. As these scenes unfolded against a background of idyllic music, the soothing narrator intoned:

"This is America, Spring of '84 . . . And this is America

. . . And this is America . . . And this . . . And this . . . And this, too, is America. Just four years ago, people were saying its problems were too big and too difficult to be handled by any one President. Yet what do we see now? Jobs are coming back. Housing is coming back. And for the first time in a long time, hope for the future is coming back. And isn't it interesting that no one is saying that the job of President is too big for one person. President Reagan is doing what he was elected to do."

The commercials, not surprisingly, came to be known as the "feel-good" ads. Their airing, as well as the themes being emphasized in the President's daily public utterances from the Oval Office or in his occasional sorties into the country, got the most careful coordination from Deaver, the keeper of the presidential body, and from Teeter, the supervisor of the Tuesday Team. Specific "issue cycles" were laid out in which one area of interest was to be exploited. Teeter said later the selected themes played so well in the polls that the cycles often were extended. It was, the cynical might have observed, like a movie held over by popular demand.

Hard-nosed professionals like Lee Atwater, however, always found something to be concerned about. He preached incessantly to the Reagan troops to beware of "the twin demons of apathy and complacency." But it was difficult under the circumstances not to crow a little. When Mondale claimed the nomination after the last round of Democratic primaries, Ed Rollins fell victim to euphoria. At a lunch he hosted at the Century Plaza in Los Angeles for political reporters who had just covered the California primary, Rollins rather indiscreetly allowed that Ronald Reagan appeared to be heading for a landslide in November.

The observation did not sit at all well at the White House, where the official word was that the President was expecting a tough fight for reelection.

"I was just reading the polls," Rollins said in his own defense much later.

But that bit of candor did not excuse him in some of his superiors' eyes for succumbing to one of the "twin demons" and thus setting a poor example for the foot soldiers of the campaign. And it was not only that. Being careless with the press was a special offense at the White House, and the "landslide" prediction was only Rollins' latest slip.

Rollins, one insider said afterward, did not have the built-in protective mechanism that other politicians automatically develop.

"Things that don't add up to a hill of beans," he said, "send somebody over at the White House up the wall. Sometimes it's Nancy Reagan, sometimes it's Jim Baker. So after a while he developed a lot of baggage; 'There goes Rollins again.' And so he lost clout."

Still, Rollins had proved by the summer of 1984 to be a strong and trusted administrator. He continued to have total control of the campaign budget and headquarters, and to be a deft and diplomatic handler of many conflicting egos. He and Atwater, who had started as "the first wave on the beach," remained as the daily operating officers of the reelection effort heading toward the Republican convention.

And as the ship's first mate, Ed Rollins was usually the one called in when there was grousing on the bridge—especially if it came from the captain's wife. One day, at a meeting at the White House of Deaver, Rollins, Atwater, Spencer and Nancy Reagan, the First Lady, began to interrogate Rollins at length about certain things in the campaign that were not quite to her liking. She inquired in her firm way why this had to be done, and not that. Rollins sat silently, knowing better than to try to defend himself. When the painful ordeal was finally over and the campaign people headed out the door, Spencer leaned over to the contrite campaign manager and whispered:

"She smelled fear all over you, Rollins!"

Such were the dimensions of the problems of those running the Reagan campaign. The President of the United States had been in charge of the country for the last three and a half years, and he was preparing to go to the country to ask for another four. In preparation, he could have created a staff to help him explain his policies in detail to the American people, and he could have used the millions of dollars in federal subsidy he received to help educate them through television on the complex problems facing the country and on how he intended to cope with them. He could have, but he didn't.

What he did do was let his politically shrewd operatives construct a campaign apparatus guaranteed to make the political trains run on time and little more. And he let his team create a Madison Avenue advertising agency to take the voters on a television trip to an imaginary America where everything was as rosy as it was in the Pepsi ads. We say he let them because there was not a trace of evidence that he ever took a hand in the direction and substance, or lack of substance, in his own campaign.

Within the rival Democratic camp at this same time, Fritz Mondale and his managers were neither so well organized nor so free of political concerns. Infinitely serious tasks required their attention now, one of which was to start organizing for a fall campaign for which President Reagan already had his political legions in place in every state in the Union. But even before Mondale could begin to address that undertaking, he first had to decide on a running mate. The way Mondale would go about the process, and the choice he would make, would soon bring a new ingredient—and new problems—into the political campaign of 1984.

15

Throwing the Long Bomb

•

FOR WALTER MONDALE and his advisers, these days after the final round of primaries should have been a time to relax and enjoy the fruits of the eighteen months that had led them to this point. On paper, at least, they were assured of those 2,008 delegates they had claimed on June 6. So there should have been time to make careful plans for the nominating convention six weeks ahead and the combat with Ronald Reagan that would follow.

In fact, the Mondale strategists recognized that their grip on the nomination was far less secure than it appeared. To blur that reality, they would send a message of their confidence by beginning a very public process of choosing a nominee for Vice President.

For several weeks Mondale had been musing over his approach to the vice presidential process. And, unsurprisingly, he was thinking of using one very much like the procedure Jimmy Carter had followed in selecting him eight years earlier. But what had been an option now became a political imperative.

"Obviously, we were doing it for a political reason," John Reilly said later. "If there was any question about whether we were the nominee, we just preempted the idea [by saying] that we were going to be seeking a Vice President."

And there plainly were reasons why there might be "any question" about Mondale's hold on the nomination.

The delegate count a few days after the last primaries by United Press International—the one the Mondale forces had anointed as the most reliable—showed him only twenty-two delegates over the top. The breakdown was: Mondale 1,989, Gary Hart 1,229,

Jesse Jackson 371, others (principally Mayor Harold Washington of Chicago and George McGovern) 58, uncommitted 201.

Moreover, now that all the votes from June 5 had been counted, it was clear that Mondale had suffered a resounding defeat in California. All the doubts about his ability to evoke enthusiasm from the electorate had been revived. There was no reason to expect a mad rush of delegates to board the train, and none developed.

Tom Donilon, Mondale's chief delegate-hunter, acknowledged later that his candidate "only had a hundred-delegate margin over what we needed going into the convention. We had successfully convinced the press and the American people that the nomination was a lock. In fact, a hundred delegates—this was, needless to say, very tight. Not that Gary Hart was close to the nomination. But any number of factors could have taken it away from Mondale, and we would have had to enter the Land of the Second Ballot, which is not a place that anybody wanted to be."

Nor was the tenuousness of Mondale's position lost on Gary Hart and his strategists.

Pudge Henkel understood that, as he put it later, "it wouldn't take something of earth-shaking significance possibly to get some of those delegates, and maybe as many as a hundred, not to vote for Mondale on the first ballot. And it was our feeling that if we could deny Mondale a first-ballot nomination, that Mondale would never win and that we would, because the convention really wouldn't have anybody to turn to. And Gary had demonstrated that he was a long-distance runner and that he was the future of the Democratic Party."

It was in this context, and under these pressures, that the Mondale campaign began the quest for a Vice President—and proceeded to make a hash of the six weeks that led up to the Democratic convention at San Francisco.

Rather than strengthening his position, Mondale and his colleagues followed a course that reinforced the picture of him as a leader of a collection of special constituencies determined to bend him to their particular demands. Rather than positioning himself for the contest ahead against the formidable Reagan, Mondale projected an image that seemed likely to make his already uphill struggle that much more difficult.

Despite the delegate counts, neither Hart nor Jackson was ready to withdraw. But Mondale and his allies began to behave as if he were the nominee, and the posture had the desired effect. When Hart went to Capitol Hill to pay his respects to the Speaker of the House, Tip O'Neill joined him in front of the cameras and said:

"You'll make a great President, but not this year."

When a delegation of Democratic state chairmen and party functionaries met with Mondale at St. Paul, the chairman of the Democratic National Committee, Charles T. Manatt, referred to him glowingly as "our nominee"—putting aside the pose of neutrality party chairmen are expected to adopt.

As the press began to focus on whom Mondale might choose for Vice President, the politicians themselves began weighing in with their own suggestions. And even some of Hart's most dedicated backers were urging him to put his campaign into neutral to avoid any risk either to Mondale or to his own chances for the vice presidency.

But the evidence of the vulnerability of Mondale's position was all around him. An analysis of ABC News exit polls in thirteen states found that Mondale had won a plurality of white voters in only three of them—New York, Pennsylvania and New Jersey. The June Gallup poll showed him trailing President Reagan by nineteen percentage points.

None of this was a secret to Mondale or his strategists. A survey conducted for the campaign by Peter Hart found Mondale fourteen points behind Reagan. And, according to several of those privy to that data, the attitudinal findings were discouraging. The voters were optimistic and pleased with the condition of the economy, and Reagan was personally popular with them. And Mondale, said one adviser, "still was not perceived as a strong leader"—an essential perception if he was to be a serious threat to Reagan.

It was in this discouraging, perhaps menacing, context that Mondale and his principal advisers faced the list of tasks they would have to perform over the next six weeks.

They had to find a formula for dealing with Gary Hart and, much trickier, Jesse Jackson. They had to deal with the preliminaries to the convention—the platform, the rules, possible credentials challenges—in a way that would assure a smooth show from San Francisco. They had to develop a plan for the general-election campaign and—above all—they had to develop a theme on which Mondale could run in the fall.

In Washington, Mondale's lieutenants were already working on compromises of the platform and rules issues at meetings of convention committees. Indeed, their control of that process, too, nourished the perception that Mondale was assured the nomination and in total control of the party apparatus.

The other problems were not so easily solved, however. And of these, none was as vexing as dealing with Jesse Jackson now that there were no longer any primaries to keep him diverted.

Jackson was plainly an aggrieved party. In interviews immediately after the final primaries, he was quick to say he still had some "grave reservations" about Mondale.

"It's not his character," he told CBS. "It's his leadership and, in some instances, his substance." To NBC, he put it this way: "We'll have to negotiate a relationship that is mutually beneficial and respectful."

In some cases, Jackson's complaints dealt quite simply with who was getting to go to San Francisco. In some of the caucus states, the Mondale managers had engineered deals on the final makeup of the delegations that gave the Rainbow Coalition a few more seats than it might otherwise have had. But Jackson was not happy that in some of the industrial states—Pennsylvania, for instance—the at-large delegate slates included blacks whom he had, in effect, defeated in the primaries.

Jackson was extremely touchy about not being accorded the proper respect, although he never quite defined what that meant. At one point, he complained privately that Tip O'Neill had met with Gary Hart but not with him immediately after the final round of primaries. What he hadn't known—and what the Mondale people rushed to tell him—was that Hart had been the one to initiate that meeting and that O'Neill was quite prepared to be even-handed.

The single vehicle that Jackson used most intensively, however, was his complaint that he didn't have as many delegates as his percentage of the popular vote might have dictated. He was particularly annoyed, the Mondale managers found, that there would be more black delegates supporting Mondale at San Francisco than himself.

The party power structure, however, was in a placatory mood. Tip O'Neill announced that he would name an advisory panel to consider whether the rules had discriminated against Jackson. And he named one of the most respected men in the party, Morris Udall, to be chairman. The Congressional Black Caucus, including its many Mondale supporters, offered its help. Bob Beckel and Bert Lance made another pilgrimage to the Howard Inn to seek a solution. But Jesse Jackson was not only complaining but threatening.

"The burden is on the Mondale campaign and the Democratic caucus [in the House] to find some remedy for that problem," he declared. "The Democratic Party will need all of its voters in November, and people locked out of the game July 15 [the eve of the convention] will not be interested in coming in on July 20 when the game is over."

Mondale was privately furious. Every day he picked up his newspaper, or turned on his television set, there was Jesse Jackson with a fresh blast that added more weight to the picture of the Democratic Party as a coalition of warring factions. But Mondale held his tongue. He was a very controlled and professional politician, and he had not come this far to destroy himself in a moment of frustration.

In contrast to Jackson, the one candidate who might still pose a direct if improbable threat to Mondale's nomination, Gary Hart, was being conspicuously circumspect.

A few days after those final primaries, he had gone home to Denver. In a speech to the faithful there that he wrote with extreme care, Hart made the point that he was not going to be a problem for his party. He insisted he would carry his campaign to the convention but added that the defeat of Ronald Reagan was "a moral imperative." Then he said:

"I am determined to meet this imperative, and I will do nothing that does not advance the purpose of defeating Ronald Reagan. I will do everything to achieve a Democratic victory in 1984."

Hart was coming under some predictable pressure to withdraw before the convention. But doing so never made any sense. Although there was no obvious opening for him, there was still a month or more to go, and there was always the chance of a Mondale gaffe or even—and no one spoke of this out loud—the possibility the presumptive nominee might die or be disabled.

The sound course for Hart was to keep his campaign alive so that his name could be placed in nomination, so that at least his followers could have their moment at San Francisco. After all, he had won eighteen primaries. Mo Udall had kept his campaign intact that way in 1976, although he had never defeated Jimmy Carter in a single primary. And now he backed Hart's decision.

"There's no need to rush to judgment," the Arizona liberal said.

It was obvious, however, that Hart had to proceed with great caution. He did not want to be seen as a spoiler; that could compromise his prospects for another presidential candidacy in 1988. He did not want to make it impossible for Mondale to consider him for Vice President. He did not want to compromise his opportunity to play a visible role in the convention.

"I was always walking a very thin line," he said later. But he was determined to keep his campaign alive because "anything might happen."

There were also what Pudge Henkel, Hart's manager, called "obvious financial implications." A report from the Federal Election Commission showed Hart had ended the primary campaign $4.7 million in debt. Although federal matching funds would cover some of that deficit, it was clear he would be ending his campaign at least $3 million and perhaps $4 million in debt. A vice presidential nomination could help immensely in retiring such a debt. And even barring that, it was important to maintain the goodwill of the presidential nominee.

So Hart continued his campaign, arguing that he would be the strongest nominee against Reagan but avoiding inflicting any fresh cuts on the bleeding Mondale.

Late in June, the détente between Mondale and Hart was ceremonialized if not formalized. John Reilly, Mondale's law partner, had been holding conversations with John McEvoy, a politically savvy Washington lawyer who had been brought into the Hart campaign too late to be much help to him. And Hart had agreed he would not challenge the 600 "tainted" delegates at the convention itself.

That concession, in turn, cleared the way for a meeting between the two candidates that the press quickly labeled a "summit." In fact, it was a good deal less momentous than that word suggests.

Hart flew into New York and drove to Arthur Krim's townhouse on the East Side for a ninety-minute breakfast with Mondale. According to staff members privy to some parts of the meeting, the two men reminisced a little about the long campaign behind them, agreed on the necessity for a strife-free convention and a strong campaign against Reagan and—without being too specific about it—made clear to one another they were willing to bury the hatchet.

It was a warm, sunny day, and the whole exercise had a festive quality. From the second-floor balcony facing on the street, the two candidates' press secretaries, Mondale's Maxine Isaacs and Hart's Kathy Bushkin, laughed together and waved to the hundred or more reporters and cameramen gathered behind police barricades below. Mondale and Hart soon appeared on the steps of Krim's house to display their amity for the television cameras, the essential proof in this age.

"We have agreed," said Hart, "to do everything within our power to see that Ronald Reagan does not have a second term in the White House."

"If the Republicans and Mr. Reagan were betting on a divided Democratic Party," said Mondale, "they can forget it."

Staff members later said Hart had remained a little testy during the meeting. But now, asked about the lasting effects of their attacks on one another, he minimized them.

"Neither of us accused each other, for example, of witchcraft," Hart said in a reference to George Bush's famous accusation four years earlier that Ronald Reagan was practicing "voodoo economics."

Then the two candidates made a show of their good humor by waving their hands in each other's faces as dozens of cameras clicked off hundreds of photographs. But the truce was genuine, if still a little uneasy. When Hart flew north to Concord, New Hampshire, that afternoon for a rally of about 600 supporters in a small downtown plaza, he made a point of saying he was there to thank the Democrats who had helped him—and of promising to start there again four years later.

Jackson, however, was still not showing any inclination to go quietly. But while he toured Central America and met with Fidel Castro, Louis Farrakhan of the Nation of Islam had touched off still another controversy and revived anew the concern over black anti-Semitism. This time Farrakhan had called Judaism "a gutter religion" and the founding of the state of Israel "an outlaw act."

As the cries of outrage mounted, Jackson finally put some genuine distance between himself and Farrakhan, denouncing his statements as "reprehensible and morally indefensible." But by this time, Jackson had been pushed off the front pages by the new attention being given to the vice-presidential question.

All through the late spring Mondale had been thinking about his choice and how he would go about making it. But he had kept the discussion close to him, reading memoranda from such longtime intimates as Johnson and Dick Moe, discussing the question with Reilly over dinner in his hotel suite late at night. And he had decided that he would follow a procedure very much like the one Jimmy Carter had used in 1976. Mondale had been happy with the result then, so why not try it again?

Reilly, the adviser closest to being Mondale's peer, was put in charge. What Reilly called "a pretty loose list" of fifteen or twenty names was drawn, and staff members were assigned to begin accumulating basic information about them, largely from public sources. Reilly decided he would not immediately seek either financial or medical information from anyone on the list. Nor would anyone be subjected to a full investigation at that point. Reilly remembered his time in the Kennedy administration Justice Department more than twenty years earlier when he had been involved in vetting people for ninety-three appointments as United States attorneys. He had learned, he said, "you were liable to damage an individual" if when you ordered a full investigation of someone, his friends and business associates learned of that investigation and then the appointment was never forthcoming. In this case, Reilly was determined that this kind of screening would apply only to those who made the "short list" of genuine possibilities.

Reilly also decided to hold off on detailed financial questionnaires because completing them could be onerous and expensive. And that was a decision, he conceded later, that he regretted.

"If I ever had it to do over again," he said, "that would be something I would change."

Meanwhile, Mondale had decided to spend this interim period before the convention at his home in North Oaks. Any candidates being seriously considered would be invited there for interviews—and this fact would be made clear to the press and public.

There was an understandable tactical reason for taking this step. The semi-public process would be another signal, if one were needed, that Mondale was in full command of the convention and the Democratic Party.

The political hazard in this particular approach was just as obvious. It would remind the press, and presumably the voters, of Mondale's history with Jimmy Carter. And everyone in the campaign understood that such a reminder wouldn't be a blessing. But after the campaign, Jim Johnson argued that refusing to use the Carter method wouldn't have solved that problem.

"We never believed that by trying to separate from Carter you were fundamentally going to alter the fact that you were Carter's Vice President," he said.

Besides, he argued, the "Plains process" used by Carter had been a popular one because it suggested a systematic and careful approach to choosing a Vice President. Moreover, Johnson said, the Mondale campaign took some soundings in a poll and found voters liked the idea.

"People thought it was a damned good way to proceed," he said.

The circumstances in which Mondale was operating were quite different, however, from those in which Carter had first used this approach. Carter had been an outsider, a former governor of Georgia with little direct and personal knowledge of the people who might be considered. By contrast, Fritz Mondale had been telling the country for almost two years now that he was the candidate of experience who knew all the players—the ones, he liked to say, "who are contemporarily relevant."

The more serious flaw, however, was the failure of Mondale and his managers to understand the difference between approval of a process and the kind of picture that process might project when it was put into practice.

Jesse Jackson, irked that he was not even being mentioned on the long lists of possibilities, quickly called the plan "a PR parade of personalities." Mondale was plainly irritated.

"I am proud of that process and, more than that, I intend to continue until I've found the very best possible running mate and the best possible Vice President and possibly the best President of the United States," he said. "I do not take this matter lightly. I take it very seriously, and I believe I know what I'm talking about because I've been there."

While Reilly began his preliminary work, there were predictable suggestions from other Democrats. Tip O'Neill had already put himself on record behind Representative Geraldine Ferraro, the three-term congresswoman from Queens who had impressed her colleagues with her drive and political acumen and was now presiding over the platform committee for the convention. At first the O'Neill endorsement was not given great weight in the political community. It was marked down as an example of the Speaker once again demonstrating loyalty to a particular favorite.

The notion of a woman also attracted a number of other Democrats, including six governors—Anthony Earl of Wisconsin, Richard Celeste of Ohio, Bob Graham of Florida, Mario Cuomo of New York, Toney Anaya of New Mexico and Michael Dukakis of Massachusetts. But those endorsements also were being taken at less than face value. Going on record for a woman, the wise guys said, was a great way for a politician to hide out on the issue for a while. And that was particularly true for those—including Graham, Cuomo and Dukakis—who themselves had appeared on various speculative lists of possible choices.

There were other groups lining up behind favorites. Bert Lance and several other state chairmen from the South were pressing hard for Senator Lloyd Bentsen of Texas. So was Jim Quackenbush, Mondale's southern coordinator. They were all convinced Mondale needed to "go South" to have a chance of winning the electoral votes in that region that would be essential if he was to have any realistic chance against President Reagan.

Other candidates were on various lists. Senator Dale Bumpers of Arkansas, a moderately liberal lawmaker held in particularly high esteem by his colleagues, was one. Senator Sam Nunn of Georgia, a more conservative Democrat who had a reputation among insiders for special expertise on national-security issues, was another. So was Senator Bill Bradley of New Jersey, the onetime basketball star who was on the way to becoming a star in Congress as well. But Nunn and Bradley made it plain from the outset that they weren't interested, and Bumpers showed little enthusiasm.

So the southern contingent formed a de facto consensus for Bentsen, who had made an abortive try for the presidential nomination himself in 1976 and clearly was interested. Moreover, Bentsen had a special political credential. In 1982 he had won a landslide reelection victory in Texas and engineered a huge voter registration campaign that was credited there with a Democratic sweep that included the replacement of a Republican incumbent governor, William Clements, by Democrat Mark White. Lloyd Bentsen had proven he could get the job done at home, and Texas would cast twenty-nine electoral votes.

At the other end of the political spectrum, there was also some vocal support for Mario Cuomo. He, too, had won in 1982, although by a relatively narrow margin, against a well-financed conservative Republican, Lew Lehrman. New York was an essential state for the Democrats, and Cuomo already had demonstrated he could be a remarkably articulate and effective candidate. But Cuomo turned the idea off from the outset, telling Mondale "I'm not free" because he had pledged to serve a full four years in Albany.

As the speculation grew and the process evolved, it became clear that a great many hard-headed Democrats believed Mondale needed to "throw the long bomb" in choosing a running mate. They were looking at those discouraging polling figures and concluding that only some dramatic choice might save the day. Even as cool a politician as Mickey Kantor, a Los Angeles lawyer and longtime Mondale backer, was arguing privately that Mondale should consider Lee Iacocca, the chairman of the Chrysler Corporation who had become such a celebrity from his success in bringing that company back from the brink and, of course, from appearing in Chrysler advertisements.

In all of this initial discussion, however, there was another common thread. The politicians who thought they knew Fritz Mondale best were absolutely certain that he was entirely too staid, too conventional, too orthodox and too cautious to make that exciting choice.

In a staff-versus-press softball game, Mondale came to bat—and bunted! The betting was that anyone who would bunt in a friendly game like that one would pick Bentsen or Bumpers, Cuomo or Hart—another man in a gray suit.

Just when Mondale began to think seriously about naming a woman was never entirely clear. The recollections of the only three people really involved in the process—Mondale, Reilly and Johnson—agreed that the time was early in the deliberations and that, in part, was a recognition of the reality of Mondale's parlous situation.

"Mondale made it clear . . . that he wanted to make it an issue that he was considering women and minorities," Reilly said later. "That was in the mix from the beginning."

But there is a great difference between making clear that you are "considering" a woman or a black for the national ticket and actually doing so. "Considering" could be just a political gesture; deciding to follow through would take something more.

The context in which Mondale was now operating, moreover, made it impossible as a practical matter not to be willing to "consider" a woman or a black. There was no great demand in the party or public for a minority candidate, but Jesse Jackson—who had been ruled out from the beginning—was still a force that had to be given some attention.

And the pressure for a woman candidate, which had been building steadily for several months, no longer could be resisted without some acceptable alternative. The activist women within the party had now seized the "long bomb" argument—the thesis that Mondale needed to make a bold move against such overwhelming odds. The more they talked about it, the more logical—even inevitable—it became in their own thinking.

Mondale, meanwhile, had begun his parade of candidates with Tom Bradley, a black who had been mayor of Los Angeles since 1973 and an early Mondale supporter this time.

Bradley was a man highly regarded within his party. But his qualifications—politically and substantively—lacked the obvious weight to make him a serious candidate in the eyes of the press and political community. He was sixty-six years old, had spent most of his life in police work and—more to the point—had just lost a gubernatorial election in California to Republican George Deukmejian. He had many good qualities, but political pizzazz was not one of them.

The result, predictably, was a skeptical press corps from the outset—and defensiveness at North Oaks. Bradley met with Mondale for three hours and then, wearing a striped tie and a broad smile, gave his friend all the best of it.

"The way I know Walter Mondale," Bradley said, "he would not engage in a charade. He would not cheapen this office of Vice President by going through a PR kind of publicity stunt."

The remark was an obvious and direct counter-thrust at Jesse Jackson.

Lloyd Bentsen and Dianne Feinstein, the mayor of San Francisco, came next later that same week. The drill in each case was roughly the same. The prospect would arrive, be photographed with Fritz and Joan Mondale in the driveway of their home, then disappear inside. Joan and the spouse would leave, perhaps to visit a museum, and Mondale and Reilly would begin the conversation with the candidate. Then Reilly would make himself scarce so that Mondale could pursue matters in which an adviser's presence might be inhibiting. Finally, after three hours or so, the group would gather again—sometimes joined by Jim Johnson—and perhaps have some lunch. Then Mondale and the prospect would hold a press conference in a schoolyard a couple of miles away.

The questions about Feinstein were different from those about Tom Bradley, but no less politically pertinent. She was Jewish, she had been married three times and her only experience was serving as mayor of a city many middle Americans regarded as a capital of social liberalism and homosexual hedonism. But she had impressed Mondale and she had shown herself to be articulate and charming in their post-meeting press conference.

"You can see why I invited her," Mondale said with obvious enthusiasm. "This is a spectacular person."

At sixty-three, Lloyd Bentsen was by no means a spectacular person. Indeed, as a presidential candidate he had been so colorless that one of us had once compared his campaign tour through a city to the passage of a piece of plate glass. He was there and he was heavy, but you couldn't see him. He did have, however, that invaluable Texas connection, and he was rated highly by his colleagues in the Senate.

The core of the problem with Bentsen, nonetheless, was that Mondale could not justify him on any but the most obvious electoral-vote grounds. He had voted for Reaganomics, which Mondale opposed. He favored the MX missile and B-1 bomber, which Mondale opposed. He opposed the nuclear freeze, which Mondale favored. And he favored covert aid to the *contras* in Nicaragua, which Mondale opposed. Beyond that, his positions on women's issues were so antithetical to the activist women in the party that the women were already sending loud—very loud—signals that his selection would cause a terrible stink at the convention.

As the full list of those Mondale would interview became apparent, the ridicule of the process mounted in quantum leaps. There were four others—Gerry Ferraro, now the obvious consensus choice of the activist women; Mayor W. Wilson Goode of Philadelphia, a black who had been elected only the previous year; Henry Cisneros, the thirty-seven-year-old Mexican-American mayor of San Antonio, and Governor Martha Layne Collins of Kentucky, the ranking Democratic woman officeholder but also elected just the previous year.

Each of them had something beyond the obvious to recommend him or her. Although Ferraro had served only three terms in the House, she was an accomplished political player. Goode was a man of obvious intelligence and judgment. Cisneros was a politician of great personal charm who had served on the Kissinger Commission studying the Central America problem. There he had caught the attention of Lane Kirkland, the president of the AFL-CIO, who had urged Mondale to take a look.

But on the basis of conventional qualifications for the presidency, none of these individuals would have been considered a prime prospect—if a prospect at all. Gerry Ferraro had three terms in the House, but so did several dozen male congressmen no one had ever heard mentioned for Vice President. Mayors of big cities had been considered in the past—Kevin White of Boston by George McGovern in 1972, for example—but they clearly lacked the foreign-policy credential to fulfill Mondale's prescription for the "best" potential President if Mondale won the election and it came to that.

So the picture—except perhaps to those three men talking to one another in North Oaks—was that of a candidate pandering to all the special constituencies, and in the most obvious way. More to the point, this was Fritz Mondale, who had been trying all year to counter his image as a captive of his own supporters, seeking to put together a patchwork that might succeed in making up a majority. The voters may have approved of the process, as Jim Johnson said, but the way the process was being used made it an easy target for every columnist and newspaper cartoonist and television comedian.

"I was taken aback by that three weeks or so of growing criticism of the process," Mondale said later, "because I thought I was doing exactly what a presidential nominee ought to do. . . . That irritated me a little bit. . . . I began to worry that it looked like we were just playing a game with the American people, that it wasn't a serious process, when in fact it was. From the beginning, I was serious in looking at a woman and was seriously looking at blacks and Hispanics because I thought this was a time to open that door. But I regret the appearance."

John Reilly also was surprised by the reaction.

"We didn't anticipate it until it began to happen," he said later.

Why the reaction should have been a surprise was never clear. There was an obvious contradiction between Mondale's saying that he wanted the "best" potential President, in terms of qualifications, and his saying that he wanted to open a door to women and minorities. Politicians who become presidential nominees always make a great point of saying they are seeking the most qualified individual when in fact they are trying to find the right political fit. In this case, Mondale was trying to make the fit in terms of race or sex rather than geography.

The ridicule might have been tempered had the parade included more obviously conventional and experienced choices—more white males with traditional political credentials. And, in fact, one of them—Mike Dukakis—was one of those considered to the very end. But he was never brought to North Oaks, even for cosmetic purposes.

"By the time there was a serious focus on Dukakis," Johnson said later, "there was a higher priority on terminating the process. It was clear to us it had to be cut off."

Mondale had told Dukakis on the telephone that he was "actively considering him" and had asked him, in essence, to remain on hold. But Mondale already knew the Massachusetts governor well, and he was reluctant to put him through the process just for appearance's sake.

"When you bring a person out there and don't select them," he said later, "there's an insult to it."

Lloyd Bentsen had taken himself out of the picture and, according to his friends in Texas, was infuriated at having been put through the whole process as the token white middle-aged male. Dale Bumpers also had declined, and he was privately fuming at stories that some of the Mondale managers had been whispering he was a political Hamlet unable to reach a decision.

Meanwhile, the activist women were turning up the heat—in a way that simply added to that picture of the embattled candidate being pushed around. The National Women's Political Caucus released a survey of delegates to the coming national convention that showed 74 percent of them in favor of a woman nominee, only 10 percent opposed.

The real crunch for Mondale came, however, when he incautiously flew to Miami Beach at the end of June for the convention of the National Organization for Women. He arrived to chants of "Run with a woman, win with a woman" and found that three prominent women Democrats in Congress—Barbara Mikulski of Maryland, Barbara Kennelly of Connecticut and Mary Rose Oakar of Ohio—had just endorsed Ferraro.

"Don't call her baby, call her Congresswoman," Mikulski told the 1,200 cheering delegates. "Don't call her baby, call her Vice President."

Mondale tried to get away with a cautious politician's promise that he was "considering a number of women" for his ticket.

"If I choose a woman," he said, "it will be because she is the best. Considering a woman is a first step, but it will not be a last. We have broken the barrier. Never again will a nominee make headlines by considering a woman. Next time headlines will be made only if women are not considered."

The peroration was neither totally convincing nor totally accurate. The fact was that at the Republican convention in Kansas City in 1976, President Gerald Ford had given very serious consideration to choosing Anne Armstrong, who had been a top Republican Party official, Cabinet-level White House adviser and ambassador to Great Britain.

Gerry Ferraro also turned up at the NOW convention and made a speech that fanned the flames just a little higher.

"Our place is in the vice presidency and the presidency . . .," she said. "I thank NOW for making dreams that once seemed impossible a reality for me."

The whole tone of the NOW convention rhetoric was not truly different from that Jesse Jackson had been using on Mondale over the last several months—in a word, threatening.

"We aren't saying, 'If there isn't a woman, we won't play,' " said NOW president Judy Goldsmith. "We're saying, 'If there isn't a woman, we don't win.' "

The day after Mondale left, the convention then passed a resolution calling for "a woman who is strong on women's issues" to be chosen—and threatening a move in that direction from the convention floor "if necessary."

Back in North Oaks, Mondale tried to pass the whole thing off, responding philosophically for public consumption that "this is politics . . . I understand that." But privately there was no mistaking his anger at the way NOW had applied such crude pressure in such a public way.

"That hurt them," Mondale said later, "and Judy knew it did."

But he insisted that the aggressiveness of the activist women never had any influence on his decision.

"I didn't feel under any pressure from organizations that told me I had to do something," he said. "What I wanted to do was to make the right decision and pick the right person, and I spent a lot of time evaluating whether the country was ready to accept a woman as Vice President."

The problem, as John Reilly saw it, was that the accusations of pandering might make Mondale reach the wrong decision.

"We considered it," he said. "It suddenly dawned on us that we weren't going to let it have the reverse effect."

And Mondale's advisers were confident the activist women could not prevent him from doing what he wanted to do.

"We always figured that if we had the delegates to be nominated," said Reilly, "we certainly had the delegates to name a Vice President."

By this point, however, it appeared—at least to those some distance from North Oaks—that the only safe alternative to a woman nominee would be either one of the minority candidates, which was unlikely, or Gary Hart, the man who had given Mondale such a tough race through the primaries.

The relative safety in choosing Hart lay simply in the fact that he had won those eighteen primaries along the way. Hart had a strong record on women's issues, essentially the same as Mondale's, and it would be difficult to justify a challenge to someone who had shown such breadth of support in the party.

The relationship between Mondale and Hart had been a difficult one. But political history was full of examples of presidential nominees putting aside their resentments and reservations to embrace an erstwhile opponent in the hope of grafting that opponent's strength onto his own. Ronald Reagan had done just that in 1980. He had serious doubts about George Bush's ability to perform under pressure, based on Bush's handling of himself at the infamous Nashua, New Hampshire, debate during the primary campaign there. But Reagan strategists believed he needed Bush to help enlist moderate Republicans, particularly in the suburbs, and talked Reagan into accepting him on the ticket.

In the case of Gary Hart, the factors in the political equation were obvious. His strength had been greatest with those young urban professionals for whom Mondale had little appeal. Indeed, polls showed many of them now intending to vote for Reagan in the general election, a trend that might have been slowed with Hart on the ticket.

"Hart was always considered very seriously by Fritz, for all the reasons you would think Fritz would consider him," Reilly said later. "There was kind of a decision going on at the time about doing a bold thing, a woman or a minority, and as we got closer and closer and closer to that, it became apparent to us that we were essentially discarding old politics and the choice of Gary was old politics."

Hart was at least willing and, by some accounts, actively interested. After the campaign he said:

"I didn't want to be Vice President, but obviously I would accept it if the collective judgment of the party leadership was that it was the best ticket. . . . You can't say, 'No, I'm not going to do it.' "

Or, more precisely, you can't refuse if you are looking down the road four years to another presidential campaign and recognize you cannot afford to be seen as a Democrat who did something less than his best for his party's presidential nominee.

The negotiations with Hart never reached the point, however, at which the nomination was offered and had to be accepted or rejected. Reilly and Hart met once on the neutral ground of a mutual friend's house in Georgetown. Hart told the Mondale agent that if he were to be considered, he would want it understood that as Vice President he wouldn't be obliged to lobby Congress on issues on which he simply didn't agree with Mondale—notably, the domestic-content bill. On the more positive side, Hart said he would like to have what he called "day-to-day responsibility" for arms control in a Mondale administration. As Reilly remembered it, that assignment would even have specified that Hart as Vice President would serve as head of the Arms Control and Disarmament Agency.

Mondale had no objections to either of these proposals, but he did have other doubts. One question in his mind, understandable in view of what had happened in the primaries, was whether Hart would stand up under the pressures of a general-election campaign. Another, given far more weight, Reilly said, was whether "how we had painted Hart" during the primaries would make it difficult to justify choosing him for the vice presidency.

As a practical matter, however, Mondale never made a final judgment on those questions. Instead, the discussions at North Oaks evolved in a way that pointed increasingly toward making a less orthodox choice.

Just when Mondale began to move beyond "considering" a woman, which was essentially meaningless, to deciding to choose one was never clear. Mondale himself recalled a group of women state senators in Florida telling him how "a hidden vote" had appeared for them in their campaigns. And he remembered Governor Rudy Perpich of Minnesota telling him that "the public liked it" when Perpich had chosen a woman to be his running mate for lieutenant governor.

"Perpich said he could feel it," Mondale said.

"I became convinced," he said, "that the public was ready for a woman, that it would create a new level of excitement, that it was an idea whose time had come."

And Mondale understood the political equities.

"It was clear to me from the beginning that this was going to be a tough year and that politics as usual would probably fail to stir the enthusiasm we needed to make a campaign out of it," he told us.

Jim Johnson put it this way:

"One of the generalized points of discussion was: To what degree will the selection of a woman change the electoral calculations? . . . Is it possible this can shuffle the deck in a fundamental way? It appeared for a time that it might do just that—

that you might unlock a level of energy and activity and pride that was not possible through any other direction."

The polling data on the impact of a woman candidate was generally inconclusive and contradictory. It was clear that some voters would resist a woman in such high office; others said they would be more inclined to vote for a ticket that included a woman. But the political professionals treated these results with skepticism. Quite possibly, they suspected, some voters would be reluctant to express a prejudice against women candidates in this age of the raised consciousness. And it was also possible that others would express support for the concept but then find a particular woman candidate lacking. The situation had no precedent, and the politicians were flying blind.

During the first week in July, Mondale met with twenty-three women leaders in the Democratic Party who pressed him to choose a woman but did not make the NOW mistake of threatening him publicly. And two days later he completed his much-lampooned parade of candidates by interviewing Martha Layne Collins.

By this point, less than ten days from the convention, Mondale, Reilly and Johnson had concluded it would be wise to make a decision and reveal it before arriving at San Francisco.

"I wanted to decide before the convention," Mondale said, "and cut off all this talk."

The political imperative was to foreclose the kind of public competition at the convention that would divide the delegates into factions, some of whom inevitably would become losers. The early decision, Reilly said later, "would avoid us going to the convention and having nothing happening in the hallways but 'Who you for?' "

So Mondale and the two senior members of "the little white boys" began several days of intense concentration on the decision. By this time, the field of realistic possibilities had been narrowed to Ferraro, Feinstein, Cisneros and Dukakis—although not necessarily in that order.

The other candidates had never been arbitrarily eliminated and crossed off some list or chart. And Reilly chafed at the notion "that we treated this as an NCAA tournament." But as the discussion became more focused, these four were the candidates being seriously considered. Their relative standings changed from day to day, sometimes from hour to hour.

"The problem is that I had good candidates," Mondale said

with the veteran politician's tact. "We spent a lot of time talking about it, coming close to a decision, then pulling back, consulting widely on the phone with political leaders."

The three men would sit in Mondale's den, then go for a walk around the three-acre grounds, then go back to the den for more talk. Mondale would throw out a name and ask his advisers to make the best possible case for that person, then cross-examine them on that case.

"We were just basically, in a fairly systematic way, tossing it around," Jim Johnson recalled. "He'd go so far he'd say, 'I think I'm going to choose so-and-so, let's sleep on it.' Then we'd come back the next day and we'd start over again."

Reilly said:

"I'd go to bed at night thinking that person's gone . . . and, hell, the next morning that person's still in the mix."

Although none of the three would put it in these terms, Michael Dukakis was obviously the safety play—the white male politician Mondale could turn to if he couldn't summon up whatever it took to make a less conventional choice. Like most Democratic leaders, Mondale knew Dukakis as an intelligent and capable public official who had overcome an inclination toward public stuffiness to become an effective campaigner as well. He had been elected governor of Massachusetts the first time in 1974, then had been upset in a 1978 primary by Edward J. King, a conservative whom he greatly underestimated. In 1982 Dukakis had returned as a much more polished politician, defeated King in a primary and won the election easily. If Mondale got into trouble on his choice, Mike Dukakis was an ideal fallback candidate.

Cisneros was sort of a wild idea, considering the shallowness of his political experience. After the fact, Johnson said he was on the list "on the basis that [he is] potentially the most exciting young political figure in America." But it probably didn't hurt that Lane Kirkland thought so highly of him.

The key element in the Cisneros case, however, was plainly the pressure to throw "the long bomb" because it was getting so late in the game and Mondale was so far behind. As was the case with a woman candidate, it seemed possible that choosing a Hispanic-American could shake up the normal electoral patterns. And there were substantial numbers of Hispanic voters in five of the largest states—California, New York, Texas, Illinois and

New Jersey—as well as several smaller states in the Far West.

As the conversations at North Oaks continued, the focus inevitably tightened on the two women—Feinstein and Ferraro. And although logic seemed to argue for Ferraro, despite her limited credentials of experience, Mondale was intrigued by Dianne Feinstein, whose credentials were even skimpier. In her interview and the subsequent press conference, he said later, "she performed brilliantly."

This interest in Feinstein was probably as good a measure as any of the distance between the Real World and North Oaks, Minnesota, at that stage in the game. Mondale told his advisers privately that her experience as mayor was "real seasoning," and they all agreed she had held the most impressive press conference of any of the possibilities. At one point, Reilly flew out to San Francisco for further conversations with the mayor covering questions that had been raised in the talks at North Oaks. And a couple of days after that, with the convention now nine days ahead, a team of lawyers was dispatched to gather her financial information.

The consideration of Ferraro was complicated by a couple of special factors. One was a story making the rounds, and finally appearing in print, that in her interview with Mondale, she had proven to be a disappointment. That story seemed to have been reinforced by one public development that clearly caused some uneasiness in the Mondale camp. At her press conference with Mondale just after the interview, Ferraro had said in her usual blunt way that she would be "amazed" if Mondale did not base his decision on a running mate on electoral-vote considerations. Because Mondale had been insisting so piously, as candidates always do, that his only criterion was the "best" person available, Ferraro's statement caused a mild stir.

Mondale always insisted that the story about Ferraro being a disappointment was completely untrue. And when it appeared in the New York *Times*, he telephoned Ferraro to reassure her.

It was not difficult to see, however, how the impression developed. Before Ferraro came out to Minnesota for the interview on the vice presidency, she had been summoned in her role as chairman of the convention's platform committee to give the prospective nominee a report. The invitation specified that there would be no discussion of the national ticket; that would come later, if she were being considered.

But Ferraro, fully awash in the speculation, had balked at that first trip because she was uncertain about how it would be viewed politically.

"She didn't like that," a Ferraro intimate said later. Ferraro, this ally said, complained privately:

"If he's going to be talking to me at all, it should be as a vice-presidential possibility."

Reilly and Johnson were obviously irked at that reluctance and made no particular secret of their feelings inside the campaign operation. And although Reilly had always been considered supportive of the idea of a woman candidate, Johnson and others had registered their reservations on more than one occasion.

"It was clear," one campaign insider said, "that many of them had their doubts about her."

The result may have been that other campaign advisers—who had been shut out of the process—then relayed the gripes to reporters as evidence that they weren't totally out of the picture.

Quite aside from this incident, however, there was some obvious reaction among the Mondale operatives to all the lobbying being done on Ferraro's behalf—particularly that threat by NOW to make a fight of it on the floor if Mondale did not yield. One way to cool down those lobbyists obviously would be to hint at a negative reaction to Ferraro inside the house on Thrush Lane.

In the critical interview, Mondale did not warm up to Gerry Ferraro as he had to Dianne Feinstein. But Mondale was impressed by the fact that Ferraro was a quick study and had the kind of street smarts he had come to value in a lifetime in Democratic Party politics. At one point in their conversation, Ferraro also asked a question none of the others had raised.

"If I am chosen and become a candidate," she asked, "how will it affect my family? Does it mean you will expect my husband to campaign separately? What about my children?" Those questions would be answered soon enough, in ways not at all to Ferraro's liking—nor to Mondale's.

The decisive factor, however, may have been the way Ferraro seemed to dovetail with Mondale's idea about what the campaign of 1984 would be all about. At the time he was holding those endless conversations with Reilly and Johnson, he was also working on the acceptance speech he intended to deliver at the convention the following week. On some occasions, while the three men talked in Mondale's den, his chief speechwriter, Marty Kaplan, was waiting elsewhere in the house for Mondale to join him on that project.

Mondale wanted to speak about the American dream, about people who had made their way, as well as those who still needed help from the government. Ferraro seemed to fit. She was the immigrants' daughter who had made her way as a prosecutor and into Congress, where she was well regarded by the other politicians. She had a strong family and religious faith.

"She was tough," Mondale said later, "and she had an ethnic background that I thought would add strength to the ticket, and [she had] federal experience. . . . She stood for a compassionate approach by government. It was a sign of respect for ethnic America, and I liked her."

Reilly said:

"Ferraro became in his mind more of a personification of what he was trying to say, or going to try to say, than did Feinstein. That's what it came down to—family, Queens, prosecutor, congressman, platform, so on, all of that."

Mike Berman, the campaign treasurer, had been dispatched to New York to meet with John Zaccaro and go over his finances, and Reilly had been sent to meet again with Ferraro to get the answers to other questions. At this point, there seemed to be no problem. So, on July 11, Mondale told Reilly and Johnson:

"I'm going to choose Ferraro."

Ferraro was in San Francisco already, presiding over the platform committee and preparing to give a speech to the World Affairs Council that night. A private jet was dispatched from Chicago to pick her up and bring her to Minnesota. And the following morning, Mondale confirmed the decision before a throng of reporters and supporters packed into a legislative chamber in the state capitol at St. Paul.

"I looked for the best Vice President and I found her in Gerry Ferraro," he said.

The scene was one of unbounded celebration coupled with a sense of history in the making. Women on the chamber floor and in the galleries hugged each other and some wiped tears from their eyes. Some women reporters, too, put aside their objectivity and grinned broadly at the political breakthrough for their sex.

Within the Mondale campaign organization—and indeed most

of the Democratic Party—there was similar jubilation. The candidate had shown himself capable of making a bold stroke that just might change the dynamics of the campaign ahead against Ronald Reagan.

"It was a great way to reshuffle the deck," Peter Hart said later. "Can you come out worse? Yes, but you take your chances."

The daring selection of Geraldine Ferraro had—for the moment, at least—papered over the failure of the Mondale campaign to use the six weeks before the convention to resolve many of the vexing questions about the campaign ahead.

Mondale still had no coherent message to present to the electorate on why he should replace President Reagan. Jesse Jackson was still muttering threats, telling black voters to "wait for my signal" before committing themselves to the Democratic ticket. A strategy for the South had still to be developed, and it was clear that Ferraro would take some selling there. The movement of uncommitted delegates to Mondale's side had been minimal, suggesting again pervasive doubts about his ability to succeed in the fall.

But, more than anything else, Fritz Mondale had seemed to add further weight to the picture of him among voters as a candidate devoted to the old-fashioned constituent politics—one who was so eager to appease women, blacks and Hispanics that he had ignored the great white middle class.

Still, Mondale had broken dramatically with tradition in the historic decision to choose a woman to run for Vice President at his side. And while he and his chief strategists now contemplated how the move would affect his chances against Reagan, women across the country—those in politics particularly—reveled in the choice itself. It was a milestone in a relatively recent campaign for political equity that already had succeeded far beyond the women's expectations.

16

What a Gas!

•

IN THE FINAL DAYS of the primary campaign, Mike Berman, one of Walter Mondale's most trusted confidants, telephoned Anne Wexler, the seasoned politician and veteran of the Jimmy Carter White House. He had, he said, a "very secret" project for her—compiling a list of women Mondale might consider for Vice President. The list, he specified, should not be limited to politicians but should include possibilities from other fields as well.

"If there's such a thing as a female Lee Iacocca," said Berman, "we'd like to know it."

Anne Wexler was obviously the logical person to ask. She had come into politics as an organizer in Connecticut for Eugene J. McCarthy in his 1968 campaign. She had been involved in every presidential campaign since that time. She had handled political contacts with public groups for President Carter. And earlier in this political cycle, she had been chairman of Fritz Mondale's "exploratory committee"—the one established in 1982 so he could act as a candidate without officially becoming one.

The critical point, however, was the fact that Wexler, who had become a successful lobbyist, was more a politician than an activist in the women's movement. She shared the feminist goals of that movement, but she was one of those rare women who was a genuine insider in the male-dominated world of politics.

Wexler agreed to the project and compiled dossiers on twenty women for Mondale's consideration. But in a covering letter she wrote:

"I have reached the inescapable conclusion that the only person you could really pick is Geraldine Ferraro."

The fact that Anne Wexler had come to that view was a reflection, first, of just how skillfully and persistently Gerry Ferraro had preempted the field of women who might be the Democratic vice-presidential nominee—in the still unlikely event that one would be chosen.

More to the point, Wexler's recommendation reflected a judgment that Ferraro came far closer than any other woman to fitting the profile the professional politicians had written long before for the first woman to run on a national ticket.

There is a significant distinction to be made here. Ferraro may have best met those specifications. But she was light-years short of meeting the hyperbolic standards that Mondale was setting for his running mate—"the best potential President." And that was a discrepancy that the voters clearly understood, even as they applauded Mondale so enthusiastically for breaking the barrier against women.

The notion of a woman on a national ticket had been treated seriously on only one previous occasion. And, although the Democrats liked to think of themselves as more advanced on women's concerns, a Republican had been the first. In 1976 Anne Armstrong had made the "final four" considered by President Gerald R. Ford in a wee-hours meeting in his hotel suite in Kansas City. The political context then was strikingly similar to the one Mondale now faced. Ford was running almost 30 percent behind Jimmy Carter in the opinion polls, and some of his advisers—including Stuart Spencer—believed he needed to take bold action. In the end, however, after pollster Bob Teeter reported his findings that indicated Armstrong might be a negative on the ticket, she was dropped from the list and Bob Dole was chosen.

In the ensuing eight years, the idea of a woman candidate had never reached a serious stage in either party. On the Republican side in 1980, there had been no obvious possibilities—nor any comparable pressure to take a chance.

But a rough consensus had developed among political professionals in both parties on the circumstances under which a woman might be chosen. It was most likely to happen if, as Teeter postulated in an interview in 1983, "a candidate thirty points behind in the polls might decide to go for the long ball."

Aside from the question of context, however, most politicians believed the first woman would have to be one who came up through the political structure, rather than out of the feminist movement. Because of the long brawls over the Equal Rights Amendment and the abortion issue, any woman from the movement was likely to carry too much political baggage. And because most of the leading women in the Democratic Party also were involved in the movement, the theory was that the first woman to be nominated would more likely be a Republican.

The consensus also held that the first woman would be one with relatively long experience in a high and visible office, as a member of the Senate or perhaps a state governor. Such prolonged exposure, the rationale went, would give the electorate time to get used to the idea that this particular woman was no different from a man in capacity for the highest office.

In the early stages of the contest for the Democratic presidential nomination, the activist women's movement was strikingly restrained in pressing for a place on the ticket, despite evidence the climate over the last two generations had become much more hospitable. A Gallup poll found 80 percent of voters surveyed answering yes when asked: "If your party nominated a woman for President, would you vote for her if she was qualified for the job?" In 1937, by contrast, only 31 percent of the voters had answered affirmatively.

There was no mystery in this apparent reluctance of the women's movement to press their case in 1982 and 1983. The movement had been jolted to its heels by the failure of ERA to achieve ratification before the deadline passed in 1982. The debate over abortion had become an emotional and scarring controversy that divided both sexes and frightened politicians on both sides of the issue. The women's rights organizations obviously lacked the kind of cohesive support that could promise to deliver an overwhelming vote for any issue or candidate.

There was also an element of caution. Most of the activist women were Democrats, and they didn't want to risk causing any rupture in their party that would make it more difficult to achieve the first imperative—the defeat of President Reagan in 1984. As former Representative Bella Abzug of New York told us at the time:

"The problem is that our people are very anxious to beat Reagan. There is tremendous unhappiness with him and his cuts in the budget affecting women."

The leaders of the movement had been impressed, however,

by the dimensions of the "gender gap"—the pronounced difference in support that women accorded Democrats over Republicans, and particularly against Ronald Reagan. Exit polls in 1980 had shown Reagan with 16 percent less support among women than among men. In the 1982 mid-term elections there was more evidence of similar but smaller gender gaps working for Democratic candidates for the House. And Democratic successes in several close Senate and gubernatorial elections in 1982 could be traced to that same preference among women.

The activist women began holding a series of meetings late in 1982 and early in 1983—largely to discuss this phenomenon. But the talks were short on specific battle plans.

"There was a lot of unstructured dialogue within the women's community," Judy Goldsmith, the NOW president, recalled.

Even when NOW called in September of 1983 for the selection of a woman for the national ticket, Goldsmith said, "we didn't make the choice of a woman the bottom line for an endorsement" of a Democratic presidential candidate. That endorsement would depend on such things as his positions on women's issues, the role given women in his campaign and his electability.

Nor was there anything approaching a consensus on any particular women as potential candidates. What discussion there was, Goldsmith said, tended to be generic.

Kathy Wilson, the chair of the National Women's Political Caucus and a Republican with a low regard for Reagan, recalled the discussion of a woman candidate evolving as a way to take advantage of Reagan's presumed weakness.

"We began talking about putting a woman on the [Democratic] ticket as a way to move the gender gap," she said, "as a way to focus attention on Ronald Reagan's insensitivity and the administration's insensitivity."

But still, even to those most interested, there was little conviction in 1983 that a woman on the ticket in 1984 was a serious possibility. And if their thinking had not reached even that level, it was obviously far too early to begin sorting out who such a candidate might be.

Meanwhile, Gerry Ferraro was pressing ahead with her own agenda—a determined application of her energies to politics with the idea of positioning herself, as she said later, "for the Senate or whatever." She had never made any bones about her interest in challenging Senator Alfonse D'Amato, the conservative New York Republican, in 1986. But if the "moving around" raised some other possibility, that was jake with her.

Almost from the moment Ferraro was first elected in 1978, she had made a more vivid impression on the political community in Washington than is usual for freshmen in Congress. She had made a friend of Tip O'Neill and, like any ambitious politician, seized every opportunity to move up in the structure. By 1983 she had a valued seat on the House Budget Committee and had become secretary of the House Democratic Caucus. Male politicians spoke of her with respect. She was, they said, "tough" and "ambitious" and "one of the boys." And, they noted, sometimes snidely, she had a particular talent for capturing press attention.

Nor had Ferraro ignored political opportunities outside the House. In 1980 she had served as one of the deputy chairmen of the Carter-Mondale campaign, whose leaders hoped she might be helpful in attracting Italian-American voters in New Jersey and Connecticut as well as New York. After the election she took a seat on the Hunt Commission that was rewriting the Democratic Party's delegate-selection rules. And, in contrast to the other congressional members of that commission, she attended almost all the meetings and took an active role in the bargaining. Like their counterparts in the House, Democratic Party officials were coming to know Ferraro as a forceful and effective politician. When the rules were finally adopted in 1982, she was credited with having been the prime agent for the provision under which 164 House Democrats would be super-delegates to the convention.

This political credential was essential. Although the activist women had no questions about her commitment to feminist goals, they recognized she had other connections in the Democratic Party equally or more important as credentials. By the time the speculation began about a woman on the ticket in 1984, those connections were an essential asset. Mondale might take a woman, but he surely could not take one handed to him by NOW, so conspicuously in the vanguard of the feminist movement.

"One of the things that, to some extent, differentiated Gerry . . . was the fact she was a party activist of a much more visible nature than some of the others," Goldsmith recalled.

By the spring of 1984, the movement—having spent much

of late 1983 assailing Reagan—was giving much more attention to the possibility of a woman becoming the Democratic nominee for Vice President.

"We got very serious about the whole notion of putting a woman on the ticket," Wilson said later.

Both the inside talk and the public dialogue became more intense. Within the women's movement the names heard most often were those of Ferraro, Representative Barbara Mikulski, the fiery inner-city Democrat from Baltimore; Representative Patricia Schroeder of Colorado; and Mayor Dianne Feinstein of San Francisco. Representative Lindy Boggs of Louisiana was also plainly interested, although the women's groups were not about to support a candidate who was not pro-choice on abortion.

But Mikulski, although one of the authentic stars of the women's movement, was not considered a realistic possibility, in part because she was so identified. Pat Schroeder was too independent for some of her sisters—and, anyway, she was identified closely with a presidential candidate, Gary Hart. Feinstein didn't have the federal experience.

But Ferraro had been "moving around" in politics for several years now, making the kind of speeches across the country that politicians with an eye for the main chance always deliver. And now when the crunch was coming in the late spring of 1984, she had used her position as chairman of the Democratic convention's platform committee to maximum political advantage. She had shown, the consensus seemed to be, that she was a capable and cool negotiator who brooked little nonsense and kept her gaze firmly fixed on the goal of a platform that would not generate political conflict within the party. Beyond that, she had a fresh and breezy—or brassy—air that communicated well on national television.

The way she came across on television was no accident, either. Earlier in the spring, when she had been named to head the platform committee, but long before there was serious talk about the vice presidency, Ferraro went to David Sawyer, the New York media consultant, and arranged to participate in some video workshops in his office.

These were mock press conference situations in which Sawyer and his staff would play the part of reporters asking the questions, which Ferraro would answer. Then Sawyer would play back the videotape and critique her performance. Then they would do the whole exercise again until they got it right.

"She didn't want to make a fool of herself," Sawyer recalled.

Meanwhile, her position began to come into sharper focus.

"We started to move to the notion of Ferraro," Kathy Wilson recalled.

For the activist women, the pivotal incident may have been one that had the potential for destroying Ferraro's chances in a moment.

On May 16 she was invited to be the guest at a "Sperling breakfast"—a Washington institution named for its founder, Godfrey (Budge) Sperling of the *Christian Science Monitor*. The breakfast met, with Sperling presiding, three or four times a week at 8:00 AM at the Sheraton Carlton Hotel. The guest would be a politician or administration official who would be questioned over bacon and eggs by twenty-five or thirty reporters and columnists from leading newspapers and magazines. Ferraro was a natural for one of these sessions because she was then presiding over the platform-committee meetings.

But, as sometimes happens to guests even under the benevolent stewardship of Budge Sperling, she made news by making a mistake.

Ferraro had been insisting that her goal was a short, thematic Democratic platform that would not be loaded down with specifics on which delegates might disagree. And in making that case that morning, she incautiously suggested that even the Equal Rights Amendment might not be mentioned by name in the document "with a capital E, capital R, capital A."

One of the reporters sitting at the table pursued the comment with several questions, any one of which Ferraro might have seized as a lifeline to extricate herself. But she didn't—and as she left the Sheraton Carlton, she realized she had made a serious mistake. Only four years earlier, the women's movement had been up in arms because the Republican Party, acceding to the wishes of Ronald Reagan, had dropped support for ERA from its platform. Reagan had argued then essentially what Ferraro was arguing now—that you could be for equal rights for women without having ERA in your platform. It was not a big story, but when a liberal Democrat with supposed feminist credentials showed any weakness on ERA, it was undoubtedly news.

When Kathy Wilson arrived at her NWPC office a little later, Ferraro already was trying to reach her. Wilson quickly called back.

"Look," Ferraro said, "I'm in hot water here."

Others received similar calls, and by noon a group of Ferraro's congressional colleagues and women's movement leaders met in a conference room at the Capitol to see what could be done. The result was a statement by Ferraro that an ERA plank would be "fully consistent with a platform which I hope will be a statement of the party's principles, priorities and policies."

But a more significant result was the demonstration by Ferraro to her colleagues that she knew how to play the pragmatic political game under stress.

"It almost became a political asset because of the way she handled it," Wilson said. "She made all the right calls. She didn't pretend she hadn't made a mistake . . . she didn't do a mea culpa or anything—just 'Help me work this out.' "

Ferraro had the problem behind her in twenty-four hours, Wilson said. "I just had some admiration. On the one hand, I said, 'Oh, my God, how could she have done it?' But on the other hand, she fixed it."

"That is the kind of thing that . . . could take on a life of its own and get to be really a nightmare," Goldsmith said. "But it was quickly contained and dealt with and straightened out."

The incident did not pass without notice in the Mondale campaign, however. That afternoon, one insider said later, Jim Johnson telephoned Anne Wexler and told her: "See, that's the problem you have with somebody like Gerry Ferraro."

Long before the flap over ERA, there had been other occasions when Ferraro had impressed the women's leaders with her skills as an effective politician. Once, after the death of efforts in 1983 to revive ERA, there was a particularly contentious press conference in which women members of Congress fell into partisan blame-placing.

The heat reached its highest level when Lynn Martin, an articulate and aggressive Republican from Illinois, declared:

"Each time it has been with a Democratic majority that we have lost, each time with a different reason."[37]

But Ferraro quickly lowered the temperature.

"We are all venting our spleen, I guess out of frustration," she said. "And I guess what happens is that we want to blame something other than the fact that we recognize there are a lot of people in this country who don't care about equal rights for women. We came up six votes short. I don't think we should blame ourselves. I think we should take a very close look at the elections in 1984 and make sure we elect people, Republicans and Democrats, who will make a difference."

Others who were there said much of the tension in the room dissolved instantly—and the women were able to move ahead without such lingering rancor.

"That's one of the reasons she became popular among all of us," Wilson said. "She was playing with the big boys."

Once the primaries ended, the feminist leaders began to be convinced that Mondale wasn't kidding with this talk about a woman on the ticket. Goldsmith met with him and Reilly and came away, she said, with "no doubt" Mondale was serious. Wilson sent Reilly a long memorandum making the case for a woman candidate, and then met with him.

"He seemed very receptive, and we were surprised," she said later.

But there were still bumps in the road. In late June, Mikulski presided over a meeting that included such leading feminists as Eleanor Smeal, past president of NOW, and Bella Abzug; such politicians as Wexler and New York City Council President Carol Bellamy; and several Democratic members of Congress—among them Barbara Kennelly of Connecticut, Sala Burton and Barbara Boxer of California, Mary Rose Oakar of Ohio. The discussion was intense as the women urgently expressed their feeling that the time had come to strike for the national ticket. Finally, they agreed to seek a meeting with Mondale to press their case. But a story also leaked out that they had talked about walking out of the convention if a woman was not chosen. The report was

37. The similarities in style between Martin and Ferraro are so striking that Martin played the part of Ferraro when Vice President George Bush was rehearsing for their debate later in the year.

quickly denied, but the Mondale strategists were, said one insider, "very angry about the story."

A more serious problem developed at the NOW convention that passed the resolution calling for a woman for Vice President and reserving the right of the women to nominate their own candidate from the floor "if necessary."

After the fact, Judy Goldsmith insisted the resolution was no more than a reflection of the "intensity" of the convention and wasn't meant to be a threat.

"We never talked about walkout," she said. "We had no interest in disrupting the convention because we didn't want a splintered party limping out of San Francisco either."

The sentiment was accurate enough. A threat to nominate a candidate from the floor is not the same as a threat to walk out of a convention. But in the political context of that meeting, the NOW action was clearly seen as an attempt to muscle Fritz Mondale, already the darling of the special interests.

But others close to the situation said later that Ellie Smeal, Goldsmith's militant predecessor, had forced the resolution over Goldsmith's behind-the-scenes objections.

"Judy really got bagged," one friend said later. "Judy didn't want this to happen. She couldn't control it. . . . She knows that confrontation is not the way to get results, and she was very upset about it."

The danger of a lasting backlash from the NOW incident was obvious. On July 4, twenty-three prominent Democratic women led by Carol Bellamy flew to St. Paul for a meeting with Mondale. They sat around a large table in a conference room at the Radisson St. Paul Hotel and each, in turn, made the case—in less demanding tones—for choosing a woman. "I had no question that he was hearing what was being said," one participant recalled later.

The subject of Ferraro never came up, however. "No names were ever mentioned, not once," Wexler said.

Indeed, by this stage, mentioning Ferraro wasn't necessary. By using the most traditional political means, Gerry Ferraro had preempted the field—at least as far as this group was concerned. Mondale himself was still considering Dianne Feinstein, but for most Democratic women the decision was already made. Ferraro had eliminated the options in much the same way Jesse Jackson had made the decision on a black candidacy for the black leaders. She was not the candidate of the women's activists per se, but every time they made their case, she was the beneficiary. Ferraro was, in short, a skilled and street-smart politician and she used those skills to reach for something no one else had ever achieved. And she got it.

Once selected by Mondale, Ferraro didn't have to worry about the fact that she lacked the political credentials ordinarily required of a vice-presidential candidate. The imperative was getting on with the campaign. And so, a few days after the convention had made her nomination official, she telephoned Anne Wexler and told her:

"I want you to be my John Reilly."

Like the relationship between old pros Mondale and Reilly, Ferraro and Wexler were a natural alliance. Ferraro had reached this point as a politician rather than as a feminist, and Wexler fit that same pattern. Ferraro was turning her attention to what any good politician does in those circumstances—prepares to make the best of the opening presented her.

We had dinner with Ferraro and Wexler one night a few weeks later at Mel Krupin's restaurant in Washington. The conversation of nearly two hours was no different from what we might have had with any Democrat from Queens, except that we were talking about a vice-presidential race rather than a contest for City Council. But what struck us most was that Ferraro was totally unabashed by the fact that she had been chosen because she was a woman—rather than because she was so well qualified she could not be resisted, which she knew she was not.

Fritz Mondale was telling the world he had chosen the "best" possible candidate. But Ferraro wasn't kidding herself. As she said herself at one point in Minnesota: "What I bring to the ticket is, first of all, a certain amount of political know-how on how to campaign. And I'm good at it."

But before getting out on the stump, there was still the ceremony of the convention and the nomination itself. And Gerry Ferraro was determined to enjoy the moment.

On the night her name went before the convention, Ferraro sat at a dining table in her hotel suite, wearing a bathrobe. She rehearsed her speech by reading it from the scroll of paper that would be run through the teleprompter just a short while later.

All was confusion. At one point, her son came in.

"Hey, Mom," he wanted to know, "what tie should I wear?"

A moment later one of her daughters trooped in.

"What do you think of this dress?" she asked, holding one up for inspection.

"It's a nice dress," Ferraro replied. "In fact, *I'm* going to wear it."

Next her husband John breezed in looking for his cuff links. And all the while, the television set in the corner of the room was showing Geraldine Ferraro being nominated at the Moscone Convention Center just outside her hotel window. But she was too busy going over the speech to watch.

Finally, she reached the critical point in her text.

"I proudly accept your nomination to run for Vice President of the United States," she read aloud.

Then she looked up, grinned and exclaimed:

"What a gas!"

17

San Francisco: Chaos and Celebration

•

WHATEVER the long-term ramifications might be of Fritz Mondale's choice of a woman to be his running mate, the action instantaneously transformed the gathering of the party clan in San Francisco from depression to celebration. Early arrivals to the Democratic National Convention had been putting the best face they could on Mondale's prospects against President Reagan, but without much conviction. But when the word of Gerry Ferraro's selection filtered out late on the Wednesday night before the convention was to open, the reaction was akin to pulling the living room drapes back and letting the sunshine in.

It was not so much that this obscure congresswoman from Queens was herself going to provide the political magic for a winning ticket. Rather, what shook the Democrats out of their doldrums was the evidence in Mondale's decision that he was not the storefront Indian he seemed to so many of them to be—dull, unimaginative, the cardboard New Dealer who dared to be cautious. Choosing a woman was not the act of a cautious man; a desperate one, maybe. But even so, how much more interesting it was, and challenging, to have a prospective presidential nominee who was swinging for the fences for a change.

The immediate uplift of mood among the arriving delegates and assorted convention hangers-on seemed to infect the whole city of San Francisco. It is not the kind of place where depression has much of a chance over the long run anyway, what with its breezy summertime climate and the high spirits the lively and cosmopolitan face of the town inspires. Although Fritz Mondale remained a longshot for the presidency, even with—or perhaps

especially with—Gerry Ferraro joining him on the Democratic ticket, the air was now festive. Parties beckoned in every major hotel and in a host of private homes, especially those of wealthy Democrats who support their political party with the regularity that ordinary folks drop dimes and dollars into their church collection basket on Sundays.

For one Democrat in particular, the gathering of the party faithful in San Francisco was a tonic—and a triumph. Charles T. Manatt, the Democratic National Chairman, an Iowa boy who made good and moved to California to make even better, was the man more than any other one person who had brought the Democratic National Convention to San Francisco. Holding the convention in California, in fact, had been a central objective of Manatt's nearly four-year tenure as national party chairman. And he had pursued it, as he pursued most things, with an intense—and to many, an oftentimes even irritating—fervor. Manatt himself lived in Los Angeles and he would have preferred seeing the convention held there. But for at least two years the city had been booked for the summer of 1984 for the XXI Olympiad, and so San Francisco was the obvious second choice. The city had an attractive woman mayor, Dianne Feinstein, and enough tourist attractions and bright lights to keep the most wide-eyed boondocks delegates awestruck and occupied.

What's more, San Francisco and California seemed delighted to have the Democratic convention. It meant business and money, but it meant more than that. Californians love to believe that there on the western edge of the continent they are also on the cutting edge of change and trends. So where better for a party to come to suggest it was alive, well and looking ahead—even with a near-certain nominee who was undeniably old hat and peddled his experience as his major ticket to the future?

The city's, and the state's, gratitude fell happily at the feet of the man who had made it all possible—Chuck Manatt. There was in the phenomenon a certain justice, but a certain irony as well. Although Manatt represented the Golden State very effectively, he was in many ways the personification of small-town, Kiwanis Club America. He was a kind of combination of Sinclair Lewis's George Babbitt and Budd Schulberg's Sammy Glick, full of pride and almost obnoxiously ambitious. Manatt was, in fact, what Babbitt surely would have admiringly called a "go-getter," and Glick would have so envied him as to have been driven to cut the legs out from under him.

There was no denying, though, that Chuck Manatt had delivered, and so he was—at least until the prospective nominee would arrive in the convention city—the man of the hour. Hostesses vied for his presence as guest of honor at their elegant Nob Hill and Pacific Heights dinner parties, and none laid on the ritz thicker for him than Ann Getty, the oil heiress reputed to be one of the wealthiest women in America. So determined was she, in fact, to demonstrate to Manatt and to the convention's most prominent players San Francisco's appreciation that she gave not one but two lavish parties for him on successive Friday and Saturday evenings before the opening of the convention.

On Friday night, the assembled guests were the dons and duchesses of American journalism—publishers, editors, columnists, Washington bureau chiefs, star reporters and, above all, anchormen from the major television networks—all the usual suspects. It was, beyond question, a night of luminaries, and Chuck Manatt, the kid from Iowa who came West and struck gold, was at the center of it all.

Manatt came into the posh Getty residence overlooking San Francisco Bay in his usual fashion, wearing his Kiwanis smile and being his usual overly solicitous self and, as always, the picture of preening self-confidence. But as he made the rounds of the room during the cocktail hour, greeting and chatting with the journalistic elite, his heart was heavy with a piece of information that before the night was over would be the principal fare of Ann Getty's already exquisite dinner menu. For Chuck Manatt knew, at that moment of his personal triumph, that he had just been—as they say over in San Francisco's seedy Fillmore district—shitcanned.

The fact was, Fritz Mondale and—most significantly the men closest to him in his campaign—did not like Chuck Manatt all that much. He was, they had to concede, a hell of a fund-raiser and an operator, but he wasn't their style. They had decided long before that Manatt would have to go once Mondale had the nomination. But events had conspired to make it seem essential to

Mondale and his "little white boys"—as his tight group of advisers were called inside the campaign—that Manatt go at once.[38]

With the selection of Ferraro, a northerner, as Mondale's running mate, the nominee and his coterie decided he would have to placate the South in some way, and the obvious bone to throw Dixie was the national party chairmanship. And so it was, Thanks a lot, Chuck, and see you around.

It is not unusual for a presidential nominee to choose his own national chairman as he approaches the fall campaign. But it is customary to let the outgoing chairman have his moment in the sun by keeping him in place until the day after the convention, at which time the national committee traditionally reorganizes. But Fritz Mondale was in a particular hurry, and the fact that Chuck Manatt was in the midst of his big moment of glory in his own state didn't make a whit of difference. In fact, the Mondale strategists decided they wanted to have Manatt's successor in place at the convention so he could play an integral part in shaping what they thought was essential to Mondale's election chances–a southern strategy for the campaign.

Indeed, as Manatt was walking around Ann Getty's living room with his political head already severed from his body, that successor was arriving in San Francisco, ready to take over. And firing Manatt in his own backyard at his moment in the sun was, the world was soon to learn, only the half of it. The man Mondale had chosen to replace him was Jimmy Carter's old crony who had been driven out of Washington on charges of serious banking irregularities and later indicted—Bert Lance![39]

The reaction among the assembled stunned Democrats was perhaps best summed up by another California party fund-raiser, Duane Garrett.

38. The term "little white boys" was a carryover from the 1980 Ted Kennedy campaign—the monicker hung on Kennedy's elite inner circle by women staffers shut out of the action. The label was easily transferred to the all-white, all-male inside group around Mondale—Johnson, Reilly, Berman, Beckel, Kaplan, Donilon, Leone. The only woman in a ranking job was Mondale's longtime press aide Maxine Isaacs as press secretary, but she was never regarded as a policy-maker. A similar term also was used by Mayor Andrew Young of Atlanta to describe the Mondale inner circle.

39. Lance resigned as Carter's director of the Office of Management and Budget on September 21,1977. He was indicted on May 23, 1979, on thirty-three counts of conspiring to obtain illegal loans from forty-one banks from 1970 through 1978. In April 1980 he was acquitted on nine counts and a mistrial was declared on three others. The Justice Department dropped all remaining charges in June 1980.

"What's the matter?" he asked. "Wasn't Billie Sol Estes available?"[40]

Suddenly, the euphoria created by Mondale's choice of a woman to be his running mate was shattered by the twin bombshell. Kicking Manatt out in his own state at his own convention was bad enough. But Bert Lance! Surely it couldn't be true. That, at least, was the immediate reaction of the incredulous Democrats. But it was true, and more than any other event in this stormy and folly-ridden election year, it cast grave doubts on the competence and wisdom of the man the Democrats were about to send into the fray against Ronald Reagan. How it happened is a classic case of the perils of the isolated and insulated candidate, and the possibilities for self-destruction in a campaign battered and exhausted by a nomination process that leads smart men to make dumb decisions.

It all really started in late June when Manatt went to North Oaks, in conjunction with a meeting of Mondale and the Democratic state chairmen. Manatt had been touching base regularly with Mondale as well as with the other candidates all through the primary/caucus period, and it was obvious to all he wanted to stay on as national chairman. The day after the state chairmen's meeting, campaign manager Bob Beckel took Manatt out to Mondale's house. According to Beckel, Manatt told Mondale he thought he had done a good job and wanted to continue in his post.

Mondale, Beckel recalled, said "I'm not going to make any commitments to you. I want to be able to have my options open to me." And Manatt said he understood that Mondale had the right to select his own chairman, Beckel said.

While there was anti-Manatt sentiment among some insiders, Beckel said, replacing him "wasn't a burning issue" at that juncture. Others said they had the impression Manatt didn't pick up on Mondale's hint of things to come and thought he would be able to stay on. Manatt told us later that was his "assumption."

As the discussions at North Oaks advanced on the vice-presidential selection and it became clear a southerner would not be chosen, the notion that Manatt should be replaced by a southerner became an almost automatic alternative.

"There was always in our minds," Johnson said later, "a belief,

40. Billie Sol Estes, a Texas Democrat with alleged ties to then Vice President Lyndon B. Johnson, was convicted and jailed in 1963 in a massive farm-mortgage swindle.

without being pressed, that if we did not go to a southern running mate, that clear and strong immediate steps would need to be taken to make it clear to people that this did not mean in any sense that we were writing off the South; or that we did not see an important role for them in the general-election campaign. In that sense, there were companion discussions [about a running mate and a new national chairman]."

There was also a sense, Johnson said, that Mondale would want his own party chairman for the general election, and so "the decision around Manatt was something that had come to be assumed"—by the Mondale people, anyway, if not by Manatt. As for the timing, Johnson said, the idea was to permit Manatt to hold the job through the convention "as a last step." But it was felt it would be an advantage, Johnson said, "to have the chairman who was going to be in place during the general election known and be able to work on the general election during that convention."

Besides, Johnson said, Manatt at his meeting with Mondale at North Oaks had said "he would be more than happy to cooperate in whatever we wanted to do, including graciously stepping down." If that was the case, though, Manatt was about to give new meaning to both words—"happy" and "graciously."

The idea of Lance originated, according to Beckel, with campaign chairman Jim Johnson in a conversation with Beckel "a couple of weeks" before Mondale decided on Ferraro as his running mate.

Beckel said he raised with Johnson "that if Mondale did not go with a southerner as Vice President, which was becoming increasingly less likely, we had to think about the South in the chairmanship."

"Johnson said," he recalled, " 'What do you think about Bert?' And my reaction was, 'I think it's a good idea.' "

Concerning Lance, Beckel confessed it was a matter of "puppy love" with him, his respect for Lance was that high. Beckel had been through the Super Tuesday war with Lance, in which the Georgian had been an effective and aggressive Mondale supporter, and Lance had played a key role in helping Beckel deal with Jesse Jackson.

"Well," Johnson said to Beckel, "let's raise it with Mondale."

Johnson did so, and reported back to Beckel that the candidate also liked the idea, provided he did decide to change chairmen and "go South."

To most of the rest of the Western world, Bert Lance may have been a political pariah after the banking irregularity charges that forced him to resign as Jimmy Carter's budget director in 1977 and his subsequent indictment in 1979. He was acquitted of most of the charges in 1980 and the Justice Department dropped the rest, but Lance nevertheless was widely regarded as a political negative on the national scene. Also, some later business and banking deals made him suspect to many. But in the eyes of those who had served with him in the Carter administration—and that included Mondale and Johnson, who was one of Mondale's chief aides as Vice President—he was a smart, loyal and honest associate.

Beyond that positive view of him, Mondale, Johnson and Mike Berman knew Lance, who was now the Democratic Party chairman in Georgia, to be an effective and shrewd politician and—above all—a good friend to Mondale. In the campaign's darkest hours after Hart's New Hampshire and Maine upsets, when Mondale desperately needed to win in the South on Super Tuesday, Lance had pitched in and helped Mondale squeak through in the Georgia primary. And since then, he had been a rock of support among the southern state chairmen, whom he had organized and now led, and had done yeoman work as a go-between with Jesse Jackson, with whom he had developed a special rapport.

"When everybody else was heading South," Mike Berman said later, meaning they were deserting Mondale, "Bert was heading North."

Nobody appreciated Lance's efforts more than Mondale. He told Johnson and other close aides that he owed Lance a great deal for the way he had stuck with him in those days and nights of early March when the lights almost went out on the Mondale campaign.

Mondale himself said after the election:

"I really like Bert. . . . He had gone through that heartache earlier and cleared himself. He had been very, very helpful to me throughout the nominating process and throughout the South. He had tried as hard as anybody down there. He gave me strength I needed in the South, and leadership."

These attitudes clearly blurred the vision of Mondale and the others about Lance, or at least about the way he was perceived outside their closed little circle. The man after all had been acquitted of the charges against him, and he had resurrected himself to the degree that he had become Georgia Democratic chairman.

"I don't think anybody was, is, unrealistic about public attitudes [about the Carter administration]," Berman said. But, he added, Mondale and his chief aides had "a great deal of affection" for Carter for the generous and open manner in which he dealt with his Vice President.

They all had been close to another Minnesotan, Hubert Humphrey, when he was Vice President under Lyndon Johnson, and they knew all the horror stories about the indignities inflicted on Humphrey. On the few occasions when Carter staff people tried to crowd the Mondale staffers, Berman said, Mondale went right to Carter and the President stopped the intrusions. Mondale appreciated that, and so "the Carter connection" that was seen by others to be a political kiss of death was not enough to cause Mondale to turn his back on somebody like Lance.

"Were we blinded? Oh, we were blinded," Berman said later, "but I don't think you would hold it against Bert that he too was part of that whole thing we were all part of. . . . He was a hell of a nice guy. And he was for us."

Although the principals also said then and later that the decisions on Ferraro, Manatt and Lance were not parts of a neatly tied "package" deal, it was demonstrably true that the factors determining the personnel decisions were so inexorably linked as to make them all but inevitable once Mondale decided on Ferraro. That choice triggered the "southern strategy," which meant that Manatt had to go, and once the strategists talked "going South," the only name seriously considered was the loyal and, they all believed, politically influential and effective Lance.

Even as Mondale was getting down to the final cut on the vice-presidential selection, he set in motion the "southern strategy." On the Monday a week before the convention was to open, he dispatched Johnson to Atlanta for an unpublicized meeting with Lance at the airport. In that meeting, Johnson broached the notion to him of replacing Manatt.

According to Lance, in advance of this meeting he had told Mondale, Johnson and Beckel "that they ought not to make any move about trying to replace Manatt, if that in fact was what they were going to do, until after the election. That politically there was no upside to it at all. It was all downside. That Manatt was in place, and for whatever reason they may have been unhappy with him, which I never did really understand or know, that it just didn't make any sense. That there just wasn't anything to be gained by it."

Again in the airport meeting with Johnson, Lance said, "I made it very clear that I thought it was a mistake to do anything, certainly during the convention week," and at least not "until Mondale was nominated in actuality."

But by this time, he said, Johnson was firm on Manatt's departure. "Johnson told me it didn't make any difference what I did or didn't do, that they were going to make a change."

Lance said he also warned Johnson about what he called "my negatives" and that, if they still wanted to go forward, it would be necessary to "do the outreach efforts" to make it work—that is, touch base with any of those other Democrats who might be expected to oppose his appointment or possibly try to scuttle it.

As Lance recalled the conversation later, Johnson asked him how he felt about the proposition "on a scale of one to ten."

"About a six and a half," Lance told him.

"Well," Johnson said, "I'm disappointed in that. I was hoping it would be closer to a nine and a half."

Lance said later that Johnson did not tell him who Mondale had selected or was leaning toward selecting for Vice President, and he intentionally did not ask because he wanted true deniability against press inquiries. At the same time, however, he said, he understood from the very fact that he was being approached to be party chairman that it was likely Mondale was not going to choose a southerner—Lloyd Bentsen had been Lance's preference—as his running mate. He told Johnson as much but added that if the choice was going to be a woman, "then once more you need to think the whole thing through."

Johnson then asked him, Lance recalled, what did he think of the choice of either Dianne Feinstein or Geraldine Ferraro?

"I'll tell you honestly," he told Johnson. "I think if you pick Dianne you'll lose by thirty points and if you pick Geraldine you'll lose by twenty."

He didn't hold that view, Lance told us, "because they were women. It was just the fact that there was no balancing in the process, and the elected officials in the South were going to run from that sort of ticket."

Over the next day or so, Lance said, he talked to Mondale by phone, reiterating his cautions. He talked to no one else about his prospective appointment, he insisted, by direction of the Mondale campaign. And as far as he knew, he said, neither did Mondale nor any of the few in the inner circle who knew about the idea. Ironically, here was the candidate tagged as the tool of the special interests who wouldn't go to the bathroom without asking their permission, and he never even sounded out his strongest allies—not even Lane Kirkland, his Geppetto to hear Mondale's critics talk—about the critical move.

By Wednesday night, when Geraldine Ferraro was flying to North Oaks from San Francisco to meet the Mondales and prepare for the announcement of her selection the next morning, Lance had agreed to take over as national party chairman. And early the next afternoon, shortly after the press conference with Ferraro at the state capitol in St. Paul, Mondale called an unsuspecting Manatt and broke the news.

The call came, Manatt told us later in his precise way, at 2:20 PM Pacific Daylight Time. He had just watched the Ferraro announcement on television, and for openers he congratulated Mondale on his choice. Toward the end of a conversation of "eight or ten minutes," Manatt recalled, Mondale informed him that because of that choice "we have to look South for a party chairman."

"Well, gee, obviously I'm surprised," Manatt said he replied, "and I just need to simply know who it is we're talking about."

Mondale did not tell him, Manatt said, nor did he himself say, as others reported later, that he would step aside for "anybody but Lance." Mondale did inform him, Manatt said, that he wanted him to take on a new assignment. It turned out to be a proposal that he become head of a coordinated Democratic fund-raising campaign committee pulling together the resources of the House and Senate campaign committees and the Democratic gubernatorial candidates as well as the DNC. Manatt had always been an excellent fund-raiser, and apparently the Mondale inner circle saw nothing wrong with taking the best of Manatt and throwing out the rest. Mondale said he would send Mike Berman, his campaign treasurer and chief money man, to San Francisco to work out the details.

Others told us, however, that Manatt dug in his heels from the start, proposing to Mondale that some way be worked out enabling him to stay on in a recognizable party leadership position. Mondale, these other sources said, felt no malice toward Manatt and was willing to work out something that would provide him a graceful exit from the party chairmanship. But Mondale didn't calculate Manatt's determination not to be bounced at his own convention in his own state.

The Mondale campaign did not seem to have an inkling of the "firestorm"—Mondale's own description later—it was about to ignite. One of us had taken a red-eye flight from San Francisco to St. Paul on Wednesday night to cover the Ferraro announcement and the next afternoon flew back to San Francisco on the same plane with Beckel. He had promised to come back and talk once we were airborne—something he ordinarily would want to do, because his fear of flying exceeds even Erica Jong's. But he was so exhausted, he explained later, that he slept all the way to San Francisco. We stopped at the airport there and had a drink, but he said nothing about Manatt or Lance, and we didn't ask. Surely Mondale wouldn't dump Manatt in San Francisco before the convention had even started. And Lance? Don't be ridiculous.

On Friday morning, Manatt met with Berman to see what could be worked out concerning the general-campaign fund-raising effort. Manatt asked Berman again "who it was going to be," he recalled, "and he wasn't in a position to say." They had a second meeting late in the afternoon, according to Manatt, at which time Berman broke the news to him that his successor was going to be Lance. But again, Manatt said, Berman was not able to elaborate.

With this humiliation now inflicted upon him, Manatt went off to the dinner party in his honor at Ann Getty's with what the tabloids always call the giants of journalism. When it came to loving publicity, Chuck Manatt never took a back seat to anybody, and he proceeded to put up a good front. But even before the party had begun, word was reaching San Francisco that the Atlanta *Constitution* and the Los Angeles *Times* were coming out with the Lance-for-Manatt story. As it trickled in to the guests, the swank little dinner party was soon buzzing with nothing but questions: Why Manatt? Why now? Why Lance? And, most important, what could Mondale have been thinking of to spring such a piece of political insanity?

While Manatt talked with Katharine Graham of the Washington *Post* at their table, some of the Democratic Party's most generous contributors sitting at about a dozen other tables expressed their incredulity, and their anger, at Mondale bouncing one of their own so unceremoniously—and for Bert Lance of all people.

After one of them complained bitterly and profanely at some length, we asked:

"You sound like you have a personal stake in this."

"I've raised $185,000 for Fritz Mondale this year," he said.

Chuck Manatt, if the truth be known, was not a great favorite in the party, because of his Rotarian ways. But Fritz Mondale in a single blow had made a political martyr of him, and suddenly the whole Democratic world in San Francisco seemed to be coming to his defense.

That Friday night, Manatt said afterward, was for him "an evening of agony and ecstasy." He admitted he was "punchy" from the developments of the last two days, but he fielded questions from those reporters who knew what was happening and took some phone calls from allies like Walter Shorenstein, a major San Francisco contributor, during the evening. Manatt insisted later that the forces that began rallying to his side—contributors, labor leaders and members of the DNC's Business Council—were self-starters.

"Don't for a minute think I orchestrated what happened," he said. "I didn't really have to." But Mondale insiders were convinced that Manatt himself had already begun to shake the bushes.

"I think he clearly started a backfire," Beckel said later, "and I don't blame him. I don't think he started a backfire with the intention of being chairman again, I don't think he thought he was going to do that. But he and his people [on the committee], all of their situations were jeopardized by it."

At any rate, Beckel began to feel the heat almost at once. When Lance arrived in San Francisco that Friday night, he went to Beckel's suite at the Meridien Hotel, and the two of them went over a list of party leaders who would have to be called in advance of the expected Saturday announcement of Lance's appointment. But already Beckel's political instincts, inexplicably anesthetized during the process of settling on Lance, were picking up bad vibes.

Suddenly there was a knock on Beckel's door. He stepped outside and into a buzz saw. John Perkins, the AFL/CIO's political director, proceeded to read Beckel the riot act. The party didn't need another fight going into the convention, and why did Manatt have to get the ax in his own state? Reports that Manatt was on his way out had been in the press for months, with no groundswell of protest. But now, in this place, all hell was breaking loose on his behalf.

"I got decidedly worried," Beckel said. "My phone kept ringing and I had my guys out talking to people." They came back with an avalanche of complaints and second-guessing from the hotel lobbies, parties and a fund-raising boat ride. "You could tell when the conventional wisdom started to take over. . . . It kind of settled on, 'How could you guys be so dumb to do it in this guy's backyard?' "

Beckel phoned Johnson, who was now at Lake Tahoe, where Mondale was in a holding pattern before coming into the convention city to be nominated. He told Johnson a bad political situation had erupted and he doubted whether they had the votes to put Lance over.

"Don't you think you're overreacting on this a little bit?" he recalled Johnson saying.

Beckel said no. "This is just the wrong mix," he said. "The chemistry is bad."

Beckel held a conference with the assembled Mondale campaign staffers to check out his instincts, and they all agreed with him. The consensus was that, yes, it was serious, but it would be worse if at this juncture Mondale changed his mind and backed off.

On Friday night, though, there didn't seem to be much danger of that happening. In Tahoe, Mondale and Johnson didn't seem to understand what all the fuss was about. Shortly after midnight, one of us encountered Mondale's deputy press secretary, Dayton Duncan, in the lobby of the Meridien, the Mondale headquarters hotel. He had just come in from Tahoe, and when we asked him about the big flap, he registered surprise. It was no big deal, he said. It would all blow over in a day or two. But after he had spent several hours in San Francisco, he changed his mind.

"It happened about like I thought it would happen," Lance

said later, recalling that he had warned Mondale against removing Manatt before the convention. Manatt was not going quietly, and that was the fly in the ointment. But it was questionable whether the party would swallow Lance in any event.

In all this, Chuck Manatt was coming out a hero. And there was no denying that he was being treated shabbily. Even Lance said so. "It was something that shouldn't have been done to him," he told us later. "He was deserving of better than that."

At the same time, however, Manatt had been around long enough to understand not only that a party nominee had the right to pick his own chairman but that the last thing Mondale needed was a divisive fight over what essentially was a backwater political post in a presidential election year. It didn't seem to bother Manatt a bit to know he wasn't wanted. And apparently it didn't occur to him simply to step aside in the interest of protecting the nominee.

Both Beckel and Lance went to bed that night knowing Saturday would be no day at the beach. At 2:30 AM Beckel set his alarm for five o'clock and turned in. He got up at five and phoned Johnson again. The Lance-for-Manatt swap was just not going to go down, he said. Beckel called Lance and told him to hold off on his calls, and nobody had to draw Lance a picture to explain what that meant.

In Tahoe, Mondale at first didn't comprehend the furor. "I was astonished by the public reaction," he told us. But he valued Lance's loyalty highly, and so when Johnson told him of Beckel's warnings from San Francisco, Mondale said, as Johnson recalled:

"That doesn't bother me. I'm willing to make that fight."

Early Saturday morning, Mondale called Lance and asked him to come over to Tahoe. It was decided that Manatt's ouster would stick, but what about Lance? He had egg on his face, and Mondale still felt that debt to him. Something else would have to be worked out. What had started out as a bold move that would demonstrate that Fritz Mondale was in charge had now turned instead into a classic demonstration of bad political judgment. And the debacle was not yet over.

At a tense meeting at Tahoe at which Mondale and the Lance family agonized over what was to be done—amid desperate phone conversations between Beckel and Johnson—a patchwork solution finally was dreamed up. Beckel announced in a press conference that Manatt was out but that Lance's role was still being defined, which was true enough. Mondale was solicitous of Lance's feelings and those of his family. At one point he asked Lance's son, Beverly, what he thought, and the young man gave the presumptive Democratic presidential nominee an earful about how shabbily his father was being treated.

Lance was plainly unhappy but said he would do whatever Mondale wanted. The reason, he told us later, was that had he stormed out in a huff at that point, in his view the fiasco would have cost Mondale the nomination.

"I didn't want to do that," he said. "I didn't want to be responsible for that. I think if I had walked away and said in effect, 'This whole campaign is the super-wimp of all times,' then I don't think he would have been the nominee. I felt he was still vulnerable."

Whether that was so or not, Lance once again played the good soldier for Mondale—not for his aides, whom Lance plainly felt had hosed him. He agreed to be named general chairman of the Mondale campaign—not of the Democratic National Committee—with nebulous duties. But, he said later, he knew the appointment was mere window dressing until such time as he could be dumped out of the heavy spotlight of publicity that now shone down on him. Mondale announced Lance's new title at a press conference in Tahoe, with Lance at his side.

The fire, however, was far from out. Back in San Francisco, the Democratic state chairmen met, and Dick Moe, Mondale's former chief of staff, was deputized to face them.

"They gave me unshirted hell," he recalled. "They thought it was the dumbest thing. They were right."

The press was excluded from the meeting, but Matt Flynn, the Wisconsin state chairman, told us before he went in:

"They say Lance has never been convicted. We need a chairman who's never been indicted."

Mondale's strategists were warning him at the same time that the fiasco could cost him delegates, and just possibly the nomination. Tom Donilon called Tahoe from San Francisco and told him he feared his delegate totals were "being imperiled by this thing."

One Mondale delegate, Dick Koster from Panama, who had been credited by some as the one who put Mondale over the top at 11:59 on the morning of June 6, was particularly outraged, and he declared himself unpledged. In finally giving Mondale his vote and bringing other Democratic delegates from Panama into the Mondale camp with him, he said, he had elicited Mondale's promise that he would make no change in the party leadership without consultation. Now Mondale had welshed on that pledge.

"There is only one person pleased by this," Koster said, "and that's Bert Lance. It's a hell of a price to pay to do that. This puts the monkey of the Carter administration back on Mondale's back, after Mondale had some success distancing himself from that fiasco. It's so stupid. Everybody was so high on the Ferraro appointment, and then comes this."

Lane Kirkland, who had told Mondale he would support whatever choice he made on the vice-presidential nomination, was not so quiescent on this one. He called Mondale two or three times to dissuade him after the word was out, but without success. Mondale told him Lance could be a great help to him in the South and that, Kirkland recalled, "he didn't think he could put together the electoral votes without some southern states."

Kirkland told us later: "I argued strenuously against it. We needed that like a hole in the head."

Manatt meanwhile was waltzing around San Francisco still playing the belle of the ball. While his staff was, in Berman's words, "out waging war," Manatt attended a day of meetings with supporters, some cocktail receptions and the second of Ann Getty's swish dinner parties.

By Sunday morning, the day before the convention was to open, the Manatt-Lance flap was consuming all political talk in San Francisco. Lance himself, and Representative Tony Coelho of California, chairman of the Democratic Congressional Campaign Committee, moved in forcefully to try to resolve the impasse. One thing was dead certain, at least in Chuck Manatt's mind. He would not be moved.

"I always had the same mission," he said later, "I never changed. I signed on, moved my family back East, tried to get the party in shape in a four-year engagement. . . . It's not accurate for anyone to say that I ever said they didn't have the right to pick their chairman." But he was mightily embarrassed by the treatment he had received, and hundreds of Democrats he had involved in the convention were coming to San Francisco, and he said he was concerned their reaction would damage the convention.

Coelho's suite at the Fairmont Hotel became the bunker at which the last chapter of the fiasco was played out. John White, a former Democratic national chairman and friend of both Lance and Manatt, got them together, and they were joined in time by Beckel and Marty Franks of the Congressional Campaign Committee. Beckel by this time was at the end of his rope. He still had to deal with Gary Hart and Jesse Jackson on other convention matters and had wasted enough time trying to extricate the Mondale campaign from its self-inflicted dilemma. He had already called Johnson and urged him to fly over from Tahoe.

"Let's get this thing behind us," he told Johnson.

The previous day, Mondale had made Lance the head of a search committee to find a new national chairman, and it was pretty clear he didn't have to look very far. Chuck Manatt was ready and willing, and he offered the easiest—if most embarrassing—out.

When Johnson arrived, there ensued several hours of uncomfortable and at times tense negotiations, with Manatt remaining unshakable. Now that Lance was not going to be his successor, he saw an opening and moved quickly into it.

"I never backed off," he told us later. "Once Bert was no longer going to be in the assignment"—that's the way Chuck Manatt talks—"I was just consistent in my position wanting to stay on. I just told Bert and John that whatever had happened had happened, but I felt I just wanted to continue on with the assignment irrespective of what had happened."

You would have thought the surrender at Appomattox was being re-enacted in Coelho's suite, with appropriate security.

"The minute anybody came into the room, he was quarantined," Manatt recalled. And Lance said: "I ended up being held hostage all day."

The negotiators moved in and out of the living room into the adjoining bedroom in twos and threes, trying to come up with something that would satisfy everybody. Phone calls were made back and forth between Mondale and John Reilly in Tahoe and Johnson and Beckel in Coelho's suite. Trays of cheeseburgers were brought in but went untouched as the powers of the Democratic Party sought to work out this earth-shaking matter. The Mondale side wanted to make sure it had control of how the national committee's money was spent, and so it was finally agreed that Berman would move in as executive director—and Manatt would stay on as chairman.

Berman was elsewhere at the time, but he was summoned. When he arrived, Johnson motioned him into the bedroom, along with Beckel and Lance. Johnson explained what had been worked out.

"Is this what Mondale wants?" Berman asked, wondering how he had been sandbagged.

"Yes," Johnson said.

"And so," the portly Berman told us later, "we then went out and they all started working on a statement—and I ate three cheeseburgers."

Johnson, Manatt and Lance broke the news to the press. As for the harried Beckel, "I went out and went to a gin mill," he said.

Thus was the stage set for what Mondale had hoped would be a convention that could catapult him to within shouting distance of Ronald Reagan. Instead, he came into San Francisco bloodied by his own poor political judgment and—now—evidence that he was a pushover to boot. He couldn't even depose the party chairman. And in the failed effort, he had violated a cardinal rule of politics: Never step on your own good story. His selection of Geraldine Ferraro to be his running mate had electrified the party and the country, but almost at once he had short-circuited the charge with the Lance-for-Manatt debacle.

Mondale had broken new political ground in choosing a woman to join him on the Democratic ticket. But in another sense he had dug himself into a deep hole by then falling back onto the dictates of old mossback politics. He had picked a woman to run for Vice President, which would not be popular in the South, and so he felt he had to select a southerner to be his national party chairman, even if it meant creating resentment and uproar on the eve of the convention.

The notion that the identity of the national chairman would make any difference in how the South voted in the general election was laughable on its face. There was ample conjecture as it was on the question of whether the vice-presidential nominee won any significant number of votes, be the choice male or female.

At a time Mondale had the unchallenged attention of the American electorate as at no previous time in this election year, he was wasting it on a petty game of musical chairs.

Mondale himself had the last word on the whole affair.

"It was my mistake," he told us after the election. "He [Lance] warned me at the time. I said, 'No, Bert, I think everything's fine.' "

Many in and out of the Mondale campaign saw other culprits, however. They blamed "the little white boys," the tight band of white, male advisers who counseled Mondale and played their cards close to the vest.

Jim Johnson was both the leader and epitome of the little white boys—a comfortably well-off forty-year-old bachelor who, one campaign staffer said, "went home every night and turned on his three television sets to the seven o'clock news"—implying he was out of touch with what average Americans thought and felt. In addition, this staffer said, "Jim had Mondale all to himself for twenty years" and was neither accustomed nor willing to cut others into the decision-making. He had an office at the campaign headquarters but seldom used it, preferring to work out of his own secluded office at the Mondale law firm. Johnson, the subordinate said, "assembled a bunch of very talented people and then put them into cubby holes" where they were supposed to tend to their own knitting only.

One other member of the hierarchy, Beckel, acknowledged openly that he had agreed that Lance was a good choice, out of admiration for the man, having worked closely with him on political problems. Others of the little white boys, however, were against the selection from the start, including John Reilly and Dick Leone, Johnson's old college buddy from Princeton. But the problem, at the core, was that the Mondale campaign was a closed shop—closed even to its strongest supporters, individuals like Lane Kirkland and Mike Dukakis.

Johnson insisted after the election that he had discussed the Lance idea "fairly widely" and that while "a couple said they thought it was a bad idea, several others thought it was a good idea." If so, though, that was a mighty short line that stood up behind the forthright Beckel to be counted.

But the Manatt-Lance affair was now behind the Democrats, and they were determined to have a productive convention. The history of such events was that the nominee enjoyed a significant boost in the polls from his convention, and Mondale certainly needed one. And for all the misfortunes that had come his way en route to San Francisco, he had reason to hope this convention might yet be a tonic. He did, after all, have the delegates in hand he needed to be nominated, and a chance that the two contending Democrats remaining in the race against him—Gary Hart and Jesse Jackson—would by nominating time fall into line behind him.

To Hart, the whole hassle over the party chairmanship was, in his words, "a tempest in a teapot" that may have said something about Mondale's management abilities but was not, he contended later, "the kind of ideological fight that could blow the convention open." Although there were some Mondale delegates like Koster who were going over the side because of Lance, most were holding—while simultaneously holding their noses.

Some of Hart's advisers, including Frank Mankiewicz and Pat Caddell, however, saw the fiasco as a possible wedge, along with the delegate-committee issue and the possibility of challenging the "tainted" delegates. But Hart himself, while not throwing in the towel, clearly had his eye on the road ahead—to 1988 and a second bid for the Democratic nomination. He described himself later to us as having been on a "tightrope" dealing with a "tough, tricky situation."

"On the one hand I had to keep open the possibility with our own people that I could win, and [on the other] not be a divisive figure," he said.

The closest he came to criticizing Mondale directly from the end of the primaries to the convention, Hart said, was in raising the issue of "electability." And even in that argument, he noted, he never said that Mondale couldn't be elected; rather, that he himself had a better chance to beat Reagan.

He also hung in, he said, because Jesse Jackson remained in the race as a "wild card" who might create some dynamic that would upset what seemed to many the inevitable nomination of Mondale. And, finally, there was always the possibility Mondale might screw up in a more serious way than he had yet done—a possibility certainly not diminished by the manner in which he had botched the Manatt-Lance affair.

Concerning the "tainted" delegates, Mankiewicz later pointed out a practical reason it would have been difficult, and probably very divisive, for Hart to have challenged them as a way of denying Mondale his majority.

"The problem was that the delegates themselves were not tainted," Mankiewicz noted. "It was the method of their election that was tainted, and they didn't know that. And unfortunately, to make a challenge at the convention or before the credentials committee . . . you have to challenge individual delegates. You can't say, 'There were thirty-eight [tainted] delegates in New York, so give me thirty-eight.' It isn't just numbers. What it comes down to is, 'Take this delegate out and put somebody else in.' And the delegates who had been elected by those illegal committees were, unfortunately, pretty goddamned good people. I mean, it would have meant challenging Carol Bellamy, Bobby Abrams, Mario Cuomo [in New York]. Major figures in the party were the tainted delegates, in New York, Pennsylvania, Ohio and elsewhere. That was the problem, and how would that look?"

And so, Mankiewicz said of Hart, "he went down lookin'."

Hart, in fact, had already formally abandoned any fight on tainted delegates before the convention opened. In a letter to Manatt, Hart wrote that while such a challenge could "significantly" alter the delegate totals, "yet it would surely, whether successful or not, splinter Democrats at this critical juncture. Therefore, for the good of our party and our chances this fall, my campaign will make no challenge before the committee or at the convention to these delegates."

Whether Hart would have been so ready to give up this fight had the matter of the "stolen records" in Philadelphia been known, and had it hurt Mondale in the subsequent primaries, was irrelevant. He didn't know and neither did the voters, and Mondale was coming into the convention with the delegates he needed for the nomination. In any event, in choosing not to make a no-holds-barred effort to block Mondale, Hart removed the last possible obstacle to keeping the party from going down the same old New Deal road. To have made that effort, however, would have jeopardized his own political future, and that he clearly was unwilling to do.

Pudge Henkel, Hart's campaign manager and close friend, said later that the idea of making a fight for delegates on the issue that some 600 of Mondale's were tainted, or on some other grounds, was very tantalizing, because the Hart campaign believed Mondale was only seventy or seventy-five delegates over the number he needed for nomination.

Tom Donilon's acknowledgment later that Mondale "only had a hundred-delegate margin over what we needed" and that his campaign feared entering "the Land of the Second Ballot" indicated that the Hart campaign's estimate was not far off.

Nevertheless, a heavy debt was hanging over the Hart campaign, and conversations had already begun with the Mondale campaign on joint debt reduction, as well as the vice presidency. And above all, Henkel said, there was 1988.

"Because we had to start thinking in terms of 1988 at that point realistically," he said, "and not 1984, we didn't want Gary or the campaign to do anything which could be characterized as Gary in the role of a spoiler, ruining Mondale's nomination for him."

And in that same regard, Henkel said Hart did not want "to so pollute the environment, particularly the relationship between the Mondale campaign and our own, so our role in the convention would become insignificant." As Hart's subsequent convention speech clearly indicated, while Mankiewicz may have been right in observing that his candidate "went down lookin'," he did not intend 1984 to be his last time at bat.

Jackson was another matter. He was playing to a much narrower constituency, and he always stepped up swinging for the fences. The knowledge of that fact worried Mondale and Company right to the last. They already had ample evidence of Jackson's focus in the long battle of the primaries and later in the party's platform, rules and credentials committee hearings in Washington. Jackson had used the hearings as a sounding board for his complaints about the way the primaries had been run, and as a warning shot across Mondale's bow and the party's that unless he received satisfaction, they would have problems with him. There was always that nebulous warning, but it was almost always enough to assure that he was treated like a porcupine being picked up by a zookeeper.

The convention opened, however, with only a relatively few potential land mines in Mondale's way. His operatives had navigated a safe course through those earlier committee deliberations in Washington, to the point where all credentials challenges were dropped and only five minority reports were filed, compared to thirty-three at the 1980 Democratic convention. At the outset of the drafting of the platform, when the Hart and Jackson forces had attempted to work their will, the Mondale operatives, holding eight votes on the committee to a combined seven for Hart and Jackson, gave the opposition a simple lesson in basic arithmetic.

"They came in on their high horse," said Paul Tully, chief of the Mondale platform team. "They were sparring, getting the lay of the land. Well, they got the lay of the land. I got eight, and they got seven."

Once that class was out, however, all sides settled down to a more accommodating mood, though Jackson as always continued his confrontational rhetoric.

In San Francisco, one of the five minority planks, supported by Hart, was finally accepted by Mondale to avoid the embarrassment of a possible defeat on the convention floor. It put the party on record against use of unilateral military involvement abroad where American interests and objectives were not clear, meaning the Persian Gulf, where Hart observed the British and French were more dependent on its oil than was the United States.

The other four minority reports were all Jackson's. The one with the highest priority for Jackson, on affirmative action, was compromised by strengthening the supportive language and dropping a specific reference to the party "rejecting quotas," a particular sore point with Jackson. That deal was struck, however, only after a heated telephone conversation between Mondale and Jackson.

"Ronald Reagan is going to enjoy this day," said Mondale, often criticized through 1984 for not standing up to the demanding Jackson, according to an insider present.

The Mondale campaign's designated hitter in dealing with Jackson, Beckel, was subjected to Jackson's political gamesmanship up to the very end. On the night before Jackson was to address the convention, Beckel, worried about what Jackson was going to say, told him:

"You've really got to give a great speech. I've got a lot invested in you."

Jackson replied:

"That's when you'll know, Beckel, whether you're a chimp, a champ or a chump. You'll know when I give my speech."

Mondale did not buckle, however, on three other Jackson pro-

posals the prospective nominee felt were essential to block. All three were soundly defeated: abolition of the runoff primary and dual voter registration, a reduction in defense spending and a call for no first use of nuclear weapons.

Jackson and Hart also were very unhappy about the rules under which the 1984 nomination fight had been waged. But by this time the Mondale forces had already thrown them a bone by agreeing to creation after the election of a "Fairness Commission" that would consider various reforms the two defeated candidates wanted.

Jackson was seeking an end to all state caucuses and the choosing of unpledged delegates. Hart wanted the percentage of unpledged "super-delegates" cut from the 14.5 percent allocated in 1984 to 5 percent, and he urged that none be selected in any state until most of the pledged delegates in that state had been picked—a way to prevent a candidate from turning the super-delegate selection into "the first primary," the way Mondale had effectively done. Hart also wanted later filing deadlines for candidate slates, and he proposed that thresholds to qualify for delegates in a primary or caucus be made optional. If they were used, he said, the threshold should not be higher than 15 percent, compared to the 20 percent required in 1984.

In accepting the "Fairness Commission," Mondale wasn't giving up anything. The party always had the power to rewrite its rules. And besides, nothing would be considered until after the election. The main thing was to clear the decks for the convention.

The voting rights matters remained central, however, to Jackson's complaint that the electoral process was rigged against black candidates, and the floor debate on the issue provided the most heated moments of the convention. When Mayor Andy Young, one of the leaders of the major civil-rights battles in the South in the 1960s and now a Mondale ally, argued that the majority plank language on voting rights already protected minority voting rights, he was booed by some black delegates.

"Shame on you!" came cries from the floor toward a man who had marched at the side of Martin Luther King, Jr., and had been in some of the bloodiest trenches of the civil-rights fight. And that was among the milder epithets.

The next day, at a meeting of the convention's black caucus, Coretta Scott King, widow of the slain civil-rights leader, admonished those delegates who had booed Young.

"Those of you who wronged Andy Young need to say, 'I'm sorry,' " she said. But all she got for her troubles were more boos countering the cheers of other blacks.

Jackson finally intervened with an emotional scolding of the black delegates who booed Young and Mrs. King.

"When I think about the roads I've walked with Andy," he said, "and the leadership of Mrs. King—her home bombed, her husband assassinated, her children raised by a widow—she deserved to be heard," he said. He went on:

"I know the reason so many of you are in a foul mood. It doesn't have anything to do with what Andy did or Mrs. King did. . . . You're all mad because you came out here and the women got the Vice President and the South got Bert Lance . . . and Manatt got the DNC and you ain't got nothing. You all are upset because you can't get no respect."

Indeed, in his pre-nomination negotiations with Beckel, Jackson repeatedly argued that "we gotta get something" that black delegates could take home to demonstrate that their political efforts had borne some fruit. But, the Mondale operatives said, they could never seem to satisfy Jackson and he was elusive on what that "something" he wanted was.

At the black caucus meeting, Jackson made an impassioned plea to its members to cast a vote for him on the first ballot.

"How are you going to explain it to your grandchildren," Jackson inquired, "if they ask, 'When the roll was called, where were you?' "[41]

Later, when Mondale and Ferraro appeared before the same group, chants of "Jess-ee! Jess-ee!" for a time prevented their speaking.

By this time, however, the Mondale forces—with Andy Young, Dick Arrington and other major black figures playing a pivotal role—had their troops in line, and Jackson's appeal posed no serious threat to Mondale's first-ballot nomination. Neither did a brief effort to have members of the Hispanic caucus abstain on the first ballot as pressure on Mondale to oppose passage of the Simpson-Mazzoli immigration bill, regarded as heavily discriminatory against Hispanics. In that case too, allies of Mondale within the caucus were able to hold the line.

41. Jackson finally got 466.5 votes on the presidential roll call, far more than had been predicted for him.

All that remained now was a carefully orchestrated effort to show the American voters, watching on television, that the Democratic Party was neither divided nor moribund. In the attempt, the party's most illustrious political stars were trotted out, and they delivered.

Governor Mario Cuomo of New York came through with a brilliant keynote speech that played on all the familiar Democratic heartstrings going back to the early days of the New Deal.

Ridiculing Reagan's repeated references to America as "a shining city on a hill, Cuomo said "this nation is more *A Tale of Two Cities*." Beyond the view "the President sees from the portico of the White House and the veranda of his ranch," the governor said, "there are people who sleep in the city's streets, in the gutter, where the glitter doesn't show." And, as if addressing Reagan directly, he went on:

"Maybe, Mr. President, if you asked a woman who'd been denied the help she needs to feed her children because you say we need the money to give a tax break to a millionaire or to build a missile we can't even afford to use—maybe then you'd understand."

Cuomo adapted his successful theme describing his own constituents as "the family of New York" to talk of "the family of America," and said:

"The Republicans believe the wagon train will not make it to the frontier unless some of our old, some of our young and some of our weak are left behind by the side of the trail. . . . We Democrats believe that we can make it all the way with the whole family intact."

What the Democrats had to do, he said, was "get the American public to look past the glitter, beyond the showmanship" of Reagan and his image-shapers and focus on the real America of inequities and social problems.

The speech clearly thrilled the assembled party activists, but it was another question how it played out in the country, in the living rooms of the greatly expanded middle class to whom the old New Deal rhetoric had lost its appeal, and where Reagan's "feel-good" ads and speeches were effective soothing syrup.

Nevertheless, Cuomo's ringing oratory was the right tonic for the immediate audience at hand, and the delegates left the hall feeling better than most of them thought they had any right to expect after the fiasco of the previous weekend.

Subsequent speeches by Hart and especially Jackson added to the upbeat atmosphere. Hart pledged his "every waking hour and every ounce of energy" to the defeat of Reagan—but not before he unmistakably served notice that he had not given up his presidential ambitions.

"This is one Hart you will not leave in San Francisco," he said on opening. Listeners were free to assume that he meant he would march with the party against Reagan, but they were free as well to take the remark as his own marching orders for another try in 1988. Almost as if he, not Mondale, were the nominee, Hart said:

"I see an America too young to quit, too courageous to turn back, with a passion for justice and a program for opportunity; an America with unmet dreams that will not die. Tonight the torch of idealism is lit in thousands of towns and tens of thousands of lives, among the young in spirit and the young in age. It will not go out. It will continue to burn. And because of that fire of commitment and hope, we will change the world. . . . So we will never give up . . . If not now, someday, we must prevail. If not now, someday, we will prevail."

But it was Jackson who really ignited the convention. With electrifying eloquence and passion, he sounded all the familiar demands for social justice that had marked his campaign oratory. But then, to the surprise of the assembled delegates and the immense relief of the Mondale forces, Jackson made a direct apology to American Jews for his earlier transgressions.

"If in my low moments, in word, deed or attitude, through some error of temper, taste or tone," he said, "I have caused anyone discomfort, created pain or revived someone's fears, that was not my truest self. If there were occasions when my grape turned into a raisin and my joy bell lost its resonance, please forgive me. Charge it to my head and not to my heart. . . . I am not a perfect servant. I am a public servant, doing my best against the odds as I develop and serve. Be patient. God is not finished with me yet."

And as the crowd roared its approval, Jackson added:

"We are much too intelligent, much too bound by our Judeo-

Christian heritage, much too victimized by racism, sexism, militarism and anti-Semitism, much too threatened as historical scapegoats to go on divided from one another."

This presentation of a penitent Jackson preaching togetherness buoyed the delegates, perhaps more than the reality of the political situation warranted. But after all the turmoil, they could be forgiven excessive exhilaration and exuberance, as Jackson himself might have put it.

The emotional high continued the next night with the nomination of Geraldine Ferraro as the first woman to run on a national ticket. Her presence at the microphone in that historic capacity, more than what she said, sent a wave of emotionalism through the hall.

"By choosing a woman to run for our nation's second-highest office," she said, "you send a powerful signal to all Americans. There are no doors we cannot unlock. We will place no limit on achievement. If we can do this, we can do anything. Tonight we reclaim our dream. We're going to make the rules of American life work fairly for all Americans again."

Mondale, as expected, was nominated on the first ballot, with Hart and Jackson calling for Mondale's nomination by acclamation as he went over the top on the roll call of states. He appeared briefly before a cheering convention as the "1812 Overture" boomed out over the hall. And by the final night of the convention, the delegates were in a stomping, placard-pumping mood as he appeared before them to accept the party's greatest prize. A band played triumphantly, and a voice boomed out, exhorting the delegates to "Celebrate good times, come on!" Determined not to allow the Republicans to corner the patriotism market, American flags were distributed to the delegates, and the convention floor became a sea of Old Glorys waving to and fro.

Mondale was a beaming, happy warrior as he addressed a convention that almost miraculously had been resurrected from its disastrous beginnings. From the outset, he was bent on projecting himself as the antithesis of Roy Spence's description as the man "who dares to be cautious." He was going to tell it with the bark off, and let the chips fall where they might. He was far behind Reagan and he knew it, and to win he was going to have to take chances. The first and biggest one the delegates had already witnessed and acclaimed: the choice of a woman running mate.

"Tonight, we open a new door to the future," he said. "Mr. Reagan calls that 'tokenism.' We call it America."

The delegates cheered wildly. Now Mondale told them the party in nominating him had endorsed "a new realism"—about itself and the voters. And he proceeded to prove it. Of his unsuccessful reelection campaign at the side of Jimmy Carter, he said:

"In 1980, Ronald Reagan beat the pants off us. So tonight, I want to say something to those of you across our country who voted for Mr. Reagan—to Republicans, to independents, and, yes, to some Democrats: I heard you. And our party heard you. After we lost, we didn't tell the American people that they were wrong. Instead, we began asking you what our mistakes had been."

In the last four years, he said, he had traveled "what seemed like every acre of America" and had learned. To prove it, he said, "Look at our platform. There are no defense cuts that weaken our security; no business taxes that weaken our economy; no laundry lists that raid our Treasury. We are wiser, stronger and focused on the future. If Mr. Reagan wants to rerun the 1980 campaign, fine. Let them fight over the past. We're fighting for the American future—and that's why we're going to win."

The remarks clearly were an attempt to cut off at the pass an obvious Reagan strategy—to put Jimmy Carter on Mondale's back and keep him there all fall. But Mondale's words seemed to indicate something more: that he had learned that the old New Deal formula didn't work anymore, that it didn't appeal to enough Americans to win an election, and that the Democrats had better wise up to that fact. They still had their obligations to the downtrodden, to be sure, and they wouldn't run away from them. But first they had to win.

In a few more minutes, however, Fritz Mondale's determination to be the candidate of candor moved him to make a statement that in a flash conveyed to voters that he wasn't any different after all from the long line of New Deal Democrats from which he had so conspicuously descended. And in that flash of candor, his slim chances to upset Reagan very probably went down the drain.

"Here is the truth about the future," he began. "We are living on borrowed money and borrowed time. These deficits hike interest rates, clobber exports, stunt investment, kill jobs, undermine growth, cheat our kids and shrink our future. Whoever is inaugurated in January, the American people will pay Mr. Reagan's bills. The budget will be squeezed. Taxes will go up. And anyone who says they won't is not telling the truth."

Then the candidate of candor said flat out:

"I mean business. By the end of my first term, I will cut the deficit by two-thirds. Let's tell the truth. Mr. Reagan will raise taxes, and so will I. He won't tell you. I just did."

The statement did not cause much stir in the convention hall, but at the White House and wherever the Reagan strategists were watching and listening, the impact was electric.

Mondale went on:

"There's another difference. When he raises taxes, it won't be done fairly. He will sock it to average-income families again, and leave his rich friends alone. I won't. To the corporations and freeloaders who play the loopholes or pay no taxes, my message is: Your free ride is over.

"To the Congress, my message is: We must cut spending and pay as we go. If you don't hold the line, I will. That's what the veto is for.

"Now that's my plan to cut the deficit. Mr. Reagan is keeping his secret until after the election. That's not leadership; that's salesmanship. I challenge Mr. Reagan to put his plan on the table next to mine—and debate it with me on national television. Americans want the truth about the future—not after the election, but now."

At his home in Washington, Lee Atwater, the deputy manager of the Reagan campaign, was stretched out in front of a television set being worked over by a masseur when he heard Mondale's bolt of candor.

"I was just bone-tired," Atwater recalled, and he had had the masseur come in for the first and only time in his life. "I was half-asleep. The masseur suggested I not even watch TV. I was half-delirious and heard him say that. Coming from my region [the South] and my political background, I knew a tax increase is just outlandish. I never will forget. I thought I was dreaming. I thought I had literally fallen asleep and was dreaming. I sat up and asked my wife and the masseur, 'Did he really say what I thought he said?' "

The next morning, when the Atwaters were watching the news on television, Atwater said to his wife, Sally:

"Well, he's getting an A-plus for boldness, but he's going to get an F-minus in the end."

Paul Laxalt, the campaign chairman, vacationing with friends on Fire Island in New York, recalled: "I was incredulous that that was even being seriously considered, much less adopted."

Mondale's allies outside the circle of the "little white boys" were equally surprised as the Reagan folks, but not nearly so gleeful. The labor people were especially jolted, because they knew how their rank-and-file felt about more taxes. What they wanted to hear about was a jobs program or talk about attacking the deficit through full employment and economic growth, producing more taxpayers—which, ironically, was what Reagan pitched in the fall.

Kirkland told us later that he had never been consulted on the tax-increase decision. It required almost "a diplomatic mission" to break into the inner councils, he said. Had he been consulted on the acceptance speech, he said, he would have reminded Mondale that two Democratic state senators had been recalled in Michigan for voting for Democratic Governor James Blanchard's tax increase, and that Governor Dick Celeste in Ohio was also in hot water for raising taxes.

But the Mondale strategists who dreamed up the tax-boost gambit were not thinking about such cautions. Dick Leone, who had joined the inner circle after the New Jersey primary, had been a principal figure in another Democratic campaign in which the candidate successfully used candor on a tax-increase issue. When Democrat Brendan Byrne was elected governor of New Jersey in 1973, he ran on a no-income-tax pledge. But afterward he sought and won enactment of the state's first such tax. He plunged in the polls, but when he ran for reelection in 1977, he was counseled by his state treasurer, Leone, to deal boldly with the issue, telling the voters he did an unpopular thing because it was required. Byrne was reelected. Similarly now, Leone figured there was no sense ducking the issue. Mondale in fact had said in a speech in January that he would raise taxes to cope with the mushrooming budget, but few seemed to have recalled that bit of candor.

"Mondale expected Reagan would attack him on that," Leone

said later. "So the question was whether to make a virtue of candor, or weasel on it."

Besides, he said, polls indicated that the voters believed taxes would go up, and they knew Mondale was more in favor of social programs than Reagan was.

Once again, according to other insiders, there was hardly any discussion of the bold move, either among the staff or among outside allies.

"They didn't do the politics around it," one of those left in the dark said afterward, meaning the appropriate bases were never touched to get reaction or to pave the way. And making the declaration was one thing, this insider said, "but to make it so high profile" was just begging for the Republicans to shoot at it. Earlier Mondale had talked about cutting the deficit in half in his first term. Now he was saying he'd reduce it by two-thirds. Some of his political advisers were incredulous.

"What additional voters did he pick up there?" one asked in exasperation later.

But Mondale was determined to draw the line on the tax increase. Marty Kaplan said later that in writing the speech draft, Mondale went over and over the formulations with him because he wanted it to hit hard.

"He knew what he was getting into," Kaplan said. Convinced to the core that Reagan would have to raise taxes, he said, to Mondale "it became an issue of who was telling the truth."

After the election, Mondale told us that "perhaps the central domestic objective of a Mondale administration was to get the debt down, to get the interest rates down and to restore American exports. . . . I had to make it clear to Democrats, and then to the American people, that I not only believed that but was prepared to get it done."

Furthermore, he said, "I was convinced that the presidency was worthless without a mandate, and I still think it is, particularly if you have to do something tough. I wanted the public to elect me knowing they'd authorized certain things to be done that would permit me to get it done, because I would have the imprimatur of the American people, and the mandate I needed. So I decided to spell it out accurately and try to make not only a deep reduction in the deficit commitment tangible but also make an issue on fairness in taxes, so that people of middle and moderate income could see that they were being dealt with more fairly than Reagan would. So I did it the way I did it."

In so doing, in fact, Mondale did throw the Reagan strategists off balance for a time, for all their assurances later that Mondale's call for a tax increase was manna from heaven for them. But only for a time.

Still, the Democrats left San Francisco feeling remarkably good about themselves. Their convention, for all the early tumult, had indeed become a celebration of party unity—on the surface anyway—that few would have foretold only a few days earlier. Now it was the Republicans' turn as their convention in Dallas approached, and they would not have to search nearly so hard to find something to celebrate about.

18

Dallas: Winners and Losers

•

FOR THE REPUBLICANS, Walter Mondale's pronouncement at San Francisco that he planned to raise taxes was a gift from the gods.

"I was in ecstasy," Stu Spencer recalled. "The political graveyard is full of tax increasers."

Just as the experts had expected, the massive press attention given to the Democratic convention had reduced President Reagan's lead in the public-opinion polls. Indeed, one survey—a special Gallup poll done for *Newsweek* magazine immediately after adjournment at San Francisco—showed the race essentially even. And although few professionals in either camp accepted that finding at face value, there was reason to believe the contest had become closer, if only for the moment.

And Fritz Mondale had used the climactic moment of his convention for political self-immolation.

With the polls tightening, Spencer said, "that was a dramatic error. At the most public moment of his campaign, he came out with an issue that was very important to the American public, but he was on the other side of it. I just thought it was foolish."

The amazement and delight ran through the Reagan campaign, and strategist Bob Teeter quickly saw the political value to the President.

"All it did was reinforce the stereotype of Mondale," he recalled. "It was perfect. It did for us what we couldn't have done with advertising. . . . He just proved himself to be the classic, big-spending, liberal, New Deal, old-time Democrat."

If Mondale wanted to break out of the mold that he had been identified with for years, Teeter said, "what they should have said was, 'We're gonna reach a balanced budget by cutting government spending.' They really thought they were going to break the stereotype, increase his credibility. . . . All they did was reinforce what everybody already knew about him. That's the way Mondale's guys had solved economic problems for thirty years, and that's what we were trying to tell people."

The President himself, watching Mondale's acceptance speech on television at the White House, told us later he had kind of a "double reaction."

"The first reaction was that he stated this position and I thought that very definitely it was the wrong position, which was encouraging," Reagan said in an interview in the Oval Office after the election.

"But then the double reaction came . . . when he so flatly declared that I, too, would raise taxes, only I would lie about it . . . [that] I wouldn't say so. I felt that was something I was darn sure going to rebut."

And Reagan, like his most astute advisers, was convinced the Mondale initiative was poor politics.

"He hadn't read the public right," he said.

Stu Spencer put it more forcefully.

"This guy is either breaking new ground," he recalled thinking to himself, "or he's the dumbest bastard I've ever seen."

But for all of the satisfaction the Republican candidate and his strategists drew from the Mondale declaration, it clearly threw them off stride over the next three weeks. And although their awkwardness in handling the issue never threatened Reagan's primacy, that awkwardness did demonstrate chinks in Reagan's positions on issues that might be exploited if Mondale could press him closely enough.

As Teeter recognized, the tax issue was not a strong card for a liberal Democrat to play. Mondale would not simply be obliged to persuade the voters that Reagan indeed had "a secret plan" for raising taxes too. He would also have to make the case that Reagan would raise them as much as Mondale and that Mondale would use the increased revenue for deficit-reduction rather than more traditional Democratic spending.

This complication was not lost on many Democrats. At the National Governors' Association's annual meeting in Nashville a week after the convention, there was obvious unease among Democratic politicians. Governor Bill Clinton of Arkansas, a strong Mondale supporter, told us that Mondale needed to detail his plans for putting the additional revenue in a trust to be used only for deficit reduction. If he didn't do so, Clinton argued, the voters would believe the Democrats simply intended to spend the money on more social programs. Governor John Carlin of Kansas had a similar concern—that Mondale needed to make it clear he would not raise taxes more than Reagan.

Vice President George Bush, out of Washington for a non-partisan ceremony, recalled encountering a Democratic Senate candidate, who told him:

"Can you imagine how we felt when Mondale came out and said we were going to raise everybody's taxes?"

But Reagan's position was also awkward. He was confronting federal deficits of $200 billion a year as far as the eye could see. He was insisting on further huge increases in defense spending. If he took a rigid position against higher taxes, how would he ever reach that balanced budget he kept preaching about?

At the White House, a key adviser there told us, the suspicion was that Mondale was trying to lead Reagan into a trap.

"My reaction was, 'They're trying to snooker us into an absolute, categorical, never-never so they could hit us on Social Security,' " this adviser said, meaning that if the President were to take a completely uncompromising stand against any tax increases, the Democrats might argue he would certainly have to cut Social Security and Medicare spending. The move, he said, was "dumb."

Spencer agreed.

"We could see what Mondale politically was possibly trying to do," he said, "and that was walk us into a trap—Social Security and all those things. That's why we knew we had to have wiggle room . . . that was the fear."

Spencer felt that Reagan's hostility to taxes was so well established he would get credit for agonizing before he would ever raise taxes. The polling data suggested, he said, that "people expected Ronald Reagan to raise taxes but . . . they didn't want somebody to tell them that."

The core of the problem for the White House, however, was that Mondale had touched a nerve. There was a continuing debate within the administration and within the Republican Party between the ideologues of supply-side economics who opposed all tax increases and the pragmatists who wanted to leave that wiggle room.

"We were very confused on the tax issue there," Spencer recalled. "We didn't have a consensus . . ."

Moreover, Reagan himself was ambivalent. Although the pragmatists—Jim Baker being the most prominent—might be able to persuade Reagan of the necessity for an escape hatch, his own inclination would have been to take a hard line against taxes. As Stu Spencer put it:

"That's where his instincts were."

The result was a series of small missteps on the issue that in another campaign situation might have been far more serious.

"I guess it wasn't a crisis," Teeter said later. "But it was a feeling that we've got a big problem and we need to get everybody singing off the same sheet of music."

When Reagan held a press conference in Washington a few days after the Democratic convention, he was quickly asked about Mondale's charge that he was secretly plotting to raise taxes.

"I have no plans for a tax increase," the President replied. "I believe it would be counter-productive with regard to the present recovery or expansion. Indeed, I believe that the tax cut that we had is largely responsible for the recovery that we're having."

That observation was something less than an ironclad promise. Anyone familiar with political rhetoric knows that when a politician says he has "no plans" to do something, he is by no means making a firm pledge. And a few minutes later Reagan seemed to open the door a little wider. He said:

"Now, if, after all our best efforts, if we have gotten government costs down to the point at which we say they cannot go any lower and government still meet its responsibilities and provide the services that are required of it—and that is still then above the percentage taken by taxes—then you would have to look at the tax structure in order to bring that up, to meet that minimum level of government expenditures."

Ten days later, Reagan added another small stick to the fire. In a radio broadcast from Santa Barbara, he said Mondale's plan for raising taxes would cost the average American family $1,500 a year, and he pledged anew that there would be no increase in "individual income taxes." That formulation raised predictable questions about whether Reagan meant he was not ruling out some kind of business, excise or sales taxes as an alternative.

Meanwhile, George Bush was encountering persistent questions about taxes on the campaign trail and finding it difficult to deflect them.

"It's Mondale who wants to raise everyone's taxes," he told reporters at the Seattle airport. "It's Mondale who says we have a secret plan. Go ask him about it."

Bush went over the Reagan ground—that he would consider taxes only if every other method failed to reduce the budget adequately and there still was not enough revenue for essential services.

"If under all those circumstances when [the President] has cut as much as he can, revenues don't add up and you're still in deficit, then he will consider revenue increases," Bush said.

On the face of it, this statement would have seemed to be about as much reassurance as the taxpayer might expect from any politician. But every entrail of every position was being closely examined, because bickering continued in Washington about what the Republican platform should say on the matter.

While the pragmatists such as Jim Baker were trying to keep their "wiggle room," the supply-siders were insisting on an absolute declaration against any taxes. Representative Jack Kemp, the leading theologian of the supply-side movement, was a case in point.

"I hope the Republican Party will speak with one voice and oppose any tax increase, no matter how it is disguised," he told Fred Barnes, then of *The Baltimore Sun*.[42]

The controversy reached its most serious level when Bush went to Santa Barbara for lunch with the President at the Reagan ranch. As the two men passed the press corps, the ubiquitous Sam Donaldson of ABC News called out another question about taxes. Reagan replied:

"Walter Mondale is not telling the truth. I've said before and I will say it again and no matter how many of you try to put in a hedging line, we have no plans for nor will I allow any plans for a tax increase. Period."

But, meeting the press after lunch, Bush found himself still beset, and he responded incautiously. There was always the pos-

42. Barnes moved to *The New Republic* magazine in March 1985.

sibility that conditions might "change dramatically," he said, so "any President would keep his options open."

"Including this one?" a reporter asked.

"Sure, I'd say so," Bush replied.

It was, once again, a small matter, but one magnified by the context. Spencer recalled the incident this way:

"Then Bush goes out there and meets the man and comes down off the hill and capitulates on the tenth time they asked him the same question. He gave them what they wanted and that was division [in Republican ranks]. . . . Then we realized we had a potential problem."

Bush himself was irked at the flap and testy with the press about it.

"Anytime I try to clarify something," he said, "a group of people jump out and say there are differences. There are not differences. The President knows there are not differences."

The press, the Vice President advised, should simply take its reading from what Reagan had to say. He was through talking about the subject, and he dismissed it in classic Bush patois:

"No more nit-picking. Zippity doo-dah. Now it's off to the races."

Long after the fact, Bush recalled:

"I said . . . he'll never say never, and that was interpreted by some as away from what the President's new position was, and I knew in my heart of hearts that it wasn't. But it took about a week to sort it out. It didn't amount to anything in terms of substance."

The final "sorting out" took place a few days later after Reagan had met with Baker and Spencer. The result was a statement—curiously written as a colloquy in which the President answered questions put to him by his press secretary Larry Speakes—spelling out a "first resort, last resort" formula.

"My opponent," said Reagan, "has spent his political life supporting more taxes and more spending. For him, raising taxes is a first resort. For me, it is a last resort."

With that one deft sentence, Reagan managed to demolish the grand Mondale strategy of candor on taxes.

In the end, the controversy over Reagan's intentions turned out to be little more than a mid-summer diversion, soon overtaken by other events. In politics, it's often as good to be lucky as smart, and 1984 was a year in which everything seemed to come up roses for Ronald Reagan.

On the same day that the Reagan statement was being released, Geraldine Ferraro was setting off another brouhaha. Leaving for California on her first solo campaign trip, the Democratic vice-presidential nominee told reporters at National Airport in Washington that, contrary to her earlier assurances, her husband John Zaccaro had decided he would not make his income tax returns public.

"My husband feels, quite frankly, that his business interests would be affected," she said. "His reaction was, 'Gerry, I'm not going to tell you how to run the country. Don't tell me how to run my business.' "

And when reporters pressed in with more questions, she added: "If you're married to an Italian man, you know what it's like."

As happens so often in politics, the importance—or at least newsworthiness—of the decision was greatly enhanced by the context. Shortly after Ferraro was chosen, it was disclosed that she had paid a civil fine levied by the Federal Election Commission for irregularities in the financing of her first campaign for the House of Representatives in 1978.

Then word came that when Ferraro had entered the House she had signed a waiver rather than disclose all of her husband's assets. That option was available for members of Congress who could claim that they had no knowledge of their spouse's holdings and derived no benefit from them. But the House Committee on Standards of Official Conduct—the so-called Ethics Committee—had issued guidelines that said the benefit test "should be interpreted very broadly."

Considering that the Ferraro-Zaccaro family lived a lifestyle of obvious affluence—they owned one vacation home on Fire Island and another in the Caribbean, for example—Ferraro's claim of "no benefit" seemed to defy reason. And, although there was no suggestion Ferraro had been guilty of any conflict of interest, there were predictable howls from conservatives demanding an investigation.

The disclosures conditioned the press and perhaps the electorate to wonder why Ferraro was now reneging on the promised tax returns. The political community and then the press were shot through with speculation about what Zaccaro or Ferraro had to "hide." The most obvious theory was a huge income and a small tax bill. Ferraro kept insisting the whole thing would become clear when she made her disclosure statement as a vice-presidential candidate later that month. But the promise of answers a week or ten days in the future did nothing immediately to satisfy her critics or the curiosity of the press.

Meanwhile, the Republicans were gathering in Dallas for the preliminaries to their convention. The principal business was the final preparation of the Republican Party platform to be adopted there. And the Reagan strategists were plainly delighted to turn attention away from their own differences on taxes to the question of Gerry Ferraro's financial disclosure.

Although some like William Timmons, the Reagan-appointed convention manager, felt the best tactic was to leave Ferraro alone, other Republicans such as Senators Bob Dole and Paul Laxalt held press conferences in Dallas raising pious questions about financial disclosure. Laxalt killed two Democrats with one stone by expressing sympathy for Ferraro because she had been "badly served by the Mondale campaign," which was supposed to have experts on disclosure requirements.

Ferraro's latest woes "pretty well became the story of the week," Lee Atwater, the Reagan deputy campaign manager, said later. "The tax thing then got lost in the shuffle."

That view may have been a slight exaggeration, but it was true that the platform deliberations never received the kind of full-bore attention they might have been given in the absence of the Ferraro-Zaccaro story.

It is a cliché to say that party platforms are meaningless. And, like some clichés, that one is essentially accurate. Presidential candidates feel free to pay as much or as little attention as they like to platforms. Other party officeholders generally ignore them. Very few people ever read a platform all the way through to the end, although the document can reveal at least the general direction in which a political party is moving.

But for the activists within a party, the platform-writing process offers opportunities to make a point or build a reputation among insiders.

In the final writing of the 1984 Republican platform, both of these factors were operating. And the protagonists were the conservatives of the so-called New Right. Jack Kemp was the leading figure, but the noisiest was a three-term congressman from Georgia, Newt Gingrich. They were determined to put the party firmly on record against tax increases, for significant military buildup and for the conservative position on a variety of social concerns. They coined the label "The Opportunity Society" to describe their focus on a free-enterprise economy, and their efforts clearly had 1988 in mind, when they hoped to succeed Reagan with one of their own as party leader.

For the White House, the whole platform process posed an awkward political dilemma. On the one hand, the Reagan strategists understood all along that the President wouldn't be held to the platform by the voters and could go his own way during the campaign. A ranking White House aide, in fact, told us at the time that Reagan would not feel bound to any part of the platform he didn't like. On the other hand, these strategists also recognized that it was important to avoid any scarring split with those Republicans who might consider the platform worth an argument.

During the early stages of the platform-writing the White House had ventured into the process fairly aggressively. But that involvement had caused some testy reactions. The chairman of the committee, Representative Trent Lott of Mississippi, had let it be known at one point that he would not welcome any suggestions from Dick Darman, the White House pragmatist considered so suspect by the New Right.

In the end, the White House limited itself to damage control. Drew Lewis, the highly regarded political operator representing the White House, tried to influence the tone of the document without having the White House flat-out repudiated by the committee. Rick Robb, a longtime political associate of Lewis who also worked on the platform, said their challenge was like "holding a sparrow in your hand. You can't squeeze it too hard or you'll kill it. And you can't hold it too loosely or it will fly away."

But the political operatives from the Reagan campaign were generally contemptuous of the whole exercise. Stuart Spencer said later he thought the platform was "kind of screwy." But his interest had been strictly in getting the convention behind the campaign without serious political mishap.

"We just wanted to get out of there with our life," he said.

Timmons felt the same way. Of the haggling over platform language, he said, "I couldn't get very excited over nouns and verbs. We wanted to come out [of the convention] unified, and we did."

However good a face the White House tried to put on the situation, it was nonetheless clear in the end that the Republican Party had adopted a politically extreme platform—on social and policy questions. The document went further on some questions than the pragmatists in the administration preferred.

The tax plank was the most obvious case—flat opposition to increases, with no wiggle room. It read:

"Our most important economic goal is to expand and continue the economic recovery and move the nation to full employment without inflation. We therefore oppose any attempts to increase taxes, which would harm the recovery and reverse the trend to restoring control of the economy to individual Americans."

Another section satisfied the lust of the supply-siders to take a swipe at Paul Volcker, the chairman of the Federal Reserve Board and, by their lights, the chief obstacle to the kind of monetary policy they were convinced was required. That passage referred to the Fed's "destabilizing actions."

Most of the document, however, was a compendium of all the rightist causes carried to the ultimate. One example: The platform called not just for a constitutional amendment to forbid abortion but for a position against abortion as a qualification for appointment to the federal judiciary.

There was a small dissident group—an ad hoc "Republican Mainstream Committee" led by Representative Jim Leach, a moderate from Iowa. But it enlisted only the well-known dissenters from the Republican move to the right over recent years. Some of them were maverick scolds, such as Senator Lowell Weicker of Connecticut and Mary Dent Crisp, the onetime vice chairman of the party who had been squeezed out four years earlier for aggressively supporting retention of an ERA platform plank. A few were long-established party regulars, such as Mary Louise Smith of Iowa, once the party's national chairman but later bounced from the U.S. Civil Rights Commission by the Reagan administration.

Hard-line conservatives in the party, who had held their own during the Nixon years, had begun to dominate in the mid-1970s and gained great steam with Reagan's election in 1980. Now they had reached the point at which distinctions were being drawn on the degree of conservatism that would be acceptable. At the same time, the infamous "eastern liberal establishment"—the wing of the party whose tenure had started with Thomas E. Dewey and ended with Nelson A. Rockefeller—had atrophied.

But in the eyes of some Reagan strategists the New Right domination of the platform process—particularly on such things as the abortion and school prayer issues—was an undisguised blessing.

"I was tickled to death," Atwater said. "What I wanted that convention to do was totally nail down the Sun Belt . . . and the conservative tilt of that convention, I think, iced the cake in the West and the South."

The platform was not, however, the only element of the Dallas convention that reinforced Reagan's position against Walter Mondale in the Sun Belt. An equally significant factor was the very visible presence of a group of prominent religious fundamentalists—television evangelists who reached large audiences of followers in much of the country.

The fundamentalists had been a largely untapped resource in secular American politics until Ronald Reagan claimed the leadership of the Republican Party in 1980. He was, after all, the first presidential candidate of modern times to suggest publicly, as he did that year, that he had his own doubts about the theory of evolution. And in that election there was evidence, although it was never quantified with any precision, that the fundamentalist churches had been an important factor in registering new voters and Reagan supporters in the South and parts of the Midwest and Far West.

As a result, the evangelists had suddenly found themselves treated by conservative Republican politicians as another resource in the mainstream of American politics. And that new respect was evident for all to see at the Dallas convention.

With one obvious exception, the evangelists were not given high-profile roles in the convention itself. The Reverend Jerry Falwell, the leader of the Moral Majority, was chosen to deliver the benediction closing the Wednesday night session in which Reagan was renominated, before a national television audience expected to be at its peak. But other fundamentalists, though less conspicuous, had been very active all through the convention, testifying before platform subcommittees, holding press conferences and doing broadcasts of their own. They included Dr. M. G. (Pat) Robertson, whose Christian Broadcasting Network claimed one of the largest audiences across the nation; the Reverend Jimmy Swaggart; the Reverend James Robison and Dr. Greg Dixon.

Moreover when the platform was finally written, the fundamentalists could and unhesitatingly did claim credit for great success. They had their way not only on such obvious goals as a prayer amendment and an amendment prohibiting abortion. They also won out on planks denying homosexual rights, favoring tuition tax credits for private schools, calling for strict laws against pornography and making opposition to abortion a requisite for appointment to the federal bench. Unsurprisingly, Falwell called the document "a platform we really could not find fault with."

But the climactic event was the President's speech before a prayer breakfast crowd of more than 10,000 people at the Reunion Arena the morning after his nomination.

"Today there are those," he said, "who are fighting to make sure voluntary prayer is not returned to the classrooms. And the frustrating thing for the great majority of Americans who support and understand the special importance of religion in the national life . . . is that those who are attacking religion claim they are doing it in the name of tolerance, freedom and open-mindedness." Then he paused and added:

"Question: Isn't the real truth that they are intolerant of religion? They refuse to tolerate its importance in our lives."

The passage that caused the greatest stir came a moment later when Reagan ventured into the thicket of the relationship between government and religion:

"There are, these days, many questions on which religious leaders are obliged to offer their moral and theological guidance. And such guidance is a good and necessary thing. To know how a church and its members feel on a public issue expands the parameters of debate. It does not narrow the debate. It expands it.

"The truth is, politics and morality are inseparable. And as morality's foundation is religion, religion and politics are necessarily related. We need religion as a guide. We need it because we are imperfect. And our government needs the church because only those humble enough to admit they're sinners can bring to democracy the tolerance it requires in order to survive."

In a single stroke, the President had seemed to give the fundamentalists a legitimacy in the political process far beyond what they had enjoyed in the past. And although Reagan's words alarmed and outraged many voters, particularly Jewish voters, his campaign strategists were delighted.

One of them explained to us later that Jews represent only 2 percent of the population and they are concentrated in states—such as New York, Pennsylvania and Illinois—the Republicans weren't counting on winning anyway.

Concerning the fundamentalists, Timmons said, "we did want to highlight that natural constituency of Ronald Reagan." As long as the Democrats with Jesse Jackson's help were registering blacks in the South, he said, the fundamentalists had to be energized to register their congregations for Reagan. The convention's Christian religious atmosphere, Timmons said, "probably cost us some Jewish votes, but the test of the pudding was in the eating, and it ate pretty well."

Mondale over the next few weeks moved quickly to exploit the issue of religious intrusion in politics; so quickly that Reagan himself apparently was taken aback by the criticism.

"Yes," he told us, "I was surprised and that they were, again, demagoging, because I saw the reaction at the prayer breakfast. I couldn't have been better received."

Moreover, the President argued, anyone who had read the speech would have seen that he was not advocating violation of the separation of church and state but simply objecting to those who wanted more state influence.

"I thought it was unfair and unjust," he said.

One Reagan strategist said later he originally thought the President had "gone too far" on the issue but later concluded it was Mondale who damaged himself by trying to press the case in areas of the country with a large fundamentalist population.

"They spent two weeks hammering that issue [and] he damaged himself beyond redemption in the South," this Reagan operative said. "We made one mistake by doing it. They made a bigger mistake by keeping it alive for two or three weeks."

With so much attention focused on ancillary events, the convention itself seemed to be a curiously flat celebration—perhaps because there was so little to do until Reagan would appear three days into the week. The hotels and restaurants of Dallas were jam-packed with well-dressed, obviously affluent Republicans, and there were dozens of parties on the social calendar every day. In the hotel lobbies the delegates traded reviews of the previous night's speeches, swapped campaign pins and speculated about how long it would be before Fritz Mondale had to drop Gerry Ferraro from the Democratic Party's ticket. But there was none of the life that would have been expected if there had been some semblance of a contest.

After the Democratic convention and the Olympics on television, Timmons said, "we knew people were going to have square eyeballs watching the tube." The Republican convention for a while considered encouraging some dissension, he said, but that notion was quickly rejected as too risky. And so there was an atmosphere in Dallas more suitable to a coronation than to a nominating convention. Other conventions in both parties had been devoid of a contest, but at least there usually was some issue of contention to provide some spark. There simply wasn't any this time at this harmonious gathering in Dallas.

Even the much-touted demonstrations against the Republicans never amounted to much. City officials had set aside a campground in a flat along the Trinity River near the arena and convention center. But the temperature was running close to 100 degrees, and the number of demonstrators never exceeded a thousand people. After a day or two, even they packed up and left.

Republican conventions are generally duller than those of the Democrats, anyway. For one thing, the population of party activists is much more homogenous than that of the Democratic Party. Less than 5 percent of the delegates and alternates were black, and the same percentage applied to Hispanics. More than half of the 2,235 delegates were white-collar professionals.

This time the Republicans made a special effort to choose more women as delegates in a transparent effort to close the gender gap. The result was that almost half—44 percent compared to 29 percent four years earlier—were women. But they were generally middle-aged, middle-class white folks who had come to Dallas to wear cowboy hats and wave signs and cheer, not to bargain for greater influence for themselves within the party or to make the case for women's issues. There was only a murmur of protest when the party platform, as in 1980, failed to include support for the Equal Rights Amendment.

Although the convention opened as a relatively subdued affair, the decibel level in the Dallas Convention Center mounted during the week as the Republican speakers seemed to be vying to outdo one another in bashing Fritz Mondale and the Democrats.

One reason, Timmons offered, was that the Republican delegates had sat on the sidelines all during the primaries and caucuses, while the Democrats clobbered each other—and Reagan. The Republicans, he said, "were behind the curve, and ready to go bananas. There was a lot of pent-up emotion."

Reagan campaign strategists insisted there was never any carefully drawn plan for the rhetoric. Instead, they said, the tough talk developed out of individual Republicans "proving their mettle" by their attacks on Mondale before a sea of waving American flags. It was simply the thing to do. Or, as Stuart Spencer put it, "That's what conventions are for—bashing."

There was, however, a common theme of denigration—capsulized on the first day when Paul Laxalt in a press conference described Mondale as "a born loser."

Democrats were depicted as weak, fearful and pessimistic, implying always that those voters who wanted to identify with the strong, brave and optimistic winners in our society would vote for Ronald Reagan rather than Walter Mondale. That line ran all through the Republican rhetoric.

Katherine Davalos Ortega, the Treasurer of the United States, set the tone in her keynote speech, describing the Democrats as "the party of doomsayers, the party of demagogues, who look to America's future with fear, not hope.

"We have come a long way in four years—from the shame of Tehran to the brave rescue of American students in Grenada. We have come from the weak leadership of the Carter-Mondale administration to the strength of the Reagan-Bush administration. We have come a long way, and we are not going back."

"All he has to offer," said former President Gerald R. Ford of Mondale, "is fear itself. . . . Their theme seems to be that America's future belongs to the wishers, the wasters, the wanters, the whiners and the weak."

Laxalt derided Mondale as weak on national security issues.

"Let me ask the American people," he said, "whom you would rather have sit down at the bargaining table and negotiate a responsible arms-reduction agreement with the Soviet Union? A tough confident leader like Ronald Reagan, eyeball to eyeball with the steely-eyed Soviet masters, or Walter Mondale?"

Even Howard H. Baker, Jr., the Senate majority leader with a long-established reputation as a voice of sweet reason, joined the pack.

"Misery has become very important to Walter Mondale," Baker said. "When he's in office, he creates it. When he's out, he invents it, because Walter Mondale has nothing to offer a successful America."

Until Reagan himself finally arrived in Dallas, the speaker who evoked the greatest enthusiasm among the Republicans was a Democrat, United Nations Ambassador Jeane J. Kirkpatrick. She denounced what she called the "blame-America-first crowd" that, she said, had captured her party. The Democrats "behaved less like a dove or a hawk than an ostrich" trying to shut out the real world.

"It was not malaise that we suffered from, it was Jimmy Carter—and Walter Mondale," Kirkpatrick said. "And so, in 1980, the American people elected a very different President. The election of Ronald Reagan marked an end to the dismal period of retreat and decline."

Reagan himself arrived on Wednesday to a huge rally in the atrium of the shiny new Loew's Anatole Hotel, just off a freeway a few miles from the convention center. There several thousand exuberant supporters chanting "Four more years! Four more years!" packed the atrium floor and lined the balconies that looked down on it. Behind the podium a ten-story American flag and perhaps 200 hand-lettered signs, many of them on bedsheets, formed a background for the President. Below the flag, a large banner read: "Bringing America Back—Prouder, Stronger and Better."

Reagan himself took up the assault on the Democrats.

"Lately it looks like that *D* in their name," he said, "has come to stand for defeatism, decline, dependency, doom and despair."

Nor was that all simply pro forma rhetoric, at least on Reagan's part. Watching the Democratic convention back in Washington, Reagan had remarked on Mario Cuomo's tough speech, telling an adviser the following morning:

"He really was out there kicking my brains out last night."

And by the time he reached Dallas, Reagan was primed to retaliate. As one insider put it, "He worked one up pretty good."

Perhaps equally important, Nancy Reagan also had been put out by the rhetoric of Tip O'Neill and Ted Kennedy. The morning after the Kennedy speech, she telephoned old friend Laxalt and asked:

"Did you hear that?"

"Nancy was really irked," Laxalt said later. "Her competitive juices were really flowing."

Never a shrinking violet privately, in political affairs affecting her husband Nancy Reagan played an unusual public role at the Dallas convention. A film prepared by the Tuesday Team just about her was shown to cheering delegates, who also were treated to a clever electronic cameo of the continuing romance of Nancy and Ronnie. On a huge television screen above the convention podium facing the delegates, the President appeared when his wife finished speaking. She turned and waved at the image, and when Reagan, watching his own television screen in his hotel suite, saw her he grinned broadly and waved back. Republican hearts fluttered across the convention hall, and probably around the nation as well.

The gimmick was a small part of an elaborate private television network run by the Republicans themselves. They had one of their own cameras in the suite with the President and others around the hall, providing live gavel-to-gavel coverage for any of the hundreds of independent television stations covering the convention who wanted it for modest plug-in cost. The major commercial networks had decided against gavel-to-gavel coverage, so the Republican Party simply stepped in and filled the void.

The week's theme of optimism versus pessimism, winners and losers, was never more apparent than in an emotional film documentary of the President, also produced by the Tuesday Team for $500,000, and then in Reagan's acceptance speech on the final night of the convention.

"America is presented with the clearest political choice of half a century," he told the cheering delegates. "The distinctions between our two parties and the different philosophy of our political opponents are at the heart of this campaign and America's future . . .

"The choices this year are not just between two different personalities or between two political parties. They are between two different visions of the future, two fundamentally different ways of governing—their government of pessimism, fear and limits or ours of hope, confidence and growth.

"Their government sees people only as members of groups. Ours serves all the people of America as individuals. Theirs lives in the past, seeking to apply the old and failed policies to an era that has passed them by. Ours learns from the past and strives to change by boldly charting a new course for the future. Theirs lives by promises, the bigger the better. We offer proven, workable answers."

In this speech, too, Reagan most obviously co-opted the Olympics, just completed in Los Angeles, for his own use during the rest of the campaign.

"Now it's all coming together," he said. "With our beloved nation at peace, we are in the midst of a springtime of hope for America. Greatness lies ahead of us. Holding the Olympic games here in the United States began defining the promise of this season."

Then he described in some detail the course the Olympic torch had followed across the country earlier in the year.

"All along the way, that torch became a celebration of America," he said, "and we all became participants in the celebration."

Indeed, the Republican-Olympic connection had been one the convention had been making all week. At the slightest provocation, cadres of young Republicans would flood the aisles, pumping their arms in the air and shouting, "U.S.A.! U.S.A.!"—the chant that had risen so often from the crowds at Los Angeles to cheer another medal for the Americans. The rush of exuberant youth was hardly spontaneous. Scores of college students wearing convention passes bearing the word "Re-admit" would move on and off the floor on the signal of an official with a convention script in hand.

At the same time, signs were prepared in advance of Reagan's speech using key phrases right out of his speech text and passed out to the delegates. When Reagan read one of the phrases off the teleprompter, television cameramen, alerted by the Reagan forces, would scan the delegates and zero in on the appropriate sign. With the Reagan crowd, thorough planning was always the trademark, even in spontaneous audience reaction.

There wasn't anything new in a President, or any other politician, trying to associate himself with the warm feelings toward winners of sports events. Indeed, when those chants of "U.S.A." first were heard in 1980, they were being sounded for the underdog United States hockey team that defeated the Russians and then the Finns to win a gold medal at Lake Placid. Both Carter and Mondale had moved quickly to milk that success of whatever political value it might have.

This time there had been no comparable American successes at Los Angeles. Although the United States athletes won the lion's share of the medals, the boycott by the Soviet Union and so many of its allies from Eastern Europe had taken some of the gloss off that success.

But the Olympics came along at just the right moment, as had the invasion of Grenada almost a year earlier, for Reagan to use as hard evidence that "America is back" and "America is standing tall."

The national response to Grenada ten months earlier had been astonishing. The United States had used a heavy military force to crush a tiny enemy on a mission whose justification had never been fully established. Yet the country greeted the feat with macho cries of "We're Number One." There had been a few carping complaints, but even many liberals had gone along with the theory that it was essential to draw a line in the sand against Communist encroachment in the Western Hemisphere.

Now there had been a similar outpouring of nationalism from the successes at Los Angeles. And it all fit perfectly the thesis of Ronald Reagan that there was a "new patriotism" abroad in the land.

In retrospect, the phenomenon does not seem such a mystery. Americans had been through a series of disheartening events and discoveries. The United States had lost a war in Vietnam. A President had been forced from office in disgrace. So had a Vice President. The country had discovered that the American economy could not be directed at will by Americans but had become dependent on others abroad. The nation suffered the ultimate humiliation of the hostages being taken in Iran—and the United States powerless for a full year to do anything about it.

All of this pre-Reagan recent history created a perfect context in late summer of 1984 for the picture of Ronald Reagan's Republican Party as the place for the "winners" in the electorate. And that was the message from Dallas: If you join us, you can be as white and affluent and successful as we have been. If you join Fritz Mondale, you are allying yourself with the losers in this society.

Closely examined, the message of the convention was shallow in its political content and shabby in the attitude it conveyed toward those less successful than these smug Republicans with a twenty-point lead in the public-opinion polls.

But the message also avoided any necessity for facing up to the genuine issues that would confront the country over the next four years. If you can get by with rhetoric about "standing tall," there's no need to explain what you intend to do about the federal deficit or toxic wastes or growing poverty. It might be true—and it clearly was at this point—that a permanent underclass of Americans was being defined and locked into place.

But, reading the polls, it was clear as well that Ronald Reagan and the Republicans didn't need such people to sail through the campaign to the promised land on November 6. Although the surveys showed only a slight lift from the events at Dallas, the Republicans had other things going for them. And the most important was still more trouble in the campaign of Walter Mondale and Geraldine Ferraro.

19

Damage Control

•

ON AUGUST 1, Walter Mondale and Geraldine Ferraro flew to Jackson, Mississippi, to begin their general-election campaign.

Mississippi was, on the face of it, a peculiar place for two northern liberals to launch their attempt to defeat President Reagan. Although blacks now made up 31 percent of the population and were an important element of the electorate, the white voters in the state were notoriously conservative. They were not totally different from those who had supported Barry Goldwater with 87 percent of their vote in 1964 and George C. Wallace with 63 percent four years later. And, anyway, the state would cast only seven electoral votes.

But the opening in Mississippi seemed to be a success where it mattered—on the network television news reports that evening. Several thousand people showed up for a rally downtown that used the white antebellum governor's mansion for a backdrop. And their response to Gerry Ferraro in particular was enthusiastic. When her turn came to speak, the crowd began a chant that would become a staple of the entire campaign:

"Ger-ry! Ger-ry!"

Moreover, before the Jackson visit was over, it had produced a vignette that showed Ferraro—and the whole notion of a woman candidate—to best advantage.

Visiting a farm outside the city, Ferraro had encountered a Central Casting white southern male, Jim Buck Ross, the seventy-year-old state commissioner of agriculture.

"Can you bake a blueberry muffin?" Ross asked.

"Sure," Ferraro replied in high good humor. "Can you?"

"Down here in Mississippi, the men don't cook," he replied.

Then he added: "Do you know here in Mississippi we've had three Miss Americas? We have the prettiest women here."

Ferraro managed to carry that off with a lift of her eyebrows and subsequently told reporters:

"I guess I was the first female vice-presidential candidate he ever met."

Later on the same trip, Mondale and Ferraro flew on to Texas for stops at Austin, Houston and San Antonio. The crowds were consistently impressive and obviously curious about this odd phenomenon of a woman on a national ticket. And Fritz Mondale responded with exuberant appeals.

"We need your help," he told a rally in Austin. "We can't do it alone. We need Texas. We need the South."

By every calculation, Mondale's assessment was clearly accurate. There was indeed no realistic scenario under which he could hope to accumulate the necessary 270 electoral votes without winning some from the South. But the decision by the Democratic candidate to endow the South with the special visibility that goes with the de facto opening of a campaign became the center of an intense debate among political professionals during and after the campaign itself. And that debate grew as Mondale spent much of the next three weeks in the region.

Jim Johnson, the author of the strategy, had calculated the numbers and found that if Mondale carried "every conceivable" state in the Northeast and Midwest, he would have only 248 electoral votes. And some of those states, such as New Jersey and Connecticut, were distinctly longshots. It was far more likely, then, that the optimum would be 200 electoral votes and then only if "everything was going well, even really well."

"It was totally obvious to me that we had to win some states in the South and West to get our 270," he said later.

This premise translated, Johnson believed, into the necessity of winning both Texas and California and a few southern states. And if either Texas or California proved beyond reach, then additional southern votes would be required.

The controversy never centered on that imperative. Instead, the debate was focused on how to go about it. And Johnson and Mondale decided the South should get the first priority.

"It was also my belief," Johnson said, "that it was not possible to do the South second. If we ignored the South and West during that early period, there would be an enormous amount made of our ignoring it."

The alternative, and more conventional approach, would have been for Mondale to give his early attention to firming up his base in the more hospitable industrial states. Then, that base locked in, he could try to expand his appeal by concentrating on the South and West.

Johnson said he went to Mondale and told him:

"We are going to pursue a strategy that gives us a chance to win."

This approach, he added, made it "extremely unlikely" Mondale would end up losing with a respectable 150 to 200 electoral votes. The strategy meant that Mondale, unless he won the election, would be more likely to end up with 50 than with 150 votes because of the way he was spreading his effort. There would be no face-saving; it was an all-or-nothing proposition.

"It was a conscious decision on his part," Johnson said of Mondale. "He said, 'I have no interest in preserving a 150-vote electoral performance.' "

Mondale recalled the decision much the same way.

"The question," he said, "was whether for appearance purposes we'd spend our time early in our natural base to make certain that was solidified or whether we'd move rapidly to create a national campaign that had a chance of winning . . . and I said, 'By all means, this is a campaign to win.' So I think we did the right thing. We went to the South, to the West a lot, and if we had been able to get some movement, particularly in the West . . . we would have drawn Reagan west a lot. So I have no regrets about that."

The strategy did not sit well with some professionals inside the Mondale campaign or with many labor and political leaders in the Midwest and Northeast. Although Johnson told us after the election that "I don't think there was any perception in the North that anybody was being ignored," reporters in these areas constantly heard bitter complaints from these leaders that the Mondale approach was risking the heart of his support. And the leaders were clearly concerned that a weak performance by the national ticket in their states might doom some of their own candidates for the Senate and House and for local offices. There was also, predictably, carping from armchair quarterbacks who had been dealt out of any role in the Mondale campaign.

"There was a lot of huffing and puffing about it in Washington," Johnson said later. "I never considered it to be a choice because I knew what the reaction would be in the South if we ignored them and then came around in October. I knew that there would be the potential for high-level defections if we didn't handle the politics of the South properly, as there had been in previous years."

Nor did Johnson give any credence to the thesis of the Republicans that any successful campaign had to rest on a "geopolitical" foundation—the accumulation of electoral votes—rather than demographics—an attempt to enlist particular elements of the electorate wherever they could be found.

Johnson had been charting and averaging out the national opinion polls all year. He had seen Reagan's lead rise steadily from ten percentage points in the spring to twelve in the early summer and now, with the Democratic convention past, to fourteen. As he saw it, arguments over geopolitics were "absolute nonsense" at that stage.

"When you're fourteen points behind with sixty days to go, with very limited financial resources, financial resources which basically allow you to move your vice-presidential and presidential candidates around and put up $20 million on television, the notion that somehow you are making geopolitical refinements in your national campaign strategy is bullshit," he said.

It was easy enough for the Republicans, sitting smugly on a huge lead and a huge treasury of "soft" money, to be giving advice. But with President Reagan as their candidate, they were under no pressure to establish the basic credibility of their campaign.

"For us, there was one overwhelming challenge and that was to get in the race," Johnson said. "We weren't going to get into the race through boosting up our natural vote in Cuyahoga County [Cleveland] 4 percent and boosting up our natural vote in Nassau County [Long Island] from, you know, 31 percent to 34 percent. We were going to get into the race through the national dialogue or we weren't. I find almost all of the geopolitical, electoral college stuff to be beside the point. That was not what the challenge was for us."

Perhaps the single most pertinent question about Johnson's approach was a different one, however. Could a concentrated effort by Mondale on friendly ground have tightened the race in the national polls and thus given him greater credibility everywhere? Might the shape of the campaign have been changed if the story being told by the networks every night was a tale of Mondale "steadily gaining" and "closing the gap" to less than, let's say, ten points?

That kind of progress was just what Johnson was seeking "through the national dialogue." But he was also convinced that he could not risk conspicuous defections across the South.

This concern had some obvious validity. To win in the South, Mondale would need at least 30 to 35 percent of the white vote even in those states—such as Alabama and Mississippi—in which the black vote was substantial. And for a ticket of two northern liberals to capture a significant share of the white vote, it was essential that white Democratic leaders give those two liberals the respectability that would come with their active approval and effort. Moreover, those white party leaders prepared to make that kind of effort needed quick attention from the candidates to validate their decisions.

Texas was a case in point. The treatment of Senator Lloyd Bentsen in the vice-presidential selection had left bruised feelings there, but most party leaders were prepared to make a genuine effort for the ticket. And that sentiment included Democrats across a fairly wide ideological band—from the moderately conservative Governor Mark White to such liberals as State Treasurer Ann Richards and State Agriculture Commissioner Jim Hightower. The state party apparatus also made a full commitment by setting out to raise almost $1 million for voter registration and turnout efforts. Mondale's co-chairmen in the state, Railroad Commissioner Buddy Temple and former state party chairman Calvin Guest each contributed $25,000 of his own for that campaign.

The southern states that seemed to offer the best opportunities for Mondale were Alabama, Arkansas, Tennessee and Kentucky. And they had that common element—the likelihood of genuine support from the Democratic Party leadership that might give Mondale and Ferraro the hope of acceptance by white voters.

The reverse was true in other southern states, where the party leaders were either silent or making a point of putting distance between themselves and the national ticket. The most obvious, unsurprisingly, was Georgia. This was the state that had saved Fritz Mondale's hide back in the Super Tuesday primaries against Gary Hart on March 13. But now the treatment given Bert Lance had created a clearly hostile political environment.

The Lance episode finally played itself out on August 2 when campaign manager Bob Beckel met with the Georgia party chairman in a New York hotel to discuss how to put an end to all "the Lance stories" that continued to plague the campaign. There was only one way out and Lance took it, submitting his resignation so that he would no longer be what he called "a source of diversion."

But the anger among the Georgia Democrats still boiled—to the point that it badly tarred one of Mondale's southern trips during this period. After cutting his ties to the Mondale campaign, Lance left the country for ten days. On his return he found a telephone message from Mondale. When Lance called back, Mondale apologized profusely for the whole affair and asked for Lance's help. He wanted to do an event in Macon, Georgia, Mondale said. Would Lance be willing to appear with him?

Lance agreed. But two days later he phoned Mondale again and said he had changed his mind. He couldn't make the date and neither could Governor Joe Frank Harris nor Lieutenant Governor Zell Miller. Moreover, as it happened, both Jimmy Carter and Senator Sam Nunn had genuine schedule conflicts that would make it impossible for them to appear.

Alarm bells rang within the Mondale operation. Jim Quackenbush, the campaign's southern coordinator and a close friend of Lance, had never thought there was much political sense in a visit to Macon, a center of conservatism and Reagan support. He argued vehemently that—with this new prospect of a public embarrassment—the stop should be canceled. But Dick Leone countered that the visit to Macon would make "a good hit" in terms of television coverage. Finally, Quackenbush arranged for his assistant, Chip Carter, to get his father Jimmy on the telephone with Bob Beckel. The former President urged the campaign manager to cancel the event and promised he would appear himself at another one later.

Beckel took that advice. But Mondale suffered political damage anyway. The story of the threatened boycott leaked out, and Joe Frank Harris made clear to the press he had intended his absence to be a message of displeasure. Zell Miller, who had been Mondale's campaign chairman back during the primaries, made his priorities clear by announcing he couldn't go to Macon because he had an important meeting "with some poultry folks."

This incident was just the kind of thing that could seriously undermine Fritz Mondale's campaign at the outset. His self-destructive mistakes may not have been as damaging as those that crippled George McGovern so early in his campaign in 1972. But such unsympathetic treatment by fellow Democrats, if allowed to spread unchecked, could soon undercut his entire campaign by giving the voters the idea there was "something wrong" here.

Other factors made it equally difficult for Mondale to establish his credibility during these early stages of the general-election campaign. And none was more significant than the controversy that developed around Geraldine Ferraro.

In the first weeks after the Democrat from Queens was chosen to be the nominee for Vice President, the euphoria of the San Francisco convention seemed to infect the whole electorate. On that first southern trip, the crowds were substantially larger than Mondale alone might have expected. And Ferraro had handled her enormous instant celebrity with the kind of good-humored self-assurance that communicated itself easily through the television cameras.

No one could predict with any confidence just how that appeal would translate into votes. The consensus among the political professionals in both the Mondale and Reagan operations seemed to be, however, that Ferraro could be a definite asset among the yuppies—the young urban professionals whom Mondale had lost in large numbers to Gary Hart. But there was also the hope in the Mondale camp that Ferraro could mobilize a hidden vote among women who would cross normal party and issue lines. And some Mondale strategists believed she might be especially helpful with the Italian-American voters who comprised an important element of the electorate in such key—and, for the Democrats, difficult—states as New Jersey and Connecticut.

The Republican professionals were less concerned about the appeal of Ferraro to Italian-Americans, a group that had been growing increasingly conservative and Republican in its voting pattern over the previous several elections. There was ample evidence by this time that Italian-American candidates didn't necessarily attract significantly disproportionate support from Italian-American voters. As Roger Stone, the northeast coordinator for Reagan, put it:

"The idea that Italians vote Italian is nonsense."

But although the Republicans talked a good game, they were not sure how Ferraro might affect women voters, particularly in light of the gender gap that favored Democrats in the 1980 and 1982 elections and had continued to be seen in opinion polls in 1984. A woman on the national ticket was brand new, and who could say how the phenomenon might skew voting patterns?

The one point of agreement among professionals in both parties was that Ferraro's effect on the campaign, if any, would depend on whether she could establish her credibility for the office. And that outcome, in turn, might depend on whether she made any serious gaffes as the campaign progressed.

Ferraro, a ringwise politician despite her limited experience, was well aware of all of this speculation. So, in approaching the campaign, she colored her customary breezy self-confidence with caution. These were big stakes; Gerry Ferraro wasn't going to screw up.

Mondale and his managers discovered just how serious Ferraro was when both candidates and their principal advisers met at Mondale's home in North Oaks the day after that first joint southern swing. The meeting had been convened to talk about campaign schedules and planning, and Johnson wanted Ferraro to make her first solo trip to the West Coast three days later. But Ferraro still didn't have her staff in place and didn't feel prepared to take the risks of going out on her own.

Anne Wexler, the political veteran who had signed on as Ferraro's John Reilly, understood this reluctance.

"You can't expose a candidate like that without guaranteeing that they would do something terrible," she said later, "and Gerry was very concerned about not making a mistake."

The issue came to a head when Johnson produced two large charts showing the campaign schedules for Mondale and Ferraro for August and September, Mondale's in green, Ferraro's in red.

'Why is it in ink?" Ferraro asked immediately. "Why isn't it in pencil?"

Johnson, ignoring the question, outlined the rationale for the early trip to the West Coast. The goal was to hit some of these states at the outset and get a foothold.

"I'm not going to do this," Ferraro said. "I'm not ready."

Then, looking at Mondale, Wexler recalled, she added:

"I'm going to be very cooperative. I'm really going to try to take all your suggestions and work very closely with your people on the schedule and I'll go wherever you want me to go. Certainly it's important for us to work this out together. But I'm not ready."

Mondale, apparently nonplussed, said nothing. Johnson called on Dick Leone and then Paul Tully to explain why it was so important to start early. But Ferraro would not cave in.

"I told you that I'm not going until I'm ready," she said.

And with that, the meeting broke up with an obviously irritated candidate for Vice President. She was particularly irked at the idea of being lectured by Tully, whom she had last seen as a staff man on the platform committee.

The following morning the group met again to talk about issues. When the session was over, Ferraro managed to get Mondale aside.

"Your people wouldn't treat Lloyd Bentsen like that," she said.

"You're absolutely right," Mondale replied. "Don't let my people push you around. I don't want you to go out before you're ready."

So the trip to California was put off for another week to give Ferraro time to finish assembling her staff and do the kind of planning that could avoid a serious mishap. Meanwhile, the issue of Ferraro's financial affairs was developing in a way that would lead to a world-class political mistake.

The Mondale managers were having some second thoughts about the process they had followed in clearing Ferraro for the ticket. But they had no reason to believe her history was going to be a serious burden as the campaign went on.

The conservatives were howling about Ferraro's failure to disclose her husband's assets on the House Ethics Committee form, but the complaint didn't appear to be the kind of thing that could be sustained and converted into a major issue.

"We knew it," John Reilly said later. "We probably should have spent more time as to whether that was going to look legitimate or not. But, standing alone, it didn't appear to be much."

There were some surprises, however. The Mondale managers had not known about Ferraro's having filed papers with the state insurance agency showing her as an officer of her husband John Zaccaro's real estate management company. That fact made it somewhat more difficult to sustain the claim that she had no knowledge of his business affairs. But the operative point was that the disclosure requirement had been established in the first place to detect potential conflicts of interest. And there was no evidence of such a conflict in her voting record. On the contrary, the pattern was, if anything, hostile to the real estate interests.

As Anne Wexler put it later:

"They didn't think that it was a big deal."

Nor were the Mondale insiders concerned about a 1978 violation of the campaign finance laws that had been settled with a civil penalty. But they had never thought to ask where Ferraro obtained the $100,000 used by her campaign committee to repay the loan from her husband that the Federal Election Commission had ruled was a violation of the statute. Now it had been disclosed that the money came through the sale of a property to Zaccaro's business partner.

Now there was a series of stories in the press—some containing allegations that might be serious, others that were obviously trivial. But all of them taken together were politically upsetting.

One of the tenants in a Zaccaro-managed building was a pornography distributor. The Zaccaro family had once owned a building that had been listed as the residence address of an organized crime figure. Zaccaro had borrowed $100,000—the amount later proved to be $175,000—from the trust of a widow for whom he had been appointed a conservator by the courts. All the money had been repaid with interest, but the political damage from that kind of thing was obvious. And no one in the Mondale hierarchy could see how the problem might reasonably have been avoided.

"I don't know what question we could have asked Zaccaro," Reilly said later, "to find out that he had mixed up some conservator funds."

The whole problem of how far you should be expected to go in investigating the husband of a female candidate was obviously brand new, and there were no easy answers.

At this point, nonetheless, Ferraro and the Mondale managers were confident that all the questions would be resolved when she made her financial disclosure in late August, right after that first trip to California. While eating dinner at Mel Krupin's a few days before that trip, Ferraro conceded to us that she was irked by all the stories. But she said she was confident the disclosure would go so far beyond the requirements that it would satisfy any reasonable person.

But there was another problem. In her original statement promising disclosure, Ferraro had specified that it would include both her own and Zaccaro's tax returns covering her years in Congress. On the eve of the trip to Mississippi, however, Ferraro told Wexler:

"John's not going to release his returns."

"You said he would," Wexler replied. "You released a statement."

"He's not going to do it," Ferraro insisted.

"Well, I think he's going to have to," Wexler said.

Wexler quickly called Mike Berman, the Mondale campaign treasurer, and told him of "the problem." Berman would have to impress on Zaccaro, they agreed, that he had to make the disclosure.

Berman, who had conducted the original inquiry into the Ferraro-Zaccaro finances, now had teams of lawyers and accountants working in Washington and New York, going over every document—including Zaccaro's tax returns—line by line. Ferraro would be in California for most of the week before the disclosure date, and that interval would allow enough time for them to persuade Zaccaro he had to agree to release the returns.

"We were counting on the financial-disclosure team taking care of this problem while we were in California," Wexler recalled later.

Ferraro, meanwhile, was planning a press conference at National Airport the morning of her departure. And a briefing paper was prepared advising her simply to finesse questions about the financial disclosure by pointing out once again that all the facts would be available within a few days.

But when the time came, Ferraro dropped her political bomb: Her husband wouldn't be releasing his returns after all, she said. Those of you who are married to Italian men would understand that.

Now there was no mistaking the political damage. Stories like this one often percolate along on the inside pages but then explode into full-fledged controversies when some development crystallizes all the questions that have been raised. That was what happened in this case. Suddenly, the question was no longer simply how much money Geraldine Ferraro possessed or even how much in taxes she had paid. Instead it was: What does she have to hide?

The Mondale insiders were no longer sanguine about the whole thing.

"It was gratuitous," Reilly recalled. "When we heard that morning that she'd done it, we almost died."

Tom Donilon, the young Mondale delegate-hunter, remembered the questions suddenly raised inside the campaign. No one knew, he said, "how deep" the problem might go.

Ferraro clearly had not understood how the game was played. Her campaign manager, John Sasso, said later that she "believed she was going to produce so much information" that the absence of Zaccaro's returns wouldn't make any difference in the long run. But this was the short run and Gerry Ferraro, who had gone to such lengths to be careful, had made a serious political mistake by drawing the press' attention to her husband's resistance.

The furor was immediate and probably excessive. At Dallas, the Republicans enjoyed her problems immensely, fanning the story whenever they could do so. All the obvious comparisons were drawn between Ferraro and Tom Eagleton, the senator from Missouri forced to step aside as George McGovern's running mate after disclosure that he had been subjected to electric shock treatments for emotional depression.

In this case, barring some felony-sized finding about Ferraro, there never was any realistic possibility she would be dropped from the ticket. One of the lessons of the Eagleton case had been that trying to fix something so major could cause more problems than the original one. The very last thing Fritz Mondale could do now would be to admit he had made a serious error in judgment.

Ferraro, meanwhile, was living through an extremely confusing trip to the West Coast. On the one hand, at every opportunity the press was besieging her with questions about the tax returns. On the other, huge crowds of enthusiastic people were turning out to cheer her along the campaign trail. In that particular, her experience was not unlike Eagleton's had been. While the political professionals were making the pragmatic decision to replace him, the crowds he encountered were wildly supportive.

"She was in a cocoon," Wexler said later. "It was an interesting experience because she was having big crowds and enormous enthusiasm. And all that stuff was going on out there while the rest of us were watching the thing crumble before our eyes and spending all the time on the telephone trying to keep it together."

For Mondale, this week at his home in North Oaks was what became known inside the campaign as "the bunker period." By all accounts, Mondale was consistently supportive. He telephoned Ferraro at least three times to express his confidence, as did Johnson, Berman and—on one occasion—Reilly. And whenever Mondale would encounter the press, he would repeat that he had full confidence in Gerry Ferraro, and that she would make a great Vice President.

But those who spent time with Mondale then also believed he did not want to intrude himself on the situation.

"He never wanted to do something that was going to injure or affect the type of person that she was, or fit her into a mold," Reilly said later.

This restraint, however, contributed to a picture of the presidential candidate as essentially a passive bystander while his running mate was fighting her way out of a burning building. That picture may not have been an accurate one, but in politics perception is often more important than reality.

According to some insiders, in fact, at one point there was discussion high in the Mondale campaign about taking Ferraro's name off the campaign logo; that is, campaign signs would no longer say "Mondale-Ferraro," although she would remain on the ticket. But cooler heads prevailed.

Also shunted aside was an offer by a Republican media consultant, Mal MacDougall, to get about fifty prominent Republicans to run an ad in the New York *Times* that would say that enough had been made of Ferraro's financial problems and that it was time to get on with the substance of the campaign. The offer was recognized by the Democrat who received it as a potential disaster for Mondale, because it would only have highlighted the perception that he was leaving his running mate in the lurch.

This Democrat, who is close to Ferraro, recalled later:

"I said, 'Well, gee, that's interesting, Mal.' And I'm thinking at the time, 'Please, Mal, don't do that. Please don't do that. If you do that, Mondale's gone.' "

By week's end, Ferraro was back in New York preparing with the lawyers and accountants for the press conference at which she would make her disclosure the next Tuesday. On Friday Zaccaro finally yielded to the pressure and agreed to release the tax returns.

Now it was a question of seizing the public-relations initiative. On Saturday a statement was released announcing Zaccaro's decision, and Sunday morning Ferraro appeared on the ABC-News program, *This Week with David Brinkley*, to begin changing the perception of the whole situation.

Her husband had changed his mind, she said, because "people were jumping to the most outrageous conclusions" about what the returns might include.

Beyond that, she suggested at one point that stereotypical bias against Italian-Americans might have played a part in some of the stories about their financial affairs.

"You know," she said, "a lot of us have grown up with vowels at the end of our names, and there has been a lot of discussion and we've grown up accepting it. . . . For anybody to imply, just because we're Italian-Americans, that we're connected to organized crime is appalling."

The next day Ferraro spent ten full hours preparing for the press conference that now had assumed such outsized proportions in the campaign of 1984. There were, one participant in those sessions said later, some surprises for Ferraro.

"This was the day," this insider said, "she found out a lot of things she didn't know . . . found out a lot of things about her husband's business."

Ferraro sailed into the press conference with her self-assurance and style intact. She knew she and her husband had, contrary to the speculation, paid enough income taxes to shut off that speculation. In fact, the accountants had discovered the Zaccaros owed another $53,000 in back taxes, which they were now paying. And Ferraro knew there had been no conflict of interest in her congressional voting.

"She didn't feel as if she had to apologize for anything," Wexler recalled.

The press conference at the Viscount Hotel at John F. Kennedy Airport was a remarkable tour de force. Ferraro's tax advisers answered questions for eighty minutes, going over details of the disclosure form. Then Ferraro herself took questions for an hour and fifty minutes from a mob of reporters. Most of the conference ran live on cable television, and the networks carried substantial chunks. They showed a candidate dealing firmly and in remarkable good humor with the sometimes ill-mannered pack—a politician confident enough to make the occasional quip or turn to her lawyers and accountants for answers she couldn't produce herself.

When one reporter droned on interminably, she interrupted:

"Are you making a speech or a statement, or do you have a question?"

At another point she made a wisecrack about her accountants, then turned to them with a grin and said:

"I'm only kidding, guys."

At still another, she was asked about her reaction when she learned of the amount of money involved in one transaction—"surprised, startled, aghast or suspicious . . . ?"

"How about, None of the above?" Ferraro replied.

The press conference did not answer every question raised about the finances of Ferraro or Zaccaro. Nor, of course, could it have anticipated further "disclosures" later in the campaign. It was reported the next week, for example, that as a congressional candidate Ferraro had received $700 in contributions from a man who had been convicted of labor racketeering.

But for political purposes, Ferraro had essentially put the issue behind her for the rest of the campaign. There were more stories—including one beauty about her parents' having been charged with taking bets in their store forty years earlier—but never anything that threatened her continued viability as a candidate. That much was apparent in the chastened reaction of the Republicans in Dallas, whose gloating over the Ferraro problem was considerably muted after they watched the press conference.

As Anne Wexler said later, "The networks pronounced her innocent."

Ferraro had proved once again that, as was so often said about her, she could play with the big boys. As John Sasso said later:

"I think lesser politicians would have folded under that pressure."

But the cost was high. Ferraro herself had been transformed by the whole controversy over her financial affairs, in Peter Hart's formulation, from "Joan of Arc to just another politician."

"We paid a terrible price for it," Wexler said later. "It was the one thing she feared more than anything else, which was making a mistake. She didn't want to make a mistake."

Fritz Mondale also paid a price. He and his strategists always measured the damage largely in terms of campaign time lost to a distraction. But the time itself was probably less important than the opportunity for the challenging candidate to take the initiative and set the agenda for the general-election campaign.

For Mondale, the entire summer seemed to be a time of reeling from one crisis to another when he should have been preparing themes for the campaign against Ronald Reagan. Even as Labor Day approached, the Democratic nominee was still involved in the kind of basic credentialing that should have been completed weeks or months before.

During the final week of August, Mondale was still holed up in North Oaks, holding meetings with groups—Democratic governors, Democratic mayors and black leaders—whose roles in the campaign and support ordinarily would have been fixed much earlier in the game. And in the case of the black leaders and Jesse Jackson, the most that could be said was that Mondale escaped with the best of a bad deal.

Despite Jackson's conciliatory speech at San Francisco, he had continued to resist an official endorsement of Mondale—the "signal" he had promised his followers as a guide to their own effort in the fall campaign. On Mondale trips through the South in August, Jim Quackenbush had been assiduous in arranging "unity meetings" involving his candidate, blacks who had supported him during the primaries and caucuses, and leaders of the Rainbow Coalition. And in several of these states, deals had been struck for cooperative efforts in the general-election campaign.

But Jackson himself had held back, and his recalcitrance was threatening to give Mondale the worst of two worlds. In the view of many southern white Democratic leaders, their presidential nominee already had given the impression of putting up with too much nonsense from Jackson. At the same time, however, Jackson was giving the impression that he needed still more concessions before he would make a full commitment to the ticket.

Nor was the situation being helped along by Jackson's friend, Minister Louis Farrakhan. On the contrary, at the end of July, at a time the Mondale strategists were hoping Jewish voters might have forgotten Farrakhan, the leader of the Nation of Islam caused a fresh cut in a speech at the National Press Club in Washington.

Mondale, he said, "does not intend to honor his debt to black people who helped him get the nomination and whom he needs to get elected."

In the final week of August, the campaign brought together in St. Paul more than fifty black leaders—including many prominent in the Jackson campaign—for a day of meetings designed to produce a united front of blacks behind Mondale. Jackson, however, insisted on having his own private meeting with the candidate. He was still miffed at not having been given the full treatment accorded those considered for Vice President earlier in the summer.

He arrived at North Oaks about two hours late and several hours after the larger meetings had begun at the Radisson Hotel downtown. Following the pattern he had used with other prominent visitors, Mondale invited Jackson to take a walk while staff members waited at the house.

"I need you now and I can't let this thing go on much longer," Mondale told him.

They returned to the house, continuing the discussion about an endorsement and Jackson's role in the campaign. Then, again following the pattern with other distinguished visitors, they drove to a schoolyard nearby where several dozen reporters and television crews waited.

There was every reason to believe that Jackson was now prepared to give Mondale his full support. The alternative now, after all, was Ronald Reagan and four more years of an administration that blacks all over the country considered implacably hostile to their concerns. But Jackson confounded Mondale once again by refusing, in response to repeated questions, to use the word "endorse" in expressing his support.

"We have embraced the mission and support the Mondale-Ferraro ticket with great fervor," he said. "My support will be wide-based, deep and intense."

At another point, he said:

"We will campaign together and present the solid front we need for victory."

But, asked if this meant there would be no further attacks on Mondale, Jackson was less than reassuring.

"I have not been attacking [Mondale]," he said, "but I will always reserve the right to challenge him. I have not taken a vow of silence or put an anesthetic on my conscience."

To any rational person outside the world of politics, the refusal of Jackson to say he was "endorsing" Mondale might seem to be splitting hairs. He was, after all, "embracing" the ticket and promising "support." But there are well-established conventions in politics, and reporters knew this balkiness on Jackson's part was no accident.

Mondale knew it, too. Standing off a few feet from Jackson's side, but well within camera range, he was clearly discomfited. The broad grin he wore when the press conference began had faded to a fixed smile, then vanished entirely. He stared down at the ground.

"It was very embarrassing," Mondale said later. "I didn't know what he was going to do and I tried to put the best face on it. Later that evening he did endorse, but you know that was awful late to have to be talking about endorsements. I was irritated."

When the session in the schoolyard ended, Mondale's agents tried a little "spin control" with the press.

"We consider this an endorsement," Jim Johnson said. "We are very pleased."

In fact, Mondale and his managers were furious. And Mondale himself was not just irritated. As one insider said later:

"Mondale was madder than hell."

Bob Beckel, who had been the principal liaison with Jackson all along, was obviously on the spot and clearly stunned.

"I thought he was ready to go," Beckel said. "It was such a foregone conclusion I thought he'd do it right. We went in there with the assumption that we were going to get an endorsement. Instead, we got a lukewarm whatever-you-call-it."

The press conference over, Mondale and Jackson climbed into separate cars and drove to the St. Paul Hotel for a reception and meeting with all the black leaders that was supposed to bring the whole exercise together for the Democratic ticket. But Jackson's attitude in the schoolyard was threatening to turn that meeting into still another political disaster.

Beckel rode downtown with Jackson, telling him:

"Time is running out here. This is a bad situation. The press roll on this thing is going to be that you didn't endorse him."

Jackson insisted later the whole matter was a misunderstanding—"strictly mechanical," he said. He didn't want to go the last mile until he could confer again with his followers who had spent several hours at the Radisson and were now waiting at the St. Paul.

"Many of the leaders had unanswered questions about Fritz and his jobs commitment and some other concerns," Jackson told us. "I didn't want them to hear I had already made a full commitment."

Mondale, riding downtown with Johnson, had a different view. Once again, he thought, Jesse Jackson had demonstrated that he was more interested in the games he was playing for his own purposes than he was in whether Fritz Mondale defeated Ronald Reagan.

For Beckel, the imperative now was to bring the black leaders together in a show of unanimity behind Mondale that Jackson could not avoid joining, or risk being blamed for undercutting the Democrat trying to replace Reagan. But Beckel—and Mondale—walked into a meeting at the St. Paul so contentious that there was serious doubt they could achieve their goals.

Jackson arrived and spoke briefly about how he hoped they could all "get together." Then, typically, he left for a rally of his own followers in Minneapolis.

But Jackson supporters in the meeting were aggressively demanding that Mondale make a specific commitment to promulgate a huge federal jobs program if elected. Mayor Richard Hatcher of Gary, Jackson's prime supporter from the outset, pressed the case intensely. So did Arthur Eves, a prominent black legislative leader from Buffalo and an important Jackson ally in the New York primary four months earlier. The message seemed to be that Fritz Mondale had to demonstrate his bona fides.

"They were jumping all over him," Beckel said later.

Mondale himself was steaming. The blacks were asking the classic question of politicians in such a situation: "What can I take home to my people?" But Mondale was thinking, one adviser said later, "I've been killing myself forever for these guys."

More to the point, Mondale clearly understood that a commitment to a broad multi-billion-dollar jobs program would totally destroy the credibility of his argument that he intended to use revenues from a tax increase to cut the federal deficit. Even the hint of such a program would be seized by the Republicans as the final proof that Mondale was still the liberal politician of the past determined to retreat to the liberal programs of the past.

"A lot of them understood what I was up to," Mondale said later of the black leaders. "But some of them wanted me to come out with some kind of massive multi-billion-dollar program and I said, 'I'm not going to do it. I got nominated on this program. I'm going to stand for reduction of these deficits. The only way we're going to get hope for black America and the rest of America is to get these deficits down. You're the ones who are paying the big price, and I'm not going to do it.' It got pretty hairy but I refused to budge."

In fact, it got hairy enough that some of the Mondale loyalists in the room wanted to say the hell with Jesse Jackson and walk out. Joe Reed, the leader of the Alabama Democratic Conference whose support had been so critical in the Alabama primary, was one of them. At one point, he pulled Beckel aside and told him:

"Why sit here and take this stuff any longer? Let's get up and leave."

But Beckel knew leaving wasn't an option. He had sent word to Jackson that his presence was essential. Jackson finally returned at a point when the meeting seemed ready to dissolve into chaos—and without any agreement that everyone would endorse Mondale. Beckel got Jackson into a corner of the room and told him:

"This has come too far too long, and it's got to end tonight."

Others who were in the meeting told us later that Beckel, never known for a long fuse, was red and shaking with anger as he talked to Jackson.

At the last minute, even after there had been a move to adjourn the meeting, Maynard Jackson took the floor and, by all accounts, saved the day for Mondale.

Maynard Jackson, who had been practicing law in Atlanta and Chicago since leaving as Atlanta's mayor, had a special status in that group. Many of the black political leaders would have preferred to see him, rather than Jesse Jackson, as the first serious black presidential candidate. But he had declined and supported Jesse Jackson all through the contest for the Democratic nomination. Now he had agreed to join the Mondale campaign as a senior adviser, and he was not going to let the whole thing disintegrate before his eyes.

Maynard Jackson began to talk. Exactly what he said was never recorded, but those who were in the room that night were virtually unanimous in remembering it as very much like a trial lawyer's summation to the jury. He went through a question-and-answer session, largely with himself, recalling all the issues on which Walter Mondale had been an ally and friend of black Americans. The time had arrived, he said, at which the struggle over the nomination should be forgotten and the black leaders, regardless of their previous alliances, should recognize the alternative and get behind this man. And they should leave that room prepared to make that position clear.

The presentation by Maynard Jackson changed the mood. And Jesse Jackson recognized it, finally speaking once more himself and, as several participants recalled it, telling the black leaders:

"I think we all ought to go out there as brothers and sisters and make this unanimous."

Looking back on the scene later, Jesse Jackson said he was prompted most by the recognition that there was so much at risk for blacks in the election, not just at the presidential level but in legislative and congressional contests.

"I finally concluded," he said, "that we had more at stake than just Fritz."

Twenty-five or thirty of the black leaders filed into an adjoining room where the reporters and television cameras waited. The blacks lined up around Mondale and declared their unanimous endorsement. And Coleman Young, the mayor of Detroit who had been the black politician most outspokenly hostile to Jesse Jackson all year, made a big show—grinning broadly if perhaps sardonically—of throwing his arm around Jackson's shoulders and helping affix a Mondale-Ferraro button to his jacket.

Beckel obviously was greatly relieved. In the St. Paul Hotel's bar an hour later, he downed three quick belts of Johnny Walker Black Label and marveled at how close the campaign had come to a political debacle in that meeting room that night.

Beckel's relief was understandable. If the meeting had come apart without that tableau of black unity for the television cameras, Mondale would have been seen as a candidate who had spent the whole year playing to Democratic constituency groups, only to be rebuffed by the leaders of the single bloc that was most reliably Democratic.

But the success the Mondale forces enjoyed in stapling together the show of support was by no means an unalloyed triumph. Labor Day—the traditional starting point for general election campaigns—was only four days away. Long before this point, Mondale should have solved whatever problems he had with party constituencies. More to the point, by this time Mondale should have been carrying a thematic message to the mainstream of the national electorate about why he should replace Ronald Reagan.

Instead, Mondale was coming to the end of the preliminaries still reinforcing that destructive image of himself as a candidate of the special interests—in this case, black leaders—rather than projecting a new image as a candidate of the broad middle class.

Meeting with twenty Democratic mayors the day after that tumultuous session with the black leaders, Mondale told reporters:

"This campaign is now ready to move. We have our coalition together. Our case is strong. The contrasts couldn't be more basic."

But a consistent theme for the Mondale campaign still had not been found—or, at the least, conveyed to the waiting electorate. Mondale was still talking about deficits and fairness, excoriating the Reagan administration as "government of the rich, by the rich and for the rich." But he was also trying to raise the salience of the church-state issue drawn from the Republican convention.

Speaking to a fund-raiser in Dallas in that final week before Labor Day, Mondale put it this way:

"In America, our faith is personal and honest and uncorrupted by political influence. May it always be thus."

But Geraldine Ferraro was involved in a running feud with the Roman Catholic hierarchy—and most especially Archbishop John J. O'Connor of New York—over her unwillingness to translate her personal opposition to abortion into a political position against choice. And although the polls showed most voters agreed with her on that position, there was little reason to believe that this issue was the kind on which a liberal woman from Queens was going to broaden her base of support.

Within the campaign operation, there was a recognition that Mondale still needed a coherent message to have any realistic chance of cracking a Reagan lead that now had reached sixteen to eighteen percentage points.

Peter Hart, the campaign's respected polling consultant, had written a memorandum urging Mondale to "stop careening from issue to issue." Hart told Mondale he needed to be "ruthlessly single-minded" in choosing one or two issues and sticking with them. But Hart was plainly dismayed because Pat Caddell, despite all the history of his aggressive posture against Mondale earlier in the year, also had been invited into the campaign and asked for his ideas on strategy.

In a 106-page memorandum, Caddell recommended what he called "a strategy of indirect approach"—that is, one that would avoid the pitfall of frontal attack on the popular Reagan. Instead, Caddell said, the aim should be to make the election less a choice between candidates than a referendum on "larger questions" about the future.

In the plan's first stage, Caddell called for contrasting "the real America . . . with the pollyanish view of America that was proclaimed in Dallas." In other words, the targeted voters—weak Democrats, young people and women—would be reminded of the hard realities of American life Reagan had been glossing over. Then, under the Caddell formulation, the campaign would "bring to saliency" all the concerns about the future in light of those glaring realities.

As we shall see, there was some evidence of the advice of both Hart and Caddell later in the Mondale campaign. But at this point there was clearly no consensus throughout the campaign on either theme or strategy.

Within the party and, to some extent, the Mondale organization itself, the level of second-guessing and complaint was mounting. Intramural arguments and rivalries always develop in campaigns in trouble, and this one was no exception. And Jim Johnson, whose primacy in the campaign no one questioned, was the target.

Johnson had many admirers in the campaign. He was an intelligent man who had the experience of working at levels of steadily increasing responsibility in four presidential campaigns before this one. He was cool and analytical—some said too much so—and highly regarded for his ability to face crisis situations calmly and seek solutions objectively.

But other staff members groused that he limited the access to Mondale to too narrow a circle of advisers and failed to reach out to good minds in the Democratic Party or even in his own campaign organization. The decision on Bert Lance had been made essentially without consulting anyone other than Mondale and

John Reilly. The decision to go ahead with the tax-increase plan in the acceptance speech also had been closely held. There had been no effort, for example, to solicit the estimate of possible political consequences from Lane Kirkland or John Perkins. Not even Peter Hart had been informed of the tax initiative until the day before the speech was to be delivered, too late to have any influence on it.

"You knew," Hart said later, "that fight had already been hashed out."

Johnson's tight control of the campaign also was causing ripples of discontent among longtime Mondale supporters around the country. As we traveled from state to state all through the late summer and fall, the complaints were the kind you always hear about a campaign in trouble. Even governors complained they couldn't get through to Johnson, let alone Mondale. Many of the complainers tried to get a hearing by going through Dick Moe, the longtime Mondale political operative who had been Democratic state chairman in Minnesota and chief of staff while Mondale was Vice President. Moe was widely known in the party and had a reputation for political acumen. But Mondale was a politician who had one chief adviser at a time. It had been Mike Berman at one point and then Dick Moe. But now it was Jim Johnson, and Moe was effectively shut out of any influence or even genuine access.

At one point, Johnson recognized the level of muttering, particularly from Democratic heavyweights in Washington who were not part of the campaign apparatus. So he created an "advisory committee" headed by Bob Strauss that met late on Monday afternoons for several weeks during the fall. Although Johnson attended the meetings, he never took the committee seriously. It was, as Strauss also recognized, a bit of window dressing—a device to neutralize campaign critics by bringing them into the tent, or at least appearing to do so.

The charade was never more evident than in one incident when the group was formed. On the day the announcement was to be made, Strauss was scheduled to go to a press breakfast at the Sheraton Carlton to explain the whole arrangement. The goal clearly was to convey the impression through the press to Democratic leaders around the country that this group of party leaders was now weighing in with Mondale with sound advice on some regular basis.

The day before the breakfast, Strauss told Johnson that he needed to speak to Mondale on the telephone. They had not talked at all since the morning after the California primary when Strauss had been the middle man in getting that critical endorsement from Representative Gillis Long of Louisiana. Johnson questioned the necessity of the call, and Strauss replied that the matter of his access to Mondale might come up at the breakfast. So, with Johnson showing some reluctance, the call was arranged. About 7:30 the next morning, Strauss and Mondale talked briefly on the telephone. Then, when a reporter asked at that breakfast how often Strauss conferred with Mondale, Strauss made a show of looking at his watch and replied:

"Oh, it's been about forty-five minutes since I last talked to him."

There was never any pattern of consultation from these advisory-committee meetings. In fact, as some of the participants recalled, at one session on which they agreed on what they considered a significant recommendation to Mondale, they spent most of their time discussing who might have the best chance of getting through to the candidate. They finally decided on Lane Kirkland, but by that time the picture of the closed campaign was accepted throughout the party.

It would be a mistake, however, to believe that the troubles burdening Mondale as he approached Labor Day were largely the product of Jim Johnson's management style or the bickering that developed within the campaign and within the Democratic Party. The weaknesses were more basic than that. Almost the entire summer had been spent in the kind of political patching and filling that should have been completed before the Democratic convention at San Francisco. And now there was no further time to make repairs.

20

You Ain't Seen Nothin' Yet

•

LABOR DAY in New York is like Labor Day in many other American cities and towns across the country. Officially, it's a day set aside as a legal holiday to honor the nation's working men and women. But in practical terms for most working men and women who have the day off, it is first and foremost a day to sleep in. Or perhaps it is a day to get chores done around the house before embarking on the day's special activities, like a picnic, or going to a ball game—or watching a parade.

That elemental bit of American behavior apparently had been overlooked, however, as Walter Mondale and Geraldine Ferraro—with an embarrassed Governor Mario Cuomo, Senator Pat Moynihan and AFL-CIO President Lane Kirkland at their sides—marched up Fifth Avenue at 9:30 on Labor Day morning. Instead of the din of crowds lining the sidewalk four or five deep, as often is the case for Manhattan's famous parades, the Democratic candidates for President and Vice President could hear their heels click on the pavement as they walked through a canyon of relative emptiness.

It was not that the Democratic nominees had no friends in New York. On the contrary, the governor and the heads of the largest and most important labor unions in the state had strongly urged Mondale and Ferraro to stage the traditional Labor Day kickoff of the campaign in New York. But not at 9:30 in the morning. In the early days of television there had been a show about New York called *The Naked City*, and never did the description seem more appropriate.

Clear across the country, Ronald Reagan kicked off his campaign for reelection under dramatically different circumstances.

At a rally scheduled for the civilized hour of 11:00 AM in a spacious Orange County park, a veritable sea of California supporters—police set the figure at an incredible 69,000—turned out to see and hear their home-state President. At least fifty-five buses brought in people of all ages who then waited an hour or longer in a hot sun to pass through one of thirteen metal detectors manned by security officers.

What the two scenes a continent apart might tell about the outcome of the election two months later was too early to say. But they did speak volumes about the organizational ability—and common sense—of the individuals who planned the Mondale and Reagan campaign kickoffs. The event on the East Coast was an unmitigated political disaster; the one on the West Coast an almost unparalleled triumph.

Why the absence of a large crowd in New York, and the presence of one in California, should have been so important was a commentary on the way positive television coverage had become the yardstick of successful campaigning. Crowds, after all, had little to do with the quality of the candidates' views or the speeches they gave. But through the prism of a television camera's eye, a large crowd helped make a candidate look successful, and a sparse one could suggest failure. For that reason, the well-orchestrated campaign these days always gave "the visual"—how an event would look on television—the highest priority. In this regard, the Reagan campaign rated an A-plus, the Mondale campaign an F. And the New York debacle and the Orange County gala, each in its own way, revealed in cameo the essence of its campaign's political strategy and style.

Mondale, in starting off in New York's Labor Day parade at 9:30 in the morning, had hoped to play the television time-zone game: a "hit" in three time zones in a single day by jetting across the country ahead of the sun. The day was carefully choreographed to draw television coverage in the East, the Midwest and on the West Coast, and also to target on urban America (midtown Manhattan), rural America (Merrill, Wisconsin, population 9,500) and suburban America (Long Beach, California).

Democrats used to kick off their presidential campaigns in Cadillac Square in Detroit, but New York was chosen because it always has a big Labor Day parade and was a more convenient takeoff point for the cross-country swing. Merrill, Wisconsin, in dairy-farming country, was selected because it too had a Labor Day parade. As for Long Beach, the Mondale planners wanted to cast their candidate as an aggressive campaigner going fearlessly right into the heart of "Reagan Country."

The only trouble with the Mondale plan was that New Yorkers don't get up early on holidays to go to parades—even to see presidential candidates. The union and political organizers of the Labor Day parade knew that fact well enough and told the Mondale braintrusters. But in order to play the time-zone game, they insisted that the starting time of the parade be moved up more than an hour, and they wouldn't take no for an answer.

So the parade began at 9:30. Reporters observing the anemic turnout asked Cuomo: "Where's the crowd?"

"They're all in church," he answered, smiling. But it was Monday, not Sunday, and even New Yorkers aren't all that pious.

Kirkland, recalling the episode with chagrin later, called it "a classic" screwup in which Mondale and the accompanying press corps came and went before the crowd arrived.

"If you read the press of that period," he said, "there was no Labor Day parade. It was a flop. We were unable to turn out people. The truth of the matter was that there were half a million people at that parade. It went from nine-thirty in the morning until four o'clock in the afternoon. It was probably the largest Labor Day parade we've had in New York, and we've had some big ones. . . . The start of the parade was moved up to accommodate [Mondale's] desire to go coast-to-coast on Labor Day. At 9:30 in the morning on Labor Day, nobody's on the sidewalks. By eleven o'clock there were a lot of people on the sidewalks."

By that time, however, Mondale and his entourage were well on their way to Wisconsin. Had Mondale stayed only two or three hours, Kirkland argued, "the television picture would have been of an enormous parade with people marching by and chanting 'We Want Fritz!' That would have been an enormous plus for him."

To make matters worse, the Wisconsin skies rained on the Merrill parade and rally as Mondale spoke. And Ferraro told the voters they would be "making history when I stand in the Capitol and take the oath as the first woman President of this great nation." It was that kind of day.

For more than a month after Mondale's own nomination, he

had been pointing toward the Labor Day kickoff. But when it came, he offered absolutely nothing new. When Pat Caddell, late of the Hart campaign, had submitted his strategy memo, Mondale had liked it. He told Marty Kaplan, the speechwriter, to scrap the Labor Day text he had written for Merrill and write one based on the Caddell memo. But when Mondale saw that text he rejected that one too, and as a result gave a speech containing mostly warmed-over ideas and lines—on the one day since his nomination that he had prime national news media attention. Starting too early in New York was not the only blunder of that opening day.

When an exhausted Mondale and Ferraro arrived in Long Beach several hours late, the crowd waiting at the suburban airport had dwindled and grown testy. Capping everything off, the public-address system broke down, obliging Mondale to use a bullhorn. And then, in the midst of his speech, someone in the crowd fainted from the heat.

"We need a medic!" Mondale shouted. "We need a medic right over here! Quick! . . . Can we get a medic over here, please?"

He was calling on behalf of the victim, but the appeal could just as well have been made for his own campaign. He hurried through the speech, then turned to Alan Cranston and Gary Hart, who were there to greet him, and said:

"Boy, this is a real hazard course."

After the rally, the Mondale entourage retreated to the *Queen Mary*, the great old Cunard luxury liner anchored in Long Beach harbor and converted into a hotel and tourist attraction. In its halcyon days before World War II, the giant ship plied the Atlantic with the most famous names of the day. Now blowup photographs of them—Winston Churchill, Clark Gable, Fred Astaire, Bette Davis—along the *Queen*'s spacious decks brought back the days when Franklin D. Roosevelt was the only American politician who mattered, and when his New Deal was seen by millions as the hope of the future. There was a certain irony in Mondale's spending his first night of the general-election campaign in such surroundings. And after the day he had put in, he could have been excused had he slipped into one of the ship's sumptuous old Art Deco bars where in the old days Adolphe Menjou might have had a nightcap before turning in.

Reagan's opening day, in contrast, went off without a hitch. Rather than worrying about time zones and urban-rural mixes, the Reagan planners settled on two events and executed them to perfection. The first and larger was the outdoor rally at Mile Square Regional Park in Fountain Valley, several miles due south of Disneyland. Although the event was not to start until eleven o'clock, people were converging on the large cricket field in the park three hours earlier; apparently they don't sleep so late on Labor Day in sunny California. Many toted lawn chairs and coolers or pushed infants in strollers. At the rally site, two large bleachers had been erected in front of a broad platform with a high blue backdrop, which shielded huge plastic bags holding hundreds of helium-filled red, white and blue balloons that were released into the sky after Reagan spoke. This balloon gimmick has become commonplace at Republican rallies, but this one was the classic of them all.

Before the President arrived, little girls in red leotards performed dance routines and waved pom-pons for the crowd. High-school bands blared out patriotic songs. Hollywood stars Charlton Heston, Mike Connors and Don Defore, and Reagan's daughter Maureen, warmed up the audience.

Reagan finally made his grand entrance amid much fanfare, including the inevitable "Ruffles and Flourishes" and "Hail to the Chief." To Americans who have never seen the arrival of a President, there is nothing to match it—the line of sleek black limousines rolling silently in, the somber Secret Service agents jumping out and briskly clearing the way, the White House flunky rushing up to the podium to hang the Presidential Seal on it before the President speaks. And the great man himself, waving and smiling, modestly accepting the thunderous cheers.

From his first words, it was vintage Reagan:

"You'll forgive me a little home-state pride, but I can't help but thank you for giving me an opportunity to get away from those puzzle palaces on the Potomac to return home to kick off our campaign."

No matter how many times he uttered that tired old line about the "puzzle palaces on the Potomac," and it had to be up in the hundreds by now, he always made it sound as if the phrase was crossing his lips for the first time. And the fact that he had now been in charge of those puzzle palaces for nearly four years didn't deter him either.

In what came to be his standard campaign speech, Reagan

proceeded to deliver a sermon on what was right about America, conceding only that there was more work to be done.

"The great crusade we began [in 1981] really never ended," he said. "We are just beginning. . . . This election is about the clear choices that will be before the American people. . . . We present to the people of America a sparkling vision of tomorrow—a belief that greatness lies ahead, only waiting for us to reach out for it."

His four specific objectives, Reagan said, were maintaining "sustained economic growth without inflation," ensuring that the country "remains today and forever prepared for peace," preserving "the rich traditional values that fill our lives and have permitted our nation to endure" and seeking "uncharted frontiers."

Reagan went on in that generalized vein until the end, when he quoted Dwight Eisenhower telling about a newly arrived government worker in Washington who went by the National Archives in a cab and asked the cabbie what the inscription, "What Is Past Is Prologue," meant.

"Oh, that," Reagan quoted the driver as saying, "that's bureaucrat talk. What it really means is, 'You ain't seen nothin' yet.' "

"Well," Reagan went on, "as far as I'm concerned, that's America's message to the world. We've got everything before us. . . . That's our message this year. We will carry it across America. You ain't seen nothin' yet!"

The crowd roared its approval, and up, up and away went the hundreds of red, white and blue balloons, as the bands played and the assorted politicians on the platform pumped the President's hand. Then the majestic ritual began in reverse: the agents clearing the way, the President moving quickly out and to his awaiting limousine and off, leaving the huge audience in an afterglow of patriotic stirrings. No doubt about it, it was a great show.

One woman in the audience, Marcia Forbes of Orange, was quoted in the Long Beach *Press-Telegram:*

"First the Olympics, now this. I'm just OD-ing on pride in America."

Ronald Reagan had credited Eisenhower and that Washington cabbie with the punch line, but it really came from the old jazz singer of the 1930s, Al Jolson. Reagan no doubt meant the phrase to convey the idea that his administration was only beginning to get to work on building a better America. But as far as the rest of his campaign was concerned, with the exception of his two debates with Mondale, the punch line was exactly wrong. Anyone who saw that rally in Orange County, in person or later on television, and the second one that day at De Anza Community College in Cupertino, saw and heard pretty much all there would be to see and hear from the Reagan reelection campaign, and it was intentionally so.

Just as in those "Spring in America, '84" television ads shown before the summer, the Reagan strategy for the fall campaign called for heavy doses of mood music and lulling lyrics, dished out in a studiously controlled environment. That formula had been used effectively in the past, most notably by Richard Nixon in winning reelection against George McGovern in 1972. But Nixon's instinct for the jugular and his zeal for a landslide victory had led to some fiercely negative commercials against McGovern. That approach was not Ronald Reagan's style. His managers would be happy to let him shower feel-good generalities on the voters, with television commercials by the Tuesday Team to match.

Reagan did go on the offensive briefly in his speech in Cupertino, near San Jose, but it was very mild stuff. Not mentioning Mondale by name but clearly referring to his tax-increase proposal, Reagan said the Democrats "intend to fund their campaign promises by raising taxes more than $1,500 per household. Is this your vision of what America's future should be?" By now, the Reagan team had its ducks in a row on the tax issue, and it was the same old refrain that had served Republicans well in the past: Fritz Mondale was just another old tax-and-spend Democrat.[43]

The Cupertino speech also introduced another staple of the Reagan pitch—invoking the names of great Democrats to win converts.

"To all those Democrats," Reagan said, "who were loyal to the party of FDR, Harry Truman and JFK but who see that its current leaders have changed it; that they no longer stand firmly for America's responsibilities in the world; that they no longer protect the working people of this country—we say to them: You are not

43. Generally overlooked was the fact that in this speech Reagan was the first of the candidates to raise the "age issue" in the campaign. "Trouble is," he said, "our opponents treat each new idea the old-fashioned way: They spurn it. I hate to say this, but the age factor may play a part in this election. Their ideas are just too old."

abandoned; our arms are open. Join us. Come walk with us down the new path of hope and opportunity."

This appeal to Democrats on the very first day of the general-election campaign was a measure of how secure the Reagan strategists already felt. The Orange County extravaganza was an undiluted rally of the faithful, and its overwhelming success was a solid indication that Reagan did not have to work overtime shoring up his base in the Republican Party. And convinced as deputy campaign manager Lee Atwater was that the convention in Dallas had "nailed down" the Sun Belt, Reagan could now go directly to the task of making inroads among the Democrats, which any Republican presidential candidate had to do to win. Reagan had been extremely successful in that endeavor in 1980 against Jimmy Carter, and he was picking up right where he had left off.

A basic and essential difference between the Mondale and the Reagan strategies from the very start was that the Mondale forces had no firm and dependable road map for the 270 electoral votes required for election on November 6; Reagan had one that charted the course down to the last detail. The Mondale plan of early courtship of the South and West—both strong Reagan areas—had the companion premise of a late "snapback" of traditional Democratic voters in the northern and midwestern industrial states if Mondale was able to show strength in the South and West. And that concept relied on the ultimate loyalty of the old coalition—blacks, labor, Jews and ethnics—often described in politics as an appeal to, and reliance on, "demographics," or the makeup of the electorate.

The Reagan plan, on the other hand, relied in a much more clean-cut fashion on arithmetic and geography: how many electoral votes in which states had to be corralled to reach the magic number of 270. Bob Teeter said later that the one question he always asked himself, and inquiring reporters, was "Show me any conceivable way Mondale gets 270." The Reagan forces ridiculed what Stuart Spencer called the Mondale campaign's "total emphasis on demographics, ignoring geographics. Geographics isn't everything," he said, "it's the only thing that counts in the electoral college. We had a 270 electoral strategy that we pretty well stuck to."

On July 23, four days after the close of the Democratic convention, Atwater wrote this memo:

"We now have a lock on an electoral majority. In a very real sense, the election is over. What we do now will determine the shape and size of our victory—but barring a major catastrophe, President Reagan is assured of reelection. By choosing a northern liberal as a running mate, Mondale has sealed his own electoral inferiority. The last time the Democrats ran a North-North ticket was 1968, and they lost, taking just one southern state; not since 1944 have they won with this combination. Mondale-Ferraro is a Snow Belt ticket, exclusively, which is not smart. They are conceding the Sun Belt to the President: South, 155 electoral votes, West 111 electoral . . . [for] 266, four short of a majority."

Atwater postulated that even in the event the Democrats were able to pick off the most liberal western states outside Reagan's own California—Washington, Oregon and Hawaii—he still was sure to win six Snow Belt states that had gone Republican in seven of the previous eight elections—North and South Dakota, Nebraska, Kansas, Indiana and New Hampshire—with a total of 34 electoral votes. Adding them to the Sun Belt pool would give Reagan 279 electoral votes—nine more than he needed for reelection.

"Remember," Atwater wrote, "this is a worst-case scenario. The President carried forty-four states in 1980, and is likely to go from his initial landslide to an even bigger landslide the second time around—just like Eisenhower did . . . I call 279 a conservative estimate of our electoral strength. But we haven't yet considered seven states in the Snow Belt that Gerald Ford carried in 1976, and we have a good shot in all of these." He ticked off Iowa, Illinois, Michigan, New Jersey, Connecticut, Vermont and Maine, for another 83 electoral votes.

"With 307 electoral votes," Atwater wrote, "Mondale could steal Arkansas, Mississippi, Alabama and Georgia from our southern base—and we'd still win. It's over, folks . . . The Democrats have chosen a strategy based on demographics, not geopolitics. Already, they have chosen a strategy that is virtually a repeat of 1968, when an all Snow-Belt ticket [Humphrey and Edmund Muskie of Maine] was virtually shut out of the Sun Belt. . . . From now on they're playing catch-up, and Ferraro may not be the godsend they think she is."

In basing the Reagan strategy on geopolitics, the President's men operated on the premise that the race would be close—though they really didn't believe it. And so they focused on the states they calculated they needed to garner 270 electoral votes. And again some of them turned to Richard Nixon for counsel. According to Roger Stone, who handled the northeast region, Nixon advised the campaign to select one northern industrial state, "one that we had our best chance to win in, and make an all-effort to deny that state to Mondale," since he would in all likelihood need a sweep of the Rust Belt to get 270 himself. Nixon recommended Ohio, and it received maximum attention.

"In essence, by picking off Ohio and putting as much resources in there as we did," Stone said later, "we really were just trying to construct a hole card just in case Mondale drew to an inside straight. If there'd been any chance of Mondale sweeping the industrial Northeast and the Midwest, we had one hole card there that we knew he couldn't get. And there we could deny him the 270 if this thing ever became tight."

Actually, senior adviser Charlie Black said, three states were selected at first for that treatment—Ohio, Michigan and Missouri—and only later was Ohio singled out by campaign manager Ed Rollins and senior strategist Stu Spencer. Its Republican tradition, a major controversy over a tax increase imposed by the Democratic governor, Richard Celeste, a strong ethnic Catholic population in and around Cleveland—all these factors led to the choice of Ohio. The state ultimately received more resources proportionately than any other, Stone said.[44]

With the arithmetic of the election confidently in place, the remaining question for the Reagan strategists was what their candidate, and his television commercials, should say to make sure he, and they, did not rock the smoothly sailing boat.

The four basic themes of the campaign had been summed up back in January in Reagan's State of the Union address proclaiming that "America is back." He touched on all four in his Orange County kickoff and would continue to do so through election day: assuring strong economic growth, peace through strength, building on traditional values and pioneering new frontiers. Aides emphasized the last two ideas as ways to present the seventy-three-year-old President as forward-looking. And he was counseled

44. One Reagan ad made especially for Ohio played on Celeste's very unpopular tax increase and Mondale's tax proposal. The tag line was: "If you like Celeste, you'll love Mondale."

not only to use the name of John Kennedy, as he did at De Anza College, but also to make repeated references to the space program, which would be forward-oriented—and reminiscent of JFK.

All through 1984 leading up to this point, one insider said, "we were associating ourselves with the future through symbols, like 'We're for high tech, not high taxes.' " Without such a focus, he said, the voters would have seen "a seventy-three-year-old man re-creating Dixon, Illinois," Reagan's boyhood hometown, and "if you don't have some claim to the future, you're not going to win."

The Reagan strategists, however, were willing to focus on the future only up to a point. When it came to discussing in specific terms what the President intended to do in another four years—where he would take the country in coping with the mushrooming federal deficit, for example—that was another matter entirely.

In the 1980 campaign, one of Reagan's top campaign managers told us after the election, Reagan could easily run on the Kemp-Roth tax cut, which promised a very attractive 30 percent tax cut. But in 1984, he said candidly, the administration was contemplating a simplification of the tax code. And that idea was hardly a vehicle for rounding up votes, he said, "because it kicks as hard as it bites. You start getting specific there, you get every interest group in the world out there. As a general proposition, simplifying the tax code is a good idea. But when you start pointing out to people that they're going to lose their deductions in exchange for that rate reduction, they all come down on you." As far as other matters were concerned, he insisted, the administration had been very specific over the previous four years.

Also, another insider noted, it didn't pay to get too specific when the President was still running, quite successfully, as an outsider trying to stop bad things from happening in those "puzzle palaces on the Potomac"—when in reality he had been Mr. Inside himself in Washington for the last four years.

Finally, there was one other reason some in the White House preferred to keep Reagan on the shortest leash possible. That reason was his propensity for the wisecrack, quip or just plain unthinking remark that could get him in political trouble. Only recently, in mid-August, while the President was being checked for a voice level for his weekly radio broadcast, an open microphone caught him saying:

"My fellow Americans. I am pleased to tell you I just signed legislation outlawing Russia forever. The bombing begins in five minutes."

Unfortunately for Reagan, the remarks were recorded and became public, to the great consternation of the White House. It was all a joke, everybody would understand that, a spokesman said. But commenting on that episode, one White House insider told us:

"We are a mistake-prone operation. He [Reagan] is a chronic [user of the] one-liner. He can't go five minutes without one. You have the equivalent of the bomber line twenty-five times a day. You can't forget that that can happen."

Such comments as the bomb joke could be particularly damaging to the President, this insider said, because of what he called Reagan's "cowboy problem"—that many feared he had Wild West instincts—a concern others less favorably disposed to the President preferred to call his "mad bomber" image. For this reason, Reagan's strategists felt that a foreign-policy environment free of crisis was of considerable importance to running the kind of programmed campaign they had in mind. Assuring that environment, however, was beyond even the control of these masters of campaign management.

There were, nevertheless, some in the Reagan inner circle who thought the President could not rest on his first-term record. He had to tell the voters, they felt, what he would do in a second term, and that the vision ought to be futuristic. Dick Darman was in the forefront of those pushing this view, with pollster Dick Wirthlin warning that Reagan was "losing on the future."

The debate went on through the summer, until Mondale helped settle it with his acceptance speech in San Francisco saying he would raise taxes to cut the deficit down to size. After being knocked off stride briefly by the declaration, the Reagan strategists soon realized that, as one of them put it later, "we had somewhat of a godsend."

To Atwater, the Mondale tax increase "was the single biggest mistake of the whole campaign. That just fell right into our trap of keeping the campaign on the economy." In the end, he said, "we basically took the school of thought that, look, let's run on our record. We don't have to make any outward promises for the future to speak of. We've got a good record."

By the time Mondale finally unveiled his deficit-cutting plan on September 10 in a speech in Philadelphia, the Reagan campaign had its "last resort" formulation in place. With the bark off, it told the voters that Reagan might have to raise taxes sometime, but he sure as hell didn't want to, whereas Mondale would do it right off, first thing. And before Mondale knew it, there he was—the challenger, on the defensive. He had been in political life for more than thirty years, long enough to know that was exactly where a challenger should never be.

Mondale did the best he could to put the deficit ball in Reagan's court. Laying out his proposal in great detail, he said he would cut the deficit by two-thirds by 1989 by slashing government spending $92 billion and by raising taxes on families making $25,000 a year or more. To Reagan, he said:

"Mr. President, all my cards are on the table—face up. Americans are now calling your hand. Let's see it. Let's debate it."

The President, however, had no intention either of showing his hand or debating the merits of Mondale's. Asked about his opponent's challenge at a White House picture-taking session—a "photo opportunity" in Nixonese—Reagan told reporters:

"This is nothing new. He told us several weeks ago he was going to raise the people's taxes, and now he's repeating it."

A horde of Republican voices joined the chorus in the obvious effort to paint the Mondale plan as just another Democratic big-tax, big-spending proposal. Mondale had hoped, by carefully including several important caveats, to blunt this broad-brush GOP characterization. But as an experienced politician he should have known better.

His proposal specifically stated that no household earning less than $25,000 a year would pay a dime more in taxes. Those making between $25,000 and $35,000 would have their tax bill raised less than two dollars a week, and those making up to $45,000 would pay four dollars a week more, with most of the burden borne by people in the higher brackets. The plan just as specifically said that the money raised through the tax increase would go into a trust fund to be used only for deficit reduction. And while his plan did propose $30 billion in new spending to restore some of Reagan's social-service cuts, Mondale at the same time proposed additional savings to cover those increased costs.

Mondale's accompanying rhetoric was tough, even bombastic, as he tried to throw Reagan on the defensive. He called the President "the biggest spender in American history" and said he was "neither a moderate nor a conservative, he's a radical." The Reagan debt, he said, was the largest "in the history of humanity" and was "the hydrogen bomb issue for domestic America." Yet Reagan, he said, "whistles right along" conducting a "happy-talk campaign" while refusing to say how he planned to "sock it to" Americans of middle income after the election with a national sales tax.

But all those details of the Mondale plan were in the fine print, and they had been too long in coming. Anyway, most voters unfortunately did not often take the time to look at the fine print. Presidential campaigns, except perhaps in the final days, were very low on their list of items that demanded their close and undivided attention. Still, had Mondale been prepared to lay out all the details of his deficit-reduction plan in his acceptance speech, and had he adequately highlighted the fact that the poor would pay no new taxes and middle-income Americans very little more, his plan might have been somewhat better received. Instead, his failure to offer specifics until nearly two months after his nomination gave the Reaganites plenty of time to develop their "last resort" formulation—and to cast Mondale's proposal in the simplistic terms of tax and spend. There aren't many constants in politics, but one of them is that voters hate taxes.

Two days after Mondale unveiled his plan, Reagan summed up the issue—and the bottom line of the campaign as Mondale chose to contest it—with these lines at one of his standard flag-waving, "New Patriotism" rallies in Endicott, New York:

"The American people aren't undertaxed. The government is overfed. The main difference between ourselves and the other side is that we see an America where every day is the Fourth of July. They see an America where every day is April Fifteenth."

So much for serious discussion of the major issue of a federal deficit out of control. But a political campaign, this one anyway, was not a seminar on economics, though Mondale tried his damnedest to make it one. He was convinced to his core that the deficit problem was a cancer on the body politic; if only the voters could be made to see how its mushrooming growth would affect their lives and the lives of their children, surely they would come to their senses and vote for him. Sure they would.

The whole matter of making deficit reduction the centerpiece had triggered an intense argument within the Mondale campaign.

Outside advisers, including New York television admakers David Sawyer and Scott Miller, late of the Glenn campaign, argued strongly that Mondale should take a quick shot at the deficit issue and then get off it, because the Republicans after their initial stumbling had gotten a firm handle on the issue. But others in the campaign, including Dick Leone and admaker Roy Spence, were convinced the deficit issue was a ten-strike.

The trouble, said one of the critics, was that "Mondale said taxes in the speech, but I don't think he really understood that the idea was to be talking about candor, and not taxes, and he kept talking about taxes." And with a well-established image as a spender, that emphasis worked against him. Still, the advocates of the deficit issue pressed on.

In one meeting around this time, one of the proponents was reported to have said:

"We're going to make Reagan eat that deficit. If we can give Mondale credibility on the deficit, we can do it on anything."

To which one of those who opposed the single-issue focus replied:

"If you can give Mondale credibility on the deficit, I'll eat that conference table."

Nevertheless, the focus on the deficit issue went forward. Mondale continued to drone on about deficits, and at the same time his television ads hammered at them. The first of the Spence ads for the fall went directly at the deficit. The ad showed well-dressed individuals leaving the Treasury Building in Washington and piling into sleek limousines as a voice-over said:

"In this building, Mr. Reagan's people are borrowing the money that's putting each of us $18,000 in debt. And who walks away with the money? Ninety thousand profitable corporations that pay no taxes, defense contractors on bloated budgets, foreign interests who make money on our debt. What the deficit really means is that you're paying for their free ride."

Another, made by Sawyer and Miller at the campaign's request and the only one of theirs used, showed a roller-coaster climbing to the peak of an amusement-park ride, then plunging downward. The narrator said:

"Nineteen eighty-two. Reaganomics takes our country into its worse recession and unemployment in fifty years. Now Ronald Reagan says the economy is moving up. It is—up on a mountain of debt and record-breaking deficits; more borrowing than all the other Presidents in history combined. That'll drive interest rates up, slow the economy down, and then [the roller-coaster plunges] . . . if you're thinking of voting for Ronald Reagan in 1984, think of what will happen in 1985."

The ad was extremely graphic, but the problem was, the issue made voters' eyes glaze over. The Republicans, in thirty years of trying to hang a much smaller federal debt and deficit spending around the Democrats' necks, had long since learned that these were matters too remote and complex for the average voter to worry much about. By now, the voters could reason, hadn't the Republicans been crying for years that the sky was falling over debts and deficits, and didn't life go on?

Still, the proponents of the deficit issue insisted they had the means with which to undermine Reagan's credibility. Leone, described by another insider as "an intellectual Hamlet," was now in charge of coordinating the campaign message—in the candidate's speeches, in advertising and in dealing with the news media. But, this insider and others testified later, Leone seemed incapable of making decisions, preferring to get into long discussions with Mondale on how awful the deficit was.

Staffers at the Mondale headquarters in Washington joked about what they called "The Leone Zone." It was like the Bermuda Triangle, they said. If you sent an idea into Leone's office, it was never heard from again. And on top of that, Leone himself was seen by other staffers, as one of them put it, as "arrogant and contemptuous of the rest of the staff." Some referred to him as "L'One." They saw his friendship with Johnson as his only credential, though some allowed that the job of pulling together all the aspects of the campaign message was not an easy one.

The Reagan campaign, meanwhile, underwent no great soul-searching on its message. Darman did some quick arithmetic on the back of an envelope and came up with a ballpark figure that Reagan could use as the average cost of Mondale's plan to the taxpayer. It varied from $1,500 on up, and the Mondale forces cried foul, saying whatever figure was used was wrong and misleading. But if the campaign was no economics seminar, it wasn't a class in advanced mathematics either. The point the Republicans wanted to make was, There goes the old Democratic tax-and-spend formula again. And Reagan's credibility was his best defense.

Voters were just not going to believe Mondale, a White House insider reasoned, when he told them:

"This guy you've been watching on television for thirty years [Reagan] and believing, he's a liar."

Bob Teeter agreed emphatically. He counseled all through the fall that the best thing that could happen for Reagan would be if the election was seen as a referendum on him. For all the complaints about the lack of specifics in Reagan's speeches and ads, Teeter said, the American people felt they knew Reagan well—and liked what they felt. Certainly if it came to taking his word against Mondale's on whether they needed to be taxed more, the decision was an easy one for most of them.

Within the White House, Mondale's attempts at decisiveness and candor, as in the Lance affair and then the tax increase proposal, only brought him ridicule. One Reagan aide referred to Mondale in internal memos as "Wimp II"—"Wimp I" having been, in this view, Jimmy Carter.

Another factor keeping the Mondale campaign on the deficit was Reagan's deft handling of foreign policy as an issue. As Mondale sought to make capital of the fact that Reagan, alone among recent Presidents, had not met with his counterpart in the Soviet Union, the Reagan administration simply arranged a high-profile meeting with Soviet Foreign Minister Andrei Gromyko. Mondale countered by scheduling his own session with Gromyko. But that move did not alter the fact that Reagan had blunted one of Mondale's most insistent complaints—that the President could not move arms control forward if he refused even to meet with the Russians.

The Reagan-Gromyko meeting was in itself no big deal. Gromyko was the foreign minister, not the Soviet head of state. And he had been in the United States many times during Reagan's four years to attend sessions of the United Nations in New York, which in fact was the main reason for his presence this time. But the Reagan image-shapers milked all they could out of Gromyko's White House visit. In advance, Reagan delivered a notably conciliatory speech at the UN, with Gromyko in the audience, saying the United States was "ready for constructive negotiations" with the Soviet Union.

Mondale promptly charged that Reagan, who earlier had labeled Moscow the "focus of evil," had "changed his tune" for domestic political reasons.

"Why this change now, forty-two days before the election?" Mondale inquired. "He should have been saying that six weeks after he took office rather than six weeks before the election."

Mondale's lament did nothing to take the positive public-relations edge off the Reagan-Gromyko meeting, and neither did Gromyko's own rather sour report on its outcome. The talks, he said in a statement released by Tass, "do not, unfortunately, warrant a conclusion about practical positive changes in the U.S. administration's foreign-policy course." Well, voters were likely to say, Reagan tried, but he's right that you can't do business with the Russians.

The pumped-up Gromyko visit also served to take the spotlight off an event eight days earlier that, had it occurred in a vacuum, might have caused considerable political problems for Reagan. On September 20, a van laden with explosives blew up outside the American Embassy annex northeast of Beirut, killing at least eight persons and injuring the American and British ambassadors, among others. The bombing was the third attack on American facilities in Lebanon in seventeen months, rekindling the debate about American security measures and about the basic justification for the continued presence of U.S. troops in the country.

Reagan responded, as he had on the other occasions, that the United States would not be intimidated by terrorism. But again there was no retaliation, in spite of Reagan's warnings when he first took office that the days were over when terrorists could attack Americans with impunity. None of the hostages held in Tehran during Jimmy Carter's last year had been killed, yet he caught hell for the whole episode. But Ronald Reagan was the Teflon President. His "explanation" for the failure of ordered security measures to have been put in place at the embassy annex, probably would have been a scandal had it come from Carter.

"Anyone that's ever had their kitchen done over," he said, "knows that it never gets done as soon as you wish it would."

But that was Reagan for you. The Democrats jumped all over that line, but it got them nowhere.

Carter, on the other hand, was everybody's punching bag. Reagan, answering a student's question at Bowling Green State

University in Ohio, in fact seemed to blame the Carter administration for the latest Beirut attack.

"We're feeling the effects today of the near-destruction of our intelligence capability in recent years before we came here," the President said. There seemed to be a public attitude then, he said, that "spying is somehow dishonest and let's get rid of our intelligence agents."

The Democrats, predictably, cried foul again and Mondale said the remark was "inexcusable." Even Reagan's own CIA director, William Casey, said through a spokesman that neither agency funds nor personnel were unduly cut by Carter. Reagan brushed aside the criticism, saying his remarks had been "distorted" by the press. It was truly amazing how frequently the press, armed with the latest electronic recording apparatus, and television, equipped with the most advanced cameras and tapes to record both his image and his voice, managed to "distort" the things he said.

Carter himself was irate over the apparent charge.

"For more than three and a half years," Carter said, "I have listened with disappointment and some degree of anger to a stream of false assertions made by President Reagan in his attempt to blame his every mistake and failure on me and others who served before him in the White House. This series of tragedies in the Middle East has been brought about by the President's own deeply flawed policy and inadequate security precautions in the face of proven danger. His frivolous reference to tardy kitchen repairs is indicative of his refusal to face the reality of his own responsibility."

A couple of days later, Reagan phoned Carter and, according to a White House spokesman, told him his remarks had been "misinterpreted." There was the news media screwing up again. Didn't they ever get anything right?

Fortunately for the President, he didn't have to rely on the press to get his message to the American people. He had the Tuesday Team—that blue-ribbon collection of Madison Avenue advertising wizards brought together just to merchandise Ronald Reagan to the electorate.

In conveying the Reagan message, according to Teeter, overseer of the Tuesday Team, the central point was "controlling the agenda"—making sure that the message focused on what the

Reagan strategists wanted said, not what Mondale wanted to debate. And in pursuing this objective, Teeter said, it was essential that the speeches of Reagan, George Bush and all the surrogates, and the television commercials, be carefully coordinated to strike the same themes at the same times. To this end, specific "issues cycles" were set. These were periods of time in which one issue would be emphasized by all components of the campaign, then put aside by all and the next issue picked up and trumpeted.

About ten days after Labor Day, the Reagan campaign kicked off its advertising effort with an unprecedented thirty-minute buy of all three major television networks, plus the major independent television stations in all the major city markets, for the simultaneous showing of a documentary on Reagan. The device is called a "roadblock" in the television advertising business, and never before had one been thrown up on this scale for a political commercial. The documentary was an extended version of the film shown at the Republican convention, complete with travelogue scenes of Reagan on the Normandy beach and the rest.

Also run in September were two commercials of the same "feel-good" tone of the spring flight of ads. They were cut from the same cloth—inspirational, with down-home images, dreamy music and vacuous messages. One, called "America Is Back," showed children riding their bikes on a placid small-town street, a young family toting furnishings into a home, a man showing off a new truck, working men and women walking into a plant, a barber at work, a teenager polishing a car and an elderly couple strolling along licking ice cream cones, while the syrupy-sounding narrator intoned:

"In a town not too far from where you live, a young family has just moved into a new home. Three years ago, even the smallest house seemed completely out of reach. Right down the street, one of the neighbors has just bought himself a new car, with all the options. The factory down by the river is working again. Not long ago, people were saying it probably would be closed forever. Just about everyplace you look, things are looking up. Life is better. America is back. And people have a sense of pride they never felt they'd feel again. And so it's not surprising that just about everyone in town is thinking the same thing. Now that our country is turning around, why would we ever turn back?"

Another, called "It's Morning Again," showed cattle feeding, a white farmhouse at dawn, a happy wedding party, an elderly man raising the American flag while trusting young faces peered up at it until the flag filled the screen. With more misty music in the background, the same syrupy announcer said:

"It's morning again in America. Today, more men and women will go to work than ever before in our country's history. With interest rates at about half the record highs of 1980, nearly two thousand families today will buy new homes, more than at any time in the past four years. This afternoon, sixty-five hundred young men and women will be married, and with inflation at less than half of what it was just four years ago, they can look forward with confidence. It's morning again in America. And under the leadership of President Reagan, our country is stronger, and prouder, and better. Why would we ever want to return to where we were less than four short years ago?"

In the next two weeks, inflation and employment were the two issues cycled on the stump and in the television ads, and they were the first using Reagan or his voice on the screen, with the same "America is back" message. In the last week in September, the next issue cycle dealt with peace. And in close coordination with Reagan's stump speeches touting what came to be called "the New Patriotism," the commercials were full of flags—flags being raised, flags fluttering in the breeze, little kids sitting on a curb with tiny flags in their hands, watching a parade go by.

One ad in this cycle showed the Roosevelt Room in the White House, a large rectangular room only steps from the Oval Office, with an oblong conference table and off in one corner the flags of each of the American armed services. Reagan did the narration himself:

"Four times in my life, America's been at war. Such a tragic waste of lives. It makes you realize how desperately the world needs a lasting peace. Just across the hall here in the White House is the Roosevelt Room. And often as I meet with my staff, I gaze up at the five service flags, each representing one of the five military services. Draped from each flag are battle streamers signifying every battle campaign fought since the Revolutionary War, each ribbon a remembrance of a time when American men and women spilled their blood into the soil of distant lands. My fondest hope for this presidency is that the people of America give us the continued opportunity to pursue a peace so strong and so lasting that we never again have to add another streamer to those flags."

While Americans were watching and listening to such ads, those who were seeing and hearing the President on the campaign trail, either on the spot or by way of the television news, were being given the same heavy dose of "the New Patriotism." Borrowing from the Olympics that had just fanned the same emotions, Reagan developed a little ritual with the crowds. He would tell them he was going to give them a little test. Then he would proceed to ask them what country had cut inflation, interest rates and unemployment. He was not going to give them the answer, he would say, but he would tell them it was known by three initials.

The audience, and particularly the young people in the crowd, invariably would start the chant used in a previous Olympics to cheer the American hockey team gold-medal winners, and carried over at the Summer Olympics in Los Angeles: "U.S.A.! U.S.A.! U.S.A.!" A vote for Ronald Reagan clearly was a vote for your country.

Although Reagan clearly and openly was the cheerleader for this particular patriotic yell at his rallies, he apparently preferred to remember the enthusiasm of American youth as completely self-starting. In an interview we had with him in the Oval Office after the election, he had this to say:

"For someone who had known the youth of America as I knew them when I was governor back there in the sixties, when they were burning the flag and burning me in effigy and a few things like that, you couldn't help but see that something had happened out there. And those young people made up so much of the crowd at our rallies. And the enthusiasm, the patriotism that showed wasn't just enthusiasm for me. It was that thing about America. How many times I'd have to stop speaking to listen to the chant of 'U.S.A.!' like they did for the Olympics."

On the stump as on television, Reagan was distinctly a non-threatening individual. Very seldom did he harangue a crowd; rather, his style was quietly conversational, firm yet breezy, flavored with humorous and self-deprecating asides and very human. He flubbed a lot of lines for a professional actor, but he always recovered with wit and aplomb. And above all he had the ability to deliver the same tired lines over and over again and make them sound as if he had never set eyes on them before.

Against this campaign phenomenon who functioned equally well on platform and on camera, the Mondale campaign had a candidate who on the stump came over on his best days as an angry, even petulant, scold and who was extremely uncomfortable appearing on television. He was convinced that he was not suited for the television era, and some of his most influential aides agreed with him. As a result, most of the Mondale commercials—in which the staff could present him in his best light, since the campaign was producing and paying for them—never showed Mondale.

"People around him," Leone said later, "tended to reinforce his view of how bad he was. He only agreed twice to be televised [for a commercial]. He didn't like it."

Particularly, Leone said, Mondale didn't like being told to look a certain way or say something a certain way, as if he were an actor.

"He didn't like to be talked to in those terms. It made him more likable to be saying, 'This is bullshit,' " his message man said, but that attitude also made it near-impossible to get Mondale to be cooperative. The problem even reached the point, Leone said, that the campaign would not even use the candidate to do the voice-over on his own commercials, when Mondale "was better than the guy we were using."

Further stiffening Mondale's resistance was his conviction that the Reagan commercials were trivializing the election. So he continued through most of September hammering away at the deficit issue and, in the process, driving his supporters around the country to distraction. As he talked about such things as "the misalignment of currency" to blue-collar audiences, eyes rolled en masse toward the ceiling.

In mid-September, another bitter debate broke out within the campaign over the continued focus on the deficit. Democratic media advisers brought in on a contract basis found themselves in limbo when they suggested, as did outside Democratic leaders, that maybe there was something else just as important to raise in the campaign.

"Could the theme honestly be the deficit?" one of them said he asked himself incredulously after that focus had been going on for weeks. "Could the message honestly be that Mondale is going to deal with deficit, the most pressing problem facing America? Things are worse than you think? That's our message against Reagan? We couldn't believe it."

At this point came the ubiquitous Patrick Caddell, pushing hard for Mondale to drop the focus on deficit reduction and taxes, and move onto themes of fairness and understanding, without attacking Reagan personally. Caddell, who a few months earlier was imploring Gary Hart to beat Mondale's brains out for his support of the Vietnam war, was now in the Mondale ranks. Johnson had resisted his entry, knowing what a divisive force he could be in a campaign with his temperamental and insistent ways. But John Reilly and Paul Tully persuaded Johnson to listen to Caddell's analysis of the Democratic plight. In advance they counseled Caddell, however, to curb his customary tantrums if he hoped to make a contribution. For once, Mondale insiders said, Caddell did just that and was instrumental in getting the candidate off the deficit kick and onto a more aggressive tack against Reagan.

The accomplishment was not, however, without the usual internal uproar that seemed to occur whenever Caddell put his nose under a political tent. His recommended strategy flew directly in the face of that focus on the deficit as pushed by Dick Leone, who, one insider said later, "went bananas" over Caddell's recommendations. The matter came to a head in mid-September, with most of the polls showing Mondale trailing Reagan by about twenty percentage points.

At a meeting in Bob Beckel's office, Caddell was astonished to hear reports that Mondale was closing the gap. He openly took issue with that optimistic view and informed those present that Mondale was the first challenger to an incumbent in political history who was losing ground in September. Johnson decided to have Caddell and Peter Hart each do additional polling to check again whether Mondale was that bad off. After much hassling, a decision was reached to refocus the campaign away from the deficit argument, but with no unanimity about what it should focus on. The top-level strategists were now splitting roughly into two camps, with Johnson, Leone and Hart in one and Reilly, Donilon and Tully supporting Caddell's call for radical change.

Mondale was scheduled to speak at George Washington University in Washington the next week and the forum was opportune for him to make his fresh start. But because of the attention being given to the Gromyko talks, Johnson and Leone were determined that Mondale have a "foreign-policy week" on the stump, and they wanted the GW speech to concentrate on that area. To Caddell, such a focus was madness, because it would do nothing to give Mondale a new look. When Caddell started to talk to Marty Kaplan about writing the GW speech, Leone—whose campaign mandate was overseeing "the message"—again went "bananas." The Mondale campaign was rapidly going under but, as one of the insiders put it, "guerrilla warfare" was being waged by Leone to protect his turf.

A core element in Caddell's concept, insiders said, was his conviction that Mondale needed to stir the consciences and party loyalties of older Democrats, and in the process achieve a "snap-back" to the Democratic ranks. It was Caddell's notion, Johnson said, that "somehow if you got a few code words out there, either around the right-wing agenda issue, in which case you snap back culturally sensitive people who previously had Democratic inclinations, or if you talked about the standard old Democratic themes about compassion and other things, there would be a snapback of the blue-collar vote."

This appeal, however, had to be made deftly, always bearing in mind Reagan's great personal popularity. Caddell's formulation, one insider said, was that "on all these things, it's not that Reagan is a bad man or chooses always the wrong policies. But he can't seem to see, he doesn't seem to realize that not everybody's rich, and that not everybody's comfortable."

On the basis of this formulation, Sawyer and Miller produced a proposal for an ad campaign called "The Other America" that said essentially, according to Miller, that "out there, beyond the TV lights, beyond the teleprompter and the tight choreography of the Reagan campaign, there's another America. And it's not just the walking wounded, but it's people who struggle and work two jobs to get by. . . . We just wanted to go and picture the real America the way it was and say Reagan can't relate to it, and he can't relate to your future."

The Sawyer-Miller proposal was shelved, but the Mondale campaign did do a so-called compassion ad that, critics said, focused on the wrong target—on the poor, rather than the middle class—and in so doing just reinforced Mondale's old New Deal image.

"I saw it," said one Mondale campaign associate, "and I thought it was a United Way commercial. It had people on crutches and in hospital beds and elderly people, and it was really saying, 'There's another America out there, and it's the poor, the sick and the elderly. And Mondale represents these people.' "

The trouble was, he said, the forty-year-old blue-collar worker the campaign should have been courting was neither poor, nor sick, nor elderly. He could agree with Mondale that these people needed help, but then go and vote his self-interest, which he saw in Reagan.

The eventual result of Caddell's arrival, and the ensuing debate over "deficits or compassion," was a very hard-hitting speech by Mondale at George Washington, finally delivering a message that Democrats could rally around. Mondale went directly at Reagan on two fronts—his campaign shift to more centrist positions and his insulated, sloganeering campaign format.

Dubbing the President "the new Reagan," Mondale said of his conciliatory speech at the UN:

"Gone is the talk of nuclear warning shots. Gone is winnable nuclear war. Gone is the evil empire. After four years of sounding like Ronald Reagan, six weeks before the election he's trying to sound like—Walter Mondale."

Then Mondale ticked off the full indictment:

"The new Reagan supports economic aid to the developing world. The old Reagan slashed it. . . . The new Reagan praises international law. The old Reagan jumped bail from the World Court. The new Reagan criticizes South Africa. The old Reagan cozied up to apartheid. The new Reagan calls for peace in Central America. The old Reagan launched an illegal war in Nicaragua. . . . The new Reagan worries about soaring arms sales. The old Reagan sold almost anything to nearly everyone. The new Reagan warns about nuclear proliferation. The old Reagan said it was none of our business and opened the sluice gates on materials to make the bomb. . . . To those who welcome the new Reagan, I say this: My dad was a Methodist minister, and he once told me, 'Son, be skeptical of deathbed conversions.' I asked why. And he said, 'Because sometimes they get well.' "

Having thus gone to the edge of accusing the President of deception, Mondale piously went on:

"I have been told to attack Mr. Reagan personally. My answer is no. I did not enter this race to tear down a person. I entered it to fight for our future. I have been advised to ignore issues, to choose slogans over substance. My answer is no. There is a big distance between Pennsylvania Avenue and Madison Avenue. And there ought to be a big difference between a presidential election and a pep rally."

After weeks of riding the deficit horse, Mondale mentioned deficits only in passing. Instead, he went right to the heart of the Reagan "feel-good" campaign format, charging that the Reagan strategists were underestimating the concern and the intelligence of American voters, especially the young. To the college students before him, Mondale said:

"You have probably heard the conventional wisdom about your generation. You are said to be self-content, materialistic and devoid of social commitment. You are supposed to have no sense of history. You are accused of having an attention span no longer than a television commercial. That's quite an indictment. I don't believe it. But suppose some people did. Imagine a presidential campaign based on those assumptions about your generation.

"Believing you to be selfish, they would pander to your supposed greed. Their message would be: Be glad for what you have—and be blind to those who have little. Believing you to have no memory, they would exploit your alleged amnesia. Their message would be: History is bunk. Republicans are Democrats. And in 1984, the year of Orwell and doublespeak, the MX missile is renamed the 'Peacekeeper.' Believing you to be shallow, they would manipulate your rumored gullibility. Their message would be all sizzle and no substance; all happy-talk and no straight talk; all blue skies and no blueprint; all television and no vision."

The Democratic candidate was presenting a pretty fair picture of what the conventional wisdom about American youth indeed was—and of how the Reagan campaign was playing on it.

"I don't know which is worse," Mondale continued, "the emptiness of such a campaign or the cynicism about the American people that it implies. I do not know which is more damning, their contempt for the issues or their condescension toward our people. They underestimate you. They're betting that Americans are not smart. That's a bad bet."

Again he returned to the "feel good" Reagan campaign:

"This crowd doesn't want you to think about the stakes in this contest. They want to trivialize it. That is arrogance. We are in an American presidential election. . . . This election is not about jelly beans and pen pals. It is about toxic dumps that give cancer to our children. This election is not about country music and birthday cakes. It is about old people who can't pay for medicine. This election is not about the Olympic torch. It is about the civil-rights laws that opened athletics to women and minorities who won those gold medals. . . . This election is not about slogans, like 'standing tall.' It is about specifics, like the nuclear freeze—because if those weapons go off, no one will be left standing at all."

The speech was by far Mondale's best rhetorical strike of the campaign. For one thing, after weeks of frustrating many Democratic leaders and angering others with his harping on the deficit that highlighted his unpopular call for new taxes, Mondale was plucking a chord to which the party faithful could respond.

But the practical political question remained: Was Mondale right about the American people, or were Reagan and his slogan-masters? Against Mondale's impassioned plea for Americans to be their brothers' keeper, Reagan's question in his 1980 debate against Carter had been dusted off and raised again: "Are you better off than you were four years ago?" And the answer seemed to be coming back, resoundingly, "Yes."

One thing the George Washington speech did achieve for Mondale was to remind voters that he was at the head of the Democratic ticket, not Geraldine Ferraro. On Labor Day, she had accompanied him on that politically disastrous cross-country sprint—to give her exposure, some on the Mondale team said. As the first woman on a national ticket, however, she was a drawing card in her own right, and the reception she received in Mondale's company sometimes created the impression that the ticket had been turned around. In fact, buttons that read "Ferraro-Mondale" began to sprout in the crowds, especially on women. She consistently outdrew her Republican counterpart, George Bush, as well, though he far outdistanced her in the polls. One, by ABC News and the Washington *Post*, showed her trailing Bush by nearly two to one—but with a more favorable rating than Mondale.

Ferraro, however, was far from an unvarnished blessing for the Democratic ticket. Her husband's financial problems continued to plague her as the press uncovered new allegations of wrongdoing in Zaccaro's real estate dealings. And now she was in the soup with the hierarchy of her Catholic church. Her position on abortion—personally opposed, but that as a public official she would not impose her religious views or those of her church on other Americans—greatly disturbed Archbishop O'Connor, among others.

O'Connor in early September publicly alleged that Ferraro had "said some things about abortion relative to Catholic teaching which are not true." He specifically said he would not "tell anybody in the United States you should vote for or against Geraldine Ferraro or anybody else." But the archbishop's words served as a catalyst for anti-abortion forces to zero in on her.

The specific cause of the row was a letter Ferraro wrote in 1982 inviting about fifty colleagues in Congress to a pro-choice briefing she said would show that "the Catholic position on abortion is not monolithic and there can be a range of personal and political responses to the issue." O'Connor took that letter, surfaced by the anti-abortionists, to mean she was challenging the Church's official view that, as O'Connor quoted Pope John Paul II, "abortion is death" and "the killing of an innocent creature."

The row brought religion further into the campaign. The subject had already been injected—at least in the Democrats' view—by the involvement of Jerry Falwell and other evangelists at the Republican convention and by Reagan's own remarks there. Mondale had been trying to capitalize on what he thought to be a broad public revulsion to mixing religion and politics, and Ferraro's problems with the archbishop only confused things.

To make matters worse, the release of Ferraro's 1982 letter came on the very day Mondale was making public his detailed plan for federal deficit reduction. Her day on the stump was supposed to be strictly subordinate to that event, but the clash with the archbishop became a competing news story. She phoned O'Connor directly and told him, she reported, "that I have never made a public statement describing or misrepresenting the teachings of my church." But the controversy continued to follow her.

The next day she said, "I'd quit my job" if she couldn't reconcile her religious beliefs with her constitutional obligations as Vice President to uphold the separation of church and state. Still the issue clung. Later, when pro-life groups began to picket her, she professed to see the hand of the Reagan campaign in their actions, and at one point challenged the opposition to "come out and fight like men."

Although Ferraro was the first woman on a national ticket, she played the standard role of a vice-presidential candidate: She attacked the opposition vigorously. She went after Reagan on arms control, lack of compassion and the whole panoply of Democratic complaints against the incumbent. She proved to be feisty but appealing, with a street-smart manner punctuated by her distinct New York accent and colloquialisms. Speaking to a group of elderly citizens at the governor's mansion in Columbus, Ohio, for instance, she noted that her own mother was "a senior citizen," although the elder Mrs. Ferraro "is not too nuts about" that label.

Part of the attention paid her no doubt was that accorded to any new celebrity. People wanted to see the attractive woman who had begun to come into their living rooms regularly via the television nightly news. But a lot of her appeal clearly was in the fact that she represented history in the making. She liked to tell audiences about how, on her first trip south as the nominee, she saw "a lot of young men holding up their baby girls and saying things like, 'Touch her.' It was an absolutely incredible thing."

Ferraro was clearly touched herself by the outpouring of affection and pride she elicited in American women. She told one crowd of radiant women in Columbus that "it's absolutely marvelous to have people shouting, 'Gerry! Gerry!' " There was a note of wonder in her voice as she said it. She liked the feeling so much, she said, she had suggested that her children start greeting her in the same way when they came down for breakfast in the morning. Their response, she reported, was: "Oh, Mom!"

Very quickly, Ferraro mastered the knack of giving no quarter in her traditional role as running mate, while retaining feminine appeal. At a stop in Toledo on the same mid-September trip, some schoolchildren presented her with a handmade Hungarian vest. She slipped it on, then turned a circle to let everyone in the school auditorium see how well it fit. The gesture was an improvement on the standard politician's move of accepting a football jersey with his name and the number "1" on it, holding it up in front of him, then tossing it to an aide in charge of collecting football jerseys with the number "1" on them.

By early October, Ferraro had hit her stride, even to the point where she was making Mondale's best arguments better—or at least more directly—than he was. During a tour of a Chrysler Corporation plant in Belvidere, Illinois, she point-blank asked members of the United Auto Workers, which had endorsed Mondale, why they were going to vote for Reagan.

"What I'm here for," she said, "is not to learn how to torque a car, not for a photo opportunity. We're running a campaign, and five weeks from today you're going to make a decision on who's going to run the country. I want to know why, why one-third of you are going to vote for Ronald Reagan."

A poll among UAW workers showing Reagan running strongly "absolutely floored" her, she said. Would "someone, anyone," tell her why they would do so? The answers came back:

"We blame Jimmy Carter for a lot of the problems . . . Iran, weak foreign policy. . . . What Reagan has done, he's said the things the working man believes. I think the average working man is against the welfare system the way it's run now."

Ferraro reminded the workers that "fifty-two hostages came home alive" from Iran, and she asked:

"Have those people who are still worrying about Iran seen what's happened in Beirut recently? Three bombings. . . . Are we standing tall in Lebanon with a President who doesn't take responsibility for what happened?"

As for the complaint against the welfare system, she said:

"What Reagan has done, very successfully, is say that we must cut programs in which there is waste, like food stamps. You know how big the food stamp program is? Eleven billion dollars. You could eliminate the whole program and you wouldn't even do anything about budget deficits. There may be some cheating, but it doesn't hold a candle to the waste and cheating that's going on in the Defense Department."

And she reminded the UAW workers that she and Mondale had supported the Chrysler bailout, which Reagan at first opposed but finally backed during the 1980 Republican primary in Michigan, the UAW headquarters state. All in all, Ferraro's performance was, more than one Democratic politician observed, one Mondale could well copy.

George Bush, meanwhile, was campaigning as the loyal Vice President, and there probably never had been one more loyal. On the same day Ferraro was grilling the UAW workers in Illinois, Bush was taking off the gloves against Mondale in Lubbock, Texas. To the Democratic nominee's criticism of security measures in the latest Beirut bombing and Reagan's failure to resume arms-control negotiations with the Soviet Union, despite the meeting with Gromyko, Bush said:

"We've seen Walter Mondale take a human tragedy in the Middle East and try to turn it to personal political advantage. . . . There's not one positive idea contained in all of Walter Mondale's carping and criticism, not one idea worthy of a man running for the highest office in the land."

Mondale's only idea, raising taxes, Bush said, "bombed so badly he doesn't even talk about it anymore." As a Texan, the Vice President said, he knew Texans would "never vote for a weak leader, a tax raiser, a more-government-handout promiser like Walter Mondale." The Democrats, he charged, were "looking for a way to get their dragging campaign off its backside.'"

Bush also made good use of the favorite Republican buzz words—Tip O'Neill—who in the GOP's hands had been molded from the benevolent if out-of-date old liberal that he was into the devil incarnate. Liberals like O'Neill and Mondale, he said, "have had their chance, and now all they can see in this great country of ours is gloom and disaster [as they seek to] scare, frighten, whine and carp, and hope something goes wrong so they can get back in office." In truth, O'Neill and Mondale *were* claiming to see gloom and disaster, and Bush certainly was right saying they were trying to get the White House back.

George Bush was not one, himself, to see gloom and disaster in the world according to Ronald Reagan. Not now, anyway. His perspective on that world had changed radically, in fact, in his four years as Vice President—since those days in the spring of 1980 when he was competing with Reagan for the Republican nomination and dubbing his rival's tax and budget cut plans "voodoo economics." In the last four years, indeed, Bush had been such a fawning Vice President that he was known in and out of his party as the GOP's prime "cheerleader," and the label was not always bestowed in admiration. He had the reputation of being a bootlicker, and his conduct in office did nothing to diminish it.

But Bush was a smart and disciplined politician, and he understood that his own political future required that, as they used to say, he knew his place. Never during his four years as Vice President did he allow himself any public criticism of Reagan. That comportment was not so unusual for someone in his position. But neither did he ever allow himself even any private criticism of the sort that Lyndon Johnson and Nelson Rockefeller had circulated in their time as the number-two men.

Some predecessors champed at the restraints the office placed on them, but not Bush. He had lunch weekly with the President, at which time he had ample opportunity to air his views, including criticisms, and that was good enough for him. And on Reagan's part, he treated Bush with respect and cordiality and gave him responsibilities in the same manner than Carter had dealt with Mondale in the previous administration. Bush knew, as Mondale was finding out this year if he didn't fully appreciate the fact already, that a Vice President can't run away from the President under whom he served. And obviously it never entered Bush's mind to try.

As for the "cheerleader" label, Bush told us after the election:

"Fine, I plead guilty to that. . . . That's the way I've been in this job, and that's the way I'm going to stay . . ."

He was surprised at the emphasis placed on the label during the campaign, Bush said, "because I've always done it. I've been supportive of the President for four years. If I have some difference with him, I'll tell him what it is, and he'll tell me if he agrees or not. But I don't think cheerleading is a bad thing to do. What do they expect you to do?"

At the time of Mondale's selection of Ferraro as his running mate, there was great speculation about the way Bush would campaign against her, and whether the feisty lady from Queens would run over him. He got much mail from friends and supporters warning him he was in "a no-win situation."

Because Bush was always the gentleman, the expectation was that he would treat her with great deference, or even gushiness. The "preppy" label also clung to him after four years as Vice President and a continuing stream of preppy locutions from him. To give just one example, we accompanied him on a political trip to South Carolina about halfway into the first Reagan term. He was asked at a press conference whether he thought the President would seek a second term and, if not, whether he would seek the White House himself. Bush's answer to the first part was: "I hope to heck he does," and he dodged the second. Bush was not the type to beat up on a woman, even oratorically. He solved the dilemma essentially by saying very little about Ferraro on the stump and focusing his fire at Mondale.

The prospect of a Bush-Ferraro debate drew particular interest, not only because that confrontation would pit a man against a woman but because the chemistry seemed so loaded against Bush. Yet there never was any question that they would debate. Bush's press secretary, Peter Teeley, said Bush always wanted to debate Ferraro, and the only complication was that, as Teeley put it later, Bush was "a bargaining chip" in the negotiations over the presidential debates. Mondale said he wanted six, but he knew he would never get them. Reagan had said early he would debate and he thought two would be about right. The vice-presidential debate was thrown in as part of the deal.

The Bush-Ferraro confrontation had to wait, however, until after the first debate between the presidential nominees, scheduled for the night of October 7 in Louisville. And the Reagan brain-trusters, always with a plan, sought to condition the viewing public for the debate, on domestic policy, with the first somewhat negative television commercials of the fall Reagan campaign. Three nights before the debate, the ads ran. Most eye-catching was an almost playful commercial that nevertheless made its point emphatically. The ad, again by the Tuesday Team, showed several average citizens each being asked a question by a silky-voiced off-screen interrogator. After each question, the citizens—a sweat-stained construction man wielding a pickax, a housewife making lunch, a farmhand loading hay—just looked at the camera in utter, utter disgust. The questions went:

"Walter Mondale thinks it would be nice if you put in some more overtime and help pay for his promises with your taxes. What do you think? . . . Walter Mondale thinks you can squeeze some more tax money out of your household budget. What do you think? . . . Walter Mondale thinks if you stay out in the fields a little more each day, you can pay the higher taxes he needs for his promises. What do you think? . . . Walter Mondale thinks if you work a little harder and get into a little higher tax bracket, you'll be able to pay the higher taxes he needs for all his promises. Vote for President Reagan. For one thing, his leadership is working.

For another, you have better things to do with your money than pay for Walter Mondale's taxes."

If there had been any doubts before this commercial ran that Reagan was primed to take Mondale to the cleaners on his bold proposal for a tax increase, the ad eradicated them. The way the campaign was going, it almost didn't seem fair.

The President, in addition to having all the advantages of incumbency, had enjoyed the luxury of an unchallenged renomination and vastly greater financial resources. While Mondale thrashed about winning his own nomination, sorting out all the various party squabbles and enduring the unexpected consequences of selecting Geraldine Ferraro as his running mate, the Reagan team had been able to put a political juggernaut in place. And now it seemed about to run over Mondale.

Here was the incumbent President, the renowned "Great Communicator" on television, getting ready to debate a man who by his own admission loathed television appearances. And to make matters worse, Reagan was miles and miles ahead in the polls—55 percent to 37 in the ABC News–Washington *Post* poll released two days before the event. Poor Fritz Mondale. By the time the debate was over, it might well be lights out for him.

21

A Real Bump in the Road

•

For weeks in advance, Fritz Mondale knew that his chances to get back into the race against Ronald Reagan would rest, barring some Republican catastrophe, on how well he stood up to the incumbent President in their two debates. And Mondale knew as well that unless he scored heavily in the first of them, what happened in the second two weeks later probably wouldn't matter. So he threw himself into the preparations for that first debate with the zeal of an undergraduate determined to be the first in his class in final examinations.

"Mondale was obsessed by the idea of these debates from the beginning," aide Tom Donilon said later. "He knew that if he was going to win the general election it would have to be in a face-to-face confrontation with Ronald Reagan. That became particularly true as we went into September and saw the Reagan strategy of non-engagement with Mondale, of treating Mondale like he did not exist."

Half a dozen times in the weeks before the first debate in Louisville on October 7, Donilon said, Mondale insisted on reviewing his minute-by-minute schedule "to make sure that nobody, as he put it, 'snuck' anything in that would interfere with his preparation schedule. Mondale chewed my ass out more times about his debate preparation schedule than he had about any single issue since I'd known him. He knew how important it was."

The emphasis on thorough preparation was vintage Mondale, Jim Johnson said. "In that sense he's the traditional lawyer," he said. "He wants to learn all the facts first. He wants to study and form in his mind the strongest possible arguments, and then he views the tone and presentation and tactics as fine tuning, which he may or may not be able to use."

To one of the Mondale debate advisers, however, tone and presentation had to be much more than mere fine tuning. Pat Caddell figured they could be the ballgame. The internal antagonism toward Caddell on the part of Johnson and Leone, however, kept Caddell out of the debate preparation until about a week before the first debate, at which time he submitted a fifty-five-page strategy memo for this critical encounter with Reagan.

The central point of the proposal was surprise—have Mondale conduct himself in a way so unanticipated that Reagan's own preparations would be inadequate to help him, and he would be thrown off balance, increasing the chances for error or erratic performance. Caddell suggested two ingredients for pulling off that surprise. First, because the Reagan advisers were probably expecting Mondale to come out throwing verbal haymakers, Mondale should be cool and deferential. Second, Mondale uncharacteristically should adopt a physically dominant posture, which could also disorient Reagan.

The memo, dated September 30, was blunt about Mondale's own inadequacies up to this point:

"The greatest opportunity for Mondale is to reveal to voters a 'different' Mondale than that they have seen and judged through the prism of campaign events and news coverage to date. . . . However, if the result of the debate is a reinforcement of the voters' perception of this election and a Walter Mondale that they have found wanting, then the event will serve to effectively close down the election rather than recasting it."

But if Mondale could jolt Reagan, he could jolt the viewing audience, including the news media, as well:

"The critical element to making the debate an overwhelming success is surprise. Surprise Reagan and throw him off stride. Surprise voters and overturn their set perceptions. Surprise the media and their pat formulations. . . . Mondale must succeed at surprising these elites by the scope and depth of his showing. He must shake their smug pack-like notions . . ."

Simply getting the better of the President, however, would not be enough, considering how far back Mondale was in the polls:

"A real victory cannot be achieved by outpointing Reagan, besting his arguments or looking good. A victory on points will be a defeat in disguise—a winning of the battle while losing the war. Mondale must rout Reagan."

However, Caddell warned at the same time, Mondale could not afford, considering Reagan's personal popularity, to hit him too straightforwardly or too hard. Mondale's tactics should be, the memo said, "distraction and dislocation" along the "lines of least expectation and least resistance." Caddell emphasized the importance of Mondale's being properly deferential toward the occupant of the White House while criticizing his views. The political climate was such, all of the Mondale strategists knew, that their man would only hurt himself if he went at Reagan like a "lawnmower," as John Reilly put it.

Still, Caddell wrote in his memo, because viewers usually decide early in a debate who is "winning," Mondale had to "hit the ground running, dominate from the outset." Not only that, he had to "shock Reagan," the memo said, by actually making physical moves that would so surprise the President and the audience that Mondale would remain the dominant figure on the screen, while rattling Reagan. The memo went on:

"Ronald Reagan will be heavily 'scripted.' His side will prepare him to deal with the 'Fighting Fritz' Mondale that they and all expect. They will prepare as they did in 1980—Stockman will know all Mondale's lines and approaches and parrot them. Reagan will prepare to parry and cut to ribbons that approach. He will polish his high-ground themes that are at the heart of his beliefs. What they will not consider or prepare for is getting a 'different' Mondale . . .

"One of Reagan's secrets is his ability to physically dominate a setting—TV speech, press conference or debate. It is the enduring value of his acting background. He uses body movement, head movement and shifting weight to convey the body language of being relaxed, in charge and strong. From his stationary position he makes all suffer by comparison. However, I believe that Mondale, by device and through practice, can come to dominate the debate in a physical sense and thus visually convey a sense of strength, of being in charge, of dominance. The idea is to utilize the stage as a performance arena—like an actor."

Here was the ultimate irony. Here was Mondale, the candidate who had spent a whole year telling the voters that "what you see is what you get," and who had repeatedly ridiculed his opponent as a puppet on a string, being advised in the very way he criticized those who advised Reagan. Here also was the candidate who said he deplored the gimmickry of television and would have nothing to do with it. But such are the pressures exerted on a man approaching perhaps the most critical moments of his bid for the presidency that Mondale not only entertained the advice—he bought it.

The Caddell memo was explicit in how Mondale could best gain the upper hand physically during the debate:

"The candidates will be only nine feet apart—not across the stage. Mondale would have two pieces to every presentation: (1) to talk directly to Reagan and (2) to speak directly to the country. Thus Mondale, when addressing Reagan, would turn, pivot and take one step toward Reagan, moving from behind the podium. He would engage Reagan. Then Mondale would step back, pivot back, face the audience, and address the country.

"The visual effect would be stunning. Mondale, by moving from the podium (which no candidate has ever done) and stepping toward Reagan, would in effect 'violate' Reagan's 'space'—an act that on television conveys confidence, strength and domination. . . . Lapel mikes are critical—wireless if possible. This cannot work if the mikes are mounted on podiums. . . . Thus we need our negotiators to get the physical arrangements desired without tipping our hand. . . . Mondale must practice the device of turn and pivot in mock debates—he cannot expect to be comfortable with it on the night of the debate."

Part of all this emphasis on rattling Reagan, Caddell noted specifically in the memo, was to raise questions about his age:

"An increase of the saliency of Reagan's age could prove decisive. . . . This is a tricky but potentially powerful area. Reagan has been so cocooned that the public may not realize that Reagan is having more difficulty hearing, following arguments, etc., than he did several years ago. If the rumors around are true, there may be more deterioration than anyone suspects. If so, he will be super-scripted by the White House—which makes the surprise strategy even more relevant."

This memo was the very essence of political hardball. Running for the White House was no gentlemen's exercise; it was warfare, as this excerpt particularly underscores:

"Mondale could, if not too obvious, probe the extent of Reagan's infirmities. Changing voice level, turning away as he speaks, pressing Reagan suddenly, are possible devices. If Reagan stumbles, appears out of it, then the potent latent concern over age could be brought to saliency."

Caddell also recommended that Mondale take "the gold watch approach"—New York media adviser Scott Miller's memorable phrase; "that Reagan did fine or [the] best he could, or tried sincerely . . . but [it's] time to move on now. Sort of embracing a grandfather and gently pushing him aside." In fact, Caddell proposed that Mondale at the outset of the debate "take the initiative of greeting Reagan in a friendly, humorous fashion. He might even consider giving Reagan a humorous gift." Caddell stopped short, however, of suggesting a gold watch.

Above all, the memo concluded in the best tradition of *Mission Impossible*, "the strategy in this paper if adopted depends on absolute secrecy. The whole cake falls if word gets out that Mondale is not going to be the 'expected' Mondale or if the tactical device leaks. Thus it must be held closely." Caddell even suggested that for secrecy's sake the debate preparation be concluded out of Washington.

"It is like preparing a boxer for a title match," the memo said. "Distractions are reduced and the whole mental attention can be thrown into peaking for the event." And in dealing with the press, Caddell wrote, "the key backgrounders must engage in a pantomime of deception. If expectations are to be overturned, then they must be built up to a maximum degree. The strategy must be protected by a 'Bodyguard of Lies.' We want the Republicans, the press and the political community to believe that Mondale is (a) coming after Reagan hammer and tong and (b) is going to make it a debate on issues and Reagan's record."

Caddell was hardly the only one in the Mondale camp who appreciated the importance of handling Reagan with kid gloves.

"Most of the conversation on the first debate," Johnson said, "was on finding the right chemistry of graciousness and engagement and toughness, so that you didn't build up a sympathy for the President."

At the same time, speechwriter Marty Kaplan said, Mondale "approached the debates in his classic lawyerly fashion, as a prosecutor getting ready for a trial. He wanted to be sure that his case against Reagan was airtight, and it was by the time we were done doing the work."

Some in the campaign, including Kaplan, thought that this approach, while commendable, missed the point about political debates. That point, Kaplan said, was "that no one cared about his case against Reagan. It would not be on the basis of the six reasons to be against Reagan's foreign policy that they were going to choose him or not; that it's going to be on things like leadership, strength, personal attractiveness, Reagan's being out of it or not—those kinds of questions. The public is not a jury, I always believed. They're consumers of products. Reagan always treated them as such, with some success."

Caddell made the same basic point in his memo:

"Voters don't remember specific issues, they remember the 'feel' of the candidate—his values, his passions, his competence, his persona. . . . The worst potential trap for Mondale, given his disposition, is to make this debate a battle over his view of the issues, his positions versus Reagan's program failures, a comparison of programs and plans. If Mondale does this he will be slaughtered by Reagan. This approach did not work in the first three weeks of September and it will not work in the debate."

Intentionally or not, these observations were a solar-plexus blow at the "intellectual Hamlets" like Leone who liked to think of presidential debates as exercises of the mind and showcases of erudition. To Caddell, though, the debates were verbal fifteen-rounders in which being able to jab and feint, and to use deft footwork, was just as important as the quality of the answers.

Caddell also knew the audience for this first debate with Reagan would be immense, and therefore offered a great opportunity for a candidate far behind in the polls and with low expectations about him. Many Americans, preoccupied with other matters until late in a presidential campaign, see an opening debate as perhaps their first and only chance to sit down and take a long and sober look at the candidates. So they watch—or endure—ninety minutes of talk in order to learn about them or just satisfy their curiosity about them.

There was a particularly good reason this year to watch Reagan and Mondale debate. Up to this point, the incumbent's television and in-person messages had been heavy on feel-good generalities and light on substance. And the challenger had been incapable of forcing him to join any serious dialogue. If there was going to be any real exchange of views and positions on which voters could appraise the two men, it would have to come in this debate in Louisville and the second one two weeks later in Kansas City.

In the early preparations for the Louisville confrontation, Caddell was not involved. Mondale's fact-oriented approach worried those on his staff who felt the politics of the debates, as opposed to the factual content, was not being adequately emphasized. Reilly and Tully lobbied Johnson to bring Caddell in for this reason. Johnson was reluctant but finally agreed.

Until Caddell's late arrival, however, the lawyerly style had prevailed in the debate preparations. They had begun in late August even before the debates had been agreed upon and were, in Kaplan's word, "endless."

In September, once Mondale started stumping regularly, most of the preparation took place in the dining room of his Washington home, which was set up as a studio, complete with videotape camera and lights and two podiums. Written questions prepared by David Lillehaug, Mondale's young issues researcher, and Lew Kaden, a friend of Leone's from Princeton, were fired at Mondale over and over by Lillehaug, until Mondale was satisfied with his answer. The answers were videotaped and replayed immediately so that the candidate and his aides could assess his performance.

Mondale would watch himself on instant replay "three, four, five, six times, the same sets of questions," Donilon recalled. "He'd say, 'Give it to me again, give it to me again. I can do better than that.' "

Later, Mondale engaged in mock debates, with Michael Sovern, president of Columbia University and another Leone friend, playing Reagan. Mondale not only rehearsed his answers but also the manner and tone in which he would deal with the incumbent President.

When Caddell finally was brought in and was given a copy of the Mondale debate briefing book, he called campaign manager Bob Beckel in distress.

"My reaction was, We're going to lose," Caddell recalled. "It's Reagan's best arguments against our best arguments. That's when I really panicked. I said, 'We're losing in our own goddamned debate book.' "

When Mondale finally saw Caddell's debate strategy memo, he asked the pollster to meet him at Mondale's home in Washington, where the mock debates were being staged. Leone, Kaden and other members of the preparation team were there and they discussed the memo. Mondale even got up at one point and began to rehearse "the pivot" toward Reagan on the makeshift set. At any rate, Caddell was now brought into the actual debate-preparation drills, setting the stage for yet another blowup in the continuing guerrilla war between Leone and friends and Caddell.

Mondale had a habit after each day of preparation to take a long, leisurely walk. After one session, he asked Caddell to accompany him. The gesture itself surprised—and upset—some of the others on the Mondale team. They knew very well the history of personal animosity that existed between Mondale and Caddell going back to the Carter administration and highlighted by Caddell's vigorous involvement in the Gary Hart challenge to Mondale. And in the existing climate, Mondale's "walk in the woods" with Caddell took on a significance among the assorted tongue-waggers in the Mondale campaign rivaling the significance afforded that other more highly publicized "walk in the woods" between arms-control negotiators Paul Nitze and Yuli Kvitsinsky in July 1982.

"By the time we're back from the walk," Caddell recalled, "it's all over the campaign headquarters, because it's one of those man-bites-dog stories."

While Mondale, amid such continuing infighting, got ready for his crucial confrontation with Reagan, the President, in a more placid environment, was getting psychologically worked up for the meeting. For the first half of the year, he had sat benignly on the sidelines while the Democrats, competing for their party's nomination, pounded him and his policies. And then when the time came to join the battle, his strategists determined that he should campaign in a thematic rather than specific way, pretty much ignoring Mondale.

The strategy was good politics but personally frustrating because there were things the Democrats and Mondale had said about Reagan that he felt were untrue and unfair. He ached to set the record straight. And the only forum in which he would have a chance to do so, considering the limitations imposed on him by his own campaign strategy, would be the debates.

"The President," a ranking White House aide said later, "had spent a fairly extended period in that campaign not responding to Mondale attacks, which was what we thought we should do, not respond, and it was singularly successful. But it was eating on him . . . and what he wanted to do was rebut and answer."

One Democratic harangue particularly disturbed him—the continuing effort to paint him as the implacable foe of Social Security bent on killing the system. Discussing the matter with us in the Oval Office after the election, the President complained about how the Democrats, first in the 1982 congressional campaign and again in 1984, were "trying to revive the feeling on the part of the senior citizens that I did nurse some plot to do away with Social Security."

The Democrats "in their demagoguery" had denied in the 1982 campaign, he said, that the system was in fiscal trouble. But his administration had saved it, he said, with the subsequent creation of a bipartisan commission and the enactment of its recommendations.

"But they brought it up again and tried to make it an issue in the campaign," Reagan said, "even if it was to the extent of only reminding people that somehow I had a plot to do away with this. It bugged me, I must say."

Accordingly, the President said, he was torn between responding to the allegation and thus heightening the issue and making "it look debatable . . . or do you just ignore it?" But if he ignored the whole matter, he said, "are there a lot of people out there whose memories are going to be such" that they might put credence in the Democrats' charge?

One who recognized that there would indeed be such people was Reagan's own crafty political adviser Stu Spencer. Spencer well knew that Reagan's public observations about the Social Security system over the previous twenty years had given senior citizens cause to worry. Going all the way back to 1964, there was that famous televised speech for Barry Goldwater in which Reagan backed Goldwater's then politically disastrous suggestion that Social Security be made voluntary. And since then, Reagan had said and done plenty more to make the elderly nervous, including the proposal by his first Secretary of Health and Human Services, Richard Schweiker, in May of 1981, to cut Social Security benefits $46 billion over five years. That one never got to first base, with the Republican-controlled Senate rejecting it resoundingly, 96–0. Even discussing Social Security was a no-win situation for Reagan and Spencer knew it.

"He feels he got a bum rap [on Social Security]," Spencer said candidly, "and he hasn't."

For that reason, Spencer said, in the debate preparations "his instructions were to ignore it." In general, in fact, Spencer said, "we tried to get Reagan to dodge" Mondale's accusations and, rather than try to rebut them, concentrate on making the points he himself wanted to make.

"But Reagan's a guy," Spencer said, "if you ask him a question, [he thinks] you deserve an answer."

That natural attitude, plus the fact that the President was champing at the things Mondale and other Democrats had said about him, affected his own debate preparations.

"By that time," Reagan said in the Oval Office interview, "not only that [Social Security], but there were so many other things in which I thought there had actually been misstatements of fact about figures and so forth, and what had been accomplished, that I set out to cram. I thought that the debate might then offer me an opportunity to rebut a good many of these things. And, you know, it is true you don't rebut them . . . in the sense of simply going out and saying, 'Hey, I didn't say that.' Then you do look defensive, and you're giving the other fellow a rehash of what he's said. But I thought at the debate that it might very likely come up, more of that face to face, and I wanted to be ready to make sure I had everything at my fingertips. . . ."

While the President was busy cramming facts and figures into his head, he underwent the same kind of mock debates that had prepared him so well for his confrontation with Jimmy Carter in 1980. Budget director David Stockman took the part of the Democratic nominee, just as he had done in 1980, and from all reports he handled the assignment brilliantly—and very aggressively. Approaching the debates, one of Reagan's strategists said, "we anticipated two versions of Mondale, and we thought the higher odds were that we would get 'Fighting Fritz' [rather than] 'Fatuous Fritz.' " In most of the Democratic primary debates that had been taped for Reagan's scrutiny, Mondale had been aggressive, so Stockman pulled out all the stops in the mock debates. But the

Reagan coaches insisted that Reagan was prepared for the softer Mondale as well.

"Stockman just did a hell of a job," Paul Laxalt acknowledged later. "If Stockman had been the candidate in that debate, it would have been something else. Stockman really got into Mondale's head. He took every Reagan position and gave it the worst possible characterization, and really did a number. He really did."

A couple of times, in fact, Stockman angered the President, he was so tough.

"He [Reagan] knew he [Stockman] was playing a role," Laxalt said, "but he hit him where he hurt. And no one likes to get embarrassed, especially if you're a sitting President in the presence of staff. . . . But Stockman was loaded up. It wasn't a fair fight. . . . He knew Mondale inside-out, and he knew the Reagan record too. He knew just exactly where all the warts were in the Reagan record. He'd been exposed to it himself. It was a masterful performance."

Stockman, another of those present said, "was much better than Mondale. He pulverized him [Reagan]. We thought Mondale wouldn't be that tough. Reagan watched Mondale [on the videotapes] and found Stockman tougher. And Stockman was reading his questions, and the President knows [had to know] Mondale can't be that good."

Although Reagan wanted and got a lot of facts, this insider said, the briefing book prepared for him was not as thick as the one he had for the 1980 debate with Carter. It ran only about twenty-five pages and included anticipated questions, themes to emphasize, some one-liners, general strategy points and a two-page closing statement.

The final mock debate took place at Camp David the day before the actual debate in Louisville, and when the exchanges between Reagan and Stockman were over, Reagan didn't bother to rehearse his closing statement. He told his coaches, one of them recalled, "that he had it under control. And Ronald Reagan has a photographic memory. When he says he's going to do it, it's done."

For all the cramming of facts, this aide said, Reagan really was "underprepared" for the first debate, because in his combativeness he focused on those facts, went into the debate eager to rebut all those "misstatements" and wasn't properly prepared for the tactical side of the debate.

Beyond that, Laxalt said later, October 7, 1984 was just not Ronald Reagan's night.

"I came down with the President as he walked onto that stage in Louisville," he recounted. "And I looked into his eyes and they were just flat. That really bothered me. Ordinarily, you know, they sparkle. But they were just flat. . . . He tends to get awfully quiet before a debate, and he was quiet then."

Laxalt wasn't the only one there who noticed Reagan's demeanor. When Mondale shook hands with him, the President seemed somehow disoriented. But when the first question of the debate was addressed to him, from James Wieghart of the Scripps-Howard News Service, Reagan handled it routinely. Wieghart wanted to know whether Reagan had a "secret plan" to balance the budget, which he had pledged to do in his 1980 campaign. Reagan gave the boiler-plate Reaganomics answer that by cutting inflation, interest rates and taxes, the nation's economic growth would erase the federal deficit, which he said was caused by "excessive government spending" and not his tax cuts.

Mondale, in his first turn, was not the "Fighting Fritz" most of the Reagan strategists had expected. Instead, acting on the Caddell battle plan, he prefaced his remarks with deferential words toward the President—before saying in more polite phrases that Reagan didn't know what he was talking about.

"One of the key tests of leadership is whether one sees clearly the nature of the problems confronted by our nation," Mondale said. "And perhaps the dominant domestic issue of our times is, What do we do about these enormous deficits? I respect the President. I respect the presidency, and I think he knows that. But the fact of it is, every estimate by this administration about the size of the deficit has been off by billions and billions of dollars. As a matter of fact, over four years, they have missed the mark by nearly $600 billion . . ."

Well, Wieghart asked, shouldn't a Democratic candidate show leadership by encouraging "responsible reductions in spending and thereby reduce the deficit?"

Mondale agreed, saying he had proposed "over $100 billion in cuts in federal spending over four years." And then he added: "But I am not going to cut it out of Social Security and Medicare and student assistance and things that people need . . ."

There was applause from the audience, but Ronald Reagan was not amused. There was Mondale raising the old Social Security bugaboo again. Indeed, the bait was out there, and Reagan could not resist snapping it up at his next opportunity. After taking an easy shot at Mondale—"I don't believe that Mr. Mondale has a plan for balancing the budget; he has a plan for raising taxes"—the President plunged in:

"With regard to Social Security, I hope there will be more time than just this minute to mention that, but I will say this: a President should never say never. But I'm going to violate this rule and say never. I will never stand for a reduction of the Social Security benefits for the people that are now getting them."

There was applause for Reagan this time, in spite of an earlier admonition against it from moderator Barbara Walters of ABC News. But the interruption didn't cause Mondale to miss a step.

"Well," he said, seeing his opening, "that's exactly the commitment that was made to the American people in 1980—he would never reduce benefits. And of course, what happened right after the election, they proposed to cut Social Security benefits by twenty-five percent, reducing the adjustment for inflation, cutting out minimum benefits for dependents [of] . . . widows trying to get them through college. Everybody remembers that. People know what happened. There is a difference. I have fought for Social Security and Medicare and for things to help people who are vulnerable all my life. And I will do it as President of the United States."

The debate had barely begun, and already Mondale had forced Reagan onto the defensive and out of the strategy his advisers had crafted for him—to ignore Mondale's charges and to make his own points rather than trying to rebut Mondale's.

The Democratic challenger was firmly taking charge of the debate. Asked by Diane Sawyer of CBS News about personal leadership, Mondale brushed aside the fact that this first debate was supposed to focus on domestic policy; he raised the matter of Reagan's responsibility in the series of terrorist attacks on American facilities in Lebanon.

"There's a difference between being a quarterback and a cheerleader," Mondale said, "and when there's a real problem, a President must confront it. . . . I believe that a President must command that White House and those who work for him. It's the toughest job on earth, and you must master the facts and insist that things that must be done are done."

Translation: Ronald Reagan is all words and no action. What's more, he's putty in the hands of the men around him. And on top of that, he doesn't know what's going on and he's a weak taskmaster.

Still, Reagan was not getting into the game. Instead, he was off rebutting that same dead horse:

". . . Incidentally, I might say that, with regard to the twenty-five percent cut to Social Security . . . the only twenty-five percent cut that I know of was accompanying that huge 1977 tax increase, was a cut of twenty-five percent in the benefits of every American who was born after 1916."

Reagan was referring here to an obscure fine point in the Social Security Act that could only confuse viewers who were not already confused.

On rebuttal, Mondale pressed the attack again:

"I guess I'm reminded a little bit of what Will Rogers once said about Herbert Hoover. He said, 'It's not what he doesn't know that bothers me, it's what he knows for sure that just ain't so.' The fact of it is, the President's budget sought to cut Social Security by twenty-five percent. It's not an opinion, it's a fact. And when the President was asked the other day, 'What do you want to cut in the budget?' he said, 'Cut those things I asked for and didn't get.' That's Social Security and Medicare."

Reagan really had the bait swallowed whole now.

"Well, let me just respond with regard to Social Security," he said. And he replied with essentially the same answer he later gave us in our interview in the Oval Office—that the system was "due to go bankrupt before 1983," that the Democrats had demagogued the issue in the 1982 campaign and that the bipartisan commission he appointed had put the system "on a sound basis now for as far as you can see into the next century."

The President clearly was convinced that he had been wronged again, and that he had set the whole matter straight once and for all. But the candidates were now well into the debate, and Reagan had yet to initiate any major points of his own.

As the debate proceeded on such various questions as the candidates' personal attitudes toward religion and religion in politics, abortion, the future of the Democratic Party and who had the better right to invoke the name of John F. Kennedy, Reagan was doing no better than holding his own. He began to spout statistics in every answer in an increasingly confusing fashion. Even when he resorted to that well-remembered line from his 1980 debate with Jimmy Carter—"There you go again"—Mondale was ready to turn it back on him.

In defending his own proposal to raise taxes as part of a comprehensive deficit-reduction plan, Mondale repeated the flat accusation he had made in his acceptance speech in San Francisco.

"Mr. Reagan," he said, "is going to have to propose a tax increase." And, Mondale warned, it was likely to be a national sales tax that would "hit middle- and moderate-income Americans and leave wealthy Americans largely untouched."

Reagan responded, amid laughter:

"You know, I wasn't going to say this at all, but I can't help it. There you go again. I don't have a plan to tax or increase taxes. I'm not going to increase taxes. I know why you are, Mr. Mondale, because as a senator, you voted sixteen times to increase taxes . . ."

On Mondale's next turn, he picked Reagan up on the phrase. Pivoting at the podium so that he faced Reagan directly—an integral part of the pre-planned stagecraft—he commented almost conversationally:

"Now, Mr. President, you said, 'There you go again.' Right? Remember the last time you said that?"

Reagan: "Um-hmm."

Mondale: "You said it when President Carter said that you were going to cut Medicare. And you said, 'Oh no, there you go again, Mr. President.' And what did you do right after the election? You went right out and tried to cut $20 billion out of Medicare. And so, when you say, 'There you go again,' people remember this, you know. And people will remember that you signed the biggest tax increase in the history of California and the biggest tax increase in the history of the United States. And what are you going to do? You've got [a] $260 billion deficit. You can't wish it away. You won't slow defense spending. You refuse to do that."

Reagan once again responded very defensively:

"With regard to Medicare, no. But it's time for us to say that Medicare is in pretty much the same condition that Social Security was. And something is going to have to be done in the next several years to make it fiscally sound. And, no, I never proposed any $20 billion should come out of Medicare."

The President was beginning to sound incoherent.

"I have proposed that the program we must treat with that particular problem," he said, whatever that meant.

A few minutes later, he was asked about a remark he had made in an area of very high unemployment in Texas, that man does not live by bread alone. Might not that remark have been better addressed to an affluent audience? Reagan replied:

"That had nothing to do with the other thing of talking about their needs, or anything. I remember distinctly, I was seguing into another subject. I was talking about the things that have been accomplished, and that was referring to the revival of patriotism and optimism, the new spirit that we're finding all over America, and it is a wonderful thing to see when you get out there among the people. So, that was the only place that that was used. I did avoid, I'm afraid, in my previous answer also, the idea of uneven . . . yes, there is no way that the recovery is even across the country, just as in the depths of the recession there was some parts of the country that were worse off, but some that didn't even feel the pain of the recession. We're not going to rest, are not going to be happy until every person in this country who wants a job can have one, until the recovery is complete across the country."

Mondale, rather than pouncing on Reagan at this point, followed the game plan and was conciliatory. Asked what was "the most outrageous thing" Reagan had said in the debate, he chose instead to say a few nice things about him. The President, he said, "has done some things to raise the sense of spirit, morale, good feeling in this country. He is entitled to credit for that." And when Reagan "lectured the country about the importance of discipline" in education, Mondale said, "I didn't like it at first, but I think it helped a little bit. . . . I like President Reagan. This is not personal. These are deep differences about our future, and that's the basis of my campaign."

Still, Mondale took one more whack at Reagan's vulnerability on Social Security—and Reagan took the bait again. Rather than talking about economic growth as the answer to the deficit, Mondale said, "Give us a plan. What will you cut? Whose taxes will you raise? Will you finally touch that defense budget? Are you going to go after Social Security, and Medicare, and student assistance, and the handicapped again, as you did last time?"

Reagan replied once more with a defense on Social Security. The most outrageous thing from Mondale, he said, "is the continued discussion and claim that somehow I am the villain who is going to pull the Social Security checks out from those people who are dependent on them. And why I think it is outrageous—first of all, it isn't true—but why it is outrageous is because, for political advantage, every time they do that, they scare millions of senior citizens who are totally dependent on Social Security, have no place else to turn. And they have to live and go to bed at night thinking, Is this true? Is someone going to take our check away from us and leave us destitute? And I don't think that that should be a part of political dialogue."

Here was Reagan using a very considerable chunk of his valuable debate time repeating—in the most graphic terms—the indictment Mondale was laying on him! The President went on to explain how "Social Security has nothing to do with the deficit." He talked all about "general funds" and "the Social Security trust fund"—as eyes glazed over from coast to coast.

At this point the moderator, Walters, got mixed up on the order of responses and rebuttals, and when she offered to give Reagan more rebuttal time, this exchange occurred:

REAGAN: No, I might as well just go with what I—
WALTERS: Do you want to go with your—
REAGAN: I don't think so.
WALTERS: Do you want to wait?
REAGAN: I'm all confused now.

And so it seemed to many in the hall and in living rooms across the country watching the debate on their television screens. The impression grew even more strongly as the President went into his closing statement. He began with yet another memorable line from his 1980 debate with Carter, the one many credited later with sewing up the election for him: "Are you better off than you were four years ago?" Then he went on to say, in often disjointed and sometimes contradictory sentences, that while he knew most Americans were better off, some weren't and therefore his task was undone. But, he said, America was better off, and he launched into a long string of statistics to prove his point:

"In the first half of 1980, gross national product was down, a minus three point seven percent. First half of '84, it's up eight and a half percent. Productivity in the first half of 1980 was down a minus two percent. Today it is up a plus four percent. Personal earnings after taxes, per capita, have gone up almost three thousand dollars in these four years. In 1980 or 1979, a person with a fixed income of eight thousand dollars would . . . was five hundred dollars above the poverty line. And this maybe explains why there are the numbers still in poverty. By 1980, that same person was five hundred dollars below the poverty line . . ."

Mondale, in his closing remarks, was contrastingly crisp. He thanked Reagan for debating—"he didn't have to, and he did, and we all appreciate it"—and then took his parting shots.

"I would rather lose a campaign about decency than win a campaign about self-interest," he said, and for good measure he slapped the Reagan administration for a "mean-spirited" assault on Social Security and Medicare. There was nothing confused about Mondale's concluding statement. And so the debate ended, ten minutes over the alloted ninety, as it had started—with the President of the United States on the defensive.

"God, I was awful," he told Spencer immediately afterward.

And he told us later:

"I left my fight in the locker room. I knew when I stood out there that I was flat. I wasn't really ready or up to it."

As the President was leaving the stage, his good friend Paul Laxalt tried to console him.

"This was your first shot," Laxalt told him. "Hell, you haven't been in the ring like Mondale has. Mondale's in condition. He's been out there. You haven't done anything in four years."

Over in the other corner of the ring, Mondale was euphoric at his own performance—and shocked at Reagan's. Later, Mondale declined to comment on that moment for the record, but Tom Donilon said that Mondale remarked to him about the President as he came off the stage:

"This guy is gone. It's scary. He's really not up to it."

And Mondale told another aide later:

"Reagan is really old. I don't know if he could have gone another fifteen minutes. I could see him tiring."

The mood in the two staff rooms at the hall, adjoining each other, provided as good a yardstick on how the debate had gone as anything did. The Mondale room was jubilant; the Reagan room controlled, but the Reaganites could hear the celebration next door.

When Mondale came into the staff room, speechwriter Marty Kaplan recalled, "his first words were, 'Mike Sovern [who had played Reagan in the mock debates] was a lot better than that guy!' And it wasn't a crack on Mondale's part. He was just shaking his head. There was no question that Reagan had lost it in the debate . . . and there was no question on balance that he [Mondale] had scored in a major way."

One of those Mondale phoned to thank from Louisville that night was Caddell, who had watched the debate on television back in Washington, where he had been exiled on debate night, he said, by Jim Johnson. It would have been too much to say that Caddell's strategy was at the core of Reagan's bad night, but that battle plan certainly helped Mondale capitalize on the President's poor performance.

The debate, Kaplan said, "gave us the sense, 'Who knows? Maybe we can do it.' " And so Mondale and entourage headed back onto the campaign trail with an enthusiasm they hadn't enjoyed since he had claimed the Democratic nomination back in July. Indeed, when one of us encountered Mondale in the lobby of the Bellevue Stratford in Philadelphia the next night, he was buoyant. His face was flushed and he wore a broad grin.

"It's all different now," he said. "We're rolling."

At the hall in Kansas City on debate night, however, the Reagan strategists were preparing to put the best face on the situation. About fifteen minutes before the debate ended, they had started drawing up a list of about half a dozen "talking points" for the "spin patrol" exercise in the press room afterward—arguments to persuade the assembled reporters and columnists that Reagan really had won. Then the aides flooded in on the deadline-harassed writers, along with a similar Mondale team of persuaders, accentuating the positive to reporters who crowded around them. Both candidates, it was obvious from this exercise, had "won." The invaders supplied the reasons, in the event the reporters hadn't noticed the strong points of their man.

This exercise was more than merely putting up a good front. The political operatives in both camps well knew, as Caddell's memo emphasized, that what would be written out of this room, and by other reporters around the country watching on television, could have an important—even critical—influence on the public perception of the debate. A considerable history already had developed of public-opinion polls finding one viewpoint immediately after a televised debate and another after the news media had chewed that debate over. The prime example had come in 1976, when President Ford made that now-famous denial of Soviet domination of Eastern Europe in one of his debates with Jimmy Carter. In a poll by Bob Teeter right after the debate, 11 percent more voters said Ford had won it than thought Carter did. But succeeding polls through the next day, as the news media analysis of Ford's "gaffe" or "blunder" circulated, showed a precipitous drop for him, until the polls were saying Ford had lost the debate by an incredible forty-five points.

The clear consensus on this night in the press room, regardless of the efforts of the Reagan "spin patrol," was that Mondale had performed well but that, more important, Reagan was, as in his own word to Spencer, awful. And Jim Baker, the White House chief of staff and a firm disciplinarian of any loose tongues in the campaign, firmed up that view when he violated his own rule in press briefings by allowing that the President had not done as well as expected.

"He didn't have the discipline to keep up saying we had won," an associate said later. Baker was guilty, in other words, of the very sin for which he and others had criticized campaign manager Ed Rollins in his earlier prediction of a landslide.

In any event, regardless of what the Reagan strategists were telling the outside world, the most astute insiders realized almost at once what they were up against. While some talked themselves into thinking Reagan had not done poorly, the resident hard-head, Stu Spencer, saw immediately that the debate would surface questions about Reagan's age and competence.

"That first debate was a real bump in the road," he told us later.

Dick Wirthlin, the pollster, made the same reading. Jim Lake, the campaign press secretary, went to him right afterward and asked:

"Dick, what do you think?"

"It's going to raise the age issue," Wirthlin said.

Spencer and Wirthlin were right, but it was interesting that questions about the President's age did not spring forth that night.

None of the resident political trend-seekers of the press or television, certainly including us, raised it in print or on the tube until a day or so later. So much for the much-maligned news media penchant for instant analysis.

The flight back East from Louisville aboard Air Force One the next morning was not exactly festive. Nancy Reagan, for one, was not pleased, and she told Laxalt so. The fault, in her eyes, lay not with her "Ronnie"—it never did. So it had to be the aides who had failed to prepare him properly.

Laxalt himself was concerned. He ran into a group of veteran Washington reporters before leaving Louisville, he recalled, "and God, it was just thumbs down, it was a disaster." Whether or not the debate really had been a disaster for the President was immaterial at this point, he said. Although one network poll had Reagan winning by a hair the night of the debate, he said, "once analysis set in, I could see what happened. By the time the media pros analyzed the goddamned thing, [I realized] that bad things were going to happen. There's a second stage to these things, and that's precisely what happened. . . . So I figured that if the reaction among the media people was uniform as it was that Reagan hadn't done well, that he really had lost the debate, and it was bad."

Sure enough, a Gallup poll for *Newsweek* immediately after the debate found that 54 percent thought Mondale had won, to only 35 percent for the President.

Back in Washington, Laxalt was already getting phone calls from worried Reagan supporters around the country.

"Is the old man slipping?" Laxalt said he was being asked. To which he would reply:

"Hell, it wasn't him. He's in great shape. It's the goddamned process that did it."

Laxalt was beginning to reflect on those debate preparations in which Stockman had hammered at Reagan so fiercely, and he was concluding that they had so beaten him down that his performance had been affected. And neither Laxalt nor Nancy Reagan was particularly high on Dick Darman, who was heavily involved in the substantive issue side of the preparations.

While Laxalt was thus musing about what had gone wrong, the news media were beginning to put into print and on the air the same question the senator from Nevada was getting: Was the old man slipping? The *Wall Street Journal* fired the first shot in an article two mornings after the debate headlined "New Question in Race: Is Oldest U.S. President Now Showing His Age?" And that night, all three major television networks weighed in with a sledgehammer examination of "the age issue."

The coverage was absolutely devastating. Predictably, they reran segments of the Louisville debate showing Reagan's obvious uncertainty and the agonizing pauses in some of his answers. But these snippets were only for openers. One evening news show aired footage of the President dozing off in the presence of Pope John Paul II. Another showed a most damaging tape of Reagan trying to dodge a question from a reporter at an impromptu outdoor encounter, with Nancy Reagan at his side. The tape showed, and a microphone picked up, the President's wife whispering an answer to him—and Reagan then repeating her suggested response word for word.

The networks also trotted out doctors and psychiatrists to discuss the signs and impairments of senility. The Reagan strategists thought this exercise was such a low blow that White House chief of staff Jim Baker filed a protest with one of the "offenders," ABC News.

Reagan himself told us that while this tack "might have bothered me one time, it didn't, because by this time I have to tell you I'd become convinced in my own mind that no one had been able to make that issue sell."

The President's success in politics stood as clear evidence that he was right on the point. As far back as 1966, when he first ran for governor of California at the age of fifty-five, questions were repeatedly being raised, not about his age at that time but about a matter usually associated with age—his stamina and staying power. Sacramento became awash with rumors about how then Governor Reagan shut off appointments in the early afternoon so that he could take a nap and make it to quitting time at five o'clock or so.

By the time Reagan made his first serious run for the presidency in 1976 (he took a feeble feint at it in 1968), he was then sixty-five and questions about his energy level and willingness to work had already graduated to "the age issue." To knock it in the head at once, his campaign manager at the time, John Sears, scheduled him into a very heavy sunup-to-sundown daily pace for the New

Hampshire primary, and the questions quickly faded. They continued to surface as one year after another passed, however, in spite of the fact that his advancing age appeared to take no toll on his physical appearance, other than those conspicuous wattles around his neck. Again, in Reagan's 1980 campaign, when he was sixty-nine years old, a running joke on his press plane was the inclusion of "staff time" on his afternoon schedule. His aides once acknowledged that Reagan would get into pajamas to "rest"—not nap.

In 1981, his resilience in recovering from the near-fatal attempt on his life underscored that this man was indeed a rare physical specimen. And that evidence served to quiet questions about his age and ability to perform, although Democrats continued trying to get a handle on both by using such code words as "competence."

Reagan himself took the age issue lightly. At the Gridiron Club dinner in Washington in 1983, he joked that he was glad White House staff squabbling was being brought under control because it had been robbing him of "a good afternoon's sleep."

This time, though, the age issue did not seem to be a laughing matter. In the Reagan strategists' carefully orchestrated campaign, in which nothing had been left to chance, about the only things that could upset their plans, and that they could not prevent happening, were some kind of serious foreign-policy crisis or the President suddenly "showing his age" in a debilitating way. And even in a foreign-policy crisis, the history had been for the American voters to rally to an incumbent President, especially in the early phases. With only six weeks to go until election day, surely he could ride out almost any problem of that nature. But the age issue was something else again. If the voters judged that Ronald Reagan at seventy-three had suddenly gone around the bend, they could well decide that reelecting him was too great a risk to take.

This question, indeed, was now dominating the news when, on the fourth day after the debate, Laxalt held a press conference in Washington. The ostensible purpose was to disclose plans for a Republican "truth squad" of leading GOP senators to take the road to rebut campaign statements by Mondale, now busy pressing his advantage. He was accusing Reagan of, among other things, having "a secret plan" to cut Social Security benefits after the election, and the White House's flat denials were doing nothing to stop Mondale from probing that open wound among the elderly.

The assembled reporters at Laxalt's "truth squad" press conference, however, were interested in only one "truth": Was the old man slipping?

"The first goddamned question is addressed immediately to me and it's about Reagan's age and performance in the debate," Laxalt recalled. "So I figured I'd better hit it frontally, and I did."

Laxalt conceded that the President had "had an off night," but he said the reason "wasn't because of any physical or mental deficiency. He was brutalized by a briefing process that didn't make any sense."

The provocative remark chagrined the debate coaches, and Darman particularly, not only because it dumped the blame for Reagan's poor performance on them but because in their view Laxalt's remarks only served to keep the problem on page one. One of the coaches did concede, however, that it "helped smooth up the Teflon coating"—that if the coaches were at fault, then the President wasn't.

When we asked Jim Baker later whether it wasn't true that Laxalt's blast, whether intentionally or not, did draw some of the heat away from Reagan and onto the debate coaches, he smiled and said:

"You've just discovered the secret of the Teflon presidency."

Darman was determined not to be pushed out of the action as a result of the Laxalt broadside. But another insider said that after that first debate "Darman jumped back as if he'd touched a hot plate." At any rate, regardless of who was at fault, the time had come to take another look at the well-oiled Reagan machine and at the fuel on which it ran, particularly the feel-good television ads.

Ed Rollins decided with his customary thoroughness, Jim Lake said later, "to take the whole engine apart and look at every bearing." All the regional directors were contacted and told to make a thorough review of their state organizations to find any possible problems.

At the same time, Laxalt, officially the campaign chairman, moved in. He told Darman and the others getting ready to prepare Reagan for the second debate in two weeks that he was taking personal responsibility for the failure and was determined there would be no repetition.

Two immediate questions were raised: What had to be done to combat the age issue? And what could be done to "pile up Mondale's negatives"—that is, to tear him down? The polls had shown Reagan's lead slipping—from eighteen points in the ABC–Washington *Post* survey before the debate to fifteen after it, and even lower in others. Wirthlin's polling showed a precipitous dip from an eighteen-point Reagan lead going into the first debate to twelve two days later.

In the campaign's efficient way, some highly visible events already had been scheduled to take place after the first debate, in case it did not go all that well. One was an old-fashioned whistlestop train trip through western Ohio during which the President made frequent appearances and remarks from the rear car's platform—and was seen and heard to be in good shape. With the extra pizzazz that attention to detail, and money, can bring, the Reagan campaign located and brought north at considerable expense the same car used by Harry Truman in 1948 in his storied "give 'em hell" comeback campaign. The car had been sitting in a railroad museum in Florida. The Reagan campaign helped pay its leasing and transportation costs by soaking the traveling press for the privilege of going along and reporting that Ronald Reagan was alive and well and campaigning in Ohio.

Concerning the television commercials, two moves were made to "pile up Mondale's negatives." One was to bring in Ken Khachigian, Reagan's speechwriter, to write the text for some "talking head" ads, showing the President looking right into the camera and addressing the voters. The Tuesday Team's feel-good ads were fine, but the time had come for Mr. Credibility himself to take over with a little mild "Mondale-bashing," as one insider put it. In a typical talking head, Reagan was seen and heard saying:

"The American people have a very clear choice this year about their economic future. And it's a very simple choice, between our opponent's old policies and our new policies. When you hear their prescription for the economy—higher taxes, bigger government, sure-to-follow high inflation, it makes you wonder if they remember how things used to be. There's a better life ahead, but only if we look ahead."

There remained, however, one product of the Tuesday Team that had been sitting on the agency's shelves for several months, awaiting just the right time for its use. It was a foreign-policy ad, and with that area to be discussed in the second debate, the time had arrived. The ad had been dreamed up and produced at the very start of the Tuesday Team's formation. Its author was one of the premier makers of product commercials, Hal Riney, a Californian who had done such prominent ads as the Gallo wine commercials, which he also narrated. His brainstorm was the thirty-second "bear ad"—the image of a large, very menacing brown bear roaming through the woods, as Riney himself intoned:

"There is a bear in the woods. For some people, the bear is easy to see. Others don't see it at all. Some people say the bear is tame. Others say it's vicious, and dangerous. Since no one can really be sure who's right, isn't it smart to be as strong as the bear—if there is a bear?"

The bear, obviously, was the Soviet Union, and at the ad's end, as the bear reached the top of a hill, a solitary hunter with a rifle slung over his shoulder stood watching him. And if you wanted to imagine that the hunter was Ronald Reagan, well, it was a free country.

Riney had thrown the ad together back in the spring, using stock footage of a bear, just to give the campaign hierarchy an idea of the kind of thing he could do. The ad wowed the Reagan strategists, as well as voter focus groups to whom it was shown. In fact, it got higher rates on approval and recall, the Reagan team said later, than any other television commercial ever made. It was deemed so powerful, however, that the Reagan planners were uncertain about what its impact would be, and so they saved it for when it might really be needed.

"At first we thought it was a little risky," Lake said later, "because the first focus group [thought it was] so different and so unique." Of ten ads they were shown, the bear ad was the only one the focus participants wanted to talk about, he said, and "we knew we were going to run that ad" before the campaign was over.

Teeter particularly loved the bear ad, and he was determined to get it on the air. He decided the ad was ideal as a prelude to the debate on foreign policy, and he started running it on the Friday night before that second debate in Kansas City. It ran exclusively for five straight days.

For Rollins, who shared the enthusiasm about the commercial, the first debate was not a complete loss.

"It let us go with the bear ad," he said.

The first version on storyboards was even better than the finished product, Rollins said. It had the hunter raising his rifle and taking aim and the bear stepping back. But Riney used a trained bear in the final version, Rollins said, "and the owner said he wasn't going to have anyone aiming a gun at his bear."

The first debate also had some other hidden benefits for the Reagan managers, or so they persuaded themselves. Charlie Black, one of the senior political advisers, said that although the campaign had laid plans for a close race, Reagan's huge lead in the polls had made it difficult "to retain enthusiasm" and curb complacency.

"But we got a little bit of a break with the news coming out of the first debate," he said. "It energized our people."

The surfacing of the age issue, another insider said, "sure did lower what we had to do in the way of performance in the second debate. All he [Reagan] had to do was show he wasn't too old to be President."

There was another break for Reagan too in the scheduled debate between the vice-presidential candidates, George Bush and Geraldine Ferraro, only four nights after the first Reagan-Mondale confrontation, although the Reagan forces didn't see it as a break going in. The conventional wisdom dictated that because the Democratic nominee was a woman, and because Bush was such a proper fellow, the scrappy New Yorker would mop up the floor with him in the Philadelphia theater chosen for the debate. Indeed, at our dinner with Ferraro earlier, she had contended she could hit him as hard as she liked, and he would not be able to return her fire in kind for fear of being cast as a bully. Such was the ability of Gerry Ferraro the pol to size up the situation.

But Bush, too, was well aware of the special chemistry that would be at work. While he was determined to focus his attacks on Mondale, it became clear to him very early that his conduct would be under particular scrutiny because his opponent was a woman. After a trip with Reagan to Texas in late July during which the two Republican candidates were photographed with some Texas cheerleaders, Jack Nelson of the Los Angeles *Times* went to see Bush and asked him whether that kind of scene wouldn't have to be avoided. Bush said no, "but it signaled to me that something was quite different when a serious reporter of that nature thought that it was going to change a lot of things."

Preparing for the debate, however, a New York advertising

woman, Susan Gianinno, advised him: "Your assignment is to win, but not have her lose."

"I don't think they would have said that," Bush told us later, "if I had been debating Tony Coelho or somebody else. And it was pretty good advice. . . . I thought about it an awful lot and tried to keep it in mind as I rehearsed with Lynn Martin."[45]

Bush's press secretary, Pete Teeley, said his boss got a stream of letters from his friends warning him that he was facing "a no-win situation" going into the debate. But there never was any question that Bush would, and wanted to, debate Ferraro.

The Democratic nominee, for her part, was not setting out in her own preparations to make mincemeat of Bush with her New York feistiness. Rather, her strategists determined that what she needed to establish in the debate was her own readiness for national office and, hence, her grasp of the major issues.

"This was not show business," Anne Wexler said later. "This was heavy politics." Voters who were already for Ferraro would enjoy seeing her push Bush around, she said, "but they were not the ones we were going after." Ferraro had to show she was "not just a lippy dame from New York," her political adviser said.

That much Gerry Ferraro did show in the debate, and she demonstrated a good grasp of the issues. And Bush, after a rather frenzied start in which he played the cheerleader for Reagan, displayed his own extensive knowledge of governmental affairs, especially in the field of foreign policy. To the surprise of nobody who knew the Vice President at all, he went down the line for his boss from the very start. He recited the Reagan record of economic recovery and the Reagan rhetoric that "America is back." And he declared:

"Of course I support the President's economic program, and I support him in everything else."

The only real tension in the debate came during an exchange on the American role in Lebanon and the U.S. reaction to the terrorist attacks on American facilities there. Ferraro recalled Reagan's pledge to "stand tall" after the American hostages were

45. Lynn Martin, a congresswoman from Illinois, played Ferraro in Bush's debate preparations. After the election, Bush hosted a lunch for Ferraro at which both debate stand-ins went along, Martin and Washington lawyer Bob Barnett, who Bush identified to us as "the guy who played me—the preppy guy."

returned from Iran and noted he had done nothing in response to those subsequent terrorist attacks in Lebanon. In his response, Bush said:

"... Let me help you with the difference, Mrs. Ferraro, between Iran and the Embassy in Lebanon. In Iran, we were held by a foreign government. In Lebanon, you had a wanton terrorist action where the government opposed it. We went to Lebanon to give peace a chance, to stop the bombing of civilians in Beirut, to remove 13,000 terrorists from Lebanon. We did—we saw the formation of a government of reconciliation. And for somebody to suggest, as our two opponents have, that these men died in shame—they better not tell the parents of those young Marines. They gave peace a chance, and our allies were with us: the British, the French and the Italians."

Through this answer, Ferraro seethed. Responding, she snapped:

"Let me just say, first of all, that I almost resent, Vice President Bush, your patronizing attitude that you have to teach me about foreign policy. I've been a member of Congress for six years. I was there when the embassy was held hostage in Iran, and I have been there, and I have seen what has happened in the past several months, seventeen months, with your administration. Secondly, please don't categorize my answers either. Leave the interpretation of my answers to the American people who are watching this debate."

The audience interrupted her with applause, but she pressed on:

"And let me say further that no one has ever said that those men who were killed—through the negligence of this administration and others—ever died in shame. No one who has a child who's nineteen or twenty years old—a son—would ever say that about the loss of anybody else's child."

The exchanges went on through a series of other issues—Central America, relations with the Soviet Union, nuclear-arms control and national defense—and Ferraro held her own with the more experienced former ambassador and CIA director. Yet in a curious way Bush may have come out ahead in the expectations game. Except for that one lapse into patronizing his opponent, Bush was not particularly deferential to her, as many had predicted he would be. And in Ferraro's determination to demonstrate that she belonged on the same platform with the Vice President, she seemed to surrender some of the buoyancy that made her such a hit on the campaign trail.

At any rate, the Reagan camp saw the vice-presidential debate as a net plus if only because it diverted attention from Reagan's age issue and helped put the Republican train back on track. Teeter for one held that view strongly. And Bush said later:

"Lots of people wrote me and told me, 'You stopped the bleeding, you turned things around.' "

The Mondale forces, still aglow over Mondale's performance against Reagan in the first debate, had hoped for a similar triumph by Ferraro. While most felt she had handled herself well, they recognized she had not hit anything close to a home run.

"I can be funny anytime," she said after the debate. "I can be flippant. I did exactly what I wanted to do—talk to the American people."

Two things Bush said, however, one during the debate and one the next day, did give the Democrats ammunition to fire at the Republican ticket for the next several news cycles.

The first was his remark that Mondale and Ferraro had said American Marines had "died in shame" in Lebanon. Mondale branded the statement "unpardonable" and demanded that Bush apologize. If he didn't, Mondale said, he would raise the issue directly with Reagan in their second debate on the approaching Sunday night. Bush refused, and the issue faded.

The second thing he said, however, did not vanish so quickly. The morning after the debate, Bush went over to Elizabeth, New Jersey, for a rally with longshoremen. On leaving, he turned to a man in the crowd and a boom microphone picked up his voice saying "we tried to kick a little ass" in the previous night's debate. When Bush saw the mike, he exclaimed:

"Whoops! Oh, God, he heard me! Turn that thing off!"

When reporters asked Bush about the remark, he called it "an old Texas football expression" but declined to repeat it or apologize. The matter became a classic campaign tempest in a teapot. A day or two earlier, Bush's wife Barbara had characterized Ferraro as "a four-million-dollar—I can't say it but it rhymes with rich," and Teeley had described her as "too bitchy." Here, certainly, a major campaign issue was building.

After the election, Bush gave us this version of how his remark was really inspired by a man in the crowd who held up a sign:

"Here was a guy standing on the dock, 'You kicked ass, George,' or something . . . an enthusiastic guy. . . . So I got up and spoke with no reference to that. It was kind of a rah-rah thing for a few minutes; finished the deal, climbed off the platform . . . shook a lot of hands walking down a long rope line, got down to the end, and here was this guy again with his sign, 'You kicked ass,' and yelling it too. I mean, an enthusiastic fellow. And I got down to the end of it, and in a moment of great exuberance, I was just about to get in the car, I saw this fellow, and I leaned over to the guy and said something like that. Then I saw this boom sticking in there."

But to have the incident "made into a piece that there's been a whole shift on the Bush campaign to have a macho image," he said, "I thought for people to seriously come up with that in the opposition was the most dumb thing I've ever heard of."[46]

By the time this monumental controversy began to subside, the second presidential debate was at hand. Reagan's preparation this time was distinctly less intense. Mike Deaver, the prime guardian of the Reagan image, took a more active hand. Stockman again played Mondale, but with a muzzle on, and the number of mock debates was reduced. The President was warned, as one aide put it, "not to fall into the rebuttal trap." Roger Ailes, the New York television specialist, was brought in as an adviser. Reagan himself was determined not to cram so many facts into his head that he would be stupefied by them, and the coaches decided the better approach was to encourage him, rather than hammer at him.

Jim Lake, the campaign press secretary, recalled that in 1980, after Reagan had been upset by Bush in the Iowa caucuses, he was very depressed and not up to par in his first New Hampshire appearances. Lake and a press associate, Linda Gosden, went into Reagan's room and told him so. Nancy Reagan was present, and as Lake and Gosden left, she went out with them and told them that was definitely not the way to handle her husband. He needed to be built up, she said, not knocked down.

46. Readers of the New York *Times* who relied on that august publication for all their information about the campaign had to guess the next day what Bush had said. The *Times* story said only that "as he left the docks, he whispered a locker-room vulgarity to a union official." Fortunately for American journalism and the public, there are still standards in some newsrooms.

Laxalt agreed. "Ronald Reagan is the type, like most political types, he doesn't need to get battered and bruised," he said. "There's enough of that going on anyway. He's a very sensitive man. More than anything else he needs to be reinforced, and certainly not overcoached. His natural instincts are very, very reliable."

Above all, Reagan knew he had done poorly in the first debate and he was eager for a second shot. Concerning Laxalt's charge that the President had been "brutalized" by his debate coaches, Reagan told us later:

"Well, maybe we overdid it in some ways, but again I think the main factor was myself. I brutalized myself with my cramming . . . I had myself so filled up with trying to remember facts and figures for whatever might be raised that I wasn't really thinking and responding to what he [Mondale] was saying there when we were face to face."

At the same time, though, Reagan said he was "not particularly" surprised at Mondale's soft approach to him, except "maybe to the extent that a lot of the analysis of it had been that he was easily aroused and that he might come storming back. So I'd been prepared if he'd done that, and he didn't." In other words, the President said his performance was not the result of Caddell's strategy of surprise as much as it was of his own determination to smother Mondale with facts.

Going into the second debate, the President said, "there was a matter of personal pride, yes. When you know you've done badly, I suppose if you're doing a show and you know you weren't hot one night, why, you decide to make up for it the next night."

In light of the way Reagan had messed up his closing statement in the first debate, in which he seemed bent on cramming in all the statistics he hadn't used, this time he rehearsed his close carefully. On the flight out to Kansas City on Air Force One, he sat in his seat with a stopwatch, timing himself as he read.

"I'm sixteen seconds over," he told Deaver.

"Don't worry about it," Deaver replied. "They won't cut off the President of the United States." In time, the comment would prove that they didn't know everything in the Reagan White House.

In all the careful preparation, however, there was one thing this political operation, which usually left no stone unturned, failed to do. It never considered or rehearsed what the President might say if asked about the one question on which the whole debate, and perhaps the campaign itself, now centered—the age issue.

"I guess it was on faith," Lake said. "All of us knew Reagan would be all right."

All of them knew it, but a couple of them—Atwater and Spencer—being hard-nosed pros decided to plan ahead, just in case the President bombed again. Spencer came into Atwater's office the Friday morning before the second debate, and together they planned a memo for their own eyes only they called "The Great American Fog Machine."

The memo, written by Atwater, in six pages illustrated in astonishing directness how one overriding rule governed the task of winning the presidency in 1984, even in the camp of an incumbent still far ahead in all the polls. And the rule was, Anything goes. Anticipating that Ronald Reagan might fare poorly in the second debate, the memo laid out a specific counterstrategy that would have done justice to Machiavelli himself.

First, what the memo called a "SWAT team" of the Reagan administration's top foreign-policy experts would be quickly dispatched to come to the President's rescue. The memo listed Secretary of State George Shultz, Secretary of Defense Caspar Weinberger, UN Ambassador Jeane Kirkpatrick, White House national security adviser Robert McFarlane and his predecessor, Secretary of Interior William Clark, as the front-line troops. Behind them would come former Secretary of State Henry Kissinger, former Secretary of Defense Donald Rumsfeld, former national security adviser Brent Scowcroft and Senate Armed Services Committee Chairman John Tower. Not only did the memo thus ignore the long-standing tradition against use of the secretaries of state and defense in political campaigns, it specifically said:

"We should not hesitate to violate protocols by enlisting top Pentagon brass to help."

At the same time Reagan's foreign-policy views were being defended, the memo said, Mondale's would have to be torn down:

"If it's clear that the President did badly, then it's our job to obscure the result. The single most important mission of the fog machine will be to shift the emphasis to Mondale, and to drive up his negative rating."

Three leading Republicans—former President Ford, Senator

Bob Dole and Reagan himself—would have to lead the attack on paid television, the memo said, and it provided a rationale for using each of them.

First, Ford in a five-minute spot would be ideal for dusting off "the Carter connection" as a weapon against Mondale, because his experience against Carter in their 1976 debate could be used as a warning. The memo said:

"If the Great Communicator loses the debate, then for purposes of the campaign, he is no longer the Great Communicator. We will be in a situation similar to '76, when the Republican incumbent was a nice guy with a good record, who unfortunately could not get his message out to the American people. So the incumbent, Jerry Ford, was defeated, and we got Jimmy Carter. Who better to warn the American people against being swayed by words than Ford himself? . . . Ford would tell the American people that he lost the debates in 1976, and he lost the presidency to Jimmy Carter. But the American people lost a lot more. They lost four years to malaise, inflation and the shame of Iran. Let's not let that crew get control of the White House again and lead us back down that same road! Don't find out the hard way what four years of liberal Democratic policies would do to your paycheck, your job, your security and your future."

Second, Dole—who lost his vice-presidential candidates' debate with Mondale in 1976—would put Mondale down in another five-minute spot as no more than a glib loser. He would point out, the memo said, that "while Ronald Reagan was bringing down inflation . . . engineering the economic recovery . . . rolling back communism in Grenada . . . leading America back to greatness," Mondale "was making a fortune as a Washington lawyer and doing a lot of talking." The memo offered this argument for Dole:

"Walter Mondale wants you to base your decision as to who will lead this country for the next four years on the basis of 90 or 180 minutes of television. He wants you to forget the last four great years for America and the previous four years of disaster. That's 180 minutes of television versus eight years of history."

Third, Reagan himself would have to be trotted out to show "that he is in full command." The memo proposed that he go on nationwide network television for thirty minutes and deal with all aspects of his domestic and foreign policies, as well as his "plans for the future"—a subject that had been avoided like a plague as long as Reagan seemed safely ahead.

The memo went on to offer a series of alibis for Reagan's poor debate performances. First of all, the process could be blamed:

"TV debates are artificially contrived 'pressure cookers' which do not coincide with the actual pressures that confront a President. . . . There is something fundamentally degrading about the entire process. Most if not all civilized nations manage to select their leaders without subjecting them to this bizarre ritual. . . . Many of the world's greatest visionaries and leaders would not hold up well in a TV debate. This does not diminish Lech Walesa, Andrei Sakharov, etc."

Another alibi would be the old national-security dodge:

"In the foreign-policy debate in particular, there was a lot the President could not talk about."

Still another would play on public animosity toward the press. Reagan defenders, the memo said, could argue that "the debates seem to have become a forum for the press to display its arrogance and to exert their control over the nation's leaders." And Ford could help out in the press-bashing by recalling how, after his 1976 debate gaffe in which he denied there was Soviet domination of Eastern Europe, it was post-debate press criticism that turned the polls around against him.

"Everyone knows that the Big Media, especially the networks, have been out to get Ronald Reagan since day one," the memo said. "Recount how the polls as to who won and who lost in Louisville were relatively even, until the media did its hatchet job on the President."

A second Reagan debate flop, in other words, would trigger full-speed-ahead scapegoating—of the televised debates, of Mondale as all talk and no substance, and of the press. Here was the campaign that had used television, and the lulling quality of slick words, as relentlessly and as ruthlessly as any in American history. The contradiction was obvious, but the memo proposed how to deal even with that problem:

"There is, of course, an irony in the above counterstrategy. The media will notice that for the first time we are minimizing the importance of words and television; but they will just have to understand, along with the voters, that Ronald Reagan takes the presidency and his incumbency seriously, and he is not going to take time out from his job as leader of the free world to polish his lines the way Mondale did."

Perhaps even more ironic was still another planned rap at the debates if the second one didn't go well for Reagan. The memo said his troops could also alibi that "debates can be and frequently are misleading and deceptive: Winning a debate often depends more upon an effective 'cheap shot' than anything else." Or, the memo might well have added, a clever one-liner that would reduce a serious discussion to frivolity.

The memo went on to talk in the most direct terms about how Vice President George Bush would have to deliver if Reagan stumbled again:

"If things go badly in Kansas City, then the Vice President's relative importance to the ticket goes way up. As we all know, he kicked Ferraro's ass in Philadelphia. Since the age issue is sure to resurface in the aftermath of a disappointing performance on the twenty-first, the image of an active, aggressive, youthful Vice President will be reassuring to the American people."

Also, the memo said, the "Reagan-Bush team" would have to be emphasized, and the more popular Republican governors and members of Congress would have to be put on paid television to shore up the sagging President:

"By developing the 'team' concept, we emphasize that the voters aren't just choosing between Ronald Reagan and Walter Mondale, but between the good people associated with Reagan and the bad people associated with Mondale. This is tricky, but it fits into our strategy of driving up Mondale's negative rating."

The memo dismissed concerns about a possible backlash in attacking Mondale too hard. It would be too late and too urgent to fret about such things:

"We won't be able to worry much about charges of 'desperation.' We will have to clobber Mondale on the following, plus anything else we can think of: Waltergate [unexplained in the memo]; delegate committees; Ferraro; income-tax discrepancies [unexplained]; patsy for the Soviets; pal of Jesse Jackson, Teddy Kennedy, Bert Lance, Tip O'Neill and George McGovern; associates with known alumni of the Carter administration—this last point focuses on the contrast between the 'Reagan-Bush team' and the 'Mondale-Carter' team."

Nor was intentionally divisive politicking to be eschewed if Reagan's reelection suddenly was in jeopardy:

"We'd like to win the country, but we only have to win a little over half of it. Indeed, given the vagaries of the popular vote, we can win with a minority of the popular vote. Therefore we shouldn't hesitate to polarize, play the South against the North, the West against the East, and so on."

Reagan's use of Harry Truman as a model, the memo said, would have to be discarded and he would have to adopt a new hero—Dwight D. Eisenhower—for a bizarre reason: Ike too was an aging verbal bumbler but was overwhelmingly reelected:

"They used to say that Eisenhower 'couldn't talk his way out of a paper bag.' Yet he led America through eight years of peace, progress and prosperity, in spite of a heart attack, ileitis, etc. The RR-Truman parallelism will in any case have to go."

Finally, the memo proposed applying a dramatic tourniquet that would surely stop the political bleeding. Noting how the voters had rallied to Eisenhower in the final days of the 1956 election during a crisis over the Suez Canal, and how Kissinger's assurance that 'peace is at hand' helped Nixon in the 1972 campaign, the memo said:

". . . Incumbents always look their best while decisively handling a crisis. We should certainly consider a trip to Grenada on October 25, the first anniversary of the liberation."

Beyond the sheer audacity of the proposals, the memo was a measure of how some in the Reagan campaign hierarchy, behind their facade of confidence, feared a recurrence and deepening of the age issue and all it implied about Reagan's ability to serve four more years. They knew that issue, in fact, was the only one that stood in the way of his reelection, and that the second debate was probably the last obstacle to clear in disposing of it.

The Mondale strategists, meanwhile, were in another of their internal squabbles over what advice to give the candidate and who should give it. Caddell was kept out of the preparations until the final days, and his champions in the campaign were beside themselves. They feared Mondale was being coached by Leone and his friends into making the second debate an issues seminar instead of the political battle royal they felt it had to be if he was to have a chance for an upset.

Caddell did write a second-debate strategy memo, this one

of thirty-eight pages, dated October 16, five days before the event, and as usual he proposed bold moves. His recommendation was for Mondale to come out smoking, moving very aggressively to get Reagan off his script and to impress the viewing audience at once that they were seeing something extraordinary. Unless Mondale did so, Caddell argued, Reagan would get by, because the voters were watching to see whether he would fall apart or whether he could function adequately. Mondale simply had to make the case persuasively that Reagan, no matter how amiable and well-intentioned a man, was not up to the challenges of the future.

Once again, Caddell's memo underscored his view that Mondale had to win the second debate decisively, fanning the age issue in the process, or the election would be over:

"From the outset we must recognize that our electoral position requires not just a decisive victory but a knockout. Debate I served to loosen Reagan's political grip; Debate II must break it. The opening we were given was age. If Reagan stumbles badly in this debate, then Debate I will not be written off as a fluke and the concerns raised then could become operational, moving the election beyond the normal definitions of party, candidate and issues. Thus the Mondale strategic imperative must be to ignite the age concern to a salient firestorm."

Again, as in his memo on the first debate, Caddell by implication challenged the preparation approach of the "intellectual Hamlets," Leone and his friend Kaden:

"For Walter Mondale, this debate is only secondarily a debate on foreign policy; it is primarily a debate on Reagan's age, his grasp and his ability. Foreign policy is the strategic vehicle, not the strategic objective and thus in preparing for this debate must take a backseat, albeit an important one. A major debate victory on the substance of foreign policy could help our electoral position and serve to assist in closing the vote margins. However, if we can win a major debate victory on age, then the prospect of blowing open the election emerges.

"In truth, this debate is a big chess match rather than a policy forum, and it must be approached as such. The preparation to date indicates the reverse perception may be prevalent. We must out-think, out-maneuver and outwit our opponent rather than simply outpoint him on arguments. . . . Reagan can afford to lose the debate on 'points' and still probably secure reelection if he can come across as aggressive, in charge, thematic, energetic and 'with it.' "

Mondale also had to keep the element of surprise, and he could do so this time, the memo said, by switching back to "Fighting Fritz." He had to behave, Caddell wrote, in the manner of a courtroom lawyer ruthlessly trying to crack a witness. The memo went on:

"The overriding objective of this debate must be to 'break' Reagan—hurt him on age, on his lack of knowledge, on his grasp of issues. Mondale must not simply beat Reagan, he must take him apart. From the very first moment he must engage, disorient, pick Reagan apart and put him on the defensive. This does not mean Mondale can brutalize, insult or attack Reagan's motives or sincerity. . . . Instead we want voters not to turn on Reagan but to decide that he must be retired despite liking him and appreciating his efforts to date."

To come on too strong, Caddell wrote, "would likely backfire and perhaps cause a sympathy backlash for Reagan. . . . The key is nuance. Mondale must go after Reagan aggressively but almost impersonally, although the object of the attack is clearly personal. It must not seem so. Mondale, in effect, should strive to be like a lawyer breaking a witness on the stand for that witness' own good; educating and bringing the jury along to the necessary but sad verdict. The weapons are not anger, abuse, contempt, self-righteousness or hostility. Instead they are incredulity, disdain, indignation, disbelief, incomprehension, contradiction, light ridicule, lecturing, pity and a tone of in-sorrow-more-than-in-anger. The object is not to destroy but to expose. The weapons must be sheathed in sympathy, respect and even occasional kindness. Reagan's motives and sincerity must be acknowledged and even hailed."

Caddell even supplied the proper rhetorical devices to get across the point to voters that their President was out of it:

"Mr. President, I don't think you understand . . . I think you missed the point . . . I think you are confused. . . . You've got your facts mixed up . . ."

Once again, however, Caddell had to be shoehorned into Mondale's debate preparation. Not until the Friday night before the Sunday event was he allowed in the presence of the candidate, at the insistence of Reilly. Having Caddell, Johnson said later, wasn't always worth "the general wear and tear" that went along with his participation. He tried, for example, "to supersede" Peter Hart as the campaign pollster, Johnson charged.

One Mondale insider put the anti-Caddell view this way:

"Caddell's most important liability is that he drives an organization to total distraction. Nobody talks about anything but Caddell once Caddell arrives on the scene. It just wasn't worth the effort."

Caddell, though, and others like Reilly, Tully and Donilon felt that the advice Caddell had provided for the first debate was ample proof that he was worth "the general wear and tear" he brought with him.

As for Caddell's view of the Johnson leadership, he said later that the Mondale campaign was "a bureaucratic campaign in which processes dominate action and thinking. You can't break through those things." The heavy emphasis on substantive foreign-policy themes in the second-debate preparation, and the neglect of tactical political thinking, proved his point, he said.[47]

The Reagan strategists, for their part, always knew what was important in putting their candidate's best foot forward. On the afternoon of the debate, Deaver and other Reagan aides went onto the set and insisted on some adjustments in the lighting. Later, Mondale aides suggested that the adjustments may have been responsible for making their candidate look haggard, especially around his eyes. Also, Deaver insisted that the room temperature be raised. He was taking no chances on the conditions not being exactly right for his principal.

Even before the debate began, however, and with the age issue still widely under discussion, voters already seemed to be pushing aside their doubts about Reagan. His lead in the Gallup poll had moved up from 17 percent after the first debate to 20 percent

47. In an interview after the election, Johnson said: "For better or for worse, bad decisions, good decisions, it was a remarkably hierarchical campaign. There was remarkably little sitting around sort of voting on decisions. Mondale made the decisions he wanted to make, which principally had to do with substance, I made the decisions I wanted to make, and Beckel made all the others. Not all the others, but major decisions . . ." Except for what Johnson called "the Caddell morass," he said, "there was never a time really when there was any ambiguity about control. . . . If I said it's going to be X, I don't know of a single time in the four years when somebody tried to go to Mondale to make it Y."

on the eve of the second and it was up to 25 percent in the NBC News poll even before then. A late New York *Times*-CBS News survey, though, had Reagan ahead by "only" 13 percent going into the Kansas City confrontation.

Finally, the starting time arrived. Mondale, greeting the President on the stage, saw a different Ronald Reagan from the one he had encountered in the first debate.

"I knew he was moving," Mondale said. The difference between Reagan's appearance before the first debate and then, he said, was "night and day . . . I knew we were in for a debate at least."

Soon the debate was on, and Mondale began to feel more confident. Perhaps Reagan looked better, but his answers weren't any better. In short order, Reagan alluded to the CIA head in Nicaragua as "the man in charge"; he floundered in the face of Mondale's allegations that he thought land-based missiles were recallable; he shunted responsibility for the basing of American Marines in Lebanon on the local commander. Mondale, while not being as aggressive as Caddell had hoped, was scoring points in rapid succession.

But then came that question from *The Baltimore Sun's* Henry Trewhitt, reminding the seventy-three-year-old President of the terrible pressure John F. Kennedy had faced in the Cuban missile crisis and inquiring whether "you would be able to function in such circumstances." And in reply came that mock-serious pledge from Reagan that "I will not make age an issue in this campaign. I am not going to exploit, for political purposes, my opponent's youth and inexperience."

Suddenly, that was the election. Of that cute one-liner that convulsed the audience and shattered Walter Mondale's hopes of an upset, Reagan told us after the election:

"That just came. That was the thing I was incapable of doing in the first one because I crammed myself dry. It just seemed like a fine answer . . ."

And that may have been the understatement of the 1984 presidential campaign. After all the millions of dollars spent and all the creativity and energies of the high-priced talent in Washington and on Madison Avenue, Ronald Reagan's favorite weapon, the old reliable one-liner, had come through for him once again.

"To me, it was Nashua all over again," said Laxalt, referring to Reagan's "I'm paying for this microphone" line that turned Reagan's debate against Bush in Nashua, New Hampshire, in 1980 into a rout.

Some, though, like Mondale's campaign manager, Jim Johnson, did not make much of the wisecrack.

"That's an obvious joke," he said after the election. "I didn't see it as a great blockbuster."

Maybe Johnson didn't, but to millions of viewers around the country, the one-liner likely told them that, like America itself, The Gipper was back—back in form; the easygoing, take-it-in-stride confident leader they liked. Never mind that the answer was a dodge and as empty of content as an air bubble. It signaled the answer they wanted to hear: the old man wasn't slipping after all.

Caddell said later Reagan's salvation was not so much the joke itself but the fact that leading up to it he had looked and sounded "with it," even though his substantive answers were poor. "It wasn't the joke that did it," he said. "It was the fact that he didn't look ga-ga in the first twenty minutes." Mondale, he said, did not pursue sufficiently the openings that Reagan's answers had offered him.

As the debate proceeded, however, Reagan again began to ramble as he had in the first encounter. In his closing statement, which he had timed on Air Force One and found to be sixteen seconds too long, he seemed to get lost. He started talking about having been asked several years earlier to write a letter to be placed in a time capsule that would be opened a hundred years later.

"I remember driving down the California coast one day," he said. "My mind was full of what I was going to put in that letter about the problems and the issues that confront us in our time and what we did about them. But I couldn't completely neglect the beauty around me: the Pacific out there on one side of the highway, shining in the sunlight, the mountains of the coast range rising on the other side. And I found myself wondering what it would be like for someone . . . wondering if someone, a hundred years from now, would be driving down that highway, and if they would see the same thing . . ."

Reagan went on in that vein, talking about the task such a letter posed for him, because its readers would know the problems faced by Americans at the time it was written and how they had solved them. And then he went on to talk about "our rendezvous with destiny"—that very same phrase Reagan had used in the close of his famous 1964 appeal for Barry Goldwater that had launched him into national politics. And he said what a wonderful experience the campaign had been for him, meeting "young America . . . we have met your sons and daughters—"

Edwin Newman, the moderator, broke in—on the President of the United States, contrary to Mike Deaver's assurance.

"Mr. President, I am obliged to cut you off there under the rules of the debate. I'm sorry," he said.

Reagan seemed flustered.

"All right," he said. "I was just going to . . . All right."

Was the old man slipping again, after all? It didn't matter one way or the other. After that earlier one-liner that had demonstrated he still had his wits about him, it would take more than a little rambling at the end to get him into trouble again.

After the election, Mondale himself conceded as much.

"His answers on the second debate were in many ways worse than the first debate," he said, "but he looked alive, and I think that's what people were really watching. . . . I knew when that debate was over, probably the campaign was over, because he had reassured Americans that he could carry on in the presidency. I believe if it hadn't been for the first debate, the reports on my performance in the second debate would have been far better. But I think the contrast between the two—all he had to do was stay on his feet the second time around."

Jim Baker remarked later that it was a good thing a second debate had been agreed upon. But it was unlikely no matter what happened that Reagan would have been beaten in 1984.

As for Spencer, he breathed a sigh of relief.

"I don't feel home free until that guy is off the tube," he said with his customary frankness afterward.

Reagan himself said he didn't think the debates were all that decisive.

"What we know now is that the debates aren't the campaign," he said later. "They're kind of a minor thing. . . . They're not like the Lincoln-Douglas debates. They're not in debate form."

Nevertheless, another poor performance by him certainly could have put some spark in the final two weeks of the campaign. And if, as the President said, the debates were "a minor thing," it was legitimate to ask what then was the substance in the campaign? Certainly it wasn't all those feel-good television commercials and their functional equivalents on the campaign stump, those meticulously orchestrated presidential pep rallies with kids responding on cue as if they were at the Olympics, "U.S.A.! U.S.A.!"

On the flight back from Kansas City, Darman, everybody's favorite goat for what happened in the first debate, penned a gag memo to Laxalt. In the form of a meeting of the campaign strategy group, it observed that Darman, in anticipating the possible downside risks of the campaign, noted the possibility that Reagan would do so well in the first debate that he would be competing against his own impossibly high standard in the second. Therefore Darman had recommended that Reagan take a dive in the first, that his performance be blamed on his "brutalization" by his staff and that he then come off the floor and triumph in the second debate. The trip home this time, clearly, was quite different from the one two weeks earlier.

For the Mondale staff, it was wishful-thinking time. The usual talking points were worked up, the prime one of which was an assault on a Reagan comment after the show-stopping one-liner that if the United States could develop the so-called Star Wars missile defense system he advocated, he would demonstrate it and offer it to the Soviet Union as a move toward world peace. The Mondale strategists convinced themselves they had a hot issue to exploit and sent their spin patrol to the press room to try to peddle that one. But they were kidding themselves. The next morning, Jim Johnson held a press briefing before leaving Kansas City and, incredibly, proclaimed:

"I think we have this election just where we want it now."

In a day or so, the Mondale campaign started running an anti–Star Wars commercial using a clip from the debate in which Mondale chided Reagan for saying he didn't know what the system would be but was for developing it. Wirthlin, the Reagan pollster, tested the public reaction and found the Mondale ad helped Reagan and hurt Mondale.

As for the Reagan television campaign, it went back to the feel-good ads, featuring the President speaking from the Oval Office, with a warm fireplace blazing behind him, saying things like "Let America be America again" and "With you back in charge, America is on the move again."

In the end, Mondale was reduced to what Democrats have always done at the close of presidential elections in recent years—going back to their traditional base. In Youngstown, Ohio, and later in Ann Arbor, Michigan, Mondale quoted a letter Reagan had written to Richard Nixon in 1960 comparing John F. Kennedy's economic ideas to those of Karl Marx and Adolf Hitler. The letter said in part:

"Under the tousled boyish haircut it is still old Karl Marx—first launched a century ago. There is nothing new in the idea of a government being Big Brother to us all. Hitler called his 'State Socialism' and way before him it was 'benevolent monarchy.' "

Reagan had been peddling himself as a convert from the Democratic Party, invoking the names of Roosevelt, Truman and Kennedy in his effort to lure Democrats into his fold. In a close election, the letter about JFK might have been a bombshell, bringing Democrats "home" in droves. In this one, it was an amusing sidelight.

Meanwhile, Peter Hart was polling nightly and finding, Johnson said, that Reagan was maintaining a lead in the neighborhood of twenty percentage points. Three nights after the debate, Johnson took a plane to Milwaukee and talked turkey with his candidate. He told him there had been "a dramatic change" since the second debate and a backlash to the attacks "on Reagan's personal inadequacies." The time had come, Johnson told him, to "go back to basics that we stand for as Democrats and what you stand for, Walter Mondale, and want to be remembered for in this race."

Mondale asked him if he saw any chance to win, and Johnson said he couldn't tell him what the formula was to do so. And so Mondale went down talking like the old New Deal Democrat that he was—and feeling exceedingly comfortable about it. Among other things, Mondale had always been particularly conscious of the way his family—his wife Joan, his daughter Eleanor, his two sons, Ted and Bill—would assess his conduct in politics. In these final days, then, he felt a special pressure to be true to the principles and ideas that had always been most important to him.

On election night, the outcome was worse for Mondale than all but the most pessimistic Democrats expected. Reagan in carrying every state but Mondale's home base of Minnesota won the largest electoral-college victory in the country's history—525 to 10 for Mondale, who also carried the District of Columbia. The President won 59 percent of the vote to 41 for the Minnesotan.

In many ways, the election was one of the most effortless for the winner and one of the most exhausting for the loser in the nation's history. Reagan had breezed through to an unopposed nomination and an election that was never seriously challenged. Mondale, on the other hand, had slugged and skidded his way to the Democratic nomination, only to stagger through a hapless fall campaign in which he never came close to his opponent and was afforded a ray of hope only because that opponent had one off night.

Now, finally, the long journey was over. Reagan, at the very end, was the unruffled performer. When he appeared before cheering supporters in the ballroom of his Los Angeles hotel to claim the victory and the crowd chanted "Four more years! Four more years!" he had another one-liner ready.

"I think that's just been arranged," he said.

What a guy.

As for Mondale in St. Paul, he congratulated the winner, thanked the American people for hearing him out and concluded:

"I'm at peace with the knowledge that I gave it everything I've got."

It remained, however, for Geraldine Ferraro in New York, in a phone call with Mondale, to provide the human touch. Ever since he had selected her as his running mate, they had been careful to avoid anything but the most professional political association and certainly to avoid doing or saying anything that might breach the notion that she was on the Democratic ticket because she was "the best potential President" and not because she was a woman. But in this last phone call as partners on the ticket, she asked him:

"When I see you tomorrow, can I kiss you?"

22

Few Heroes, Many Villains

•

ON NOVEMBER 13, 1984, just seven days after the election, David Stockman, President Reagan's budget director, disclosed that the federal deficit in the next fiscal year was now expected to be $210 billion, not the $175 billion the Reagan administration had previously estimated. The situation was so dire, Stockman made clear, that further radical measures would be required to correct it.

This "November surprise" inspired no little cynical comment in Washington. The basic premise of President Reagan's campaign had been that we were all heading down the glory road to peace and prosperity without pain.

But few in the capital were really surprised. Nearly everyone knew that Ronald Reagan had been just blowing smoke. Now that the presidential election was finally over, it was time to return to the real world.

The shamelessness with which the White House now addressed the deficit question was a telling comment on the quality of the political campaign that had culminated on November 6 with Reagan's landslide reelection.

The campaign had been so sterile that there never was any occasion on which Reagan felt obliged to deal with the hard questions about the federal deficit—or, for that matter, about any issue of the future. Instead, the President had buried Walter Mondale under a mountain of votes evoked by feel-good television commercials and Reagan's own remarkable ability to persuade the electorate that "America is back" had some serious meaning.

And, for his part, the Democratic nominee for President had run a campaign that so misjudged the voters' concerns that he never put enough pressure on Reagan to force a serious dialogue on the issues. The only uncertain moment in the campaign had been that brief period of uneasiness about whether Reagan, soon to be seventy-four years old, still had the capacity and stamina for the office.

The campaign of 1984 cannot reasonably be assessed, however, in simple terms of winners or losers.

Ronald Reagan, merely by capturing the most votes, didn't warrant undiluted praise. The President was a man of sincere beliefs and genuine commitments to his political goals. But he had lent himself willingly to a mindless campaign to convince his fellow Americans that their nation faced no problems that could not be solved with slogans about "standing tall." Reagan was just fulfilling what Adlai Stevenson once called the first duty of any politician—getting elected.

Nor did Walter Mondale warrant unremitting condemnation because he had mounted a campaign wretched enough to suffer such a political debacle. Fritz Mondale was a decent man who had represented values of generosity and compassion. His sin, instead, was his failure to understand how the world had turned during his lifetime in politics.

The real losers—and deservedly so—were the people of the United States, and that was the case without regard to which candidate they had supported. They had just dozed through a process that is supposed to be the ultimate of democratic exercises—the choice of one candidate over another for the most powerful office in the free world. But they had settled for an empty contest of images on their television screens that told them essentially nothing about the decisions that would be made for their future.

Moreover, because the campaign was so devoid of content, the results told them nothing reliable about the shape of American politics in the years ahead.

Once the returns were calculated, there were predictable Republican claims that a significant "political realignment" was in the making. And there appeared to be strong evidence to support that contention in Reagan's remarkably strong performance among young voters and among white southerners and middle-class working people who previously had allied themselves with the Democrats.

A better case, however, could be made that this election was a polarizing one. According to the New York *Times*/CBS News exit poll, Mondale had won a majority only among blacks, Hispanic-Americans, Jewish voters, the unemployed, women with less than a high school education, voters with annual incomes under $12,500, and voters from households with union members. If the election was not precisely a triumph of the society's haves over its have-nots, the class, cultural and economic distinctions were approximate enough. For all the talk about one America, the Reagan campaign seemed to advocate the tyranny of the majority.

Despite the breadth and diversity of the support for Reagan, it could not be argued logically that this was a realigning election. That term suggests a thoughtful decision made on the basis of some set of policies the President had espoused—and the voters had chosen. In 1984, there was never the kind of political dialogue that would be required for such decisions. Would anyone argue that Republican policies and programs were so well understood and popular that the 49-state landslide result would have been the same had the Republican nominee been George Bush rather than Ronald Reagan?

It was, then, a campaign with few heroes, and many villains—the process itself, the politicians, the press and, finally, the people.

At first blush, the weaknesses of the process seemed largely confined to the Democratic Party. Certainly that is where flaws were most obvious in this campaign.

From the outset, the activist Democrats in their latest reforms made it even more difficult for their eventual nominee to have a realistic chance against an incumbent President in the general election. The rules for delegate selection written in 1981 and 1982 were a reaction against the disasters of the past: the nomination of one candidate on the ideological fringe, George McGovern in 1972, and then of a total outsider, Jimmy Carter in 1976, who committed the unpardonable sin of losing the White House as an incumbent.

But these Democratic insiders, in their zeal to keep a tight control on the process and choose a candidate of their own, followed an essentially self-defeating course. Rather than designing a system that would attract the mainstream of the electorate, they plotted to make it possible for someone—either Ted Kennedy or

Fritz Mondale in the original planning—to capture the nomination by winning the party's activist constituencies, eschewing the great unwashed mass of voters.

The insiders also established thresholds of voter support that candidates needed in primaries and caucuses to obtain delegates to the national convention. The requirement was poison to longshot candidates, Jesse Jackson particularly, in their efforts to gain a toehold in the nominating process. The insiders' goal was to wrap up the campaign for the nomination before the primary and caucus voters in most states ever had a chance to express their views. The rationale was that a drawn-out process would be too debilitating to the eventual nominee. The scheme to end the campaign on Super Tuesday in March didn't succeed, but it was no less real.

More successful was the manner in which the Mondale campaign subverted the intent of the Democratic reform creating "superdelegates." These officeholders were supposed to be party wise men who would exercise sober and reflective judgment of a nominee after the primaries and caucuses were held. Instead, even before the first delegate-selecting events took place, many of them were pressured into publicly committing to Mondale.

The preliminaries to the 1984 campaign that ran all through 1983 were, as we have seen, essentially meaningless inside games the Democratic politicians played with one another. But neither the politicians nor the press could ever resist the temptation to treat those straw votes and candidate forums as serious exercises. If success in, let's say, the straw vote in Wisconsin would earn you a day or two of attention from the television networks, then winning the support of the two or three thousand local people involved was worth any sacrifice of money and time and emotional commitment.

The 1983 preliminaries were all the more self-destructive for the Democrats because their candidates spent almost all that time bickering among themselves about the past. Woe betide the candidate who had cast an incautious vote on some aspect of Reaganomics or failed to pass the litmus test for devotion to arms reduction. Those questions may have been all-consuming to liberal activists or labor skates, but there was little reason to believe they critically engaged the average voter.

The Republicans escaped this trap, but only because there

never was any genuine doubt about the makeup of their ticket. It should not be forgotten that the precedent for the Democratic follies of 1983 was set by the Republicans in a very similar series of divisive and debilitating straw votes and forums in 1979.

There was, however, one highly destructive element of the Democratic situation peculiar to the Democrats—the role of the activist groups within their party. Each of its principal constituencies—blacks, labor, feminists, Jewish voters, Hispanic-Americans—had its own agenda. More to the point, each insisted that any candidate with any hope of winning its support would be obliged to accept that entire agenda.

Again, this dilemma did not confront the Republicans because they had no contest. The seeds of similar problems were obvious for them, too, in the rigidity of the New Right on taxes and in the militancy of the fundamentalists on such issues as abortion and school prayer. But in 1984 the Republicans, with Ronald Reagan as unifier, could smugly enjoy the spectacle of Democratic candidates trying to hold their battered old coalition together for just one more election.

That the Democrats would have to begin the campaign of 1984 in January of 1983 was, on the face of it, ridiculous. But there were factors built into the process that made that early start essential for most of the candidates, even if the voters were so obviously less engrossed.

One was money. Since the campaign of 1976, the federal government has provided matching funds for presidential candidates who raise at least $5,000 in each of twenty states in amounts of $250 or less. Once that standard is met, the candidate receives public money dollar for dollar for each contribution of up to $250—to a maximum of about $10 million under the 1984 formula. None of the federal money was to be disbursed until January of 1984, shortly before the caucuses and primaries would begin. But—and this was the critical point—any money raised by a candidate at any point in 1983 was eligible to be matched.

The standard plan for each candidate thus became essentially the same: raise as much as possible during 1983, take the matching money as soon as possible, then pour it into television advertising that would lead to a big score in those first caucuses and primaries.

But to raise the money, the candidates had to reach the point at which they were "taken seriously." And to achieve that elusive stature, most of them spent everything they raised all through 1983 and then borrowed more against their assured matching funds. And so they ran out of money by the start of 1984, just when they needed it. They spent it all, moreover, on those inside games among themselves that never reached most of the electorate.

One move might help shorten the process somewhat, or at least delay its intensity. Congress could postpone for six or eight months the starting date for raising money to qualify for matching funds, from January 1st of the year preceding the presidential election year to July 1st or September 1st. To compensate for this loss of fund-raising time, Congress could also double the limit on individual contributions from $1,000 to $2,000 and raise the qualifying ceiling from $250 to $500. Candidates still would be free to campaign earlier, but they would be less obliged to do so than they are now.

The fact that the 1984 campaign started so early and went on so long, with so few voters seriously involved, resulted in a related distortion—far too much attention to the public-opinion polls.

Political professionals and the press always are ambivalent about polls, and 1984 was no exception. On the one hand, the politicians and the reporters understood that there were clear limits to the validity of early polls taken before most voters were interested in the campaign. Throughout 1983, the results reflected how well the candidates' names were known, rather than any considered public judgment about the candidates. And knowledgeable people within the political community accepted that fact, at least intellectually.

But even the politicans and political reporters who fully understand these limits cannot resist the "scientific" findings of the polls. The surveys are beguiling because they impose a kind of order on a situation that, in itself, is necessarily lacking in form. Thus, in this case, John Glenn was automatically appraised the most credible challenger to Mondale, ahead of Gary Hart and the others who were simply unknown quantities to most voters. Glenn held that status, moreover, long after most of the political professionals had concluded his campaign was a failure.

This combination of polls and money propelled the politics of

1984. Candidates felt obliged to take part in intrinsically insignificant events, thinking they might earn attention on the television networks, which have become the single most important force in American politics. Then, if they earned that attention, the candidates would become better known and perhaps their stock would rise in the polls. And if that goal also was achieved, the candidates could expect to find it easier to raise more campaign money and could compete more effectively in still more intrinsically insignificant events.

This bizarre cycle was intensified by the primary process itself. After 1980, the Democrats went through the obligatory hand-wringing over the flaws in the nominating system. But the plan they produced was not really any improvement. The primaries and caucuses still came at a dizzying pace—sometimes singly, sometimes in clusters. The pace never allowed the press or politicians, let alone the poor voters, time to figure out what was happening. The result was wild swings of sentiment from Mondale to Hart, back to Mondale and then to Hart again, based on nothing more substantial than a one-liner, a fortuitous moment on television or a minor gaffe by an exhausted candidate. In addition, states with populations in the tens of millions got short shrift, while very small states whose only attraction was their early date on the political calendar were inundated with candidate and news-media attention.

In many respects, the primaries can be valuable learning experiences for the voter. They do provide insight into how candidates will behave under stress and into which candidates may have leadership ability. But in the Democratic primaries of 1984, the one most obvious lesson was ignored. And that was the continuing evidence that Fritz Mondale was the "wrong" candidate for the times. It was not because he wouldn't have made a capable President but because he carried so much political baggage that he permitted Ronald Reagan to cast the campaign as a referendum on the "Carter-Mondale" past rather than on the future.

Under ideal circumstances, the primaries also can validate or disprove the underlying premises of the competing candidates. But that surely didn't happen in 1984. On the contrary, there was never any serious examination or disclosure of what commitments Mondale had made or hadn't made to Democratic constituencies. Instead, there was the picture of Mondale as the "candidate of the special interests." Nor was there ever a serious examination of whether Gary Hart really was or was not presenting genuine programmatic alternatives to Mondale. Instead, there was the derision of Hart as the "candidate of new ideas" who couldn't get a television commercial pulled in the Illinois primary.

The intense primary/caucus schedule, and federal limits on how much could be spent overall and in each state, also led in 1984 to major efforts to circumvent the law. On a simple level, candidates and their staffs stayed in motels across state lines from the state in which they were campaigning, so that their expenses would not be billed against that state's spending limit. This evasion had been used in earlier campaigns and was relatively harmless.

A new and more insidious wrinkle was the creation and extensive use of delegate committees by the Mondale campaign. They not only skirted the spirit if not the letter of the law but also led to serious ethical and possibily legal offenses against the whole process. While these excesses cannot be excused, the stringent and, in many cases, unrealistic financial restrictions imposed on campaigns often persuade candidates or their managers, in desperate straits, to resort to desperate measures. Ironically, the federal regulations that permitted creation of the delegate committees were intended to encourage and increase grass-roots political activity. A simpler way would be to require the television networks to provide a limited amount of free time to qualified, serious candidates and prohibit purchase of any more. That step alone would free up millions of dollars and likely persuade campaign managers to put their campaigns back into storefronts on the Main Streets of America, where they could be seen and where average citizens could participate, as in pre-television days.

Short of that kind of reform, raising the individual contribution limit would help, and might lessen the temptation of campaigns to exploit loopholes such as the delegate committee option. The language authorizing such committees needs tightening, as well, to discourage continued abuse. Campaign material distributed to elect delegates should have to bear the delegates' names and only incidentally include those of the candidate they support, and such committees should be limited to individuals actually running for delegate. They should not be allowed for at-large committees whose eventual delegates, for example, don't appear on any ballot and are appointed only after a state primary.

Congress ought to consider some way too get a handle on the "independent expenditure" committees that in 1984 spent some $17,000 in the presidential campaign, more than $16,000 of it in behalf of President Reagan. While this one-sided advantage apparently had little decision effect in so lop-sided an election, it could be critical in a closer race in 1988. The Supreme Court's early 1985 decision declaring any limit on spending by such committees an abridgement of the free-speech amendment to the Constitution threatens to distort the process even more, inviting a further escalation of the campaign alms race. And it will not be easy for Congress to find an approach that will satisfy this court, especially, on the First Amendment question. But both major parties have expressed concern that such free-lancing committees are not acceptable to the presidential campaigns they seek to benefit, and hence hold a potential for abuse by engaging in activities not necessarily in the best interest of the candidate.

Some alternative proposals for the primary schedule also make sense. The best, in our view, would set aside four or five Tuesdays over a four- or five-month period on which all states would be obliged to hold their primaries or precinct caucuses. A variation would provide for regional voting—all the primaries and caucuses in the East on one Tuesday, all those in the South on another and so on. The common element in these proposals is that there would be enough time for press, the politicians and hopefully even the voters to gain some understanding of their options.

But the state party leaders—Republican and Democratic alike—have never shown much interest in such rationality. For them, the usual goal has been to set their dates at a time giving their states maximum attention from the candidates and the national press—and not necessarily in that order.

Once again, this primary madness was exclusively a Democratic problem in the campaign of 1984. But there is no reason to believe the Republicans will escape it in 1988. Then, presumably, with President Reagan completing his second term, they will face the same obstacle course with a multi-candidate field.

The imperative of being "taken seriously" had another debilitating effect on the Democratic candidates in 1983 and early 1984.

Many of them, men with good reputations acquired over years in American politics, bent themselves out of shape in trying to corner a share of the market that might be reflected in the polls.

Alan Cranston's contention that he gave a higher priority than the other candidates did to arms control and peace was nonsense. In these times, any candidate for President in either party is certain to make national security his first priority. But there was Cranston telling audiences all over the country that he had some special claim to be "the peace candidate" because he had once known Albert Einstein.

Reubin Askew was another example of a candidate whose image became skewed by the process. As governor of Florida and later United States trade ambassador, he had won a deserved reputation as a candidate of serious purpose. But in trying to gain a foothold in the Iowa caucus campaign, he embraced an issue, the opposition to abortion, that in other times he would have disdained as having little to do with qualifying for the presidency.

The campaign also led the candidates into attacks on one another most of them never would have made without that pressure to gain a hearing and an advantage. The bitter warfare between Glenn and Mondale and, later, Mondale and Hart left wounds not likely ever to heal completely. Did Walter Mondale really believe Gary Hart lacked the compassion to fill the needs of black Americans? Did Hart really believe Mondale could be held accountable for "days of shame" in the Iran hostage crisis? There have always been harsh words between candidates involved in intraparty contests as well as in general elections. But the voters' willingness in 1984 to respond to such shallow gimmicks as "Where's the beef?" nourished the compulsion to score with a "good hit" on television.

But if the process and politicians were culpable in making the 1984 campaign such an unrewarding experience, so was the news media. And, because of television's enormous influence on all aspects of American life, that fact was particularly true of the networks.

Over the last four presidential elections, the influence and authority of television in politics has grown in quantum leaps—just as it has in most facets of American life. During much of this period, television's coverage of politics was derivative. Its characterizations of political situations were more often made first by newspapers, then accepted by the networks. But that dependency began to change as the networks employed more sophisticated reporters and the politicians made a greater effort to tailor their campaigns to the medium.

In the campaign of 1984, there was no doubt that the single most important objective for a candidate was scoring well on the evening news shows on a particular night. Campaign managers closed their office doors at 6:30 or 7:00 every night to watch what "really" had happened that day. And if an event didn't happen on television, it didn't happen at all.

The Gary Hart phenomenon after his second-place finish in Iowa was fueled by his extraordinary coverage over the next several days by the networks and the Boston stations viewed by New Hampshire voters. In the same way, Mondale revived his campaign by conveying an image on television as the "Fighting Fritz" who had made a great comeback on Super Tuesday—by winning but two of the nine contests that day. Again, in the final round of primaries, Mondale could claim the nomination because television was able to report his triumph in New Jersey but, because of the time difference, the networks didn't catch up with Hart's overwhelming victory in California.

Later, beginning the general-election campaign, Mondale suffered what was widely accepted as a political disaster when he arranged his Labor Day schedule for the parade in New York that looked so bad on television. The decision to do so, though, was the Mondale campaign's, so he could only blame his own staff—and its insatiable appetite for network television coverage.

Television's growing influence was not matched by a corresponding ability to convey nuance. Nor was it matched by a willingness on the part of television news directors to resist the good "visual"—the kind of staged events that Ronald Reagan's managers used so effectively to present his campaign appearances as so little different from his campaign commercials.

In a bizarre irony, the Reagan television commercials became the reality of what the 1984 Reagan campaign was all about, and the actual Reagan rallies merely parroted them.

Nor did the print press distinguish itself in 1984; on the contrary, many newspaper and magazine reporters seemed reluctant to defy the judgments of the networks about what was really happening. There were, to be sure, many stories that examined and found the flaws in Mondale, Hart and, later, Reagan. But on too many occasions reporters went along with the flow of excitement engendered by television rather than standing apart from it or disputing it. Jesse Jackson got a free ride for much of his campaign because many in the press were reluctant to risk being accused of racism. The choice of Geraldine Ferraro as Mondale's nominee for Vice President was treated far less critically than would have been the case with some male three-term member of the House of Representatives.

But the most serious flaw in the whole system of communicating information to the voters was its failure to provide a rounded picture of the candidates and the differences of their views of the world. In the best of political worlds, candidates for President would be accorded some regular access to television in a way that might make them as well known as a minor character in *Hill Street Blues*. But that didn't happen in 1984 and is probably a pipe dream.

The shallowness of the communications process was never shown more clearly than in the contrast between the most effective political commercials and the reality.

During the primary period, by most professional assessments, the single most effective television spot was the "red telephone" ad prepared by Roy Spence for Mondale against Hart. The message was unmistakable: Mondale had the credentials of experience to be a safe custodian of the "nuclear button," but Hart was so "untested" he would represent a risk in the Oval Office. But no one ever examined the validity of that premise. What evidence was there to suggest that Hart would be more inclined than Mondale to respond improperly in a crisis? The answer was nothing more substantial than a couple of gaffes during the Illinois primary. But in the puerile politics of 1984, that "evidence" was enough.

The one television commercial the politicians considered the most effective in the general-election campaign was the "bear in the woods" ad run by the Reagan campaign. The implication was that Reagan's defense policy would guard the nation if the Soviet Union was aggressively hostile, but that Mondale might not even accept the fact of the Soviet threat. But there was never any serious political dialogue between the two nominees for President that exposed the full dimensions of their views on the dangers of nuclear war and the measures necessary to prevent it.

There were, of course, those two debates in Louisville and

Kansas City arranged by the League of Women Voters, the self-anointed promoters of "discussions of the issues" in presidential politics. It was fair to say that those debates were better than nothing in giving the voters material for comparisons. But they weren't much better. The President, leading overwhelmingly in the opinion polls, held all the high cards in the negotiations on the format. The result was so structured that, had the President not stumbled in the first debate in Louisville, the two encounters would have been largely repetitions of their daily campaign rhetoric.

There isn't any reason the two political parties could not commit themselves long ahead of the next campaign to a series of presidential-candidate debates using different—and potentially more revealing—formats.

The debates among the Democratic hopefuls in 1983 and 1984 that most approximated direct exchanges, without the distraction of questioning panelists, proved to be the most revealing. With a fair, firm but inobtrusive moderator in charge, they give the candidates the best opportunities to demonstrate tactical debating skills and grasp of subject matter. Also, those debates limited to discussion in depth of a single topic, as in the 1983 forums in Iowa on arms control and farm policy require the candidates to reveal breadth of knowledge and ability to build a persuasive case in detail. The critical presidential debates surely should accomplish no less. Three 90-minute exchanges, each covering two specific subjects for 45 minutes, or even three for 30 minutes each, could be much more enlightening than were the scatter-shot debates of 1984.

This possibility is particularly realistic in a situation in which presumably there will be no incumbent running in 1988 with the special leverage that circumstance implies. But there has been no great popular demand for a more intelligent process and, lacking that demand, no such change is likely.

The discouraging impression, based on what happened in the campaign of 1984, is that the voters just don't give much of a damn about the quality of a presidential campaign. They will take whatever they are given.

Voter turnout did increase slightly in 1984, reversing a trend of ever-lower participation since 1960. But the increase over 1980—only 0.7 percent—was miniscule, especially when viewed against the intensive efforts of both parties and perhaps a dozen other organizations to increase registration and voting.

And surely there was no evidence in 1984 of growing sophistication on the part of the electorate. On the contrary, too many voters seemed smugly willing to make their judgments based on those flickering images on their television screens. We have become a society with an attention span roughly comparable to that of a twelve-year-old, and we demand instant and easy answers to complex and vexing questions.

So, in overwhelming numbers, the voters accepted Ronald Reagan's assurance that they could "stand tall" and "go for the gold" if they returned him to the White House for four more years. They didn't ask him just what he intended to do. They didn't make much effort to find out how that view of the future differed from Walter Mondale's. That would have been boring, time-consuming and taxing. They accepted the Republicans' judgment that Fritz Mondale was a loser beneath their consideration.

And so, on January 21, 1985, Ronald Wilson Reagan was sworn in for a second term as President of the United States before a thousand elite officials and friends in the Rotunda of the Capitol. The exercise was peculiarly appropriate as a final act in the presidential election campaign of 1984; it was a totally staged event, principally for television. Reagan, in private, had actually taken the oath the previous day, as required by the Constitution.

But, as they say, that's show business.

Index